Guide to Periodicals in Education and Its Academic Disciplines

Second Edition

by

WILLIAM L. CAMP

and

BRYAN L. SCHWARK

The Scarecrow Press, Inc.

Metuchen, N. J.   1975

Library of Congress Cataloging in Publication Data

Camp, William L
  Guide to periodicals in education and its
academic disciplines.

  Published in 1968 under title: Guide to periodicals
in education.
  Includes indexes.
  1. Education—Periodicals—Bibliography.
2. Periodicals—Bibliography. I. Schwark, Bryan L.,
joint author. II. Title.
Z5813.C28 1975 [LB1025] 016.37'05 75-6784
ISBN 0-8108-0814-5

Dedication

This work is dedicated to all those who search and strive toward the further advancement of learning and knowledge, but especially to those who have spent and are spending valuable time to refine past achievements and to make new discoveries; all of which they document and pass on to others through the unselfish publication of their research and knowledge in journal literature.

WLC
BLS

TABLE OF CONTENTS

PREFACE

The second edition of <u>Guide to Periodicals in Education and Its Academic Disciplines</u> contains information obtained from editors and publishers of 602 nationally distributed education and education-related periodicals issued in the United States. It is intended to provide authors, educators, and researchers with detailed data necessary for the preparation of manuscripts to be submitted for publication. Individuals who wish to follow scholarly reporting in specific areas of education will find the <u>Guide</u> helpful in acquainting them with periodicals available in specialized and interdisciplinary educational fields. Students, librarians, publishers, and others interested in education or education-related journals will find valuable reference material concerned with journal content and publication information contained in this second edition of the <u>Guide.</u>

Information was obtained by means of questionnaires sent to editors and publishers, personal examination of the periodicals when necessary, and from other sources. Publications which were used to obtain current addresses for mailing of the questionnaire to publishers and editors for this edition were <u>Ulrich's International Periodicals Directory</u>, Fifteenth Edition, 1973-1974, 1973; <u>Magazines for Libraries,</u> edited by Bill Katz, Second Edition, 1972; <u>Standard Periodical Directory</u>, edited by Leon Garry, Fourth Edition, 1973; <u>Ayer Directory of Publications,</u> 105th Edition, 1973, as well as publishers' announcements and the periodicals themselves. Because journal titles, editors, publishers, publishers' addresses, prices, and publication policies are constantly changing, the compilers have done their very best to provide the reader with the most accurate and up-to-date information available.

The editors of the <u>Guide</u> wish to express their sincere thanks to all the editors, publishers and others who responded to requests for current policies and information. Without these contributions, preparation of the second edition would not have been possible. The Guide contains 373 of the 449 titles which were listed in the first edition. A number of periodicals from that edition have ceased publication. Two-hundred and twenty-nine new titles, including titles that appeared in the first edition and which have changed title, bring the total number of entries in the second edition to 602.

Exclusion from the Guide does not necessarily imply rejection since approximately 100 new queries to be considered for inclusion went unanswered. Due to the changing nature of journal literature and because of time limitations, all the vital information for these journals could not be obtained for this edition. The editors of the Guide encourage journal editors and publishers who wish their journals to be considered for the next edition to contact the Guide's editors through Scarecrow Press.

The editors wish to acknowledge the valuable typing and editorial assistance provided by Mrs. Jane Schwark who devoted countless hours in preparation of the final manuscript.

William L. Camp, Ph. D.

Bryan L. Schwark, M. S.

INTRODUCTION

Six-hundred and two journal entries are arranged alphabetically within the general subject categories listed in the Table of Contents. Abbreviations are listed first. A Master List of Subject Headings is included to provide assistance in locating subjects used in the Subject Index. A Table of Contents, a Subject Index, and a Title Index provide three methods of entry into the data included in the Guide. A list of style manuals cited by the journal editors is also included as an aid to prospective authors. Each journal entry contains subscription information, editorial address, a statement of editorial policy, information on manuscript preparation and disposition, copyright, and additional significant information.

No attempt has been made to include most regional, state or local publications or alumni magazines, handbooks, student publications, annual reports, transactions and proceedings, college bulletins, or monographs in series.

Fifty-five periodicals which never or only occasionally accept unsolicited manuscripts are identified with an asterisk (*) which precedes the title. A dagger symbol (†) preceding an entry indicates that the editor or publisher of that periodical did not respond to a questionnaire mailed to the editorial office or office of publication. In these cases information was obtained directly from a recent issue of the journal or some other reliable source.

This Guide is intended to provide the most complete and current data obtainable regarding nationally distributed publications which relate directly to education and its academic disciplines. The editors believe this guide will serve as a complete summary of current periodical information required by authors who plan submission of a manuscript to one of the periodicals listed in the Guide. However, prospective contributors should consult a recent issue of the journal under consideration whenever possible. When an entry is marked with an asterisk, communication with the journal editor regarding editorial policy concerning unsolicited articles should be initiated prior to submission of the completed manuscript.

WLC
BLS

THE GUIDE

ADMINISTRATION AND SUPERVISION

ADMINISTRATIVE SCIENCE QUARTERLY

Subscription Data:
   Published by the Graduate School of Business and Public Administration, Cornell University, Malott Hall, Ithaca, New York 14850. Issued quarterly, in March, June, September, and December. Advertising is accepted. Circulation: 4,400. Subscription: $12.00 per year; $20.00 to institutions; $9.00 to students. Founded: 1956.

Editorial Address:
   The Editor, Administrative Science Quarterly, Cornell University, Malott Hall, Ithaca, New York 14850.

Editorial Policy:
   Includes manuscripts combining empirical and theoretical data dealing with the behavior of organizational and administrative structures. The reading audience includes academic and non-academic persons interested in administration. Unsolicited manuscripts are welcome. Eight to ten major articles are published per issue. Book reviews are included.

Manuscript Preparation:
   Accepted manuscripts average 25 to 35 double-spaced typewritten pages. Three copies are required. Return postage and a self-addressed envelope are not required. Bibliographical procedure should follow a style sheet which is available through the office of the editor. List footnotes on a separate page. Use wide margins on both sides, double-space, and use only one side of the paper. A background or explanatory cover letter and an outline, summary, or abstract are required. Biographical information about the author is required. Illustrations, pictures, graphs, etc., may be included, but should be on separate pages. No payment is made for accepted manuscripts. Reprints are available from the business manager.

Manuscript Disposition:
   Receipt of a manuscript is acknowledged. Editorial decisions are made within 3-1/2 months. Accepted articles usually appear in print within four or five months after acceptance. Unaccepted manuscripts are returned with criticism and/or suggestions.

Copyright:
   Held by Cornell University.

ADMINISTRATOR'S NOTEBOOK

Subscription Data:
   Published by the Midwest Administration Center, University of

Chicago, 5835 Kimbark Avenue, Chicago, Illinois 60637. Issued nine times each year, September through June. Advertising is not accepted. Circulation: 3,000. Subscription: $3.00 per year. Founded: 1952.

Editorial Address:

The Editor, Administrator's Notebook, Midwest Administration Center, University of Chicago, 5835 Kimbark Avenue, Chicago, Illinois 60637.

Editorial Policy:

Includes articles and research reports on educational administration. The reading audience includes school superintendents, principals, state officials, and professors of educational administration. Unsolicited articles are welcome. One major article is published per issue. Book reviews and major essay reviews are occasionally published.

Manuscript Preparation:

Accepted manuscripts average 12 to 15 double-spaced typewritten pages. Three copies are required. Return postage and a self-addressed envelope are desired. Bibliographical style should follow the Turabian Manual for Writers. Use one inch margins and double-space throughout. Place all footnotes at the end of the article in numerical sequence. A background or explanatory cover letter about the article is desired, but not an outline or summary. Biographical information about the author is unnecessary. Graphs and tables should be kept at a minimum. No payment is made for accepted articles; however, authors receive 50 free reprints.

Manuscript Disposition:

Receipt of a manuscript is acknowledged. Editorial decisions are made within four weeks. Accepted articles usually appear in print from two to four months after acceptance. Unaccepted manuscripts are returned without criticism or suggestions.

Copyright:

Held by the Midwest Administration Center, University of Chicago.

AMERICAN SCHOOL AND UNIVERSITY

Subscription Data:

Published by the North American Publishing Company, 134 North Thirteenth Street, Philadelphia, Pennsylvania 19107. Issued monthly, 12 months a year. Advertising is accepted. Circulation: Controlled, Non-Qualified 4,500, Qualified 42,000. Subscription: $15.00 per year; $28.00 for two years; $39.00 for three years. Founded: 1927.

Editorial Address:

The Editor, American School and University, 134 North Thirteenth Street, Philadelphia, Pennsylvania 19107.

Editorial Policy:

Includes articles and reports on building, planning, operating, maintaining, and equipping schools. The reading audience includes administrative, business and plant management personnel in public, private and parochial schools, junior colleges and universities. Unsolicited manuscripts are welcome. Six major articles are published per issue. Book reviews are sometimes included.

Manuscript Preparation:
Accepted manuscripts average 1,500 words. One copy is required. Return postage and a self-addressed envelope are required. Footnotes should not be used. Use one inch margins and double-space. A background or explanatory cover letter is required and an outline, summary, or abstract is suggested. Biographical information about the author should include a summary of present position and professional background. Illustrations, pictures, and graphs are requested. Payment is made for accepted manuscripts under some circumstances. Reprint costs vary with article length and number ordered.

Manuscript Disposition:
Receipt of a manuscript is acknowledged. Editorial decisions are made within eight weeks. Accepted articles usually appear in print within 12 months. Unaccepted manuscripts are returned on request, sometimes with criticism and/or suggestions.

Copyright:
Held by the North American Publishing Company.

AMERICAN SCHOOL BOARD JOURNAL

Subscription Data:
Published by the National School Boards Association, 800 State National Bank Plaza, Evanston, Illinois 60201. Issued monthly. Advertising is accepted. Circulation: 50,000. Subscription: $12.00 per year. Founded: 1891.

Editorial Address:
The Editor, American School Board Journal, 800 State National Bank Plaza, Evanston, Illinois 60201.

Editorial Policy:
Includes articles on the philosophy of public education; politics of public education; articles on policy making and administrative techniques for operating public schools. The reading audience includes members of public elementary and secondary boards of education, professional administrators and business executives of schools, school architects and principals, and professors of education. Unsolicited manuscripts are welcome. Ten to twelve major articles are published per issue. Book reviews are included.

Manuscript Preparation:
Accepted manuscripts should not exceed 1,200 words. One copy is required. Return postage and a self-addressed envelope are preferred. Bibliographical procedure should generally follow the University of Chicago Manual of Style. No preference is given to special manuscript footnoting and manuscript margin and spacing recommendations as long as it is clear what is meant and is readable. A background or explanatory cover letter and an outline, summary, or abstract of the article are helpful. Brief

biographical information about the author is required. Illustrations, pictures, graphs, etc., are acceptable. Payment for accepted manuscripts is made on commission. Reprints are available.

Manuscript Disposition:
Receipt of a manuscript is acknowledged. Editorial decisions are made within eight weeks. Accepted articles usually appear in print within 10 to 12 months. Unaccepted manuscripts are returned, often with criticism and/or suggestions.

Copyright:
Held by the National School Boards Association.

COLLEGE MANAGEMENT

Subscription Data:
Published by Macmillan Professional Magazines, Inc., One Fawcett Place, Greenwich, Connecticut 06830. Issued monthly, except bimonthly June-July, August-September, and November-December. Advertising is accepted. Circulation: 26,000. Subscription: $11.25 per year; $18.75 foreign. Founded: 1965.

Editorial Address:
The Editor, College Management, Macmillan Professional Magazines, Inc., One Fawcett Place, Greenwich, Connecticut 06830.

Editorial Policy:
Includes articles which summarize topics of interest to college administrators. Most articles are case histories presented in a practical way. The reading audience includes top college executive officers including deans and registrars, business and operational managers, and off-campus specialists such as educational architects, consultants, and foundation and governmental officials. Unsolicited articles are welcome. Five to ten major articles are published per issue. Book reviews are not included.

Manuscript Preparation:
No limitations are placed upon manuscript length. One copy is required. Return postage and a self-addressed envelope are unnecessary. Use one inch margins and double-space. Use footnotes only when absolutely necessary and list them in chronological order at the end of the article. A background or explanatory cover letter about the article is desired. No summary or outline of the article is required, but outlines submitted in advance will be evaluated by the editor. Biographical information about the author is desired and should include a summary of his written works and professional experience. Illustrations, pictures, and graphs are designed to highlight articles. Payment is made for accepted articles with rates dependent upon length, subject, and amount of time the editors must spend reworking the manuscript. Reprints are available with costs varying with article length.

Manuscript Disposition:
Editorial decisions are made within 30 days. Time from acceptance of a manuscript to its appearance in print varies with subject and number of articles set for publication. Unaccepted

manuscripts are returned, occasionally with suggested changes
or criticism.
Copyright:
Held by Macmillan Professional Magazines, Inc.
Additional Information:
The editor is interested in current practice and innovation.
Case histories are acceptable, but strictly theoretical work is
usually rejected.

EDUCATIONAL ADMINISTRATION QUARTERLY

Subscription Data:
Published by the University Council for Educational Administra-
tion, 29 West Woodruff Avenue, Columbus, Ohio 43210. Issued
three times each year, in January, April, and October. Adver-
tising is not accepted. Circulation: 2,000. Subscription:
$7.50 per year, with reduced rates for full-time students.
Founded: 1965.
Editorial Address:
Donald Carver, Editor, Educational Administration Quarterly,
Graduate School of Education, University of Illinois, Urbana,
Illinois 61801.
Editorial Policy:
Includes articles on topics and problems of both a speculative
and an empirical nature which are directly related to educational
administration. The primary purpose of the Quarterly is to pro-
vide a forum for discourse and dialogue, including constructive
controversy, among students of educational administration. The
reading audience includes research-oriented school administrators, graduate students, professors of educational administration,
and other behavioral scientists. Unsolicited articles are welcome. Seven or eight major articles are published per issue.
Solicited book reviews are included.
Manuscript Preparation:
Accepted manuscripts average from 15 to 20 double-spaced typewritten pages. Three copies are required. Return postage and
self-addressed envelope are unnecessary. Bibliographical procedure should follow the Turabian Manual for Writers. Use
1-1/2 inch margins and double-space throughout. All footnotes
should be listed at the end of the manuscript. A brief background or explanatory cover letter about the article is desired,
but not an outline or summary. Biographical information about
the author is desired and should include present position and
title. Graphs and charts may be used. No payment is made
for accepted articles. Twenty-five free reprints are mailed to
each author. A reprint cost summary is available through the
office of the publisher.
Manuscript Disposition:
Receipt of a manuscript is acknowledged. Editorial decisions
are usually made within two months. Accepted articles usually
appear in print from three to six months after acceptance. Unaccepted manuscripts are returned with criticism or suggestions.

Copyright:
Held by the University Council for Educational Administration.
Additional Information:
A detailed document entitled "Information for Contributors" is available through the office of the editor.

EDUCATIONAL LEADERSHIP

Subscription Data:
Published by the Association for Supervision and Curriculum Development, 1201 Sixteenth Street, N. W., Washington, D. C. 20036. Issued eight times each year, October through May. Advertising is accepted. Circulation: 18, 837. Subscription: $8.00 per year. Founded: 1943.
Editorial Address:
The Editor, Educational Leadership, 1201 Sixteenth Street, N. W., Washington, D. C. 20036.
Editorial Policy:
Articles in each issue are usually organized around a theme based upon the expressed interests and concerns of the membership. Feature articles by leading educators, news of curriculum developments, reviews of significant books and booklets, and reports of curriculum research are included. The reading audience includes teachers, supervisors, curriculum workers, administrators, college and university professors, librarians, instructional materials specialists, directors of curriculum projects and research labs, etc. Unsolicited articles are welcome. Five to ten major theme articles are published per issue. Book and booklet reviews are included.
Manuscript Preparation:
Accepted manuscripts average 1,400 to 1,500 words. Two copies are required. Return postage and a self-addressed envelope are required. Complete and accurate bibliographical information is necessary. Use wide margins and double-space throughout. A background or explanatory cover letter about the article is not desired nor is an outline or summary. Biographical information about the author is unnecessary. Photographs and illustrations are welcome. No payment is made for accepted articles. Reprints are not available through ASCD, but may be obtained from University Microfilms, Ann Arbor, Michigan 48106.
Manuscript Disposition:
Receipt of a manuscript is acknowledged. Editorial decisions are made rather promptly. Time from acceptance of a manuscript to its appearance in print varies depending upon the topic being treated in a particular issue and space available. Unaccepted manuscripts are returned without critical comment.
Copyright:
Held by the Association for Supervision and Curriculum Development.

MODERN SCHOOLS

Subscription Data:
Published by Electrical Information Publications, Inc., 2132 Fordem Avenue, Madison, Wisconsin 53701. Issued nine times each year, September through May. Advertising is accepted. Circulation: 30,000. Subscription: $2.50 per year. Founded: 1955.

Editorial Address:
Ellen J. Hoelster, Editor, Modern Schools, Electrical Information Publications, Inc., 2132 Fordem Avenue, Madison, Wisconsin 53701.

Editorial Policy:
Includes articles related to electric comfort, conditioning, lighting, unusual construction, and school lunch programs. The reading audience includes school administrators, utility executives, teachers, and educators. Unsolicited articles are welcome. Three or four major articles are published per issue. Book reviews are not included.

Manuscript Preparation:
Accepted manuscripts average 2,000 words. One copy is required. Return postage and a self-addressed envelope are required. Bibliographical procedure should follow any standard form of style. Use wide margins and double-space. A background or explanatory cover letter and an outline or summary of the article are required. Biographical information about the author is required. Use black and white glossies only; graphs are acceptable. No payment is made for accepted articles. Reprints are available; author must pay for reprints.

Manuscript Disposition:
Receipt of a manuscript is acknowledged. Editorial decisions are made within three weeks. Time from acceptance of a manuscript to its appearance in print varies according to edit calendar. Unaccepted manuscripts are returned if author encloses a stamped self-addressed envelope. Criticism or suggestions are not provided.

Copyright:
Held by Electrical Information Publications, Inc.

NATIONAL ASSOCIATION OF SECONDARY SCHOOL PRINCIPALS. BULLETIN

Subscription Data:
Published by the National Association of Secondary School Principals, 1904 Association Drive, Reston, Virginia 22091. Issued monthly, September through May. Advertising is accepted. Circulation: 30,000. Subscription: Available only as part of annual $30.00 membership to the Association; $2.00 per single copy. Founded: 1917.

Editorial Address:
    The Editor, Bulletin of the National Association of Secondary School Principals, 1904 Association Drive, Reston, Virginia 22091.

Editorial Policy:
    Includes articles which relate to all aspects of secondary education. The reading audience includes junior and senior high school principals and other school administrators. Unsolicited manuscripts are welcome. Eight to twelve major articles are published per issue. Book reviews are included.

Manuscript Preparation:
    Accepted manuscripts average from 2,500 to 4,000 words. The original and one clear copy are required. Return postage and a self-addressed envelope are required. Bibliographical procedure should contain for book--author's name, name of book; city, state, and name of publisher; year date; chapter title and page reference (if needed); for publication--author's name, title of article, name of publication, date, and page reference. Footnotes should appear at the bottom of each page. Use one inch margins and double-space. A background or explanatory cover letter is not required nor is an outline, summary, or abstract. Biographical information about the author is required. Illustrations may be used only if they are necessary to clarify the text. No payment is made for accepted manuscripts. Reprints are available at cost and each author receives two free copies of the Bulletin.

Manuscript Disposition:
    Receipt of a manuscript is acknowledged. Each issue is based upon a central theme. Because articles are not selected until three months prior to publication, editorial decision time and time of appearance of an article in print varies greatly. Unaccepted manuscripts are returned, often without criticism or suggestions.

Copyright:
    Held by the National Association of Secondary School Principals.

Additional Information:
    The NASSP does not endorse, except by official action of the Executive Committee, any individual, group, organization, opinion, idea, proposal, or judgment published in the Bulletin.

NATIONAL ELEMENTARY PRINCIPAL

Subscription Data:
    Published by the National Association of Elementary School Principals, 1801 North Moore Street, Arlington, Virginia 22209. Issued six times each year, in September, October, November, January, February, and April. Advertising is accepted. Circulation: 30,000. Subscription: $20.00 per year included as part of membership dues; $2.00 per issue. Founded: 1921.

Editorial Address:
    The Editor, National Elementary Principal, National Association of Elementary School Principals, 1801 North Moore Street, Arlington, Virginia 22209.

Editorial Policy:
   Includes articles on all phases of early childhood, elementary,
   and middle school education; school administration; and social
   issues affecting education. The reading audience includes elementary and middle school principals, supervisors, superintendents, and professors of education and educational administration.
   Unsolicited manuscripts are welcome. Eight to fifteen major
   articles are published per issue. Book reviews are included.
Manuscript Preparation:
   Accepted manuscripts average from 2,000 to 3,500 words. The
   original and two carbon copies are required. Return postage
   and a self-addressed envelope are desired. Any widely used
   footnoting procedure is acceptable, but complete information is
   required. Manuscripts should be double-spaced and have 40
   characters per line. Type footnotes separately at the end of the
   article. A background or explanatory cover letter is not required, but may be supplied at author's discretion. An outline,
   summary, or abstract of the article is not required. Biographical information about the author is required and should include
   full title and place of employment. Illustrations, pictures, and
   graphs may be used. No payment is made for accepted manuscripts. Reprints are available at cost, with price dependent
   upon article length.
Manuscript Disposition:
   Receipt of a manuscript is acknowledged. Editorial decisions
   are made within approximately six weeks. Accepted articles
   usually appear in print within two to twelve months. Unaccepted
   manuscripts are returned, without criticism or suggestions.
Copyright:
   Held by the National Association of Elementary School Principals.

NATION'S SCHOOLS

Subscription Data:
   Published by McGraw-Hill, Inc., 230 West Monroe Street, Chi-
   cago, Illinois 60606. Issued monthly. Advertising is accepted.
   Circulation: 30,000. Subscription: $25.00 per year; $2.50
   per issue. Founded: 1928.
Editorial Address:
   The Editor, Nation's Schools, 230 West Monroe Street, Chicago,
   Illinois 60606.
Editorial Policy:
   Includes articles on all phases of school administration. The
   reading audience includes school superintendents and their as-
   sistants, school business officials, high school principals, and
   school architects. Unsolicited articles are welcome. Ten to
   eighteen major articles are published per issue. Book reviews
   are included.
Manuscript Preparation:
   Accepted manuscripts average 1,200 words. One copy is required. Return postage and self-addressed envelope are unnecessary. Use wide margins and double-space. Avoid use of
   footnotes when possible. A background or explanatory cover

letter about the article is not desired nor is an outline or summary. Biographical information about the author is required.
Illustrations, pictures, and graphs may be used. Payment is
made only for commissioned articles. Reprint costs vary with
order volume.

Manuscript Disposition:
Editorial decisions are made within two to four weeks. Accepted articles appear in print from one to eighteen months after
acceptance. Unaccepted manuscripts are returned with criticism
or suggestions.

Copyright:
Held by McGraw-Hill, Inc.

OASCD CURRICULUM BULLETIN (formerly Curriculum Bulletin)

Subscription Data:
Published by the Oregon Association for Supervision and Curriculum Development, Box 421, Salem, Oregon 97308. Issued
bimonthly, in January, March, May, July, September, and November. Advertising is not accepted. Circulation: 1,000.
Subscription: $5.00 per year. Founded: 1939.

Editorial Address:
The Editor, OASCD Curriculum Bulletin, Box 421, Salem, Oregon 97308.

Editorial Policy:
Includes research-based articles which relate to curriculum,
grades K through 12 and community college, plus related topics.
The reading audience includes administrators, supervisors, and
teachers. Unsolicited articles are welcome. One major article
is published per issue. Book reviews are not included.

Manuscript Preparation:
Accepted manuscripts average from 10,000 to 25,000 words.
One copy is required. Return postage and a self-addressed
envelope are unnecessary. Use standard margins and double-
space. Bibliographical procedure should follow the Education
Index style or any other standard guide. Place footnotes at the
end of the article. A background or explanatory cover letter,
an outline or summary of the article, and biographical information about the author are desired. All illustrations must be
prepared in black and white. No payment is made for accepted
articles. Five free reprints are mailed to authors; additional
copies may be obtained at cost if ordered in advance.

Manuscript Disposition:
Receipt of a manuscript is acknowledged. Editorial decisions
are made within four to eight weeks. Accepted articles usually appear in print from two to three months after acceptance. Unaccepted manuscripts are returned with minimum comment.

Copyright:
Not copyrighted.

*SCHOOL ADMINISTRATOR

Subscription Data:
   Published by the American Association of School Administrators,
   1801 North Moore Street, Arlington, Virginia 22209. Issued
   every four weeks, 13 per year. Advertising is not accepted.
   Circulation: 20, 000. Subscription: Free with membership in
   the American Association of School Administrators. Founded:
   1943.
Editorial Address:
   The Editor, School Administrator, American Association of
   School Administrators, 1801 North Moore Street, Arlington, Vir-
   ginia 22209.
Editorial Policy:
   Includes reports and news items of interest to school administra-
   tors. The reading audience includes school administrators at
   all levels. Unsolicited articles cannot be used. One major
   article is published per issue. Book reviews are included.
Manuscript Preparation:
   Length of accepted manuscript is stated when invitation is ex-
   tended. Permission for reprint is granted if credit is given to
   School Administrator.
Copyright:
   Held by the American Association of School Administrators.

SCHOOL BUSINESS AFFAIRS

Subscription Data:
   Published by the Association of School Business Officials of the
   United States and Canada, 2424 West Lawrence Avenue, Chicago,
   Illinois 60625. Issued monthly. Advertising is accepted. Cir-
   culation: 5, 000. Subscription: $9. 00 per year to Association
   members; $30. 00 per year to non-members. Founded: 1935.
Editorial Address:
   Dwight B. Esau, Managing Editor, School Business Affairs, As-
   sociation of School Business Officials of the United States and
   Canada, 2424 West Lawrence Avenue, Chicago, Illinois 60625.
Editorial Policy:
   Includes articles on all phases of school business, including research. The reading audience includes school business officials
   and their associates. Unsolicited articles are welcome. From
   three to ten major articles are published per issue. Book reviews are occasionally included.
Manuscript Preparation:
   Accepted manuscripts average from two to seven double-spaced
   typewritten pages. Two copies are required. Return postage
   and a self-addressed envelope are not required. Footnoting
   and other bibliographical procedure should follow the University
   of Chicago Manual of Style. Use 1-1/2 inch margins and double-
   space throughout. A background or explanatory cover letter

about the article is desired. An outline or summary of the article is desired in advance of or with submission of the finished manuscript. Biographical information about the author is required. Use of illustrations, pictures, graphs, etc., is encouraged. No payment is made for accepted articles. Reprints are available, and additional copies of the journal may be purchased.

Manuscript Disposition:
Receipt of a manuscript is acknowledged. Editorial decisions are made immediately. Time from acceptance of a manuscript to its appearance in print varies. Unaccepted manuscripts are returned with a rejection note.

Copyright:
Not copyrighted.

SCHOOL MANAGEMENT

Subscription Data:
Published by Macmillan Professional Magazines, Inc., One Fawcett Place, Greenwich, Connecticut 06830. Issued monthly, except bimonthly June-July, August-September, and November-December. Advertising is accepted. Circulation: 45,000. Subscription: $11.25 per year; $18.75 for two years; $18.75 foreign. Founded: 1957.

Editorial Address:
The Editor, School Management, One Fawcett Place, Greenwich, Connecticut 06830.

Editorial Policy:
Includes articles on topics of interest to public school administrators, with special emphasis placed on case histories presented in a practical way. The reading audience includes elementary and secondary school administrators, school architects and consultants, educational association administrators, school supply dealers and manufacturers, and government administrators of educational agencies. Unsolicited articles are welcome. Five to nine major articles are published per issue. Book reviews are not included.

Manuscript Preparation:
No limitation is placed upon manuscript length. One copy is required. Return postage and a self-addressed envelope are unnecessary. Use one inch margins and double-space. Use footnotes only when absolutely necessary, then place them in chronological order at the end of the article. A background or explanatory cover letter about the article is desired. No summary or outline is required, but outlines submitted in advance of articles will be evaluated by the editor. Biographical information about the author is required and should include a summary of his or her written works and related experience. Illustrations, pictures, and graphs may be used. Payment is made for accepted articles at rates which vary with length, subject, and amount of time the editors must devote to editing the manuscript. Reprint costs are determined by article length; two free copies are mailed to the author.

Manuscript Disposition:
   Editorial decisions are made within 30 days. Time from accept-
   ance of a manuscript to its appearance in print varies with the
   subject and number of articles set for publication. Unaccepted
   manuscripts are returned, occasionally with suggestions or criti-
   cism.
Copyright:
   Held by Macmillan Professional Magazines, Inc.
Additional Information:
   The editor is interested in happenings and in research findings.
   Case histories are acceptable, but strictly theoretical work will
   be rejected.

*TRENDS

Subscription Data:
   Published by the National School Public Relations Association,
   1801 North Moore Street, Arlington, Virginia 22209. Issued
   monthly, September through July. Advertising is not accepted.
   Circulation: 3,200. Subscription: $8.00 per year; Free with
   Association membership. Founded: 1946.
Editorial Address:
   The Editor, Trends, National School Public Relations Association,
   1801 North Moore Street, Arlington, Virginia 22209.
Editorial Policy:
   Includes articles which deal with all phases of school public relations. The reading audience includes school public relations
   directors and school administrators. Unsolicited articles cannot
   be used, but news reports which relate to public relations in
   schools are often accepted for publication. The number of articles published per issue varies widely. Book reviews are included.
Copyright:
   Held by the National School Public Relations Association.

ADULT EDUCATION

*ADMINISTRATOR'S SWAP SHOP (formerly Swap Shop)

Subscription Data:
> Published by the National Association for Public Continuing and
> Adult Education, 1201 Sixteenth Street, N. W., Washington, D. C.
> 20036. Issued six times each year, in October, November,
> December, February, March, and April. Advertising is not ac-
> cepted. Subscription: $5.00 per year. Founded: 1960.

Editorial Address:
> David A. Puddington, Editor, Administrator's Swap Shop, Na-
> tional Association for Public Continuing and Adult Education,
> 1201 Sixteenth Street, N. W., Washington, D. C. 20036.

Editorial Policy:
> Includes articles on basic education, the dropout, crimes around
> the country, etc. The reading audience includes administrators
> of adult education programs. Unsolicited articles can occasional-
> ly be used. One article is published per issue. Book reviews
> are not included.

Copyright:
> Held by the National Association for Public Continuing and Adult
> Education.

ADULT EDUCATION

Subscription Data:
> Published by the Adult Education Association of the United States
> of America, 810 Eighteenth Street, N. W., Washington, D. C.
> 20006. Issued quarterly, in November, February, May, and
> August. Advertising is accepted. Circulation: 4,500. Sub-
> scription: $11.00 per year; $3.00 per issue. Founded: 1950.

Editorial Address:
> Dr. Dwight D. Rhyne, Editor, Adult Education, University of
> North Carolina, Chapel Hill, North Carolina 27514.

Editorial Policy:
> Includes scholarly reports and articles regarding adult education
> agencies, students, personnel, finance, and programs. The
> reading audience includes both scholars and practitioners in adult
> education. Unsolicited articles are welcome. Four to six major
> articles are published per issue. Book reviews are included.

Manuscript Preparation:
> Accepted manuscripts average from 1,000 to 3,500 words. One
> copy is required. Return postage and a self-addressed envelope
> are not required. Bibliographical procedure should follow the
> Turabian Manual for Writers. Use wide margins and double-

space. A background or explanatory cover letter about the article is desired, but not an outline or summary. Biographical data about the author is unnecessary. Graphs, pictures, and illustrations may be used only when they are necessary to clarify points made in the article. No payment is made for accepted articles. Reprints are available at cost if ordered in advance of publication.

Manuscript Disposition:
Receipt of a manuscript is acknowledged. Editorial decisions are made within six weeks. Accepted articles usually appear in print from one to twelve months after acceptance. Unaccepted manuscripts are returned without criticism or suggestions.

Copyright:
Held by the Adult Education Association of the United States of America.

ADULT JEWISH EDUCATION

Subscription Data:
Published by the National Academy of Adult Jewish Studies of the United Synagogue of America, 218 East Seventieth Street, New York 10021. Issued intermittently. Selected advertising is accepted. Circulation: 2,000. Subscription: $1.50 per four issues; $.50 per issue. Founded: 1953.

Editorial Address:
The Editor, Adult Jewish Education, 218 East Seventieth Street, New York, New York 10021.

Editorial Policy:
Includes articles which deal with ideas, practice, and projects in the field of adult Jewish education. The reading audience includes Rabbis, adult educators, members of congregations, adult education committee-members, and others interested in the field of adult Jewish education. Unsolicited articles are welcome. Three major articles are published per issue. Book reviews are included by invitation only. No abstracts are published.

Manuscript Preparation:
Accepted manuscripts range from 1,800 to 5,000 words. Two copies are required. Return postage and a self-addressed envelope are desired. Bibliographical procedure should follow the U.S. Government Printing Office Style Manual or Words Into Type. Use wide margins and double-space. A background or explanatory cover letter about the article is desired, but not an outline or summary. Biographical information about the author is desired and should include a summary of his present position. Illustrations, pictures, and graphs are not often used. No payment is made for accepted articles. Authors receive 10 free copies of each issue which contains their work. Limited numbers of additional copies are also available.

Manuscript Disposition:
Receipt of a manuscript is acknowledged within one week. Editorial decisions are made within one month. Time from acceptance of a manuscript to its appearance in print varies with the

number of accepted articles being held for publication. Unaccepted manuscripts are returned, occasionally with criticism and/or suggestions.

Copyright:

Held by the National Academy for Adult Jewish Studies.

Additional Information:

Opinions and views expressed in this journal are those of the individual authors and do not necessarily represent those of the National Academy for Adult Jewish Studies or the United Synagogue of America.

ADULT LEADERSHIP

Subscription Data:

Published by the Adult Education Association of the USA, 810 Eighteenth Street, N. W., Washington, D. C. 20006. Issued monthly, September through June. Advertising is accepted. Circulation: 7,500. Subscription: $13.00 per year. Founded: 1950.

Editorial Address:

Dr. Nicholas P. Mitchell, Editor-in-Chief, Adult Leadership, Division of Educational Services, University of South Carolina, Columbia, South Carolina 29208.

Editorial Policy:

Adult Leadership prefers general "how to do it" articles in all fields of adult education, but also carries historical and other material. The reading audience includes adult educators in all fields, formal and informal. Unsolicited manuscripts are welcome. Eight to ten major articles are published per issue. Book reviews are included.

Manuscript Preparation:

Accepted manuscripts average from 1,000 to 4,000 words. Two copies are required. Return postage and a self-addressed envelope are preferred, but are not required. MLA Style Sheet is preferred. Double-space manuscript and omit the use of footnotes when possible. A background or explanatory cover letter and an outline, summary, or abstract are helpful, but not required. Biographical information about the author includes only a short blurb. Illustrations, pictures, graphs, etc., are used occasionally, but are usually avoided because of limited budget. No payment is made for accepted manuscripts. The journal provides reprints on order at slightly over their cost.

Manuscript Disposition:

Receipt of a manuscript is acknowledged. Editorial decisions are made within two months. Accepted articles usually appear in print within one to twelve months. Unaccepted manuscripts are returned, usually without criticism and/or suggestions.

Copyright:

Held by the Adult Education Association of the USA.

CONTINUING EDUCATION

Subscription Data:
  Published by the Pennsylvania Research Associates, Inc., 1428
  Ford Road, Cornwells Heights, Pennsylvania 19020.   Issued
  quarterly, in January, April, July, and October.   Advertising
  is accepted.   Circulation: 1, 200.   Subscription: $35.00 per
  year; $62.00 for two years; $85.00 for three years.   Founded:
  1968.
Editorial Address:
  The Editor, Continuing Education, Pennsylvania Research Associates Inc., 1428 Ford Road, Cornwells Heights, Pennsylvania
  19020.
Editorial Policy:
  Includes articles in all areas of adult education: business and
  technical training, continuing education in the professions, planning, and participation in conferences, and short courses.   The
  reading audience includes administrators, personnel managers,
  inservice training directors, and librarians.   Unsolicited manuscripts are welcome.   One to three major articles are published
  per issue.   Book reviews are occasionally included.
Manuscript Preparation:
  Accepted manuscripts average 1, 000 to 5, 000 words.   One copy
  is required.   Return postage and a self-addressed envelope are
  not required.   List footnotes on a separate page and double-
  space manuscript.   A background or explanatory cover letter is
  not required nor is an outline, summary, or abstract.   A photograph and biography is required if the manuscript is accepted.
  Illustrations, pictures, graphs, etc., are acceptable and include
  line-drawings or glossy photographs.   No payment is made for
  accepted manuscripts.   Reprints are provided to authors on request at cost.
Manuscript Disposition:
  Receipt of a manuscript is acknowledged.   Editorial decisions
  are made within four weeks.   Accepted articles usually appear
  in print within three to six months.   Unaccepted manuscripts
  are returned, sometimes with criticism and/or suggestions.
Copyright:
  Held by the Pennsylvania Research Associates, Inc.

JOURNAL OF EXTENSION

Subscription Data:
  Published by the American Printing and Publishing, 2909 Syene
  Road, Madison, Wisconsin 53701.   Issued quarterly, in March,
  June, September, and December.   Advertising is not accepted.
  Circulation: 6, 100.   Subscription: $7.00 per year to the
  United States and Canada; $13.00 for two years; $18.00 for
  three years; $8.00 foreign; $16.00 for two years; $24.00 for
  three years.   Founded: 1963.

Editorial Address:
 Pat Borich, Editor, Journal of Extension, Editorial Office, 260
 Coffey Hall, University of Minnesota, St. Paul, Minnesota 55101.
Editorial Policy:
 Includes articles based on research, articles based on creative
 thought, and case studies in which an experience is looked at in
 reference to theory. The reading audience includes extension
 and adult educators. Unsolicited manuscripts are welcome. Approximately four major articles are published per issue. Book
 reviews are included.
Manuscript Preparation:
 Accepted manuscripts average eight to twelve double-spaced,
 typewritten pages. Four copies are required. Return postage
 and a self-addressed envelope are not required. Bibliographical
 procedure should follow the University of Chicago Manual of
 Style. Type all footnotes on a separate page at the end of the
 manuscript. Use normal manuscript margins and spacing. A
 background or explanatory cover letter is not required, but an
 outline, summary, or abstract is required. Biographical information about the author is required. Illustrations, pictures, graphs,
 etc., should include a camera-ready copy. No payment is made
 for accepted manuscripts.
Manuscript Disposition:
 Receipt of a manuscript is not acknowledged. Editorial decisions are made within six to eight weeks. Accepted articles
 usually appear in print within four to six months. Unaccepted
 manuscripts are not returned. Criticism and/or suggestions
 are provided for manuscripts that are to be resubmitted.
Copyright:
 Held by the Extension Journal, Inc.

NUEA SPECTATOR

Subscription Data:
 Published by the National University Extension Association, One
 Dupont Circle, Suite 360, Washington, D.C. 20036. Issued
 quarterly. Advertising is accepted. Circulation: 3,500. Subscription: $7.50 per year; $5.00 to libraries and member institutions. Founded: 1925.
Editorial Address:
 The Editor, NUEA Spectator, Division of Extension, University
 of Missouri, 5100 Rockhill Road, Kansas City, Missouri 64110.
Editorial Policy:
 Includes scholarly articles and reports of university extension
 programs. The reading audience includes adult educators in extension and continuing education. Unsolicited articles are welcome. Six major articles are published per issue. Book reviews are not included.
Manuscript Preparation:
 Accepted manuscripts average five to six double-spaced typewritten pages. Two copies are required. Return postage and
 a self-addressed envelope are desired. Use wide margins and

double-space. A background or explanatory cover letter about
the article is desired, but not an outline or summary. Biographical information about the author is desired and should include a summary of formal education and professional experience.
Photographs considered for publication with reports or articles
are returned upon request. No payment is made for accepted
articles. Reprints are not available.

Manuscript Disposition:
Receipt of a manuscript is acknowledged. Editorial decisions
are made as soon as possible. Accepted articles usually appear
in print within one year after acceptance. Unaccepted manuscripts are returned, sometimes with suggestions.

Copyright:
Held by the National University Extension Association.

TECHNIQUES FOR TEACHERS OF ADULTS

Subscription Data:
Published by the National Association for Public Continuing and
Adult Education, 1201 Sixteenth Street, N. W. , Washington, D. C.
20036. Issued eight times each year. Advertising is not accepted. Circulation: 6, 000. Subscription: $5. 00 per year;
$.40 per issue. Founded: 1960.

Editorial Address:
The Editor, Techniques For Teachers of Adults, Suite 429, 1202
Sixteenth Street, N. W. , Washington, D. C. 20036.

Editorial Policy:
Includes articles and reports of practical ideas for the teaching
of adult student, especially tried and proven methods. The
reading audience includes teachers of adults and administrators
of adult education programs. Unsolicited manuscripts are welcome. The number of major articles published per issue varies.
Book reviews are not included.

Manuscript Preparation:
No limitations are placed upon manuscript length. One copy is
required. Return postage and a self-addressed envelope are desired. Use one inch margins and double-space. A background
or explanatory cover letter about the article is required. Biographical information about the author is desired and should include his full name, position, and the name of his school. Illustrations are not often used. No payment is made for accepted
articles. Each author may request free copies of the issue in
which his article appears.

Manuscript Preparation:
Receipt of a manuscript is acknowledged. Editorial decisions
are made as soon as possible. Accepted manuscripts usually
appear in print within six months after acceptance. Unaccepted
manuscripts are returned, often with criticism.

Copyright:
Not copyrighted.

ANTHROPOLOGY AND ARCHAEOLOGY

AMERICAN ANTHROPOLOGIST

Subscription Data:
Published by the American Anthropological Association, 1703 New Hampshire Avenue, N. W. , Washington, D. C. 20009. Issued four times each year. Advertising is accepted. Circulation: 11, 000. Subscription: $21. 00 per year to Association members; $30. 00 to institutions; $16. 00 to students. Founded: 1889.

Editorial Address:
Robert A. Manners, Editor, American Anthropologist, Department of Anthropology, Brandeis University, Waltham, Maryland 02154.

Editorial Policy:
Includes a quarterly journal devoted to cross-field and theoretical articles, review articles, book and audiovisual reviews, obituaries, and discussion and debate items. The reading audience includes a general anthropological audience. Unsolicited articles are welcome. Book reviews are included.

Manuscript Preparation:
Accepted manuscripts average 10 to 30 double-spaced typewritten pages on noncorrasable bond paper. One original plus two copies are required. Return postage and a self-addressed envelope are not required. See a recent issue for bibliographical procedure and footnoting recommendations. Use one inch margins on the left and right. A background or explanatory cover letter is not required; however, an outline, summary, or abstract of the article is required. The abstract should contain 50 to 75 words. Biographical information about the author is not required. Illustrations, pictures, graphs, etc. , must be submitted suitable for publication without redrawing. No payment is made for accepted manuscripts. Reprints are available only to authors and must be on order prior to publication.

Manuscript Disposition:
Receipt of a manuscript is acknowledged. Editorial decisions are usually made within six weeks. Accepted articles usually appear in print within six to twelve months after acceptance. Unaccepted manuscripts are returned with criticism and suggestions.

Copyright:
Held by the American Anthropological Association.

AMERICAN ANTIQUITY

Subscription Data:
Published by the Society for American Archaeology, 1703 New
Hampshire Avenue, Washington, D. C. 20009. Issued quarterly,
in January, April, July, and October. Advertising is accepted.
Circulation: 4, 000. Subscription: $15.00 per year; $20.00
to institutions. Founded: 1935.

Editorial Address:
Frank Hole, Editor, American Antiquity, Department of Anthropology, Rice University, Houston, Texas 77001.

Editorial Policy:
Includes original articles on the archaeology of the new world
and closely related subjects. The reading audience includes
professionals and students of archaeology, anthropology, and related disciplines. Unsolicited articles are welcome. Three to
five major articles and some reports, reviews, current research,
and comments are published per issue. Book reviews are included.

Manuscript Preparation:
Accepted manuscripts may not exceed 20 double-spaced typewritten pages. One original and two copies are required. Return postage and a self-addressed envelope are desired. Bibliographical procedure and style should follow "Notice to Authors"
on each issue's inside front cover. Double-space only on one
side of the sheet. A background or explanatory cover letter
about the article is unnecessary. A short abstract, which is
published with the article, is required with the manuscript. Biographical information about the author is not required. Camera-
ready illustrations, pictures, graphs, etc., may be used. No
payment is made for accepted articles. Reprints are available
at cost.

Manuscript Disposition:
Receipt of a manuscript is acknowledged. Editorial decisions
are made within four to six weeks. Accepted articles usually
appear in print from three to six months after acceptance. Unaccepted manuscripts are returned with criticism and/or suggestions.

Copyright:
Held by the Society for American Archaeology.

ARCHAEOLOGY

Subscription Data:
Published by the Archaeological Institute of America, 260 West
Broadway, New York, New York 10013. Issued quarterly, in
January, April, July, and October. Advertising is accepted.
Circulation: 14, 000. Subscription: $8.50 per year; $15.00
for two years; $22.00 for three years. Founded: 1948.

Editorial Address:
  The Editor, Archaelogy, 260 West Broadway, New York, New York 10013.
Editorial Policy:
  Includes articles and reports on archaeology and related disciplines. The reading audience includes interested laymen, students, and professional archaeologists. Unsolicited manuscripts are welcome. Seven or eight major articles are published per issue. Book reviews are included.
Manuscript Preparation:
  Accepted manuscripts average six to ten double-spaced typewritten pages. One copy is required. Return postage and a self-addressed envelope are unnecessary. Bibliographical procedure should follow any widely used style manual. Avoid the use of footnotes wherever possible. Use wide margins and double-space throughout. A background or explanatory cover letter is desired, but not an outline, summary, or abstract. Biographical information about the author is required and should include a summary of his formal education and professional background. Use of illustrations and pictures are encouraged. Payment of $6.00 per printed page is made for accepted manuscripts. One-hundred free copies are mailed to the author; cost of additional reprints varies with article length and order volume.
Manuscript Disposition:
  Receipt of a manuscript is acknowledged. Editorial decisions are made as soon as possible. Accepted articles usually appear in print within six to twelve months. Unaccepted manuscripts are returned, sometimes with criticism and/or suggestions.
Copyright:
  Held by the Archaeological Institute of America.
Additional Information:
  The article must be written so that it is understood by untrained laymen and students who are not familiar with technical terminology of archaeology. The editorial staff often does extensive rewriting, subject to the author's approval.

CURRENT ANTHROPOLOGY

Subscription Data:
  Published by the University of Chicago Press, 5801 South Ellis Avenue, Chicago, Illinois 60637. Sponsored by the Wenner-Gren Foundation for Anthropological Research. Issued quarterly, in March, June, September, and December. Advertising is accepted. Circulation: 7,047. Subscription: $21.00 per year; $7.00 special rate including associates. Founded: 1957.
Editorial Address:
  Sol Tax, Editor, Current Anthropology, 1126 East Fifty-ninth Street, Chicago, Illinois 60637.
Editorial Policy:
  Includes review articles and research reports as inclusive, international, and interdisciplinary as the sciences of man as these are defined by the changing community of associates. The

reading audience includes anthropologists and professionals of related disciplines. Unsolicited manuscripts are welcome. Approximately four major articles are published per issue. Book reviews are included.

Manuscript Preparation:

One copy is required. Return postage and a self-addressed envelope are not required. Bibliographical procedure should follow the University of Chicago Manual of Style or a style sheet that is available from the editor upon request. Footnotes, numbered in sequence throughout the paper, should be listed together at the end of the article. Acknowledgments, if any, should be the first footnotes with the identifying number attached to the title of the paper. Use standard margins and double-space. A background or explanatory cover letter is required, and an abstract of less than 200 words is required. Biographical information about the author is not required. Tables and figures should be numbered with Arabic numerals, provided with captions, cited in the text, and grouped following the references and footnotes. Photographs should have a glossy finish and high contrast; where it is relevant, the scale should be indicated in the photograph itself or in the caption. Drawings should be in India ink on white paper; if they are not of high enough quality for printing, the author will be asked to improve them or (at his option) to bear the cost of such improvement. No payment is made for accepted manuscripts. Twenty-five free reprints are given to authors of major articles.

Manuscript Disposition:

Receipt of a manuscript is acknowledged. Editorial decisions are made within six weeks. Accepted articles usually appear in print within nine months. Unaccepted manuscripts are returned with substantive comments that may be useful to the author.

Copyright:

Held by the Wenner-Gren Foundation for Anthropological Research.

AMERICAN ARTIST

Subscription Data:
    Published by Billboard Publishing Company, Inc., 1515 Broad-
    way, New York, New York 10036. Issued monthly. Advertising
    is accepted. Circulation: 70,000. Subscription: $12.00 per
    year; $1.25 per issue. Founded: 1937.
Editorial Address:
    The Editor, American Artist, Billboard Publishing Company,
    Inc., 1515 Broadway, New York, New York 10036.
Editorial Policy:
    Includes reports of working methods and techniques used by art-
    ists in all graphic and sculptural media. The reading audience
    includes artists, teachers of art, and art students. Most but
    not all articles and other contributions are written on assign-
    ment by a board of contributing editors and resident staff. Let-
    ters of inquiry concerning proposed articles are invited and
    should be sent to the editor. Authors who submit unsolicited
    manuscripts must have technical background and teaching ex-
    perience in art, and familiarity with the periodical. Six to
    eight major articles are published per issue. Book reviews are
    included.
Manuscript Preparation:
    Manuscripts should average 2,500 words. The original and one
    clear carbon are required. Return postage and a self-addressed
    envelope are desired. An outline or summary should be sub-
    mitted to the editor in advance of the finished manuscript. Use
    wide margins, double-space, and use footnotes sparingly. A
    background or explanatory cover letter about the article is de-
    sired and should include educational and professional biographi-
    cal data about the author, and his picture. Pictures, illustra-
    tions, and graphs may be used. Payment of $75.00 is made
    upon publication of an article. Reprints are not available.
Manuscript Disposition:
    Receipt of a manuscript is acknowledged. Editorial decisions
    are made within one month. Accepted articles usually appear
    in print within three to four months after acceptance. Unac-
    cepted manuscripts are returned.
Copyright:
    Held by Billboard Publications, Inc.

ART EDUCATION

Subscription Data:
    Published by the National Art Education Association, 1201

Sixteenth Street, N. W. , Washington, D. C. 20036. Issued nine
times each year, September through May. Advertising is accepted. Circulation: 10, 000. Subscription: $15. 00 per year.
Founded: 1948.
Editorial Address:
The Editor, Art Education, National Art Education Association,
1201 Sixteenth Street, N. W. , Washington, D. C. 20036.
Editorial Policy:
Includes articles on current trends, problems, philosophies,
and issues in art education, from preprimary through university
levels. The reading audience includes art teachers and supervisors; art education students; university art education professors; museum educators. Unsolicited manuscripts are welcome.
Six major articles are published per issue. Book reviews are
included.
Manuscript Preparation:
Accepted manuscripts average eight to fourteen double-spaced
pages. One copy is required. Return postage and a self-addressed envelope are not required. List footnotes on reference
page at the end of the article. A background or explanatory
cover letter is not required nor is an outline, summary, or abstract. Biographical information about the author is required
and should include one line stating the author's present title and
position, school, city, and state. Black and white glossy photographs may be included, preferably eight by ten inches. No
payment is made for accepted manuscripts.
Manuscript Disposition:
Receipt of a manuscript is acknowledged. Editorial decisions
are made within three months. Accepted articles usually appear
in print within 12 months. Unaccepted manuscripts are returned,
sometimes with criticism and/or suggestions.
Copyright:
Held by the National Art Education Association.

ART JOURNAL (formerly College Art Journal)

Subscription Data:
Published by the College Art Association of America, Inc. , 16
East Fifty-second Street, New York, New York 10022. Issued
quarterly, in spring, summer, fall, and winter. Advertising
is accepted. Circulation: 7, 000. Subscription: Available
through membership in the College Art Association; $5. 00 per
issue for non-members.
Editorial Address:
The Editor, Art Journal, 16 East Fifty-second Street, New
York, New York 10022.
Editorial Policy:
Includes articles and reports on the teaching of art and related
subjects, and general art history with emphasis on modern art.
The reading audience includes college art teachers and art col-
lectors. Unsolicited articles are welcome. Six to eight major

articles are published per issue. Book reviews are included.

Manuscript Preparation:
Accepted manuscripts range from 1,100 to 4,000 words. One copy is required. Return postage and a self-addressed envelope are desired. Bibliographical procedure should follow the University of Chicago Manual of Style. Use wide margins and double-space. Place all footnotes at the end of the article. A background or explanatory cover letter about the article is not desired nor is an outline or summary. Biographical information about the author is desired, but should be limited to 100 or fewer words. Illustrations may be used. No payment is made for accepted articles. Reprints are available; 10 free copies are mailed to the author.

Manuscript Disposition:
Receipt of a manuscript is acknowledged. Editorial decisions are made within four to six weeks. Accepted articles usually appear in print within six weeks after acceptance. Unaccepted manuscripts are returned with suggestions.

Copyright:
Held by the College Art Association of America, Inc.

†ART NEWS

Subscription Data:
Published by Art News Subscription Service, 121 Garden Street, Marion, Ohio 43302. Issued monthly, December through May, and quarterly in June, July, and August. Advertising is accepted. Circulation: 38,000. Subscription: $15.00 per year; $17.00 foreign; $1.50 per issue. Founded: 1902.

Editorial Address:
The Editor, Art News, 750 Third Avenue, New York, New York 10017.

Editorial Policy:
Includes information which relates to painting, sculpture, and the fine arts. The reading audience includes art collectors, artists, art teachers, and art students. Unsolicited articles and photographs are welcome, but must be accompanied with return postage. Eight to ten major articles are published per issue. Only book reviews prepared upon assignment by the editors are included.

Manuscript Preparation:
Manuscripts may be of any reasonable length. Two copies are required. Return postage and a self-addressed envelope are desired. Use one inch margins and double-space. Avoid use of footnotes. A background or explanatory cover letter about the article is desired, but not a summary or abstract. Biographical information about the author is desired. Illustrations, pictures. graphs, etc., may be used. No payment is usually made for accepted articles. Reprints are sometimes available.

Manuscript Disposition:
Receipt of a manuscript is acknowledged. Editorial decisions

are made as soon as possible. Accepted articles usually appear in print within six weeks after acceptance. Unaccepted manuscripts are returned.

Copyright:

Held by Art News Associates.

Additional Information:

Art News is intended for a knowledgeable rather than a popular audience. Its articles are written by recognized professional authorities and are therefore often commissioned in advance by the editors. In the case of unsolicited contributions it is recommended that a brief letter be sent in advance, informally describing the article proposed, so that the editors may exercise their discretion in guiding the respective author as to length, illustrations, etc. When articles or photographs are unsuitable for publication, every care is exercised toward their return. Under no circumstances will any unsolicited art object be accepted for inspection.

ART QUARTERLY

Subscription Data:

Published by the Founders Society, Detroit Institute of Arts, 5200 Woodward Avenue, Detroit, Michigan 48202. Issued quarterly, in June, September, December, and March. Advertising is accepted. Subscription: $16.00 per volume (four issues). Founded: 1938.

Editorial Address:

The Editor, Art Quarterly, 5200 Woodward Avenue, Detroit, Michigan 48202.

Editorial Policy:

Includes articles and reports on all phases of art history. The reading audience consists of scholars in art history: university and college teachers, museum curators, connoisseurs and collectors, and students. Unsolicited articles are welcome. Four to six major articles are published per issue. Book reviews are included.

Manuscript Preparation:

Accepted manuscripts range from five to forty double-spaced typewritten pages, including footnotes. One copy is required. Return postage and a self-addressed envelope are desired. Bibliographical procedure should follow the MLA Style Sheet. Use 1-1/4 inch margins and double-space throughout. List footnotes at the end of the manuscript. A background or explanatory cover letter about the article is desired, but not an outline or summary. Biographical information about the author is unnecessary. Illustrations, pictures, graphs, etc., may be used. Authors may submit clear glossy photographs as part of articles, but must secure permission for their publication. Payment is made for accepted articles at rates of $50.00 to $200.00 depending on article length and number of photographs used. Reprints are available; 25 are mailed free to authors with additional copies available at below cost.

Manuscript Disposition:
  Receipt of a manuscript is acknowledged. Unaccepted manu-
  scripts are returned with criticism or suggestions.
Copyright:
  Not copyrighted.

ARTS AND ACTIVITIES

Subscription Data:
  Published by Publishers' Development Corporation, 8150 North
  Central Park Avenue, Skokie, Illinois 60076. Issued monthly,
  September through June. Advertising is accepted. Circulation:
  40,000. Subscription: $9.00 per year. Founded: 1937.
Editorial Address:
  The Editor, Arts and Activities, Editorial Department, 8150
  North Central Park Avenue, Skokie, Illinois 60076.
Editorial Policy:
  Includes articles on all phases of art education. The reading
  audience includes art instructors at all levels and elementary
  school teachers. Unsolicited articles are welcome. Eight major
  articles are published per issue. Book reviews are included.
Manuscript Preparation:
  No limitations are placed upon manuscript length. One copy is
  required. Return postage and a self-addressed envelope are desired. Use wide margins and double-space. Avoid footnotes
  where possible. A background or explanatory cover letter about
  the article is desired, but not an outline or summary. Biographical information about the author is required and should include indication of the grade level he/she teaches and the school
  at which he/she teaches if they are an educator. Illustrations,
  pictures, graphs, etc., may be used to show procedures, finished
  products, etc. Payment for accepted articles averages from
  $35.00 to $50.00.
Manuscript Disposition:
  Receipt of a manuscript is acknowledged. Editorial decisions
  are made within 30 days. Accepted articles usually appear in
  print within nine months after acceptance.
Copyright:
  Held by Publishers' Development Corporation.
Additional Information:
  Brochures which provide detailed manuscript preparation information are available to authors.

ARTS MAGAZINE

Subscription Data:
  Published by Art Digest, Inc., 23 East Twenty-sixth Street, New
  York, New York 10010. Issued eight times each year, in December-January, February, March, April, May, June, September-October, and November. Advertising is accepted. Circulation: 20,000. Subscription: $16.00 per year. Founded: 1926.

Editorial Address:
   The Editor, Arts Magazine, 23 East Twenty-sixth Street, New
   York, New York 10010.
Editorial Policy:
   Includes essays on modern aesthetics, art historical reevalua-
   tion, monographs on major modern artists, studies of trends,
   issues relevant to the art world and interviews with artists. The
   reading audience includes art scholars, art teachers, art students, artists, and collectors. Unsolicited manuscripts are welcome. Eight to ten major features are published per issue.
   Book reviews are not included.
Manuscript Preparation:
   Accepted manuscripts average from 1,500 to 4,000 words. One
   copy is required. Return postage and a self-addressed envelope
   are required. Bibliographical procedure should follow the University of Chicago Manual of Style. List footnotes on a separate
   page. Use wide margins and double-space. A background or
   explanatory cover letter and an outline, summary, or abstract
   of the article are required. Biographical information about the
   author is required. Authors are expected to supply all illustrations. Payment is made for accepted manuscripts. Reprint
   costs are variable.
Manuscript Disposition:
   Receipt of a manuscript is not acknowledged. Editorial decisions
   are made within two weeks. Accepted articles usually appear in
   print within two months. Unaccepted manuscripts are returned
   with criticism and/or suggestions.
Copyright:
   Held by Art Digest, Inc.

DESIGN

Subscription Data:
   Published by the Phyllis L. Thom, Review Publishing Company,
   1100 Waterway Boulevard, Indianapolis, Indiana 46202. Issued
   bimonthly September through June. Advertising is accepted.
   Circulation: 11,000. Subscription: $7.00 per year; $13.50
   for two years; $19.50 for three years; Canadian and foreign:
   add postage. Founded: 1899.
Editorial Address:
   The Editor, Design, 1100 Waterway Boulevard, Indianapolis,
   Indiana 46202.
Editorial Policy:
   Includes articles on all phases of art and design. Articles are
   edited to provide the out-of-the-ordinary projects and techniques
   which are educational and informative to the amateur and the
   professional. The reading audience includes 80% schools, art
   teachers, and libraries, and 20% craftsmen and art hobbyists.
   Unsolicited manuscripts are welcome. At least 12 major articles
   are published per issue. Book reviews are included.
Manuscript Preparation:
   Accepted manuscripts average 900 words. One copy is required.

Return postage and a self-addressed envelope are required. Use one inch margins and double-space. A background or explanatory cover letter is not required nor is an outline, summary, or abstract. Biographical information about the author is not required. Illustrations, pictures, graphs, etc., may be used. Payment is made for accepted manuscripts of approximately $.03 per word. Reprints are available.

Manuscript Disposition:
Receipt of a manuscript is not acknowledged. Editorial decisions are made within eight weeks. Accepted articles usually appear in print within four months. Unaccepted manuscripts are returned if a self-addressed envelope is included. Criticism or suggestions are not provided.

Copyright:
Held by Design.

Additional Information:
Design seeks articles in all fields of creative art: painting, handcrafts, sculpture, glass, ceramics, enameling, graphics, and teaching methods.

*DESIGN QUARTERLY

Subscription Data:
Published by the Walker Art Center, Vineland Place, Minneapolis, Minnesota 55403. Issued quarterly. Advertising is not accepted. Circulation: 6,000. Subscription: $5.00 per year. Founded: 1946.

Editorial Address:
The Editor, Design Quarterly, Walker Art Center, Vineland Place, Minneapolis, Minnesota 55403.

Editorial Policy:
Includes articles on all phases of design. The reading audience includes professionals and others interested in design, education, architecture, and/or visual communication. Unsolicited manuscripts cannot be used. One or two major articles are published per issue. Book reviews are not included.

Copyright:
Held by the Walker Art Center.

JOURNAL OF AESTHETICS AND ART CRITICISM

Subscription Data:
Published by the Waverly Press, Mount Royal and Guiford Avenues, Baltimore, Maryland 21202. Issued quarterly, in February, May, August, and November. Advertising is accepted. Circulation: 2,600. Subscription: $15.00 per year; $16.00 foreign. Founded: 1941.

Editorial Address:
John Fisher, Editor, Journal of Aesthetics and Art Criticism, Department of Philosophy, Temple University, Philadelphia, Pennsylvania 19122.

Editorial Policy:
Includes articles and reports on aesthetics and criticism of art, music, and literature. The reading audience includes university professors, critics, artists, students, and musicians. Unsolicited articles are often used. Nine or ten major articles are published per issue. Book reviews are included.

Manuscript Preparation:
Accepted manuscripts average less than 25 double-spaced typewritten pages. Two copies are required. Return postage and a self-addressed envelope are necessary. Bibliographical procedure should follow the University of Chicago Manual of Style. Use two inch margins and double-space throughout. Footnotes should be placed at the end of the article. A background or explanatory cover letter about the article is not desired nor is an outline or summary. Biographical information about the author is solicited after acceptance of a manuscript. Illustrations, pictures, graphs, etc., may be used. The author must obtain permission to use all pictures submitted. No payment is made for accepted articles. Reprints are available; 50 free copies are mailed to the author.

Manuscript Disposition:
Receipt of a manuscript is acknowledged. Editorial decisions are made within two months. Accepted articles usually appear in print 12 to 18 months after acceptance. Unaccepted manuscripts are returned, sometimes with criticism and/or suggestions.

Copyright:
Held by the American Society for Aesthetics.

POPULAR CERAMICS

Subscription Data:
Published by William H. Geisler, Popular Ceramics Inc., 6011 Santa Monica Boulevard, Los Angeles, California 90038. Issued monthly. Advertising is accepted. Circulation: 51,790. Subscription: $7.50 per year; $14.00 for two years; $19.00 for three years; foreign add $.75 each year. Founded: 1949.

Editorial Address:
The Editor, Popular Ceramics, 6011 Santa Monica Boulevard, Los Angeles, California 90038.

Editorial Policy:
Includes articles on new styles and developments and approaches in the field of ceramics and material that will aid and inspire the reader's creative endeavors. Articles fall into three categories: instructive (step-by-step), technical and human interest. The reading audience includes thousands of readers involved in all aspects of the hobby ceramic world. Unsolicited manuscripts are welcome. Twelve to twenty major articles are published per issue. Book reviews are included.

Manuscript Preparation:
Accepted manuscripts average 600 to 1,000 words. One copy is required. Return postage and a self-addressed envelope are

required. All material should be typewritten and double-spaced. Paragraphs should be indented. Please check for proper grammar and correct spelling. Simplicity and clarity are of utmost importance, particularly in an instructive article. A background or explanatory cover letter is not required nor is an outline, summary, or abstract. Biographical information about the author is required with head cuts. All pictures must be sharp and clear, preferably shot against a plain background. All photographs published become the property of Popular Ceramics, however, if you wish a photograph returned, enclose return postage. If diagrams or illustrations accompany the article, they must be sharp and clear and rendered in India ink. Use only black and white glossy prints in either four by five or eight by ten inch sizes. Use few color reproduction prints. No payment is made for accepted manuscripts. Reprints are not available.

Manuscript Disposition:

Receipt of a manuscript is acknowledged. Since the editorial department works several months in advance, it may be quite some time between acceptance of an article and its publication. Manuscripts on seasonal articles must be in the office at least ninety days prior to the date of publication. Unaccepted manuscripts are returned with criticism and/or suggestions.

Copyright:

Held by Popular Ceramics Publications, Inc.

Additional Information:

Popular Ceramics is constantly in search of ceramists with new ideas and new techniques, who are willing to tell the readers how they can become better ceramic hobbyists.

SCHOOL ARTS MAGAZINE

Subscription Data:

Published by Davis Publications, Inc., 72 Printers Building, Worcester, Massachusetts 01608. Issued 10 times each year, September through June. Advertising is accepted. Circulation: 33,000 plus. Subscription: $8.00 per year; $9.00 foreign including Canada.

Editorial Address:

George Horn, Editor, School Arts Magazine, 8809 Oakleigh Road, Baltimore, Maryland 21234.

Editorial Policy:

Includes reports of art and craft teaching, and other related educational topics. The reading audience includes art, craft, and classroom teachers in public elementary and secondary schools. The journal is sometimes used as a text in teachers college. Unsolicited articles are welcome. Fourteen major articles are published per issue. Book reviews are included.

Manuscript Preparation:

Accepted manuscripts average 1,000 words. One copy is required. Return postage and a self-addressed envelope are desired, but not mandatory. See a recent issue for footnoting and

other bibliographical procedure. Use wide margins and double-space. A background or explanatory cover letter about the article is not desired nor is an outline or summary. Biographical information about the author is necessary. See articles for reference. Illustrations, pictures, graphs, etc., may be used. Payment for accepted articles is made upon publication.
Manuscript Disposition:
Receipt of a manuscript is acknowledged. Editorial decisions are made within 90 days. Accepted articles usually appear in print within one year after acceptance. Unaccepted manuscripts are returned without criticism or suggestions.
Copyright:
Held by School Arts Magazine.

†STUDIES IN ART EDUCATION

Subscription Data:
Published by the National Art Education Association, 1201 Sixteenth Street, N. W., Washington, D. C. 20036. Issued three times each year, in fall, winter, and spring. Advertising is accepted. Circulation: 2, 800. Subscription: $15.00 per year; $5.00 per issue. Founded: 1959.
Editorial Address:
Dr. Marylou Kuhn, Senior Editor, Studies in Art Education, Department of Art Education, Florida State University, Tallahassee, Florida 32306.
Editorial Policy:
Includes articles and reports of philosophical, historical and empirical study concerning art education. Studies in Art Education is devoted to the scholarly examination of research and issues in the field of art education. The journal welcomes thoughtful manuscripts dealing with significant problems in the field and invites workers in areas other than art education to contribute. The journal is interested in philosophical and historical materials, as well as empirical studies. Papers which develop new theoretical approaches to the understanding of issues in art education are especially welcome. The reading audience includes college and university faculty, students, art supervisors, and classroom teachers. Unsolicited articles are welcome. Five major articles are published per issue. Book reviews are included.
Manuscript Preparation:
Accepted manuscripts average 4,500 words. An original and three copies are required. Return postage and a self-addressed envelope are unnecessary. Footnoting and other bibliographical procedure should follow the APA Publication Manual. Type should be double-spaced for all copy including quotations and references. Line length should contain 52 characters. A background or explanatory cover letter about the article is not desired nor is an outline or summary. Biographical information about the author is desired and should include a summary of his recent professional positions. Tables should be typed on a

separate sheet. Graphs, charts, and drawings should be on heavy bond in India ink with legend typed in place on a separate sheet. Photographs should be in black and white with a glossy finish. No payment is made for accepted articles. Reprints are available.

Manuscript Disposition:
Receipt of manuscript is acknowledged. Editorial decisions are made as soon as possible; time required varies with appropriateness, quality, need, and time submitted. Accepted articles usually appear in print within six months after acceptance. Unaccepted manuscripts are returned, often with criticism and/or suggestions.

Copyright:
Not copyrighted.

BIOLOGY

AMERICAN BIOLOGY TEACHER

Subscription Data:
    Published by the National Association of Biology Teachers, Inc.,
1420 N Street, N.W., Washington, D.C. 20005. Issued monthly,
September through May. Advertising is accepted. Circulation:
15,000. Subscription: $15.00 per year. Founded: 1938.
Editorial Address:
    Jack L. Carter, Editor, American Biology Teacher, Colorado
College, Colorado Springs, Colorado 80903.
Editorial Policy:
    Includes articles covering all kinds of biologic education. The
reading audience includes college, high school, and elementary
school science teachers. Unsolicited manuscripts are welcome.
Ten major articles are published per issue. Book reviews are
included.
Manuscript Preparation:
    Accepted manuscripts average from 3,500 to 5,000 words. One
copy is required. Return postage and a self-addressed envelope
are required. Footnoting and other bibliographical procedure
should follow the "Suggestions for Contributors" that are published in each issue--usually carried in the latter half of the
magazine. A background or explanatory cover letter is desired,
but not an outline or summary. Biographical information about
the author will be required by the editor upon acceptance of the
manuscript. Illustrations, pictures, graphs, are subject to following the "Suggestions for Contributors" that are published in
each issue. No payment is made for accepted articles.
Manuscript Disposition:
    Receipt of a manuscript is acknowledged. Editorial decisions
are made within 120 days. Accepted articles usually appear in
print within four months after acceptance. Unaccepted manuscripts are returned, often with criticism and/or suggestions.
The editor suggests when revisions should be made. About one-
third of the authors whose manuscripts are rejected are requested
to resubmit their articles back to the editor after revision.
Copyright:
    Held by the American Biology Teacher.

ANIMAL BEHAVIOUR

Subscription Data:
    Published jointly by the Association for the Study of Animal

Behaviour (United Kingdom) and the Animal Behavior Society (United States and Canada). Printed by Bailliere Tindall, 7 and 8 Henrietta Street, Covent Garden, London, England. Issued quarterly, in February, May, August, and November. Advertising is accepted. Circulation: Not known. Subscription: $37.40 per year; Members of the Association obtain journal at lower rate. Founded: 1952.

Editorial Address:
Dr. Jack P. Hailman, Editor, Animal Behaviour, Department of Zoology--Birge Hall, University of Wisconsin-Madison, Madison, Wisconsin 53706.

Editorial Policy:
Includes papers on all aspects of behavior in any animals. The reading audience includes ethologists, psychologists, zoologists, and some anthropologists. Unsolicited manuscripts are welcome. Approximately 25 to 30 major articles are published per issue. Book reviews are included.

Manuscript Preparation:
No limitations are placed upon manuscript length. A minimum of two copies are required. Return postage and a self-addressed envelope are not required. Bibliographical procedure should follow a guide which is published in Animal Behaviour, Volume 18, Part 3 which is available from the editor. Footnotes should be used extremely sparingly for such things as change of address. Footnotes should not be used to embellish the text nor for material that could go in the acknowledgments. Use wide margins and double-space; typescript is required. A background or explanatory cover letter is not required, but a 120 word abstract is required. Biographical information about the author is not required. All illustrations, except color plates, are considered. Each table should be typed on a separate sheet and its place in the text indicated in the lefthand margin at the appropriate position on the manuscript. Tables should be as simple as possible, with minimum rules and footnotes. Figures (line drawings and photographs) are numbered consecutively in Arabic numerals. Legends should be typed on a separate sheet. No payment is made for accepted manuscripts. Fifty reprints of each article are supplied free of charge; additional reprints may be purchased, and orders for these should be sent to the publishers when the proofs are returned.

Manuscript Disposition:
Receipt of a manuscript is acknowledged. Editorial decisions are made within approximately 12 to 15 weeks. Accepted articles usually appear in print within nine to twelve months after acceptance of the final version. Unaccepted manuscripts are returned with complete criticisms from at least two outside referees.

Copyright:
Held by the Association for the Study of Animal Behaviour.

Additional Information:
Manuscripts originating in North America must go to the American editor; those from elsewhere must go to the editor in England.

†AUDUBON MAGAZINE

Subscription Data:
Published by the National Audubon Society, 950 Third Avenue, New York, New York 10022. Issued six times each year, in January, March, May, July, September, and November. Advertising is accepted. Circulation: 260,000. Subscription: $10.00 per year. Founded: 1899.

Editorial Address:
The Editor, Audubon Magazine, 950 Third Avenue, New York, New York 10022.

Editorial Policy:
Includes articles on nature, conservation, ornithology (popular), zoology, botany, biology, wildlife preservation, and ecology. The reading audience includes those interested in conservation of wildlife, man's balance with nature; also for the layman and those who appreciate good photographic representation. Unsolicited manuscripts are welcome; however, most of the articles are assigned in advance by the editor. Six to ten major articles are published per issue; also included is an environmental section in the back of the magazine, devoted to ecological happenings, domestic plus international, litigations, etc. Book reviews are included when possible.

Manuscript Preparation:
Accepted manuscripts average 1,000 to 3,000 words. One copy is required. Return postage and a self-addressed envelope are required. No special bibliographical procedure is required. Double-space and use 1-1/2 inch margins. A background or explanatory cover letter and an outline, summary, or abstract of the article are required, but strongly recommend that editor first be queried about the article idea. Interested in black and white photographs and transparencies of any size. Payment is made for accepted manuscripts. No reprints are available and permission must be requested for any reprinting or reproduction done by readers.

Manuscript Disposition:
Receipt of a manuscript is not acknowledged. Editorial decisions are made within two to four weeks. Accepted articles usually appear in print within two years. Unaccepted manuscripts are returned if stamped self-addressed envelope is enclosed. Criticism and/or suggestions are provided only when time permits.

Copyright:
Held by the National Audubon Society.

BIOMETRICS

Subscription Data:
Published by the International Biometric Society, Institute of Statistics, P.O. Box 5962, Raleigh, North Carolina 27607. Issued quarterly. Advertising is accepted. Circulation: 6,300. Subscription: $10.00 per year to members; $15.00 to nonmembers. Founded: 1945.

Editorial Address:
   The Editor, Biometrics, Department of Statistics, Colorado
   State University, Fort Collins, Colorado 80521.
Editorial Policy:
   Includes articles and reports on mathematics and statistics as
   applied to biology. The reading audience includes graduate students, statisticians, and biologists. Unsolicited manuscripts are
   welcome. Twelve to fifteen major articles are published per
   issue. Book reviews are included.
Manuscript Preparation:
   No restriction on length of manuscripts. Three copies are required. Return postage and a self-addressed envelope are not
   required. Bibliographical procedure should follow the Harvard
   Style Guide or some other similar style manual. Double-space
   manuscript and use 1-1/2 inch margins. A background or explanatory cover letter is not required. A summary, with a
   maximum of 150 words, is required. Biographical information
   about the author is not required. Tables should be typed on
   separate sheets, and identified by arabic numbers and by a short
   descriptive title. Tables cannot include any handwritten material.
   Illustrations should also be identified by arabic numbers and by
   a brief caption. (Captions should not be included on illustrations,
   but should be typewritten collectively on an accompanying sheet.)
   Originals should be approximately 8-1/2 by 11 inches. The
   original of each chart, diagram, or graph should be executed in
   black on white drawing paper or board, or blue tracing linen,
   or on coordinate paper ruled in blue only; coordinate lines to be
   reproduced should be ruled in black. For printing, illustrations
   may be reduced to 1/2 or 1/3 original dimensions. Lines
   should therefore be of sufficient thickness, and decimal points,
   periods, and dots should be large enough to reproduce well.
   Lettering and numerals should be at least one mm. high when
   reproduced in a cut three inches wide. Besides that intended
   for the printer, two additional copies of each illustration should
   be sent; these need not be of reproduction standard. All tables
   and illustrations should be located in the text. No payment is
   made for accepted articles. Reprints are available for a minimal charge.
Manuscript Disposition:
   Receipt of a manuscript is acknowledged. Editorial decisions
   are made within three to six months. Accepted articles usually
   appear in print within 18 to 21 months. Unaccepted manuscripts
   are returned with criticism and/or suggestions.
Copyright:
   Held by the Biometric Society. Reprint permission is freely
   given.

*BOTANICAL REVIEW

Subscription Data:
   Published by the New York Botanical Garden, Bronx, New York
   10458. Issued quarterly. Advertising is accepted. Circulation:

2, 500.   Subscription: $14. 00 per year; $15. 00 foreign.
Founded: 1935.

Editorial Address:
 Arthur Cronquist, Editor, Botanical Review, The New York Botanical Garden, Bronx, New York 10458.

Editorial Policy:
 The function of the Review is to present syntheses of the state
 of knowledge and understanding of individual segments of botany.
 It is to be hoped that these syntheses can be read and understood by other botanists less well informed than the authors.
 New information can and sometimes should be incorporated into
 the articles, but Botanical Review is not the place for articles
 primarily concerned with presenting a limited set of new data.
 Most articles are solicited or arranged in advance, but unsolicited manuscripts are also considered and sometimes published.
 All manuscripts are subject to critical review before acceptance,
 but is is to be expected that most solicited manuscripts will in
 fact be acceptable.

Manuscript Preparation:
 Manuscripts should be double-spaced on good quality paper, with
 margins adequate for editorial annotation.   Two copies should
 be provided, but the second set of illustrations need not be in a
 form suitable for reproduction.   Contributors should follow the
 general style of recent issues of the Review, both as to text and
 as to bibliography.   A table of contents should be provided at the
 beginning.   The author or authors should be indicated for any
 specific or infraspecific name the first time the name is used in
 the manuscript.   Citations of periodical literature should be in
 general conformity with those given in Botanico-Periodicum-
 Huntianum, a publication of the Hunt Botanical Library, Pittsburgh, Pennsylvania.

Copyright:
 Held by the Botanical Review.

†ECONOMIC BOTANY

Subscription Data:
 Published by the New York Botanical Garden, Bronx, New York
 10458.   Issued quarterly, in March, May, August, and November.   Advertising is accepted.   Circulation: 2, 000.   Subscription: $15. 00 per year in the United States and Canada; $16. 00
 foreign.   Founded: 1947.

Editorial Address:
 Richard E. Schultes, Editor, Economic Botany, Botanical Museum of Harvard University, Cambridge, Massachusetts 02138.

Editorial Policy:
 Includes articles and reports on botany and related sciences.
 The reading audience includes professional botanists, agricul-
 turists, and students.   Unsolicited articles are welcome.   Five
 major articles are published per issue.   Book reviews are included.

Manuscript Preparation:
No limitations are placed upon manuscript length. Two copies are required. Return postage and a self-addressed envelope are desired. See a recent issue for footnoting procedure. Other bibliographical procedure should follow the Council of Biology Editors Style Manual. Use one inch margins and double-space. A background or explanatory cover letter about the article is required. An outline or summary is desired with submission of the finished manuscript. Biographical information about the author is unnecessary. Illustrations, pictures, graphs, etc., may be used and will be returned if requested. Reprints are available.

Manuscript Disposition:
Receipt of a manuscript is acknowledged. Editorial decisions are made within three months. Accepted articles usually appear in print from nine to twelve months after acceptance. Unaccepted manuscripts are returned, often with criticism and/or suggestions.

Copyright:
Not copyrighted.

JOURNAL OF HEREDITY

Subscription Data:
Published by the American Genetic Association, Thirty-second Street and Elm Avenue, Baltimore, Maryland 21211. Issued six times each year. Advertising regarding scientific publications is accepted. Circulation: 4,500. Subscription: $15.00 per year in the United States; $16.00 elsewhere. Founded: 1903.

Editorial Address:
The Editor, Journal of Heredity, American Genetic Association, Thirty-second Street and Elm Avenue, Baltimore, Maryland 21211.

Editorial Policy:
Includes articles on plant, animal, and human genetics. The reading audience includes professors, researchers, laboratory personnel, physicians, and other scientists. Unsolicited articles are welcome. Twelve to fifteen major articles and six to ten "notes" are published per issue. Book reviews are included.

Manuscript Preparation:
Accepted manuscripts average from 12 to 20 double-spaced typewritten pages, or from 4 to 6 Journal pages. Two copies are required. Return postage and a self-addressed envelope are desired. Bibliographical procedure should follow the Council of Biology Editors Style Manual. Use one inch margins and double-space throughout. Avoid use of footnotes where possible. A background or explanatory cover letter about the article is desired, but not an outline or summary. Biographical information about the author is required and should include a summary of present position. Illustrations, tables, and graphs are used freely. No payment is made for accepted articles. Contributors

are assessed $50.00 per page for accepted manuscripts. Reprints are available at cost; a cost summary is available through the office of the editor.

Manuscript Disposition:
Receipt of a manuscript is acknowledged. Editorial decisions are made by an editorial board as soon as possible. Accepted articles usually appear in print from two to six months after acceptance. Unaccepted manuscripts are returned, often with criticism and/or suggestions. Occasionally the editor will refer an article to another publication.

Copyright:
Held by the American Genetic Association.

QUARTERLY REVIEW OF BIOLOGY

Subscription Data:
Published by the Stony Brook Foundation, Inc., State University of New York, Stony Brook, New York 11790. Sponsored by the American Society of Naturalists. Issued four times each year, in March, June, September, and December. Advertising is accepted. Circulation: 3,100. Subscription: $15.00 per year in the United States and Canada; $15.00 foreign. Founded: 1926.

Editorial Address:
The Editor, Quarterly Review of Biology, State University of New York, Stony Brook, New York 11790.

Editorial Policy:
Includes articles which cover the major areas of biological research in the biological sciences. The reading audience includes professional biologists, lay biologists, teachers, and researchers. Unsolicited articles are welcome. Two to four major articles are published per issue. Approximately 200 book reviews are included per issue.

Manuscript Preparation:
No policy has been established regarding manuscript length. Three copies are required. Return postage and a self-addressed envelope are desired. Bibliographical procedure should follow the Council of Biology Editors Style Manual. Use 1-1/2 inch margins and double-space. Use no footnotes; footnote material should be written into the text or may be bracketed as part of the text. A background or explanatory cover letter about the article is desired. An abstract of 200 or fewer words is required. Illustrations, pictures, graphs, etc., may be used. Prepare all line-drawings in India ink or as glossy prints or half-tones. No payment is made for accepted articles. Authors are charged for excessively long articles. Reprints are usually available.

Manuscript Disposition:
Receipt of a manuscript is acknowledged. Editorial decisions are made as soon as possible. Accepted articles usually appear in print within one year after acceptance. Unaccepted manuscripts are returned, often with criticism and/or suggestions.

BUSINESS EDUCATION

BALANCE SHEET

Subscription Data:
> Published by the South-Western Publishing Company, Inc., 5101 Madison Road, Cincinnati, Ohio 45227. Issued seven times each year, September through April with combination December-January issue. Advertising is not accepted. Circulation: 135,000. Subscription: Free to teachers of business education, distributive education, and economics. Founded: 1919.

Editorial Address:
> The Editor, Balance Sheet, South-Western Publishing Company, Inc., 5101 Madison Road, Cincinnati, Ohio 45227.

Editorial Policy:
> Includes articles on all phases of business and economics education. The reading audience includes business education, distributive education, and economics teachers. Unsolicited articles are welcome from teachers of business, economics, and related disciplines. Approximately seven major articles are published per issue. Book reviews are included, but are prepared in-house.

Manuscript Preparation:
> Manuscripts should not exceed 2,500 words. One copy is required. Return postage and a self-addressed envelope are unnecessary. Use one inch margins and double-space. See a recent issue for footnoting and other bibliographical procedure. A background or explanatory cover letter about the article is desired, but not an outline or summary. Use of illustrations, pictures, graphs, etc., should be selective. No payment is made for accepted articles.

Manuscript Disposition:
> Editorial decisions are made within three weeks. Accepted articles usually appear in print within nine months after acceptance. Unaccepted manuscripts are returned, usually without criticism or suggestions.

Copyright:
> Not copyrighted.

BALL STATE JOURNAL FOR BUSINESS EDUCATORS

Subscription Data:

> Published by the Business Education and Office Administration Department, College of Business, Ball State University, Muncie,

Indiana 47306. Issued three times each year, in November,
February, and May. Advertising is accepted. Circulation:
1, 500. Subscription: Free to in-state business education departments and libraries; $3. 00 to others. Founded: 1929.

Editorial Address:
The Editor, Ball State Journal for Business Educators, College
of Business, Ball State University, Muncie, Indiana 47306.

Editorial Policy:
Includes articles on all phases of business education. The reading audience includes business teachers at the secondary level
and teachers in training. Unsolicited articles are welcome.
Generally, three major articles are published per issue. Book
reviews are not included.

Manuscript Preparation:
Accepted manuscripts average from 3, 000 to 3, 500 words.
Three copies are required. Return postage and a self-addressed
envelope are required. Manuscript organization and placement
on the page, as well as footnoting and other bibliographical procedure, may follow any commonly used format and need not follow a specific style manual. Double-space throughout. A background or explanatory cover letter about the article is required.
Biographical information about the author is desired and should
include full name, address, position, and educational background.
Illustrations, pictures, and graphs are not often used. No payment is made for accepted articles. Reprints are not available.

Manuscript Disposition:
Receipt of a manuscript is acknowledged. Editorial decisions
are made promptly. Time from acceptance of an article to its
appearance in print varies with editorial need. Unaccepted
manuscripts are returned with suggestions or other comments.

Copyright:
Not copyrighted.

BUSINESS EDUCATION WORLD

Subscription Data:
Published by the Gregg/Community College Division, McGraw-
Hill Book Company, 1221 Avenue of the Americas, New York,
New York 10020. Issued five times each school year, in Sep-
tember-October, November-December, January-February, March-
April, and May-June. Advertising is not accepted. Circulation:
100, 000. Subscription: Free to business educators. Founded:
1919.

Editorial Address:
Mrs. Susan S. Schrumpf, Editor, Business Education World,
McGraw-Hill Book Company, 1221 Avenue of the Americas, New
York, New York 10020.

Editorial Policy:
Includes articles on innovative applications of teaching methodology (simulations, block programs, individualized instruction,
etc.), educational concepts and theories in business and office

education, descriptions of new curricula, results of experiments
and their implications to the teaching community, and research
and development reports. The reading audience includes teachers, teacher educators, and administrators. Unsolicited manuscripts are welcome. About seven major articles are published
per issue. Book reviews are not included.

Manuscript Preparation:
Accepted manuscripts average from 1, 600 to 2, 500 words. Two
copies are required. Return postage and a self-addressed envelope are desirable. All footnotes should appear at the end of
the article. Manuscripts should be typed and double-spaced on
a 60-space line with the first page including the title and the
author's name and professional affiliation. A background or explanatory cover letter is required, but not an outline, summary,
or abstract. Biographical information about the author should
include his professional affiliation only. Graphs and photographs
are published when they are an integral part of the editorial content. Payment is made for accepted manuscripts. McGraw-Hill
holds all reproduction rights, but will reassign rights to author
after publication.

Manuscript Disposition:
Receipt of a manuscript is acknowledged. Editorial decisions
are made within six to eight weeks. Accepted articles usually
appear in print within six months to one year. Unaccepted
manuscripts are returned, sometimes with criticism and/or suggestions.

Copyright:
Held by McGraw-Hill Book Company.

BUSINESS HISTORY REVIEW

Subscription Data:
Published by the Harvard University Graduate School of Business
Administration, 214-16 Baker Library, Soldiers Field, Boston,
Massachusetts 02163. Sponsored by the President and Fellows
of Harvard College. Issued four times each year, in March,
June, October, and January. Advertising is accepted. Circula-
tion: 2, 000. Subscription: $15. 00 per year; $6. 00 to students
and teachers. Founded: 1926.

Editorial Address:
The Editor, Business History Review, 214-16 Baker Library,
Soldiers Field, Boston, Massachusetts 02163.

Editorial Policy:
Includes scholarly documented articles on the economic, social,
and political history of business. No geographical or chronological restrictions are made. The reading audience includes
scholars, businessmen, archivists, and students. Unsolicited
articles are welcome. Four or five major articles are published
per issue. Books prepared by the editorial staff are included.

Manuscript Preparation:
Manuscripts should not exceed 30 double-spaced typewritten pages.

One copy is required. Return postage and a self-addressed envelope are desired. Bibliographical procedure should follow the University of Chicago Manual of Style. Use 1-1/2 inch margins and double-space throughout. Place footnotes on a separate page at the end of the article. A background or explanatory cover letter about the article is desired, but not an outline or summary. Biographical information about the author is required and should include rank and institutional or business affiliation. Illustrations are not normally used and the use of graphs should be kept to a minimum. No payment is made for accepted articles. Reprints are available; 20 free copies are mailed to the author. Additional copies are available at a small charge.

Manuscript Disposition:
Receipt of a manuscript is acknowledged. Editorial decisions are made within eight to ten weeks. Accepted articles usually appear in print within one year after acceptance. Unaccepted ones are returned, usually with criticism and/or suggestions.

Copyright:
Held by the President and Fellows of Harvard College.

Additional Information:
Awards of $250.00 for the best article published and $100.00 for the best article by an author under 35 years of age are awarded annually. When published articles are reprinted in anthologies, a permission fee of $50.00 is divided equally between the publisher and the author.

†COMPASS

Subscription Data:
Published by United Business School Association, 1730 M Street, N.W., Washington, D.C. 20036. Issued monthly. Advertising is accepted. Circulation: 4,500. Subscription: $3.00 per year; $2.00 to members of the Compass Association. Founded: 1941.

Editorial Address:
The Editor, Compass, United Business Schools Association, 1730 M Street, N.W., Washington, D.C. 20036.

Editorial Policy:
Includes articles on all phases of post-secondary school business education. The reading audience includes business educators, business school administrators, and publishers of business school materials. Unsolicited articles are welcome. Three major articles are published per issue. Book reviews are included.

Manuscript Preparation:
Accepted articles may not exceed 300 words. One copy is required. Return postage and a self-addressed envelope are desired. Type 36 characters per line and double-space. Do not use footnotes. A background or explanatory cover letter about the article is desired, but not an outline or summary. Biographical information about the author is desired and should include a summary of occupation, education, and previous

employment. Illustrations and graphs may be used; glossy pictures must be submitted in black and white. No payment is made for accepted articles. Reprints are available; costs vary with number of copies ordered and article length.

Manuscript Disposition:
Receipt of a manuscript is acknowledged. Editorial decisions are made within two weeks. Accepted articles usually appear in print within two months after acceptance. Unaccepted manuscripts are returned, often with criticism and/or suggestions.

Copyright:
Held by the United Business Schools Association.

DECA DISTRIBUTOR

Subscription Data:
Published by the Distributive Education Clubs of America, Inc., 200 Park Avenue, Falls Church, Virginia 22046. Issued four times each year, in October, December, February, and April. Advertising is accepted. Circulation: 150,000. Subscription: $3.00 per year. Founded: 1947.

Editorial Address:
The Editor, DECA Distributor, 200 Park Avenue, Falls Church, Virginia 22046.

Editorial Policy:
Includes articles on career encouragement in the fields of marketing and distribution. The reading audience includes students of grades nine through fourteen and distributive education teachers. Unsolicited manuscripts are welcome. Eight major articles are published per issue. Book reviews are not included.

Manuscript Preparation:
Accepted manuscripts average 1,000 words. One copy is required. Return postage and a self-addressed envelope are not required. Use wide margins and double-space. A background or explanatory cover letter is not required nor is an outline, summary, or abstract. Biographical information about the author is required. Illustrations, pictures, graphs, etc., are used and encouraged. No payment is made for accepted manuscripts. Reprints are available.

Manuscript Disposition:
Receipt of a manuscript is acknowledged. Editorial decisions are made within four weeks. Accepted articles usually appear in print within two months. Unaccepted manuscripts are returned, if requested, with criticism and/or suggestions.

Copyright:
Held by the Distributive Education Clubs of America, Inc.

*DELTA PI EPSILON JOURNAL

Subscription Data:
Published by Delta Pi Epsilon, c/o Johnson Publishing Company, Boulder, Colorado 80302. Issued four times each year, in

February, May, August, and November. Advertising is not accepted. Circulation: 11,000. Subscription: $4.00 per year. Founded: 1957.

Editorial Address:
Doris and Floyd Crank, Delta Pi Epsilon Journal, Department of Business Education, Northern Illinois University, DeKalb, Illinois 60115.

Editorial Policy:
Includes articles and reports of research in all phases of business administration. The reading audience includes teachers of business and others interested in the field. Unsolicited articles are not often used. Four or five major articles are published per issue. Book reviews are not usually included.

Manuscript Preparation:
Accepted manuscripts range from 5,000 to 10,000 words. One copy is required. Return postage and a self-addressed envelope are not desired. Footnoting and other bibliographical procedure should follow the University of Chicago Manual of Style. Use wide margins and double-space. A background or explanatory cover letter about the article is desired, but not an outline or summary. Biographical information about the author is desired and should include educational background, research experience, and place of employment. Illustrations, pictures, graphs, etc., are occasionally used. No payment is made for accepted articles. Reprints are not available, but extra copies of each issue of the Journal may be ordered.

Manuscript Disposition:
Receipt of a manuscript is acknowledged immediately. Editorial decisions are made within one week. Accepted articles usually appear in print within one year after acceptance. Detailed suggestions are provided when alteration of an accepted manuscript is required. Unaccepted manuscripts are returned.

Copyright:
Held by Delta Pi Epsilon.

Additional Information:
The editors are especially interested in reports of significant research in business, business education, and education in general.

†EBTA JOURNAL

Subscription Data:
Published by the Eastern Business Teachers Association, Box 962, Newark, New Jersey 07101. Issued biannually, in November and May. Advertising is accepted. Circulation: 5,500. Subscription: Free to members; Nonmembers should contact the Association for information regarding procurement of single issue. Founded: 1962.

Editorial Address:
The Editor, EBTA Journal, 1368 Commonwealth Avenue, Brighton, Massachusetts 02134.

Editorial Policy:
Includes articles which relate to business education with emphasis

on methodology. The reading audience includes high school, college, and university teachers of business. Unsolicited articles are welcome. Eight to ten major articles are published per issue. Book reviews are not included.

Manuscript Preparation:
Accepted manuscripts average from 1, 200 to 1, 500 words, but none may exceed 2, 500 words. One copy is required. Return postage and a self-addressed envelope are unnecessary. Footnoting and other bibliographical procedure may follow any logical format and need not follow a specific style manual. A background or explanatory cover letter about the article is not desired nor is an outline or summary. Biographical information about the author is desired and should include his professional status and school affiliation. Illustrations, pictures, and graphs are occasionally used. No payment is made for accepted articles. Reprints are available.

Manuscript Disposition:
Receipt of a manuscript is acknowledged. Editorial decisions are made within two weeks. Accepted articles usually appear in print within six months after acceptance. Unaccepted manuscripts are returned with reasons and/or criticism.

Copyright:
Held by the Eastern Business Teachers Association.

JOURNAL OF BUSINESS EDUCATION

Subscription Data:
Published by the Journal of Business Education, 15 South Franklin Street, Wilkes-Barre, Pennsylvania 18701. Issued monthly, October through May. Advertising is accepted. Circulation: 14, 000. Subscription: $6.50 per year. Founded: 1928.

Editorial Address:
The Editor, Journal of Business Education, 15 South Franklin Street, Wilkes-Barre, Pennsylvania 18701.

Editorial Policy:
Includes articles on all phases of business education. The reading audience includes public and private junior high, secondary, and college teachers of business. Unsolicited articles are welcome. Eight major articles are published per issue. Book reviews are included.

Manuscript Preparation:
Accepted manuscripts average 1, 400 words. Use subheads every two to three hundred words. One copy is required. Return postage and a self-addressed envelope are unnecessary. Use wide margins, double-space, and avoid use of footnotes where possible. A background or explanatory cover letter about the article is desired, but not an outline or summary. Biographical information about the author is desired and should include a summary of his current position. Illustrations, pictures, graphs, etc., may be used. No payment is made for accepted articles. Reprints are not available.

Manuscript Disposition:

Receipt of a manuscript is acknowledged. Editorial decisions are made as soon as possible. Time from acceptance of a manuscript to its appearance in print varies greatly. Unaccepted manuscripts are returned with criticism and/or suggestions.

Copyright:

Held by Robert C. Trethaway.

CHEMISTRY AND PHYSICS

AMERICAN JOURNAL OF PHYSICS

Subscription Data:
  Published by the American Institute of Physics, 335 East Forty-
  fifth Street, New York, New York 10017. Issued monthly. Advertising is accepted. Circulation: 12,300. Subscription:
  $25.00 per year; $27.00 foreign; $2.50 per issue; Included in
  annual $20.00 dues of members of the Association. Founded:
  1933.

Editorial Address:
  The Editor, American Journal of Physics, Room 20B-136,
  Massachusetts Institute of Technology, Cambridge, Massachusetts
  02139.

Editorial Policy:
  Includes regular articles, letters, notes and discussions, book
  and film reviews, and occasionally resource letters. The Journal is "devoted to the instructional and cultural aspects of physical science," rather than to research. Expository, didactic articles are especially encouraged. These contributions should aid
  significantly the process of learning physics and not be simply
  a display of cleverness or erudition. Highly specialized and/or
  highly mathematical contributions are not encouraged. Topics
  from the entire field of physics and neighboring disciplines are
  appropriate; however, the mere solution of another physical
  problem, of which there are so many, seldom constitutes an acceptable contribution. The reading audience includes teachers
  and students of physics, primarily at the college and university
  level. Unsolicited manuscripts are welcome. Approximately ten
  to twelve major articles are published per issue. Book reviews
  are included.

Manuscript Preparation:
  Accepted manuscripts vary in length. Two copies are required.
  Return postage and a self-addressed envelope are not required.
  Bibliographical procedure should follow the American Institute of
  Physics Style Manual. List footnotes on a separate page at the
  end of the article. Use standard margins and double-space
  throughout. A cover letter is preferred, and a 50 to 100 word
  abstract is required for articles, but not for notes. Biographical information about the author is not required. A brief legend should be provided for every diagram and photograph, but
  it should not be made a part of the figure. All legends are set
  in type by the printer and should be gathered together on the
  final page of the manuscript. Line drawings should be made
  with black India ink. Photographs of apparatus are seldom very

useful and should generally be avoided; but when they are essential, they must have a gloss finish and must be of standard eight by ten inch size. Tables should be typed on separate sheets at the end of the running text and each should be provided with a brief title. Important equations should each appear on a separate line, with the correct punctuation placed before and after the equation. No payment is made for accepted manuscripts. Author's institution is required to pay a publication charge of $70.00 per page. If page charges are honored, 100 free reprints are offered. Additional reprints may be purchased; price depends on length of article.

Manuscript Disposition:
Receipt of a manuscript is acknowledged. Editorial decisions are made within approximately eight weeks. If page charges are honored, accepted articles usually appear in print within approximately five months from acceptance time. If page charges are not paid, accepted articles usually appear in print within approximately ten months from acceptance time. One unaccepted manuscript is returned, usually with criticism and/or suggestions.

Additional Information:
See "Information for Contributors" on inside front cover of January - 1974 issue for more procedural information.

CHEMISTRY

Subscription Data:
Published by the American Chemical Society, 1155 Sixteenth Street, N.W., Washington, D.C. 20036. Issued monthly except July-August issue. Advertising is accepted. Circulation: 35,000. Subscription: $6.00 per year; $10.50 foreign; $4.50 per issue in lots of 10 or more with single payment; $3.75 per issue in academic year of nine months and sent to a single address. Founded: 1927.

Editorial Address:
O. Theodor Benfey, Editor, Chemistry, Guilford College, Department of Chemistry, Greensboro, North Carolina 27410.

Editorial Policy:
Includes reports and articles on general chemistry and research, including: (a) reports which relate to the current levels of knowledge in specific areas of chemistry, (b) feature articles on applied chemistry, (c) articles which deal with the interactions of science and society, (d) biographical and historical material presented to help readers understand current chemical developments and to illustrate scientific methods and philosophical aspects underlying the practice of science, (e) news items to provide the reader with a clear understanding of the chemistry of recent chemical developments, and (f) summaries of experimental projects. The reading audience includes high school and first year college chemistry students and teachers. Book reviews are included.

Manuscript Preparation:
Accepted manuscripts average from 2,000 to 3,000 words.

Three copies are required. Return postage and a self-addressed envelope are unnecessary. Bibliographical procedure should follow the style used in Chemical Abstracts. Use no footnotes in the text. Use two inch margins and double-space. A background or explanatory cover letter about the article is desired, but not an outline or summary. Biographical information about the author is desired and should include information regarding educational background and current position. Illustrations, graphs, and photographs may be included. No payment is made for accepted articles. Reprints are available; costs vary with article length.

Manuscript Disposition:
Receipt of a manuscript is acknowledged. Editorial decisions usually are made within eight weeks. Accepted articles usually appear in print within ten months after acceptance. Unaccepted manuscripts are returned, often with comments.

Copyright:
Held by the American Chemical Society.

JOURNAL OF CHEMICAL EDUCATION

Subscription Data:
Published by the Division of Chemical Education of the American Chemical Society, Twentieth and Northampton Streets, Easton, Pennsylvania 18042. Issued 12 times each year. Advertising is accepted. Circulation: 28,000. Subscription: $6.00 per year; $7.00 in Canada and PUAS; $8.00 elsewhere. Founded: 1924.

Editorial Address:
W. T. Lippincot, Editor, Journal of Chemical Education, University of Arizona, Tucson, Arizona 85721.

Editorial Policy:
Includes college chemistry review articles, reports of experiments and demonstrations, and course and curriculum descriptions. The reading audience includes college and high school teachers and students. Unsolicited articles are welcome. Twenty-five to thirty-five major articles are published per issue. Book reviews are included.

Manuscript Preparation:
Manuscripts, if possible, should be no longer than 16 typewritten pages. The original and two clear copies are required. Return postage and a self-addressed envelope are not required. Use wide margins and double-space. In historical and biographical articles and in papers containing no more than five literature references, it is desirable that references be handled as footnotes. All footnotes should be placed at the end of the article in numerical order. A background or explanatory cover letter about the article is desired, but not an outline or summary. Biographical information about the author is unnecessary. Use of illustrations, pictures, graphs, etc., is encouraged. The original of all illustrations, pictures, graphs, etc., should be included with the manuscript. Line drawings should be prepared in black India ink on white drawing paper, blue tracing cloth,

or blue-lined coordinate paper twice or three times the desired
size. Photographs should have a gloss finish and be at least
postcard size. Tables should be placed on separate pages, with
location noted in text. No payment is made for accepted articles.
Reprints are available; order forms are sent with proofs.

Manuscript Disposition:
   Receipt of a manuscript is acknowledged. Editorial decisions
   are made within one to three months. Accepted articles usually
   appear in print within eight to ten months after acceptance. Unaccepted manuscripts are returned with criticism and/or suggestions.

Copyright:
   Held by the Division of Chemical Education of the American
   Chemical Society.

Additional Information:
   If the paper has been presented at a meeting, a footnote including the name of the society, date, and occasion should be included. A detailed "Notice to Authors" which provides greater
   detail regarding manuscript preparation may be obtained from the
   office of the editor.

PHYSICS TEACHER

Subscription Data:
   Published by the American Association of Physics Teachers,
   Drawer AW, Stony Brook, New York 11770. Issued monthly,
   September through May. Advertising is accepted. Circulation:
   10,000. Subscription: $10.00 per year in the United States,
   Canada, and Mexico; $14.00 in Europe, Middle East, and North
   Africa; $12.00 elsewhere. Founded: 1962.

Editorial Address:
   The Editor, Physics Teacher, Department of Physics, State University of New York, Stony Brook, New York 11790.

Editorial Policy:
   Includes articles and notes of interest to teachers of introductory
   physics at the high school and college level. The reading audience includes high school and college teachers of physics. Unsolicited manuscripts are welcome. Four or five major articles
   and seven or eight notes are published per issue. Book reviews
   are included.

Manuscript Preparation:
   Accepted manuscripts average up to 5,000 words; notes average
   approximately 1,000 words. Two copies are required. Bibliographical procedure should follow the American Institute of Physics Style Manual. Type footnotes double-spaced, grouped together in sequence at the end of the manuscript. Number them consecutively throughout the article, regardless of whether they are
   explanatory notes or literature references, except when they are
   appended to the title of an article or to author's name. The
   manuscript should be typed on white bond paper, 8-1/2 by 11
   inches, 16 pound or heavier stock. It should not be a dittoed
   or mimeographed copy. The entire manuscript including quota-

tions, tables, footnotes, and legends for figures must be typed
double-spaced. Margins of about 1-1/2 inches in width should
be left on the top, sides, and bottom. A brief legend should be
provided for every diagram and photograph, but it should not be
made a part of the figure. Line drawings should be made with
black India ink on plain white drawing paper or blue tracing
cloth. Prints and photostats are not acceptable. For presenting
apparatus, particularly if it is complicated, a line or working
drawing is almost always better than a photograph. If a graph
is drawn on coordinate paper, the paper must be blue lined.
Photographs of apparatus must have a glossy finish and must be
of standard eight by ten inch size. Tables should be typed on
separate sheets at the end of the running text. They should be
numbered consecutively with Roman numerals. Each important
equation should appear on a separate line, with the correct
punctuation placed before and after it. No payment is made for
accepted manuscripts. Reprints may be ordered at author's expense.

Manuscript Disposition:

Receipt of a manuscript is acknowledged. Editorial decisions
are made within four to six weeks. Accepted articles usually
appear in print within three to four months. Unaccepted manuscripts are returned with criticism and/or suggestions.

Copyright:

Held by the American Association of Physics Teachers.

CHILDREN AND YOUTH

ACADEMIC THERAPY

Subscription Data:
   Published by the Academic Therapy Publications, Inc., 1539
   Fourth Street, San Rafael, California 94901. Issued six times
   each year, in September, October, December, February, March,
   and June. Advertising is accepted in four issues. Circulation:
   8,700. Subscription: $6.00 per year. Founded: 1965.
Editorial Address:
   The Editor, Academic Therapy, 1539 Fourth Street, San Rafael,
   California 94901.
Editorial Policy:
   Includes articles on practical ideas, position papers, and research. The reading audience includes learning specialists,
   reading teachers, etc. Unsolicited manuscripts are welcome.
   Fifteen major articles are published per issue. Book reviews
   are included.
Manuscript Preparation:
   Accepted manuscripts average 10 to 12 double-spaced typewritten
   pages. Two copies are required. Return postage and a self-
   addressed envelope are required. Bibliographical procedure
   should follow the University of Chicago Manual of Style. Place
   footnotes on separate page. Use standard margin and spacing.
   A background or explanatory cover letter is required, but not an
   outline, summary, or abstract. Biographical information about
   the author is helpful. Clear and reproducible illustrations, pictures, graphs, etc., are acceptable. No payment is made for
   accepted manuscripts. Fifty free reprints are given to each author upon publication.
Manuscript Disposition:
   Receipt of a manuscript is acknowledged. Editorial decisions
   are made within six weeks. Accepted articles usually appear in
   print within one year. Unaccepted manuscripts are returned
   without criticism or suggestions.
Copyright:
   Held by the Academic Therapy Publications, Inc., unless previously copyrighted.

ADOLESCENCE

Subscription Data:
   Published by Libra Publishers, Inc., P.O. Box 165, 391 Willets
   Road, Roslyn Heights, L.I., New York 11577. Issued quarterly,
   in spring, summer, fall, and winter. Advertising is accepted.

Circulation: 5,000. Subscription: $10.00 per year; $18.00 for two years. Founded: 1966.

Editorial Address:

The Editor, Adolescence, Libra Publishers, Inc., P.O. Box 165, 391 Willets Road, Roslyn Heights, L.I., New York 11577.

Editorial Policy:

Includes professional articles concerning adolescence by members of the various disciplines; psychiatry, psychology, physiology, sociology, and education. The reading audience includes mostly professionals in the above disciplines plus others such as social workers, YMCA directors, and religious leaders. Unsolicited manuscripts are welcome. Approximately nine to twelve major articles are published per issue. Book reviews are included.

Manuscript Preparation:

Accepted manuscripts average between 1,200 words and 7,500 words. Two copies are required. Return postage and a self-addressed envelope are required. Bibliographical procedure should follow any widely used style sheet. List footnotes on a separate page; use wide margins and double-space. A background or explanatory cover letter is not required nor is an outline summary, or abstract. Biographical information about the author is required. Illustrations, pictures, graphs, etc., should be kept to a minimum and when submitted should be in the original, camera-ready form. No payment is made for accepted manuscripts. Reprints may be purchased.

Manuscript Disposition:

Receipt of a manuscript is acknowledged. Editorial decisions are made within two weeks. Accepted articles usually appear in print within eight to twelve months. Unaccepted manuscripts are returned with criticism and/or suggestions.

Copyright:

Held by Libra Publishers, Inc.

CHILD CARE QUARTERLY

Subscription Data:

Published by Behavioral Publications, 72 Fifth Avenue, New York, New York 10011. Issued quarterly. Advertising is accepted. Circulation: 2,000. Subscription: $12.00 per year; $25.00 to institutions. Founded: 1971.

Editorial Address:

Jerome Beker, Editor, Child Care Quarterly, 11 Ross Avenue, Spring Valley, New York 10977.

Editorial Policy:

The Quarterly is the first independent periodical dedicated to the improvement of child care practice in a variety of settings. The Quarterly is designed to serve child workers, their supervisors, agency administrators, and instructors in this rapidly accelerating field. The reading audience includes child psychiatrists, pediatricians, and psychologists. Unsolicited manuscripts are welcome. Five or six major articles are published per issue. Book reviews are included.

Manuscript Preparation:
  Accepted manuscripts should not exceed more than 20 double-
  spaced pages. Three copies are required. Return postage and
  a self-addressed envelope are required. Bibliographical procedure should follow the APA Publication Manual. Footnotes are
  discouraged. Use one inch margins on the top, sides, and bottom and double-space. A background or explanatory cover letter
  and an outline, summary, or abstract are required. Biographical information about the author is required. Illustrations, pictures, graphs, etc., should be placed on separate pages at the
  end of the manuscript and marked with Arabic numerals. No
  payment is made for accepted manuscripts. No free reprints
  are available; cost varies with length of article.
Manuscript Disposition:
  Receipt of a manuscript is acknowledged. Editorial decisions
  are made within six months to one year. Accepted articles usually appear in print within six months to a year. Unaccepted
  manuscripts are returned if postage is provided. Criticism
  and/or suggestions are provided upon request.
Copyright:
  Held by Behavioral Publications.

CHILD DEVELOPMENT

Subscription Data:
  Published by the University of Chicago Press for the Society for
  Research in Child Development, 5801 South Ellis Avenue, Chi-
  cago, Illinois 60637. Issued quarterly, in March, June, September, and December. Advertising is accepted. Circulation:
  6, 800. Subscription: $25.00 per year; $8.00 per issue.
  Founded: 1930.
Editorial Address:
  W. E. Jeffrey, Editor, Child Development, Department of Psychology, University of California, Los Angeles, California 91403.
Editorial Policy:
  Includes articles which deal with original research, reviews,
  and theory of normal child development. The reading audience
  includes research workers and college professors in the field
  of child development, psychologists, psychiatrists, pediatricians,
  educators, speech therapists, etc. Unsolicited manuscripts are
  welcome. Thirty to forty articles are published per issue.
  Book reviews are not included.
Manuscript Preparation:
  Manuscript length should be no more than 30 pages. Two copies are required. Return postage and a self-addressed envelope
  are unnecessary. Bibliographical procedure should follow the
  APA Publication Manual. Use one inch margins and double-
  space. A background or explanatory cover letter about the article is not desired, but an abstract of not more than 150 words
  is required. Biographical information about the author is unnecessary. Illustrations, pictures, graphs, etc., may be used.
  No payment is made for accepted articles. Contributors are

charged only for extraordinary tabular or graphic material, and for early publication. Reprints are available; a reprint cost sheet is available from the office of the editor.

Manuscript Disposition:
Receipt of a manuscript is acknowledged within one week. Editorial decisions are made in less than three months. Accepted articles usually appear in print within one year after acceptance. Unaccepted manuscripts are returned, often with criticism and/ or suggestions.

Copyright:
Held by the Society for Research in Child Development.

Additional Information:
The manuscript rejection rate for Child Development is more than 75 percent. Contributors should study current issues for style and content level.

CHILD STUDY JOURNAL

Subscription Data:
Published by State University College of New York at Buffalo, 1300 Elmwood Avenue, Buffalo, New York 14222. Issued quarterly. Advertising is not accepted. Circulation: 500. Subscription: $5.00 per year; $10.00 to libraries and commercial. Founded: 1970.

Editorial Address:
Donald E. Carter, Editor, Child Study Journal, State University College of New York at Buffalo, 1300 Elmwood Avenue, Buffalo, New York 14222.

Editorial Policy:
Includes theory and research on child and adolescent development, particular attention is given to articles devoted to educational and psychological aspects of human development. The reading audience includes primarily professionals, educators, and college students. Unsolicited manuscripts are welcome. Five or six major articles are published per issue. Book reviews are included.

Manuscript Preparation:
No limitations are placed upon manuscript length; however, prefer manuscripts that do not exceed 20 double-spaced typewritten pages. Two copies are required. Return postage and a self-addressed envelope are appreciated. Bibliographical procedure should follow the APA Publication Manual. Footnotes should be numbered and placed after the reference page. Use a minimum of one inch margins and double-space. A background or explanatory cover letter is not required, only author's address and affiliation (company or university) is needed. A 100 to 120 word abstract is required. Biographical information about the author is not required. Tables, graphs, etc., should be on separate sheets and be ready to print. No payment is made for accepted manuscripts. Reprints are provided for authors with no charge.

Manuscript Disposition:
  Receipt of a manuscript is acknowledged. Editorial decisions
  are made in approximately 10 to 12 weeks. Accepted articles
  usually appear in print within approximately 12 months. One
  copy of the unaccepted manuscript is returned. Criticisms and/
  or suggested revisions are provided for accepted manuscripts
  when necessary.
Copyright:
  Held by the State University College of New York at Buffalo.
Additional Information:
  The APA Publication Manual should be used to answer any questions regarding: style, format, referencing in text, bibliography,
  etc.

CHILDREN TODAY (formerly Children)

Subscription Data:
  Published by the Children's Bureau, Office of Child Development,
  U. S. Department of Health, Education, and Welfare, Washington,
  D. C. 20201. Issued six times each year, in January, March,
  May, July, September, and November. Advertising is not ac-
  cepted. Circulation: 30,000. Subscription: $3.90 per year in
  the United States and Canada; $.70 per issue. Founded: 1954.
Editorial Address:
  The Editor, Children Today, Office of Child Development, Children's Bureau, P.O. Box 1182, Washington, D.C. 20013.
Editorial Policy:
  Includes articles on a wide range of subjects, including health,
  child welfare, social work, psychology, education, and others
  related to children, youth, and their families. The reading audience includes those whose daily jobs and interest are focused
  on children, youth, and their families. Unsolicited manuscripts
  are welcome. Six major articles are published per issue. Book
  reviews are included.
Manuscript Preparation:
  Accepted manuscripts should be no longer than 3,000 words for
  major articles; from 1,000 to 2,000 words for shorter features;
  about 500 words for research summaries. Manuscripts are
  considered for publication only if they have not been previously
  published. Speeches from conferences should carry appropriate
  identification. The original and two carbons are required. Return postage and a self-addressed envelope are required. Footnotes should be listed on a separate page. Use wide margins
  and double-space. A background or explanatory cover letter is
  not required nor is an outline, summary, or abstract. A brief
  summary of professional background is required. Photographs
  to illustrate articles are desirable. No payment is made for
  accepted manuscripts. Reprints of some articles are available.
Manuscript Disposition:
  Receipt of a manuscript is acknowledged. Editorial decisions
  are made within three to eight weeks. Accepted articles usually

appear in print within three to six months. Unaccepted manuscripts are returned, usually without criticism.

Copyright:
Not copyrighted. Permission should be obtained from author to reprint and appropriate credit should be given author, journal, and Office of Child Development.

DAY CARE AND EARLY EDUCATION

Subscription Data:
Published by Behavioral Publications, Inc., 72 Fifth Avenue, New York, New York 10011. Issued bimonthly, in September, November, January, March, May, and July. Advertising is accepted. Circulation: Not determined. Subscription: $9.00 per year; $15.00 to institutions. Founded: 1973.

Editorial Address:
Joseph Michelak, Editor, Day Care and Early Education, Behavioral Publications, Inc., 72 Fifth Avenue, New York, New York 10011.

Editorial Policy:
Includes descriptions of model early childhood programs; generalized discussion articles on consequential issues in the field by academicians and others, and articles on components of early-childhood programs: curriculum, nutrition, management, health care, etc. The reading audience includes professionals and paraprofessionals in day-care and other early childhood programs. Unsolicited manuscripts are welcome. Five or six major articles are published per issue. Book reviews are included.

Manuscript Preparation:
Accepted manuscripts average approximately 2,500 words. One copy is required. Return postage and a self-addressed envelope are preferred. References should be made within the manuscript. A background or explanatory cover letter is preferred, but an outline, summary, or abstract is not required. Biographical information about the author is preferred. Any appropriate photographs or other illustrations are desired. Payment is made for accepted manuscripts.

Manuscript Disposition:
Receipt of a manuscript is not acknowledged. Editorial decisions are made immediately on unaccepted articles, but varies on material requiring consideration. Accepted articles usually appear in print within six months. Unaccepted manuscripts are returned, usually with criticism and/or suggestions.

Copyright:
Held usually by Behavioral Publications, Inc.

EARLY YEARS

Subscription Data:
Published by the Allen Raymond, Inc., Hale Lane, Darien, Connecticut 06820. Issued nine times each year, September

through May. Advertising is accepted. Circulation: 100,000.
Subscription: $8.00 per year. Founded: 1970.

Editorial Address:

The Editor, Early Years, Hale Lane, Darien, Connecticut
06820.

Editorial Policy:

Includes features, classroom management, curriculum how-to,
exceptional child material, and materials testing. The reading
audience includes classroom teachers of preschool through grade
three. Unsolicited manuscripts are welcome. Seven features
and twenty-one articles are published per issue. Book reviews
are included.

Manuscript Preparation:

Accepted manuscripts usually average 1,500 words; however,
no limitations are placed on length. One copy is required. Return postage and a self-addressed envelope are preferred. Bibliographical procedure is not stipulated since articles preferably
do not contain bibliographies. A background or explanatory cover letter is preferred, but not required. An outline, summary,
or abstract is not required. Biographical information about the
author is not required; however, author should include current
affiliation. Photographs are used if judged appropriate; art work
for illustrative material is done by the staff. Payment is made
for accepted manuscripts on publication. Permission requests
to reprint are considered separately.

Manuscript Disposition:

Receipt of a manuscript is not acknowledged. Editorial decisions are made within six to eight weeks. Time from acceptance of a manuscript to its appearance in print varies since much
of the material is school-year seasonal. Unaccepted manuscripts
are returned without criticism or suggestions.

Copyright:

Held by the Allen Raymond, Inc.

Additional Information:

Most of the material comes from the elementary classrooms
across the country; classroom tested articles and ideas are preferred.

GIFTED CHILD QUARTERLY

Subscription Data:

Published by the National Association for Gifted Children, 8080
Springvalley Drive, Cincinnati, Ohio 45236. Issued four times
each year, in fall, winter, spring, and summer. Circulation:
3,000. Subscription: $20.00 per year. Founded: 1957.

Editorial Address:

The Editor, Gifted Child Quarterly, National Association for
Gifted Children, 8080 Springvalley Drive, Cincinnati, Ohio
45236.

Editorial Policy:

Includes articles on the gifted self-concept: how to modestly
reinforce it, programs and practices for the gifted, and research

on the gifted. The reading audience includes supervisors, parents, teachers, gifted children, and adults. Unsolicited manuscripts are welcome. Eight to ten major articles are published per issue. Book reviews are included.

Manuscript Preparation:
Accepted manuscripts average five to eight double-spaced typewritten pages. Two copies are required. Return postage and a self-addressed envelope are required. See the current issue of Gifted Child Quarterly for bibliographical procedure. Avoid the use of footnotes. Use 1-1/2 inch margins. A background or explanatory cover letter and an outline, summary, or abstract of the article are required. Biographical information about the author is required. Illustrations, pictures, graphs, etc., should have wide latitude. No payment is made for accepted manuscripts. The writer grants permission to the National Association for Gifted Children for reprints.

Manuscript Disposition:
Receipt of a manuscript is acknowledged. Editorial decisions are made within four weeks. Accepted articles usually appear in print within six months. Unaccepted manuscripts are returned when stamped self-addressed envelope is enclosed. Criticism and/or suggestions are provided.

Copyright:
Held by the National Association for Gifted Children.

HISTORY OF CHILDHOOD QUARTERLY

Subscription Data:
Published by Atcom, Inc., 2315 Broadway, New York, New York 10024. Issued quarterly. Advertising is accepted. Circulation: 4,000. Subscription: $14.00 per year; $20.00 to institutions. Founded: 1973.

Editorial Address:
The Editor, History of Childhood Quarterly, Atcom, Inc., 2315 Broadway, New York, New York 10024.

Editorial Policy:
Includes articles on the history of childhood and family, psychological analysis of historical movements, and individuals. The reading audience includes historians, educators, sociologists, and psychotherapists. Unsolicited manuscripts are welcome. Six major articles are published per issue. Book reviews are included.

Manuscript Preparation:
No limitations are placed upon manuscript length. One copy is required. Return postage and a self-addressed envelope are required. Bibliographical procedure should follow the University of Chicago Manual of Style. List footnotes at end of the article. Double-space manuscript. A background or explanatory cover letter is not required nor is an outline, summary, or abstract. Biographical information about the author is required. Illustrations, pictures, graphs, etc., should be flexible. No payment is made for accepted manuscripts. Fifty free reprints are given to each author.

Manuscript Disposition:
>Receipt of a manuscript is acknowledged. Editorial decisions are made within one week. Accepted articles usually appear in print within six months. Unaccepted manuscripts are returned with criticism and/or suggestions.

Copyright:
>Held by Atcom, Inc.

PARENT COOPERATIVE PRESCHOOLS INTERNATIONAL JOURNAL

Subscription Data:
>Published by the Parent Cooperative Preschools International, 9111 Alton Parkway, Silver Spring, Maryland 20910. Issued three times each year, in October, January, and April. Advertising is accepted. Circulation: 13,000. Subscription: $5.40 per year; $2.40 to associates; $1.00 to groups; $5.40 to libraries; Free with membership in the Parent Cooperative Preschools International. Founded: 1970.

Editorial Address:
>Barbara Cantor, Editor, Parent Cooperative Preschools International Journal, 9111 Alton Parkway, Silver Spring, Maryland 20910.

Editorial Policy:
>Includes articles on preschool education, child development, child rearing, thoughts of teachers, and consumer articles (toys, etc., affecting children). The reading audience includes parents and teachers of preschoolers, professors and instructors in early childhood at universities. Unsolicited manuscripts are welcome. Approximately three major articles are published per issue. Book reviews are included, but are completed by Nancy Orr, Head Children's Librarian, Montgomery County, Maryland.

Manuscript Preparation:
>Accepted manuscripts should not exceed 1,500 to 1,800 words. One copy is required. Return postage and a self-addressed envelope are preferred. Use 80 characters per line and double-space. A background or explanatory cover letter is often helpful, but an outline, summary, or abstract is not required. Biographical information about the author is requested and should contain a short blurb of one to two sentences that follow the article. Illustrations are accepted if they are camera-ready. Photographs are credited to the photographer. No payment is made for accepted manuscripts. Authors receive copies of the magazine in which their article is published. Reprinting is permitted when requested and approved by the editorial board; however, reprints are not to be sold.

Manuscript Disposition:
>Receipt of a manuscript is always acknowledged. Editorial decisions are made within a maximum of four weeks. Unaccepted manuscripts are returned if requested. Criticism and/or suggestions are sometimes provided.

Copyright:
>Held by the Parent Cooperative Preschools International.

PARENTS' MAGAZINE

Subscription Data:
    Published by the Parents' Institute, a Division of Parents' Magazine Enterprises, Inc., 52 Vanderbilt Avenue, New York, New York 10017. Issued monthly. Advertising is accepted. Circulation: 2,150,000. Subscription: $5.95 per year; $.60 per issue. Founded: 1926.

Editorial Address:
    The Editor, Parents' Magazine, 52 Vanderbilt Avenue, New York, New York 10017.

Editorial Poli
    Includes articles on all phases of child rearing. Especially emphasized are problems and successes of preschool, school age, and adolescent children and their parents; practical guides to infant care; reports which offer constructive advice about family and marriage relationships in the United States; articles encouraging informed citizen action regarding social concerns, including international and interracial affairs; and information on new trends in education, and mental and physical health. The reading audience includes youth educators, families with young children, and others interested in the topics covered. Unsolicited articles are welcome. Seven or eight major articles are published per issue. Book reviews are included.

Manuscript Preparation:
    Accepted articles range from 2,000 to 2,500 words. Picture stories with text of approximately 1,000 words, which illustrate stages of child development or ways or handling children's problems, can also be used. One copy is required. Return postage and a self-addressed envelope are desired. Use one inch margins and double-space. A background or explanatory cover letter about the article is unnecessary. Writers should query the editor regarding article ideas, enclosing an outline and sample opening, before submitting the completed manuscript. Biographical information about the author is desired. Illustrations, pictures, graphs, and artwork may be used. Payment is made upon acceptance and varies, starting at a base of about $350.00 for full-length articles.

Manuscript Disposition:
    Receipt of a manuscript is not acknowledged. Editorial decisions are made within three weeks. Time from acceptance of manuscript to its appearance in print varies with the topic and backlog of accepted articles. Unaccepted manuscripts are returned.

Copyright:
    Held by Parents' Magazine Enterprises, Inc.

*TODAY'S CHILD NEWSMAGAZINE (formerly Today's Child)

Subscription Data:
    Published by Edwards Publications, Inc., School Lane, Roosevelt, New Jersey 08555. Issued monthly, except July and August. Advertising is not accepted. Circulation: 12,000.

Subscription: $5.00 per year; $8.00 for two years; $10.00 for three years. Founded: 1953.

Editorial Address:

The Editor, Today's Child Newsmagazine, Edwards Publications, Inc., School Lane, Roosevelt, New Jersey 08555.

Editorial Policy:

Includes news-style stories on the latest thinking and opinions of professionals in the various areas of child development. The newsmagazine does not buy or use articles, per se. The reading audience includes early childhood educators, other professionals in the area of child development, and students. Unsolicited stories cannot be used. The number of major stories published per issue varies. Book reviews are often included.

Copyright:

Held by Edwards Publications, Inc.

YOUNG CHILDREN

Subscription Data:

Published by the National Association for the Education of Young Children, 1834 Connecticut Avenue, N.W., Washington, D.C. 20009. Issued six times each year, in October, December, February, April, June, and August. Advertising is accepted. Circulation: 22,000 copies per issue. Subscription: $10.00 per year; $12.00 foreign. Founded: 1935.

Editorial Address:

The Editor, Young Children, National Association for the Education of Young Children, 1834 Connecticut Avenue, N.W., Washington, D.C. 20009.

Editorial Policy:

Includes articles which relate to children from birth to age eight. The reading audience includes teachers, administrators, parents, college professors, librarians, social workers, and others concerned with early childhood education and development. Unsolicited manuscripts are welcome. Five or six major articles are published per issue. Book reviews are included.

Manuscript Preparation:

No limitations are placed upon manuscript length. Two copies are required. Return postage and a self-addressed envelope are desired. Bibliographical procedure should follow any widely used style manual. Use wide margins and double-space. A background or explanatory cover letter is required, but not an outline, summary, or abstract. Biographical information about the author is required and should include a summary of present position, educational background, and experience with young children. Illustrations, pictures, graphs, etc., may be used; black and white photographs of children in learning situations are encouraged. Payment is not made for accepted manuscripts. Reprints are available, with costs dependent upon article length and order volume.

Manuscript Disposition:

Receipt of a manuscript is acknowledged. Editorial decisions

are made within eight to ten weeks. Accepted articles usually appear in print within two to four months after acceptance. Unaccepted manuscripts are returned, usually with criticism and/ or suggestions.

Copyright:
 Held by the National Association for the Education of Young Children.

CLASSICAL STUDIES

CLASSICAL BULLETIN

Subscription Data:

Published by the Department of Classical Languages, St. Louis University, St. Louis, Missouri 63103. Issued six times each year, November through April. Advertising is accepted. Circulation: 1,500. Subscription: $2.00 per year. Founded: 1925.

Editorial Address:

Chauncey E. Find, Editor, Classical Bulletin, Department of Classical Language, St. Louis University, St. Louis, Missouri 63103.

Editorial Policy:

Includes articles on classical Greek and Roman literature and Greek and Roman culture. The reading audience includes teachers of the classical languages. Unsolicited articles are welcome. Three major articles and several shorter articles are published per issue. Brief book summaries are included.

Manuscript Preparation:

Accepted manuscripts average eight double-spaced typewritten pages. One copy is required. Return postage and a self-addressed envelope are desired. For footnoting and other bibliographical procedure see a recent issue. Use wide margins and double-space throughout. An explanatory cover letter about the article is not desired nor is an outline or summary. Biographical information about the author is desired. Illustrations, pictures, and graphs are seldom used. No payment is made for accepted articles. Reprints are available with five free copies mailed to the author.

Manuscript Disposition:

Receipt of a manuscript is not usually acknowledged. Editorial decisions are made as soon as possible. Time from acceptance of a manuscript to its appearance in print varies widely and depends upon subject of the article and editorial needs. Unaccepted manuscripts are returned, sometimes with suggestions or other comments.

Copyright:

Not copyrighted.

CLASSICAL JOURNAL

Subscription Data:

Published by the Classical Association of the Middle West and South, Inc., Department of Classics, Florida State University,

Tallahasee, Florida 32306. Issued quarterly, in October-November, December-January, February-March, and April-May. Advertising is accepted. Circulation: 5,000. Subscription: $8.00 per year. Founded: 1905.

Editorial Address:
   The Editor, Classical Journal, Department of Classics, University of Colorado, Boulder, Colorado 80302.

Editorial Policy:
   Includes articles on the Greek and Latin classics, literature, archaeology, pedagogy, mythology and religion, and history. The reading audience includes teachers, scholars, and students on both the secondary and university level. Unsolicited articles are welcome. Six to nine major articles are published per issue. Book reviews are included.

Manuscript Preparation:
   Articles should not exceed 30 double-spaced typewritten pages. One copy is required. Return postage and a self-addressed envelope are unnecessary. Bibliographical procedure should follow the University of Chicago Manual of Style. Place footnotes on a separate page at the end of the article. Use wide margins and double-space throughout, including footnotes. A background or explanatory cover letter about the article is not desired nor is an outline or summary. Biographical information about the author is unnecessary. Illustrations, pictures, graphs, etc., are occasionally used. No payment is made for accepted articles. Ten free copies of the Journal are mailed to the author with additional copies available at modest cost.

Manuscript Disposition:
   Receipt of a manuscript is acknowledged. Editorial decisions are made within 12 weeks. Accepted articles usually appear in print within 12 months. Unaccepted manuscripts are returned with reasons for rejection.

Copyright:
   Held by the Classical Association of the Middle West and South, Inc.

CLASSICAL OUTLOOK

Subscription Data:
   Published by the American Classical League, Miami University, Oxford, Ohio 45056. Published 10 times each year, September through June. Advertising is accepted. Circulation: 6,000. Subscription: $5.00 per year. Founded: 1922.

Editorial Address:
   Konrad Gries, Editor, Classical Outlook, Queens College, Flushing, New York 11367.

Editorial Policy:
   Includes notes, articles, and verse dealing with classical antiquity in all its aspects. The reading audience includes teachers of the classics at all levels as well as people interested in the classics and the classical tradition. Unsolicited manuscripts are welcome. Two or three major articles are published per issue. Book reviews are included.

Manuscript Preparation:
Accepted manuscripts average from one to twelve double-spaced typewritten pages. One copy is required. Return postage and a self-addressed envelope are required. Bibliographical procedure should follow the MLA Style Sheet. Footnote material such as bibliographical information is to be incorporated in the text. Use one inch margins and double-space. A background or explanatory cover letter is required but not an outline, summary, or abstract. Biographical information about the author should include professional affiliation. No illustrations are accepted; graphs, tables, etc., are very rarely used. No payment is made for accepted manuscripts. Reprints are available at $.15 each.

Manuscript Disposition:
Receipt of a manuscript is acknowledged. Editorial decisions are made within two weeks. Accepted articles usually appear in print within 24 months. Unaccepted manuscripts are usually returned with critical explanation and suggestions.

Copyright:
Not copyrighted.

Additional Information:
Subscriptions, advertisements, and other business matters are handled by the Oxford, Ohio office while manuscripts and books for review, etc., are to be sent to the editor at Queens College.

CLASSICAL WORLD

Subscription Data:
Published by the Classical Association of the Atlantic States, 120 Carnegie Building, Department of Classics, University Park, Pennsylvania 16802. Issued eight times each year, September through May. Advertising is accepted. Circulation: 2,900. Subscription: $5.25 per volume or with membership in Regional Classical Associations. Founded: 1907.

Editorial Address:
The Editor, Classical World, 120 Carnegie Building, Department of Classics, Pennsylvania State University, University Park, Pennsylvania 16802.

Editorial Policy:
Includes articles, scholarly surveys, news of the classical world, reviews, and books received. The reading audience includes school and university teachers and a general audience interested in classical subjects. Unsolicited manuscripts are welcome. Two or three major articles are published per issue. Book reviews are included.

Manuscript Preparation:
Suggested maximum length should be 20 to 25 pages of typed copy, including end-notes. One copy is required. Return postage and a self-addressed envelope are not required, but are encouraged. Bibliographical procedure should follow the MLA Style Sheet and Classical World format. Use wide margins and double-space throughout, including quotations and end-notes. Place end-notes on separate pages. A background or explanatory

cover letter is not required, nor is an outline, summary, or
abstract. Biographical information about the author is not required. Illustrations, pictures, graphs, etc., are acceptable
within limits. No payment is made for accepted manuscripts.
Reprints are available.

Manuscript Disposition:

Receipt of a manuscript is acknowledged. Editorial decisions
are made within 90 days. Accepted articles usually appear in
print within one year, but this varies according to backlog. Unaccepted manuscripts are returned with criticism and/or suggestions.

Copyright:

Held by the Classical Association of the Atlantic States.

Additional Information:

No Greek font available; Greek must be transliterated. Back
issues are available.

COMMUNICATIONS

*BROADCASTING

Subscription Data:
    Published by Broadcasting Publications Inc., 1735 DeSales Street,
    N. W., Washington, D. C. 20036. Issued 51 Mondays each year,
    combined issue last two weeks of year. Advertising is accepted.
    Circulation: 35,286. Subscription: $25.00 per year. Founded:
    1931.
Editorial Address:
    The Editor, Broadcasting, 1735 DeSales Street, N. W., Washing-
    ton, D. C. 20036.
Editorial Policy:
    Includes news stories of all lengths, news interpretation, and
    articles on current trends and events. The reading audience in-
    cludes the management class, and those who aspire to it, in
    broadcasting and allied fields. Unsolicited manuscripts are not
    welcome. The magazine is entirely staff written.
Copyright:
    Held by Broadcasting Publications Inc.
Additional Information:
    Broadcasting is the news weekly, of broadcasting and allied arts.

COMMUNICATION RESEARCH

Subscription Data:
    Published by Sage Publications, Inc., 275 South Beverly Drive,
    Beverly Hills, California 90212. Issued quarterly, in January,
    April, July, and October. Advertising is accepted. Circulation:
    Not determined. Subscription: $12.00 per year; $23.00 for two
    years; $33.00 for three years; $18.00 to institutions; $35.00
    for two years; $51.00 for three years; $9.00 to students.
    Founded: 1974.
Editorial Address:
    F. G. Kline, Editor, Communication Research, Department of
    Journalism, University of Michigan, Ann Arbor, Michigan 48104.
Editorial Policy:
    Communication Research is concerned with the study of commu-
    nication processes at all levels. Within this field's rapidly ex-
    panding boundaries, the journal focuses on explication and test-
    ing of models that explain the processes and outcomes of com-
    munication. The journal has a wide scope, including such fields
    as journalism, political science, psychology, economics, sociol-
    ogy, marketing, and speech communication. A major goal is
    the unification of common communication interests across these

and other fields. Papers submitted for inclusion in the journal
should provide theoretical contributions derived from supporting
data that meet specific standards. The reading audience is
varied. Unsolicited manuscripts are welcome. Four or five
major articles are published per issue. Book reviews are included.

Manuscript Preparation:
No limitations are placed upon manuscript length. Three copies
are required. Return postage and a self-addressed envelope are
not required. Footnoting and other bibliographical procedure
should follow the Sage style sheet which is available from the
editor. All copy, including indented matter, notes and references, should be typed double-spaced on white standard paper.
Lines should not exceed six inches in length. Type only on one
side of a sheet and number all pages. A background or explanatory cover letter and an abstract are required. Biographical
information about the author is required if the article is accepted.
Type each table on a separate sheet, showing only a marginal
reference line in the text for placement. Contributors should attempt to furnish cleanly typed tables suitable for photographing
as artwork. In general, artwork should be prepared for same-
size use at a maximum size of 4-1/2 by 6 inches. Artwork
should be clean, sharp, preferably black on white paper. Most
office copying machine work reproduces very poorly and should
be avoided. Glossy photostats are best, preferably furnished
to final size. No payment is made for accepted manuscripts.

Manuscript Disposition:
Receipt of a manuscript is acknowledged. Editorial decisions
are made within eight weeks. Accepted articles usually appear
in print within four to six months. Unaccepted manuscripts are
returned with criticism and/or suggestions.

Copyright:
Presently undetermined.

EDUCATIONAL AND INDUSTRIAL TELEVISION

Subscription Data:
Published by C. S. Tepfer Publishing Company, Inc., 607 Main
Street, Ridgefield, Connecticut 06877. Issued monthly. Advertising is accepted. Circulation: 17,200. Subscription: $10.00
per year; $12.00 to Canada and Mexico; $14.00 foreign; $1.00
per issue. Founded: 1967.

Editorial Address:
The Editor, Education and Industrial Television, C.S. Tepfer
Publishing Company, Inc., 607 Main Street, Ridgefield, Con-
necticut 06877.

Editorial Policy:
Includes specific and practical articles of case studies, how-
to, etc., that will help readers do their job better, more quickly, cheaper, and easier; also gives readers ideas of areas to
explore that they are not now active in. The reading audience
includes the television professionals who use the medium for
communications, teaching, training, by broadcast, on the cable,

in schools (all levels), business, industry, hospitals, the Services, etc. Unsolicited manuscripts are welcome. Between
four and eight major articles are published per issue. Book
reviews are not included; however, available books, with a brief
note of contents, are mentioned in the literature column, with
provision for interested readers to respond.

Manuscript Preparation:
Accepted manuscripts range from 500 to 3,000 words. Two
copies are preferred. Return postage and a self-addressed envelope are not required. Footnotes and bibliographies are not
included. All references to, and quotes from other sources
should be identified in the body of the article itself. Follow the
University of Chicago Manual of Style. Use at least 10 space
margins and double-space. A background or explanatory cover
letter is not required, but is appreciated. An outline, summary,
or abstract is not required. Biographical information about the
author must include at least author's title of current position.
Illustrations, of all kinds, photographs (black and white), cartoons, diagrams, floor plans, charts, graphs, etc., are encouraged. No payment is made for accepted manuscripts. Reprints
are on special order. Authors receive ten copies (more if they
request) of the issue with their article, plus a complimentary
year's subscription.

Manuscript Disposition:
Receipt of a manuscript is acknowledged usually within 10 days
but sometimes longer. Editorial decisions are made within one
to four months depending on work load. Accepted articles usually appear in print anywhere from immediately to two years; depending upon content and emphasis of issues. Unaccepted manuscripts are returned with criticism and/or suggestions, if both
are requested. Suggested alternatives for rejected manuscripts
may be provided.

Copyright:
Held by C.S. Tepfer Publishing Company, Inc.

Additional Information:
Write in English, not in trade jargon. Use personal pronouns
(I, we, you), not "the writer" or "the reader." Be factual and
specific. Argumentative pieces are occasionally accepted, but
do not include unsupported generalities.

EDUCATIONAL BROADCASTING

Subscription Data:
Published by Brentwood Publishing Corporation, 825 South Barrington Avenue, Los Angeles, California 90049. Issued bimonthly. Advertising is accepted. Circulation: 14,412. Subscription: $20.00 per year; $35.00 for two years; $45.00 for three
years; $40.00 foreign per year. Founded: 1968.

Editorial Address:
The Editor, Educational Broadcasting, 825 South Barrington
Avenue, Los Angeles, California 90049.

Editorial Policy:
Includes feature articles stressing new and more effective appli-

cations of hardware and software for filming, transmitting and viewing, thereby making the broadcaster, as well as the audio-visual director, better informed, more efficient and effective. The reading audience includes educators, engineers and training directors who buy and use instructional services at primary, secondary and higher education levels, ETV station managers, ITV operators and directors, military instructional coordinators, government broadcasters, industrial training directors, medical education directors and audio-visual directors. Unsolicited manuscripts are welcome. Six major articles are published per issue. Book reviews are included.

Manuscript Preparation:

Accepted manuscripts should average 16 to 20 double-spaced, typewritten pages; however, longer or shorter articles are acceptable. Two copies are required. Return postage and a self-addressed envelope are not required. Bibliographical procedure should follow the style sheet which is available from the editor. All copy is to be typed on standard pica or executive typewriters, double-spaced, on white paper. A background or explanatory cover letter and an outline, summary, or abstract are required. Biographical information about the author is required and should include educational background, job affiliations and titles, major professional accomplishments and memberships in professional/ technical societies. Arrange in chronological order, include pertinent dates, and submit a recent head cut. Graphs, diagrams, photographs, or illustrations are acceptable. Illustrations cannot be redrawn; they are reproduced directly from submitted material. Accordingly, all lines must be sharply drawn, all notations legible, reproducible black should be used throughout, with everything clean and unfolded. Each table should appear on a separate sheet, clearly labeled, and bearing author's name on reverse side. When applicable, send black and white photographs with article, and clearly indicate the caption to be used with each. No payment is made for accepted manuscripts. Special arrangements will have to be made directly with the journal if more than two copies of the article are desired by each author. Address such correspondence to: Reprint Department, 825 South Barrington Avenue, Los Angeles, California 90049.

Manuscript Disposition:

Receipt of a manuscript is acknowledged. Time from acceptance of a manuscript to its appearance in print varies with editorial need. Unaccepted manuscripts are returned, sometimes with criticism and/or suggestions.

Copyright:

Held by Acalyte Publications Corporation.

JOURNAL OF BROADCASTING

Subscription Data:

Published by the Association for Professional Broadcasting Education, 1771 N Street, N.W., Washington, D.C. 20036. Issued quarterly. Advertising is not accepted. Circulation: 1,900.

Subscription: $10.00 per year; $5.00 to students. Founded: 1956.

Editorial Address:

Christopher H. Sterling, Editor, Journal of Broadcasting, Temple University, Philadelphia, Pennsylvania 19122.

Editorial Policy:

Includes articles and reports on the entire field of mass communication including issues, education, law in broadcasting, broadcast journalism, international communication, audience research, and cross media study. Several bibliographies are published each year. The reading audience includes college teachers from broadcasting and related fields, persons employed in commercial broadcasting, and researchers. Unsolicited articles are welcome. Seven to ten major articles are published per issue. Book reviews are included in extensive "Books in Review" plus "Books in Brief" sections.

Manuscript Preparation:

Accepted manuscripts average from eight to sixteen double-spaced typewritten pages. One copy is required, two if possible. Return postage and a self-addressed envelope are useful. Bibliographical procedure should follow either Campbell's Form and Style or Turabian's Manual for Writers using the general format used in recent issues. Use 1-1/2 inch margins and double-space throughout. Footnotes should be listed at the end of the article. A background or explanatory cover letter about the article is desired, but not an outline or summary. Biographical information about the author is desired and should include indication of academic training, commercial broadcasting experience, if any, and publications. Illustrations and pictures are seldom used. Charts, tables, and graphs may be used, but must be submitted on separate pages. Location of tables in the text should be indicated. No payment is made for accepted articles. Reprints are available; a detailed reprint cost sheet is available through the office of the editor. Four reprints and two copies of the issue in which the article appears are mailed to the author at no charge.

Manuscript Disposition:

Receipt of a manuscript is acknowledged. Editorial decisions are made as soon as possible, averaging from two to four weeks. Titles of accepted articles are listed in the next issue (after acceptance) and usually appear in an issue or so after that. Accepted articles usually appear in print within five months after acceptance. Unaccepted manuscripts are returned with suggestions and criticism.

Copyright:

Held by the Association for Professional Broadcasting Education.

JOURNAL OF COMMUNICATION

Subscription Data:

Published by the Annenberg School of Communications, University of Pennsylvania, and International Communication Association, 3620 Walnut Street C5, University of Pennsylvania, Philadelphia, Pennsylvania 19174. Issued quarterly, in January, April, July, and October. Advertising is accepted. Circulation: 4, 000. Subscription: $12. 00 per year. Founded: 1950.

Editorial Address:
George Gerbner, Editor, Journal of Communication, Annenberg School of Communications, University of Pennsylvania, 3620 Walnut Street C5, Philadelphia, Pennsylvania 19174.

Editorial Policy:
Includes articles on all aspects of communication: mass media, interpersonal communication, attitude and opinion research, language behavior, and other social issues of communication. The reading audience includes researchers, teachers and practitioners in all disciplines concerned with human communication. Unsolicited articles are welcome. Six to ten major articles are published per issue. Book reviews are included.

Manuscript Preparation:
Manuscript length should be consistent with importance of the topic and thoroughness of its treatment. Average length desired is 10 to 15 double-spaced typed pages. Two copies are desired. Return postage and a self-addressed envelope are required if the author wishes to guarantee the return of manuscript. Source citations should be listed alphabetically at the end of the article and referred to by number within the text. Footnotes should be used only for substantive material. Use wide margins and double-space. A background or explanatory cover letter is required, but not an outline, summary, or abstract. Biographical information about the author is required. Illustrated material is desired and authors should submit material or suggestions. No payment is made for accepted manuscripts. Reprints are available at cost from the printer. Some reprints are furnished on a complimentary basis.

Manuscript Disposition:
Receipt of a manuscript is acknowledged. Editorial decisions are made within six to eight weeks. Accepted articles usually appear in print within six months. Unaccepted manuscripts are not returned unless postpaid return envelope is provided. Criticism and/or suggestions are not usually provided.

Copyright:
Held by the Journal of Communication.

MASS COMMUNICATION REVIEW

Subscription Data:
Published by Mass Communication and Society Division of the Association for Education in Journalism, Department of Journalism, Temple University, Philadelphia, Pennsylvania 19122. Issued currently three times each year, serially. Advertising is accepted. Circulation: 700. Subscription: $6. 00 per year; $2. 00 per issue.

Editorial Address:
The Editor, Mass Communication Review, Mass Communication

and Society Division of the Association for Education in Journalism, Department of Journalism, Temple University, Philadelphia, Pennsylvania 19122.

Editorial Policy:
Includes reviews, scholarly pieces, and essays on media-related subjects. The reading audience includes journalism educators, professional journalists, and media researchers. Unsolicited manuscripts are welcome. Approximately five major articles are published per issue. Book reviews are included.

Manuscript Preparation:
No limitations are placed upon manuscript length. Three copies are required. Return postage and a self-addressed envelope are required. Bibliographical procedure may follow any style, but must be consistent. List footnotes on a separate page. Use 60 space line on a standard sheet. A background or explanatory cover letter is required, but not an outline, summary, or abstract. Biographical information about the author is required. Illustrations, pictures, graphs, etc., are used where applicable. No payment is made for accepted manuscripts. Reprints are sold on a per page basis.

Manuscript Disposition:
Receipt of a manuscript is acknowledged. Editorial decisions are made within 12 weeks. Accepted articles usually appear in print within one year or less. Unaccepted manuscripts are returned if postage is included. Criticism and/or suggestions are generally not provided.

Copyright:
Held by the author.

PUBLIC TELECOMMUNICATIONS REVIEW (formerly Educational Broadcasting Review)

Subscription Data:
Published by the National Association of Educational Broadcasters, 1346 Connecticut Avenue, N.W., Washington, D.C. 20036. Issued bimonthly. Advertising is accepted. Circulation: 4,000. Subscription: $12.50 per year. Founded: 1973.

Editorial Address:
The Editor, Public Telecommunications Review, National Association of Educational Broadcasters, 1346 Connecticut Avenue, N.W., Washington, D.C. 20036.

Editorial Policy:
Includes articles relating to public broadcasting, instructional communications, and related fields. The reading audience includes professionals in public telecommunications, scholars, lawyers, and others with interest in the field. Unsolicited manuscripts are welcome. Six to ten major articles are published per issue. Book reviews are included.

Manuscript Preparation:
Accepted manuscripts average 1,500 words for reviews and other shorter pieces to 4,000 to 5,000 words for featured articles. Two copies are required. Return postage and a self-

addressed envelope are not required. Footnoting and bibliographical procedure should follow Words Into Type. Use 1-1/2 inch margins and double-space throughout. A background or explanatory cover letter is desirable, but not an outline, summary, or abstract. Biographical information about the author should include only his current position. Illustrations, pictures, graphs, etc., may be used; camera-ready photographs are preferred. No payment is made for accepted manuscripts. Reprints are available with varying costs.

Manuscript Disposition:

Receipt of a manuscript is acknowledged. Editorial decisions are made within one month. Accepted articles usually appear in print within three months. Unaccepted manuscripts are not returned. Criticism and/or suggestions are sometimes provided for accepted manuscripts.

Copyright:

Not copyrighted.

COUNSELING, GUIDANCE, AND PERSONNEL

AMERICAN VOCATIONAL JOURNAL

Subscription Data:
Published by the American Vocational Association, Inc., 1510 H Street, N.W., Washington, D.C. 20005. Issued monthly, September through May. Advertising is accepted. Circulation: 55,000. Subscription: $6.00 per year; $8.00 foreign. Founded: 1925.

Editorial Address:
The Editor, American Vocational Journal, 1510 H Street, N.W., Washington, D.C. 20005.

Editorial Policy:
Includes articles on all phases of vocational and technical education. The reading audience includes vocational teachers and administrators at all levels. Unsolicited manuscripts are welcome with priority given to subscribers. Ten to eighteen major articles are published per issue. Staff-written book reviews are included.

Manuscript Preparation:
Accepted manuscripts average 800 to 2,000 words. Two copies are required. Return postage and a self-addressed envelope are desired. See a recent issue for bibliographical procedure. Type manuscript, use wide margins, and double-space. A background or explanatory cover letter is not required. An outline of the article is required in advance of article submission. Biographical information about the author is desired. Sharp, black and white photographs that really illustrate articles are used. Graphs are occasionally used; however, drawings are rarely used. No payment is made for accepted manuscripts. Reprints are available at cost.

Manuscript Disposition:
Receipt of a manuscript is acknowledged. Editorial decisions are made within three to four months. Time from acceptance of an article to its appearance in print varies from timeliness of the topic and backlog of accepted manuscripts. Unaccepted manuscripts are returned with reasons for rejection.

Copyright:
Held by the American Vocational Association, Inc.

COLLEGE AND UNIVERSITY PERSONNEL ASSOCIATION. JOURNAL

Subscription Data:
Published by the College and University Personnel Association, One Dupont Circle, Suite 525, Washington, D.C. 20036. Issued

quarterly, in winter, spring, summer, and fall. Advertising is
not accepted. Circulation: 3,000. Subscription: $15.00 per
year to members of the Association; $20.00 to non-members;
$5.00 per issue. Founded: 1949.

Editorial Address:
The Editor, Journal of the College and University Personnel Association, Suite 525, One Dupont Circle, Washington, D.C. 20036.

Editorial Policy:
Includes scholarly articles of interest to personnel persons and
college administrators. The articles are often written by professors, administrators, and personnel persons. The reading
audience includes personnel persons and administrators in colleges and universities, including college presidents. Unsolicited
manuscripts are welcome. Eight major articles are published
per issue. Book reviews are included.

Manuscript Preparation:
Accepted manuscripts average 10 to 50 double-spaced pages.
Three copies are required. Return postage and a self-addressed
envelope are not required. Footnoting and bibliographical procedure should follow the Turabian Manual for Writers. Double-
space and use 1-1/2 inch margins. A background or explanatory
cover letter is not required, but a two sentence summary is required. Biographical information about the author is required.
Illustrations, pictures, graphs, etc., are restricted in use, but
some are accepted. No payment is made for accepted manuscripts. Reprints are available through the publisher.

Manuscript Disposition:
Receipt of a manuscript is acknowledged. Editorial decisions
are made within four to six weeks. Accepted articles usually
appear in print within 12 months. Unaccepted manuscripts are
returned without criticism or suggestions.

Copyright:
Held by the College and University Personnel Association.

COLLEGE BOARD REVIEW

Subscription Data:
Published by the College Entrance Examination Board, Publica-
tions Office, 888 Seventh Avenue, New York, New York 10019.
Issued quarterly. Advertising is not accepted. Circulation:
20,000. Subscription: $5.00 per year; $1.25 per issue.
Founded: 1947.

Editorial Address:
The Editor, College Board Review, College Entrance Examination Board, 888 Seventh Avenue, New York, New York 10019.

Editorial Policy:
Includes articles on guidance, student admissions and placement,
and other related aspects of the educational process. The reading audience includes school counselors, administrators, and
other interested educators. Unsolicited articles are welcome.
Ten major articles are published per issue. Book reviews are
included.

Manuscript Preparation:
　　Accepted manuscripts average 2, 000 to 4, 000 words. Two copies are required. Return postage and a self-addressed envelope
are required. Use wide margins and double-space. See a recent issue for bibliographical style. A background or explanatory
cover letter about the article is desired, but not an outline or
summary. Biographical information about the author is desired.
Illustrations, graphs, etc., may be used. A head and shoulder
picture of the author of each accepted article is required. Payment is made for accepted articles. Reprints are available for
some articles.
Manuscript Disposition:
　　Receipt of a manuscript is acknowledged. Editorial decisions
are made within eight weeks. Accepted articles usually appear
in print within one year after acceptance. Unaccepted manuscripts are returned without criticism or suggestions.
Copyright:
　　Held by the College Entrance Examination Board.

COLLEGE STUDENT JOURNAL

Subscription Data:
　　Published by Project Innovation, 1402 West Capital Drive, Mil-
waukee, Wisconsin 53206. Issued quarterly. Advertisment re-
lated to college students is accepted. Circulation: 1, 500. Sub-
scription: $7. 50 per year; $10. 00 to institutions. Founded: 1966.
Editorial Address:
　　Robert E. Hoyle, Managing Editor, College Student Journal,
1402 West Capitol Drive, Milwaukee, Wisconsin 53206.
Editorial Policy:
　　Includes original investigations and theoretical papers dealing
with college student values, attitudes, opinions, and learning.
This includes graduate level schools and professional schools.
The reading audience includes college faculty, students, administrative staff, and persons interested in college students and
their educational development. Unsolicited manuscripts are
welcome. Approximately 20 to 24 articles are published per
issue. Book reviews related to college students and learning
are included.
Manuscript Preparation:
　　Accepted articles average from 2, 000 to 3, 000 words in length;
however, all lengths are considered. Two copies are required.
Return postage is necessary. Bibliographical procedure should
follow the APA Publication Manual and a style sheet available
from the editor upon request. Avoid the use of footnotes. A
cover letter is not required, but an abstract of less than 120
words is required and should follow the APA Publication Manual.
Biographical information about the author is not required. Fig-
gures, half-tones, and dense tables require lithographic plates;
cost must be covered by the author. No payment is made for
accepted manuscripts. Reprints are available from the printer
at the time of publication.

Manuscript Disposition:
  Receipt of a manuscript is acknowledged. Editorial decisions are made within four to six weeks. Accepted articles are generally printed within one year. Unaccepted articles are returned with criticisms provided if the article is publishable.
Copyright:
  Held by Project Innovation.
Additional Information:
  Monographs are published, but no more than one for each issue of the Journal. Uninvited articles and articles not considered to be "Priority" require authors to share in publication costs.

COUNSELOR EDUCATION AND SUPERVISION

Subscription Data:
  Published by the American Personnel and Guidance Association, 1607 New Hampshire Avenue, N. W., Washington, D. C. 20009. Issued quarterly, in September, December, March, and June. Advertising is accepted. Circulation: 6, 000. Subscription: $6.00 per year to non-members of the Association. Founded: 1961.
Editorial Address:
  Edwin L. Herr, Editor, Counselor Education and Supervision, 323 Social Science Building, Pennsylvania State University, University Park, Pennsylvania 16802.
Editorial Policy:
  Includes articles on research and the theoretical dealing explicitly with counselor education and/or supervision. The reading audience includes university professors of counselor education: state, national and district directors of guidance, pupil personnel services, or counseling services. Unsolicited manuscripts are welcome. Twelve to fourteen major articles are published per issue. Book reviews are not included.
Manuscript Preparation:
  Accepted manuscripts average 2, 500 words. Three copies are required. Return postage and a self-addressed envelope are requested. Bibliographical procedure should follow the APA Publication Manual. Use 1-1/2 inch margins and double-space. A background or explanatory cover letter is not required, but an abstract of the article is required. Biographical information about the author is required. No pictures, but illustrations, graphs, and tables are accepted. No payment is made for accepted manuscripts. Author receives 10 free copies of the journal in which the article appears.
Manuscript Disposition:
  Receipt of a manuscript is acknowledged. Editorial decisions are made within eight to twelve weeks. Accepted articles usually appear in print within twelve to fifteen months. All copies are returned except a file copy; criticism and/or suggestions are provided.
Copyright:
  Held by the American Personnel and Guidance Association.

ELEMENTARY SCHOOL GUIDANCE AND COUNSELING

Subscription Data:

Published by the American School Counselor Association, a division of the American Personnel and Guidance Association, 1607 New Hampshire Avenue, N.W., Washington, D.C. 20009. Issued quarterly, in October, December, March, and May. Advertising is accepted; write to George Warner, Advertising Sales Manager, c/o American Personnel and Guidance Association Press. Subscription: $8.00 per year; $6.00 per year to Association members; $2.50 per issue. Founded: 1965.

Editorial Address:

Dr. Robert D. Myrick, Editor, Elementary School Guidance and Counseling, College of Education, University of Florida, Gainesville, Florida 32611.

Editorial Policy:

Includes articles directed to the interests of educators and pupil personnel specialists involved in counseling and guidance of elementary school children of K through 8. Both research and innovative concept articles are published. The reading audience includes elementary and junior high school counselors, teachers, administrators, counselor educators, pupil personnel services directors, and state supervisors of guidance. Unsolicited manuscripts are the general rule with an editorial board reviewing the manuscripts. Five to six major articles are published per issue. Featured columns review and include contributors material in the columns as co-authors with the column editors. Book reviews are included.

Manuscript Preparation:

Accepted manuscripts should not exceed 10 pages. The original and two clear copies are required. Return postage and a self-addressed envelope are not required. Footnoting and other bibliographical procedure generally follow the APA Publication Manual. Authors should consult recent issues of the journal for more specific guidelines. Use 2-1/2 inch margins, double-space, and avoid the use of footnotes. Background information is required, but an explanatory cover letter is optional. An outline, summary, or abstract is not required. Biographical information about the author is required and should include author's identification, place of employment, and address. Camera-ready illustrations, pictures, graphs, etc., are acceptable. No payment is made for accepted manuscripts. Reprints are available through APGA Press in lots of 50 from publication sales.

Manuscript Disposition:

Receipt of a manuscript is acknowledged immediately by postcard from the editor. Editorial decisions are made within eight to twelve weeks. Accepted articles usually appear in print within four to six months. Two copies of an unaccepted manuscript are returned and one copy is retained by the editor. In most cases, critical comments are provided, sometimes in detail and sometimes in general, depending on the review board's work.

Copyright:

Held by the American Personnel and Guidance Association.

Additional Information:

> Elementary School Guidance and Counseling has approximately
> 80 pages per issue, with featured issues running 90 pages.
> Manuscripts should be typewritten and well organized. They
> should be concise so that the development of ideas is logical
> and the implications for practice are clear. Authors need not
> be school counselors, but they should speak to the school coun-
> selor as a practitioner.

*GUIDANCE EXCHANGE

Subscription Data:

> Published by Guidance Exchange, 3310 Rochambeau Avenue,
> Bronx, New York 10467. Issued annually, in February. Ad-
> vertising is not accepted. Subscription: $15.00 per year.
> Founded: 1960.

Editorial Address:

> The Editor, Guidance Exchange, 3310 Rochambeau Avenue,
> Bronx, New York 10467.

Editorial Policy:

> Guidance Exchange consists entirely of reviews of literature in
> the fields of guidance, education, and psychology. The reading
> audience includes school counselors, guidance supervisors, psy-
> chologists, teachers, and other educators. Unsolicited articles
> cannot be used. Book reviews are included.

Copyright:

> Held by Guidance Exchange.

JOURNAL OF COLLEGE PLACEMENT

Subscription Data:

> Published by the College Placement Council, Inc., Box 2263,
> Bethlehem, Pennsylvania 18001. Issued four times each year,
> in October-November, December-January, February-March, and
> April-May. Advertising is accepted. Circulation: 4,500. Sub-
> scription: Journal and another publication, Salary Survey, are
> part of one subscription package. Members of College Place-
> ment Council receive subscription as part of membership;
> $25.00 to members for additional subscriptions; $35.00 to non-
> members. Founded: 1940.

Editorial Address:

> The Editor, Journal of College Placement, College Placement
> Council, Inc., Box 2263, Bethlehem, Pennsylvania 18001.

Editorial Policy:

> Includes articles on all phases of the placement of college grad-
> uates. The reading audience includes college placement direc-
> tors and personnel representatives from business, industry, and
> government. Unsolicited articles are welcome. Nine or ten
> major articles are published per issue. Book reviews are in-
> cluded.

Manuscript Preparation:

> Accepted manuscripts average from 3,000 to 4,000 words. Two

copies are required. Return postage and a self-addressed envelope are desired. Use one inch margins and double-space. Use no footnotes or reference list. A background or explanatory cover letter about the article is required. An outline or summary of the article is desired in advance of or with submission of the finished manuscript. Biographical information about the author is required and should include a summary of educational background, recent published works, and qualifications for writing the article. Illustrations, graphs, etc., may be used. Photographs must be prepared as glossy prints; other art must be ready for the engraver. No payment is made for accepted articles. Reprints are available only on a special order basis.

Manuscript Disposition:
Receipt of a manuscript is acknowledged. Editorial decisions are made by an editorial committee within one to three months. Accepted articles usually appear in print within six months. Unaccepted manuscripts are returned, sometimes with suggestions. Amount and quantity of criticism depends upon quality of the manuscript and whether it might be acceptable for publication elsewhere.

Copyright:
Held by the College Placement Council, Inc.

JOURNAL OF COLLEGE STUDENT PERSONNEL

Subscription Data:
Published by the American Personnel and Guidance Association, 1607 New Hampshire, N. W., Washington, D. C. 20009. Issued six times each year, in January, March, May, July, September, and November. Advertising is accepted. Circulation: 8,500. Subscription: $15.00 per year. Founded: 1959.

Editorial Address:
Albert B. Hood, Editor, Journal of College Student Personnel, East Hall, University of Iowa, Iowa City, Iowa 52240.

Editorial Policy:
Includes theory and research articles which relate to college student personnel topics. The reading audience includes college student personnel workers and professors. Unsolicited articles are welcome. Twelve major articles are published per issue. Book reviews are not included.

Manuscript Preparation:
Maximum length of most manuscripts is 12 to 15 typewritten pages. Two copies are required. Return postage and a self-addressed envelope are desired. Bibliographical procedure should follow the APA Publication Manual. Use wide margins and double-space. A background or explanatory cover letter about the article is desired and a 50 word abstract is required. Biographical information about the author is desired and should include his position, title, and institutional affiliation. Illustrations, pictures, and graphs should be kept to a minimum. No payment is made for accepted articles. Reprints are available at cost; 50 free copies are mailed to the authors.

Manuscript Disposition:
Receipt of a manuscript is acknowledged. Editorial decisions are usually made within 90 days. Accepted articles usually appear in print within one year after acceptance. Unaccepted manuscripts are returned, with criticism and/or suggestions.

Copyright:
Held by the American Personnel and Guidance Association.

JOURNAL OF COUNSELING AND VALUES

Subscription Data:
Published by the National Catholic Guidance Conference, 3227 Fourteenth Avenue, Kenosha, Wisconsin 53140. Issued quarterly, in October, January, April, and July. Advertising is accepted. Circulation: 1,200. Subscription: $10.00 per year. Founded: 1955.

Editorial Address:
Donald A. Biggs, Editor, Journal of Counseling and Values, 327 Walter Library, University of Minnesota, Minneapolis, Minnesota 55455.

Editorial Policy:
Includes articles concerned with counseling and values. The reading audience includes people in education, counseling, and religion. Unsolicited manuscripts are welcome. Eighty major articles are published per year. Book reviews are included.

Manuscript Preparation:
Accepted manuscripts average approximately 15 pages. Two copies are required. Return postage and a self-addressed envelope are not required. See a recent issue for bibliographical style and footnoting. A background or explanatory cover letter is required, but not an outline, summary, or abstract. Biographical information about the author is not required. Illustrations, pictures, and graphs are unacceptable. No payment is made for accepted manuscripts. Reprints may be purchased.

Manuscript Disposition:
Receipt of a manuscript is acknowledged. Editorial decisions are made within six weeks. Accepted articles usually appear in print within 12 to 18 months. Unaccepted manuscripts are returned with criticism and/or suggestions.

Copyright:
Held by the National Catholic Guidance Conference.

JOURNAL OF EMPLOYMENT COUNSELING

Subscription Data:
Published by the National Employment Counselors Association, 1607 New Hampshire Avenue, N.W., Washington, D.C. 20009. Issued quarterly, in March, June, September, and December. Advertising is accepted. Circulation: 2,000. Subscription: $4.00 per year. Founded: 1964.

Editorial Address:
David Brenna, Editor, Journal of Employment Counseling,

National Employment Counselors Association, 1607 New Hampshire Avenue, N. W. , Washington, D. C. 20009.

Editorial Policy:

Includes articles concerning occupational psychology, industrial sociology, vocational counseling, and employment counseling in both public and private agencies. The reading audience includes professional counselors of adults, students, and counselor educators. Unsolicited manuscripts are welcome. Seven major articles are published per issue. Book reviews are not included.

Manuscript Preparation:

Accepted manuscripts average not more than 15 double-spaced typewritten pages. Return postage and a self-addressed envelope are not required. Bibliographical procedure should follow the APA Publication Manual. Use 1-1/2 inch margins and double-space. A background or explanatory cover letter is not required, but an abstract of from 100 to 120 words is required. Biographical information about the author is required for accepted manuscripts and will be obtained by the editor. Picture-ready graphs, illustrations, and pictures are welcome. No payment is made for accepted manuscripts. Ten copies of the Journal issue are given to the author with reprints available at cost.

Manuscript Disposition:

Receipt of a manuscript is acknowledged. Editorial decisions are made within seven to twelve weeks. Accepted articles usually appear in print within eight months (unless very timely). Unaccepted manuscripts are returned with criticism and/or suggestions.

Copyright:

Held by the American Personnel and Guidance Association.

MEASUREMENT AND EVALUATION IN GUIDANCE

Subscription Data:

Published by the American Personnel and Guidance Association, 1607 New Hampshire Avenue, N. W. , Washington, D. C. 20009. Issued quarterly, in April, July, October, and January. Advertising is accepted. Circulation: 3, 000. Subscription: $8. 00 per year. Founded: 1968.

Editorial Address:

Bill Mehrens, Editor, Measurement and Evaluation in Guidance, 419 North Capital Avenue, Michigan State University, Lansing, Michigan 49014.

Editorial Policy:

Includes articles dealing with theoretical and other problems of measurement. All manuscripts must have clearly described implications for the practitioner in measurement and evaluation. Unsolicited manuscripts are welcome. Six or seven major articles are usually published per issue. Book reviews are included.

Manuscript Preparation:

Accepted manuscripts should generally not exceed more than 10 double-spaced typewritten pages. One original and two copies

are required. Return postage and a self-addressed envelope
are not required, but are preferred. Bibliographical procedure
should follow the APA Publication Manual. Do not include footnotes. Use at least one inch margins and double-space. A
background or explanatory cover letter is not required, but an
abstract that does not exceed more than 175 words is required.
Biographical information about the author is required and should
include author's note with professional title and place of employment. All figures should be camera-ready. No payment is
made for accepted manuscripts. Reprints are available.

Manuscript Disposition:
Receipt of a manuscript is acknowledged. Editorial decisions
are made within two to three months. Accepted articles usually
appear in print within three to six months. Unaccepted manuscripts are returned, sometimes with criticism and/or suggestions.

Copyright:
Held by the American Personnel and Guidance Association.

NATIONAL ASSOCIATION FOR WOMEN DEANS, ADMINISTRATORS,
AND COUNSELORS. JOURNAL (formerly National Association of
Women Deans and Counselors. Journal)

Subscription Data:
Published by the National Association for Women Deans, Administrators, and Counselors, 1028 Connecticut Avenue, N.W.,
Suite 922, Washington, D.C. 20036. Issued quarterly, in fall,
winter, spring, and summer. Advertising is accepted. Circulation: 3,000. Subscription: $7.50 per year; $9.00 foreign;
$2.00 per issue. Founded: 1916.

Editorial Address:
The Editor, Journal of the National Association for Women
Deans, Administrators, and Counselors, 1028 Connecticut Ave-
nue, N.W., Suite 922, Washington, D.C. 20036.

Editorial Policy:
The Journal, with an annual total of 200 pages, publishes many
articles of special interest to women, but because most of the
readers work with both men and women students, the editors
are equally interested in articles that will be of use to personnel administrators, deans, counselors, and educators and to
graduate students in training for similar work. Unsolicited
manuscripts are welcome. Four to eight major articles are
published per issue. Book reviews are included.

Manuscript Preparation:
Articles should be from 2,500 to 3,000 words in length or from
10 to 12 double-spaced typewritten pages. Two copies are preferred. Return postage and a self-addressed envelope are not
required. Bibliographical procedure should follow the APA Publication Manual. Authors who wish to submit manuscripts should
consult current issues of the Journal to note the general trend
of style and interest. Use standard margins and double-space.
A background or explanatory cover letter is not required nor is

an outline, summary, or abstract. Biographical information
about the author is required. Tables are acceptable, but do
not include pictures, etc. No payment is made for accepted
manuscripts. Reprints are available at cost to the author.
Manuscript Disposition:
    Receipt of a manuscript is acknowledged. Unaccepted manu-
    scripts are returned with criticism and/or suggestions.
Copyright:
    Not copyrighted.

NATIONAL ASSOCIATION OF COLLEGE ADMISSIONS COUNSELORS.
JOURNAL (formerly Association of College Admissions Counselors.
Journal)

Subscription Data:
    Published by the National Association of College Admissions
    Counselors, 9933 Lawler Avenue, Skokie, Illinois 60076. Issued
    quarterly. Advertising is not accepted. Circulation: 5, 000.
    Subscription: $8. 00 per year. Founded: 1937.
Editorial Address:
    The Editor, Journal of the National Association of College Ad-
    missions Counselors, 9933 Lawler Avenue, Skokie, Illinois
    60076.
Editorial Policy:
    Includes articles on admission to colleges; transferring between
    educational institutions; financial-aid policies; and general college
    administration policies. The reading audience includes college
    admissions officers and high school counselors. Unsolicited
    manuscripts are welcome. Six to twenty major articles are pub-
    lished per issue. Book reviews are not included.
Manuscript Preparation:
    No limitations on accepted manuscripts. One copy is required.
    Return postage and a self-addressed envelope are not required.
    There is no specific policy regarding bibliographical procedure.
    Vitae is no longer published with article; only include a brief
    biographical note as it pertains to the article. Manuscripts
    should be legible. A background or explanatory cover letter is
    not required nor is an outline, summary, or abstract. Brief
    biographical information about the author is not required. Do
    not include illustrations, pictures, graphs, etc. No payment is
    made for accepted manuscripts. Reprints are arranged by in-
    dividual request; usually recommend photocopy tear sheets and
    reprint locally.
Manuscript Disposition:
    Receipt of a manuscript is acknowledged. Editorial decisions
    are made within three months. Accepted articles usually appear
    in print within three to nine months. Unaccepted manuscripts
    are returned without criticism and/or suggestions.
Copyright:
    Held by the National Association of College Admissions Counselors.

PERSONNEL AND GUIDANCE JOURNAL

Subscription Data:
Published by the American Personnel and Guidance Association, 1607 New Hampshire Avenue, N. W., Washington, D. C. 20009. Issued 10 times each year, except July and August. Advertising is accepted. Circulation: 35,000. Subscription: $20.00 per year. Founded: 1922.

Editorial Address:
The Editor, Personnel and Guidance Journal, the American Personnel and Guidance Association, 1607 New Hampshire Avenue, N. W., Washington, D. C. 20009.

Editorial Policy:
Includes manuscripts directed to the common interests of counselors and personnel workers in schools, colleges, community agencies, and government. Especially welcome is stimulating writing dealing with (1) discussions of current professional and scientific issues; (2) descriptions of new techniques or innovative practices and programs; (3) scholarly commentaries on APGA as an association and its role in society; (4) critical integrations of published research; and (5) research reports of unusual significance to practitioners. Dialogues, poems, and brief descriptions of new practices and programs are also considered. The reading audience includes school and college counselors, rehabilitation counselors, employment counselors, vocational counselors, and university professors in the area of counselor education. Unsolicited manuscripts are welcome. Five to eight major articles and two to four "In the Field" articles are published per issue. Solicited book reviews are included.

Manuscript Preparation:
Major articles average 2,000 to 3,500 words; "In the Field" articles average under 2,500 words. One original and two clear copies are required. Return postage and a self-addressed envelope are not required. Bibliographical procedure should follow the APA Publication Manual. Avoid footnotes wherever possible. Double-space all material, including references, footnotes, and quotations. Leave extra space above and below the subheads and wide margins all around. A background or explanatory cover letter is not required. An outline, summary, or abstract of the article is required for all full-length articles, but not for articles for "In the Field" section. Biographical information about the author is required. Figures must be submitted as clean, camera-ready art; photographs may accompany articles. No payment is made for accepted manuscripts. Authors receive complimentary journals (10 journals to senior author of each article) and may order paid reprints of their articles.

Manuscript Disposition:
Receipt of a manuscript is acknowledged. Two to three months may elapse between acknowledgment of receipt of a manuscript and notification concerning its disposition. Accepted articles

usually appear in print within five months from date of acceptance. Unaccepted manuscripts are returned with criticism and/
or suggestions.
Copyright:
    Held by the American Personnel and Guidance Association.
Additional Information:
    "Guidelines for Authors" appears in each issue of the Journal.

SCHOOL COUNSELOR

Subscription Data:
    Published by the American Personnel and Guidance Association,
    1607 New Hampshire Avenue, N.W., Washington, D.C. 20009.
    Issued five times each year, in September, November, January,
    March, and May. Advertising is accepted. Circulation: 18,000.
    Subscription: $8.00 per year. Founded: 1942.
Editorial Address:
    Marguerite R. Carroll, Editor, School Counselor, Fairfield Uni-
    versity, Fairfield, Connecticut 06430.
Editorial Policy:
    Includes articles on theory and practice. The reading audience
    includes school counselors and counselor educators. Unsolicited
    manuscripts are welcome. Five major articles are published
    per issue. Book reviews are included.
Manuscript Preparation:
    Accepted manuscripts average five to seventeen pages. Three
    copies are required. Return postage and a self-addressed en-
    velope are not required. Footnoting and bibliographical proce-
    dure should follow the APA Publication Manual. Use 1-1/2
    inch margins. A background or explanatory cover letter is not
    required nor is an outline, summary, or abstract. Biographical
    information about the author is not required. Illustrations, pic-
    tures, graphs, etc., are acceptable if appropriate and artistic.
    No payment is made for acceptable manuscripts. Reprints are
    available with permission of American Personnel and Guidance
    Association and author.
Manuscript Disposition:
    Receipt of a manuscript is acknowledged. Editorial decisions
    are made within four to twelve weeks. Accepted articles usual-
    ly appear in print within six months. Unaccepted manuscripts
    are returned with criticism and/or suggestions.
Copyright:
    Held by the American Personnel and Guidance Association.

STUDENT PERSONNEL ASSOCIATION FOR TEACHER EDUCATION.
JOURNAL

Subscription Data:
    Published by the American Personnel and Guidance Association,
    1607 New Hampshire Avenue, N.W., Washington, D.C. 20009.
    Issued quarterly, in fall, winter, spring, and summer. Ad-

vertising is accepted.   Circulation: 1, 000.   Subscription: $6.50
per year; $1.75 per issue.   Founded: 1961.

Editorial Address:

Dr. James Dickinson, Editor, Journal of the Student Personnel
Association for Teacher Education, College of Education, University of South Florida, Tampa, Florida 33620.

Editorial Policy:

Includes articles on research, description of practices, essays
on teacher education, selection of teachers, evaluation of inservice teachers, and counselors.   The reading audience includes college student personnel workers, college counselors,
teacher educators, and counselor educators.   Unsolicited manuscripts are welcome.   Five to six major articles are published
per issue.   Book reviews are included.

Manuscript Preparation:

Accepted articles average eight double-spaced pages; seldom
accept a single article exceeding 25 pages.   Three copies are
required.   Return postage and a self-addressed envelope are
not required.   Bibliographical procedure should follow the APA
Publication Manual.   A background or explanatory cover letter
is not required nor is an outline, summary, or abstract.   Biographical information about the author is not required.   No
photographs; print graphs and figures in form for printing are
acceptable.   No payment is made for accepted manuscripts.
The author receives five copies of the issue in which the article
appears.

Manuscript Disposition:

Receipt of a manuscript is acknowledged.   Editorial decisions
are made within eight to ten weeks.   Accepted articles usually
appear in print within three to six months.   Unaccepted manuscripts are returned with criticism and/or suggestions.

Copyright:

Held by the American Personnel and Guidance Association.

VOCATIONAL GUIDANCE QUARTERLY

Subscription Data:

Published by the National Vocational Guidance Association, 1607
New Hampshire Avenue, N. W. , Washington, D. C. 20009.   Issued
four times each year, in September, December, March, and
June.   Advertising is accepted.   Circulation: 14, 000.   Subscription: $8.00 per year.   Founded: 1952.

Editorial Address:

Daniel Sinick, Editor, Vocational Guidance Quarterly, George
Washington University, Washington, D. C. 20006.

Editorial Policy:

Includes articles which relate to all aspects of guidance and
counseling, with emphasis on those which deal with the role of
work in the life of man.   Topics such as occupational choice,
vocational development, occupational information, educational
and vocational planning, economics of the labor market,

96 / Counseling, Guidance, and Personnel

occupational trends and outlook, youth and work, and occupational adjustment of special groups are suggestive of some of the general areas of content appropriate for submission. The reading audience includes counselors at all levels in a variety of settings. Unsolicited articles are welcome. Ten major articles are published per issue.

Manuscript Preparation:

Accepted manuscripts average 1, 500 words. No manuscript, except for solicited articles and reviews of special topics, should exceed 3, 000 words. The original and two carbons are required. Return postage and a self-addressed envelope are desired. See a recent issue for referencing procedure. Use one inch margins and double-space. Biographical information about the author is desired and should include his rank or position and place of employment. Illustrations and pictures may be used. Glossy prints of attractive illustrative materials and relevant exhibits such as graphs and charts may be used. No payment is made for accepted articles. Reprints are available; a reprint cost sheet is available.

Manuscript Disposition:

Receipt of a manuscript is acknowledged. Editorial decisions are made within two to three months. Accepted articles usually appear in print within one year after acceptance. Unaccepted manuscripts are returned with criticism or suggestions.

Copyright:

Held by the National Vocational Guidance Association.

DATA PROCESSING

†DATA PROCESSING FOR EDUCATION

Subscription Data:
    Published by the North American Publishing Company, 134 North
Thirteenth Street, Philadelphia, Pennsylvania 19107. Issued
monthly. Advertising is not accepted. Circulation: 960. Subscription: $36.00 per year. Founded: 1961.

Editorial Address:
    The Editor, Data Processing for Education, North American
Publishing Company, 134 North Seventeenth Street, Philadelphia,
Pennsylvania 19107.

Editorial Policy:
    Includes articles on data processing, computers, information,
retrieval, and computer assisted instruction. The reading audience includes educators in the data processing field and in other
related areas of education. Unsolicited articles are welcome.
One or two major articles are published per issue. Book reviews are included.

Manuscript Preparation:
    Accepted manuscripts average from 1,500 to 2,000 words. One
copy is required. Return postage and a self-addressed envelope
are desired. Footnoting and other bibliographical procedure may
follow any widely used manual of style. Use wide margins and
double-space. A background or explanatory cover letter about
the article is desired, but not an outline or summary. Biographical information about the author is desired and should
include a summary of his present position. Original glossy
photographs may be used. Payment of $25.00 is made for each
article used. Reprints are sometimes available.

Manuscript Disposition:
    Receipt of a manuscript is acknowledged. Editorial decisions
are made as soon as possible. Accepted articles usually appear
in print within three months after acceptance. Unaccepted manuscripts are returned, sometimes with criticism or suggestions.

Copyright:
    Held by the North American Publishing Company.

EDUCOM BULLETIN

Subscription Data:
    Published by EDUCOM, Interuniversity Communications Council,
Inc., P.O. Box 364, Princeton, New Jersey 08540. Issued
quarterly, in March, June, September, and December. Advertising is not accepted. Circulation: 10,000. Subscription:

Free to faculty of EDUCOM member institutions; $5.00 per year to nonmember educators; $10.00 per year to others. Founded: 1965.

Editorial Address:
The Editor, EDUCOM Bulletin, Interuniversity Communications Council, Inc., P.O. Box 364, Princeton, New Jersey 08540.

Editorial Policy:
Includes articles of interest to the general reader on the application of computing and other technology for research, institutional, and administrative use in higher education. The reading audience includes primarily faculty and administrators in colleges and universities. Unsolicited manuscripts are welcome. Three major articles are published per issue. Book reviews are not included.

Manuscript Preparation:
Accepted manuscripts average 2,000 to 3,000 words. Three copies are required. Return postage and a self-addressed envelope are not required. Bibliographical procedure may follow any standard style manual. List footnotes and references on separate pages. Use one inch margins and double-space. A background or explanatory cover letter and an outline, summary, or abstract are required. Biographical information about the author is required. Original art and photographs are requested. No payment is made for accepted manuscripts. Reprints normally are not prepared; however, they will be provided upon request at cost.

Manuscript Disposition:
Receipt of a manuscript is acknowledged. Editorial decisions are made within four weeks. Accepted articles usually appear in print within six to twelve weeks. Two copies of unaccepted manuscripts are returned with criticism and/or suggestions.

Copyright:
Held by EDUCOM.

Additional Information:
Preliminary letters of inquiry regarding possible articles are welcome and will be answered within four weeks.

JOURNAL OF DATA EDUCATION

Subscription Data:
Published by the Society of Data Educators, 516 Marr Avenue, Truth or Consequences, New Mexico 87901. Issued monthly, October through May. Advertising is accepted. Circulation: 800. Subscription: $12.00 per year. Founded: 1960.

Editorial Address:
The Editor, Journal of Data Education, 516 Marr Avenue, Truth or Consequences, New Mexico 87901.

Editorial Policy:
Includes articles of interest to teachers of data processing or computer science. The reading audience includes teachers. Unsolicited manuscripts are welcome. Forty to sixty major articles are published per issue. Book reviews are included.

Manuscript Preparation:
No limitations are placed upon manuscript length. One copy is required. Return postage and a self-addressed envelope are not required. A background or explanatory cover letter is not required nor is an outline, summary, or abstract. Biographical information about the author is useful, but not required. No payment is made for accepted manuscripts.

Manuscript Disposition:
Receipt of a manuscript is acknowledged. Editorial decisions are made within one week. Accepted articles usually appear in print within four to nine months. Unaccepted manuscripts are returned with criticism and/or suggestions.

Copyright:
Held by the author.

JOURNAL OF EDUCATIONAL DATA PROCESSING

Subscription Data:
Published by the Educational Systems Corporation, P.O. Box 2995, Stanford, California 94305. Issued bimonthly. Advertising is accepted. Circulation: 1,500. Subscription: $11.00 per year; $12.00 foreign. Founded: 1964.

Editorial Address:
The Editor, Journal of Educational Data Processing, Educational Systems Corporation, P.O. Box 2995, Stanford, California 94305.

Editorial Policy:
Includes articles which report information processing techniques in all areas of education. The reading audience includes data processing specialists and others interested in the field. Unsolicited articles are welcome. Four major articles are published per issue. Book reviews are included.

Manuscript Preparation:
No limitations are placed upon manuscript length. Two copies are required. Return postage and a self-addressed envelope are desired. Bibliographical procedure should follow the AERA Style Manual. Use wide margins and double-space. Footnotes must be numbered and collected at the end of the manuscript. No background or explanatory cover letter about the article is desired, but an abstract is required with submission of the finished article. Biographical information about the author is required and should include a summary of his professional background. Illustrations, pictures, graphs, etc., are occasionally used. No payment is made for accepted articles. Reprints are available; costs must be negotiated with the printer. Additional reprint information may be obtained from the office of the editor.

Manuscript Disposition:
Receipt of a manuscript is acknowledged. Editorial decisions are made as soon as possible. Accepted articles usually appear in print from three to six months after acceptance. Unaccepted manuscripts are returned, often with suggestions.

100 / Data Processing

Copyright:
Held by the Educational Systems Corporation.

Additional Information:
Because selected issues are devoted to particular topics, correspondence with the editor prior to submission of a final manuscript is recommended.

DRAMATICS

Subscription Data:
Published by the International Thespian Society, College Hill
Station, Box E, Cincinnati, Ohio 45224. Issued eight times
each year, in October through May. Advertising is accepted.
Circulation: 55,000. Subscription: $5.00 per year, $3.00 to
students. Founded: 1929.

Editorial Address:
R. Glenn Webb, Editor, Dramatics, Box E, College Hill Station,
Cincinnati, Ohio 45224.

Editorial Policy:
Includes informative articles on various aspects of theatre with
emphasis on production; there is no script analysis. Interviews
are welcome. Original one-act plays, suitable for high school
production, are not to exceed 30 minutes running time. The
reading audience includes primarily students, teachers, and directors in high school theatre. Unsolicited manuscripts are
welcome. Six major articles are published per issue. Book
reviews are included.

Manuscript Preparation:
Accepted manuscripts average from 1,500 to 2,000 words for
regular articles and 30 minute running time for one-act plays.
One copy is required. Return postage and a self-addressed envelope are required. Bibliographical procedure should follow
the MLA Style Sheet. Use wide margins, double-space, and
place footnotes on a separate page. A background or explanatory
cover letter is not required nor is an outline, summary, or abstract. Biographical information about the author is requested.
Black and white photographs and illustrations are usually requested. Payment of up to $25.00 is usually made for accepted
manuscripts. Reprints are available from Johnson Reprints.

Manuscript Disposition:
Receipt of a manuscript is acknowledged. Editorial decisions
are made within six weeks. Accepted articles usually appear
in print within two to four months. Unaccepted manuscripts are
returned when accompanied by stamped self-addressed envelope.
Criticism and suggestions are often provided.

Copyright:
Held by the International Thespian Society.

Additional Information:
Editorial philosophy: Educational. Dramatics is often used as
a classroom and resource instructional tool for theatre and communication arts.

EDUCATIONAL THEATRE JOURNAL

Subscription Data:
  Published by the American Theatre Association, 1317 F Street,
  N. W., Washington, D. C. 20004. Sponsored by the University
  and College Theatre Association, a constituent of the American
  Theatre Association. Issued four times each year, in March,
  May, October, and December. Advertising is accepted. Circu-
  lation: 6,000. Subscription: Included with membership in the
  University and College Theatre Association; $12.00 per year to
  other constituents of the American Theatre Association; $15.00
  per year to others. Founded: 1949.
Editorial Address:
  Anthony Graham-White, Editor (1972-75), Educational Theatre
  Journal, Department of Drama, University of Texas, Austin,
  Texas 78712.
Editorial Policy:
  Includes articles on all phases of theatre and drama. The read-
  ing audience includes university, college, and secondary scholars
  as well as others interested in community theatre, children's
  theatre, and professional theatre. Unsolicited articles are wel-
  come. Seven or eight major articles are published per issue.
  Book reviews are included.
Manuscript Preparation:
  Accepted manuscripts average from 2,500 to 5,000 words. One
  copy is required. Return postage and a self-addressed envelope
  are desired. Bibliographical procedure should follow the MLA
  Style Sheet or the University of Chicago Manual of Style. Include all footnotes on a page at the end of the article. A brief
  background or explanatory cover letter about the article is desired, but not an outline or summary. Biographical information
  about the author is desired and should include indication of
  current position and place of work, plus other personal information relevant to the article. Line drawings and photographs may
  be used. No payment is made for accepted articles. A reprint
  cost sheet is available through the office of the publisher.
Manuscript Disposition:
  Receipt of a manuscript is acknowledged. Editorial decisions
  are made as soon as possible. Time from acceptance of a
  manuscript to its appearance in print varies widely and depends
  upon available space, timeliness, and relationship to other accepted articles. Unaccepted manuscripts are returned with criticism and/or suggestions given only when an article merits rewriting.
Copyright:
  Held by the American Theatre Association.

PLAYERS MAGAZINE

Subscription Data:
  Published by the National Collegiate Players, N. I. U. Theatre,
  De Kalb, Illinois 60115. Issued bimonthly, September through

August. Advertising is accepted and encouraged. Circulation: 10, 000. Subscription: $5.00 per year. Founded: 1923.

Editorial Address:

Byron Schaffer, Jr. , Editor, Players Magazine, N. I. U. Theatre, De Kalb, Illinois 60115.

Editorial Policy:

Includes articles on all aspects of American theatre and drama: history, criticism, theory, technical practice, design, information, and interview. The reading audience includes professional, academic, and community theatre workers. Unsolicited manuscripts are welcome. Seven to nine major articles are published per issue. Book reviews are included.

Manuscript Preparation:

Accepted manuscripts average 2, 000 or more words. Two copies are required. Return postage and a self-addressed envelope are required. Bibliographical procedure should follow the MLA Style Sheet. Manuscript footnoting should be listed on a separate page. A background or explanatory cover letter is not required nor is an outline, summary, or abstract. Biographical information about the author is required. Encourage the use of supporting illustrations and/or pictures. No payment is made for accepted manuscripts. Reprints are negotiable.

Manuscript Disposition:

Receipt of a manuscript is acknowledged. Editorial decisions are made within eight weeks. Accepted articles usually appear in print within two to four months. Unaccepted manuscripts are returned with criticism and/or suggestions.

Copyright:

Held by Byron Schaffer, Jr. , Editor.

PLAYS

Subscription Data:

Published by Plays, Inc. , Eight Arlington Street, Boston, Massachusetts 02116. Issued eight times each year, October through May. Advertising is accepted. Circulation: 25, 500. Subscription: $8.00 per year. Founded: 1940.

Editorial Address:

The Editor, Plays, Eight Arlington Street, Boston, Massachusetts 02116.

Editorial Policy:

Includes plays for children. The reading audience includes elementary and high school students and their teachers. Unsolicited plays are welcome. Ten plays are published per issue. Book reviews are included.

Manuscript Preparation:

Limitations are placed upon manuscript length; one act plays only. One copy is required. Return postage and a self-addressed envelope are desired. Use wide margins and double-space. A background or explanatory cover letter about the manuscript is not desired nor is an outline or summary. Biographical information about the author is unnecessary. Neither illustrations nor pictures can be used. Good payment is made for accepted plays.

Manuscript Disposition:

Receipt of a manuscript is not acknowledged. Editorial decisions are made within two to three weeks. Time from acceptance of a manuscript to its appearance in print varies widely with editorial need. Unaccepted manuscripts are returned, rarely with criticism or suggestions.

Copyright:

Held by Plays.

DRUG FORUM

Subscription Data:
Published by the Baywood Publishing Company, Inc., 43 Central
Drive, Farmingdale, New York 11735. Issued quarterly, in
spring, summer, fall, and winter. Advertising is not accepted.
Circulation: 700. Subscription: $25.00 per year; $27.00 for-
eign. Founded: 1971.

Editorial Address:
The Editor, Drug Forum, 43 Central Drive, Farmingdale, New
York 11735.

Editorial Policy:
Includes articles on drug information and research. Drug Forum
is a professional journal addressed to those charged with the responsibility of, and those vitally interested in, seeking solutions
to the problems of drug abuse. It will provide a forum for the
interchange of ideas and information among the international community of individuals involved in the many aspects of drug de-
pendency control. The reading audience includes those in drug
research and treatment programs as well as the public. Unsolicited manuscripts are welcome. Seven or eight major articles are published per issue. Book reviews are included.

Manuscript Preparation:
Accepted manuscripts average approximately 5,000 words. Two
copies are required. Return postage and self-addressed envelope are not required. Bibliographical procedure should follow
the Baywood style. List footnotes on the bottom of page. Manuscripts should be typewritten on white, 8-1/2 by 11 inch, bond
paper double-spaced. The text should be at a level compatible
with the academic background of the broad range of readers in
this professional area. The submitted paper must be an original
work, in English, never before published. A background or explanatory cover letter and a 150 word abstract are required.
Biographical information about the author is required and should
include only the author's affiliation. Illustrations, pictures,
graphs, etc., are acceptable, but should include only original
art work, not photocopies. No payment is made for accepted
manuscripts. Authors will receive 20 reprints of their paper
and a copy of the journal in which the article appears.

Manuscript Disposition:
Receipt of a manuscript is acknowledged by the editor. Editorial
decisions are made within three weeks. Accepted articles usually appear in print within three months. Unaccepted manuscripts
are returned with criticism and/or suggestions.

Copyright:
Held by the Baywood Publishing Company.

GRASSROOTS

Subscription Data:
Published by STASH Press (Student Association for the Study of Hallucinogens), 118 South Bedford Street, Madison, Wisconsin 53703. Issued monthly, January through December. Advertising is not accepted. Circulation: 2,200. Subscription: $95.00 per year. Founded: 1970.

Editorial Address:
The Editor, Grassroots, 118 South Bedford Street, Madison, Wisconsin 53703.

Editorial Policy:
The majority of articles are reprinted from other published sources. Grassroots is a new total drug information service which monthly screens, synthesizes, and digests data from such disparate sources as the underground press and professional journals and symposia proceedings. Combining the resources of the National Coordinating Council on Drug Education and the Student Association for the Study of Hallucinogens, Grassroots presents information unburdened by a moral point of view, with the ultimate aim of helping their readers to get at the roots of the "drug problem," and to search for ways to provide alternatives to drugs by humanizing the institutions. Grassroots will emphasize not only good data on the pharmacological, psychological, and sociological aspects of drug use, but will attempt to identify successful educational, preventive, and rehabilitative strategies. The reading audience includes educated laypersons and drug program administrators. Unsolicited manuscripts are welcome. Five to eight major articles are published per issue. Book reviews are included.

Manuscript Preparation:
No limitations are placed upon manuscript length. Three copies are required. Return postage and a self-addressed envelope are not required. Bibliographical procedure should follow the Index Medicus citation format. A background or explanatory cover letter and an outline, summary, or abstract are recommended. Biographical information about the author is not required. Illustrations, pictures, graphs, etc., must be submitted in a form suitable for photo-reproduction. No payment is made for accepted manuscripts. No reprints are provided to authors.

Manuscript Disposition:
Receipt of a manuscript is acknowledged. Editorial decisions are made within four to six weeks. Accepted articles usually appear in print within three months. Unaccepted manuscripts are not returned. Criticism and/or suggestions are not provided.

Copyright:
Held by STASH Press.

Additional Information:
Grassroots is co-published by STASH Press and the National Coordinating Council on Drug Education.

JOURNAL OF DRUG EDUCATION

Subscription Data:
Published by the Baywood Publishing Company, Inc., 43 Central Drive, Farmingdale, New York 11735. Issued quarterly. Advertising is accepted. Circulation: Not known. Subscription: $25.00 per year; $27.00 foreign. Founded: 1971.

Editorial Address:
Albert E. Bedworth, Editor, Journal of Drug Education, Baywood Publishing Company, Inc., 43 Central Drive, Farmingdale, New York 11735.

Editorial Policy:
Journal of Drug Education provides an international forum for the dissemination of factual drug information. Authoritative and professional in every respect, broad in scope, the Journal presents papers on every phase of drug education prepared by experts throughout the world. Designed to provide a medium for the discussion of all aspects of the drug abuse problem, the Journal addresses itself to those charged with the responsibility of disseminating responsible, accurate information on this subject to the various sectors of our society. Principal areas of investigation are: the role of the educator in drug education; innovations in drug education; school and community drug education programs; drug research information; and drug education as applied to business and industry, law enforcement agencies, the clergy, the military, and all other areas sensitive to the misuse of drugs. Unsolicited manuscripts are welcome. Eight to ten major articles are published per issue. Book reviews are included.

Manuscript Preparation:
Accepted manuscripts average 5,000 words. Two copies are required. Return postage and a self-addressed envelope are not required. Manuscripts should be typewritten on white, 8-1/2 by 11 inch, bond paper, double-spaced. The text should be at a level compatible with the academic background of the broad range of readers in the professional area. The submitted paper must be an original work, in English, never before published. A background or explanatory cover letter is not required, but an outline, summary, or abstract is required. Biographical information about the author is required. Key all photographs, line art, tables, etc., to the text. Unsolicited art is welcome. No payment is made for accepted manuscripts. Authors will receive 20 reprints of their paper and a copy of the Journal in which it appears.

Manuscript Disposition:
Receipt of a manuscript is acknowledged. Editorial decisions are made within three weeks. Accepted articles usually appear in print within three months. Unaccepted manuscripts are returned with criticism and/or suggestions.

Copyright:
Held by Baywood Publishing Company.

JOURNAL OF PSYCHEDELIC DRUGS

Subscription Data:
Co-published by STASH Press (Student Association for the Study of Hallucinogens) and the Haight-Ashbury Free Medical Clinic, 118 South Bedford Street, Madison, Wisconsin 53703. Issued quarterly, in January-March, April-June, July-September, and October-December. Advertising is accepted. Circulation: 3, 800. Subscription: $20. 00 per year; $30. 00 to institutions; $40. 00 foreign. Founded: 1967.

Editorial Address:
The Editor, Journal of Psychedelic Drugs, 118 South Bedford Street, Madison, Wisconsin 53703.

Editorial Policy:
Includes original articles that deal with drug use, drug misuse, drug abuse, drug addiction, psychoactive drugs, altered states of consciousness, or related matters. Overly technical papers will not be considered. The reading audience includes educated laypeople, drug program workers, doctors, psychologists, psychiatrists, etc. Unsolicited manuscripts are welcome. Twelve to eighteen major articles are published per issue. Book reviews are included.

Manuscript Preparation:
No restrictions are placed upon manuscript length. One original and two plain-paper carbons or Xerox copies are required. Return postage and a self-addressed envelope are not required. Bibliographical procedure should follow the Index Medicus citation format. "Suggestions to Contributors Sheet" is available on request from the editor. Manuscripts should be typed on one side of standard 8-1/2 by 11 inch noncorrasable bond typewriter paper, clearly mimeographed or multilithed. Do not use ditto. Footnotes appearing in the text should be single-item citations. A list of all footnotes in numerical order should be typed on a separate sheet and double-spaced. This sheet should be placed immediately after the text material. All material must have ample margins of two inches on each side and 1-1/2 inches on top and bottom. Double-space throughout. A background or explanatory cover letter and an abstract of 200 to 300 words are required. Biographical information about the author is not required. Illustrations must be furnished in a form suitable for photoreproduction. Tables and figures should be kept to a absolute minimum and should supplement rather than duplicate text material. Each table should be typed on a separate sheet and be placed after the references section of the manuscript. Figures should be submitted in a form suitable for photographic reproduction. Use India ink on a good grade of drawing paper. Photographs (black and white only) submitted as figures should be five by seven inch glossy prints, uncropped and marked slightly on the back with a pencil. Submit all figures, photographs, and tables in duplicate with the manuscript. No payment is made for accepted manuscripts. Fifty free reprints are given to primary authors.

Manuscript Disposition:
Receipt of a manuscript is acknowledged. Editorial decisions

are made within four to six weeks. Accepted articles usually appear in print within three to six months. Unaccepted manuscripts are not returned. A critical review by the editorial board is provided.

Copyright:
Held by the Journal of Psychedelic Drugs.

STASH CAPSULES

Subscription Data:
Published by STASH Press (Student Association for the Study of Hallucinogens), 118 South Bedford Street, Madison, Wisconsin 53703. Issued bimonthly, in January-February, March-April, May-June, July-August, September-October, and November-December. Advertising is not accepted. Circulation: 6,000. Subscription: $5.00 per year. Founded: 1968.

Editorial Address:
The Editor, STASH Capsules, 118 South Bedford Street, Madison, Wisconsin 53703.

Editorial Policy:
Includes review articles dealing with psychoactive drugs, drug use-misuses, and related topics. The reading audience includes educated laypersons, drug program workers, and doctors. Unsolicited manuscripts are welcome. One major article is published per issue. Book reviews are not included.

Manuscript Preparation:
Accepted manuscripts average 4,000 to 5,000 words. Three copies are required. Return postage and a self-addressed envelope are required. Bibliographical procedure should follow the Index Medicus citation format. Use two-inch margins throughout and double-space. A background or explanatory cover letter is recommended but an outline, summary, or abstract is not required. Biographical information about the author is not required. Use a minimum of illustrations. Payment is made for accepted articles of $150.00 per article. Twenty-five free copies are given to the author.

Manuscript Disposition:
Receipt of a manuscript is acknowledged. Editorial decisions are made within six weeks. Accepted articles usually appear in print within three or four months. Unaccepted manuscripts are not returned.

Copyright:
Held by STASH Press.

*SPEED: CURRENT INDEX TO THE DRUG ABUSE LITERATURE

Subscription Data:
Published by STASH Press (Student Association for the Study of Hallucinogens), 118 South Bedford Street, Madison, Wisconsin 53703. Issued twice monthly, on the first and fifteenth.

Advertising is not accepted. Circulation: 2, 200. Subscription: $20. 00 per year; $30. 00 foreign. Founded: 1973.

Editorial Address:

The Editor, Speed: Current Index to the Drug Abuse Literature, 118 South Bedford Street, Madison, Wisconsin 53703.

Editorial Policy:

Speed is a bibliographic index. The Index does not publish articles. The reading audience consists of people in libraries and drug program workers.

Copyright:

Held by STASH Press.

ECONOMICS

AMERICAN ECONOMIC REVIEW

Subscription Data:
 Published by the American Economic Association, 1313 Twenty-first Avenue, South, Nashville, Tennessee 37212. Issued five times each year, in March, June, September, and December, plus a Convention Proceedings issue in May. Advertising is accepted. Circulation: 26, 000. Subscription: $30. 00 per year to nonmembers; $20. 00 per year to members; a three-year junior membership of $10. 00 per year is available to registered students. Founded: 1911.

Editorial Address:
 George H. Borts, Editor, American Economic Review, Box Q, Brown University, Providence, Rhode Island 02912.

Editorial Policy:
 Includes articles on economics and related topics. The reading audience includes economists, businessmen, educators, and students. Unsolicited articles are welcome. Twelve major articles and twenty shorter articles are published per issue. Book reviews are not included.

Manuscript Preparation:
 Manuscript length should not exceed 50 pages of double-spaced typescript and should be submitted in duplicate with a submission fee of $10. 00. Return postage and a self-addressed envelope are not necessary. Bibliographical procedure should follow style instructions, available upon request to the editor. Use one inch margins and place footnotes at the end of the article. A background or explanatory cover letter about the article is desired, but not an outline or summary. Abstracts are to be furnished upon request of the editor. Biographical information about the author is not necessary. Tables and figures should be placed on separate pages at the end of the manuscript. Payment is not made for accepted articles. Reprints are available only to authors at the time of publication; fifty free copies are mailed to the author.

Manuscript Disposition:
 Receipt of a manuscript is acknowledged. Editorial decisions are made within six months. Accepted articles usually appear in print within ten to twelve months after acceptance. Unaccepted manuscripts are returned, often with criticism and/or suggestions.

Copyright:
 Held by the American Economic Association.

AMERICAN JOURNAL OF ECONOMICS AND SOCIOLOGY

Subscription Data:
Published by the American Journal of Economics and Sociology, Inc., 50 East Sixty-ninth Street, New York, New York 10021. Issued quarterly, in January, April, July, and October. Advertising is not accepted. Circulation: 2,500. Subscription: $5.00 per year. Founded: 1941.

Editorial Address:
The Editor, American Journal of Economics and Sociology, 50 East Sixty-ninth Street, New York, New York 10021.

Editorial Policy:
Includes articles which relate to synthesis and integration in the social sciences, with emphasis on economics and sociology. The reading audience includes college teachers, research workers, and public and private school administrators. Unsolicited articles are welcome. Nine major articles are published per issue. Book reviews are included.

Manuscript Preparation:
Manuscripts should not exceed 5,000 words. One copy is required. Return postage and a self-addressed envelope are desired. Bibliographical procedure should follow the MLA Style Sheet. Use wide margins and double-space. Footnotes should be placed at the bottom of each page or collected at the end of the article. A background or explanatory cover letter about the article is desired, but not an outline or summary. Biographical information about the author is desired and should include a summary of formal education and indication of current academic or professional association memberships. Illustrations and pictures of professional quality may be used. Graphs must be prepared in India ink. No payment is made for accepted articles. Reprints are available; 100 free copies are mailed to authors with additional orders provided at cost.

Manuscript Disposition:
Receipt of a manuscript is acknowledged. Editorial decisions are made within two months. Accepted articles usually appear in print within one year after acceptance. Unaccepted manuscripts are returned, usually without criticism. Articles that can be placed elsewhere are returned with specific suggestions for resubmission.

Copyright:
Held by the American Journal of Economics and Sociology. Permission to reproduce is granted only with the author's consent.

Additional Information:
A document entitled "Information for Contributions" is available upon request from the office of the editor. The Journal circulates in more than sixty countries of the world. Three microfilm, one microcard, and one offset edition are available in addition to the usual letterpress edition.

ANNALS OF REGIONAL SCIENCE

Subscription Data:
 Published by the Annals of Regional Science, Department of
 Economics, Western Washington State College, Bellingham, Washington 98225. Issued three times each year, in February, June,
 and October. Advertising is accepted. Circulation: 1,100.
 Subscription: $15.00 per year; $8.00 per issue. Founded:
 1967.
Editorial Address:
 The Editor, Annals of Regional Science, Department of Economics, Western Washington State College, Bellingham, Washington
 98225.
Editorial Policy:
 Includes articles on urban, regional, and environmental research
 and policy. The reading audience includes the academician, consultant, and the planner in both the private and the governmental
 sectors. Unsolicited manuscripts are welcome. Twelve to fifteen major articles are published per issue. Book reviews are
 included.
Manuscript Preparation:
 Accepted manuscripts average 15 to 20 double-spaced typewritten
 pages. Three copies are required. Return postage and a self-
 addressed envelope are not required. Bibliographical procedure
 should follow the MLA Style Sheet. Footnotes should be placed
 at the bottom of the respective page. An abstract, preceding
 introduction, is required. Biographical information about the
 author is required and should include a short statement of professional association. Illustrations, pictures, graphs, etc., are
 acceptable, but must be suitable for photographic reproduction.
 One copy of the final version of the approved article shall include all the supplemental materials such as diagrams, tables,
 graphs, and maps drawn in black ink on white paper in a form
 suitable for photographic reproduction, considering the possibility
 of reduction. No payment is made for accepted manuscripts.
 The Annals do not supply complimentary copies of the respective
 issue to the author nor are complimentary reprints provided.
 Authors desiring reprints of their articles should contact Union
 Printing Company, P.O. Box 127, Bellingham, Washington 98225,
 for cost estimates and terms of payment.
Manuscript Disposition:
 Receipt of a manuscript is acknowledged. Editorial decisions
 are made within two to three months. Accepted articles usually
 appear in print within six to twelve months. Unaccepted manuscripts are not returned. Criticism and/or suggestions are pro-
 vided for the revision of accepted manuscripts.
Copyright:
 Held by the Annals of Regional Science.

†ECONOMIC DEVELOPMENT AND CULTURAL CHANGE

Subscription Data:
Published by the University of Chicago Press, 5801 Ellis Avenue, Chicago, Illinois 60637. Sponsored by the Research Center for Economic Development and Cultural Change, University of Chicago, Chicago, Illinois 60637. Issued quarterly, in October, January, April, and July. Advertising is accepted. Circulation: 3,300. Subscription: $10.00 per year; $18.00 for two years; $26.00 for three years; $15.00 per year to institutions; $28.00 for two years; $41.00 for three years; $3.00 per issue; $4.00 per issue to institutions. Founded: 1952.

Editorial Address:
The Editor, Economic Development and Cultural Change, 1130 East Fifty-ninth Street, Chicago, Illinois 60637.

Editorial Policy:
Includes sociological, economic, and anthropological articles and reviews which relate to economic development and cultural change. The reading audience includes sociologists, economists, anthropologists, educators, city planners, economic developers, and other interested persons. Unsolicited articles are welcome. Five to seven major articles are published per issue. Book reviews are included.

Manuscript Preparation:
Accepted manuscripts average from 25 to 40 double-spaced typewritten pages. Two copies are required. Return postage and a self-addressed envelope are desired. Bibliographical procedure should follow the University of Chicago Manual of Style. Use wide margins and double-space throughout. Place all footnotes at the bottom of the page to which they refer. A background cover letter about the article is desired, but not an outline or summary. Biographical information about the author is unnecessary. Illustrations, pictures, graphs, etc., may not be used. No payment is made for accepted articles. Reprints are available; a cost schedule is available through the office of the editor.

Manuscript Disposition:
Receipt of a manuscript is acknowledged. All manuscripts are sent to readers whose comments are evaluated by the editor. Editorial decisions are made within three months. Accepted articles usually appear in print within eight to twelve months after acceptance. Unaccepted manuscripts are returned, often with criticism and/or suggestions based on the readers' comments.

Copyright:
Held by the University of Chicago Press.

GROWTH AND CHANGE

Subscription Data:
Published by the College of Business and Economics, University of Kentucky, 227 Commerce Building, Lexington, Kentucky 40506.

Issued quarterly, in January, April, July, and October. Advertising is not accepted. Circulation: 1,200. Subscription: $7.50 per year; $8.25 to Canada and Mexico; $8.50 to other foreign. Founded: 1970.

Editorial Address:

Executive Editor, Growth and Change, College of Business and Economics, University of Kentucky, Lexington, Kentucky 40506.

Editorial Policy:

Includes policy-related articles, usually ones which outline research and spell out the implications of the research for regional development. Interdisciplinary articles are encouraged. The reading audience includes approximately 800 university and institutional library subscriptions and 400 individuals. Unsolicited manuscripts are welcome. Seven or eight major articles are published per issue. Book reviews are included.

Manuscript Preparation:

Accepted manuscripts average 3,500 words, exclusive of footnotes, tables, and illustrations. Three copies are required with photocopies preferred, but no carbons. Bibliographical procedure should generally follow the University of Chicago Manual of Style. "Guidelines for Authors" sheet is available from the editor on request. All references must be in footnote form, numbered consecutively, double-spaced and typewritten at end of manuscript. Use at least one inch margins on both sides and type double or triple-spaced on one side of the paper only. A background or explanatory cover letter is preferred, but an outline, summary, or abstract is not required. Biographical information about the author is required and should include only author's name and occupational title. Author must supply all camera-ready copy for figures. No payment is made for accepted manuscripts. Reprints are available; 25 free copies are mailed to the author. Additional reprints are available at cost.

Manuscript Disposition:

Receipt of a manuscript is acknowledged. Editorial decisions are made within three to forty weeks. Accepted articles usually appear in print within 12 to 15 months. Unaccepted manuscripts are returned only if author provides postpaid envelope. Criticism and/or suggestions are provided in all cases in which a manuscript is reviewed.

Copyright:

Held by the University of Kentucky College of Business and Economics.

JOURNAL OF DEVELOPING AREAS

Subscription Data:

Published by Western Illinois University, 900 West Adams Street, Macomb, Illinois 61455. Issued quarterly, in January, April, July, and October. Advertising is accepted. Circulation: 1,700. Subscription: $9.00 per year to North America; $12.00 to North American institutional; $7.00 elsewhere. Founded: 1966.

Editorial Address:
   The Editor, Journal of Developing Areas, Western Illinois University, Macomb, Illinois 61455.
Editorial Policy:
   Includes geographic, economic, political, and sociological studies on development primarily, but articles from other fields (education, history, business, physical sciences, music, art, psychology, philosophy, etc.) are also welcome. The reading audience includes primarily scholars and students in the first four fields and practitioners of development in both developed and developing countries. Unsolicited manuscripts are welcome if they fall within an area of interest and are properly prepared. Approximately five major articles are published per issue. Book reviews are included.
Manuscript Preparation:
   Accepted manuscripts average 25 to 35 double-spaced pages on 8-1/2 by 11 inch paper, including double-spaced footnotes. Occasionally both shorter and longer manuscripts are accepted for publication. Three copies are required. Return postage and a self-addressed envelope are required. Bibliographical procedure should follow the University of Chicago Manual of Style. All footnotes should be double-spaced and placed at the end of the text with usually no more than one footnote number per line of text. Footnotes should be grouped as much as possible. Use one inch margins on top, bottom, and both sides and double-space throughout. A background or explanatory cover letter is required, but not an outline, summary, or abstract. Biographical information about the author is not required for submission of an article, but is required before publication. Illustrations, pictures, graphs, etc., should be kept to minimal essential levels; all illustrations (maps and diagrams) must be camera-ready. No payment is made for accepted manuscripts. Author receives two copies of the issue and 50 offprints. Other offprints may be ordered at the time of copy submission to the printer at printer's cost.
Manuscript Disposition:
   Receipt of a manuscript is acknowledged. Editorial decisions are made within 12 weeks. Accepted articles usually appear in print within 12 months. Unaccepted manuscripts are returned if postage has been provided. Criticism and/or suggestions are provided.
Copyright:
   Held by Western Illinois University.
Additional Information:
   Chapters from dissertations and papers prepared for oral presentation are not evaluated; the manuscript has to have been prepared specifically for a journal format. The editorial staff occasionally decides not to evaluate a submitted manuscript by the formal process when it is felt to lack quality. The formal process consists of independent reading by three anonymous referees; the manuscript should be prepared so that the author is also anonymous to the referees. Manuscript preparation information is available upon request.

JOURNAL OF ECONOMIC EDUCATION

Subscription Data:
   Published by the Joint Council on Economic Education, 1212
   Avenue of the Americas, New York, New York 10036.   Issued
   twice each year, in March and October.   Advertising is accepted.
   Circulation: 5, 000.   Subscription: $4. 00 per year.   Founded:
   1969.
Editorial Address:
   Dr. George C. Dawson, Managing Editor, Journal of Economic
   Education, 1212 Avenue of the Americas, New York, New York
   10036.
Editorial Policy:
   Includes articles on the teaching of economics at any educational
   level.   Papers reporting research and evaluation are preferred.
   The reading audience includes teachers of economics in colleges
   and schools and educational administrators and researchers.   Unsolicited manuscripts are welcome.   Seven or eight major
   articles are published per issue.   Book reviews are usually included.
Manuscript Preparation:
   Accepted manuscripts average 10 to 12 double-spaced typewritten
   pages.   Three copies are required.   Return postage and a self-
   addressed envelope are preferred.   Manuscripts should be double-
   spaced and this applies to straight text, footnotes, bibliography,
   and figure legends.   Bibliographical procedure and style should
   follow style sheet which is available from the office of the editor.
   Use standard 8-1/2 by 11 inch white paper and type on one side
   only.   Leave a 1-1/2 inch margin on all four sides of the text.
   Be consistent in usage of capitals, foreign expressions, italicized
   or hyphenated words, and quotation marks.   Footnotes should be
   placed on a separate page.   A background or explanatory cover
   letter is not required, but an outline, summary or abstract is
   preferred.   Give a brief summary interpretation of the article
   at the end, but for shorter articles this may not be necessary.
   Biographical information about the author is not required.   When
   tables are used, the text should not repeat the information contained in the tables, but merely refer to the table in order to
   prove or interpret a statement.   Figures should only be used if
   they present some useful data not easily conveyed by the written
   word.   Legends should be short and those that are longer than
   two lines should be rewritten as part of the text.   No payment
   is made for accepted manuscripts.   No set policy on reprints; however, prints are arranged for if authors request
   them.
Manuscript Disposition:
   Receipt of a manuscript is acknowledged.   Editorial decisions
   are made within eight to twelve weeks.   Accepted articles usually appear in print within six to eight months.   Unaccepted
   manuscripts are usually returned with criticism and/or suggestions.
Copyright:
   Held by the Joint Council on Economic Education.

JOURNAL OF MARKETING

Subscription Data:
  Published by the American Marketing Association, 222 South
  Riverside Plaza, Chicago, Illinois 60606. Issued quarterly, in
  January, April, July, and October. Advertising is accepted.
  Circulation: 29,000. Subscription: $7.00 per year to mem-
  bers; $14.00 to nonmembers; $16.00 foreign. Founded: 1936.
Editorial Address:
  The Editor, Journal of Marketing, Pennsylvania State University,
  Boucke Building 403, University Park, Pennsylvania 16802.
Editorial Policy:
  Includes articles on all phases of marketing. The primary ob-
  jective of the Journal is to make information available regarding
  new marketing discoveries, techniques, ideas, trends, views of
  old problems, and generalizations of scattered concepts. The
  reading audience includes marketing practitioners, businessmen
  interested in marketing, and teachers and students of marketing.
  Unsolicited articles are welcome. Approximately seven to nine
  major articles and two to four Marketing Notes and Communications section articles are published per issue. Book reviews
  are included.
Manuscript Preparation:
  Accepted manuscripts average 20 to 25 double-spaced typewritten pages. Marketing Notes and Communications articles average
  eight to ten double-spaced typewritten pages. Four copies are
  required. Return postage and a self-addressed envelope are unnecessary. Format should follow a recent issue. Footnoting and
  bibliographical procedure should follow the University of Chicago
  Manual of Style or the MLA Style Sheet. Footnotes must be
  placed at the bottom of each page and should be numbered consecutively. Use one inch margins and double-space throughout.
  A background or explanatory cover letter about the article and a
  150 word content summary are required. A 50 to 75 word abstract is required. Biographical information about the author is
  desired in a statement which should not exceed 150 words. Illustrations, pictures, graphs, etc., may be used. All tables
  and charts must have titles and should be numbered consecutively
  using Arabic numerals. No payment is made for accepted articles. Fifteen free reprints per regular article and five free reprints per Marketing Notes and Communications articles are
  given to the author.
Manuscript Disposition:
  Receipt of a manuscript is acknowledged. Editorial decisions
  are made within four to twelve weeks. Accepted articles usually appear in print from two to six months after acceptance. Unaccepted manuscripts are returned, often with detailed critique.
Copyright:
  Held by the American Marketing Association.
Additional Information:
  Supplementary materials, exhibits, appendixes, etc., may be deposited with the American Documentation Institute of the Library
  of Congress.

JOURNAL OF RETAILING

Subscription Data:
> Published by New York University, Institute of Retail Management, Washington Square, New York, New York 10003. Issued four times each year, in January, April, July, and October. Advertising is not accepted. Circulation: 4,000. Subscription: $7.00 per year. Founded: 1925.

Editorial Address:
> The Editor, Journal of Retailing, New York University, Washington Square, New York, New York 10003.

Editorial Policy:
> Includes articles on retailing, marketing, economics, and psychology. The reading audience includes retail executives, teachers of retailing and marketing, management consultants, advertising executives, accountants, sales training executives, and manufacturers interested in marketing. Book reviews are included.

Manuscript Preparation:
> Accepted manuscripts average from 10 to 20 double-spaced typewritten pages. Three copies are required. Return postage and a self-addressed envelope are required. Footnoting and other bibliographical procedure should follow the University of Chicago Manual of Style. Footnotes should be numbered consecutively and must appear at the bottom of the page on which the reference is made. Use 1-1/2 inch margins and double-space throughout. An abstract of approximately 150 words is desired. Biographical information about the author should include exact position and earned degrees. Illustrations, tables, and graphs may be used. No payment is made for accepted articles. Reprints are occasionally available. Authors receive an advance copy of the issue, plus five additional free copies upon publication.

Manuscript Disposition:
> Receipt of a manuscript is acknowledged. Editorial decisions are made within six months. Unaccepted manuscripts are returned with criticism or suggestions.

Copyright:
> Held by New York University.

JOURNAL OF RISK AND INSURANCE

Subscription Data:
> Published by the American Risk and Insurance Association, One State Farm Plaza, Bloomington, Illinois 61701. Issued four times each year, in March, June, September, and December. Advertising is accepted. Circulation: 2,200. Subscription: $15.00 per year. Founded: 1932.

Editorial Address:
> The Editor, Journal of Risk and Insurance, One State Farm Plaza, Bloomington, Illinois 61701.

Editorial Policy:
:   Includes original articles related to the fields of risk and insurance. The reading audience includes university teachers of insurance and others who work in the industry. Unsolicited articles are welcome. Ten major articles are published per issue. Book reviews and communications are included.

Manuscript Preparation:
:   Accepted manuscripts average from 12 to 35 double-spaced typewritten pages. Shorter works will be considered for the communications section of the Journal. Three copies are required. Return postage and a self-addressed envelope are not required. Use one inch margins. Quoted matter which runs more than 30 words should be indented and may be single-spaced. All quoted matter should be separated from other content by a triple space. Footnotes must be numbered consecutively and not more than a 150 word abstract is required. A background or explanatory cover letter about the article is desired, but not an outline or summary. Biographical information about the author will be obtained from a personnel data sheet which is sent to authors of all accepted articles. No pictures can be used, but illustrations and graphs are occasionally used. Each table or chart must appear on a separate page. Use Arabic, not Roman, numerals to identify tables and charts. The author must indicate in the body of the article where each table and chart will appear. No payment is made for accepted articles. Twenty-five free reprints are provided to authors. Other reprints may be ordered at the time of printing via cost sheet and order form which may be obtained through the office of the editor.

Manuscript Disposition:
:   Receipt of a manuscript is acknowledged. Editorial decisions are made within six to eight weeks. Accepted articles usually appear in print within nine months. Unaccepted manuscripts are returned with reasons for rejections.

Copyright:
:   Held by the American Risk and Insurance Association.

Additional Information:
:   Italics should not be used. Center all headings and subheadings.

QUARTERLY REVIEW OF ECONOMICS AND BUSINESS

Subscription Data:
:   Published by the Bureau of Economic and Business Research, College of Commerce and Business Administration, University of Illinois, Urbana, Illinois 61801. Issued four times each year, in February, May, August, and November. Advertising is accepted. Circulation: 1,700. Subscription: $6.00 per year; $8.00 to organizations. Founded: 1961.

Editorial Address:
:   The Editor, Quarterly Review of Economics and Business, 408 David Kinley Hall, University of Illinois, Urbana, Illinois 61801.

Editorial Policy:
    Includes articles on all phases of economic theory and policy.
    The reading audience includes government and business officials,
    college professors, and students. Unsolicited articles are wel-
    come. Five major articles are published per issue. Book re-
    views are included.
Manuscript Preparation:
    Manuscript length varies from 15 to 25 double-spaced typewritten
    pages; also shorter notes. Two copies are required. Return
    postage and a self-addressed envelope are unnecessary. Biblio-
    graphical procedure should follow the University of Chicago Man-
    ual of Style. Place all footnotes on a separate page. Use wide
    margins and double-space throughout. No background or ex-
    planatory cover letter about the article is required. An outline
    or summary of the article is desired with submission of finished
    manuscript. Biographical information about the author is re-
    quested on a printed form soon after an article is accepted for
    publication. Illustrations, graphs, tables, and charts may be
    used. No payment is made for accepted articles. Reprint costs
    vary with article length; 50 free copies are mailed to authors.
Manuscript Disposition:
    Receipt of a manuscript is acknowledged. Editorial decisions
    are made as soon as possible. Accepted articles usually appear
    in print from two to four months after acceptance. Unaccepted
    manuscripts are returned with criticism and/or suggestions.
Copyright:
    Held by the Bureau of Economic and Business Research of the
    University of Illinois.

REVIEW OF SOCIAL ECONOMY

Subscription Data:
    Published by the Association for Social Economics, DePaul Uni-
    versity, 2322 North Kenmore Avenue, Chicago, Illinois 60614.
    Issued twice each year, in April and October. Advertising is
    accepted. Circulation: 950. Subscription: $10.00 per year;
    $11.00 foreign. Founded: 1944.
Editorial Address:
    W.R. Waters, Editor, Review of Social Economy, DePaul Uni-
    versity, 2322 North Kenmore Avenue, Chicago, Illinois 60614.
Editorial Policy:
    Includes articles on all phases of economics and the relationship
    of economics to ethics. The reading audience includes profes-
    sional economists, professors, and students of economics and
    ethics. Unsolicited articles are welcome. Seven major articles
    are published per issue. Book reviews are included.
Manuscript Preparation:
    No policy regarding manuscript length has been established.
    Two copies are required. Return postage and a self-addressed
    envelope are unnecessary. Bibliographical procedure may fol-
    low any widely used style manual. Use wide margins and dou-
    ble-space. Place footnotes at the end of the article. A back-
    ground or explanatory cover letter about the article is not

desired nor is an outline or summary. Biographical information
about the author is desired and should include a summary of his
current position. Illustrations, pictures, graphs, etc., are
rarely used. No payment is made for accepted articles. Reprints are available at cost; 10 free copies are mailed to the
author.

Manuscript Disposition:
  Receipt of a manuscript is acknowledged. Editorial decisions
  are made as soon as possible. Time from acceptance of a manuscript to its appearance in print varies with editorial need. Unaccepted manuscripts are returned, often with criticism and/or
  suggestions.

Copyright:
  Held by Review of Social Economy.

SOUTHERN ECONOMIC JOURNAL

Subscription Data:
  Published jointly by the Southern Economic Association and the
  University of North Carolina at Chapel Hill. Issued four times
  each year, in July, October, January, and April. Advertising
  is accepted. Circulation: 3,500. Subscription: $15.00 per
  year. Founded: 1935.

Editorial Address:
  Managing Editor, Southern Economic Journal, Carroll Hall,
  Chapel Hill, North Carolina 27514.

Editorial Policy:
  Includes articles and notes on all areas of economics. The
  reading audience includes professional economists, educators,
  and students. Unsolicited articles are welcome. Fifteen major
  articles are published per issue. Book reviews are included.

Manuscript Preparation:
  Manuscripts should not exceed 25 double-spaced typewritten
  pages. Two copies are required. Return postage and a self-
  addressed envelope are unnecessary. Footnoting and other bibliographical procedure should follow the University of Chicago
  Manual of Style. Use one inch margins and double-space throughout. A background or explanatory cover letter about the article
  is unnecessary. An abstract is desired with submission of the
  finished manuscript. Biographical information about the author
  is not required. Pictures are rarely included. Illustrations,
  graphs, and charts may be used, but must be submitted in India
  ink. No payment is made for accepted articles. Reprints are
  available; 100 copies are mailed to the author with a submission
  fee of $10.00.

Manuscript Disposition:
  Receipt of a manuscript is acknowledged. Editorial decisions
  are made within two months. Accepted articles usually appear
  in print within three to six months after acceptance. Occasionally the article will appear in the following issue. Unaccepted
  manuscripts are returned, often with criticism and/or suggestions.

EDUCATION - GENERAL

*AMERICAN EDUCATION

Subscription Data:
  Published by the United States Office of Education, Department of Health, Education, and Welfare, 400 Maryland Avenue, S. W., Washington, D. C. 20202. Issued monthly, with double issues in January-February and August-September. Advertising is not accepted. Circulation: 40,000. Subscription: $7.00 per year in the United States. Founded: 1965.

Editorial Address:
  The Editor, American Education, United States Office of Education, 400 Maryland Avenue, S. W., Washington, D. C. 20202.

Editorial Policy:
  Includes articles on federal programs in the field of education. The reading audience includes educators, government officials, advanced students, and members of the general public. Unsolicited articles are rarely used. Five major articles are published per issue. Book reviews are not included.

Copyright:
  Not copyrighted; all material is in public domain.

AMERICAN TEACHER

Subscription Data:
  Published by the American Federation of Teachers, 1012 Fourteenth Street, N. W., Washington, D. C. 20005. Issued quarterly in spring, summer, fall, and winter. Advertising is not accepted. Circulation: 460,000. Subscription: $5.00 per year. Founded: 1916.

Editorial Address:
  The Editor, American Teacher, 1012 Fourteenth Street, N. W., Washington, D. C. 20005.

Editorial Policy:
  Includes articles which deal with all phases of public-school education. The reading audience includes public and private school teachers. Unsolicited articles are welcome. Seven major articles are published per issue. Book reviews are included.

Manuscript Preparation:
  Manuscripts should not exceed 2,000 words. The original and one clear carbon are required. Return postage and a self-addressed envelope are unnecessary. Bibliographical procedure should follow the MLA Style Sheet. Use two inch margins, 60-space lines, and double-space. Footnotes should appear at the bottom of the page to which they refer, but should be used

sparingly. A background or explanatory cover letter is required
and an outline, summary, or abstract is preferred. Biographical information about the author is required. Illustrations, pictures, graphs, etc., are welcome. Payment is made for accepted manuscripts. Reprints, when available, are provided at
cost.

Manuscript Disposition:
Receipt of a manuscript is not acknowledged. Editorial decisions are made within 12 to 16 weeks. Accepted articles usually appear in print within six to eight months. Unaccepted manuscripts are returned without criticism or suggestions.

Copyright:
Not copyrighted.

*ARTS IN SOCIETY

Subscription Data:
Published by Research and Statewide Programs in the Arts, University of Wisconsin-Extension, Room 728, Lowell Hall, 610
Langdon Street, Madison, Wisconsin 53706. Issued three times
each year, in April, July, and October. Advertising is accepted.
Circulation: 5,000. Subscription: $7.50 per year. Founded:
1958.

Editorial Address:
Edward L. Kamarck, Editor, Arts In Society, University of
Wisconsin-Extension, Room 728, Lowell Hall, 610 Langdon
Street, Madison, Wisconsin 53706.

Editorial Policy:
Arts in Society includes four areas: 1) teaching and learning
the arts, 2) aesthetics and philosophy, 3) social analysis, 4) examples of creative expression. The reading audience includes
arts educators, arts professionals and arts administrators, library patrons, arts institutions, and members of the general
public interested in the arts. Author should query first before
sending unsolicited manuscripts. Ten to fifteen major articles
are published per issue. Book reviews are included.

Manuscript Preparation:
Accepted manuscripts average 1,500 to 3,000 words. One copy
is required. Return postage and a self-addressed envelope are
required. Bibliographical procedure should follow the MLA Style
Sheet. Double-space manuscript. A background or explanatory
cover letter is not required nor is an outline, summary, or abstract. Biographical information about the author is required.
Illustrations, black and white photographs, and graphs are all
acceptable. Modest honorarium is paid for manuscripts. Reprints are not available.

Manuscript Disposition:
Receipt of a manuscript is not acknowledged. Editorial decisions
are made within six weeks. Time from acceptance of a manuscript to its appearance in print varies according to when articles
fit within focus of a specific issue. Unaccepted manuscripts are
not returned, but accepted manuscripts are returned if stamped

self-addressed envelope is enclosed.   Criticism and/or suggestions are not provided.
Copyright:
    Held by Arts In Society.

CHANGING EDUCATION

Subscription Data:
    Published by the American Federation of Teachers of the AFL-
    CIO, 1012 14th Street, N. W. , Washington, D. C. 20005.   Issued
    quarterly, in February, May, August, and November.   Circula-
    tion: 325, 000.   Advertising is accepted.   Subscription: $5.00
    per year in combination with the American Teacher.   Founded:
    1966.
Editorial Address:
    The Editor, Changing Education, 1012 14th Street, Washington,
    D. C. 20005.
Editorial Policy:
    Includes articles which deal with education and social change,
    teacher rights, and related topics.   The reading audience in-
    cludes classroom teachers and school administrators.   Unsolic-
    ited articles are welcome.   Twelve major articles are published
    per issue.   Book reviews are included.
Manuscript Preparation:
    Accepted manuscripts average 1, 500 words.   Two copies are
    required.   Return postage and a self-addressed envelope are
    desired.   Use wide margins and double-space throughout.   Bib-
    liographical procedure should follow the University of Chicago
    Manual of Style.   Place all footnotes at the end of the article.
    A background or explanatory cover letter about the article is re-
    quired.   An outline or summary is desired in advance of or with
    submission of the finished manuscript.   Biographical information
    about the author is desired and should include a summary of
    formal education and current employment, plus a recent photo-
    graph.   Drawings, graphs, photographs, etc. , may be used.
    Payment of up to $100.00 is made for accepted articles upon
    publication and up to $35.00 for book reviews.   Reprints are
    available; costs vary with article length.
Manuscript Disposition:
    Receipt of a manuscript is not acknowledged.   Editorial deci-
    sions are made within four months.   Accepted articles usually
    appear in print within six months after acceptance.   Unaccepted
    manuscripts are returned, often with suggestions and/or criti-
    cism.
Copyright:
    Not copyrighted.

CLEARING HOUSE

Subscription Data:
    Published by Fairleigh Dickinson University, Teaneck, New

Jersey 07666. Issued nine times each year, September through
May. Advertising is accepted. Circulation: 9,200. Subscription: $5.00 per year. Founded: 1920.

Editorial Address:
The Editor, Clearing House, Fairleigh Dickinson University,
Teaneck, New Jersey 07666.

Editorial Policy:
Includes articles which relate to junior and senior high school
programs, services, and personnel, including reports of innovation in the classroom, guidance, and administrative organization.
Articles should report current practice, interesting experiments,
research findings, or new slants on persistent educational problems. The reading audience includes junior and senior high
school, college, and university educators. Unsolicited articles
are welcome. Fourteen major articles are published per issue.
Book reviews are included.

Manuscript Preparation:
Manuscripts should not ordinarily exceed 2,500 words, although
short reports of 100 to 600 words are sometimes used. Return
postage and a self-addressed envelope are desired. Bibliographical procedure should follow the University of Chicago Manual of
Style. Use one inch margins and double-space throughout. Place
footnotes at the bottom of each page or on a separate page at
the end of the article. A background or explanatory cover letter
about the article is desired, but no outline or summary is required. Biographical information about author is desired and
should include data regarding school affiliation and current position. Graphs and tables may be used, but photographs may not.
No payment is made for accepted articles. Reprint costs vary
with article length and number of copies ordered.

Manuscript Disposition:
Receipt of a manuscript is acknowledged. Editorial decisions
are made within one to four months. Accepted articles appear
in print from three to four months after acceptance. Unaccepted
manuscripts are returned, often with criticism and/or suggestions.

Copyright:
Held by Clearing House.

Additional Information:
To tailor articles to available space, slight editorial changes
are sometimes made.

COLORADO QUARTERLY

Subscription Data:
Published by the University of Colorado, Boulder, Colorado
80302. Issued quarterly, in July, October, January, and April.
Advertising is not accepted. Circulation: 750. Subscription:
$4.00 per year. Founded: 1952.

Editorial Address:
The Editor, Colorado Quarterly, Hellems 134, University of
Colorado, Boulder, Colorado 80302.

Editorial Policy:
    Includes non-technical articles of general interest written by
specialists in all fields of education. The reading audience includes library patrons and college graduates. Unsolicited manuscripts are welcome. Six or seven major articles are published
per issue. Book reviews are not included.

Manuscript Preparation:
    Accepted manuscripts average 4, 000 to 6, 000 words. One copy
is required. Return postage and a self-addressed envelope are
required. Bibliographical procedure should follow the University
of Chicago Manual of Style. Place footnotes at the end of article. Double-space and use normal margins. A background or
explanatory cover letter is not required nor is an outline, summary, or abstract. A short biographical note about the author
is required if the manuscript is accepted. Illustrations, pictures, graphs, etc., are seldom used. No payment is made for
accepted manuscripts. Reprints of articles are furnished authors
at cost.

Manuscript Disposition:
    Receipt of a manuscript is not acknowledged. Editorial decisions
are made usually within two to three weeks. Accepted articles
usually appear in print within approximately six months. Unaccepted manuscripts are returned if stamped, self-addressed envelope is furnished. Criticism and/or suggestions are provided
if the manuscript might be acceptable with some revision, but
are not provided if the manuscript is rejected.

Copyright:
    Held by the University of Colorado.

COMMUNITY EDUCATION JOURNAL

Subscription Data:
    Published by the Pendell Publishing Company, Box 1666, Mid-
land, Michigan 48640. Issued six times each year. Advertising
is accepted. Circulation: 3, 500. Subscription: $7. 50 per
year; $18. 00 for three years; $12. 00 foreign. Founded: 1971.

Editorial Address:
    The Editor, Community Education Journal, Box 1666, Midland,
Michigan 48640.

Editorial Policy:
    Includes case histories, regional stories, etc. The reading
audience includes adult laymen and educators. Unsolicited manuscripts are welcome. Fifteen to twenty major articles are published per issue. Book reviews are included.

Manuscript Preparation:
    Accepted manuscripts average approximately 2, 500 words. One
original is required. Return postage and a self-addressed envelope are not required. Footnoting and other bibliographical
procedure is not specified. Use one inch margins on the side
and bottom, use two inch margins on the top of the first page,
and one inch margins on each successive page top. A background or explanatory cover letter is not required nor is an

outline, summary, or abstract. Biographical information about
the author is required. Black and white glossy prints or very
good Polaroids are acceptable. No payment is made for accepted
manuscripts. Reprints are made by the Journal.
Manuscript Disposition:
    Receipt of a manuscript is acknowledged. Editorial decisions
    are made within four to six weeks. Accepted articles usually
    appear in print within six to nine months. Unaccepted manu-
    scripts are returned, occasionally with criticism and/or sugges-
    tions.
Copyright:
    Held by the Pendell Publishing Company.

CONTEMPORARY EDUCATION

Subscription Data:
    Published by the School of Education, Indiana State University,
    Terre Haute, Indiana 47809. Issued quarterly, in October,
    January, March, and May. Advertising is not accepted. Circu-
    lation: 3,700. Subscription: $7.00 per year. Founded: 1929.
Editorial Address:
    The Editor, Contemporary Education, Reeve Hall, Room 201,
    Indiana State University, Terre Haute, Indiana 47809.
Editorial Policy:
    Includes articles on education/theory. The reading audience in-
    cludes teachers, administrators, and educators. Unsolicited
    manuscripts are welcome. Nine or ten major articles are pub-
    lished per issue. Book reviews are included.
Manuscript Preparation:
    Accepted manuscripts average 10 to 12 double-spaced typewritten
    pages. One copy is required. Return postage and a self-ad-
    dressed envelope are required. Bibliographical procedure may
    follow Campbell's Form and Style or APA Publication Manual
    and should be scholarly consistent. A background or explanatory
    cover letter is not required nor is an outline, summary, or ab-
    stract. Biographical information about the author is not required.
    Illustrations, pictures, photographs, etc., are acceptable, but
    should be camera-ready. No payment is made for accepted man-
    uscripts. Reprints are available.
Manuscript Disposition:
    Receipt of a manuscript is acknowledged. Editorial decisions
    are made within four weeks. Accepted articles usually appear
    in print within six months to one year. Unaccepted manuscripts
    are returned if stamped self-addressed envelope is provided.
    Criticism and/or suggestions are sometimes provided.
Copyright:
    Held by the School of Education, Indiana State University.

CRITICAL INQUIRY

Subscription Data:
    Published by the University of Chicago Press, 11030 Langley

Avenue, Chicago, Illinois 60628. Issued quarterly, in September, December, March, and June. Advertising is accepted. Circulation: Not determined, but 3,000 for first issue. Subscription: $10.00 per year; $18.00 for two years; $26.00 for three years; $14.00 to institutions; $26.00 for two years; $38.00 for three years; $8.00 to students; $7.50 to charter members; $13.50 for two years; $10.50 to charter institutions; $19.50 for two years. Founded: 1974.

Editorial Address:
Sheldon Sacks, Editor, Critical Inquiry, Wieboldt Hall, 1050 East Fifty-ninth Street, Chicago, Illinois 60637.

Editorial Policy:
Includes articles on criticism and theory of literature, music, visual arts, film, and popular culture. The reading audience includes professionals in literature, music, visual arts, film, and popular culture. Unsolicited manuscripts are welcome. Eight to ten major articles are published per issue. Book reviews are included.

Manuscript Preparation:
Accepted manuscripts have varied in length from five to ninety pages, but there is no policy on length established at this time. Two copies are required. Bibliographical procedure should follow the University of Chicago Manual of Style. Footnotes should be listed separately in order if explanatory; references to page numbers should be in brackets in text after quoted material, with a list of sources on a separate page in alphabetical order. Use 1-1/2 inch margins on the left and one inch margins on the right and double-space. A background or explanatory cover letter is recommended, but not an outline, summary, or abstract. Illustrations are accepted and should accompany articles, and should be in "ready for press" condition. Photographs are acceptable. No payment is made for accepted articles. Author retains rights to republish.

Manuscript Disposition:
Receipt of a manuscript is acknowledged. Editorial decisions are made within four to six weeks. Time from acceptance of an article to its appearance in print varies with editorial need. Unaccepted manuscripts are returned only if envelope and postage is provided by the author. Criticism and/or suggestions are provided in some cases, if requested, and if there are suggestions from readers' reports.

Copyright:
Held by the University of Chicago Press.

*EDCENTRIC

Subscription Data:
Published by the Center for Educational Reform, Inc., a nonprofit, tax exempt corporation, P.O. Box 10085, or 1802, Eugene, Oregon 97401. Issued bimonthly, in February, April, June, September, and December. Exchange advertising is accepted and is a regular policy. Circulation: 5,000. Subscription: $6.00 per year; $10.00 to institutions. Founded: 1969.

Editorial Address:
 The Editor, Edcentric, P. O. Box 10085, or 1802, Eugene, Oregon 97401.

Editorial Policy:
 Includes articles that contain analysis of both the traditional schooling system and the alternative school movement and "experiential learning" articles and reviews of current books on educational change. The articles and book reviews are supplemented by an extensive directory of educational resources, tools, groups, organizations, publications, etc. Previously Edcentric attracted radical learners and teachers, but are currently expanding to include other diverse groups interested in learning and sharing in educational change. Unsolicited manuscripts are only on rare occasions accepted, but they are still welcome. Three to seven major articles are published per issue. Edcentric also includes book reviews, current events of interest, recommended resources, and an extensive directory of new educational resources.

Manuscript Preparation:
 Accepted manuscripts should not exceed 5,000 words with an average of 10 to 15 double-spaced typewritten pages. Two copies are useful. Return postage and a self-addressed envelope are required. Bibliographical procedures are not required, but suggested readings and resource materials pertinent to article topic are very useful. Use one inch margins and double-space. A background or explanatory cover letter is not required nor is an outline, summary, or abstract, but both may be useful for review and suggested directional content. Biographical information about the author is required. Graphics, photographs, and illustrations are welcome, but payment is subject to agreement. Payment is made occasionally for solicited or exceptional manuscripts. Edcentric welcomes reprint of any information included in the magazine, but with the expressed consent of the author.

Manuscript Disposition:
 Receipt of a manuscript is acknowledged. Editorial decisions are made within four weeks. Accepted articles usually appear in print within six months, but depends upon the planned content and focus of up-coming issues. Unaccepted manuscripts are returned if stamped, self-addressed envelope is enclosed. Criticism and/or suggestions are occasionally provided if the author requests.

Copyright:
 When copyrighted, held by authors of the articles.

EDUCATION

Subscription Data:
 Published by Project Innovation, 1402 West Capital Drive, Milwaukee, Wisconsin 53206. Issued quarterly, in September-October, November-December, February-March, and April-May. Advertisement related to educational matters is accepted. Circulation: 3,500. Subscription: $7.50 per year; $10.00 to institutions. Founded: 1880.

Editorial Address:
Robert E. Hoyle, Managing Editor, Education, 1402 West Capitol Drive, Milwaukee, Wisconsin 53206.

Editorial Policy:
Includes original investigations and theoretical papers dealing with worthwhile innovations in learning, teaching, and education. The journal is primarily concerned with teacher education in all of its many aspects. The reading audience includes teachers, educators, teacher education students, and persons interested in education and learning. Unsolicited manuscripts are welcome. From 20 to 24 articles are published in each issue. Book reviews are included.

Manuscript Preparation:
The typical manuscript averages from 2,000 to 3,000 words in length. Two copies of the manuscript and return postage is required. Style sheet is available on request; follow APA Publication Manual. Footnotes are not desired. Background letter is not required. Abstract of not more than 120 words is required. Biographical information required is name and mailing address; institution affiliation is desired. Illustrations, half tones, and dense tables require lithograph plates where cost is borne by the author. No payment is made for accepted articles. Reprints are available from printer at a nominal cost.

Manuscript Disposition:
Receipt of a manuscript is acknowledged. Editorial decisions are made from four to six weeks. Accepted articles are printed generally within one year. Unaccepted articles are returned with criticism.

Copyright:
Held by Project Innovation.

Additional Information:
Articles not invited or marked "Priority" often require author to share in printing costs.

*EDUCATION DIGEST

Subscription Data:
Published by Prakken Publications, Inc., 416 Longshore Drive, Ann Arbor, Michigan 48107. Issued nine times each year, September through May. Advertising is accepted. Circulation: 54,000. Subscription: $7.00 per year. Founded: 1935.

Editorial Address:
The Editor, Education Digest, 416 Longshore Drive, Ann Arbor, Michigan 48107.

Editorial Policy:
Includes articles on all phases of education. The reading audience includes school administrators and teachers. No unsolicited manuscripts can be used. All articles are selections or condensations from other periodicals which relate to education. Sixteen to twenty major articles are published per issue. Book reviews are included.

Copyright:
Held by Prakken Publications, Inc.

EDUCATIONAL FORUM

Subscription Data:
Published by Kappa Delta Pi, Box A, West Lafayette, Indiana 47906. Issued four times each year, in January, March, May, and November. Advertising is not accepted. Circulation: 48,000. Subscription: $7.00 per issue in the United States (special rates for members); $8.00 foreign. Founded: 1935.

Editorial Address:
Harry S. Broudy, Editor, Educational Forum, Room 343, Armory, University of Illinois, Champaign, Illinois 61820.

Editorial Policy:
Includes articles on all phases of education. The reading audience includes educators at all levels in the United States and abroad. Unsolicited articles are welcome. Twelve to fourteen major articles are published per issue. Book reviews are included.

Manuscript Preparation:
Accepted manuscripts should not exceed 4,000 words. One copy is required. Return postage and a self-addressed envelope are required. Bibliographical procedure should follow the University of Chicago Manual of Style. Use two inch margins and double-space. Number footnotes consecutively and place them on a separate page. Include a word count at the end of the manuscript. A background or explanatory cover letter about the article is unnecessary. An outline or summary of the article and biographical information about the author are not required. No illustrations are to be used. No payment is made for accepted manuscripts; 100 free reprints are available.

Manuscript Disposition:
Receipt of a manuscript is acknowledged. Editorial decisions are made within three to four weeks. Accepted articles usually appear in print from 12 to 15 months after acceptance. Unaccepted manuscripts are returned without criticism or suggestions.

Copyright:
Held by Educational Forum.

EDUCATIONAL HORIZONS

Subscription Data:
Official publication of Pi Lambda Theta, 2000 East Eighth Street, Bloomington, Indiana 47401. Issued quarterly. Advertising is not accepted. Circulation: 16,500. Subscription: $5.00 per year. Founded: 1922.

Editorial Address:
The Editor, Educational Horizons, 2000 East Eighth Street, Bloomington, Indiana 47401.

Editorial Policy:
Includes articles on any aspect of education including original research and its application. The reading audience includes people in the field of education. Unsolicited manuscripts are welcome. Five or six major articles are published per issue. Book reviews are not included.

Manuscript Preparation:
 Accepted manuscripts average from 1, 500 to 2, 000 words. The original and one carbon are required. Return postage and a self-addressed envelope are desired. Bibliographical procedure should follow the University of Chicago Manual of Style. Use a 10 space left margin, a 14 space right margin, and double-space throughout. Footnotes, numbered consecutively, should appear at the bottom of each page. A background or explanatory cover letter about the article is not required nor is an outline or summary. Biographical information about the author is required. Illustrations, charts, and tables may be used. No payment is made for accepted articles. Reprints are available, but can be provided only if the author requests copies at the time of publication.

Manuscript Disposition:
 Receipt of a manuscript is acknowledged. A statement of acceptance, rejection, or need for additional editorial time is made as soon as possible. Accepted articles usually appear in print within one year after acceptance. Unaccepted manuscripts are returned, if requested, with a brief reason for rejection.

Copyright:
 Held by Phi Lambda Theta.

EDUCATIONAL PERSPECTIVES

Subscription Data:
 Published by the College of Education, University of Hawaii, 1776 University Avenue, Honolulu, Hawaii 96822. Issued four times each year, in October, December, March, and June. Advertising is not accepted. Circulation: 1, 000 to 1, 500. Subscription: $2. 00 per year. Founded: 1961.

Editorial Address:
 The Editor, Educational Perspectives, College of Education, University of Hawaii, Honolulu, Hawaii 96822.

Editorial Policy:
 Each issue is built around a theme set by an educational board. Topics such as educational TV, educational research, and policy making in education are typical. The reading audience includes educators at all levels, especially administration. Unsolicited articles are welcome. Six to eight articles are published per issue. Book reviews are occasionally included.

Manuscript Preparation:
 Accepted manuscripts average 2, 000 words. One copy is required. Return postage and a self-addressed envelope are unnecessary. Bibliographical procedure should follow the University of Chicago Manual of Style. A background or explanatory cover letter about the article is desired, but not an outline or summary. Biographical information about the author is desired and should include a summary of educational background, indication of current professional position, and a recent photograph. Illustrations, pictures, and graphs may be used. No payment is made for accepted articles. Reprints are not available.

Manuscript Disposition:
  Receipt of a manuscript is acknowledged. Editorial decisions
  are made as soon as possible. Time from acceptance of a
  manuscript to its appearance in print varies with the topic of
  the article and specific plans for future issues. Unaccepted
  manuscripts are returned, often with criticism.
Copyright:
  Held by the University of Hawaii College of Education.
Additional Information:
  The editor will supply themes for future issues upon request.

EDUCATIONAL THEORY

Subscription Data:
  Published by the John Dewey Society, Philosophy of Education
  Society, and the College of Education, Education Building, Uni-
  versity of Illinois, Urbana, Illinois 61801. Issued quarterly, in
  winter, spring, summer, and fall. Advertising is accepted.
  Subscription: $8.00 per year. Founded: 1951.
Editorial Address:
  The Editor, Educational Theory, Education Building, University
  of Illinois, Urbana, Illinois 61801.
Editorial Policy:
  Includes scholarly articles and studies in the foundations of education and in related disciplines outside the field of education
  which contribute to the advancement of educational theory. The
  general purposes of the journal are to foster the continued development of educational theory and to encourage wide and effective discussion of theoretical problems within the profession.
  The reading audience includes professors of history and philosophy of education in colleges and universities, Philosophy of Education Society members, John Dewey Society members, and
  other persons interested in the theoretical aspects of education.
  Unsolicited articles are welcome. Nine or ten major articles
  are published per issue. Book reviews are included.
Manuscript Preparation:
  Accepted manuscripts average from 3,500 to 4,000 words. The
  original and three carbons are required. Return postage and
  a self-addressed envelope are desired. Use wide margins and
  double-space throughout. No set bibliographical style is required, but all footnotes should be prepared in a consistent fash-
  ion. A background or explanatory cover letter about the article
  is required, but not an outline or summary. A brief biographical statement about the author is desired. Illustrations, pictures, and graphs are rarely used. No payment is made for
  accepted articles. Reprint costs vary with article length.
Manuscript Disposition:
  Receipt of a manuscript is acknowledged. Editorial decisions
  are made within two to four months. Manuscripts are submitted to a review board for consideration. Accepted articles
  usually appear in print from nine to eighteen months after acceptance. Unaccepted manuscripts are returned, sometimes
  with criticism and/or suggestions.

Copyright:
Held by Educational Theory. Permission will be granted if an author requests to reprint his article in a book or other publication.

EVALUATION: A FORUM FOR HUMAN SERVICE DECISION-MAKERS

Subscription Data:
Published by the Minneapolis Medical Research Foundation, 501 Park Avenue South, Minneapolis, Minnesota 55415. Issued irregularly, approximately twice a year with additional special issues. Advertising is not accepted. Circulation: 10,000. Subscription: Not determined. Founded: 1972.

Editorial Address:
The Editor, Evaluation, 501 Park Avenue South, Minneapolis, Minnesota 55415.

Editorial Policy:
Includes research project descriptions and summaries, policy statements, overviews, and theoretical concepts--all dealing with program evaluation. The reading audience includes administrators and practitioners in the human services fields. Unsolicited manuscripts are welcome. Twelve to fourteen major articles are published per issue. Book reviews are included and decided for each issue.

Manuscript Preparation:
Accepted manuscripts average under 20 double-spaced typewritten pages. One copy is required. Return postage and a self-addressed envelope are required if author wishes originals to be returned. Bibliographical procedure should follow the Turabian Manual For Writers. Only substance footnotes should be included. References to specific works should be cited in the text and completed citation will be printed in the bibliography section. Use a minimum of one inch margins on all four sides and double-space. A background or explanatory cover letter and an outline, summary, or abstract are not required, but helpful. Biographical information about the author is helpful, but not required unless article is accepted for publication. Illustrations, pictures, graphs, etc., are dependent on paper and should be kept to a minimum. No payment is made for accepted manuscripts. Reprints are made by special request only at expense of party making the request. Ten free copies of the issue in which the article is published are sent to author.

Manuscript Disposition:
Receipt of a manuscript is acknowledged. Editorial decisions are made within eight to sixteen weeks. Accepted articles usually appear in print within six to nine months. Unaccepted manuscripts are returned if stamped, self-addressed envelope is enclosed. Criticism and/or suggestions are usually provided.

Copyright:
Held by the Minneapolis Medical Research Foundation, Inc.

HARVARD EDUCATIONAL REVIEW

Subscription Data:
Published by Harvard Graduate School of Education, Cambridge, Massachusetts 02138. Issued quarterly. Advertising is accepted. Circulation: 14,500. Subscription: $12.00 per year, $3.50 per issue. Founded: 1931.

Editorial Address:
The Editor, Harvard Educational Review, Longfellow Hall, 13 Appian Way, Cambridge, Massachusetts 02138.

Editorial Policy:
Includes articles on the entire field of education, especially theoretical speculation, empirical research, and policy positions. The reading audience includes educators from all academic disciplines. Unsolicited manuscripts are welcome. Four major articles are published per issue. Book reviews are prepared upon invitation of the editor. The editorial board invites readers to react to articles through "Letters to the Editors."

Manuscript Preparation:
Accepted manuscripts average from 5,000 to 10,000 words. Two copies are required. Return postage and a self-addressed envelope are unnecessary. Bibliographical procedure should follow the University of Chicago Manual of Style. Use wide margins and double-space. A brief abstract is required. Biographical information about the author is desired. No payment is made for accepted articles. Each author receives two copies of the journal and 25 free reprints. Additional reprints may be purchased at a price which varies with article length.

Manuscript Disposition:
Receipt of a manuscript is acknowledged within one week. Editorial decisions are made within six to eight weeks. Accepted articles usually appear in print within four months after acceptance. Unaccepted manuscripts are returned, occasionally with criticism.

Copyright:
Held by the Harvard Graduate School of Education.

ILLINOIS SCHOOLS JOURNAL

Subscription Data:
Published by the Chicago State University, 95 and King Drive, Chicago, Illinois 60628. Issued quarterly. Advertising is not accepted. Circulation: 7,500. Subscription: $4.00 per year. Founded: 1906.

Editorial Address:
Dr. Virginia McDavid, Editor, Illinois Schools Journal, English Department, Chicago State University, Chicago, Illinois 60628.

Editorial Policy:
Includes articles of interest to teachers, supervisors, administrators, etc. The reading audience includes teachers, supervisors, administrators, etc. Unsolicited manuscripts are

welcome. Four or five major articles are published per issue.
Book reviews are not included.
Manuscript Preparation:
   Accepted manuscripts average 12 double-spaced pages, but this
   is flexible. Two copies are required. Return postage and a
   self-addressed envelope are required. Footnoting and other bibliographical procedure should follow the MLA Style Sheet. A
   background or explanatory cover letter is required, but not an
   outline, summary, or abstract. Biographical information about
   the author is required. Illustrations can not be used. No payment is made for accepted manuscripts. Five copies are mailed
   to the author.
Manuscript Disposition:
   Receipt of a manuscript is acknowledged. Editorial decisions
   are made within three months. Accepted articles usually appear
   in print within one year. Unaccepted manuscripts are returned
   with criticism and/or suggestions.
Copyright:
   Held by the Chicago State University.

INDEPENDENT SCHOOL BULLETIN

Subscription Data:
   Published by the National Association of Independent Schools, 4
   Liberty Square, Boston, Massachusetts 02109. Issued four
   times each year, in October, December, February, and May.
   Advertising is accepted. Circulation: 9,500. Subscription:
   $6.00 per year. Founded: 1941.
Editorial Address:
   The Editor, Independent School Bulletin, National Association
   of Independent Schools, 4 Liberty Square, Boston, Massachusetts
   02109.
Editorial Policy:
   Includes articles on all aspects of elementary and secondary
   education. The reading audience includes elementary and secondary teachers and administrators, teacher educators, parents,
   and trustees. Unsolicited articles are welcome. Fifteen to
   twenty major articles are published per issue. Only solicited
   book reviews are included.
Manuscript Preparation:
   Accepted manuscripts average from 2,500 to 3,000 words. One
   double-spaced copy is required. Return postage and a self-addressed envelope are desired. A background or explanatory
   cover letter about the article is desirable, but no outline or
   summary is required. Biographical information about the author
   is required and should include a summary of current professional
   position. Illustrations, pictures, and graphs may be submitted.
   No payment is made for accepted articles. Reprints are not
   available.
Manuscript Disposition:
   Receipt of a manuscript is acknowledged. Editorial decisions
   are made as soon as possible. Time from acceptance of a

manuscript to its appearance in print varies with editorial need.
Unaccepted manuscripts are returned, sometimes with criticism.
Copyright:
Held by the National Association of Independent Schools.

INTELLECT (formerly School and Society)

Subscription Data:
Published by the Society for the Advancement of Education, Inc.,
1860 Broadway, New York, New York 10023. Issued monthly,
October through May. Selected advertising is accepted; advertising rate-cards are available upon request. Circulation:
10,500. Subscription: $15.00 per year. Founded: 1915.
Editorial Address:
William W. Brickman, Editor, Intellect, Graduate School of Education, University of Pennsylvania, Philadelphia, Pennsylvania
19174.
Editorial Policy:
Includes articles on educational theory and criticism, humanities,
and social sciences. The reading audience includes college and
university faculty, administration, and advanced students. Unsolicited manuscripts are welcome. Ten to twelve major articles
are published per issue. Book reviews are included.
Manuscript Preparation:
Accepted manuscripts average 3,500 words maximum. One copy
is required. Return postage and a self-addressed envelope are
desired. Footnoting and bibliographical procedure should follow
Intellect's own style sheet available on request to the editor.
A background or explanatory cover letter is not required. A
one-sentence brief summary and a one-sentence brief quotation
are required. Biographical information about the author is desired and should include title, professional address, and
position. No graphs or tables can be used. No payment is
made for accepted manuscripts. Apply to the main office for
reprints.
Manuscript Disposition:
Receipt of a manuscript is not acknowledged. Editorial decisions are made within one month. Accepted articles usually
appear in print within six months. Unaccepted manuscripts are
returned if postage accompanies the manuscript. Criticism
and/or suggestions are provided.
Copyright:
Held by the Society for the Advancement of Education, Inc.

JOURNAL OF AESTHETIC EDUCATION

Subscription Data:
Published by the University of Illinois Press, University of Illinois at Urbana-Champaign, Urbana, Illinois 61801. Issued
quarterly, in January, April, July, and October. Advertising
is accepted. Circulation: 1,500. Subscription: $7.50 per
year. Founded: 1966.

Editorial Address:
    Ralph A. Smith, Editor, Journal of Aesthetic Education, 288B
College of Education, University of Illinois at Urbana-Champaign,
Urbana, Illinois 61801.

Editorial Policy:
    The Journal welcomes the following types of manuscripts: ar-
ticles devoted to an understanding of the basic problem areas
of education in the arts and the humanities (literature, music,
the visual and performing arts, etc.); articles dealing with the
aesthetic aspects of the art and craft of teaching in general;
articles devoted to the appreciation and understanding of the aesthetic character of other disciplines and subjects, such as the
sciences, mathematics, etc.; and articles treating the aesthetic
import and significance of the new communications media and
the environmental arts in their various forms. All articles
should include explicit discussions of educational relevance. Unsolicited manuscripts are welcome. Approximately seven major
articles are published per issue. Book reviews are included.

Manuscript Preparation:
    Accepted manuscripts average 4,000 to 5,000 words, but this
will vary. Two copies are required. Return postage and a
self-addressed envelope are required. Footnoting and other bibliographical procedure should follow the form sheet provided by
the Journal. A background or explanatory cover letter is not
required nor is an outline, summary, or abstract. Biographical information about the author is required. Few illustrations,
pictures, graphs, etc., are used. No payment is made for
accepted manuscripts. One hundred copies are available for
purchase by the author.

Manuscript Disposition:
    Receipt of a manuscript is acknowledged. Editorial decisions
are made within two to three weeks. Time from acceptance
of a manuscript to its appearance in print varies with editorial
need. Unaccepted manuscripts are returned, sometimes with
criticism and/or suggestions.

Copyright:
    Held by the University of Illinois Press.

JOURNAL OF EDUCATION

Subscription Data:
    Published by the Boston University School of Education, 765
Commonwealth Avenue, Boston, Massachusetts 02115. Issued
four times each year, in February, April, October, and December. Paid advertising will be accepted per approval of each
advertisement by the editorial board. Circulation: 2,500. Subscription: $5.00 per year; $1.25 per issue. Founded: 1875.

Editorial Address:
    The Editor, Journal of Education, School of Education, 765 Com-
monwealth Avenue, Boston, Massachusetts 02115.

Editorial Policy:
    Articles of generic interest to educational practitioners are

included. Articles concerning practical issues and concerns of educators around the country as highlighted by research and local situation are particularly encouraged. Purely theoretical articles are discouraged; relevance for practicing educators must be demonstrated. The reading audience includes educators in formal elementary through college institutions, public and private, as well as industrial and governmental. Unsolicited manuscripts are welcome. They are subject to a blind referee reviewing system. Approximately 10 major articles are published per issue. A book review section is a major part of the Journal. Primary contributions are accepted from the B. U. School of Education faculty although other contributors would be welcome.

Manuscript Preparation:
There is no minimum or maximum length for articles considered for publication. Clarity of expression is more important than the length of an article. Authors should submit the original typed manuscript along with two copies. Return postage and a self-addressed envelope are not required, but desirable. Footnoting and other bibliographical procedure should follow the APA Publication Manual. All manuscripts must be double-spaced and be of reputable preparation. A background or explanatory cover letter is not required unless the manuscript in entirety does not accompany submission. An abstract of 100 to 200 words in length is required. Biographical information about the author is not required. Illustrations, pictures, graphs, etc., should follow the APA Publication Manual. No payment is made for accepted manuscripts except for those requested. Reprint requests will be fulfilled at the rate of $1.25 per copy plus postage.

Manuscript Disposition:
Receipt of a manuscript is acknowledged. Editorial decisions are made within four weeks when possible. Accepted articles usually appear in print within 12 months. Unaccepted manuscripts are returned with criticism and/or suggestions provided if the article is of interest to the Journal of Education; if not, the author is so informed.

Copyright:
Held by the Trustees of Boston University. All material published in the Journal is the copyrighted property of the Journal.

JOURNAL OF SPECIAL EDUCATION

Subscription Data:
Published by Buttonwood Farms, Inc., 3515 Woodhaven Road, Philadelphia, Pennsylvania 19154. Issued four times each year, in spring, summer, fall, and winter. Advertising is accepted. Circulation: 3,500. Subscription: $15.00 per year; $16.00 Canadian and International; $10.00 to students. Founded: 1967.

Editorial Address:
The Editor, Journal of Special Education, 443 South Gulph Road, King of Prussia, Pennsylvania 19406.

Editorial Policy:
The Journal is multidisciplinary and publishes articles of

research, theory, opinion, and review respecting special education and areas of special concern to general education. It is
intended as a forum for all disciplines engaged in these areas.
The Journal is most interested in publishing articles that are
definitive and carefully documented. It is less interested in
case studies and general surveys, although articles of unusual
interest will be considered. The reading audience includes professionals in education, administration, psychiatry, psychology,
social work, and special education. Unsolicited manuscripts are
welcome. Eight to ten major articles are published per issue.
Book reviews are occasionally included.

Manuscript Preparation:
At present articles both of extended length and of a short "report" type are acceptable; in the event of any questions regarding article length, prospective authors should contact the editors.
Three copies are required; however, do not send original manuscript for it will not be returned. Bibliographical procedure
should follow wherever possible the general directions given in
the APA Publication Manual. The style of writing should be
such as to make the article comprehensible to the Journal's multidisciplinary audience. It is recommended that authors, when
using technical terms uncommon outside of their own professional
boundaries, include brief parenthetical definitions, short footnotes,
or even a glossary explaining them. A background or explanatory
cover letter is required. Each manuscript should include an abstract or summary not exceeding 300 words. Biographical information about the author is required and should include credentials
and background. Do not send original artwork; if manuscript is
accepted, artwork will then be requested. Original artwork must
be black and white, high-contrast glossies suitable for photo-
ready reproduction. No payment is made for accepted manuscripts. Every author of accepted articles will receive 20 free
reprints of their article with opportunity to order more at nominal cost.

Manuscript Disposition:
Receipt of a manuscript is acknowledged. Unaccepted manuscripts
are not returned.

Copyright:
Held by Buttonwood Farms, Inc.

MARQUETTE UNIVERSITY EDUCATION REVIEW

Subscription Data:
Published by the School of Education, Marquette University, 502
North Fifteenth Street, Milwaukee, Wisconsin 53233. Issued
twice each year, in spring and fall. Currently only advertising
pertaining to Marquette University is included. Subscription:
Free to educational institutions and organizations, libraries, and
to professional educators; $1.00 per issue. Founded: 1970.

Editorial Address:
The Editor, Marquette University Education Review, School of
Education, Marquette University, 502 North Fifteenth Street,
Milwaukee, Wisconsin 53233.

Editorial Policy:
   Includes timely and topical articles dealing with any area of education that includes reports of research, statement of opinion, comparative analysis, etc. The reading audience includes professional educators and students of education. Unsolicited manuscripts are welcome. Four to six major articles are published per issue. Book reviews are frequently included.

Manuscript Preparation:
   Accepted manuscripts average six to twelve double-spaced typewritten pages. One copy is required. Return postage and a self-addressed envelope are desired. Bibliographical procedure may follow any accepted scholarly form. Place footnotes on a separate page. Use normal manuscript margins and double-space. A background or explanatory cover letter and an outline, summary, or abstract are desired, but not required. Illustrations, graphs, etc., can be included; however, pictures with articles are not desired. No payment is made for accepted manuscripts. Fifty free copies of the issue containing their article is given each author. No reprints are available.

Manuscript Disposition:
   Receipt of a manuscript is acknowledged. Editorial decisions are made normally within two months. Accepted articles usually appear in print within one to two months. Unaccepted manuscripts are returned with criticism and/or suggestions.

Copyright:
   Not copyrighted.

Additional Information:
   Copies of back issues are available from the editor. Subscription requests are to be forwarded to the editor.

NRTA JOURNAL

Subscription Data:
   Published by the National Retired Teachers Association of the United States. Issued six times each year, in January, March, May, June, September, and November. Advertising is not accepted. Circulation: 250,000. Subscription: $2.00 per year with Association membership. Founded: 1947.

Editorial Address:
   The Editor, NRTA Journal, 215 Long Beach Boulevard, Long Beach, California 90802.

Editorial Policy:
   Includes articles on topics of interest to retired teachers. The reading audience includes retired teachers. Unsolicited articles can be used. The number of articles published per issue varies. Book reviews are not included.

Manuscript Preparation:
   Accepted manuscripts average from 500 to 2,500 words. One copy is required. Return postage and a self-addressed envelope are required. No special requirements for bibliographical style. Use standard manuscript margin and spacing. A background or explanatory cover letter is not required nor is an outline, summary, or abstract. Biographical information about the author

is not required.   Payment is made for accepted manuscripts.
Manuscript Disposition:
    Receipt of a manuscript is acknowledged.   Editorial decisions
    are made within six weeks.   Unaccepted manuscripts are re-
    turned, sometimes with criticism and/or suggestions.
Copyright:
    Held by the National Retired Teachers Association of the United
    States.

NATIONAL EDUCATIONAL SECRETARY

Subscription Data:
    Published by the National Association of Educational Secretaries,
    1801 North Moore Street, Arlington, Virginia 22209.   Issued
    four times each year, in September, December, March, and
    June.   Advertising is accepted.   Circulation: 6,500.   Subscrip-
    tion: $5.00 per year; free as part of $10.00 a year Association
    dues.   Founded: 1934.
Editorial Address:
    Miss Virginia Mathony, Editor, National Educational Secretary,
    14277 Eastridge Drive, Whittier, California 90602.
Editorial Policy:
    Includes articles on education and secretarial procedure and As-
    sociation events.   The reading audience includes members of the
    National Association of Educational Secretaries, office employees
    in school systems and other educational offices, secretarial sci-
    ence educators, and administrators.   Unsolicited manuscripts
    are welcome.   Two or three major articles and other shorter
    articles are published per issue.   Book reviews are included in
    some issues.
Manuscript Preparation:
    No limitations are placed upon manuscript length, but they should
    not exceed 1,500 words.   All manuscripts will be edited to avail-
    able space.   Two copies are required.   Return postage and a
    self-addressed envelope are required.   Footnoting and other bib-
    liographical procedure should follow the NEA Style Manual.   Use
    wide margins and double-space.   A background or explanatory
    cover letter is required, but not an outline, summary, or ab-
    stract.   Biographical information about the author is desired and
    should include author's achievements in education.   Illustrations,
    pictures, graphs, etc., are desired when they complement the
    article; use professional glossy photographs.   No payment is
    made for accepted manuscripts.   Reprints are not available.
Manuscript Disposition:
    Receipt of a manuscript is acknowledged.   Editorial decisions
    are made usually within two weeks.   Accepted articles appear-
    ance in print depends upon editorial need.   Unaccepted manu-
    scripts are returned, seldom with criticism and/or suggestions.
Copyright:
    Held by the editor in name of the National Association of Educa-
    tional Secretaries.
Additional Information:
    Material may be reprinted with permission of the editor.

NOTRE DAME JOURNAL OF EDUCATION

Subscription Data:
Published by the University of Notre Dame, P.O. Box 686,
Notre Dame, Indiana 46556. Issued quarterly, in spring, summer, fall, and winter. Advertising is accepted. Circulation:
2,000. Subscription: $9.00 per year; $16.50 for two years;
$24.00 for three years. Founded: 1970.

Editorial Address:
The Editor, Notre Dame Journal of Education, P.O. Box 686,
Notre Dame, Indiana 46556.

Editorial Policy:
Includes professional educational articles. The reading audience
includes educators, people in libraries and university libraries,
and anyone interested in professional educational readings. Unsolicited manuscripts are welcome. Approximately 10 major articles are published per issue. Book reviews are occasionally
included.

Manuscript Preparation:
Accepted manuscripts average approximately 15 typewritten pages.
One copy is required, but two are preferred. Return postage
and a self-addressed envelope are preferred. Bibliographical
procedure should follow the MLA Style Sheet. Prefer footnotes
be placed at the end of the manuscript, but any consistently
footnoted manuscript is acceptable. A background or explanatory
cover letter is not required nor is an outline, summary, or abstract. Biographical information about the author is required and
should include name, position, place of affiliation, and other publications. No payment is made for accepted manuscripts. Reprints are not available.

Copyright:
Not copyrighted.

PTA MAGAZINE

Subscription Data:
Published by PTA Magazine, Inc., 700 North Rush Street, Chicago, Illinois 60611. Issued monthly, September through June.
Advertising is accepted. Circulation: 70,000. Subscription:
$3.50 per year; $.50 per issue. Founded: 1906.

Editorial Address:
The Editor, PTA Magazine, 700 North Rush Street, Chicago,
Illinois 60611.

Editorial Policy:
Includes non-fiction articles on child and youth guidance, parent
education, home-school cooperation, and international problems
which affect children, families, and schools. The reading audience includes parents, teachers, school administrators, psychologists, psychiatrists, child guidance workers, youth leaders,
and members of the general public. Unsolicited manuscripts
are welcome. Ten major articles are published per issue.
Book reviews are not included.

Manuscript Preparation:

Accepted manuscripts average 1, 800 words. One copy is required. Return postage and a self-addressed envelope are desired. Bibliographical procedure should follow the University of Chicago Manual of Style. Use wide margins and double-space. A background or explanatory cover letter about the article is desired, but not an outline or summary. Biographical information about the author is required and should include his full name, current position, school or university, and a list of previous publications. Photographs and illustrations may be used. Contributors are usually paid between $100 and $150 per article. Each author receives three complimentary copies of the magazine.

Manuscript Disposition:

Receipt of a manuscript is not acknowledged. Editorial decisions are made within three to six weeks. Accepted articles appear in print as soon as possible. Unaccepted manuscripts are returned without suggestions or criticism.

Copyright:

Held by PTA Magazine, Inc.

PEABODY JOURNAL OF EDUCATION

Subscription Data:

Published by the George Peabody College for Teachers, Nashville, Tennessee 37203. Issued quarterly, in October, January, April, and July. Advertising is accepted. Circulation: 2, 700. Subscription: $6.00 per year; $8.00 to institutions. Founded: 1923.

Editorial Address:

Ralph E. Kirkman, Editor, Peabody Journal of Education, George Peabody College for Teachers, Nashville, Tennessee 37203.

Editorial Policy:

The Peabody Journal of Education is interdisciplinary and is designed to foster the professional development and enrichment of teachers, administrators, and other leaders in education. The Journal carries full-length articles and short contributions as well as book reviews, editorial comment, and occasional special features of interest to faculty and administrators alike. The reading audience includes educators and others interested in institutions of learning. Unsolicited manuscripts are welcome. Eight to twelve major articles are published per issue. Book reviews are included.

Manuscript Preparation:

Accepted manuscripts average six to twelve pages. Three copies are required. Return postage and a self-addressed envelope are required. Bibliographical procedure should follow the MLA Style Sheet. The author's name and institution association should be indicated on a separate page rather than on the manuscript. Footnotes should be placed on a separate page and at the end of each manuscript. Manuscripts should follow standard margins and should be double-spaced. A background or explanatory cover

letter is not required nor is an outline, summary, or abstract.
Biographical information should include, on a separate page,
author's name and institutional affiliation. Illustrations, pictures,
graphs, etc., are accepted. No payment is made for manuscripts. Contributors are given six free copies of the Journal
in which their articles appear. Reprints may be purchased at
publication cost.

Manuscript Disposition:
All manuscripts are acknowledged. Editorial decisions are made
within 45 days. Accepted articles appear in print within three
to six months. Unaccepted manuscripts are returned, provided
the authors supply stamped, self-addressed envelope. Criticism
and/or suggestions are not provided unless requested.

Copyright:
Held by the George Peabody College for Teachers.

PHI DELTA KAPPAN

Subscription Data:
Published by Phi Delta Kappa, Inc., Eighth Street and Union
Avenue, Bloomington, Indiana 47401. Issued monthly, September through June. Advertising is accepted in limited quantity
(about four pages per issue). Circulation: 105,000. Subscription: $8.00 per year; $1.00 per issue. Founded: 1915.

Editorial Address:
The Editor, Phi Delta Kappan, Eighth Street and Union Avenue,
Bloomington, Indiana 47401.

Editorial Policy:
Includes particularly those articles having to do with educational
policy, trends, significant news, and new developments of all
kinds. The reading audience includes educational leaders and
policy makers. Nearly one-half are administrators at all levels;
over one-third are connected with colleges and universities;
around 15 percent are K through 12th grade teachers. Unsolicited manuscripts are welcome. Twelve to twenty major articles
are published per issue. Book reviews are included.

Manuscript Preparation:
Accepted manuscripts average 750 to 3,500 words. One copy is
required, but prefer two. Return postage and a self-addressed
envelope are preferred. Bibliographical information about the
author is required and should include his position, title, institutional affiliation, and qualifications for writing on topic of manuscript. Illustrations, pictures, and graphs may be used. Payment is seldom made for accepted articles, never for unsolicited
materials. Photo-offset reprints of articles are available; a
price list may be obtained through the office of the editor.

Manuscript Disposition:
Receipt of a manuscript is acknowledged. Editorial decisions
are made immediately to six months. Accepted articles usually
appear in print from six weeks to one year after acceptance.
Unaccepted manuscripts are returned, sometimes with criticism
and suggestions.

Copyright:
    Held by Phi Delta Kappa, Inc.
Additional Information:
    Views expressed in articles, editorials, or reviews may either
support or oppose positions taken by Phi Delta Kappa as an
organization.

PHI KAPPA PHI JOURNAL

Subscription Data:
    Published by the Honor Society of Phi Kappa Phi, 3001 Plymouth
Road, Ann Arbor, Michigan 48105. Issued quarterly, in winter,
spring, summer, and fall. Advertising is not accepted. Circulation: 75,000. Subscription: Free with membership dues;
$3.00 to non-members.
Editorial Address:
    Robert M. Lightfoot, Jr., Editor, Phi Kappa Phi Journal,
Cullom-Davis Library, Bradley University, Peoria, Illinois
61606.
Editorial Policy:
    Includes articles and addresses dealing with education and schol-
arship. The Journal cuts across all academic fields with articles pertaining to all fields welcome; however, since readers
are not all of any one discipline, highly technical contributions
cannot be used. A few short poems are acceptable. The reading audience includes Phi Kappa Phi membership primarily, but
not entirely. Unsolicited manuscripts are welcome. Approximately 10 to 12 major articles are published per issue. Book
reviews are not included.
Manuscript Preparation:
    Accepted manuscripts average 2,000 to 4,000 words. Two cop-
ies are required. Return postage and a self-addressed envelope
are welcome, but not required. Bibliographical procedure should
follow the MLA Style Sheet or University of Chicago Manual of
Style. Type manuscript and double-space. A background or explanatory cover letter is desirable, but an outline, summary, or
abstract is not required. Biographical information about the
author is required and should include present position and Phi
Kappa Phi connection. Author's picture is customarily published,
but need not be sent until after acceptance. No payment is made
for accepted manuscripts. Each author receives 20 copies of
the article or 10 copies of the poem. Reprints are not available,
but extra copies can be provided if requested.
Manuscript Disposition:
    Receipt of a manuscript is acknowledged only if it appears that
the decision will be slow in response. Editorial decisions are
made usually within two to six weeks. Accepted articles usually appear in print within six to twelve months, but this varies
depending on timeliness and other factors. Unaccepted manuscripts are returned, sometimes with criticism and/or suggestions if it appears that some changes will make an article publishable.

Copyright:
    Held by Phi Kappa Phi. Reprint rights are normally granted on
    request if acknowledgment is made.

SCHOLASTIC TEACHER

Subscription Data:
    Published by the Scholastic Magazines, Inc. , 50 West Forty-
    fourth Street, New York, New York 10036. Issued monthly,
    September through May. Advertising is accepted. Circulation:
    440, 000 combined circulation (Elementary Teacher's Edition and
    Junior-Senior High Teacher's Edition). Subscription: $4.95 per
    year. Founded: 1946.
Editorial Address:
    The Editor, Scholastic Teacher, 50 West Forty-fourth Street,
    New York, New York 10036.
Editorial Policy:
    Helping teachers grow professionally is a primary concern of
    Scholastic Teacher. ST's editorial takes teachers beyond the de-
    tails of day-to-day classroom routines and into the "big issues"
    on the American education scene today; accountability, perform-
    ance contracting, teacher tenure, open education, ethnic studies,
    corporal punishment, compulsory education, vouchers, etc. ST
    takes its readers into model classrooms, to talk with creative
    teachers, around the country and keeps teachers in touch with
    the most recent curriculum developments and trends, the most
    provocative education controversies. Their major features are
    usually national in scope and report on controversies, trends,
    or innovations in education. Their articles are usually about
    a single innovative school program or teaching method. Also
    included are potpourri items and teaching tips. The reading
    audience includes elementary school teachers of grades one
    through six, junior and senior high school teachers of English,
    social studies, humanities and science. Unsolicited manuscripts
    are welcome, but a query letter is suggested. Five or six ma-
    jor articles are published per issue. All book reviews are as-
    signed by the review editor.
Manuscript Preparation:
    Accepted manuscripts average from 1, 000 to 2, 000 words for
    major features; 1, 500 words or less for articles; 500 words or
    less for potpourri items; 100 to 200 words for teaching tips.
    One copy is required. Return postage and a self-addressed en-
    velope are required. Short related bibliography may be added
    to the manuscript. ST prefers "original material" ... not re-
    search-type articles with lists of footnotes. The manuscript
    should be typewritten, double-spaced, and have a 76 character
    line. A background or explanatory cover letter is required, but
    not an outline, summary, or abstract. Biographical information
    about the author is required. Photographs of good quality that
    are preferably eight by ten inch glossy black and white prints
    are desired. (They are paid for separately, if used.) Payment
    is made for accepted manuscripts at the rate of $150.00 and up

for major features on assignment only; $40.00 to $75.00 for
articles upon acceptance; $10.00 and up for potpourri items
upon publication; $5.00 and up for teaching tips upon publication.
Reprints are available by special order.

Manuscript Disposition:
Receipt of a manuscript is acknowledged. Editorial decisions
are made within six weeks. Time from acceptance of an article
to its appearance in print varies widely with subject of the article and editorial needs. Unaccepted manuscripts are returned,
often with criticism and/or suggestions.

Copyright:
Held by the Scholastic Magazines, Inc.

SCHOOL AND COMMUNITY

Subscription Data:
Published by the Missouri State Teacher Association, P.O. Box
458, Columbia, Missouri 65201. Issued monthly, September
through May. Advertising is accepted. Circulation: 52,000.
Subscription: $4.50 per year, $.50 per issue. Founded: 1920.

Editorial Address:
The Editor, School and Community, P.O. Box 458, Columbia,
Missouri 65201.

Editorial Policy:
Includes articles on the entire field of education. The reading
audience includes elementary, secondary, and college teachers,
supervisors, principals, counselors, superintendents, and PTA
and school board members. Unsolicited manuscripts are welcome. Twelve major articles are published per issue. Book
reviews are not included.

Manuscript Preparation:
Accepted manuscripts average from 625 to 1,500 words. One
copy is required. Return postage and a self-addressed envelope
are desired. Use one inch margins and double-space. A background or explanatory cover letter about the article is required.
Biographical information about the author is desired and should
include his full name and position; no photograph is required.
Avoid use of illustrations. No payment is made for accepted
articles. Reprint costs vary with article length. Each author
receives five free copies of the journal.

Manuscript Disposition:
Receipt of a manuscript is acknowledged immediately. Editorial
decisions are made within one week. Accepted articles usually
appear in print within three months after acceptance. Unaccepted
manuscripts are returned, sometimes with criticism or suggestions.

Copyright:
Held by School and Community.

SCHOOL REVIEW

Subscription Data:
Published by the Department of Education, University of Chicago, 5835 Kimbark, Chicago, Illinois 60637. Issued quarterly, in spring, summer, autumn, and winter. Advertising is accepted. All advertising correspondence should be addressed to University of Chicago Press, 5801 Ellis Avenue, Chicago, Illinois 60637. Circulation: 3,800. Subscription: $10.00 per year; $14.00 to institutions; $5.00 to students; $3.00 per issue; $3.75 per issue to institutions; $2.50 per issue for bulk rate. Founded: 1893.

Editorial Address:
Editorial Office, School Review, 5835 Kimbark Avenue, Chicago, Illinois 60637.

Editorial Policy:
Includes articles on original research, philosophical discussion, and critical appraisal of all aspects of education. In addition to articles, School Review publishes book reviews, short essays, opinions, and informal expressions of original thinking. Additional discussion of provocative articles may be solicited for publication. About 70% of each issue is mailed to libraries, about 20% to schools, and about 10% to individuals. Unsolicited articles are welcome. Approximately 35 articles are published per volume; four to five major articles are published per issue. Book reviews are included.

Manuscript Preparation:
No limitations are placed on manuscript length. Three copies, return postage, and a self-addressed envelope are required. Bibliographical procedure should follow the University of Chicago Manual of Style. Use wide margins and double-space throughout. Place all footnotes and references at the end of the article. A background or explanatory cover letter is not desired nor is an outline or summary. Biographical information should include a summary of the author's professional background. Illustrations, pictures, and graphs are rarely used. No payment is made for accepted articles. Reprints are available; a cost summary may be obtained through the editorial office.

Manuscript Disposition:
Receipt of a manuscript is acknowledged. Editorial decisions are made within two to three months. Accepted articles usually appear in print within one year after acceptance. Unaccepted manuscripts are returned if postage and self-addressed envelope are provided. Criticism and/or suggestions are not regularly provided.

Copyright:
Held by the University of Chicago; however, an author may copyright his own work.

*STUDIES IN EDUCATION

Subscription Data:
Published by the College of Education of West Texas State University, Box 208, Canyon, Texas 79016. Issued once each year, in September. Advertising is not accepted. Circulation: 300. Subscription: Free as long as supply lasts. Founded: 1956.

Editorial Address:
The Editor, Studies in Education, West Texas State University, Box 208, Canyon, Texas 79016.

Editorial Policy:
Includes research articles in education. The reading audience includes public school teachers, administrators, and professors of education. Unsolicited manuscripts are not welcome. Four major articles are published per issue. Book reviews are not included.

Copyright:
Not copyrighted.

*STUDIES IN PHILOSOPHY AND EDUCATION

Subscription Data:
Published by Studies in Philosophy and Education, Inc., Southern Illinois University, Edwardsville, Illinois 62025. Issued irregularly. Advertising is accepted. Circulation: 1,500. Subscription: $8.00 per year; $9.00 to libraries; $8.50 foreign individuals; $9.50 foreign libraries. Founded: 1960.

Editorial Address:
The Editor, Studies in Philosophy and Education, Southern Illinois University, Edwardsville, Illinois 62025.

Editorial Policy:
Includes articles which relate to all phases of philosophy of education. The primary purpose of the journal is to provide a forum for advanced philosophical contemplation in the field of educational theory. The reading audience includes professional educational philosophers and others in related fields such as the foundations of education. Unsolicited articles are welcome, but most articles are written by invitation. Number of major articles varies per issue. Book reviews are included in a book review issue.

Manuscript Preparation:
Accepted manuscripts average 10,000 words with the maximum approaching monograph length. Two copies are required. Return postage and a self-addressed envelope are desired. Footnoting and other bibliographical procedure should follow the University of Chicago Manual of Style. Use wide margins and double-space. A background or explanatory cover letter about the article is not necessary nor is an outline, summary, or abstract. Ordinarily a one page prospectus should be sent to the editorial board before any major writing is undertaken. Biographical information about the author is unnecessary. Illustrations, pictures, graphs, etc., may not be used. No payment is made for accepted articles. Reprints are not available.

Manuscript Disposition:
   Receipt of a manuscript is acknowledged. Editorial decisions
   are made by members of an editorial board as soon as possible.
   Time from acceptance of a manuscript to its appearance in print
   varies with editorial need. Unaccepted manuscripts are returned,
   sometimes with suggestions and/or criticism.
Copyright:
   Held by Studies in Philosophy and Education, Inc.

TEACHERS COLLEGE RECORD

Subscription Data:
   Published by Teachers College, Columbia University, 525 West
   One-hundred and twentieth Street, New York, New York 10027.
   Issued four times each year, September, December, February,
   and May. Advertising is accepted. Circulation: 7,000. Sub-
   scription: $10.00 per year. Founded: 1900.
Editorial Address:
   The Editor, Teachers College Record, Teachers College, Co-
   lumbia University, 525 West One-hundred and twentieth Street,
   New York, New York 10027.
Editorial Policy:
   Includes articles on all aspects of education and related issues
   of public and social policy and intellectual concern. The reading audience includes professors and professionals in education
   and related fields in humanities and social sciences. Unsolicited
   articles are welcome. Seven to ten major articles are published
   per issue. Book reviews are included.
Manuscript Preparation:
   Accepted manuscripts average from 3,500 to 5,000 words, although longer articles are occasionally used. Two copies are
   required. Return postage and a self-addressed envelope are
   necessary. Bibliographical procedure should follow the University of Chicago Manual of Style or the MLA Style Sheet. List
   footnotes at the end of the article. Use wide margins and double-space. A background or explanatory cover letter about the
   article is useful, but no outline or summary is required. Biographical information about the author is not required. Graphs
   and tables may be used, but do not include any illustrations or
   pictures. No payment is made for accepted articles. Reprints
   are available; a cost summary may be obtained from the office
   of the editor. One-hundred free reprints are mailed to the author.
Manuscript Disposition:
   Receipt of a manuscript is acknowledged. Editorial decisions
   are made within two months. Accepted articles usually appear
   in print within twelve months after acceptance. Unaccepted
   manuscripts are returned, sometimes with criticism and/or suggestions.
Copyright:
   Held by Teachers College, Columbia University.
Additional Information:
   A yearly media and direct mail promotion is conducted.

*THEORY INTO PRACTICE

Subscription Data:
> Published by the College of Education, Ohio State University, 1945 North High Street, Columbus, Ohio 43210. Issued five times each year, in October, December, February, April, and June. Advertising is not accepted. Circulation: 3,200. Subscription: $5.00 per year, $9.00 for two years. Founded: 1962.

Editorial Address:
> The Editor, Theory Into Practice, College of Education, Ohio State University, 29 W. Woodruff, Columbus, Ohio 43210.

Editorial Policy:
> Includes articles on all phases of education. The reading audience includes public school teachers and administrators, and university faculty. Unsolicited articles cannot be used. From 10 to 15 articles are published per issue. Book reviews are occasionally included.

Copyright:
> Held by the Ohio State University College of Education.

THRUST (formerly Journal of Secondary Education)

Subscription Data:
> Published by the Association of California School Administrators, 1550 Rollins Road, Burlingame, California 94010. Issued six times each year, in October, November, January, February, April and May. Advertising is accepted. Circulation: 7,200. Subscription: $6.00 per year; $1.50 per issue; $6.50 foreign. Founded: 1925.

Editorial Address:
> Henry D. Weiss, Managing Editor, Thrust, Suite 50, 1550 Rollins Road, Burlingame, California 94010.

Editorial Policy:
> Includes articles on all phases of education concentrating on current management and learning process activities. The reading audience includes administrators, teachers, professors, and school board members. Unsolicited articles are welcome. Eight major articles are published per issue.

Manuscript Preparation:
> Accepted manuscripts average from 2,500 to 3,000 words. One copy is required. Return postage and a self-addressed envelope are desired. See a recent issue for bibliographical style. Use wide margins and double-space. A background or explanatory cover letter about the article is desired, but not an outline or summary. Biographical information about the author is desired and should include a summary of present position. Pictures may be used and charts and graphs are often used. No payment is made for accepted articles. Reprints are available.

Manuscript Disposition:
   Receipt of a manuscript is acknowledged. Accepted articles
usually appear in print from three to six months after acceptance. Unaccepted manuscripts are returned without criticism
or suggestions.
Copyright:
   Held by the Association of California School Administrators.

TODAY'S EDUCATION (formerly NEA Journal)

Subscription Data:
   Published by the National Education Association of the United
States, 1201 Sixteenth Street, N. W., Washington, D. C. 20036.
Issued four times a year, in September-October, November-
December, January-February, and March-April. Advertising
is accepted. Circulation: 1,500,000. Subscription: $1.05 per
year (included and available only as part of membership dues).
Founded: 1913.
Editorial Address:
   The Editor, Today's Education, National Education Association
of the United States, 1201 Sixteenth Street, N. W., Washington,
D. C. 20036.
Editorial Policy:
   Includes articles on all phases of education and service pages.
The reading audience includes educators at all levels. Unsolicited articles are welcome. Eight to twelve major articles are
published per issue. Book reviews are included.
Manuscript Preparation:
   Accepted manuscripts average from 1,500 to 1,800 words. Two
copies are required. Return postage and a self-addressed envelope are desired. All manuscripts must be prepared in Today's Education style. Use 1-1/2 inch margins and double-
space. Because all statements are checked before publication,
detailed footnotes are needed for reference purposes. A background or explanatory cover letter may accompany the manuscript if the author so desires; no outline or summary of the
article is required. Biographical information about the author
is required and should include a complete address and indication of published works and current educational position.
Illustrations, pictures, graphs, etc., may be used. No payment
is made for accepted articles. Reprint information will be supplied on request.
Manuscript Disposition:
   Receipt of a manuscript is acknowledged. Editorial decisions
are made within three months. Time from acceptance of a
manuscript to its appearance in print varies with editorial need.
Unaccepted manuscripts are returned with a letter of explanation
without criticism or suggestions.
Copyright:
   Held by the National Education Association of the United
States.

URBAN EDUCATION

Subscription Data:
 Published by Sage Publications, 275 South Beverly Drive, Beverly Hills, California 90212. Issued quarterly, in April, July, October, and January. Advertising is accepted. Circulation: 1,200 to 1,500. Subscription: $10.00 per year to individuals and professionals; $15.00 to institutions; $8.00 to full-time students. Founded: 1966.

Editorial Address:
 Warren Button, Editor, Urban Education, Foster Hall, State University of New York at Buffalo, Buffalo, New York 14214.

Editorial Policy:
 Includes articles on research and innovation related to urban education. The reading audience includes city school administrators, teachers and professors, and other interested social scientists. Unsolicited articles are welcome. Four or five major articles are published per issue. Book reviews are included.

Manuscript Preparation:
 Accepted manuscripts range from 20-25 double-spaced typewritten pages. Two copies are required. Return postage and a self-addressed envelope are desired. Bibliographical procedure should follow the special style sheet available from the editor. Footnotes and references should appear on a separate page at the end of the manuscript. Manuscripts should have a 1-1/2 inch margin, be double-spaced and typewritten. A background or explanatory cover letter about the article is desired, but not an outline or summary. Biographical information about the author is required and a summary is requested when article is accepted. Authors are required to submit camera-ready black and white art; no photographs. No payment is made for accepted articles. Two complete copies of the issue and 25 tearsheets are supplied each author without charge; an order form for additional reprints, quoting prices for quantities of 100 or more, is mailed to each author upon publication.

Manuscript Disposition:
 Receipt of a manuscript is acknowledged. Editorial decisions are made within six to eight weeks. Accepted articles usually appear in print within six months after acceptance. Unaccepted manuscripts are returned, generally with criticism.

Copyright:
 Held by Sage Publications.

*VIEWPOINTS

Subscription Data:
 Published by the School of Education, Education 109, Indiana University, Bloomington, Indiana 47401. Issued bimonthly, in January, March, May, July, September, and November. Advertising is not accepted. Circulation: 1,000. Subscription: $8.00 per year. Founded: 1924.

Editorial Address:
> The Editor, Viewpoints, Room 109, School of Education, Indiana University, Bloomington, Indiana 47401.

Editorial Policy:
> Includes scholarly essays about education that range from classroom experiences through reports of research findings. The reading audience includes a cross-section of administrators and practitioners at various levels ranging from preschool to higher education. Unsolicited manuscripts are not welcome; all the articles are commissioned. Approximately eight major articles are published per issue but this will vary. Book reviews are not included.

Manuscript Preparation:
> Reprints are not available.

Manuscript Disposition:
> Accepted articles usually appear in print within three months of receipt of manuscript. Unaccepted manuscripts are returned with criticism and/or suggestions.

Copyright:
> Held by the School of Education, Indiana University.

EDUCATIONAL RESEARCH

AMERICAN EDUCATIONAL RESEARCH JOURNAL

Subscription Data:
Published by the American Educational Research Association, 1126 Sixteenth Street, N. W., Washington, D. C. 20036. Issued quarterly, in winter, spring, summer, and fall. Advertising is accepted at the publisher's address. Circulation: 14,000. Subscription: $10.00 per year; $18.00 for two years. Founded: 1964.

Editorial Address:
Kaoru Yamamoto, Editor, American Educational Research Journal, College of Education, Arizona State University, Tempe, Arizona 85281.

Editorial Policy:
Includes original reports of empirical and theoretical studies in education. The reading audience includes members of the American Educational Research Association and other researchers in education. Unsolicited manuscripts are welcome. Up to 10 major articles are published per issue. Book reviews are included.

Manuscript Preparation:
Manuscripts should average between five and fifteen pages in length. The original and two copies are required for editorial review which usually takes two to three months. Return postage and a self-addressed envelope are not required, although highly desired. Bibliographical procedure should follow the APA Publication Manual. Manuscripts should be typed double-spaced (including quotations, footnotes, and references) on 8-1/2 by 11 inch noncorrasable bond, with ample margins. The author's name and affiliation should appear on a separate cover page, and only on this page, to insure anonymity in the reviewing process. A background or explanatory cover letter is not required. Include, on separate pages, an abstract of 100 to 120 words, and a biographical resume of the author (and all co-authors, if any) giving name, position, office address, degrees and institutions, areas of specialization, and AERA divisional membership. The format of headings, tables, figures, citations, references, and other details must follow the style described in the APA Publication Manual. All figures must be camera-ready. Manuscripts which do not conform to these specifications will be returned immediately to the author for proper style change. No payment is made for accepted manuscripts. Fifty free reprints will be provided the author, or the principal author, of each article published in the Journal. Additional reprints may be ordered at

the time galley proof is returned.

Manuscript Disposition:

Receipt of a manuscript is acknowledged. Editorial decisions are made within three weeks, if immediately unacceptable, and 15 weeks, if reviewed. Accepted articles usually appear in print within 12 months. Unaccepted manuscripts are returned with criticism and/or suggestions provided if reviewed.

Copyright:

Held by the American Educational Research Association.

CALIFORNIA JOURNAL OF EDUCATIONAL RESEARCH

Subscription Data:

Published by the California Teachers Association, 1705 Murchison Drive, Burlingame, California 94010. Issued five times each year, in January, March, May, September, and November. Advertising is not accepted. Circulation: 1,200. Subscription: $10.00 per year. Founded: 1950.

Editorial Address:

Garford G. Gordon, Editor, California Journal of Educational Research, Psychology Department, San Jose State University, San Jose, California 95192.

Editorial Policy:

Includes original research in education, critical reviews of educational research, and reports of demonstration projects based on concepts devised for research. The reading audience includes educational researchers, public school teachers, and teacher trainers. Unsolicited manuscripts are welcome. Four major articles are published per issue. Book reviews are sometimes included.

Manuscript Preparation:

Accepted manuscripts average 1,500 to 3,000 words. The original plus one copy are required. Return postage and a self-addressed envelope are required. Bibliographical procedure should follow the APA Publication Manual. A background or explanatory cover letter and a 150 word abstract are required. Biographical information about the author is required. Illustrations, pictures, graphs, etc., are accepted and should be clearly and accurately titled, inked to size, and placed within text at appropriate place. No payment is made for accepted manuscripts. Authors receive five free copies and may order additional copies from the printer.

Manuscript Disposition:

Receipt of a manuscript is acknowledged. Editorial decisions are made within four weeks. Accepted articles usually appear in print within six months. Unaccepted manuscripts are returned with criticism and/or suggestions.

Copyright:

Held by the California Teachers Association.

†EDUCATIONAL RECORDS BUREAU BULLETIN

Subscription Data:
  Published by the Educational Records Bureau, Darien Plaza,
  16 Thorndal Circle, Darien, Connecticut 06820. Issued twice
  each year. Advertising is not accepted. Circulation: 1,250.
  Subscription: Free to members of the Educational Records Bureau;
  $5.00 per year to others; $3.50 per issue. Founded: 1927.
Editorial Address:
  The Editor, Educational Records Bureau Bulletin, Educational
  Records Bureau, Darien Plaza, 16 Thorndal Circle, Darien,
  Connecticut 06820.
Editorial Policy:
  Includes articles which deal with problems in the field of educational tests and measurements. The reading audience includes
  guidance personnel and administrators of elementary and secondary schools and colleges. Unsolicited articles are welcome.
  Five major articles are published per issue. Book reviews are
  not included.
Manuscript Preparation:
  Accepted manuscripts average 1,500 words. Two copies are required. Return postage and a self-addressed envelope are unnecessary. Avoid use of footnotes when possible. Use wide
  margins and double-space. A background or explanatory cover
  letter about the article is required. An outline or summary of
  the article is desired in advance of or with submission of the
  finished manuscript. Biographical information about the author
  is desired and should summarize professional affiliations and
  pertinent experience. Illustrations, pictures, graphs, etc., may
  be used. No payment is made for accepted articles. Reprints
  are provided at cost.
Manuscript Disposition:
  Receipt of a manuscript is acknowledged. Editorial decisions
  are made within one month. Accepted articles usually appear
  in print within six months after acceptance. Unaccepted manuscripts are returned, often with criticism.
Copyright:
  Held by the Educational Records Bureau.

JOURNAL OF EDUCATIONAL MEASUREMENT

Subscription Data:
  Published by the National Council of Measurement in Education,
  Inc., Office of Evaluation Service, Michigan State University,
  East Lansing, Michigan 48823. Issued quarterly, in spring,
  summer, fall, and winter. Advertising is accepted. Circula-
  tion: 3,000. Subscription: $10.00 per year; Free to Council
  members. Founded: 1964.
Editorial Address:
  Richard M. Jaeger, Editor, Journal of Educational Measurement,
  College of Education, FAO292, University of South Florida,
  Tampa, Florida 33620.

Editorial Policy:
Includes articles on all aspects of applied educational measurement. The reading audience includes school, university, and technical school personnel. Unsolicited articles are welcome. Approximately seven articles are published per issue. Book reviews are included.

Manuscript Preparation:
No limitations are placed upon manuscript length. Three copies are required. Return postage and a self-addressed envelope are unnecessary. Footnoting and other bibliographical procedure should follow the APA Publication Manual. Use one inch margins and double-space. A background or explanatory cover letter about the article is usually unnecessary. An abstract of no more than 150 words is requested. Illustrations, pictures, and graphs may be used. No payment is made for accepted articles. Reprints are available; 50 free copies are mailed to the author. Additional reprints may be ordered at time the author returns corrected galley proofs.

Manuscript Disposition:
Receipt of manuscript is acknowledged if a stamped, self-addressed postcard is provided. Editorial decisions are made by two referees within one to three months. Accepted articles usually appear in print within six to twelve months after acceptance. Unaccepted manuscripts are returned with suggestions and/or criticism.

Copyright:
Held by the National Council of Measurement in Education, Inc.

Additional Information:
Authors are encouraged to read the statements of editorial policy for the Journal on page ii in the Spring - 1970 issue.

JOURNAL OF EDUCATIONAL RESEARCH

Subscription Data:
Published by Dembar Educational Research Services, Inc., 2101 Sherman Avenue, Box 1605, Madison, Wisconsin 53701. Sponsored by the American Educational Research Association, 1201 Sixteenth Street, N. W., Washington, D. C. 20036. Issued ten times each year, with May-June and July-August issues combined. Selected advertising is accepted. Circulation: 6,500. Subscription: $10.00 per year; $1.50 per issue. Founded: 1920.

Editorial Address:
The Editor, Journal of Educational Research, Dembar Educational Research Services, Inc., 2101 Sherman Avenue, Box 1605, Madison, Wisconsin 53701.

Editorial Policy:
Includes critiques, articles, and reports on research from the entire field of education. The reading audience includes public school, college, and university teachers, students of education, and school administrators. Unsolicited articles are welcome. Ten to fifteen major articles are published per issue. Book reviews which summarize research-based materials are included.

Manuscript Preparation:
    Accepted manuscripts average from 1,500 to 3,000 words and
    should include a statement of the problem, related research,
    population and methodology, and a summary. One copy is re-
    quired. Return postage and a self-addressed envelope are de-
    sired. Bibliographical procedure should follow the University
    of Chicago Manual of Style. A guide to manuscript preparation
    may be obtained from the office of the editor. Use wide mar-
    gins and double-space. A background or explanatory cover let-
    ter about the article is desired. An abstract of not more than
    120 words, which may be published in place of the article, with
    approval of the author, is required. The abstract should include
    a statement of the problem, method, results, and conclusions.
    In a review or discussion article, state the topics covered and
    the central thesis. A brief biographical sketch about the author
    is desired. Graphs and tables may be used, but not pictures.
    Contributors are charged $6.00 per printed page (approximately
    1,200 words) for published articles. Reprints are available at
    cost; costs vary with article length and order volume. Each
    author receives ten free copies of the Journal.
Manuscript Disposition:
    Receipt of a manuscript is immediately acknowledged. Editorial
    decisions are made within two months. Accepted articles usually
    appear in print within one year to eighteen months after ac-
    ceptance. Unaccepted articles are returned, often with criti-
    cism.
Copyright:
    Held by the Dembar Educational Research Services, Inc.

JOURNAL OF EXPERIMENTAL EDUCATION

Subscription Data:
    Published by Dembar Educational Research Services, Inc., Box
    1605, Madison, Wisconsin 53701. Issued quarterly. Advertising
    is accepted. Circulation: 2,044. Subscription: $10.00 per
    year; $3.00 per issue. Founded: 1931.
Editorial Address:
    Professor John Schmid, Editor, Journal of Experimental Educa-
    tion, Department of Research & Statistical Methodology, Univer-
    sity of North Colorado, Greeley, Colorado 80631.
Editorial Policy:
    Includes articles and reports of research from the entire field
    of education, with emphasis on specialized and technical prob-
    lems of sophisticated design. The reading audience includes
    scholars and researchers from all areas of education. Unsolic-
    ited articles are welcome. Ten major articles are published
    per issue. Book reviews are included.
Manuscript Preparation:
    Accepted manuscripts average from 3,000 to 5,000 words. One
    copy is required. Return postage and a self-addressed envelope
    are desired. Bibliographical procedure should follow A Manual
    of Form for Theses and Term Reports by Dugdale; a general
    guide may be obtained from the office of the editor. Use wide

margins and double-space. A background or explanatory cover
letter about the article is desired, but not an outline or summary. Biographical information about the author is desired.
Tables and graphs may be used. Contributors are charged $6.00
per printed page (approximately 1,200 words) for published articles. Each author receives ten free copies of the Journal. Additional copies and reprints may be ordered at cost; costs vary
with article length and order volume.

Manuscript Disposition:

Receipt of a manuscript is immediately acknowledged. Editorial
decisions are made within one month. Accepted articles usually
appear in print within nine-twelve months after acceptance. Unaccepted manuscripts are returned, often with criticism.

Copyright:

Held by Dembar Educational Research Service, Inc.

JOURNAL OF RESEARCH AND DEVELOPMENT IN EDUCATION

Subscription Data:

Published by the College of Education, University of Georgia,
Athens, Georgia 30601. Business office at 175 West Wieuca
Road, N.W., Atlanta, Georgia 30342. Issued four times each
year, in spring, summer, fall, and winter. Advertising is not
accepted. Circulation: 3,000. Subscription: $7.00 per year;
$8.00 foreign. Founded: 1967.

Editorial Address:

The Editor, Journal of Research and Development in Education,
175 West Wieuca Road, N.W., Atlanta, Georgia 30342.

Editorial Policy:

Each issue is devoted to a central theme with the editorial board
selecting the theme for each issue. Criteria for theme selection are: relevancy, breadth of interest, and availability of
scholarly collaboration on a broad geographical basis. The editorial board invites theme selection from scholars, researchers
and developers, as well as professional organizations in education. Unsolicited manuscripts must be accompanied by postage
paid return envelope if the author wishes them returned. There
is no specific number of articles in each issue, but there is a
page limitation of 110 pages for each issue. Book reviews are
not included.

Manuscript Preparation:

No limitations are placed upon manuscript length. One copy of
the manuscript must be submitted for review. Return postage
and a self-addressed envelope are required. The Journal's own
style manual is furnished to authors in the event their material
is accepted for inclusion in an issue. Manuscripts should be
accompanied by an abstract. Biographical information is required from each author. Graphs are acceptable when necessary,
but not encouraged. Illustrations, pictures, etc., are not used.
No payment is made for accepted manuscripts. Reprints are
not available.

Manuscript Disposition:

Receipt of a manuscript is acknowledged. Editorial decisions

are made within no specific time schedule. Accepted article selection is normally one year in advance of publication. Unaccepted manuscripts are returned if the author includes postage paid envelope. Criticism and/or suggestions are not provided.

Copyright:
Held by the University of Georgia.

RESEARCH IN HIGHER EDUCATION

Subscription Data:
Published by the APS Publications Inc., 150 Fifth Avenue, New York, New York 10011. Issued quarterly, in March, June, September, and December. Advertising is not accepted. Circulation: 1,000. Subscription: $12.00 per year; $20.00 to institutions. Founded: 1973.

Editorial Address:
Charles F. Elton, Research in Higher Education, College of Education, Department of Higher Education, University of Kentucky, Lexington, Kentucky 40506.

Editorial Policy:
Includes quantitative studies. The reading audience includes institutional researchers, faculty, university administrators, and student and personnel specialists. Unsolicited manuscripts are welcome. Seven or eight major articles are published per issue. Book reviews are not included.

Manuscript Preparation:
Accepted manuscripts vary in length. Two copies are required. Return postage and a self-addressed envelope are not required. Footnoting and other bibliographical procedure should follow the APA Publication Manual. A background or explanatory cover letter is not required, but a 120 word abstract is required. Biographical information about the author is not required. Illustrations, pictures, graphs, etc., are acceptable if they can be reproduced. No payment is made for accepted manuscripts. Reprints may be purchased at the time of reading galley proofs.

Manuscript Disposition:
Receipt of a manuscript is acknowledged. Editorial decisions are made within four weeks. Accepted articles usually appear in print within six to twelve months. Unaccepted manuscripts are returned with criticism and/or suggestions.

Copyright:
Held by the APS Publications Inc.

Additional Information:
Each manuscript is read by two consulting editors and is graded on a manuscript rating form on a five point scale.

REVIEW OF EDUCATIONAL RESEARCH

Subscription Data:
Published by American Educational Research Association, 1126 Sixteenth Street, N.W., Washington, D.C. 20036. Issued four

times each year. Selected advertising is accepted. Circulation: 5, 500. Subscription: $10.00 per year; $27.00 for three years; $3.00 per issue. Founded: 1930.

Editorial Address:

The Editor, Review of Educational Research, Box 2604, Princeton, New Jersey 08540.

Editorial Policy:

Publishes critical, integrative reviews of research literature bea bearing on education, including reviews and interpretations of substantive and methodological issues. Is not limited to reviews of educational research as such, but welcomes reviews of research in the social and behavioral sciences, management sciences, humanities etc., as long as they bear on educational issues. Although the Review does not publish original empirical research studies, some reporting of original research would be considered acceptable if it extends or provides closure to a broader integrative review. The reading audience includes college and public school directors of research, and college professors. The previous policy of publishing solicited review manuscripts organized around a single topic for each issue was replaced by a policy of publishing unsolicited reviews of research on topics of the contributor's own choosing. The Review will occasionally publish solicited, but carefully referred, analytical reviews of current major issues, studies, or books. Approximately six articles are published per issue. Book reviews are not included.

Manuscript Preparation:

No limitations on accepted manuscripts. Three copies are required. Return postage and a self-addressed envelope are not required. The APA Publication Manual should be consulted for bibliographical procedure. Neither a background or explanatory cover letter nor an outline, summary, or abstract are required. Biographical information about the author is required for inclusion at the end of published articles. May include camera-ready copies of graphs and charts. Payment is not made for accepted manuscripts. Author receives 50 free reprints; additional reprints charged on the basis of length of precribed paper and number of copies desired.

Manuscript Disposition:

Receipt of a manuscript is acknowledged. Editorial decisions are made in approximately 12 to 16 months. Accepted articles appear in print generally within six months from acceptance. Unaccepted manuscripts are returned with criticism and/or suggestions generally provided from referees comments.

Copyright:

Held by the American Educational Research Association.

Additional Information:

Papers submitted are reviewed by at least two referees whose recommendations are relied on heavily in their decision to accept or reject.

ELEMENTARY EDUCATION

AMS BULLETIN

Subscription Data:
  Published by the American Montessori Society, 175 Fifth Avenue, New York, New York 10010. Issued quarterly, usually in March, June, September, and December. Advertising is not presently accepted. Circulation: 3,500. Subscription: $15.00 per year as part of membership dues. Founded: 1960.

Editorial Address:
  The Editor, AMS Bulletin, 175 Fifth Avenue, New York, New York 10010.

Editorial Policy:
  Includes reports on all phases of application of Montessori methods and principles to American education and on related methods of teaching. The reading audience includes AMS members (schools, teachers, parents, etc.), other nursery schools, and libraries and universities with interest in contemporary activities of the Montessori movement in America. Unsolicited manuscripts can be considered. Approximately one or two major articles are published per issue. Book reviews are not included.

Manuscript Preparation:
  Accepted manuscripts average from 24 to 32 double-spaced pages. A minimum of two copies are required. Return postage and a self-addressed envelope are required. Submit the bibliographical procedure to be followed. Use one inch margins and double-space. A background or explanatory cover letter is required and an outline, summary, or abstract of the article is helpful. Biographical information about the author is required. Illustrations, pictures, graphs, etc., should be limited. No payment is made for accepted manuscripts. Reprints are possible.

Manuscript Disposition:
  Receipt of a manuscript is acknowledged. Unaccepted manuscripts are returned if requested. Criticism and suggestions are not provided.

Copyright:
  Held by the American Montessori Society.

AMS NEWS

Subscription Data:
  Published by American Montessori Society, 175 Fifth Avenue, New York, New York 10010. Issued quarterly, in March, May, October, and December. Advertising is not presently accepted. Circulation: 3,500. Subscription: $15.00 per year and included with membership in the Society. Founded: 1970.

Editorial Address:
 The Editor, AMS News, American Montessori Society, 175 Fifth
 Avenue, New York, New York 10010.
Editorial Policy:
 Includes articles on Montessori education in schools, special
 programs, etc., and items on related early childhood information, reports on pending legislation, society news, parents columns, etc. The reading audience includes the members of society: schools, teachers, parents, administrators, nursery
 schools, universities, libraries, and students. Unsolicited manuscripts may be considered. A variable number of major articles are published per issue. Book reviews are included.
Manuscript Preparation:
 Accepted manuscripts average 200 to 500 words. One copy is
 required. Return postage and a self-addressed envelope are required. Bibliographical procedure is not generally needed for
 this type of article. If appropriate, provide sources for quotations and references. Use 1-1/2 inch margins and double-space.
 A background or explanatory cover letter is required, but not
 an outline, summary, or abstract. Biographical information
 about the author is required. Illustrations, pictures, graphs,
 etc., may be used but are very limited. No payment is made
 for accepted manuscripts. Articles may be reprinted upon request and with due credit given.
Manuscript Disposition:
 Receipt of a manuscript is acknowledged. Unaccepted manuscripts are returned upon request, with stamped, self-addressed
 envelope. Criticism and/or suggestions are not provided.
Copyright:
 Held by the American Montessori Society.

†CHILD LIFE

Subscription Data:
 Published by M. Alice Simpson, 1100 Waterway Boulevard, Box
 567B, Indianapolis, Indiana 46202. Issued monthly, except bimonthly during June-July and August-September. Advertising is
 accepted. Circulation: 200,000. Subscription: $6.00 per year;
 $11.00 for two years; $16.00 for three years. Founded: 1922.
Editorial Address:
 E. Catherine Cummins, Editor, Child Life, 1100 Waterway
 Boulevard, Indianapolis, Indiana 46202.
Editorial Policy:
 Includes a wide variety of materials. Social studies, language
 arts, and science materials are often featured. An editorial
 staff prepares some of this material and evaluates material on
 other educational subjects from outside sources. Little-known
 anecdotes about famous persons, events, or accomplishments
 in which identity is withheld until the end, factual material of
 unique interest to children, verse, and nature articles are welcomed. Projects, especially mechanical items, which children
 can make from materials readily available at home or at school
 and which involve a minimum of adult guidance may be submitted.

Short lively plays which can be produced in a living room or
classroom with a minimum of simple props and small casts are
desired. Picture stories about children, animals, events, nature, and humor, i.e., any story that can be told better by
pictures than by words, will be considered for publication.
Please send seasonal material six months in advance. The reading audience includes children aged seven to eleven and their
teachers. Unsolicited articles are welcome. The number of
articles published per issue varies widely. Book reviews are
included.

Manuscript Preparation:
Fiction is limited to 900 words. Serials are limited to two
parts. Two copies are required. Return postage and a self-
addressed envelope are required. Use wide margins and double-
space. Avoid use of footnotes. A background or explanatory
cover letter is not desired, but an outline or summary of the
article is required. Biographical information about the author
is unnecessary. Illustrations, pictures, graphs, etc., may be
used. Payment is made for accepted articles. Payment for
photographs depends on quality, etc. Reprints are available.

Manuscript Disposition:
Receipt of a manuscript is acknowledged. Editorial decisions
are made within six weeks. Time from acceptance of a manuscript to its appearance in print varies widely with editorial
need. Unaccepted manuscripts are returned, sometimes with
criticism or suggestions.

Copyright:
Held by the Saturday Evening Post Company, Inc.

CHILDHOOD EDUCATION

Subscription Data:
Published by the Association for Childhood Education International,
3615 Wisconsin Avenue, N.W., Washington, D.C. 20016. Issued
eight times each year, October through May. Selected advertising is accepted. Circulation: 31,000. Subscription: $12.00
per year; $4.00 to undergraduate students; $1.75 per issue.
Founded: 1924.

Editorial Address:
The Editor, Childhood Education, Association for Childhood Edu-
cation International, 3615 Wisconsin Avenue, N.W., Washington,
D.C. 20016.

Editorial Policy:
Includes specific word and picture illustrations of acceptable
classroom practices; reports of research findings; articles by
leaders in education and allied fields; reports on important educational events; discussion of current issues in education; reports on education beyond the United States; human interest stories; book reviews. Emphasis throughout is on elementary education from nursery school through 8th grade. The reading audience includes teachers, parents, librarians, church school

workers, pediatricians, social workers, future teachers, and others. Unsolicited manuscripts are welcome. Six to eight major articles are published per issue. Book reviews are included (books for children and books for adults).

Manuscript Preparation:
Accepted manuscripts average from 950 to 1,950 words. Two copies are required. Return postage and a self-addressed envelope are required. Bibliographical procedure should follow the University of Chicago Manual of Style. Manuscripts should be typewritten, double-spaced, and on one side of an 8-1/2 by 11 inch paper. A background or explanatory cover letter is not required nor is an outline, summary, or abstract. Biographical information about the author is not required, except for present position. Indicate if photographs are copyrighted; photographs are returned to the author following publication. Illustrations, pictures, and graphs may be used. No payment is made for accepted manuscripts. Reprint prices vary depending on length.

Manuscript Disposition:
Receipt of a manuscript is acknowledged. Editorial decision time and time from acceptance of an article to its appearance in print varies widely. Unaccepted manuscripts are returned with criticism and/or suggestions.

Copyright:
Held by the Association for Childhood Education International.

Additional Information:
The Association for Childhood Education International Publications Committee plans each issue around a central theme, except for two non-theme issues.

*CONSTRUCTIVE TRIANGLE

Subscription Data:
Published by the American Montessori Society, 175 Fifth Avenue, New York, New York 10010. Issued quarterly, in winter, spring, summer, and fall. Advertising is not presently accepted. Circulation: 1,200. Subscription: $20.00 per year as part of Society membership. Founded: 1965.

Editorial Address:
The Editor, Constructive Triangle, 175 Fifth Avenue, New York, New York 10010.

Editorial Policy:
Includes articles written by and for Montessori teachers and presentations of varying material for the Montessori classroom. The reading audience includes primarily Montessori teachers, but also included are interested persons in Montessori schools, and universities. Unsolicited manuscripts are not welcome. Four to ten major articles are published per issue. Book reviews are sometimes included.

Copyright:
Held by the American Montessori Society.

ELEMENTARY SCHOOL JOURNAL

Subscription Data:
> Published by the Department of Education, University of Chicago, 5835 Kimbark Avenue, Chicago, Illinois 60637. Issued monthly, October through May. Selected advertising is accepted. Circulation: 20,000. Subscription: $8.00 per year. Founded: 1900.

Editorial Address:
> The Editor, Elementary School Journal, Judd Hall, 5835 Kimbark Avenue, Chicago, Illinois 60637.

Editorial Policy:
> Includes articles on all phases of elementary education including administration, research, classroom practice, curriculum, art, music, health, and conservation. The reading audience includes school principals, supervisors, curriculum planners, superintendents, and classroom teachers. Unsolicited articles are welcome. Eight major articles are published per issue. Book reviews are occasionally included.

Manuscript Preparation:
> Manuscripts should not exceed 2,000 words. Two copies are required. Return postage and a self-addressed envelope are unnecessary. See a recent issue for bibliographical procedure. Type 37 characters per line and double-space throughout. A background or explanatory cover letter about the article is desired, but not an outline or summary. Biographical information about the author should include his present position. Simple uncluttered black and white glossy prints are welcome. No payment is made for accepted articles, but 50 reprints or one year's subscription are provided free to authors. A cost schedule for additional reprints is available through the office of the editor.

Manuscript Disposition:
> Receipt of a manuscript is acknowledged. Editorial decisions are made within three to four weeks. Accepted articles usually appear in print within six months after acceptance. Unaccepted manuscripts are returned, occasionally for revision based on the editor's suggestions.

Copyright:
> Held by the University of Chicago.

Additional Information:
> Black and white glossy prints are used on the front cover and in the inside.

HIGHLIGHTS FOR CHILDREN

Subscription Data:
> Published by Highlights for Children, Inc., 2300 West Fifth Avenue, Columbus, Ohio 43216. Issued monthly, except bimonthly during June-July and August-September, and semimonthly in December. Advertising is not accepted. Circulation: 1,010,000. Subscription: $9.95 per year. Founded: 1946.

Editorial Address:
> Walter B. Barbe, Editor, Highlights for Children, 2300 West
> Fifth Avenue, Columbus, Ohio 43216.

Editorial Policy:
> Includes (1) unusual wholesome stories which appeal to both boys
> and girls--stories with strong emotional appeal, full of actions
> and word pictures, and easy to illustrate, (2) factual articles in-
> cluding history and science, and (3) descriptions of craft ideas.
> The reading audience includes children, three to twelve years of
> age, and their teachers. Unsolicited articles and stories are
> welcome. Five major articles are published per issue.

Manuscript Preparation:
> Stories vary from 500 to 1,000 words (seldom longer). One
> copy and return postage and a self-addressed stamped envelope
> are required. Use wide margins and double-space; include bib-
> liography with factual manuscript. Biographical information
> about the author is desired. Seldom use illustrations submitted
> with manuscripts unless publisher has specifically requested their
> submission. Payment of $.05 to $.15 per word is made for ac-
> cepted articles.

Manuscript Disposition:
> Editorial decisions are made in approximately six weeks. Unac-
> cepted manuscripts are returned with suggestions.

Copyright:
> Held by Highlights for Children - purchase all rights.

Additional Information:
> The editor is especially interested in:
> 1. Easy-to-read stories with strong plots. (500 to 1,000 words)
> 2. Stories in urban settings.
> 3. Stories with characters from varying ethnic groups.
> Suggestions of material reward for upward striving and sugges-
> tions of war, crime or violence, are unacceptable.

INSTRUCTOR

Subscription Data:
> Published by the Instructor Publications, Inc., Seven Bank Street,
> Dansville, New York 14437. Issued monthly, September through
> June. Advertising is accepted. Circulation: 300,000. Subscrip-
> tion: $9.00 per year; $1.25 per issue. Founded: 1891.

Editorial Address:
> The Editor, Instructor, Editorial Department, Seven Bank Street,
> Dansville, New York 14437.

Editorial Policy:
> Includes all types of articles that are of interest and help to ele-
> mentary school teachers, including classroom activities in sci-
> ence and social studies, brief accounts of creative arts activities,
> short descriptions of teaching devices or methods, stories for
> the holidays, plays, and reports of creative dramatic activities.
> The reading audience includes public and parochial elementary
> school teachers, principals, and supervisors. Unsolicited

manuscripts are welcome. Approximately 40 major articles are published per issue. Book reviews, written by the staff, are included.

Manuscript Preparation:

Accepted manuscripts average 200 to 1,300 words. One copy is required. Return postage and a self-addressed envelope are required. Bibliographical procedure should follow the University of Chicago Manual of Style. Manuscripts should be typewritten and double-spaced with one inch margins. A background or explanatory cover letter is required but not an outline, summary, or abstract. A summary of the author's present position is desired. Illustrations are often used and are usually done by the staff. Payment is made for accepted manuscripts. There is no policy of reprints; contributors receive one free copy of issue and additional copies are available at cost.

Manuscript Disposition:

Receipt of a manuscript is acknowledged. Editorial decisions are made within four months. Accepted articles usually appear in print within three to eight months. Unaccepted manuscripts are returned, occasionally with criticism and/or suggestions.

Copyright:

Held by the Instructor Publications, Inc.

LEARNING

Subscription Data:

Published by Education Today Company, Inc., 530 University Avenue, Palo Alto, California 94301. Issued nine times each year, September through May. Advertising is accepted. Circulation: 175,000. Subscription: $10.00 per year. Founded: 1972.

Editorial Address:

The Editor, Learning, 530 University Avenue, Palo Alto, California 94301.

Editorial Policy:

Includes those articles particularly pertinent to elementary school teachers. This includes public affairs matters in areas of education, behavioral science research, classroom action stories, humor, and "how-to's." The reading audience includes approximately 80% elementary school teachers and the balance are people in other educational areas or in the behavioral sciences. Unsolicited manuscripts are welcome. Seven major articles are published per issue. Book reviews are included.

Manuscript Preparation:

Accepted manuscripts average 1,500 to 4,000 words. One copy is required. Return postage and a self-addressed envelope are required. There is no bibliographical procedure to follow. Triple-space manuscript. A background or explanatory cover letter is required, but not an outline, summary, or abstract. Biographical information about the author is required. Illustrations, pictures, graphs, etc., are sometimes included, but this will vary with the article. Payment is made for accepted manuscripts. Reprint permission must be obtained in writing from the publisher.

Manuscript Disposition:

Receipt of a manuscript is acknowledged. Editorial decisions are made within one to three weeks. Accepted articles usually appear in print within two months to one year. Unaccepted manuscripts are returned with criticism and/or suggestions.

Copyright:

Held by Education Today Company, Inc.

PEOPLE WATCHING

Subscription Data:

Published by Behavioral Publications, 72 Fifth Avenue, New York, New York 10011. Issued biannually, in the academic year in fall and spring. Advertising is accepted. Circulation: 2,000. Subscription: $5.00 per year; $10.00 to institutions. Founded: 1971.

Editorial Address:

Sheldon R. Roen, Ph.D., Editor, People Watching, Human Sciences, Inc., 72 Fifth Avenue, New York, New York 10011.

Editorial Policy:

People Watching is a popular styled periodical directed mainly at the elementary school level and provides a vehicle for articles, special features, new techniques, reviews, programs, and exchange of information among teachers, curriculum developers, and researchers on the subject of behavioral science. The reading audience includes psychologists, psychotherapists, and psychiatrists. Unsolicited manuscripts are welcome. Ten major articles are published per issue. Book reviews are included.

Manuscript Preparation:

Accepted manuscripts should not exceed more than 12 double-spaced pages. Three copies are required. Return postage and a self-addressed envelope are required. Bibliographical procedure should follow the APA Publication Manual. Avoid the use of footnotes. Use one inch margins on the top, sides, and bottom and double-space. A background or explanatory cover letter is optional, but an outline, summary, or abstract is required. Biographical information about the author is required. Illustrations, pictures, graphs, etc., are to be placed on separate pages at end of the manuscript, marked with Arabic numerals, and indicated where placed in the manuscript. No payment is made for accepted manuscripts. No free reprints are available; cost varies with length of article.

Manuscript Disposition:

Receipt of a manuscript is acknowledged. Editorial decisions are made within six months to one year. Accepted articles usually appear in print within six months to one year. Unaccepted manuscripts are returned if postage is provided. Criticism and/or suggestions are provided upon request.

Copyright:

Held by Behavioral Publications.

TEACHER (formerly <u>Grade Teacher</u>)

<u>Subscription Data:</u>
Published by Macmillan Professional Magazines, Inc., 22 West Putnam Avenue, Greenwich, Connecticut 06830. Issued monthly, except July and August, combined May/June issue. Advertising is accepted. Circulation: 280,000. Subscription: $8.00 per year in the United States and Canada; $10.50 foreign and Pan American rate. Founded: 1883.

<u>Editorial Address:</u>
The Editor, <u>Teacher,</u> Macmillan Professional Magazines, Inc., 22 West Putnam Avenue, Greenwich, Connecticut 06830.

<u>Editorial Policy:</u>
Includes articles on all subjects of interest to professional, pre-school, elementary, and junior high school teachers. The reading audience includes the pre-school, elementary, and junior high school teachers, administrators, and supervisors. Unsolicited manuscripts are welcome. Twenty to twenty-five articles are published per issue. Book reviews are included.

<u>Manuscript Preparation:</u>
Accepted manuscripts should contain no more than 2,000 words. One copy is required. Return postage and a self-addressed envelope are required. Incorporate footnotes in text. Double-space manuscript and leave extra space. A background or explanatory cover letter is desired but not an outline, summary, or abstract. Biographical information about the author is not required. Illustrations, pictures, graphs, etc., are encouraged and will be purchased when appropriate. Payment is made for accepted manuscripts. Reprints are usually not available.

<u>Manuscript Disposition:</u>
Receipt of a manuscript is not acknowledged. Editorial decisions are made within six weeks. Accepted articles usually appear in print within four to twelve months. Unaccepted manuscripts are returned without criticism and suggestions.

<u>Copyright:</u>
Held by Macmillan Professional Magazines, Inc.

ETHNOLOGY AND ETHNIC GROUPS

AMERICAN ETHNOLOGIST

Subscription Data:
> Published by the American Anthropological Association, 1703
> New Hampshire Avenue, N. W., Washington, D. C. 20009. Issued
> quarterly, in February, May, August, and November. Advertis-
> ing is accepted. Circulation: 5,000. Subscription: $20.00 per
> year. Founded: 1974.

Editorial Address:
> Dr. Victoria R. Bricker, Editor, American Ethnologist, Depart-
> ment of Anthropology, Tulane University, New Orleans, Louisi-
> ana 70118.

Editorial Policy:
> Includes articles on ethnology: methodological and theoretical
> contributions, comparative studies, culture change, diachronic
> studies which relate ethnography to ethnohistory. The reading
> audience includes ethnologists and social anthropologists. Un-
> solicited manuscripts are welcome. Ten to fifteen major arti-
> cles are published per issue. Book reviews are not included.

Manuscript Preparation:
> Accepted manuscripts average 30 to 50 pages. Three copies are
> required. Return postage and a self-addressed envelope are not
> required. Bibliographical procedure should follow the format of
> American Anthropologist. List footnotes on separate page. Dou-
> ble-space manuscript and use at least one inch margins on all
> sides. A background or explanatory cover letter is not required,
> but an abstract is required. Biographical information about the
> author is not required. No payment is made for accepted manu-
> scripts. Reprints may be ordered from American Anthropolog-
> ical Association by authors only, and only prior to printing.

Manuscript Disposition:
> Receipt of a manuscript is acknowledged. Editorial decisions
> are made within eight to twelve weeks. Unaccepted manuscripts
> are returned with criticism and/or suggestions.

Copyright:
> Held by the American Anthropological Association.

AMERICAN INDIAN CULTURE AND RESEARCH JOURNAL

Subscription Data:
> Published by the Regents of the University of California -
> U. C. L. A., American Indian Culture and Research Center, Camp-
> bell Hall 3221, 405 Hilgrad, Los Angeles, California 90024.

Issued quarterly. Advertising is accepted. Circulation: Nationwide. Subscription: $4.00 per year; $1.00 per volume. Founded: 1970.

Editorial Address:

The Editor, American Indian Culture and Research Journal, Campbell Hall 3221, 405 Hilgard, University of California - U.C.L.A., Los Angeles, California 90024.

Editorial Policy:

Includes significant contributions by America's leading scholars in all academic fields that pertain to the study of the American Indian citizen. Original scholarly papers are invited on a broad range of questions involving American Indian people. Economics, political science, sociology, history, literature, and philosophy will certainly be fields of interest. While encouraging innovation, the editor will favor those articles which demonstrate rigorous and thorough research in an interdisciplinary context. The reading audience includes all people. Unsolicited manuscripts are welcome. Four or five major articles are published per issue. Book reviews are not included.

Manuscript Preparation:

Accepted manuscripts average 10 pages. Two copies are required. Return postage and a self-addressed envelope are not required. Footnoting, bibliographical procedure, and manuscript margin and spacing should follow the MLA Style Sheet. Manuscripts should be double-spaced. A background or explanatory cover letter is required, but not an outline, summary, or abstract. Biographical information about the author is required. Illustrations, pictures, graphs, etc., are acceptable. No payment is made for accepted manuscripts.

Manuscript Disposition:

Receipt of a manuscript is acknowledged. Editorial decisions are made within four weeks. Accepted articles usually appear in print within two months. Unaccepted manuscripts are not returned. Criticism and/or suggestions are provided for manuscripts that are to be resubmitted.

Copyright:

Held by the Regents of the University of California.

Additional Information:

The Journal is a vehicle through which the spectrum of topics and the areas of interest included under Indian studies may be expanded and made relevant to an ever wider American audience. It provides a quarterly forum to fill the gap between traditional materials published on the historical American Indian and the dynamic intellectual and cultural upsurge occurring throughout today's Native American community.

BLACK SCHOLAR

Subscription Data:

Published by the Black World Foundation, P.O. Box 908, Sausalito, California 94965. Issued monthly, except bimonthly December-January and July-August. Advertising is accepted.

Circulation: 20,000. Subscription: $10.00 per year; $25.00 for three years. Founded: 1969.

Editorial Address:
The Editor, Black Scholar, P.O. Box 908, Sausalito, California 94965.

Editorial Policy:
Includes well-written essays on all aspects of black community life and thought. Articles may be historical, contemporary, theoretical or speculative, but should be documented. The reading audience includes primarily black teachers, professionals, and students. Unsolicited manuscripts are welcome. Six or seven major articles are published per issue. Book reviews are published in each issue.

Manuscript Preparation:
Accepted manuscripts average six to twenty-five double-spaced typewritten pages. One copy is required. Return postage and a self-addressed envelope are required. Bibliographical procedure should follow the MLA Style Sheet. If footnotes number more than six or seven, they should be listed on a separate sheet at the end of the essay. Double-space manuscript. A background or explanatory cover letter is required, but not an outline, summary, or abstract. Biographical information about the author is required for publication with essay. Black Scholar has the capability to publish pictures and graphs when needed. No payment is made for accepted manuscripts; however, each author receives complimentary copies of the journal. Reprints are available only by special arrangement.

Manuscript Disposition:
Receipt of a manuscript is acknowledged. Editorial decisions are made generally within eight to ten weeks, depending on publication schedule. Accepted articles usually appear in print within two to six months, depending upon publication schedule. Unaccepted manuscripts are returned, occasionally with criticism and/or suggestions.

Copyright:
Held by the Black Scholar.

Additional Information:
Each issue is organized around a particular topic (Black Health, Black Family, Black Education, Economics, etc.), hence authors should examine the publishing calendar that is published in the September issue (and sometimes in subsequent issues) each year.

ETHNOLOGY

Subscription Data:
Published by the University of Pittsburgh, 234 Atwood Street, Pittsburgh, Pennsylvania 15213. Advertising is not accepted. Circulation: 3,500. Subscription: $10.00 per year. Founded: 1962.

Editorial Address:
The Editor, Ethnology, Department of Anthropology, University of Pittsburgh, Pittsburgh, Pennsylvania 15260.

Editorial Policy:

Includes articles on both social and cultural anthropology. The reading audience includes anthropologists, sociologists, and social scientists. Unsolicited manuscripts are welcome. Usually eight major articles are published per issue. Book reviews are not included.

Manuscript Preparation:

Accepted manuscripts average two to fifty double-spaced typewritten pages. One copy is required. Return postage and a self-addressed envelope are preferred. See a recent issue for bibliographical procedure. Footnotes must be used sparingly and listed separately from the text. Use reasonable margins and double-space. A background or explanatory cover letter is not required nor is an outline, summary, or abstract. Biographical information about the author is not required. Illustrations, pictures, graphs, etc., must be in the form of a glossy print suitable for photo-engraving. No payment is made for accepted manuscripts. Author may purchase 100 reprints at cost.

Manuscript Disposition:

Receipt of a manuscript is acknowledged. Editorial decisions are made within eight to ten weeks. Accepted articles usually appear in print within three months. Unaccepted manuscripts are returned, occasionally with criticism and/or suggestions.

Copyright:

Not copyrighted.

INTEGRATED EDUCATION: A REPORT ON RACE AND SCHOOLS

Subscription Data:

Published by Integrated Education Associates, School of Education, Northwestern University, 2003 Sheridan Road, Evanston, Illinois 60201. Issued six times each year. Advertising is accepted. Circulation: 4,000. Subscription: $8.00 per year. Founded: 1963.

Editorial Address:

The Editor, Integrated Education: A Report on Race and Schools, School of Education, Northwestern University, 2003 Sheridan Road, Evanston, Illinois 60201.

Editorial Policy:

Includes articles on research, action study of integration, and equality in education. The reading audience includes college teachers, school personnel, civil rights advocates, and government personnel. Unsolicited articles are welcome. Six major articles are published per issue. Book reviews are included.

Manuscript Preparation:

Accepted manuscripts average 1,500 to 2,500 words. One copy is required. Return postage and a self-addressed envelope are desired. See a recent issue for footnoting and other bibliographical procedure. Use wide margins and double-space throughout. No background or explanatory cover letter about the article is desired nor is an outline or summary. Biographical information about the author is desired and should include data regarding educational affiliations and experience. Illustrations, pictures, and graphs are occasionally used. No payment is made for accepted articles. Reprints are available; a price list will be provided upon request.

Manuscript Disposition:
Receipt of a manuscript is acknowledged. Editorial decisions are made as soon as possible. Accepted articles usually appear in print from two to four months after acceptance. Unaccepted manuscripts are returned with suggestions.

Copyright:
Held by Integrated Education Associates.

Additional Information:
Laboratory articles are particularly encouraged with emphasis on specific practices which have been successful.

JOURNAL OF AMERICAN INDIAN EDUCATION

Subscription Data:
Published by Arizona State University, College of Education, Tempe, Arizona 85281. Sponsored by the Indian Education Center of Arizona State University. Issued three times each year, in January, May, and October. Advertising is not accepted. Circulation: 2,000. Subscription: $3.50 per year. Founded: 1961.

Editorial Address:
George A. Gill, Editor, Journal of American Indian Education, Center for Indian Education, Arizona State University, Tempe, Arizona 85281.

Editorial Policy:
Includes articles which deal with Indian education as well as other areas of Indian affairs. The reading audience includes persons who work directly with Indians and their education. Unsolicited articles are welcome. From five to seven major articles are published per issue. Book reviews are included.

Manuscript Preparation:
Accepted manuscripts average 2,500 words. In special cases longer articles are divided for publication in two issues. One copy is required. Return postage and a self-addressed envelope are desired. Use wide margins and double-space throughout. A background or explanatory cover letter about the article is desired, but not an outline or summary. Biographical information about the author is desired and should include a summary of current position and educational background. Graphs and charts may be used; photographs will be considered. No payment is made for accepted articles. Reprints are sometimes available by early request.

Manuscript Disposition:
Receipt of a manuscript is acknowledged. Editorial decisions are made as soon as possible by an editorial board. Accepted articles usually appear in print within six months after acceptance. Unaccepted articles are returned with reasons.

Copyright:
Held by the Journal of American Indian Education.

JOURNAL OF BLACK STUDIES

Subscription Data:
    Published by Sage Publications, 275 South Beverly, Beverly Hills,
    California 90212. Issued quarterly. Advertising is accepted.
    Circulation: 2,000. Subscription: $10.00 per year; $15.00 to
    institutions; $8.00 to students. Founded: 1970.
Editorial Address:
    Dr. Molefi K. Asante, Editor, Journal of Black Studies, Depart-
    ment of Black Studies, State University of New York, Buffalo,
    New York 14226.
Editorial Policy:
    Includes scholarly articles dealing with all aspects of life of
    people of African descent. Journal of Black Studies is an inter-
    national scholarly journal with a multi-disciplinary focus. The
    reading audience includes academicians and students. Unsolicited
    manuscripts are welcome if they are of good quality. Seven ma-
    jor articles are published per issue. Book reviews are included.
Manuscript Preparation:
    Accepted manuscripts should not exceed 25 typewritten pages.
    The original and one copy are required. Return postage and a
    self-addressed envelope are required. Bibliographical procedure
    should follow the APA Publication Manual or Sage style sheet.
    A background or explanatory cover letter is not required, but
    an outline, summary, or abstract is recommended. Biographical
    information about the author is required. Illustrations, pictures,
    graphs, etc., should be prepared by the author. No payment is
    made for accepted manuscripts. Author receives 15 free copies.
Manuscript Disposition:
    Receipt of a manuscript is acknowledged. Editorial decisions
    are made within five weeks. Accepted articles usually appear
    in print within six months. Unaccepted manuscripts are returned
    with criticism provided by the editors.
Copyright:
    Held by Sage Publications.

JOURNAL OF ETHNIC STUDIES

Subscription Data:
    Published by the College of Ethnic Studies, Western Washington
    State College, Bellingham, Washington 98225. Issued quarterly,
    in spring, summer, fall, and winter. Advertising is accepted.
    Circulation: 600. Subscription: $8.00 per year; $4.00 to stu-
    dents. Founded: 1973.
Editorial Address:
    The Editor, Journal of Ethnic Studies, College of Ethnic Studies,
    Western Washington State College, Bellingham, Washington
    98225.
Editorial Policy:
    Includes all articles dealing with North American ethnic groups.
    Preference is given to the comprehensive approach. The read-
    ing audience includes professors, counselors, social workers,

students, and the general public who are interested in understanding ethnicity. Unsolicited manuscripts are welcome. Four major articles are published per issue. Book reviews are included.

Manuscript Preparation:
No limitations are placed on length of accepted manuscripts as quality is important. Two copies are required. Return postage and a self-addressed envelope are required. Bibliographical procedure should follow the MLA Style Sheet. List footnotes on a separate page. A background or explanatory cover letter is not required nor is an outline, summary, or abstract. Illustrations, pictures, graphs, etc., will be included, if pertinent. No payment is made for accepted manuscripts. At the present time, no reprints are available.

Manuscript Disposition:
Receipt of a manuscript is acknowledged. Editorial decisions are made within four to ten weeks. Accepted articles usually appear in print within four to six months. Unaccepted manuscripts are returned, sometimes with criticism and/or suggestions if revision is possible.

Copyright:
Held by the College of Ethnic Studies.

JOURNAL OF NEGRO EDUCATION

Subscription Data:
Published for the Bureau of Educational Research, by the Howard University Press, Howard University, Washington, D.C. 20001. Issued quarterly, in January, April, August, and October. Advertising is not accepted. Circulation: 3,000. Subscription: $6.00 per year. Founded: 1932.

Editorial Address:
Dr. Charles A. Martin, Editor-in-Chief, Journal of Negro Education, Howard University Press, Howard University, Washington, D.C. 20001.

Editorial Policy:
Includes reports of problems which relate to (1) the education of Negroes and (2) the wider context of social, cultural, and historical phases of Negro life and the lives of other minority groups. The primary goals of the Journal are to stimulate collection and dissemination of facts about the education of Negroes, to present discussions involving critical appraisals of proposals and practices relating to the education of Negroes, and to stimulate investigations of problems incident to the education of Negroes. The reading audience includes college teachers, executives, and others concerned with Negro education. Unsolicited articles are welcome. Twenty-five major articles are published per issue. Book reviews are included.

Manuscript Preparation:
Accepted manuscripts average 15 double-spaced typewritten pages. Two copies are required. Return postage and a self-addressed envelope are desired. Footnoting and other bibliographical procedure may follow the University of Chicago Manual of Style or

a good general style manual. Full bibliographic data must be
provided by the author for all references. Use wide margins
and double-space throughout. A background or explanatory cover
letter about the article is desired, but no outline or summary
is required. Biographical information about the author is not
desired except for author's official title. Tabular matter should
be held to a minimum. Tables should be typed on separate
sheets, numbered with arabic numerals, titled, and cited in the
text. Drawings, sketches, graphs and similar kinds of figures
cannot be used. No payment is made for accepted articles.
Reprints are available; an order blank for reprints accompanies
proofs.

Manuscript Disposition:
Receipt of a manuscript is acknowledged. Editorial decisions
are made within eight weeks. Accepted articles usually appear
in print from 16 to 18 months after acceptance. Unaccepted manuscripts are returned, often with criticism and/or suggestions.

Copyright:
Held by the Howard University Press.

NEGRO EDUCATIONAL REVIEW

Subscription Data:
Published by Negro Educational Review, P.O. Box 2895, West
Bay Annex, Jacksonville, Florida 32203. Issued quarterly, in
January, April, July, and October. Advertising is accepted.
Circulation: 3,000. Subscription: $7.50 per year; $2.50 per
issue. Founded: 1950.

Editorial Address:
The Editor, Negro Educational Review, P.O. Box 2895, West
Bay Annex, Jacksonville, Florida 32203.

Editorial Policy:
Includes research reports and scholarly articles which summarize current problems in the field of education. Priority is
given to articles which relate to social, economic, political, or
educational aspects of Negro life. The reading audience includes
higher education personnel, social workers, civil rights leaders,
public school teachers, government officials, and research workers. Unsolicited articles are welcome. Five major articles
are published per issue. Unsolicited book reviews are included,
but must conform to standards of the New York Times. Abstracts of reports are sometimes used, but only if they make a
definite contribution to the aims of the Review.

Manuscript Preparation:
Accepted manuscripts average 10 double-spaced typewritten
pages, 15 maximum. Two copies, a stamped self-addressed
envelope, and a cover letter are required. Bibliographical procedure should follow the University of Chicago Manual of Style,
a guide which may be obtained from managing editor, or the
10th Anniversary Edition of the Review, Volume X, Numbers 3
and 4 (July and October 1959). Use wide margins and double-

space throughout. Biographical information about the author should include only name and official title. Avoid use of illustrations. No payment is made for accepted articles. Reprints are available. Each author will receive two free copies of the Review. Additional copies may be obtained at half price.

Manuscript Disposition:
Receipt of a manuscript is acknowledged within 10 days. Editorial decisions are made by the managing editor and selected members of an editorial board within 20 to 30 days. Accepted articles usually appear in print from 16 to 18 months after acceptance. Unaccepted manuscripts are returned, often with criticism.

Copyright:
Held by Negro Educational Review.

URBAN LIFE AND CULTURE

Subscription Data:
Published by Sage Publications, 275 South Beverly Drive, Beverly Hills, California 90212. Issued quarterly, in April, July, October, and January. Advertising is accepted. Circulation: 800. Subscription: $10.00 per year; $8.00 to students. Founded: 1972.

Editorial Address:
The Editor, Urban Life and Culture, Department of Sociology, University of California, Davis, California 95616.

Editorial Policy:
Includes articles on urban ethnography. The reading audience includes sociologists, anthropologists, and other social scientists of an urban ethnographic orientation. Unsolicited manuscripts are welcome. Five major articles are published per issue. Book reviews are included.

Manuscript Preparation:
Accepted manuscripts average seven to seventy pages. Two copies are required. Return postage and a self-addressed envelope are appreciated. Bibliographical procedure may follow the APA Publication Manual, ASA Style Manual, etc. List footnotes on a separate page. A background or explanatory cover letter is not required nor is an outline, summary, or abstract. Biographical information about the author is not required. Illustrations, pictures, graphs, etc., should be camera-ready. No payment is made for accepted manuscripts. Author receives half the fee for reprints and can reprint for free in his/her own larger work.

Manuscript Disposition:
Receipt of a manuscript is acknowledged. Editorial decisions are made within two to five weeks. Accepted articles usually appear in print within six months. Unaccepted manuscripts are returned with criticism and/or suggestions.

Copyright:
Held by Sage Publications.

Additional Information:
Urban Life and Culture has a highly interdisciplinary editorial policy which invites and publishes articles from sociology, anthropology, political science, geography, criminology, and psychology, as well as from other fields oriented to the closeup study of urban settings.

GEOGRAPHY

ASSOCIATION OF AMERICAN GEOGRAPHERS. ANNALS

Subscription Data:
>Published by the Association of American Geographers, 1710
>Sixteenth Street, N. W., Washington, D. C. 20009. Issued quar-
>terly. Advertising is accepted. Circulation: 9,000. Subscrip-
>tion: $16.00 per year. Founded: 1911.

Editorial Address:
>The Editor, Annals, Association of American Geographers, 1710
>Sixteenth Street, N. W., Washington, D. C. 20009.

Editorial Policy:
>Includes articles and reports regarding study of all phases of
>geography. The reading audience includes professional geogra-
>phers, economists, educators, and advanced students. Unsolic-
>ited articles are welcome. Ten to fifteen major articles are
>published per issue. Book reviews are included.

Manuscript Preparation:
>Accepted manuscripts range from 4,000 to 25,000 words, minus
>illustrative material. One copy is required. Return postage
>and a self-addressed envelope are unnecessary. Bibliographical
>procedure should follow the Association of American Geographers
>Style Sheet (See Annals, Volume 60, Number One, March 1970).
>Use 1-1/2 inch margins and double-space. Place footnotes
>serially in a separate page. A background or explanatory cover
>letter about the article is desired. An abstract is desired with
>submission of the finished manuscript. Biographical information
>about the author is required. Black and white finished illustra-
>tions, pictures, and graphs may be used and all will be returned.
>No payment is made for accepted articles. Reprints are avail-
>able; costs vary with article length.

Manuscript Disposition:
>Receipt of a manuscript is acknowledged. Editorial decisions
>are made within three months. Accepted articles usually appear
>in print within 12 months after acceptance. Unaccepted manu-
>scripts are returned with reasons for rejection as well as occa-
>sional suggestions for improvement.

Copyright:
>Held by the Association of American Geographers.

GEOGRAPHICAL REVIEW

Subscription Data:
>Published by the American Geographical Society, Broadway at

156th Street, New York, New York 10032. Issued four times
each year, in January, April, July, and December. Advertising
is not accepted. Circulation: 7,200. Subscription: $17.50 per
year. Founded: 1916.

Editorial Address:

The Editor, Geographical Review, American Geographical Society,
Broadway at 156th Street, New York, New York 10032.

Editorial Policy:

Includes articles which relate to all aspects of geography and
tangential physical and social sciences. The reading audience
includes physical and social scientists, businessmen, government employees, educators, and students. Unsolicited articles
are welcome. Five or six major articles are published per issue. Book reviews are included.

Manuscript Preparation:

Manuscripts should not exceed 6,000 words. One copy is required. Return postage and a self-addressed envelope are unnecessary. Bibliographical procedure may follow any widely
used style manual. Use a 1-1/2 inch left margin, double-space,
and type 26 lines per page. Consecutively numbered footnotes
should be listed on a separate page at the end of the article. A
background or explanatory cover letter about the article is desired. An abstract of 100 to 150 words is required with the
finished manuscript. Biographical information about the author
is unnecessary. Illustrations may be used. Maps, graphs, and
diagrams will be redrawn by a staff cartographer; only clear
sketches are required from the author. Photographs must be
black and white five-by-seven-inch prints. No payment is made
for accepted articles. Reprints are available; 50 bound copies
are mailed to the author. A cost summary and reprint order
form may be obtained through the office of the editor.

Manuscript Disposition:

Receipt of a manuscript is acknowledged. All manuscripts are
reviewed by at least two readers. Editorial decisions are made
within two weeks. Accepted articles usually appear in print
from nine to twelve months after acceptance. Unaccepted manuscripts are returned with criticism often given; occasionally authors are referred to a more appropriate journal for resubmission.

Copyright:

Held by the American Geographical Society.

Additional Information:

Manuscripts are accepted only from professionals. Papers must
be original, authoritative, and preferably based upon field investigation. The Review is international in distribution and character; it reaches 108 different countries.

JOURNAL OF GEOGRAPHY

Subscription Data:

Published by the National Council for Geographic Education by the
University of Miami, Coral Gables, Florida 33124. Publisher's

address is 115 North Marion Street, Oak Park, Illinois 60301.
Issued monthly, September to May. Advertising is accepted.
Circulation: 8,000. Subscription: $12.00 to $16.00 per year
scaled according to subscriber's income. Founded: 1902.
Editorial Address:
Harm J. de Blij, Editor, Journal of Geography, Department of
Geography, University of Miami, Coral Gables, Florida 33124.
Editorial Policy:
The editors are especially interested in the following types of
articles: (1) papers helpful to teachers in the transmission to
students of research work by professional geographers that is of
general significance and interest, (2) research articles dealing
with the field of education in geography, and (3) articles focusing
upon geographic aspects of practical and current problems in
our society. The reading audience includes teachers, college
teachers, and university faculty. Unsolicited manuscripts are
welcome. Four to five major articles are published per issue.
Book reviews are included.
Manuscript Preparation:
No limitations are placed upon manuscript length. One original
is required. Return postage and a self-addressed envelope are
not required. See a existing copy of the Journal for bibliographical procedure. Articles should be typewritten on 8-1/2 by 11
inch bond paper. Place footnotes in the text immediately following the line of reference. A background or explanatory cover
letter is welcome. An abstract of 100 to 150 words is required
to direct the reader's attention to the salient points made by the
author; and, if appropriate, the particular relevance of the article to teachers of geography. A one sentence biography of the
author is required. Illustrations, pictures, graphs, etc., will
be published; exceptionally expensive reproduction costs must be
shared by the author. Maps and drawings should be done in
black ink and of professional quality. Photographs, if any,
should be clear and sharply focused, with good contrast and
printed on glossy, firm paper. No payment is made for accepted
manuscripts. Reprints can be ordered.
Manuscript Disposition:
Receipt of a manuscript is acknowledged. Editorial decisions
are made within a maximum of two months. Unaccepted manuscripts are returned with criticism and/or suggestions.
Copyright:
Held by the National Council for Geographic Education.

PROFESSIONAL GEOGRAPHER

Subscription Data:
Published by the Association of American Geographers, 1710
Sixteenth Street, N.W., Washington, D.C. 20009. Issued four
times each year, in February, May, August, and November.
Advertising is accepted. Circulation: 8,000 (10% foreign). Sub-
scription: $8.00 per year in the United States and Canada;
$8.50 elsewhere. Founded: New series in 1949.

Editorial Address:
  Donald J. Patton, Editor, Professional Geographer, Florida State
  University, Tallahassee, Florida 32306.
Editorial Policy:
  Includes articles on all phases of geography. The reading audience includes university and government geographers and students. Unsolicited articles are welcome. Four to eight articles
  are published per issue together with reports and letters from
  readers. Book reviews are included.
Manuscript Preparation:
  Accepted manuscripts average from five to fifteen double-spaced
  typewritten pages. One copy is required. Return postage and a
  self-addressed envelope are unnecessary. Bibliographical procedure may follow any widely used style manual. A background
  or explanatory cover letter about the article is desirable. Biographical information about the author is unnecessary. Illustrations, pictures, graphs, and line-drawings may be used, but no
  half-tones. No payment is made for accepted articles. Reprints
  are available; a cost summary is available through the office of
  the editor.
Manuscript Disposition:
  Receipt of a manuscript is acknowledged. Editorial decisions
  are made within two to three months. Accepted articles usually
  appear in print within six months after acceptance. Unaccepted
  manuscripts are returned with criticism and/or suggestions.
Copyright:
  Held by the Association of American Geographers.

*WEATHERWISE

Subscription Data:
  Distributed by the American Meteorological Society, 45 Beacon
  Street, Boston, Massachusetts 02108. Published by Weatherwise,
  Inc. All subscription correspondence to AMS, Boston, Massa-
  chusetts. Issued six times each year, in February, April, June,
  August, October, and December. Advertising is not accepted.
  Circulation: 7,000. Subscription: $8.00 per year; $5.00 per
  year to members of the American Meteorological Society.
Editorial Address:
  The Editor, Weatherwise, 230 Nassau Street, Princeton, New
  Jersey 08540.
Editorial Policy:
  Includes articles on the development of the science of meteorology
  and on current weather events. Includes a review of the month's
  weather and an individual weather map for every day of the year.
  The reading audience includes professional meterorologists,
  weather hobbyists, and high school and college students. Unso-
  licited manuscripts cannot be used. No payment is made. Four
  or five articles are published per issue. Book reviews are included.
Copyright:
  Held by Weatherwise, Inc.

AMERICAN JOURNAL OF MENTAL DEFICIENCY

Subscription Data:
    Published by the American Association on Mental Deficiency,
    5201 Connecticut Avenue, N. W., Washington, D. C. 20015. Is-
    sued bimonthly, in July, September, November, January, March,
    and May. Advertising is accepted and should be sent to the pub-
    lisher. Circulation: 14, 000. Subscription: $18. 00 per volume;
    $19. 00 foreign; $4. 00 per issue; $36. 00 to institutions and li-
    braries; $38. 00 foreign; $8. 00 foreign per issue. Founded:
    1876.
Editorial Address:
    The Editor, American Journal of Mental Deficiency, Box 503,
    Peabody College, Nashville, Tennessee 37203.
Editorial Policy:
    Publishes reports of empirical research, tightly conceived theory
    papers, and innovative reviews of the literature related to the
    field of mental retardation. The reading audience includes psy-
    chologists, educators, physicians, and social workers. Unsolic-
    ited manuscripts are welcome. Twenty major articles are pub-
    lished per issue. Book reviews are included.
Manuscript Preparation:
    Accepted manuscripts average 20 pages in length; brief reports
    average four pages; and book reviews average four pages. Three
    copies are required. Return postage and a self-addressed envel-
    ope are not required. Bibliographical procedure should follow
    the APA Publication Manual. All material must be double-
    spaced, including quotations, references, and tabular presenta-
    tions. A background or explanatory cover letter is not required,
    but an abstract is required. All figures should be professional-
    ly drawn and submitted in the form of original line drawings or
    glossies. No payment is made for accepted manuscripts. Re-
    prints may be purchased from the printer at the time of publica-
    tion of material.
Manuscript Disposition:
    Receipt of a manuscript is acknowledged. Editorial decisions
    are made within approximately eight weeks. Accepted articles
    usually appear in print within nine months. Unaccepted manu-
    scripts are returned with criticism and/or suggestions. Each
    manuscript is reviewed by at least two consulting editors. The
    anonymous reviews are enclosed with the editor's or associate
    editors' decision letter to the author.
Copyright:
    Held by the American Association on Mental Deficiency.

Additional Information:

All expressions of linear measure, weight, and volume should be in the metric system. There should be no identification of the author(s) except on the cover sheet or letter of transmittal since manuscripts are given an anonymous review.

COMMUNITY MENTAL HEALTH JOURNAL

Subscription Data:

Published by Behavioral Publications, 72 Fifth Avenue, New York, New York 10011. Issued quarterly. Advertising is accepted. Circulation: 5,000. Subscription: $12.00 per year; $25.00 to institutions. Founded: 1965.

Editorial Address:

Lenin A. Baler, Ph.D., Editor, Community Mental Health Journal, Community Mental Health Program, Room M15108, School of Public Health II, University of Michigan, Ann Arbor, Michigan 48104.

Editorial Policy:

The Journal is devoted to emergent approaches in mental health research, theory, and practice as they relate to community, broadly defined. Mental health is seen as more or less congruent with the general concept of social well being. The reading audience includes psychologists, psychotherapists, and psychiatrists. Unsolicited manuscripts are welcome. Nine or ten major articles are published per issue. Book reviews are included.

Manuscript Preparation:

Articles should not exceed 3,500 words or 20 double-spaced typed pages (including tables, figures, and references). Three copies are required. Return postage and a self-addressed envelope are required. Bibliographical procedure should follow the APA Publication Manual. Footnotes are not allowed. Use one inch margins on the top, sides, and bottom and double-space. A background or explanatory cover letter is optional, but a 100 word abstract is required. Biographical information about the author is required. Tables and figures should be numbered separately. Figures, which includes graphs and diagrams, should be photographed or on separate sheets drawn in India ink on good quality heavy white paper or tracing paper. Table format should be as simple as possible. Illustrations, pictures, graphs, etc., are to be placed on separate pages at the end of manuscript, marked with arabic numerals, and indicated where placed in the manuscript. No payment is made for accepted manuscripts. No free reprints are available; cost varies with length of article.

Manuscript Disposition:

Receipt of a manuscript is acknowledged. Editorial decisions are made within six months to one year. Accepted articles usually appear in print within six months to one year. Unaccepted manuscripts are returned if postage is provided. Criticism and/or suggestions are provided upon request.

Copyright:

Held by Behavioral Publications.

EXCEPTIONAL CHILD EDUCATION ABSTRACTS

Subscription Data:
    Published by the Council for Exceptional Children, 1920 Association Drive, Reston, Virginia 22091. Issued quarterly, in spring, summer, fall, and winter. Advertising is not accepted. Circulation: 800. Subscription: $50.00 to institutions; $25.00 to members of the Council. Founded: 1969.
Editorial Address:
    The Editor, Exceptional Child Education Abstracts, Council for Exceptional Children, 1920 Association Drive, Reston, Virginia 22091.
Editorial Policy:
    Includes professional texts, journal articles, research reports, and curriculum guides concerned with the education of handicapped and gifted children and youth. The reading audience includes primarily the college and university, and school districts. Unsolicited manuscripts are welcome. Seven-hundred and fifty major articles are published per issue. Book reviews are included.
Manuscript Preparation:
    Two copies are required. Return postage and a self-addressed envelope are not required. A background or explanatory cover letter and an outline, summary, or abstract are required. Biographical information about the author is not required. Camera-ready illustrations, pictures, graphs, etc., are acceptable. No payment is made for accepted manuscripts. Permission is required to quote or to reprint.
Manuscript Disposition:
    Receipt of a manuscript is acknowledged by copy of abstract if accepted. Editorial decisions are made within three to four weeks. Accepted articles usually appear in print within four months. Unaccepted manuscripts are not returned.
Copyright:
    Held by the Council for Exceptional Children.

JOURNAL FOR SPECIAL EDUCATORS OF THE MENTALLY RE-
TARDED (formerly Digest of the Mentally Retarded)

Subscription Data:
    Published by the Journal for Special Educators of the Mentally Retarded, Inc., Center Conway, New Hampshire 03813. Issued three times each year, in fall, winter, and spring. Advertising is accepted. Circulation: 5,000. Subscription: $7.00 per year. Founded: 1964.
Editorial Address:
    The Editor, Journal for Special Educators of the Mentally Retarded, 107-20 One-hundred twenty-fifth Street, Richmond Hill, New York 11419.
Editorial Policy:
    The Journal includes original articles concerned with the education, broadly defined, of the mentally retarded child. Articles concerned with pilot studies, classroom work and innovations at the local level are encouraged. The reading audience includes

teachers of the mentally retarded and college staffers who are
with the special education department. Unsolicited manuscripts
are welcome. Fifteen major articles are published per issue.
Book reviews are included.

Manuscript Preparation:
Accepted manuscripts average 3, 000 words. Manuscripts should
be submitted with an original and carbon copy, double-spaced,
with generous margins. Return postage and a self-addressed envelope are required. Bibliographical procedure should follow the
MLA Style Sheet. References, if any, should be cited in the text
and not by footnotes. A background or explanatory cover letter
is not required nor is an outline, summary, or abstract. Biographical information about the author is not required. Use of
illustrations, pictures, graphs, etc. , is optional. No payment
is made for accepted manuscripts.

Manuscript Disposition:
Receipt of a manuscript is acknowledged. Editorial decisions
are made within four weeks. Unaccepted manuscripts are sometimes returned.

Copyright:
Held by the Journal for Special Educators of the Mentally Retarded.

MENTAL RETARDATION

Subscription Data:
Published by the American Association on Mental Deficiency,
5201 Connecticut Avenue, N. W. , Washington, D. C. 20015. Issued bimonthly. Advertising is accepted. Circulation: 11, 500.
Subscription: $15. 00 to non-members; $17. 00 foreign non-members. Founded: 1963.

Editorial Address:
The Editor, Mental Retardation, 765 Commonwealth Avenue,
Boston University, Boston, Massachusetts 02215.

Editorial Policy:
Includes articles on new approaches in methodology; critical summaries; program descriptions; case studies illustrating philosophy
or theory; research reports; interpretation of essays or current
topics. The reading audience includes psychologists, superintendents of residential facilities, and all people in the field of
mental retardation. Unsolicited manuscripts are welcome. Ten
to twelve major articles are published per issue. Book reviews
are included.

Manuscript Preparation:
Accepted manuscripts average up to 10 double-spaced pages.
Three copies are required. Return postage and a self-addressed
envelope are not required. Bibliographical procedure should follow the APA Publication Manual. Use 1-1/4 inch margins and
double-space. A background or explanatory cover letter is not
required, but an outline, summary, or abstract is required.
Biographical information about the author is required. Tables
and graphs should be self-explanatory and not completely repeated

in text. Authors may be asked to bear costs of extensive tables.
Photographs should be of professional quality, preferably eight
by ten inches, with caption on reverse side. Use glossy prints
that can be photographed. No payment is made for accepted
manuscripts. Reprint order forms are sent to the author with
the edited manuscript.

Manuscript Disposition:
Receipt of a manuscript is acknowledged. Editorial decisions
are made within one to two months. Accepted articles usually
appear in print within three to six months. Unaccepted manuscripts are returned with criticism and/or suggestions.

Copyright:
Held by the American Association on Mental Deficiency.

MENTAL RETARDATION NEWS (formerly Children Limited)

Subscription Data:
Published by the National Association for Retarded Children,
2709 Avenue E East, Arlington, Texas 76011. Issued 10 times
each year. Advertising is not accepted. Circulation: 180,000.
Subscription: $3.50 per year; $4.50 foreign. Founded: 1952.

Editorial Address:
The Editor, Mental Retardation News, P.O. Box 6109, 2709
Avenue E East, Arlington, Texas 76011.

Editorial Policy:
Includes news articles which report new developments in the
field of mental retardation and programs of care and treatment
for the mentally retarded. Fields represented include: medicine,
research, education, social work, psychology, psychiatry, recreation, vocational rehabilitation and employment, legislation,
and residential care. The reading audience includes parents of
retarded children, professional people concerned with mental retardation, and citizens interested in the field. Unsolicited articles are welcome. Several major articles are published per issue. Book reviews are included.

Manuscript Preparation:
Accepted manuscripts average 600 words. One copy is required.
Return postage and a self-addressed envelope are desired. Bibliographical procedure may follow any widely used manual of
style. Place all footnotes in alphabetical order at the end of the
article. A background or explanatory cover letter about the article is desired. A summary is required in advance of the finished manuscript. Biographical information about the author is
desired and should include a summary of his/her present position and all other information which establishes his/her authority
regarding the topic about which they have written. Illustrations,
pictures, graphs, etc., may be used. Action pictures may be
used when submitted as sharp, clear, black and white glossy
prints. No payment is made for accepted articles. Reprints
are available; costs vary with article length and number ordered.

Manuscript Disposition:
Receipt of a manuscript is acknowledged. Editorial decisions

are made as soon as possible. Time from acceptance of a manuscript to its appearance in print varies widely. Unaccepted manuscripts are returned without criticism or suggestions.

Copyright:
Not copyrighted; however, the editor should be notified when articles are reprinted.

POINTER

Subscription Data:
Published by the New Readers Press, Box 131, Syracuse, New York 13210. Issued three times each year, in fall, winter, and spring, plus index. Advertising is accepted. Circulation: Very wide readership on an international level. Subscription: $4.50 per year. Founded: 1955.

Editorial Address:
The Editor, Pointer, 111 Alta Vista Drive, Grass Valley, California 95945.

Editorial Policy:
Includes articles on special education, with focus on the mentally retarded, emotionally disturbed, neurologically handicapped, and all areas of learning disabilities. The reading audience includes teachers, psychologists, reading specialists, parents, doctors, speech therapists, and is available in public libraries, colleges, and universities. Unsolicited articles are welcome. Fifty or more articles are published per issue. Book reviews are included.

Manuscript Preparation:
No restrictions are placed upon manuscript length. One copy is required. Return postage and a self-addressed envelope are desired. Footnoting and other bibliographical procedure may follow any widely used manual of style. Use wide margins and double-space. A background or explanatory cover letter about the article is not desired nor is an outline, summary, or abstract. Biographical information about the author is unnecessary. Illustrations, pictures, graphs, etc., are used. Pictures are gladly accepted in black and white. No payment is made for accepted articles. Reprints are available for some articles.

Manuscript Disposition:
Receipt of a manuscript is acknowledged. Editorial decisions are made within two to three weeks. Time from acceptance of a manuscript to its appearance in print varies with the subject of the article and the amount of editing time required. Unaccepted manuscripts are returned with suggestions.

Copyright:
Held by the New Readers Press.

Additional Information:
Articles based on practical and successful special education classroom experience and practice are especially welcome. All issues are available on microfilm; there are several foreign editions. The Pointer, for special class teachers and parents of the handicapped, has received over 20 awards, representing a wide range of endeavors.

TRAINING SCHOOL BULLETIN

Subscription Data:
Published by the American Institute for Mental Studies, Training School Unit, 1667 East Landis Avenue, Vineland, New Jersey 08360. Issued quarterly, in February, May, August, and November. Advertising is not accepted. Circulation: 10,000. Subscription: $4.00 per year; foreign add $2.50 per year for postage. Founded: 1904.

Editorial Address:
The Editor, Training School Bulletin, American Institute for Mental Studies, Training School Unit, 1667 East Landis Avenue, Vineland, New Jersey 08360.

Editorial Policy:
Includes articles on or closely related to the field of intellectual impairment and mental retardation. The reading audience includes medical personnel, teachers, and other professional workers in the field of mental retardation and related fields. Unsolicited articles are welcome. Seven to eight major articles are published per issue. Book reviews are sometimes included.

Manuscript Preparation:
Accepted manuscripts average 10 double-spaced typewritten pages. The original and one carbon are required. Return postage and a self-addressed envelope are desired. Bibliographical procedure should follow the APA Publication Manual. Use wide margins and double-space throughout. A background or explanatory cover letter and an outline, summary, or abstract of the article are required. Biographical information about the author is required. Illustrations, pictures, and graphs may be used. Contributors may be asked to share part of publication cost in cases of extensive use of illustrations or tabular material. No payment is made for accepted manuscripts. Twenty-five free copies of the Bulletin are mailed to each author; additional copies may be purchased at $1.00 each. Contact the printer: Standard Publishing Company, 308 South Eighth Street, Vineland, New Jersey 08360.

Manuscript Disposition:
Receipt of a manuscript is acknowledged. Editorial decisions are made within one month. Accepted articles usually appear in print within four months after acceptance. Unaccepted manuscripts are returned with reasons, criticism, and/or suggestions.

Copyright:
Not copyrighted.

AMERICAN ANNALS OF THE DEAF

Subscription Data:
Published by the Conference of Executives of American Schools for the Deaf, and the Convention of American Instructors of the Deaf, 5034 Wisconsin Avenue, N. W., Washington, D. C. 20016. Issued six times each year, in February, April, June, August, October, and December. Advertising is accepted. Circulation: 6, 300. Subscription: $12.50 per year. Founded: 1847.

Editorial Address:
The Editor, American Annals of the Deaf, 5034 Wisconsin Avenue, N. W., Washington, D. C. 20016.

Editorial Policy:
Includes educational and research articles that are related to the education of the deaf. The reading audience includes anyone interested in the education of the deaf. Unsolicited manuscripts are welcome. Five or six major articles are published per issue. Book reviews are included.

Manuscript Preparation:
Include a good original and two copies, typewritten on 8-1/2 by 11 inch heavy duty, white, bond paper. All copy must be double-spaced, including references, legends, footnotes, and quoted material. Allow margins of at least 1-1/2 inches at top, bottom and left, and one inch at right. The reference bibliography will be critically examined at time of review for acceptance. Personal communications and unpublished data should not be included. The following minimum data should be typed double-spaced: names of authors, complete title of the work cited in text, publication, volume number, and year of publication. References should be arranged according to the order in which they are cited in the text, not alphabetically. All references must be numbered consecutively and typewritten on a separate sheet. All original articles must be accompanied by a synopsis abstract typed on a separate sheet of paper. The abstract replaces the summary from which it differs in that 1) it should not exceed 135 words in length, and 2) it is placed at the beginning of the article, rather than at the end. Include only essential features of the report, emphasizing data and avoiding generalizations. Do not repeat the title of the manuscript. Illustrations consist of all material which cannot be set in type, such as photographs, line drawings, graphs, charts, and tracings. Tables will be set in type and should be included on separate sheets of paper. Omit all illustrations which fail to increase understanding of the text. For drawings and graphs use only black India ink on illus-

tration board or on a good grade of white drawing paper. Illustrations should be numbered and cited in the text; legends must accompany each and should be typed double-spaced on a separate sheet, not on separate sheets for each figure. Reprints are available according to price schedule.

Manuscript Disposition:
Receipt of a manuscript is acknowledged. Editorial decisions are made as soon as possible. Time from acceptance of a manuscript to its appearance in print varies with editorial need. Unaccepted manuscripts are returned without criticism or suggestions.

Copyright:
Held by the Conference of Executives of American Schools for the Deaf, Inc., and Convention of American Instructors of the Deaf, Inc.

AMERICAN JOURNAL OF OCCUPATIONAL THERAPY

Subscription Data:
Published by the American Occupational Therapy Association, Inc., 6000 Executive Boulevard, Rockville, Maryland 20852. Issued 10 times each year. Advertising is accepted. Circulation: 16,118. Subscription: $10.50 per year to United States, Canada, and Mexico; $12.50 to institutions; $12.50 to foreign individuals; $14.50 to foreign institutions. Founded: 1947.

Editorial Address:
The Editor, American Journal of Occupational Therapy, 6000 Executive Boulevard, Rockville, Maryland 20852.

Editorial Policy:
Manuscripts accepted for publication are of a professional and scientific nature which pertain to occupational therapy and include new approaches and techniques of practice, development of theory, research and educational activities, and professional trends. Unsolicited manuscripts are welcome. Approximately seven major articles are published per issue. Book reviews are included.

Manuscript Preparation:
Accepted manuscripts average no more than 15 double-spaced typewritten pages. One original and two copies are required. Return postage and a self-addressed envelope are not required. Bibliographical procedure should follow the University of Chicago Manual of Style and the "Guide to the Preparation of Manuscripts"; the latter is published within the Journal. A cover letter and an outline, summary, or abstract of the article are required. No payment is made for accepted manuscripts. Permission of the editor is not required to photocopy or reproduce up to 100 copies of an article as it appears in American Journal of Occupational Therapy if such prints are distributed free of charge within an organization or classroom. Permission for reprinting or other distribution of articles must be obtained from the editor.

Manuscript Disposition:
Receipt of a manuscript is acknowledged. Editorial decisions are made within two months. Accepted articles usually appear

in print within six months. Unaccepted manuscripts are returned
with criticism and suggestions.

Copyright:
Held by the American Occupational Therapy Association, Inc.

Additional Information:
Neither the statements of authors nor the claims of advertisers
necessarily carry endorsement of the American Occupational
Therapy Association unless set forth by adopted resolution or
policy statement.

EDUCATION OF THE VISUALLY HANDICAPPED

Subscription Data:
Published by the Association for Education of the Visually Handicapped, 1604 Spruce Street, Philadelphia, Pennsylvania 19103.
Issued quarterly, in March, May, October, and December. Advertising is not accepted. Circulation: 3, 300. Subscription:
$6.00 for ink print; $10.00 for braille; $6.45 foreign. Founded:
1969.

Editorial Address:
Dr. Don L. Walker, Editor, Education of the Visually Handicapped, University of Virginia, Department of Special Education, Charlottesville, Virginia 22903.

Editorial Policy:
Includes: 1) research, practices, and approaches in education
of visually impaired children, and 2) methods and materials for
education of visually impaired. The reading audience includes
teachers and administrators in education of visually impaired,
teacher trainees, and teacher educators, and a few parents of
visually impaired children. Unsolicited manuscripts are welcome. Four to six major articles are published per issue.
Selected book reviews are included, but these are usually solicited.

Manuscript Preparation:
Manuscripts may vary in length depending on the nature and
content of the article, but should be no less than 500 words and,
in most instances, should not exceed 2, 500 to 3, 000 words.
Two copies are required. Return postage and a self-addressed
envelope are required only if unaccepted manuscript return is
desired. Footnoting and other bibliographical procedure should
follow the APA Publication Manual. Manuscripts should be submitted on 15 or 20 pound bond on 8-1/2 by 11 inch paper. Pica
type is preferable to elite type. Manuscripts should be double-
spaced, with left margin of 1-1/2 inches and all others one
inch. Footnotes are discouraged; use only if absolutely necessary. A background or explanatory cover letter is required,
but not an outline, summary, or abstract. Biographical information about the author is required and should include a brief
statement of position. Illustrations, pictures, graphs, etc.,
are acceptable and should follow the APA Publication Manual.

No payment is made for accepted manuscripts. Reprints are
available at the following rates: $.13 a page for 100 sets and
$.14 a page for 50 sets.
Manuscript Disposition:
  Receipt of a manuscript is acknowledged. Editorial decisions
  are made usually within six to eight weeks. Accepted articles
  usually appear in print within three to six months. Unaccepted
  manuscripts are returned if postage paid envelope is enclosed
  with manuscript. Criticism and/or suggestions are usually provided.
Copyright:
  Held by the Association for Education of the Visually Handicapped.

EXCEPTIONAL CHILDREN

Subscription Data:
  Published by the Council for Exceptional Children, 1920 Association Drive, Reston, Virginia 22091. Issued eight times each
  year, September through May, excluding December. Advertising
  is accepted. Circulation: 58,000. Subscription: $12.50 per
  year. Founded: 1934.
Editorial Address:
  The Editor, Exceptional Children, 1920 Association Drive, Reston,
  Virginia 22091.
Editorial Policy:
  Includes articles on research and application of methods for
  teaching children who are exceptional (retarded, gifted, blind,
  handicapped in vision or hearing, etc.). The reading audience
  includes teachers, teacher educators, administrators, psychologists, and parents of exceptional children. Unsolicited manuscripts are welcome. Four to six major articles are published
  per issue. Book reviews are included.
Manuscript Preparation:
  Accepted manuscripts average from 10 to 25 double-spaced pages.
  The original plus three copies are required. Return postage
  and a self-addressed envelope are not required. Bibliographical
  procedure should follow the APA Publication Manual or the University of Chicago Manual of Style. Footnotes should be avoided
  when possible; when they are necessary include them within the
  text. A cover letter and an outline, summary, or abstract of
  the article are required. Biographical information about the
  author is required. Glossies are required; photographs are encouraged. No payment is made for accepted manuscripts. "Request for Permission to Reprint" blank may be obtained from
  the editor.
Manuscript Disposition:
  Receipt of a manuscript is acknowledged. Editorial decisions
  are made within six to twelve months. Unaccepted manuscripts
  are returned with criticism and/or suggestions.
Copyright:
  Held by the Council for Exceptional Children.

EXCEPTIONAL PARENT

Subscription Data:
      Published by the Psy-Ed Corporation, 264 Beacon Street, Boston,
      Massachusetts 02116. Issued bimonthly. Advertising is accepted.
      Circulation: 15,000. Subscription: $10.00 per year; $18.00
      for two years; $24.00 for three years. Founded: 1971.
Editorial Address:
      Stanley D. Klein, Ph. D., Editor-in-Chief, Exceptional Parent,
      P. O. Box 101, Back Bay Annex, Boston, Massachusetts 02117.
Editorial Policy:
      Includes articles on practical guidance for parents and profes-
      sionals concerned with the care of children with disabilities.
      The reading audience includes parents and professionals. Unso-
      licited manuscripts are welcome. Twelve major articles are
      published per issue. Book reviews are rarely included.
Manuscript Preparation:
      Accepted manuscripts should not exceed 2,400 words. One copy
      is required. Return postage and a self-addressed envelope are
      required. Bibliographical procedure should follow the MLA
      Style Sheet. Type and double-space manuscript. A background
      or explanatory cover letter is not required, but an outline, sum-
      mary, or abstract is helpful. Biographical information about the
      author is required. Payment is made for accepted manuscripts.
      Fifty free reprints are given to the author.
Manuscript Disposition:
      Receipt of a manuscript is acknowledged. Editorial decisions
      are made within eight weeks, but this varies considerably. Time
      from acceptance of a manuscript to its appearance in print varies
      with editorial need. Unaccepted manuscripts are returned, some-
      times with criticism and/or suggestions.
Copyright:
      Held by the Psy-Ed Corporation.
Additional Information:
      Editors suggest an outline be sent, before preparation of an ar-
      ticle, for feedback from editors and editorial advisory board.

HEARING AND SPEECH NEWS

Subscription Data:
      Published by the National Association of Hearing and Speech
      Agencies, 814 Thayer Avenue, Silver Spring, Maryland 20910.
      Issued six times each year, in January, March, May, July,
      September, and November. Advertising is accepted. Circula-
      tion: 13,000. Subscription: $5.00 per year; $2.50 to librar-
      ies. Founded: 1926.
Editorial Address:
      The Editor, Hearing and Speech News, National Association of
      Hearing and Speech Agencies, 814 Thayer Avenue, Silver Spring,
      Maryland 20910.
Editorial Policy:
      Includes articles on all aspects of hearing and speech, especially

clinical practice, research, and program administration. The
reading audience includes audiologists, speech pathologists, otolo-
gists, and other professionals as well as lay persons, hearing
handicapped, speech handicapped, parents, and students. Unsolicited articles are welcome. Three or four major articles are
published per issue. Book reviews are included.

Manuscript Preparation:
  Accepted manuscripts average from 1, 500 to 2, 000 words. One
  copy is required. Return postage and a self-addressed envelope
  are desired. Use two inch side margins and double-space.
  Footnoting and other bibliographical procedure should follow a
  recent issue. A background or explanatory cover letter about
  the article is desired, but not an outline or summary. Biographical information about the author is desired and should include
  information on his work and educational experience which quali-
  fies him as knowledgeable in the area represented in the article.
  A picture of the author is desired. Illustrations, pictures,
  graphs, etc., will be used only if essential to clarity of the text.
  No payment is made for accepted articles. Reprint costs vary
  with article length and number ordered.

Manuscript Disposition:
  Receipt of a manuscript is acknowledged. Editorial decisions
  are usually made within two weeks. Time from acceptance of a
  manuscript to its appearance in print varies with the date the
  manuscript is received. Unaccepted manuscripts are returned
  with reasons and suggestions. When possible, the author is
  directed to another journal for which the material may be more
  appropriate.

Copyright:
  Held by the National Association of Hearing and Speech Agencies.

INTERNATIONAL REHABILITATION REVIEW

Subscription Data:
  Published by the International Society for Rehabilitation of the
  Disabled, 219 East Forty-fourth Street, New York, New York
  10017. Issued quarterly. Advertising is accepted. Circulation:
  14, 000 internationally. Subscription: $5. 00 per year. Founded:
  1949.

Editorial Address:
  The Editor, International Rehabilitation Review, International So-
  ciety for Rehabilitation of the Disabled, 219 East Forty-fourth
  Street, New York, New York 10017.

Editorial Policy:
  Includes articles which report general rehabilitation activities of
  all types, including special education for handicapped children
  and adolescents. The reading audience includes educational and
  vocational personnel at all levels. The number of major articles
  published per issue varies. Book notices are included.

Copyright:
  Held by the International Society for Rehabilitation of the Disabled.

JOURNAL OF LEARNING DISABILITIES

Subscription Data:
  Published by Professional Press, Inc., 5 North Wabash Avenue,
  Chicago, Illinois 60602. Issued monthly, with June-July and
  August-September combined. Paid advertising is accepted. Cir-
  culation: 14,500. Subscription: $10.00 per year in the United
  States and Canada; $18.00 foreign. Founded: 1968.
Editorial Address:
  P.E. Lane, Editor-in-Chief, Journal of Learning Disabilities,
  5 North Wabash Avenue, Chicago, Illinois 60602.
Editorial Policy:
  Includes articles on practical and theoretical problems of dealing
  with individuals with learning disabilities: basic and applied research, clinical case studies, administrative problems, reviews
  of research and remedial programs and assessment techniques.
  The reading audience includes special educators, psychologists,
  physicians, and allied professions working with learning disability children. Unsolicited manuscripts are welcome. Seven or
  eight major articles are published per issue. Book reviews are
  included.
Manuscript Preparation:
  Accepted manuscripts average approximately 15 double-spaced
  typewritten pages. Three copies are required. Return postage
  and a self-addressed envelope are not required. Footnoting and
  other bibliographical procedure should follow the "Counsel to
  Contributors" that is available from the publisher. A background
  or explanatory cover letter is not required, but a summary or
  abstract is required. Biographical information about the author
  is required only upon acceptance of the article. Illustrations,
  pictures, graphs, etc., should follow the "Counsel to Contributors." No payment is made for accepted manuscripts. Five
  copies are free to the author and large quantities are available
  at cost depending on length of paper and quantity ordered. Author may reprint the article if credit is given to the Journal.
Manuscript Disposition:
  Receipt of a manuscript is acknowledged. Editorial decisions
  are made usually within eight to ten weeks. Accepted articles
  usually appear in print within eight to ten months after acceptance. Rejected manuscripts are returned to author, usually
  with criticism and suggestions.
Copyright:
  Held by Professional Press, Inc.

JOURNAL OF REHABILITATION

Subscription Data:
  Published by the National Rehabilitation Association, 1522 K
  Street, N.W., Washington, D.C. 20005. Issued six times each
  year, in January/February, March/April, May/June, July/
  August, September/October, and November/December. Advertising is accepted. Circulation: 35,000. Subscription: $5.00
  per year. Founded: 1935.

Editorial Address:
    The Editor, Journal of Rehabilitation, National Rehabilitation Association, 1522 K Street, N.W., Washington, D.C. 20005.
Editorial Policy:
    Includes articles and reports on all phases of human rehabilitation. The reading audience includes state and federal rehabilitation employees, physicians, nurses, psychologists, occupational therapists, social workers, educators, and students. Unsolicited articles are welcome. Twelve major articles are published per issue. Book reviews are included.
Manuscript Preparation:
    Manuscripts may not exceed 12 double-spaced typewritten pages. Two copies are required. Return postage and a self-addressed envelope are unnecessary. Bibliographical and format style should follow a recent issue. Use wide margins and double-space throughout. Keep use of footnotes to a minimum. A background or explanatory cover letter about the article is not desired nor is an outline or summary. Biographical information about the author is desired and should include a summary of academic background, current position, and field of specialization. Illustrations, pictures, graphs, etc., must be submitted as glossy prints. No payment is made for accepted articles. Reprints are not often available.
Manuscript Disposition:
    Receipt of a manuscript is acknowledged. Editorial decisions are made as soon as possible. Accepted articles usually appear in print within six to twelve months after acceptance. Unaccepted manuscripts are returned, occasionally with criticism and/or suggestions.
Copyright:
    Held by the National Rehabilitation Association.

JOURNAL OF SPEECH AND HEARING DISORDERS

Subscription Data:
    Published by the American Speech and Hearing Association, 9030 Old Georgetown Road, Washington, D.C. 20014. Issued four times each year, in February, May, August, and November. Advertising is not accepted. Circulation: 14,000. Subscription: $23.00 per year; $6.25 per issue. Founded: 1935.
Editorial Address:
    Elizabeth Carrow, Editor, Journal of Speech and Hearing Disorders, Baylor College of Medicine, Texas Medical Center, Houston, Texas 77025.
Editorial Policy:
    Includes unpublished articles concerning theory, clinical interpretations of research findings, evaluation and remedial procedures, case studies, counseling, and other related matters in the field of speech pathology and audiology. Reporting research design and results should not be the principal purpose of the article. The reading audience includes physicians, speech clinicians, and others interested in speech and hearing problems.

Unsolicited manuscripts are welcome. Approximately 15 major articles are published per issue. Book reviews are not included.

Manuscript Preparation:

No limitations are placed upon manuscript length. Three copies are required. Return postage and a self-addressed envelope are not required. Double-space manuscript and use a minimum of footnotes. Footnotes should be included in the text, if possible. Statistical data should not be presented in great detail; descriptive headings which indicate the scholarly nature of the article are preferable to "Methods" etc. as headings. A background or explanatory cover letter and an abstract of the article are required. Biographical information about the author is required if the article is to be published. Illustrations, pictures, graphs, etc., must be originals. No payment is made for accepted manuscripts. Requests should be addressed to author for reprints or permission to reprint.

Manuscript Disposition:

Receipt of a manuscript is acknowledged. Editorial decisions are made within two months. Accepted articles usually appear in print within six to twelve months. Unaccepted manuscripts are returned with criticism and/or suggestions.

Copyright:

Held by the American Speech and Hearing Association.

JOURNAL OF SPEECH AND HEARING RESEARCH

Subscription Data:

Published by the American Speech and Hearing Association, 9030 Old Georgetown Road, Washington, D.C. 20014. Issued quarterly, in March, June, September, and December. Advertising is not accepted. Circulation: 25,000. Subscription: $23.00 per year; $26.00 foreign. Founded: 1958.

Editorial Address:

Dr. Thomas J. Hixon, Editor, Journal of Speech and Hearing Research, Department of Communicative Disorders, University of Wisconsin - Madison, Madison, Wisconsin 53706.

Editorial Policy:

Includes research reports and theoretical articles dealing with normal and disordered language, speech, and hearing. The reading audience includes members of the American Speech and Hearing Association plus researchers and students in the areas of interest. Unsolicited manuscripts are welcome. Twenty to twenty-five major articles are published per issue. Book reviews are not included.

Manuscript Preparation:

Since the American Speech and Hearing Association publishes a monograph series, manuscripts of monograph length are not accepted. Three copies are required. Return postage and a self-addressed envelope are required. Do not use footnotes. Use 8-1/2 by 11 inch paper, with 1-1/4 inches, one inch, one inch, and one inch margins and double-space throughout. A 200 word abstract is required. Biographical information about the author

is not required.   Use only high-quality graphs; see a recent issue of the Journal.   No payment is made for accepted manuscripts, but $50.00 per page, voluntary page charge.   Reprints
may be purchased from the publisher.

Manuscript Disposition:
   Receipt of a manuscript is acknowledged.   Editorial decisions
   are made within 12 to 16 weeks.   Accepted articles usually appear in print within six months.   Unaccepted manuscripts are
   not returned, unless postage is provided by the authors.   Criticism and/or suggestions are provided.

Copyright:
   Not copyrighted.   Articles may be reproduced with permission
   of the editor and the author.

REHABILITATION LITERATURE

Subscription Data:
   Published by the National Easter Seal Society for Crippled Children and Adults, 2023 West Ogden Avenue, Chicago, Illinois
   60612.   Issued monthly.   Advertising is not accepted.   Circulation: 3,200.   Subscription: $10.00 per year.   Founded: 1940.

Editorial Address:
   The Editor, Rehabilitation Literature, National Easter Seal So-
   ciety for Crippled Children and Adults, 2023 West Ogden Avenue,
   Chicago, Illinois 60612.

Editorial Policy:
   Includes articles on all aspects of rehabilitation of the handicapped
   and disabled.   The reading audience includes students and professional personnel in all areas of rehabilitation.   Unsolicited articles are welcome.   Twelve to sixteen major articles are published
   per issue.   Book reviews are included.

Manuscript Preparation:
   Manuscripts should not exceed 6,000 words, or 17 elite double-
   spaced typewritten pages.   Two copies are required.   Return
   postage and a self-addressed envelope are unnecessary.   Footnoting and other bibliographical procedure may follow any widely
   used manual of style.   Footnotes should appear at the bottom of
   the page to which they refer.   All other references must be alpha-
   betized and typed on a separate page.   Use wide margins and
   double-space throughout.   A background or explanatory cover letter about the article is desired.   An outline or summary is required with submission of the finished article.   Biographical information about the author is desired and should contain a summary of his educational background, professional experience, and
   membership in professional organizations.   These data will be
   used in the preparation of a short biographical statement which
   will appear on page one of the published article.   A glossy photographic print of the author, suitable for reproduction, is requested.
   Illustrations, pictures, graphs, etc., are not often used.   No payment is made for accepted articles.   Reprints are available
   through the office of the editor.

Manuscript Disposition:
   Receipt of a manuscript is acknowledged.   Editorial decisions

are made within two weeks. Accepted articles usually appear
in print within three to five months after acceptance. Unaccepted
manuscripts are returned, sometimes with criticism and/or suggestions.

Copyright:
    Held by the National Easter Seal Society for Crippled Children
    and Adults.

Additional Information:
    In each issue an "Article of the Month," which summarizes cur-
    rent knowledge and recent developments in a specific subject
    field, is featured.

SIGHT-SAVING REVIEW

Subscription Data:
    Published by the National Society for the Prevention of Blind-
    ness, Inc., 79 Madison Avenue, New York, New York 10016.
    Issued quarterly. Selected advertising is accepted. Circulation:
    6,000. Subscription: $7.00 per year; $2.00 per issue. Founded:
    1931.

Editorial Address:
    Editor-in-Chief, Sight-Saving Review, National Society for the
    Prevention of Blindness, Inc., 79 Madison Avenue, New York,
    New York 10016.

Editorial Policy:
    Includes articles on causes of blindness and trends in the blind-
    ness rate in the United States; advances in research and in the
    treatment of the blinding eye diseases; safety legislation and pre-
    vention of eye injuries; governmental and voluntary prevention of
    blindness programs; recommendations for screening techniques.
    The reading audience includes eye physicians, general practi-
    tioners, optometrists, opticians, teachers of partially seeing,
    administrators in public health, welfare and medical social work
    and safety engineers. Unsolicited manuscripts are welcome.
    Five to seven major articles are published per issue. Book re-
    views are included.

Manuscript Preparation:
    Accepted manuscripts average four to ten printed pages. Ref-
    erences, footnotes, figure captions, and tables should be typed
    double-spaced on separate sheets of paper. The original and
    one copy are required. Return postage and a self-addressed en-
    velope are not required. Bibliographical procedure should fol-
    low the list of journals indexed in Index Medicus and the Univer-
    sity of Chicago Manual of Style. Use Webster's Third Una-
    bridged New International Dictionary as a guide for spelling,
    hyphenation, compounding, and division. Cite using the following
    order of symbols: asterisk, dagger, double dagger. The aster-
    isk is repeated for each new page. Double-space manuscript on
    8-1/2 by 11 inch typewritten pages on sturdy opaque white paper.
    A background or explanatory cover letter is not required, nor is

an outline, summary, or abstract. Biographical information
about the author is required. Tables, graphs, or illustrations
should be mounted on the same size paper as typing paper and
numbered in sequence. Show position in manuscript. No payment is made for accepted manuscripts. The author is given
25 free reprints and three copies of the journal.

Manuscript Disposition:
 Receipt of a manuscript is acknowledged. Editorial decisions
 are made within four weeks. Accepted articles usually appear in
 print within ten months. Unaccepted manuscripts are returned
 with criticism and/or suggestions.

Copyright:
 Held by the National Society for the Prevention of Blindness,
 Inc.

Additional Information:
 A complete and accurate reference must be provided for published
 material that is cited. Journal articles are to be cited in text
 by superscript Arabic numbers in order of appearance giving the
 abbreviation of journal title.

SPECIAL CHILDREN

Subscription Data:
 Published by the American Association of Special Educators,
 107-20 One-hundred and twenty-fifth Street, Richmond Hill, New
 York 11419. Issued three times each year. Advertising is ac-
 cepted. Circulation: 4,000. Subscription: $7.00 per year.
 Founded: 1973.

Editorial Address:
 The Editor, Special Children, American Association of Special
 Educators, 107-20 One-hundred and twenty-fifth Street, Richmond
 Hill, New York 11419.

Editorial Policy:
 Includes articles relating to the problems of special children.
 The reading audience includes special educators: professionals
 involved with the handicapped; also parents, and students in special education. Unsolicited manuscripts are welcome. Approximately 15 major articles are published per issue. Book reviews
 are included.

Manuscript Preparation:
 Accepted manuscripts average 2,000 to 3,000 words. Two copies
 are required. Return postage and a self-addressed envelope are
 required. A background or explanatory cover letter is not required.

Manuscript Disposition:
 Receipt of a manuscript is acknowledged. Editorial decisions
 are made within approximately one month. Unaccepted manuscripts are sometimes returned.

Copyright:
 Not copyrighted.

TEACHING EXCEPTIONAL CHILDREN

Subscription Data:
  Published by the Council for Exceptional Children, 1920 Association Drive, Reston, Virginia 22091. Issued quarterly, in September, December, February, and May. Advertising is accepted.
  Circulation: 51,000. Subscription: $4.00 per year with Council
  membership; $7.50 per year without membership; $8.00 postal
  union countries; $8.50 other countries; $2.00 per issue. Founded:
  1968.
Editorial Address:
  The Editor, Teaching Exceptional Children, Council for Exceptional Children, 1920 Association Drive, Reston, Virginia 22091.
Editorial Policy:
  The general purpose of Teaching Exceptional Children is to provide information that is of practical value to those who work
  with exceptional children and adults. This purpose is accom-
  plished through the journal by highlighting specific instructional
  methods and materials that have potential value for educational
  programs; by interpreting and translating theory and research
  findings from various disciplines into implications for classroom
  application; by presenting methods for the evaluation of students
  on educational relevant variables. The reading audience includes
  administrators, teachers, parents, teacher-trainers, and students. Unsolicited manuscripts are welcome. Six major articles
  are published per issue. Book reviews are not included.
Manuscript Preparation:
  No limitations are placed upon accepted manuscripts. One copy
  is required. Return postage and a self-addressed envelope are
  not required. Bibliographical procedure should follow the APA
  Publication Manual. Avoid the use of footnotes; explanatory material should be incorporated within the text with a reference
  list at the end of the article. Use 1-1/2 inch left hand margins
  and one inch margins for all others. Double-space all material,
  including quotes and references. A background or explanatory
  cover letter is not required nor is an outline, summary, or abstract. Biographical information about the author is required.
  Illustrations, pictures, graphs, etc., can be freely included.
  No payment is made for accepted manuscripts. The Council for
  Exceptional Children maintains all publication rights, including
  reprints.
Manuscript Disposition:
  Receipt of a manuscript is acknowledged. Editorial decisions
  are made within 12 weeks. Accepted articles usually appear in
  print within six months after acceptance. Unaccepted manuscripts
  are returned without criticism and/or suggestions.
Copyright:
  Held by the Council for Exceptional Children.
Additional Information:
  Guide for "Preparing Your Manuscript for Teaching Exceptional
  Children" is available upon request.

VOLTA REVIEW

Subscription Data:
> Published by the Alexander Graham Bell Association for the
> Deaf, Inc., 3417 Volta Place, N.W., Washington, D.C. 20007.
> Issued monthly, except June, July, and August. Advertising is
> accepted. Circulation: 7,000. Subscription: $15.00 per year;
> $10.00 to students. Founded: 1899.

Editorial Address:
> The Editor, Volta Review, Alexander Graham Bell Association
> for the Deaf, Inc., 3417 Volta Place, N.W., Washington, D.C.
> 20007.

Editorial Policy:
> Includes educational, medical, scientific, and parent-oriented
> articles which relate to the hearing impaired. The reading au-
> dience includes teachers and parents of hearing impaired chil-
> dren, doctors, audiologists, therapists, rehabilitation workers,
> and hearing-aid dealers. Unsolicited articles are welcome.
> Five major articles are published per issue. Book reviews are
> included.

Manuscript Preparation:
> Accepted manuscripts average from 500 to 2,500 words. The
> original and two carbons are required. Return postage and a
> self-addressed envelope are not required. For footnoting and
> other bibliographical procedure see a recent issue of the Review.
> Use one inch margins and double-space. A background or ex-
> planatory cover letter about the article is desired. An abstract
> of the article is desired in advance of or with submission of
> finished manuscript. Biographical information about the author
> is required and should include the complete name of the organiza-
> tion or school with which he is associated, a summary of posi-
> tions he has previously held, a summary of his education and
> significant accomplishments, and his current mailing address.
> Illustrations, pictures, graphs, etc., may be used. No payment
> is made for accepted articles; however, free copies of the Re-
> view and an author's discount on reprints are provided. Reprint
> costs vary with article length and number of copies ordered. A
> detailed reprint cost summary is available through the office of
> the editor.

Manuscript Disposition:
> Receipt of a manuscript is acknowledged. Editorial decisions
> are made within 60 to 90 days. Accepted articles usually ap-
> pear in print within six to eight months. Unaccepted manuscripts
> are returned. Criticism and/or suggestions are usually not pro-
> vided unless specifically requested by the author.

Copyright:
> Held by the Alexander Graham Bell Association for the Deaf, Inc.

HEALTH

AMERICAN JOURNAL OF NURSING

Subscription Data:
  Published by the American Journal of Nursing Company, 10
  Columbus Circle, New York, New York 10019. Sponsored by
  the American Nurses Association. Issued monthly. Advertising
  is accepted. Circulation: 280,000. Subscription: $8.00 per
  year. Founded: 1900.
Editorial Address:
  The Editor, American Journal of Nursing, 10 Columbus Circle,
  New York, New York 10019.
Editorial Policy:
  Includes articles in all phases of nursing including current pro-
  fessional developments and clinical material. The reading audience includes professional nurses in hospitals, schools, industry,
  etc., nursing educators, and student nurses. Unsolicited arti-
  cles are welcome. Fifteen to twenty articles are published per
  issue. Book reviews are included.
Manuscript Preparation:
  Accepted manuscripts should average 1,500 to 2,000 words.
  The original and one carbon are required. Return postage and
  a self-addressed envelope are unnecessary. Footnoting and
  other bibliographical procedure should follow the University of
  Chicago Manual of Style. Use wide margins and double-space.
  A background or explanatory cover letter about the article is required. An outline or summary of the article is desired. Biographical information about the author is required. Illustrations,
  pictures, graphs, etc., may be used. Each photograph must be
  accompanied by a full description, including identification of all
  persons pictured and their permission slips or a note as to
  where they are filed. Rough line-diagrams are also satisfacto-
  ry, and can be redrawn by an AJN staff artist. Photographs
  and/or artwork supplied by the author will be returned as soon
  as possible following publication. Payment of $20.00 per printed
  page or 100 reprints for exclusive use of material is made for
  accepted articles. Reprints can be substituted for payment or
  are available to author at a reduced price.
Manuscript Disposition:
  Receipt of a manuscript is acknowledged. Editorial decisions
  are made within twelve weeks. Accepted articles usually appear
  in print within two to twelve months after acceptance. All unaccepted manuscripts are returned, usually without criticism or
  suggestions.

Copyright:
    Held by the American Journal of Nursing.
Additional Information:
    About 80% of article content is reserved for clinical, technical, or nursing service material.

AMERICAN JOURNAL OF PHARMACEUTICAL EDUCATION

Subscription Data:
    Published by the American Association of Colleges of Pharmacy, 8121 Georgia Avenue, Silver Spring, Maryland 20910. Issued five times each year, in February, May, August, November, and December. Advertising is not accepted. Circulation: 2,000. Subscription: $10.00 per year. Founded: 1937.
Editorial Address:
    C. Boyd Granberg, Editor, American Journal of Pharmaceutical Education, College of Pharmacy, Drake University, Des Moines, Iowa 50311.
Editorial Policy:
    Includes articles which deal with all phases of pharmaceutical education and with education in general. The reading audience includes pharmaceutical and other educators, scientists in related fields, government and industrial pharmacists, practicing pharmacists, and advanced students. Unsolicited articles are welcome. Twelve to fifteen major articles are published per issue. Book reviews are included.
Manuscript Preparation:
    Accepted manuscripts average 4,000 words. Two copies are required. Return postage and a self-addressed envelope are desired but not required. Style to be followed is outlined in Instructions to Authors which is printed in the Announcements section of the February issue of each volume. Use 1-1/2 inch margins and double-space. A background or explanatory cover letter about the article is required. An outline or summary is desired prior to or with submission of the finished article. Biographical information about the author is desired and should include professional title and the location of employment or practice. Illustrations, pictures, graphs, tables, etc., may be used but costs of cuts and of setting tabular material must be borne by the author. No payment is made for accepted articles. Reprints are available; a schedule of reprint costs may be obtained from the office of the editor.
Manuscript Disposition:
    Receipt of a manuscript is acknowledged. All articles are submitted to review and decisions are generally made within three weeks. Accepted articles usually appear in print from three to six months after acceptance. Unaccepted manuscripts are returned with reviewers' comments.
Copyright:
    Held by the American Association of Colleges of Pharmacy.

AMERICAN JOURNAL OF PUBLIC HEALTH

Subscription Data:
  Published by the American Public Health Association, Inc.,
  1015 Eighteenth Street, N. W., Washington, D. C. 20036. Issued
  monthly, plus special issues. Advertising is accepted. Circulation: 30,000. Subscription: $20.00 per year; $22.00 foreign.
  Founded: 1911.

Editorial Address:
  The Editor, American Journal of Public Health, 1015 Eighteenth
  Street, N. W., Washington, D. C. 20036.

Editorial Policy:
  The Journal publishes reports of original research, demonstrations, evaluation, and other papers covering the current aspects
  of public health. Includes articles on environment, family planning, community health planning, nursing, laboratory, etc. The
  reading audience includes a wide variety of people involved in
  public health. Unsolicited manuscripts are welcome. The number of major articles varies each year. Book reviews are included.

Manuscript Preparation:
  Accepted manuscripts average 5,000 words. Two copies are required. Return postage and a self-addressed envelope are not
  required. Bibliographical procedure may follow any widely used
  style manual. Footnotes should be kept to a minimum and typed
  at the foot of the appropriate page, separated from the text with
  a horizontal line. Double-space manuscript on 8-1/2 by 11 inch
  bond paper. A background or explanatory cover letter is not required, but an outline or summary is required with the finished
  article. Biographical information about the author is required
  and should include address, degrees, and professional affiliation.
  Illustrations, pictures, graphs, etc., may be used. Illustrative
  material should be prepared as glossy prints. No payment is
  made for accepted articles. Reprints are available; form and
  cost sheets are provided when galley proofs are sent for author's
  approval.

Manuscript Disposition:
  Receipt of a manuscript is acknowledged. Editorial decisions
  are made within eight to ten weeks. Unaccepted manuscripts
  are returned, sometimes with criticism and/or suggestions.

Copyright:
  Held by the American Public Health Association, Inc.

JOURNAL OF DENTAL EDUCATION

Subscription Data:
  Published by the American Association of Dental Schools, 1625
  Massachusetts Avenue, N. W., Washington, D. C. 20036. Issued
  monthly. Advertising is accepted. Circulation: 3,200. Subscription: $15.00 per year to United States and Canada; $20.00
  foreign. Founded: 1926.

Editorial Address:
> Dr. Erling Johansen, Editor, Journal of Dental Education, Department of Dental Research, University of Rochester, 260 Crittenden Boulevard, Rochester, New York 14642.

Editorial Policy:
> Includes articles on dentistry and dental education. The reading audience includes deans, department heads, faculty members, students, and others. Unsolicited manuscripts are welcome. Usually eight to twelve major articles are published per issue. Book reviews are sometimes included.

Manuscript Preparation:
> Accepted manuscripts average 20 double-spaced typewritten pages. The original and two copies are required. Return postage and a self-addressed envelope are not required. Footnotes should be incorporated into the text wherever possible. Double-space and use 8-1/2 by 11 inch paper; margins should be one inch at the top, bottom, and right and 1-1/2 inches at the left. A background or explanatory cover letter is not required nor is an outline, summary, or abstract. Biographical information about the author is required and should include the author's name, academic degrees, institution, title, and academic rank. A reasonable number of illustrations, pictures, graphs, etc., are allowed without cost to the author. Drawings should be professionally done in black and white; they will not be returned. No payment is made for accepted manuscripts. Reprints are available from the American Association of Dental Schools' Washington office.

Manuscript Disposition:
> Receipt of a manuscript is acknowledged. Editorial decisions are usually made within eight weeks. Accepted articles usually appear in print within six to twelve months. Unaccepted manuscripts are returned with criticism and/or suggestions.

Copyright:
> Held by the American Association of Dental Schools.

Additional Information:
> All papers presented at meetings of the AADS are the property of the Association and are considered for publication in the Journal, and may not be published elsewhere without written consent.

JOURNAL OF MEDICAL EDUCATION

Subscription Data:
> Published by the Association of American Medical Colleges, One Dupont Circle, N. W., Washington, D. C. 20036. Issued 12 or more times each year, occasionally published in two parts. Advertising is accepted. Circulation: 6,900. Subscription: $15.00 per year in the United States, Latin America, and Canada; $18.00 foreign; $10.00 to students. Founded: 1926.

Editorial Address:
> Merrill T. McCord, Editor, Journal of Medical Education, One Dupont Circle, N. W., Washington, D. C. 20036.

Editorial Policy:
>   Includes articles on medical education including preparation for
>   medical study, the medical school experience, intern and resi-
>   dent education, and graduate and postgraduate medical education.
>   The editorial board recognizes that medical education includes
>   the activities of faculty, students, and administrators and those
>   of the practicing professions who also teach and learn.   Thus,
>   it invites communications from any of these sources.   Eight or
>   nine major articles are published per issue.   Book reviews are
>   included.

Manuscript Preparation:
>   The Journal publishes three types of articles.   Main articles
>   consist of reflective, perspective writings with broad reader ap-
>   peal and documented reports on major studies involving medical
>   education.   Both types of articles should not run more than 15
>   double-spaced manuscript pages, and each article must include
>   an abstract of not more than 150 words.   "Communications"
>   articles are used for the purpose of providing a medium for
>   rapid publication of new ideas regarding programs and techniques
>   and of preliminary findings in education experiments.   Articles
>   for this section are absolutely limited to four double-spaced
>   manuscript pages.   Article titles must not run more than two
>   Journal lines, and all articles should contain subheads of two or
>   three words.   "Letters to the Editor" are especially welcomed
>   and should not be more than four double-spaced manuscript
>   pages.   Manuscripts should be written in the third person and
>   should be submitted in duplicate.   Return postage and a self-
>   addressed envelope are not required.   All authors should be
>   fully identified.   All copy, including references, tables, and leg-
>   ends, should be typed double-spaced.   Each table, diagram,
>   graph, or photograph should have a brief legend.   Each table
>   should be typed on a separate sheet of paper.   All illustrations
>   must be professionally drawn and lettered.   Only published ma-
>   terial specifically cited in the text should be listed as references.
>   References must be submitted in accordance with the style fol-
>   lowed in current issue of the Journal, including, in order: au-
>   thor, title, journal abbreviation (Index Medicus citation format),
>   volume number, inclusive page numbers, and year; book refer-
>   ences should also include editors, edition, publisher, and place
>   of publication.   No payment is made for accepted articles.   Re-
>   print order forms are sent to the author at the same time as
>   galley proofs.   Reprints may be ordered in multiples of 100;
>   prices depend on the length of the article.

Manuscript Disposition:
>   Receipt of a manuscript is acknowledged.   Editorial decisions
>   are usually made within 30 days.   All manuscripts are reviewed
>   by an editorial board before acceptance for publication.   Accepted
>   articles usually appear in print within six months after accept-
>   ance.   Unaccepted manuscripts are returned, occasionally with
>   criticism or suggestions.

Copyright:
>   Held by the Association of American Medical Colleges.

JOURNAL OF NURSING EDUCATION

Subscription Data:
Published by the Blakiston Publications, McGraw-Hill Book Company, 1221 Avenue of Americas, New York, New York 10020. Issued quarterly, in January, April, August, and November. Advertising is not accepted. Circulation: 5,000. Subscription: $6.00 per year; $8.00 foreign. Founded: 1962.

Editorial Address:
Mary A. Murray, Managing Editor, Journal of Nursing Education, 1221 Avenue of Americas, New York, New York 10020.

Editorial Policy:
Includes articles which relate to nursing education programs and curriculum. The reading audience includes nursing educators and professionals in related disciplines. Unsolicited articles are welcome; new writers are encouraged. Six major articles are published per issue. Book reviews are not included.

Manuscript Preparation:
Accepted manuscripts average from 10 to 20 double-spaced typewritten pages. Two copies are required. Return postage and a self-addressed envelope are desired. See a recent issue for bibliographical procedure. Use 1-1/2 inch right and left margins and one inch top and bottom margins. Double-space all material including quotations. List footnotes at the end of the article. A background or explanatory cover letter about the article is not desired nor is an outline or summary. Biographical information about the author is desired and should include a summary of professional background. Glossy black and white photographs, charts, and graphs prepared on white paper in indelible black ink may be used. No payment is made for accepted articles. Reprints are not available.

Manuscript Disposition:
Receipt of a manuscript is acknowledged. Editorial decisions are made by an editorial board within six months. Accepted articles usually appear in print within a year after acceptance. Unaccepted manuscripts are returned with reviewers' comments. Suggestions for rewriting are made only if recommended for resubmission by reviewers.

Copyright:
Held by the McGraw-Hill Book Company.

Additional Information:
A detailed guide to manuscript preparation is available through the office of the editor.

JOURNAL OF NUTRITION EDUCATION

Subscription Data:
Published by the Society for Nutrition Education, 2140 Shattuck Avenue, Suite 1110, Berkeley, California 94704. Issued quarterly, in January-March, April-June, July-September, and October-December. Advertising is accepted. Circulation: 8,500.

Subscription: $8.00 per year; $9.00 to Canada and Pan America; $9.50 other foreign; $12.00 to institutions, corporations, and libraries. Founded: 1969.

Editorial Address:
The Editor, Journal of Nutrition Education, 2140 Shattuck Avenue, Suite 1110, Berkeley, California 94704.

Editorial Policy:
Includes new findings in the field of nutrition education: research, critique, reviews, and program or activity reports. The reading audience includes professionals and paraprofessionals involved in nutrition education: nutritionists, dietitians, home advisors, teachers, physicians, food editors, home economists, etc. Unsolicited manuscripts are welcome. Five to eight major articles are published per issue. Book reviews are included.

Manuscript Preparation:
Accepted manuscripts should not exceed 12 pages. Four copies are required. Return postage and a self-addressed envelope are not required. "Information for Contributors" is available upon request. Cite references by number in the order in which they are cited using Chemical Abstracts for journal abbreviation. List footnotes and tables on separate sheets and double-space. Use 1-1/2 inch left and right margins. A background or explanatory cover letter and an outline, summary, or abstract are not required. Biographical information about the author is required and should include only current position or title and work address. Illustrations, pictures, graphs, etc., are welcomed if professionally prepared. Author must pay $110.00 per page if manuscript is more than four pages. Reprints can be provided at cost to the author in quantities of 100 or more. Prices are available on request.

Manuscript Disposition:
Receipt of a manuscript is acknowledged. Editorial decisions are made within eight weeks. Accepted articles usually appear in print within four to six months. Unaccepted manuscripts are returned. Criticisms and suggestions from a review panel are always provided for both accepted and rejected manuscripts.

Copyright:
Held by the Society for Nutrition Education.

Additional Information:
Includes occasional supplements on special subjects. Single back issues are available for $2.00. Nutrition educators may apply for membership in the Society for Nutrition Education. Journal subscription is included with dues along with reference lists published by the National Nutrition Education Clearing House. A catalog of services is available on request.

JOURNAL OF SCHOOL HEALTH

Subscription Data:
Published by the American School Health Association, Kent, Ohio 44240. Issued monthly, September through June. Adver-

tising is accepted. Circulation: 12,000. Subscription: $15.00
per year. Founded: 1927.

Editorial Address:
Delbert Oberteuffer, Ph.D., Editor, Journal of School Health,
337 West Seventeenth Avenue, Ohio State University, Columbus,
Ohio 43210.

Editorial Policy:
Includes articles which relate to all aspects of school health education. The reading audience includes school nurses, school
physicians, and teachers. Unsolicited articles are welcome.
Six major articles are published per issue. Book reviews are
included.

Manuscript Preparation:
Accepted manuscripts average from 2,000 to 2,500 words. Manuscripts should be submitted to the editor in the original with a
duplicate copy. Return postage and a self-addressed envelope
are unnecessary. The Journal uses the reference format of the
Council of Biology Editors Style Manual. Bibliographical procedure may follow any widely used manual of style. Manuscripts
must be typewritten on 8-1/2 by 11 inch white bond paper. All
copy must be double-spaced on one side of the paper only and
generous margins provided on each side and at the top and bottom of each page. The title of the manuscript should be clearly
stated in capital letters at the top of the first page and preferably should not exceed 80 type characters. A sub-title in lower
case may also be used. Acknowledgements to persons or organizations should be stated as footnotes at the bottom of the first
page of the manuscript. Authors' names, degrees, and professional affiliations should be given directly under the title of the
manuscript. If additional information about the author is desired, it should be carried in a footnote at the bottom of the
first page of the manuscript. Some indication should be made
either on the manuscript or in the cover letter to identify the
senior author or the person with whom the editor should correspond concerning the manuscript and to whom galley proof
should be sent for reading. Illustrations such as photographs,
line drawings, graphs, charts, tracings, etc., will be used at
the discretion of the editor. Authors often are asked to keep
such illustrations at a minimum and to interpret such illustrations in prose. If illustrations are submitted, they should be
submitted in duplicate on glossy prints. Each illustration must
be numbered and cited in the text at the spot where it should
be used. At the time of publication each author will receive
two complimentary copies of the Journal in which his manuscript
appears. Accompanying these will be an order blank for reprints. Reprints must be ordered at the time the copies are
received.

Manuscript Disposition:
Receipt of a manuscript is acknowledged. Editorial decisions
are made within three weeks. Accepted articles usually appear
in print within six months after acceptance. Unaccepted manuscripts are returned, often with suggestions.

Copyright:
    Not copyrighted.

LIFE AND HEALTH

Subscription Data:
    Published by the Review and Herald Publishing Association,
    6856 Eastern Avenue, Washington, D. C. 20012.   Issued monthly.
    Limited advertising is accepted.   Circulation: 157, 000.   Sub-
    scription: $6. 00 per year.   Founded: 1884.
Editorial Address:
    The Editor, Life and Health, Review and Herald Publishing As-
    sociation, 6856 Eastern Avenue, Washington, D. C. 20012.
Editorial Policy:
    Includes articles which relate to general health with emphasis
    on prevention of disease.   The reading audience includes a broad
    spectrum.   Unsolicited articles are accepted.   Five to six major
    articles are published per issue.   Book reviews are occasionally
    included.
Manuscript Preparation:
    Accepted manuscripts vary up to 2, 000 words.   One copy is
    required.   Return postage and a self-addressed envelope are re-
    quired.   Articles must be thoroughly researched and documented.
    A background or explanatory cover letter is welcome, but not
    required; an outline, summary, or abstract of the article is not
    required.   A brief is required.   Illustrations, pictures, and
    graphs are frequently used.   Payment of up to $150. 00 is made
    for accepted manuscripts.
Manuscript Disposition:
    Receipt of a manuscript is acknowledged.   Accepted articles
    usually appear in print within six months.   Unaccepted manu-
    scripts are returned, seldom with criticism or suggestions.
Copyright:
    Held by the Review and Herald Publishing Association.

PHYSICAL THERAPY (formerly American Physical Therapy Association. Journal)

Subscription Data:
    Published by the American Physical Therapy Association, 1156
    Fifteenth Street, N. W. , Washington, D. C. 20005.   Issued month-
    ly.   Advertising is accepted.   Circulation: 21, 500.   Subscrip-
    tion: $12. 00 per year; $15. 00 foreign.   Founded: 1921.
Editorial Address:
    The Editor, Physical Therapy, American Physical Therapy As-
    sociation, 1156 Fifteenth Street, N. W. , Washington, D. C. 20005.
Editorial Policy:
    Includes articles and reports on basic science and research
    which pertain to physical therapy.   The reading audience includes
    physical therapists, physical therapy students, orthopedic sur-
    geons, and medical educators.   Unsolicited articles are wel-

come. Six major articles are published per issue. Book reviews and abstracts are included.

Manuscript Preparation:
No limitations are placed upon manuscript length. The original and one carbon copy are required. Return postage and a self-addressed envelope are unnecessary. Bibliographical procedure should follow the Physical Therapy Style Manual. Use one inch margins and double-space throughout. A background or explanatory cover letter about the article is desired. A 100 word abstract is required for submission of the article. Biographical information about the author is required and should include a summary of current position, academic degrees, and indication of where degrees were taken. Illustrations, pictures, figures, and graphs may be used; release slips must be attached to pictures. No payment is made for accepted articles. Reprints are available through the author; the reprint order form is mailed to each author at the time the article is on galleys.

Manuscript Disposition:
Receipt of a manuscript is acknowledged. Editorial decisions are made by a journal committee within four to six weeks. Accepted articles usually appear in print within six months after acceptance.

Copyright:
Held by the American Physical Therapy Association.

SCHOOL HEALTH REVIEW

Subscription Data:
Published by the American Association for Health, Physical Education, and Recreation, 1201 Sixteenth Street, N. W., Washington, D. C. 20036. Issued bimonthly, January-February, March-April, May-June, July-August, September-October, and November-December. Advertising is not accepted. Circulation: 9,000. Subscription: Available to Association members with $25.00 dues. Founded: 1969.

Editorial Address:
The Editor, School Health Review, American Association for Health, Physical Education, and Recreation, 1201 Sixteenth Street, N. W., Washington, D. C. 20036.

Editorial Policy:
Includes articles on all aspects of school health education. All types of articles including practical, theoretical, technical, philosophical, and inspirational are suitable. The reading audience includes educators at all levels. Unsolicited articles are welcome. Ten to twelve major articles are published per issue. Book reviews are included.

Manuscript Preparation:
Accepted manuscripts average three to six double-spaced typewritten pages or approximately 750 to 1,500 words; longer articles are considered only if quality warrants. One copy is required. Use one inch margins and double-space throughout. Documentation is not encouraged. A background or explanatory

cover letter about the article is not desired nor is an outline or summary. A brief biographical summary about the author is desired. Illustrations, photographs, and diagrams may be used. Photographs should, where possible, be glossy eight by ten inch prints and should be accompanied by captions which provide complete information about content of the picture as well as credit lines. Indicate which photographs are copyrighted; no photograph payment is made. Photographs are returned only at the author's request. No payment is made for accepted articles, but the author receives two advance copies of the journal.

Manuscript Disposition:
Receipt of a manuscript is acknowledged. Editorial decisions are made within two months. Accepted articles usually appear in print within one year after acceptance. Galley proofs are sent only upon written request. Unaccepted manuscripts are returned without criticism or suggestions.

Copyright:
Held by the American Association for Health, Physical Education, and Recreation.

*SOCIAL HEALTH NEWS

Subscription Data:
Published by the American Social Health Association, 1740 Broadway, New York, New York 10019. Issued monthly, except July and August. Advertising is not accepted. Circulation: 2,000. Subscription: $10.00 per year with Association membership. Founded: 1930.

Editorial Address:
The Editor, Social Health News, American Social Health Association, 1740 Broadway, New York, New York 10019.

Editorial Policy:
Includes articles and reports on venereal disease, drug misuse, and related topics. The reading audience includes civic leaders, health administrators, and social workers. Unsolicited articles cannot be used. Two to three major articles are published per issue. Book reviews are occasionally included.

Copyright:
Held by the American Social Health Association.

*TODAY'S HEALTH

Subscription Data:
Published by the American Medical Association, 535 North Dearborn Street, Chicago, Illinois 60610. Issued monthly. Advertising is accepted. Circulation: 610,000. Subscription: $5.00 per year. Founded: 1923.

Editorial Address:
The Editor, Today's Health, American Medical Association, 535 North Dearborn Street, Chicago, Illinois 60610.

Editorial Policy:
Looks for family angle wherever possible and covers such subjects areas as: nutrition, recreation, child development, ecology, and other health-related community problems and the latest
developments in the treatment of major diseases. Also includes
fresh insights on improving the way people interact, health angles
on major news events and personalities, and well-documented
pieces crusading for better, healthier living. The reading audience includes the general public as well as educators and students
interested in health. Unsolicited articles are not welcome. Elev-
en major articles are published per issue. Book reviews are
not included.

Manuscript Preparation:
Accepted manuscripts average from 2,500 to 3,000 words. One
copy is required. Return postage and a self-addressed envelope
are required. Use no footnotes, use wide margins, and double-
space. A background or explanatory cover letter about the article is required, but not an outline or summary. Biographical
information about the author is unnecessary. Illustrations, pictures, and graphs may be used when necessary. Payment for
accepted articles range from $500.00 to $1,000.00. Reprint
permission is granted pending author's permission and payment
agreements to assist in public health education. Permission is
not granted for use of article in a commercial way or for endorsement.

Manuscript Disposition:
Receipt of a manuscript is not acknowledged. Editorial decisions
are made within two to four weeks. Time from acceptance of a
manuscript to its appearance in print varies with editorial need.
Unaccepted manuscripts are generally returned without criticism
or suggestions.

Copyright:
Held by the American Medical Association.

HIGHER EDUCATION

AAUP BULLETIN

Subscription Data:
  Published by the American Association of University Professors, One Dupont Circle, Washington, D. C. 20036. Issued quarterly, in March, June, September, and December. Advertising is accepted. Circulation: 90,000. Subscription: $10.00 per year. Founded: 1915.

Editorial Address:
  The Editor, AAUP Bulletin, Department of English, University of Nebraska, Lincoln, Nebraska 68508.

Editorial Policy:
  Includes articles on all phases of higher education. The reading audience includes college and university professors, and administrators. Unsolicited articles are welcome. Two major articles are published per issue. Book reviews are included.

Manuscript Preparation:
  Manuscripts may be of any reasonable length. Two copies are required. Return postage and a self-addressed envelope are desired. Footnotes should be placed at the bottom of each page. Use wide margins and double-space. A background or explanatory cover letter is not desired nor is an outline or summary. Biographical information about the author including his faculty affiliation or position is desired. Few illustrations can be used. No payment is made for accepted articles. Reprint costs vary with article length and order volume.

Manuscript Disposition:
  Receipt of a manuscript is acknowledged. Editorial decisions are made within one month. Accepted articles usually appear in print within three to six months after acceptance. Unaccepted manuscripts are returned, rarely with criticism and/or suggestions.

Copyright:
  Held by the American Association of University Professors.

*AAUW JOURNAL (formerly American Association of University Women. Journal)

Subscription Data:
  Published by the American Association of University Women, 2401 Virginia Avenue, N. W., Washington, D. C. 20037. Issued seven times a year, two issues--substantive articles, five issues --member news and information. Advertising is accepted on a

very limited basis. Circulation: 180, 000. Subscription: $4. 00 per year; $4. 50 foreign. Founded: 1911.

Editorial Address:
The Editor, AAUW Journal, American Association of University Women, 2401 Virginia Avenue, N. W. , Washington, D. C. 20037.

Editorial Policy:
Includes articles on education, world and domestic affairs, and cultural interests including science and art. The reading audience includes educators, university educated laymen, and community leaders. Unsolicited articles are rarely used, but will be considered. Approximately ten major articles are published per issue.

Manuscript Preparation:
Accepted manuscripts average 2, 000 words. Many articles are precommissioned. The original and one clear carbon, return postage and a self-addressed envelope are required. Use one inch margins and double-space. Footnotes and bibliographies should not be used. A background or explanatory cover letter about the article is desired. Biographical information about the author is required and should include information regarding her competence to write on the subject covered and a summary of her professional position. Small payment is made for accepted articles. Reprint costs vary with article length.

Manuscript Disposition:
Receipt of a manuscript is not acknowledged. Accepted articles appear in print as soon as space permits. Unaccepted manuscripts are returned with limited comment.

Copyright:
Held by the American Association of University Women.

ASSOCIATION OF COLLEGE UNIONS-INTERNATIONAL. BULLETIN (formerly Association of College Unions. Bulletin)

Subscription Data:
Published by the Association of College Unions-International, Box 7286, Stanford, California 94305. Issued five times each year, in October, December, February, March, and June. Advertising is not accepted. Circulation: 5, 000. Subscription: available to members only. Founded: 1932.

Editorial Address:
The Editor, Bulletin of the Association of College Unions-International, Box 7286, Stanford, California 94305.

Editorial Policy:
Includes articles on activities in campus centers, management, programs (including cinema, lectures, concerts, forums, debates, social programs, bowling, billiards), and building construction and maintenance. The reading audience includes the staffs of campus centers, student programmers, and policy makers, faculty advisers, deans of students, and college business managers. Unsolicited manuscripts are welcome. Two or three major articles are published per issue. Book reviews are included.

Manuscript Preparation:
Accepted manuscripts average 500 to 1,500 words. One copy is required. Return postage and a self-addressed envelope are not required. Bibliographical procedure should follow the New York Times Style Book. Use 1-1/2 inch margins, double-space, and type manuscript. A background or explanatory cover letter is not required nor is an outline, summary, or abstract. Biographical information about the author is not required. Illustrations, pictures, graphs, etc., are used. No payment is made for accepted manuscripts. A limited number of reprints are available.

Manuscript Disposition:
Receipt of a manuscript is acknowledged. Editorial decisions are made within six weeks. Accepted articles usually appear in print within two or three months. Unaccepted manuscripts are not returned. Criticism and/or suggestions are sometimes provided for manuscripts that are to be resubmitted.

Copyright:
Held by the Association of College Unions-International.

CHANGE MAGAZINE

Subscription Data:
Published by Educational Change, Inc., NBW Tower, New Rochelle, New York 10801. Issued 10 times each year, with two combined issues of July-August and December-January. Advertising is accepted. Circulation: 28,000. Subscription: $12.00 per year. Founded: 1969.

Editorial Address:
The Editor, Change Magazine, Educational Change, Inc., NBW Tower, New Rochelle, New York 10801.

Editorial Policy:
Includes lively, timely articles and reports dealing with all aspects of higher education. The reading audience includes the academic community--faculty, administrators, government policy makers, and interested laymen. Unsolicited manuscripts are welcome. Forty major articles are published per issue. Book reviews are included.

Manuscript Preparation:
Accepted manuscripts average 2,000 to 5,000 words. One copy is required. Return postage and a self-addressed envelope are required. Bibliographical procedure should follow the University of Chicago Manual of Style. Do not use footnotes. Use normal margins and double-space. A background or explanatory cover letter is not required nor is an outline, summary, or abstract. Biographical information about the author is required. Artwork is commissioned by the magazine separately, but photographs are welcome. Payment is made for accepted manuscripts. Publisher holds reprint rights. Permission for reprints is usually granted, but payment is required from commercial enterprises and author shares payment.

Manuscript Disposition:
Receipt of a manuscript is acknowledged. Editorial decisions

are made within four to five weeks. Accepted articles usually
appear in print within two to three months. Unaccepted manuscripts are returned, sometimes with criticism and/or suggestions.
Copyright:
    Held by Educational Change, Inc.

*CHRONICLE OF HIGHER EDUCATION

Subscription Data:
    Published by the Editorial Projects for Education, Inc., 1717
    Massachusetts Avenue, N.W., Washington, D.C. 20036. Issued
    weekly, except biweekly in summer (42 issues per year). Ad-
    vertising is accepted. Circulation: 26,484. Subscription:
    $21.00 per year if billed; $20.00 per year if payment accom-
    panies order. Founded: 1966.
Editorial Address:
    The Editor, Chronicle of Higher Education, 1717 Massachusetts
    Avenue, Washington, D.C. 20036.
Editorial Policy:
    Includes articles on all phases of higher education; book reviews;
    news from all over the United States; Canadian and foreign news;
    texts of major documents affecting higher education; a "fact-file"
    of statistics, etc. The reading audience includes college and
    university faculty members and administrators. Inquiries should
    be made in advance as paper is mostly staff-written. Thirty
    to forty major articles are published per issue. Book reviews
    are included.
Copyright:
    Held by the Editorial Projects for Education, Inc.

COLLEGE AND UNIVERSITY

Subscription Data:
    Published by the American Association of Collegiate Registrars
    and Admissions Officers, One Dupont Circle, N.W., Suite 330,
    Washington, D.C. 20036. Issued quarterly, in fall, winter,
    spring, and summer. Advertising is not accepted. Circulation:
    5,500. Subscription: $8.00 per year. Founded: 1926.
Editorial Address:
    The Editor, College and University, Office of the Secretary of
    the University, Ohio University, Athens, Ohio 45701.
Editorial Policy:
    Includes articles on higher education administration, financial
    aids, institutional research--with emphasis on fields of records,
    registration, and admissions. The reading audience includes
    higher education administrators; these include particularly regis-
    tration, personnel, admissions, records, student personnel, fi-
    nancial aids, and research personnel. Unsolicited manuscripts
    are welcome. Six to eight major articles are published per is-
    sue. Book reviews are included.

Manuscript Preparation:
    Accepted manuscripts average eight to ten typewritten pages.
    One copy is required. Return postage and a self-addressed en-
    velope are required. Bibliographical procedure should follow
    the MLA Style Sheet. A background or explanatory cover letter
    is not required nor is an outline, summary, or abstract. Bio-
    graphical information about the author should include his name
    and position. Graphs and illustrations are accepted. No pay-
    ment is made for accepted manuscripts. Reprints are available
    from the publisher.
Manuscript Disposition:
    Receipt of a manuscript is acknowledged. Editorial decisions
    are made within four weeks. Accepted articles usually appear
    in print within four months. Unaccepted manuscripts are re-
    turned, normally without criticism and/or suggestions.
Copyright:
    Not copyrighted.

*COLLEGE AND UNIVERSITY BULLETIN

Subscription Data:
    Published by the American Association for Higher Education,
    One Dupont Circle, Suite 780, Washington, D.C. 20036. Issued
    monthly, September through June. Advertising is not accepted.
    Circulation: 8,500. Subscription: $10.00 per year; Free to
    Association members. Founded: 1948.
Editorial Address:
    The Editor, College and University Bulletin, American Associa-
    tion for Higher Education, One Dupont Circle, Suite 780, Wash-
    ington, D.C. 20036.
Editorial Policy:
    Includes articles on "Research Currents," short four page re-
    views on recent research on current issues in higher education;
    book reviews; association news; and short news stories on var-
    ious higher educational topics. The reading audience includes
    professors, college and university administrators, and others in-
    volved in higher education. Unsolicited articles cannot be ac-
    cepted. Five to seven major articles are published per issue.
    Book reviews are included.
Copyright:
    Held by the American Association for Higher Education.

COLLEGE AND UNIVERSITY BUSINESS

Subscription Data:
    Published by McGraw-Hill, Inc., 230 West Monroe, Suite 1100,
    Chicago, Illinois 60606. Issued monthly. Advertising is ac-
    cepted. Circulation: 15,000. Subscription: $15.00 per year,
    payable in advance. Founded: 1946.
Editorial Address:
    The Editor, College and University Business, 230 West Monroe,
    Suite 1100, Chicago, Illinois 60606.

Editorial Policy:
Includes articles which relate to college and university administration, with a business and operational emphasis. The reading
audience includes college presidents, treasurers, purchasing
agents, and deans. Unsolicited articles are welcome; query preferred. Twelve to fourteen major articles are published per issue. Book reviews are included.

Manuscript Preparation:
Accepted manuscripts average 2,500 words. One copy is required. Return postage and a self-addressed envelope are required. See a recent issue for bibliographical procedure. Use
1-1/2 inch margins and double-space. Avoid use of footnotes
when possible. A background or explanatory cover letter about
the article is desired, but not an outline or summary. Biographical information about the author is desired and should include a summary of his current professional position. Illustrations, pictures, and graphs may be included. No payment is
made for accepted articles. Reprints are sometimes available.

Manuscript Disposition:
Receipt of a manuscript is acknowledged. Editorial decisions
are made as soon as possible. Time from acceptance of a manuscript to its appearance in print varies with the topic of the article and the manuscript backlog. Unaccepted manuscripts are
returned without criticism or other comment.

Copyright:
Held by McGraw-Hill, Inc.

COLLEGE AND UNIVERSITY JOURNAL

Subscription Data:
Published by the American College Public Relations Association,
One Dupont Circle, Suite 600, Washington, D.C. 20036. Issued
five times each year, in January, March, May, September, and
November. Advertising is accepted. Circulation: 4,600. Sub-
scription: $9.50 per year. Founded: 1962.

Editorial Address:
The Editor, College and University Journal, American College
Public Relations Association, One Dupont Circle, Suite 600,
Washington, D.C. 20036.

Editorial Policy:
Includes articles on all phases of college and university advancement. Most of the articles are of higher education in regard to
institutional advancement (development, public relations, etc.).
The reading audience includes college and university personnel,
including public relations specialists, and students of public relations. Unsolicited manuscripts are welcome. Six or seven
major articles are published per issue. Book reviews are seldom included.

Manuscript Preparation:
Accepted manuscripts average up to 3,000 words. Two copies
are required. Return postage and a self-addressed envelope are
preferred. Bibliographical procedure should follow references
in the text. Use large margins and double-space. A background

or explanatory cover letter is not required nor is an outline, summary, or abstract. Biographical information about the author should include name, job, and place of employment. Illustrations, pictures, graphs, etc., are most welcome. No payment is made for accepted manuscripts. Reprints are available at cost.

Manuscript Disposition:

Receipt of a manuscript is acknowledged. Editorial decisions are made within six to eight weeks. Accepted articles usually appear in print within four months. Unaccepted manuscripts are returned, without criticism and/or suggestions.

Copyright:

Held by the American College Public Relations Association.

COLLEGE PRESS SERVICE (formerly Collegiate Press Service Journal)

Subscription Data:

Published by the College Press Service, Inc., 1452 Pennsylvania Street, Denver, Colorado 80203. Issued twice each week with eight-page releases, on Wednesday and Saturday, September through May. Advertising is not accepted. Circulation: 400 subscribing papers in 47 states. Subscription: $50.00 per year to libraries; papers should contact College Press Service for sliding scale based on frequency of publication. Founded: 1961.

Editorial Address:

The Editor, College Press Service, 1452 Pennsylvania Street, Denver, Colorado 80203.

Editorial Policy:

Coverage includes events on individual campuses; curricular and educational reform; campus trends; conferences and activities of national education and student groups; governmental activity affecting higher education; alternative coverage of national and international affairs; no opinion articles. The reading audience includes junior colleges, four year colleges, technical schools, graduate schools, campus student governments, higher education foundations, and libraries. Unsolicited manuscripts are welcome. Six to ten major articles are published per issue. Staff written book reviews are usually included.

Manuscript Preparation:

Accepted manuscripts average 300 to 1,200 words. One copy is required. Return postage and a self-addressed envelope are required. Avoid use of footnotes and bibliography; style is similar to Associated Press Style Book. Use one inch margins and double-space. A background or explanatory cover letter is required, but not an outline, summary, or abstract. Biographical information about the author is required. Illustrations, pictures, graphs, etc., are used, but they should be camera-ready and not exceed eight by five inches. Payment of $5.00 to $25.00 is usually made for accepted articles. In rare cases, College Press Service will accept articles printed elsewhere first; back issues or sample copies are available upon request.

Manuscript Disposition:
Receipt of a manuscript is not acknowledged. Editorial decisions are usually made within four to five weeks. Time from acceptance of an article to its appearance in print varies with editorial need. Unaccepted manuscripts are returned if accompanied by stamped, self-addressed envelope. Criticism and/or suggestions are sometimes provided if writer shows promise for future stronger work.

Copyright:
Articles are usually not copyrighted; however, CPS sometimes buys first or second serial rights in rare cases.

Additional Information:
CPS publishes twice-weekly releases of eight pages each (six of copy and two of graphic art and editorial cartoons) for reproduction by subscriber papers. CPS has subscribers in 47 states for a total readership of 1.2 million. Writers include young professionals with a background in educational reform, student rights, military counseling, sociological study, and consumerism. CPS maintains the only nationwide center for censorship counseling, and is the campus censorship representative of the Reporters Committee for the Freedom of the Press.

COLLEGE STORE JOURNAL (formerly College Store)

Subscription Data:
Published by the National Association of College Stores, Inc., 55 East College Street, Oberlin, Ohio 44074. Issued six times each year. Advertising is accepted. Circulation: 4,200. Subscription: $9.00 per year. Founded: 1934.

Editorial Address:
Max L. Williamson, Editor, College Store Journal, National Association of College Stores, 55 East College Street, Oberlin, Ohio 44074.

Editorial Policy:
Includes technical articles which deal with management, design, service, promotion, and other topics of interest to college store and distribution personnel, and college business managers. Unsolicited articles are welcome, although a majority of published articles are solicited by the editor. Normally a potential author will submit his idea to the editor for consideration, with specific assignment made when feasible. From 12 to 20 major articles are published per issue.

Manuscript Preparation:
No limitations are placed upon manuscript length. One copy is required. Return postage and a self-addressed envelope are desired. See a recent issue for footnoting procedure and article format. Use one inch margins and double-space. A background or explanatory cover letter about the article is desired, but not an outline or summary. A recent photograph is required for use with accepted articles. Illustrations, pictures, graphs, etc., may be used. Payment for accepted articles is made by special arrangement only. Reprints are sometimes available.

Manuscript Disposition:
    Receipt of a manuscript is acknowledged. Editorial decisions
    are made as soon as possible. Accepted articles usually appear
    in print within two to four months after acceptance. Unaccepted
    manuscripts are returned with criticism and/or a brief explana-
    tion of rejection.
Copyright:
    Held by the National Association of College Stores.

COMMUNITY AND JUNIOR COLLEGE JOURNAL (formerly Junior
College Journal)

Subscription Data:
    Published by the American Association of Community and Junior
    Colleges, One Dupont Circle, N. W. , Washington, D. C. 20036.
    Issued nine times each year, monthly with combined August-
    September, June-July, and December-January. Advertising is
    accepted. Circulation: 48,000. Subscription: $7.00 per year.
    Founded: 1930.
Editorial Address:
    The Editor, Community and Junior College Journal, American
    Association of Community and Junior Colleges, One Dupont
    Circle, N. W. , Washington, D. C. 20036.
Editorial Policy:
    The reading audience includes faculty, deans, presidents, and
    counselors in areas of higher education. Unsolicited manuscripts
    are welcome. Eleven to fifteen major articles are published per
    issue. Book listings are included.
Manuscript Preparation:
    Accepted manuscripts should average five to seven double-spaced
    pages. Two copies are required. Return postage and a self-
    addressed envelope are required. Bibliographical sources should
    be included within the text. Avoid the use of footnotes. Use 70
    characters per line, 25 lines per page. A background or ex-
    planatory cover letter is required, but not an outline, summary,
    or abstract. Biographical information about the author is re-
    quired. Policies concerning illustrations, pictures, graphs, etc.,
    are flexible. No payment is made for accepted manuscripts.
    Reprints are available.
Manuscript Disposition:
    Receipt of a manuscript is acknowledged. Editorial decisions
    are made within two weeks. Accepted articles usually appear
    in print within one year. Unaccepted manuscripts are returned
    with criticism and/or suggestions.
Copyright:
    Held by American Association of Community and Junior Colleges.

COMMUNITY COLLEGE REVIEW

Subscription Data:
    Published by the North Carolina State University, P. O. Box

5504, Raleigh, North Carolina 27607. Issued quarterly, in spring, summer, fall, and winter. Advertising is accepted. Circulation: 10,000. Subscription: $4.00 per year; group rates available. Founded: 1973.

Editorial Address:

Ken B. Segner, Editor, Community College Review, P.O. Box 5504, Raleigh, North Carolina 27607.

Editorial Policy:

Includes articles presenting ideas and research on community college education, including adult basic education, occupational education, general or liberal arts education, teaching methodologies, and administrative problems. The reading audience includes circulation in 50 states and Canada consisting of administrators, teachers, trustees, libraries, university faculty preparing teachers and administrators for the field, and graduate students in the field. Unsolicited manuscripts are welcome. Approximately eight major articles are published per issue. Book reviews are not presently included, but will be in the future.

Manuscript Preparation:

Accepted manuscripts average 1,500 to 2,000 words, but no limitations are placed on length. One copy is required. Return postage and a self-addressed envelope are not required. Bibliographical procedure should follow the Turabian Manual for Writers. Double-space manuscript. A background or explanatory cover letter and an outline, summary, or abstract are preferred. Biographical information about the author is preferred. Illustrations, pictures, graphs, etc., are acceptable, but prefer that charts or graphs be summarized in words. No payment is made for accepted manuscripts. Reprints are available with no set price.

Manuscript Disposition:

Receipt of a manuscript is acknowledged. Editorial decisions are made within three months. Accepted articles usually appear in print within six months. Unaccepted manuscripts are returned, without criticism and/or suggestions, unless manuscript has some potential.

Copyright:

Held by the North Carolina State University.

Additional Information:

Material published provides very diverse interests beneficial to the broad field of community college education. Concentration of the style of articles is clear and readable and may include controversial viewpoints.

EDUCATIONAL RECORD

Subscription Data:

Published by the American Council on Education, One Dupont Circle, Washington, D.C. 20036. Issued quarterly, in winter, spring, summer, and fall. Advertising is not accepted. Circulation: 9,500. Subscription: $10.00 per year; $2.50 per issue; $16.00 foreign; $4.00 per issue. Founded: 1920.

Editorial Address:
<u>The Editor, Educational Record,</u> American Council on Education,
One Dupont Circle, Washington, D.C. 20036.
Editorial Policy:
Includes articles on all phases of higher education and public affairs. The reading audience includes administrators and other
executive officers of accredited colleges, universities, and professional and scholarly organizations. Unsolicited articles are
welcome. Fifteen to eighteen articles are published per issue.
Book reviews are included in each issue.
Manuscript Preparation:
Manuscript length should not exceed 20 double-spaced typewritten
pages. One copy is required. Return postage and a self-addressed envelope are unnecessary. Editorial style should follow
the University of Chicago <u>Manual of Style.</u> An explanatory cover
letter about the article is desired, but an outline is not required.
Biographical information about the author is required and should
include indication of his current position and title. Graphs and
tables should be used only occasionally. No payment is made
for accepted articles. Reprint costs vary with article length and
number of copies ordered. Author receives 100 gratis reprints.
Manuscript Disposition:
Receipt of a manuscript is acknowledged. Editorial decisions
are made within one to three months. Accepted articles usually
appear in print within two to six months after acceptance. Unaccepted manuscripts are returned without suggestions or criticism.
Copyright:
Held by the American Council on Education.

IMPROVING COLLEGE AND UNIVERSITY TEACHING

Subscription Data:
Published by the Graduate School of Oregon State University,
Oregon State University Press, 101 Walso Hall, Corvallis, Ore-
gon 97331. Issued quarterly, in winter, spring, summer, and
fall. Advertising is accepted. Circulation: 3,000. Interna-
tional--goes to 40 countries, all states and provinces of the
United States and Canada. Subscription: $6.00 per year; $9.00
for two years; $12.00 for three years. Founded: 1953.
Editorial Address:
The Editor, <u>Improving College and University Teaching,</u> 101
Waldo Hall, Oregon State University, Corvallis, Oregon 97331.
Editorial Policy:
Includes articles on college and university teaching written by
college and university teachers. The reading audience includes
college and university faculty and students. Unsolicited manu-
scripts are welcome. About 30 major articles are published per
issue. The winter issue includes an extensive book section.
Manuscript Preparation:
The preferred length of a manuscript is 1,500 words but longer
and shorter articles are used. One copy is required. Return

postage and a self-addressed envelope are not required. Bibliographical procedure should follow any style if consistently followed. Footnotes are usually printed at the end of an article.
Manuscripts should be double-spaced on 8-1/2 by 11 inch paper,
ribbon typing. A background or explanatory cover letter is not
required nor is an outline, summary, or abstract, but both are
usually helpful. Biographical information should include author's
professional or academic title or position, degrees held and
sources. Illustrations, pictures, graphs, etc., are used where
message of article requires. A small portrait of the author is
usually used with an article. No payment is made for accepted
manuscripts. Authors receive a reasonable number of copies
of the issue in which the article is printed.

Manuscript Disposition:
Receipt of a manuscript is acknowledged. Editorial decisions
are made in approximately four weeks. Time from acceptance
of the article to its appearance in print varies greatly. Unaccepted manuscripts are returned with criticism and/or suggestions sometimes provided. Authors are expected to be agree-
able to editorial improvement of readability, but revisions are
subject to the author's approval.

Copyright:
Held by the Oregon State University.

Additional Information:
A plan is under consideration for an Improving College and University Teaching imprint series for the prompt printing of urgent
articles that may soon be out of date.

JGE: JOURNAL OF GENERAL EDUCATION

Subscription Data:
Published by the Pennsylvania State University Press, 215 Wagner
Building, University Park, Pennsylvania 16802. Issued quarterly,
in April, July, October, and January. Advertising is accepted.
Circulation: 1,900. Subscription: $9.00 per year. Founded:
1946.

Editorial Address:
The Editor, JGE: Journal of General Education, Pennsylvania
State University Press, 215 Wagner Building, University Park,
Pennsylvania 16802.

Editorial Policy:
Includes articles that contribute fresh ideas and insights concerning general education of students in junior colleges, colleges, and
universities. The reading audience includes teachers and individuals. Unsolicited manuscripts are welcome. Seven major
articles are published per issue. Book reviews are included.

Manuscript Preparation:
No limitations are placed on manuscript length. One copy is
required. Return postage and a self-addressed envelope are
required. Bibliographical procedure should follow the University
of Chicago Manual of Style. A background or explanatory cover
letter is not required nor is an outline, summary, or abstract.

Biographical information about the author is required after acceptance of the article. Do not include pictures; simple tables and graphs are acceptable. No payment is made for accepted manuscripts. Twenty-five free reprints are given to each author; no additional reprints are available.

Manuscript Disposition:

Receipt of a manuscript is acknowledged. Editorial decisions are made within four weeks. Accepted articles usually appear in print within 12 months. Unaccepted manuscripts are returned without criticism and/or suggestions.

Copyright:

Held by Pennsylvania State University.

JOURNAL OF HIGHER EDUCATION

Subscription Data:

Published by the Ohio State University Press, 2070 Neil Avenue, Columbus, Ohio 43210. Issued monthly, except July, August, and September. Advertising is accepted. Circulation: 6,200. Subscription: $10.00 per year; $12.00 to libraries. Founded: 1930.

Editorial Address:

Robert Silverman, Editor, Journal of Higher Education, 2070 Neil Avenue, Columbus, Ohio 43210.

Editorial Policy:

Includes data based articles which have operational significance for members of the academic community. The reading audience includes college and university administrators and faculty. Unsolicited manuscripts are welcome. Five to six major articles are published per issue. Book reviews are included.

Manuscript Preparation:

Accepted manuscripts should average 15 to 18 pages. Two copies are required. Return postage and a self-addressed envelope are required. Bibliographical procedure should follow the University of Chicago Manual of Style. Use wide margins and double-space on non-corrasable paper. A background or explanatory cover letter is not required, but an abstract is required. Biographical information about the author is required. Illustrations, pictures, graphs, etc., may be used sparingly. No payment is made for accepted manuscripts. Reprints are available through the Journal's printer.

Manuscript Disposition:

Receipt of a manuscript is acknowledged. Editorial decisions are made within four to six weeks. Accepted articles usually appear in print within four to six months. Unaccepted manuscripts are returned with criticism and/or suggestions provided if requested.

Copyright:

Held by the Ohio State University Press.

*JOURNAL OF TEACHER EDUCATION

Subscription Data:

Published by the American Association of Colleges for Teacher Education, One Dupont Circle, Washington, D. C. 20036. Issued quarterly, in spring, summer, fall, and winter. Advertising is accepted. Circulation: 12, 000. Subscription: $10. 00 per year; $25. 00 for three years. Founded: 1950.

Editorial Address:

The Editor, Journal of Teacher Education, American Association of Colleges for Teacher Education, One Dupont Circle, Washington, D. C. 20036.

Editorial Policy:

Includes articles on issues of current and future interest in teacher education; short, controversial; some research articles are also included. The reading audience includes teacher educators. Some unsolicited manuscripts are accepted. Eight to ten major articles are published per issue. Book reviews are included.

Manuscript Preparation:

Accepted articles average 10 double-spaced typewritten pages. Two copies are required. Return postage and a self-addressed envelope are desired. Bibliographical style and footnoting should follow the University of Chicago Manual of Style. Footnotes should be on a separate page. A background or explanatory cover letter is not required, but an outline, summary, or abstract of the article is recommended. Biographical information about the author is required. There are no policies concerning illustrations, pictures, graphs, etc. No payment is made for accepted manuscripts. Reprints are available at cost; must order a minimum of 100.

Manuscript Disposition:

Receipt of a manuscript is acknowledged. Editorial decisions are made within three months. Accepted articles usually appear in print within one year. Unaccepted manuscripts are returned, if requested, without criticism and suggestions.

Copyright:

Held by the American Association of Colleges for Teacher Education.

LIBERAL EDUCATION

Subscription Data:

Published by the Association of American Colleges, 1818 R Street, N. W. , Washington, D. C. 20009. Issued four times each year, in March, May, October, and December. Educational and fund raising advertising is accepted, but commercial advertising is not. Circulation: 4, 000. Subscription: $5. 00 per year; $2. 50 to Association members. Founded: 1915.

Editorial Address:
The Editor, Liberal Education, Association of American Colleges, 1818 R Street, N. W., Washington, D. C. 20009.

Editorial Policy:
Includes articles on all phases and fields of education. The reading audience includes college administrators and faculty members, staff members of educational organizations and charitable foundations, and business leaders. Unsolicited articles are welcome. Twelve to fourteen major articles are published per issue. Book reviews are occasionally included.

Manuscript Preparation:
Accepted manuscripts average 3, 000 words. One copy is required. Return postage and a self-addressed envelope are unnecessary. Use the University of Chicago Manual of Style for special footnoting recommendations. Use wide margins and double-space. A background or explanatory cover letter about the article is not desired nor is an outline or summary. Biographical information about the author is required for publication. No illustrations, pictures, graphs, etc., are used. No payment is made for accepted articles. Reprints are available on order by the author.

Manuscript Disposition:
Receipt of a manuscript is acknowledged. Editorial decisions are made within two to three months. Time from acceptance of a manuscript to its appearance in print varies with editorial need. Unaccepted manuscripts are returned without suggestions or criticism.

Copyright:
Held by the Association of American Colleges.

UNIVERSITY COLLEGE QUARTERLY

Subscription Data:
Published by Michigan State University, East Lansing, Michigan 48823. Issued four times each year, in November, January, March, and May. Advertising is not accepted. Circulation: 4, 600. Subscription: Free to educators. Founded: 1956.

Editorial Address:
The Editor, University College Quarterly, 240 Bessey Hall, Michigan State University, East Lansing, Michigan 48824.

Editorial Policy:
Includes articles which deal with general education, educational administration, the status of teaching, new developments in education, subject matter, and special educational programs. Poetry is also occasionally published. The reading audience includes professors, teachers, and administrators in all fields. Unsolicited articles are welcome. Five to eight major articles are published per issue. Book reviews are included.

Manuscript Preparation:
Accepted manuscripts average from six to twelve double-spaced typewritten pages. One copy is required. Return postage and a self-addressed envelope are desired. Bibliographical proce-

dure should follow the MLA Style Sheet. Footnotes should be
avoided where possible or incorporated as brief citations placed
within parentheses in the text. Use wide margins and double-
space throughout. A background or explanatory cover letter
about the article is not desired nor is an outline or summary.
Biographical information about the author is desired and should
include title, academic rank, institution, and location. Illustrations, pictures, graphs, etc., are occasionally used. No payment is made for accepted articles. Twenty free reprints are
mailed to each author; additional copies may be ordered at a
nominal cost.

Manuscript Disposition:

Receipt of a manuscript is acknowledged. Editorial decisions
are normally made within one week. Accepted articles appear
in print within twelve months after acceptance. Unaccepted manuscripts are returned, sometimes with criticism given and occasionally with the suggestions that another publication be considered.

Copyright:

Held by Michigan State University.

Additional Information:

Keep articles short and write with educated general reader in
mind. Place emphasis on results and significance. In addition
to traditional articles, occasional ironic, satiric, editorial, or
semi-fiction pieces can also be considered.

HISTORY

AMERICAN HISTORICAL REVIEW

Subscription Data:
  Published by the American Historical Association, 400 A Street,
  S. E., Washington, D. C. 20003. Issued five times each year, in
  February, April, June, October, and December. Advertising is
  accepted. Circulation: 17,000 members, 6,000 institutional sub-
  scriptions. Subscription: $15.00 per year; $20.00 to institu-
  tions; $10.00 to students and emeriti; $25.00 to full professors
  and non-academic individuals; $400.00 for life membership.
  Founded: 1884.
Editorial Address:
  The Editor, American Historical Review, 400 A Street, S. E.,
  Washington, D. C. 20003.
Editorial Policy:
  Includes scholarly articles of historical nature. The reading audience includes professional historians, educators, and others interested in history. Unsolicited articles are welcome; book reviews and review articles are not welcome. Four to five major
  articles are published per issue. Book reviews are included.
Manuscript Preparation:
  Accepted manuscripts average 40 double-spaced typewritten pages,
  including footnotes. One copy is required. Return postage and
  a self-addressed envelope is not required but appreciated. Bibliographical procedure should follow the University of Chicago
  Manual of Style. Footnotes should be on separate pages following
  the text. Manuscripts should be double-spaced and have generous
  margins. A background or explanatory cover letter is not required nor is an outline, summary, or abstract. Illustrations,
  pictures, and graphs are accepted. Payment is not made for accepted manuscripts. Authors of articles receive 100 free reprints and may order more at cost.
Manuscript Disposition:
  Receipt of a manuscript is acknowledged. Editorial decisions
  are made within two to three months. Accepted articles usually
  appear in print in about a year. Unaccepted manuscripts are
  returned, usually with criticism and/or suggestions.
Copyright:
  Held by the American Historical Association unless special agreement to transfer copyright to the author is made.

AMERICAN JEWISH HISTORICAL QUARTERLY

Subscription Data:
  Published by the American Jewish Historical Society, 2 Thornton

Road, Waltham, Massachusetts 02154. Issued quarterly, in September, December, March, and June. Advertising is accepted. Circulation: 3, 600. Subscription: $15.00 per year. Founded: 1893.

Editorial Address:
  The Editor, American Jewish Historical Quarterly, American Jewish Historical Society, 2 Thornton Road, Waltham, Massachusetts 02154.

Editorial Policy:
  Includes articles and reports on American and Western Hemisphere Jewish history. The reading audience includes educators and students who are interested in American Jewish historical research. Unsolicited, fully annotated and documented, objectively presented articles are welcome. Three or four major articles are published per issue. Book reviews are included.

Manuscript Preparation:
  Accepted manuscripts average from 10 to 40 double-spaced typewritten pages, or from 3, 000 to 12, 000 words. Return postage and a self-addressed envelope are desired. See a recent issue for format and bibliographical procedure. Use 1-1/2 inch margins and double-space throughout. Footnotes should be placed on a separate page at the end of the article. A background or explanatory cover letter about the article is desired. Biographical information about the author is desired and should include an indication of academic background and previous publications. Illustrations, pictures, graphs, etc., may be used. No payment is made for accepted articles. Reprints are available; costs vary with article length and order volume. Fifty free reprints are mailed to the author.

Manuscript Disposition:
  Receipt of a manuscript is acknowledged. Editorial decisions are made as soon as possible. Each manuscript is evaluated by three readers. Accepted articles usually appear in print within six to twelve months after acceptance. Unaccepted manuscripts are returned, often with suggestions and/or criticism.

Copyright:
  Held by the American Jewish Historical Society.

Additional Information:
  Each contributor should indicate whether or not the article is based upon original research, the published and unpublished sources used, and ways in which the work extends existing knowledge in the field covered.

HISTORY OF EDUCATION QUARTERLY

Subscription Data:
  Published by the School of Education of New York University, School of Education, New York University, Washington Square, New York, New York 10003. Issued quarterly, in spring, summer, fall, and winter. Advertising is not accepted. Circulation: 1, 800. Subscription: $15.00 to institutions; $12.50 per year to individual subscribers who are members of the History of Education Society. Founded: 1961.

Editorial Address:
  The Editor, History of Education Quarterly, Room 737, 239
  Green Street, New York University, Washington Square, New
  York, New York 10003.
Editorial Policy:
  Includes articles on the history of education. The reading audi-
  ence includes scholars interested in history and the history of
  education. Unsolicited articles are welcome. Five major articles are published per issue. Book reviews are included.
Manuscript Preparation:
  No limitations are placed upon manuscript length. Two or more
  copies are required. Return postage and a self-addressed envelope are desired. Footnoting and other bibliographical procedure should follow the University of Chicago Manual of Style.
  Use wide margins and double-space. A background or explanatory cover letter about the article is desired, but not an outline
  or summary. Biographical information about the author is desired. Illustrations, pictures, and graphs are seldom used. No
  payment is made for accepted articles and full issues must be
  purchased.
Manuscript Disposition:
  Receipt of a manuscript is acknowledged. Editorial decisions
  are made as soon as possible. Time from acceptance of a manuscript to its appearance in print varies with editorial need.
  Unaccepted manuscripts are returned with criticism and/or suggestions.
Copyright:
  Held by New York University.

INDIAN HISTORIAN

Subscription Data:
  Published by the American Indian Historical Society, 1451 Masonic Avenue, San Francisco, California 94117. Issued quarterly, in January, April, July, and November. Advertising is not
  accepted. Circulation: 5,500. Subscription: $6.00 per year.
  Founded: 1964.
Editorial Address:
  The Editor, Indian Historian, 1451 Masonic Avenue, San Francisco, California 94117.
Editorial Policy:
  The reading audience includes the educational community including students, professors, etc. Unsolicited manuscripts are
  welcome, but the editor will not be responsible for them. Eight
  major articles are published per issue. Book reviews are included.
Manuscript Preparation:
  Accepted manuscripts average 20 to 40 double-spaced typewritten
  pages. Two copies are required. Return postage and a self-
  addressed envelope are required. Bibliographical procedure
  should follow the MLA Style Sheet. List footnotes on a separate
  page. Use two inch margins on each side. A background or

explanatory cover letter is required, but not an outline, summary, or abstract. Biographical information about the author is required. Illustrations, pictures, graphs, etc., are acceptable. No payment is made for accepted manuscripts. Copyright permission for reprints is usually granted.

Manuscript Disposition:
Receipt of a manuscript is acknowledged. Editorial decisions are made within eight weeks. Accepted articles usually appear in print within six months. Unaccepted manuscripts are returned without criticism and/or suggestions.

Copyright:
Held by the American Indian Historical Society.

JOURNAL OF AMERICAN HISTORY

Subscription Data:
Published by the Organization of American Historians, 112 North Bryan Street, Bloomington, Indiana 47401. Issued quarterly, in March, June, September, and December. Advertising is accepted. Circulation: 12,500. Subscription: $12.00 per year; $15.00 to institutions; $6.00 to students. Founded: 1913.

Editorial Address:
Martin Ridge, Managing Editor, Journal of American History, 702 Ballantine Hall, Indiana University, Bloomington, Indiana 47401.

Editorial Policy:
Includes scholarly articles on all phases of American history. The reading audience includes professional historians and teachers. Unsolicited articles are welcome. Five or six major articles are published per issue. Book reviews are included.

Manuscript Preparation:
Accepted manuscripts average 7,500 words, including footnotes. One copy is required. Return postage and a self-addressed envelope are desired. Footnoting and other bibliographical procedure should follow a recent issue. Footnotes should be double-spaced and placed at the end of the manuscript. Use 20 space lines and double-space throughout. A background or explanatory cover letter about the article is desired, but not an outline or summary. Biographical information about the author is unnecessary. Illustrations, pictures, graphs, etc., may be used. Payment is made for accepted articles. Reprints are available; a cost schedule for authors is available through the office of the editor.

Manuscript Disposition:
Receipt of a manuscript is acknowledged. Editorial decisions, based upon comments of several referees, are made within two months. Accepted articles usually appear in print within three months after acceptance. Unaccepted manuscripts are returned, often with criticism and comments.

Copyright:
Held by the Organization of American Historians.

JOURNAL OF INTERDISCIPLINARY HISTORY

Subscription Data:
Published by the Massachusetts Institute of Technology Press,
28 Carleton Street, Cambridge, Massachusetts 02142. Issued
quarterly, in June, September, December, and March. Advertising is accepted. Circulation: 1,800. Subscription: $12.50
per year; $16.50 to institutions. Founded: 1970.

Editorial Address:
The Editor, Journal of Interdisciplinary History, E53-490.
Massachusetts Institute of Technology, Cambridge, Massachusetts
02139.

Editorial Policy:
Includes methodological and substantive articles devoted to the
application of other disciplines and branches of learning to research in history, without limit of geographical bound or chronological period. The reading audience includes historians, political scientists, and psychologists. Unsolicited manuscripts are
welcome. Eight to ten major articles are published per issue.
Book reviews are included.

Manuscript Preparation:
Accepted manuscripts average 30 double-spaced typewritten pages.
Two copies are required. Return postage and a self-addressed
envelope are requested. Footnotes should be listed at the end
of the text and typed double-spaced. Use 1-1/4 inch margins
and double-space. A background or explanatory cover letter is
requested, but an outline, summary, or abstract is not required.
Biographical information about the author is required. Graphs
and figures are used, but illustrations are rarely used. No
payment is made for accepted manuscripts. Authors of major
articles receive 25 free offprints.

Manuscript Disposition:
Receipt of a manuscript is acknowledged. Editorial decisions
are made within four to six weeks. Accepted articles usually
appear in print within 10 months. Unaccepted manuscripts are
returned with criticism and/or suggestions.

Copyright:
Held by the Massachusetts Institute of Technology and the editors
of the Journal of Interdisciplinary History.

JOURNAL OF NEGRO HISTORY

Subscription Data:
Published by the Association for the Study of Negro Life and
History, Inc., 1407 Fourteenth Street, N.W., Washington, D.C.
20005. Issued quarterly, in January, April, July, and October.
Advertising is accepted. Circulation: 7,000. Subscription:
$10.00 per year; $10.50 foreign; $3.00 per issue. Founded:
1916.

Editorial Address:
The Editor, Journal of Negro History, P.O. Box 7694, Baltimore, Maryland 21207.

Editorial Policy:
  Includes scientific historical articles which treat definitely the
  history of the Black man in the United States and throughout the
  world. The reading audience includes students and scholars at
  college level and beyond. Unsolicited manuscripts are welcomed
  and considered carefully. Usually five or more major articles
  are published per issue. Book reviews are included.
Manuscript Preparation:
  Accepted manuscripts average no more than 30 double-spaced
  typewritten pages. Shorter articles and documents are accepted,
  depending upon their merit and editorial decisions. An original
  and two carbon copies are required. Return postage and a self-
  addressed envelope are required. Manuscript articles must conform reasonably in size, format, and excellent quality of copy
  as shown in recent issues. Footnotes must be numbered consecutively on a separate page at the end of the manuscript. Manuscript margins should be no less than 1-1/2 inches wide according to standard arrangements. A background or explanatory
  cover letter is not required nor is an outline, summary, or abstract. Biographical information about the author is required.
  Illustrations are not used and any graphs sent should follow
  standard procedures. No payment is made for accepted manuscripts. Five copies of the issue in which a manuscript is published are sent to the author. Reprints must be requested prior
  to printing; a fee is charged for this service.
Manuscript Disposition:
  Receipt of a manuscript is acknowledged. Editorial decisions
  are made usually within four weeks. Time of acceptance of an
  article to its appearance in print varies with editorial need. Unaccepted manuscripts are returned, rarely with criticism and/or
  suggestions.
Copyright:
  Held by the Association for the Study of Negro Life and History,
  Inc.

JOURNAL OF SOUTHERN HISTORY

Subscription Data:
  Published by the Southern Historical Association, Tulane Univer-
  sity, New Orleans, Louisiana 70118. Issued quarterly, in Feb-
  ruary, May, August, and November. Advertising is accepted.
  Circulation: 4,900. Subscription: $10.00 per year. Founded:
  1935.
Editorial Address:
  Managing Editor, Journal of Southern History, Rice University,
  Houston, Texas 77001.
Editorial Policy:
  Includes articles on the history of the southern United States and
  related topics. The reading audience includes historians, edu-
  cators, and students. Unsolicited manuscripts are welcome.
  Four or five major articles are published per issue. Book re-
  views are included.

Manuscript Preparation:

Accepted manuscripts average approximately 6, 500 to 12, 000 words. Two copies are preferred. Return postage and a self-addressed envelope are not required. Bibliographical procedure should follow Webster's Third New International Dictionary and University of Chicago Manual of Style; but do not follow for footnote form. Consult recent issues for special manuscript footnoting recommendations. Footnotes should be double-spaced and placed on separate pages at the end of article. Do not use periods after numerals and indent first line; do not use op. cit. or loc. cit. Double-space manuscript and use 1-1/2 inch margins. A background or explanatory cover letter is not required nor is an outline, summary, or abstract. Biographical information about the author should include identification of present position. Halftones will not reproduce, but line cuts are acceptable and may be used when necessary. No payment is made for accepted articles. Authors receive 100 free offprints. Reprinting of articles in anthologies requires approval of author, who may set a fee in addition to the $100 fee required by the Association. Bobbs-Merril reprints with a royalty of five percent to author and two and one-half percent to Association.

Manuscript Disposition:

Receipt of a manuscript is acknowledged. Editorial decisions are made normally within three to six weeks. Accepted articles usually appear in print within 9 to 18 months, but depends on backlog and nature of article. Unaccepted manuscripts are returned, many with criticism and/or suggestions.

Copyright:

Held by the Southern Historical Association.

JOURNAL OF THE HISTORY OF IDEAS

Subscription Data:

Published by City University of New York, 33 West Forty-second Street, New York, New York 10036. Issued quarterly, in January, April, July, and September. Advertising is accepted. Circulation: 4, 000. Subscription: $7. 50 per year; $10. 00 to libraries. Founded: 1940.

Editorial Address:

Philip P. Wiener, Editor, Journal of the History of Ideas, Temple University, Philadelphia, Pennsylvania 19122.

Editorial Policy:

Includes articles on the cultural and intellectual history of science, philosophy, and social thought. The reading audience includes scholars and students. Unsolicited research articles are welcome. Eight to ten major articles are published per issue. One book review per issue covering several recent books on intellectual history is preferred.

Manuscript Preparation:

Accepted manuscripts average 10, 000 words maximum, including footnotes for articles and 1, 500 to 4, 000 words maximum, including footnotes for shorter notes. One copy is required. Re-

turn postage and a self-addressed envelope are desired. Bibliographical procedure should follow the University of Chicago Manual of Style. Use two inch margins and double-space. Footnotes
should be numbered consecutively on a separate page. A background or explanatory cover letter about the article is not desired
nor is an outline or summary. Biographical information about
the author is unnecessary. Illustrations, pictures, graphs, etc.,
may not be used. No payment is made for accepted articles.
Reprints are available; 25 to 50 free copies are mailed to the
author. More reprints can be ordered at author's expense.

Manuscript Disposition:
Receipt of a manuscript is acknowledged. Editorial decisions
are made within 10 weeks. Accepted articles usually appear in
print within 24 to 27 months. Unaccepted manuscripts are returned, often with criticism and/or suggestions.

Copyright:
Held by the Journal of the History of Ideas, Inc.

Additional Information:
Articles should deal with the history of ideas within two or more
disciplines.

WISCONSIN MAGAZINE OF HISTORY

Subscription Data:
Published by the State Historical Society of Wisconsin, 816 State
Street, Madison, Wisconsin 53706. Issued quarterly. Advertising is not accepted. Circulation: 5,530. Subscription: $7.50
per year. Founded: 1919.

Editorial Address:
The Editor, Wisconsin Magazine of History, State Historical Society of Wisconsin, 816 State Street, Madison, Wisconsin 53706.

Editorial Policy:
Includes original studies in aspects of Wisconsin, Mid-western,
and national history. The reading audience includes professional
historians, college-trained readers with an interest in history,
and the general public. Unsolicited manuscripts are welcome.
Two to six major articles are published per issue. Book reviews are included.

Manuscript Preparation:
Accepted manuscripts should not exceed more than 8,000 words.
Two copies are required. Return postage and a self-addressed
envelope are not required. See a recent issue for bibliographical procedure. Footnotes should be listed separately at the end
of the article. Use one inch margins and double-space. A
background or explanatory cover letter is not required nor is an
outline, summary, or abstract. Biographical information about
the author is required. Suggestions are welcome concerning illustrations, pictures, graphs, etc. No payment is made for accepted manuscripts. Twenty-five copies are furnished to each
author.

Manuscript Disposition:
Receipt of a manuscript is acknowledged. Editorial decisions

are made within two to six weeks. Accepted articles usually appear in print within six months. Unaccepted manuscripts are returned with criticism and/or suggestions.

Copyright:

HOME ECONOMICS

FORECAST FOR HOME ECONOMICS (formerly <u>Practical Forecast</u>
<u>for Home Economics</u>)

<u>Subscription Data:</u>
  Published by Scholastic Magazines, Inc., 50 West Forty-fourth
  Street, New York, New York 10036. Issued nine times each
  year, September through May-June. Advertising is accepted.
  Circulation: 70,000 (50,000 to home economics teachers in
  secondary schools). Subscription: $6.00 per year. Founded:
  1906.
<u>Editorial Address:</u>
  The Editor, <u>Forecast for Home Economics</u>, Scholastic Magazines,
  Inc., 50 West Forty-fourth Street, New York, New York 10036.
<u>Editorial Policy:</u>
  Includes articles on all areas of home economics. The reading
  audience includes home economists, both practitioners and teachers. Unsolicited articles are welcome. Eight to ten major articles are published per issue. Staff-written book reviews are
  included.
<u>Manuscript Preparation:</u>
  Accepted manuscripts average from 1,000 to 2,000 words. One
  copy is required. Return postage and a self-addressed envelope
  are desired. Footnoting and other bibliographical procedure may
  follow any widely used style manual. Use one inch margins and
  double-space. A background or explanatory cover letter about
  the article is desired. An outline or summary of the article is
  required in advance of submission of the finished manuscript.
  Biographical information about the author is desired and should
  include sufficient background information to establish his or her
  authority in the field. Sharp black and white photographs should
  accompany articles which require illustration. Payment for accepted articles varies with length and quality, but averages from
  $50.00 to $100.00. Reprints are available; individual arrangements must be made through the office of the editor.
<u>Manuscript Disposition:</u>
  Receipt of a manuscript is not acknowledged, but articles are
  immediately returned if they are not acceptable. Accepted articles appear in print from four months to two years after acceptance. Unaccepted articles are returned, sometimes with
  criticism and/or suggestions.
<u>Copyright:</u>
  Held by Scholastic Magazines, Inc.

JOURNAL OF HOME ECONOMICS

Subscription Data:
  Published by the American Home Economics Association, 2010
  Massachusetts Avenue, N. W. , Washington, D. C. 20036. Issued
  monthly, except June, July, and August. Advertising is accepted.
  Circulation: 50,000. Subscription: $12.00 per year; $22.00
  for two years. (Limited to members or those not eligible for
  membership in AHEA.) Founded: 1909.
Editorial Address:
  The Editor, Journal of Home Economics, 2010 Massachusetts
  Avenue, N. W. , Washington, D. C. 20036.
Editorial Policy:
  Includes articles on art, family economics and home manage-
  ment, family relations and child development, home economics
  education, housing and household equipment, food and nutrition,
  and textiles and clothing. The reading audience includes workers
  in home economics and related fields. Unsolicited articles are
  welcome. Seven or eight major articles are published per issue.
  Book reviews are included.
Manuscript Preparation:
  Accepted manuscripts range from two to ten double-spaced typewritten pages. One original and one carbon are required for
  feature articles. One original and three carbons are required
  for research articles. Return postage and a self-addressed envelope are desired. See a recent issue for format and bibliographical procedure. Type approximately 50 characters per line
  and double-space throughout. Biographical information about the
  author is desired and should include a summary of current position. A background or explanatory cover letter about the article
  is not desired nor is an outline or summary. Illustrations,
  graphs, etc. , may be used. Clear glossy picture prints may be
  used and will be returned; credit lines must be complete. Charts
  must be drawn in India ink with lettering done using a mechanical
  lettering device. All charts and tables must be prepared on separate pages, with placement indicated in the text. No payment
  is made for accepted articles. Authors receive two free copies
  of the issue in which their article appears. Reprints are available; costs vary with article length and order volume.
Manuscript Disposition:
  Receipt of a manuscript is acknowledged. Editorial decisions
  are made as soon as possible. Accepted articles appear in
  print from three months to three years after acceptance. Unaccepted manuscripts are returned, often with criticism and/or
  suggestions.
Copyright:
  Held by the American Home Economics Association.
Additional Information:
  A document entitled "Information for Authors" is available through
  the office of the editor.

INDUSTRIAL EDUCATION (formerly Industrial Arts and Vocational Education)

Subscription Data:
Published by the Macmillan Professional Magazines, Inc., One Fawcett Place, Greenwich, Connecticut 06830. Issued nine times each year, September through May/June. Advertising is accepted. Circulation: 33,000. Subscription: $7.00 per year. Founded: 1914.

Editorial Address:
Howard Smith, Editor, Industrial Education, One Fawcett Place, Greenwich, Connecticut 06830.

Editorial Policy:
Articles are oriented to needs of the shop/lab teachers in industrial arts, vocational, industrial, and technical education. They include shop activities and how-to, safety, methods and curriculum in the areas circumscribed by industrial arts, trade and industrial (vocational education) and the science and engineering-related technical education (technician training). The reading audience includes instructors and administrators in the areas previously mentioned. Unsolicited manuscripts are welcome. Thirteen to nineteen major articles are published per issue. Book reviews are included.

Manuscript Preparation:
Accepted manuscripts average six to eight double-spaced type-written pages. One copy is required. Return postage and a self-addressed envelope are required. Manuscripts should be double-spaced. A background or explanatory cover letter is usually desirable, but an outline, summary, or abstract is not required. Biographical information about the author is not required. Use black and white photographs. Drawings can be in pencil or ink as they are redrawn and relettered. Payment is made for accepted manuscripts. Offer own reprints on selected articles with reprinting permitted. Check with the editor for permission prior to reproducing the article.

Manuscript Disposition:
Receipt of a manuscript is acknowledged. Editorial decisions are made within four to six weeks. Accepted articles appearance in print varies according to circumstances, usually from three months to one year. Unaccepted manuscripts are returned if the author includes return postage. Criticism and/or suggestions are sometimes provided. Manuscripts suitable for revision are critiqued for resubmission.

Copyright:
Held by Industrial Education.

JOURNAL OF INDUSTRIAL TEACHER EDUCATION

Subscription Data:
 Published by the National Association of Industrial and Technical
 Teacher Educators, Michael Golden Labs, Purdue University,
 West Lafayette, Indiana 47907. Issued quarterly, in fall, winter, spring, and summer. Advertising is not accepted. Circulation: 1,600. Subscription: $6.00 per year to Association
 members; $10.00 to non-members. Founded: 1962.

Editorial Address:
 H. C. Kazanas, Editor, Journal of Industrial Teacher Education,
 103 Industrial Education Building, University of Missouri, Columbia, Missouri 65201.

Editorial Policy:
 Includes articles of research and philosophy of industrial, technical, and vocational education. The reading audience includes
 teachers, teacher educators, researchers and administrators in
 industrial, technical, and vocational education and related fields.
 Unsolicited manuscripts constitute a primary source of material.
 Ten to fifteen major articles are printed per issue; a yearly index is provided in each fall issue. In rare occasions, book reviews may be included.

Manuscript Preparation:
 Accepted manuscripts average 12 to 18 double-spaced typewritten
 pages. Three copies are required. Return postage and a self-
 addressed envelope are not required. Footnoting and other bibliographical procedure should follow the APA Publication Manual.
 Use wide margins and double-space. A background or explanatory cover letter about the manuscript is desired, but not an
 outline, summary, or abstract. Biographical information about
 the author is required. Illustrations, graphs, and half-tones
 are occasionally used and the author must provide clear copies
 of them. No payment is made for accepted manuscripts. Reprints are available on request by the author and at his expense.
 The Journal does not provide free reprints except for four copies of the issue sent to the author.

Manuscript Disposition:
 Receipt of a manuscript is acknowledged. Editorial decisions
 are made as soon as the reviewed manuscripts are returned to
 the editor by the editorial reviewers. Time from acceptance
 of a manuscript to its appearance in print varies with editorial
 need and nature of manuscript. Unaccepted manuscripts are
 returned with criticism and/or suggestions.

Copyright:
 Held by the National Association of Industrial and Technical
 Teacher Educators.

MAN/SOCIETY/TECHNOLOGY

Subscription Data:
 Published by the American Industrial Arts Association, 1201
 Sixteenth Street, N. W., Washington, D. C. 20036. Issued eight

times each year, in September-October, November, December,
January, February, March, April, and May-June. Advertising
is accepted. Circulation: 10,000. Subscription: Free to members in the Association; $9.00 to libraries. Founded: 1940.

Editorial Address:
  The Editor, Man/Society/Technology, American Industrial Arts
  Association, 1201 Sixteenth Street, N.W., Washington, D.C.
  20036.

Editorial Policy:
  Includes articles related to industrial arts education; there is a
  theme schedule, but random-interest articles are used as well.
  The reading audience includes industrial arts teachers, college
  teachers, and supervisors. Unsolicited manuscripts are welcome.
  Six to eight major articles are published per issue. Book reviews are included.

Manuscript Preparation:
  Accepted manuscripts average usually between 12 to 16 double-
  spaced pages. Two copies are required. Return postage and a
  self-addressed envelope are required for return of manuscript.
  Bibliographical procedure may follow any accepted style. Footnotes should be listed separately at the end of the article. Use
  one inch margins and double-space. A background or explanatory
  cover letter is appreciated, but not required. An outline, summary, or abstract is not required. Minimal, one-sentence biographical information about the author is required. Camera-
  ready, black and white illustrations, pictures, and graphs should
  be supplied by the author. No payment is made for accepted
  manuscripts. Reprints are available on request at author's expense.

Manuscript Disposition:
  Receipt of a manuscript is acknowledged. Editorial decisions
  are made usually within eight weeks, although reviewers take
  longer to report. Time from acceptance of a manuscript to its
  appearance in print depends on the schedule of themes; list is
  available on request. Unaccepted manuscripts are returned if
  envelope is supplied. Criticism and/or suggestions are provided if reviewers want revision before publication.

Copyright:
  Held by the American Industrial Arts Association.

SCHOOL SHOP

Subscription Data:
  Published by Prakken Publication, Inc., 416 Longshore Drive,
  Ann Arbor, Michigan 48107. Issued monthly, September through
  June. Advertising is accepted. Circulation: 44,000. Subscrip-
  tion: $8.00 per year. Founded: 1941.

Editorial Address:
  The Editor, School Shop, P.O. Box 623, Ann Arbor, Michigan
  48107.

Editorial Policy:
  Includes articles on all phases of industrial and technician

education. The reading audience includes teachers of industrial
and technical education, and federal, state, and local directors
and supervisors of industrial education programs. Unsolicited
articles are welcome. Fifteen major articles are published per
issue. Staff-written book reviews are included.

Manuscript Preparation:

Accepted manuscripts average from 300 to 1,800 words. One
copy is required. Return postage and a self-addressed envelope
are desired. Footnoting and other bibliographical procedure may
follow any widely used style manual. Use wide margins and
double-space. Avoid use of footnotes when possible. A background or explanatory cover letter about the article is required.
An outline or summary of the article is desired in advance of
or with submission of the finished manuscript. Biographical
information about the author is desired and should include a summary of present position. Illustrations, pictures, graphs, etc.,
are extensively used. Payment is made for accepted articles.
Reprints are available; costs vary with article length and order
volume.

Manuscript Disposition:

Receipt of a manuscript is acknowledged. Editorial decisions
are made within two to four weeks. Time from acceptance of
a manuscript to its appearance in print varies with editorial
need. Unaccepted manuscripts are returned, sometimes with
suggestions and/or criticism.

Copyright:

Held by Prakken Publications, Inc.

Additional Information:

When describing the construction of projects, please keep procedures to a minimum. Describe only those construction steps
that are complicated or that might need clarification. When
writing about a project emphasize the instructional values of the
project; i.e., indicate in detail what the student will learn when
he makes the project described. A document entitled "Pointers
on Writing for School Shop" is available through the office of the
editor.

INSTRUCTIONAL MEDIA AND TECHNIQUES

AV COMMUNICATION REVIEW

Subscription Data:
  Published by the Association for Educational Communications
  and Technology, 1201 Sixteenth Street, N. W., Washington, D. C.
  20036. Issued quarterly, in spring, summer, fall, and winter.
  Advertising is accepted (whole page or one-half page). Circulation: 8,000. Subscription: $13.00 per year; $14.00 foreign;
  $3.50 per issue. Founded: 1953.
Editorial Address:
  Dr. Robert Heinich, Editor, Professor of Education, AV Communication Review, Bloomington, Indiana 57401.
Editorial Policy:
  Includes articles on educational communication, educational media,
  theory, development, and research related to technological proc-
  esses in education. The reading audience includes leaders in the
  field of instructional technology, school administrators, teachers,
  researchers, and behavioral scientists. Unsolicited manuscripts
  are welcome. Four to eight major articles are published per issue. Book reviews are included. Send books for review to Dr.
  John B. Haney, Center for Instructional Development, Queens
  College of CUNY, Flushing, New York 11367.
Manuscript Preparation:
  Accepted manuscripts average approximately eight to thirty double-spaced typewritten pages. Three copies are required. Return postage and a self-addressed envelope are required. Bibliographical procedure should follow the APA Publication Manual.
  Footnotes must be numbered consecutively and placed at bottom
  of each page. Use 8-1/2 by 11 inch white paper with 1-1/2
  to two inch margins at the left and top. Submission of a background or explanatory cover letter is optional. An abstract of
  the article is required, but should be very short (three or four
  summarizing sentences). Biographical information about the
  author is required on a separate sheet. Finished artwork, illustrations, pictures, and graphs may be used; prefer camera-
  ready material. No payment is made for accepted manuscripts.
  The author receives three copies of the issue in which the article appears; author may buy reprints by special arrangement
  with the publisher. Publisher permits nonprofit organizations
  to reprint articles for noncommercial purposes; publisher asks
  reprinter to obtain permission of author.
Manuscript Disposition:
  Receipt of a manuscript is acknowledged. Editorial decisions
  regarding rejects are made quickly; usually takes three to six
  months for decisions on possible acceptance. Accepted articles

usually appear in print within three months to one year. Unaccepted manuscripts are returned with suggestions if article requires revision.

Copyright:
Held by the Association for Educational Communications and Technology.

†AV GUIDE: THE LEARNING MEDIA MAGAZINE (formerly Educational Screen and Audio-Visual Guide)

Subscription Data:
Published by H. S. Gillete, 434 South Wabash Avenue, Chicago, Illinois 60605. Sponsored by Educational Screen, Inc., Publication Office, Louisville, Kentucky 40202. Issued monthly. Advertising is accepted. Circulation: 12,000. Subscription: $6.00 per year; $10.00 for two years; $13.00 for three years; $6.50 Canada; $7.00 foreign. Founded: 1922.

Editorial Address:
The Editor, AV Guide, 434 South Wabash Avenue, Chicago, Illinois 60605.

Editorial Policy:
Includes articles on audio-visual materials and equipment, theory, and application of audio-visuals in education. The reading audience includes educators interested in or working with audio-visual aids. Unsolicited articles are welcome. Six or seven major articles are published per issue. Book reviews are sometimes included.

Manuscript Preparation:
Accepted manuscripts average from six to eight typewritten double-spaced pages at 250 words per page. One copy is required. Return postage and a self-addressed envelope are desired. Use one inch margins and double-space throughout. See a recent issue for bibliographical procedure. A background or explanatory cover letter about the article is desired but not required. No outline or summary of the article need be submitted. Biographical information about the author is required and should include a summary of his present position. No payment is made for accepted articles, but 10 free copies of the issue in which his article appears are mailed to the author. Pictures and illustrative material are welcome with feature articles. Reprints are available at standard rates which vary with article length, number ordered, and number of colors used.

Manuscript Disposition:
Receipt of a manuscript is acknowledged. Editorial decisions are made within three to six weeks. Accepted articles usually appear in print within six months after acceptance. Unaccepted manuscripts are returned with criticism and suggestions.

Copyright:
Held by Educational Screen, Inc.

Additional Information:
The editor attempts to provide up-to-date information on learning theory, A-V materials, and equipment to educators in all fields

who are responsible for the selection, evaluation, application, promotion, and purchase of audio-visual materials, equipment, and services. The editor strives to present not only a picture of what is available, but also specific information about the use of audio-visual tools in education.

AUDIOVISUAL INSTRUCTION

Subscription Data:
Published by the Association for Educational Communications and Technology, 1201 Sixteenth Street, N. W., Washington, D. C. 20036. Issued monthly, September through June. Advertising is accepted. Circulation: 19,000. Subscription: $12.00 per year; $13.00 foreign. Founded: 1956.

Editorial Address:
The Editor, Audiovisual Instruction, AECT, 1201 Sixteenth Street, N. W., Washington, D. C. 20036.

Editorial Policy:
Includes articles, reports, and other information concerning the improvement of instruction through more effective use of learning materials and educational technology. Each issue contains a number of articles devoted to a single theme. The reading audience includes media directors, school administrators, teachers, and librarians. Unsolicited manuscripts are welcome. Approximately 10 major articles are published per issue. Book reviews are included.

Manuscript Preparation:
Accepted manuscripts average from 1,200 to 1,500 words. Two copies are required. Return postage and a self-addressed envelope are not required. Bibliographical procedure should follow the APA Publication Manual. Footnotes are not encouraged, only references. Manuscripts must be typed double-spaced on 8-1/2 by 11 inch white paper throughout, including quoted material. Manuscripts should be typed to an average character width of 35 characters. Paragraphs should be indicated by a five-character indentation. A background or explanatory cover letter is required. A brief summary is encouraged, but not required. Biographical information should include title of article, author's name and affiliation, and the full address (including zip code) to which correspondence should be sent; information must be included on a separate sheet. All manner of visuals are strongly encouraged. Photographs and artwork should be submitted with the manuscript. If such materials are to be returned, the name and address to which they are to be sent must be clearly marked on the back of each piece. No payment is made for accepted manuscripts. Unless previously copyrighted, manuscripts accepted for publication are copyrighted by the publisher, and become the exclusive property of the publisher.

Manuscript Disposition:
Receipt of a manuscript is acknowledged. Editorial decisions are made within no set time; also there is no set time when

accepted articles usually appear in print. Unaccepted manuscripts are returned without criticism and suggestions.

Copyright:
Held by the Association for Educational Communications and Technology.

Additional Information:
Mimeographed, duplicated, or single-spaced manuscripts are not acceptable. They will be returned immediately.

*†EDUCATIONAL EQUIPMENT AND MATERIALS

Subscription Data:
Published by Communications Seminars, Inc., 60 East Forty-second Street, New York, New York 10017. Issued quarterly. Advertising is accepted. Circulation: 6,000. Subscription: $3.00 per year; $1.00 per issue.

Editorial Policy:
The Editor, Educational Equipment and Materials, Communications Seminars, Inc., 60 East Forty-second Street, New York, New York 10017.

Editorial Policy:
Includes articles and reports on educational equipment and materials and their use. The reading audience includes school administrators and business officials. Unsolicited articles are sometimes used. Ten to twelve major articles are published per issue. Book reviews are included.

Manuscript Preparation:
Accepted manuscripts average two to four journal pages in length. Two copies are required. Return postage and a self-addressed envelope are desired. Use wide margins and double-space. Format should follow a recent issue. A background or explanatory cover letter about the article is desired, but not an outline or summary. Biographical information about the author is desired. Illustrations, pictures, graphs, etc., may be used. No payment is made for accepted articles. Reprints are sometimes available.

Manuscript Disposition:
Receipt of a manuscript is acknowledged. Editorial decisions are made as soon as possible. Accepted manuscripts appear in print as needed. Unaccepted manuscripts are returned, sometimes with suggestions.

Copyright:
Held by Robinson-Phillips, Inc.

EDUCATIONAL TECHNOLOGY

Subscription Data:
Published by Educational Technology Publications, 140 Sylvan Avenue, Englewood Cliffs, New Jersey 07632. Issued monthly. Advertising is accepted. Circulation: 10,000. Subscription: $21.00 per year; $75.00 for five years. Founded: 1961.

Editorial Address:

The Editor, Educational Technology, Educational Technology Publications, 140 Sylvan Avenue, Englewood Cliffs, New Jersey 07632.

Editorial Policy:

Includes articles on all phases of programmed instruction, use of computers in education, audio-visual aids, learning psychology, films, and educational research. The reading audience includes professors of education, school administrators, and audio-visual directors. Unsolicited articles are welcome. Fifteen to twenty major articles are published per issue. Book reviews, learning systems, cybernetics, instructional innovation, individualized instruction, behavioral objectives, competency-based education, PPBS, cost-effectiveness of education, and management systems are included.

Manuscript Preparation:

Accepted manuscripts average from 2,500 to 5,000 words. One copy is required. Return postage and a self-addressed envelope are desired. Footnoting and other biographical procedure may follow any widely used manual of style. Use wide margins and double-space. A background or explanatory cover letter about the article is desired, but not an outline or summary. Biographical information about the author is desired and should include a short summary of his professional training and experience. Illustrations, pictures, graphs, etc., may be used. No payment is made for accepted articles. Reprint costs vary with the quantity ordered.

Manuscript Disposition:

Receipt of a manuscript is acknowledged. Editorial decisions are made within two weeks. Accepted articles usually appear in print within six months after acceptance. Unaccepted manuscripts are returned with suggestions.

Copyright:

Held by Educational News Service. A liberal policy on release of rights has been established.

Additional Information:

The readership of this journal is extremely interested in educational innovation. The journal is "The Magazine for Managers of Change in Education."

FILM NEWS

Subscription Data:

Published by the Film News Company, Rohama Lee, 250 West Fifty-seventh Street, New York, New York 10019. Issued six times each year, in February, April, June, September, October, and December. Advertising is accepted. Circulation: 11,000. Subscription: $6.00 per year; $7.00 foreign (abroad). Founded: 1939.

Editorial Address:

Rohama Lee, Editor-Publisher, Film News, 250 West Fifty-seventh Street, New York, New York 10019.

Editorial Policy:
Includes articles on the use of audiovisual media; historical regarding the audiovisual field, film, and people; "What They Are
Showing" (program suggestions); a new films section; film and
TV press; equipment news, calendar, and previews of films and
film strips. The reading audience includes users of audiovisual
(especially films and strips) in school, public libraries, government, and the trade. Unsolicited manuscripts are welcome, but
query first. An average of three major articles are published
per issue. Book reviews are included.

Manuscript Preparation:
Accepted manuscripts vary in length. One copy and one carbon
copy are required. Return postage and a self-addressed envelope are required. Bibliographical procedure to follow will be
sent on request. Use adequate margins and double-space. A
background or explanatory cover letter is required, but not an
outline, summary, or abstract. Biographical information about
the author is required. Pictures and some graphs are used.
Payment is not made for accepted manuscripts. Reprints must
be by permission.

Manuscript Disposition:
Receipt of a manuscript is acknowledged. Editorial decisions
are made as soon as possible. Time of acceptance of article
to appearance in print varies. Unaccepted manuscripts are
returned with criticism and/or suggestions.

Copyright:
Held by Rohama Lee doing business as Film News Company.

FILM QUARTERLY

Subscription Data:
Published by the University of California Press, Berkeley, Cali-
fornia 94720. Issued quarterly, in September, December,
March, and June. Advertising is accepted. Circulation: 8,500.
Subscription: $5.00 per year; $9.00 to institutions; $1.00 more
for foreign subscriptions. Founded: 1945.

Editorial Address:
The Editor, Film Quarterly, University of California Press,
Berkeley, California 94720.

Editorial Policy:
Includes articles which contain criticism and comment on the
use of motion pictures as an art. The reading audience includes
film-makers, students, audio-visual directors, etc. Unsolicited
articles are welcome. Four major articles plus reviews of six
to ten films are published per issue. Book reviews are included.

Manuscript Preparation:
Manuscripts should not exceed 9,000 words. One copy is required. Return postage and a self-addressed envelope are desired. Bibliographical procedure should follow the University
of Chicago Manual of Style. Use wide margins and double-
space; carbons are unacceptable. A background or explanatory
cover letter about the article is desired. An advance outline

is desired to minimize risk of rejection. Biographical information about the author is required and should include a summary of his educational and professional background, and his current film-related activities. Illustrations, pictures, graphs, etc., are welcome. Payment of approximately $.01 per word is made upon publication. Reprints are not available. Two free copies of the journal are mailed to authors; additional copies are available at $.75 each.

Manuscript Disposition:
Receipt of a manuscript is acknowledged. Editorial decisions are made at quarterly meetings. Accepted articles usually appear in print within three to six months after acceptance. Unaccepted manuscripts are returned sometimes with criticism. Suggestions for revision are made when an article is recommended for resubmission.

Copyright:
Held by the University of California Press.

Additional Information:
Personality pieces and news articles cannot be used. The editor is especially interested in documentation, interviews, re-evaluations of older films, and reports of issues which relate to the aesthetics of films and the current circumstance of the film artist. Prompt replies are made to writers who wish to obtain advance reaction to a proposal.

INTERNATIONAL JOURNAL OF INSTRUCTIONAL MEDIA

Subscription Data:
Published by the Baywood Publishing Company, Inc., 43 Central Drive, Farmingdale, New York 11735. Issued four times each year. Advertising is not accepted. Circulation: 600. Subscription: $25.00 per year; $27.00 foreign excluding Canada. Founded: 1972.

Editorial Address:
Phillip J. Sleeman, Editor, International Journal of Instructional Media, 14 Eastwood Road, Storrs, Connecticut 06268.

Editorial Policy:
Includes articles that discuss specific applications and techniques. Helping students learn more effectively, encouraging individualism, irrespective of where the learning process occurs--in the classroom, in the study hall, in the library, and at home--is the fundamental philosophy of the Journal. Papers by individuals currently utilizing instructional media in their work are presented. The papers reflect experimental testing as well as proven, effective programs in instructional media. All articles are designed to shed light, provide new ideas, and encourage the broader use of media in education. The reading audience includes audio-visual directors, curriculum and media directors, educational TV personnel, data processing directors, and programmed instruction directors. Unsolicited manuscripts are welcome. Eight to ten major articles are published per issue. Book reviews are included.

Manuscript Preparation:

Accepted manuscripts average 5,000 words. Two copies are required. Return postage and a self-addressed envelope are not required. Bibliographical procedure should follow the Baywood style sheet. Manuscripts should be typewritten on white, 8-1/2 by 11 inch, bond paper and double-spaced. The text should be at a level compatible with the academic background of the broad range of readers in the professional area. The submitted paper must be an original work and in English. A background or explanatory cover letter and an abstract are required. Biographical information is required and should include author's affiliation. Original drawing and art work are acceptable, but no photographs. No payment is made for accepted manuscripts. Twenty free reprints are given to the author and orders are taken for authors.

Manuscript Disposition:

Receipt of a manuscript is acknowledged. Editorial decisions are made within three weeks. Accepted articles usually appear in print within three months. Unaccepted manuscripts are returned, without criticism and/or suggestions, unless manuscript is to be resubmitted.

Copyright:

Held by the Baywood Publishing Company, Inc.

*†JEWISH AUDIO-VISUAL REVIEW

Subscription Data:

Published by the National Council on Jewish Audio-Visual Materials, American Association for Jewish Education, 101 Fifth Avenue, New York, New York 10003. Issued once each year. Advertising is accepted. Circulation: 2,500. Subscription: $4.00 per year. Founded: 1949.

Editorial Address:

The Editor, Jewish Audio-Visual Review, National Council on Jewish Audio-Visual Materials, 101 Fifth Avenue, New York, New York 10003.

Editorial Policy:

Includes reviews of films, filmstrips, and related materials. The reading audience served includes principals, teachers, Rabbis, group workers, etc. Unsolicited articles cannot be used. The number of articles published per issue varies. Book reviews are not included.

Copyright:

Held by the National Council on Jewish Audio-Visual Materials.

JOURNAL OF EDUCATIONAL TECHNOLOGY SYSTEMS

Subscription Data:

Published by Baywood Publishing Company, Inc., 43 Central Drive, Farmingdale, New York 11735. Issued quarterly. Circulation: Not determined. Subscription: $27.50 per year; $29.50 foreign. Founded: 1972.

Editorial Address:
___
The Editor, Journal of Educational Technology Systems, Baywood
Publishing Company, Inc., 43 Central Drive, Farmingdale, New
York 11735.

Editorial Policy:
___
Includes original, factual, informative articles on the approaches
and techniques of using technology as an aid to instruction. Articles describe actual practice and experimentation in various
educational applications of modern technology. The reading audience includes educators. Unsolicited manuscripts are welcome.
Eight to ten major articles are published per issue. Book reviews are included.

Manuscript Preparation:
___
Accepted manuscripts average 2,000 to 5,000 words. Two copies
are required. Return postage and a self-addressed envelope are
required. Manuscripts should be typewritten on white 8-1/2 by
11 inch bond paper, double-spaced. The text should be at a level
compatible with the academic background of the broad range of
readers in the professional area. The submitted paper must be
an original work, in English, never before published. A background or explanatory cover letter is not required, but an outline, summary, or abstract is required. Biographical information about the author is required. Key all photographs, line art,
tables, etc., to the text. No payment is made for accepted manuscripts. Authors will receive 20 reprints of their paper.

Manuscript Disposition:
___
Receipt of a manuscript is acknowledged. Editorial decisions
are made within three weeks. Accepted articles usually appear
in print within three months. Unaccepted manuscripts are returned with criticism and/or suggestions.

Copyright:
___
Held by Baywood Publishing Company, Inc.

†VISUAL COMMUNICATIONS JOURNAL

Subscription Data:
___
Published by the International Graphic Arts Education Association, 1025 Fifteenth Street, N.W., Washington, D.C. 20005. Issued four times each year, in September, December, March,
and May. Advertising is accepted. Circulation: 6,000. Subscription: $7.50 per year. Founded: 1965.

Editorial Address:
___
The Editor, Visual Communications Journal, International Graphic
Arts Education Association, 1025 Fifteenth Street, N.W., Wash-
ington, D.C. 20005.

Editorial Policy:
___
Includes articles and reports on all phases of visual communication. The reading audience served includes graphic arts and
printing teachers, and others interested in the field. Unsolicited
articles are welcome. Twelve major articles are published per
issue. Book reviews are included.

Manuscript Preparation:
___
Manuscripts should not exceed two typewritten double-spaced

pages. One copy is required. Return postage and a self-addressed envelope are required. Footnoting and other bibliographical procedure may follow any widely used style manual. A background or explanatory cover letter about the article is not desired nor is an outline or summary. Biographical information about the author is unnecessary. Illustrations, pictures, graphs, etc., are rarely used. No payment is made for accepted articles. Reprints are usually not available.

Manuscript Disposition:

Receipt of a manuscript is not acknowledged. Editorial decisions are made approximately one month prior to publication. Unaccepted manuscripts are returned, sometimes with suggestions.

Copyright:

Held by the International Graphic Arts Education Association.

INTERNATIONAL EDUCATION

*CHINESE EDUCATION

Subscription Data:
   Published by the International Arts and Science Press, 901 North
   Broadway, White Plains, New York 10603.   Issued quarterly.
   Advertising is accepted at the rate of $100.00 per page.   Circu-
   lation: 500.   Subscription: $65.00 per year.   Founded: 1968.
Editorial Address:
   The Editor, Chinese Education, International Arts and Science
   Press, 901 North Broadway, White Plains, New York 10603.
Editorial Policy:
   Includes translations of articles on Chinese education.   The read-
   ing audience includes educators.   Unsolicited manuscripts are
   not welcome.   Seven major articles are published per issue.
   Book reviews are not included.
Copyright:
   Held by the International Arts and Science Press.

COMPARATIVE EDUCATION REVIEW

Subscription Data:
   Published by the Comparative and International Education Society,
   Dean Thomas J. La Belle, Graduate School of Education,
   U.C.L.A., 405 Hilgard Avenue, Los Angeles, California 90024.
   Issued three times each year, October, February, and June.
   Advertising is accepted.   Circulation: 3,000.   Subscription:
   $10.00 per year to Society members; $5.00 to students.   Founded:
   1957.
Editorial Address:
   Professor Andreas M. Kazamias, Editor, Comparative Education
   Review, Box 71, Education Building, University of Wisconsin -
   Madison, Madison, Wisconsin 53706.
Editorial Policy:
   The Review publishes analytic and/or interpretative articles deal-
   ing with all aspects of education across nations and cultures.
   Unsolicited manuscripts are welcome.   Six or seven major arti-
   cles are published per issue.   Book reviews are included.
Manuscript Preparation:
   Accepted manuscripts average 15 to 30 double-spaced typewritten
   pages including notes.   Three copies are required.   Return
   postage and a self-addressed envelope are required if the manuscript is to be returned.   Bibliographical procedure should follow
   the University of Chicago Manual of Style.   Footnotes should be

double-spaced within each note and triple-spaced between the notes; they should be typed separately and inserted at the end of the manuscript. Each table should be typed on a separate page; tables and notes should be numbered consecutively. A background or explanatory cover letter is not required. A summary paragraph of not more than 150 words is required. Biographical information about the author is required if the manuscript is accepted for publication. Illustrations, pictures, graphs, etc., are used at the editor's discretion. No payment is made for accepted manuscripts. The authors receive five copies of the issue in which the article appears. Reprints are not available.

Manuscript Disposition:
Receipt of a manuscript is acknowledged. Editorial decisions are made within 12 weeks. Unaccepted manuscripts are returned if a stamped self-addressed envelope is provided. Criticism and/or suggestions are provided.

Copyright:
Held by the Comparative and International Education Society.

*SOVIET EDUCATION

Subscription Data:
Published by the International Arts and Sciences Press, 901 North Broadway, Whiteplains, New York 10603. Issued quarterly, in spring, summer, fall, and winter. Advertising is accepted at $100.00 per page. Circulation: 500. Subscription: $100.00 per year. Founded: 1958.

Editorial Address:
The Editor, Soviet Education, International Arts and Sciences Press, 901 North Broadway, Whiteplains, New York 10603.

Editorial Policy:
Includes translation articles of Soviet authors in education. The reading audience includes educators. Unsolicited manuscripts are not welcome. Seven major articles are published per issue. Book reviews are not included.

Copyright:
Held by the International Arts and Sciences Press.

*WESTERN EUROPEAN EDUCATION

Subscription Data:
Published by the International Arts and Sciences Press, 901 North Broadway, Whiteplains, New York 10603. Issued quarterly. Advertising is accepted at $100.00 per page. Circulation: 500. Subscription: $55.00 per year. Founded: 1969.

Editorial Address:
The Editor, Western European Education, International Arts and Sciences Press, 901 North Broadway, Whiteplains, New York 10603.

Editorial Policy:
Includes translations of articles appearing in the European

journals.   The reading audience includes educators.   Unsolicited manuscripts are not welcome.   Seven major articles are published per issue.   Book reviews are not included.

Copyright:
      Held by the International Arts and Sciences Press.

JOURNALISM

COLUMBIA JOURNALISM REVIEW

Subscription Data:

Published by the Graduate School of Journalism, Columbia University, New York, New York 10027. Issued six times each year. Advertising is not accepted. Circulation: 23,000. Subscription: $9.00 per year. Founded: 1961.

Editorial Address:

The Editor, Columbia Journalism Review, 700 Journalism Building, Columbia University, New York, New York 10027.

Editorial Policy:

Includes articles on newspaper, magazine, broadcast, and related journalism. The primary goals of the Review are to assess the performance of journalism in all its forms, call attention to its shortcomings and strengths, and help define and redefine standards of honest responsible service in ways which will help to stimulate continued improvement in the profession. The reading audience includes professional journalists, educators, and students. Unsolicited articles are welcome. Four to eight major articles are published per issue. Book reviews are included.

Manuscript Preparation:

Accepted manuscripts range from 1,000 to 6,000 words. One copy is required. Return postage and a self-addressed envelope are desired. Footnotes and information notes may be used. Use wide margins and double-space. A background or explanatory cover letter about the article is required. An outline or summary of the article is desired in advance of or with submission of the finished manuscript. Biographical information about the author is desired and should include indication of professional affiliations, position, and recent works. Illustrations, pictures, graphs, etc., are usually prepared by the editorial staff, but should be enclosed if available. Payment of $.10 per word is made for accepted articles. Reprints can be made available, but are not often requested.

Manuscript Disposition:

Receipt of a manuscript is acknowledged. Tentative editorial decisions are made within two weeks; scheduling decisions are made bimonthly. Accepted articles usually appear in print within five to twelve weeks after acceptance. Extended criticism of unaccepted articles cannot be made, but explanation of rejection and alternate placement possibilities are often provided.

Copyright:

Held by the Graduate School of Journalism of Columbia University.

JOURNALISM QUARTERLY

Subscription Data:
  Published by the Association for Education in Journalism, School
  of Journalism, University of Minnesota, Minneapolis, Minnesota
  55455. Issued quarterly, in February, May, August, and November. Advertising is accepted. Circulation: 4,000. Subscrip-
  tion: $10.00 per year. Founded: 1924.
Editorial Address:
  Guido H. Stempel III, Acting Editor, Journalism Quarterly,
  School of Journalism, Ohio University, Athens, Ohio 45701.
Editorial Policy:
  Includes articles on research in mass communication. The reading audience includes 25% AEJ members; rest are other academicians and professional journalists. Unsolicited manuscripts
  are welcome. Fifteen major articles are published per issue.
  Book reviews are included.
Manuscript Preparation:
  Accepted manuscripts average 12 to 16 pages. Three copies are
  required. Return postage and a self-addressed envelope are not
  required. Bibliographical procedure should follow the Journalism
  Quarterly style sheet. Use footnotes, not references, and place
  all on the same page. Use standard margin and double-space.
  A background or explanatory cover letter is not required, nor is
  an outline, summary, or abstract. Biographical information
  about the author is required. Illustrations, pictures, graphs,
  etc., are used when pertinent. No payment is made for accepted manuscripts. Reprints are sold to authors, but must be
  ordered when proofs are sent to the author.
Manuscript Disposition:
  Receipt of a manuscript is acknowledged. Editorial decisions
  are made within 15 weeks. Accepted articles usually appear in
  print within nine to twelve months. One copy is returned with
  criticism and/or suggestions.
Copyright:
  Held by the Association for Education in Journalism.

SCHOLASTIC EDITOR GRAPHICS/COMMUNICATIONS (formerly Scholastic Editor)

Subscription Data:
  Published by Otto W. Quale, 18 Journalism Building, University
  of Minnesota, Minneapolis, Minnesota 55455. Issued monthly,
  except bimonthly in September-May, December-January. Adver-
  tising is welcome. Circulation: 3,500. Subscription: $5.75
  per year; $10.00 for two years; $14.00 for three years; $1.00
  per issue. Founded: 1921.
Editorial Address:
  The Editor, Scholastic Editor Graphics/Communications, 18
  Journalism Building, University of Minnesota, Minneapolis,
  Minnesota 55455.
Editorial Policy:
  Includes articles which relate to the publication of high school

and college yearbooks, newspapers and magazines and also occasional articles on classroom TV, filmmaking photography, and other forms of graphic communications. The reading audience includes high school and college publications editors, staffs and advisers and those interested in scholastic communication. Unsolicited manuscripts are welcome. From four to five major articles are published per issue. Book reviews are included.

Manuscript Preparation:
Accepted manuscripts average from 500 to 4,000 words. Only the original manuscript is required. Return postage and a self-addressed envelope are preferred, but are not required. Bibliographical material is not generally published with the article. Double-space all copy and avoid the use of footnotes. A background or explanatory cover letter is desired, but not an outline, summary, or abstract. Enclose a short biography and a recent picture of the author with the manuscript for possible publication with the article. Illustrations, pictures, graphs, etc., are highly desired since this is a graphics-oriented publication. Payment for regular articles is usually in the form of five contributor's copies upon publication. Reprints are negotiable.

Manuscript Disposition:
Receipt of a manuscript is not acknowledged until accepted or rejected. Editorial decisions are made within two to three weeks. Time from acceptance of a manuscript to its appearance in print varies with editorial need. Unaccepted manuscripts are returned only if accompanied by a stamped self-addressed envelope with sufficient postage. Criticism and/or suggestions are provided only if requested by the author.

Copyright:
Held by Scholastic Editor Graphics/Communications.

Additional Information:
First serial rights are generally purchased. All other rights revert to the author.

SCHOOL PRESS REVIEW

Subscription Data:
Published by the Columbia Scholastic Press Association, Box 11, Central Mail Room, Columbia University, New York, New York 10027. Issued eight times each year, October through May. Advertising is not accepted. Circulation: 3,000. Subscription: $4.50 per year; $.50 per issue (except April which is $1.00). Founded: 1925.

Editorial Address:
The Editor, School Press Review, Box 11, Central Mail Room, Columbia University, New York, New York 10027.

Editorial Policy:
Includes articles on all aspects of scholastic journalism. The reading audience includes student editors and advisers to student publications and others interested in scholastic journalism. Unsolicited manuscripts are welcome. At least two major articles are published per issue. Book reviews are included.

Manuscript Preparation:
Accepted manuscripts average 1,200 words. One copy is required. Return postage and a self-addressed envelope are desired. Bibliographical procedure may follow any widely used style manual. Place footnotes on a separate sheet. Use wide margins and double-space. A background or explanatory cover letter is not required, nor is an outline, summary, or abstract. Biographical information about the author is desired and should include a statement of his relationship to, or experience in scholastic journalism. Illustrations, pictures, graphs, etc., are rarely used. No payment is made for accepted manuscripts. Reprint orders can be filled prior to publication.

Manuscript Disposition:
Receipt of a manuscript is not acknowledged. Editorial decisions are made as soon as possible. Accepted articles usually appear in print within one year after acceptance. Unaccepted manuscripts are returned, rarely with suggestions and/or criticism.

Copyright:
Held by the Columbia Scholastic Press Association.

Additional Information:
Liberal permission is granted for other uses of contents of magazine, but full credit must be given.

AMERICAN JOURNAL OF COMPARATIVE LAW

Subscription Data:
  Published by the American Association for the Comparative Study
  of Law, Inc., School of Law (Boalt Hall), University of California, Berkeley, California 94720. Issued quarterly in winter,
  spring, summer, and autumn. Advertising is not accepted.
  Circulation: 2,000. Subscription: $12.50 per year. Founded:
  1951.

Editorial Address:
  The Editor, American Journal of Comparative Law, School of
  Law (Boalt Hall), University of California, Berkeley, California
  94720.

Editorial Policy:
  Includes articles which deal with comparison of laws and the
  latest developments in domestic and foreign law. The reading
  audience includes law teachers, practitioners, and students.
  Unsolicited articles are welcome. Five major articles and two
  or three shorter current reports are published per issue. Book
  reviews are included.

Manuscript Preparation:
  Major articles range from 7,500 to 8,000 words or from 20 to
  25 printed pages, with reports ranging from 2,000 to 3,000
  words or from five to ten printed pages. One copy is required.
  Return postage and a self-addressed envelope are desired. Footnoting and other bibliographical procedure should follow the Harvard Style Guide. Contributors from outside the United States
  may use the style to which they are accustomed. Use wide
  margins and double-space throughout. A background or explanatory cover letter about the article is desired, but not an outline
  or summary. Biographical information about the author is required and should include a summary of present occupation and
  credentials for writing the article. Illustrations, pictures,
  graphs, etc., are occasionally used. No payment is made for
  accepted articles. Reprints are available; 50 free copies are
  mailed to the author.

Manuscript Disposition:
  Receipt of a manuscript is acknowledged. Editorial decisions
  are made as soon as possible. Accepted articles usually appear
  in print from three to six months after acceptance. Unaccepted
  manuscripts are returned, often with criticism and/or suggestions.

Copyright:
  Held by the American Association for the Comparative Study of
  Law, Inc.

AMERICAN JOURNAL OF INTERNATIONAL LAW

Subscription Data:
  Published by the American Society of International Law, 2223
  Massachusetts Avenue, N. W., Washington, D. C. 20008. Issued
  four times each year, in January, April, July, and October,
  plus a September issue containing the PROCEEDINGS OF ASIL.
  Advertising is accepted. Circulation: 9,000. Subscription:
  $30.00 per year. Founded: 1907.
Editorial Address:
  The Editor, American Journal of International Law, 2223 Massachusetts Avenue, N. W., Washington, D. C. 20008.
Editorial Policy:
  Includes material dealing with international law, international
  relations, and the areas peripheral thereto. The reading audience includes lawyers, professors of law and political science,
  government personnel, and students. Unsolicited manuscripts
  are accepted for examination. The number of major articles
  varies, usually about three or four, depending on other contents
  of issue. Book reviews and a list of books received are published regularly.
Manuscript Preparation:
  Accepted articles average approximately 15,000 words. Return
  postage and a self-addressed envelope are desired, but not required. Bibliographical procedure should follow the Harvard
  Law Review Style Sheet or a recent issue of the American Journal of International Law for style. Harvard citation system is
  used. Footnotes should be listed at the bottom of each page of
  manuscript or numerically on a separate sheet. Use one inch
  side margins, type, and double-space. An outline, summary,
  or abstract of the article is desired, but not necessary. Biographical information about the author is required. Illustrations,
  pictures, graphs, etc., should be limited and be used only if
  really necessary or pertinent. Payment is not made for accepted
  manuscripts. Fifty free reprints are available to authors; additional copies are available at reasonable rates.
Manuscript Disposition:
  Receipt of a manuscript is acknowledged. Review is made by the
  editor-in-chief and several editors of the Journal. Decision on
  publication is made as soon as possible, but usually within three
  months. Accepted articles usually appear in print within four
  months. Unaccepted manuscripts are returned to the author,
  usually with criticism and/or suggestions.
Copyright:
  Held by the American Journal of International Law.

COLUMBIA LAW REVIEW

Subscription Data:
  Published by Columbia University, New York, New York 10027.
  Issued eight times each year, October through May. Advertising
  is accepted. Circulation: 4,000. Subscription: $15.00 per
  year. Founded: 1901.

Editorial Address:

The Editor, Columbia Law Review, 435 West One-hundred and sixteenth Street, New York, New York 10027.

Editorial Policy:

Includes articles and reports on all phases of the law. The reading audience includes practicing lawyers, law educators, and students. Unsolicited articles are welcome. Two or three major articles are published per issue. Book reviews are included.

Manuscript Preparation:

Manuscripts may not exceed 100 triple-spaced typewritten pages. One copy is required. Return postage and a self-addressed envelope are unnecessary. See a recent issue for footnoting and other bibliographical procedure. Use one inch margins and triple-space throughout. A background or explanatory cover letter about the article is desired, but not an outline or summary. Biographical information about the author is unnecessary. Illustrations, pictures, graphs, etc., are seldom used. No payment is made for accepted articles. Reprints are available; a cost summary may be obtained from the office of the editor.

Manuscript Disposition:

Receipt of a manuscript is acknowledged. Editorial decisions are made within three to five weeks. Time from acceptance of a manuscript to its appearance in print varies with editorial need.

Copyright:

Held by Columbia Law Review.

ENVIRONMENTAL AFFAIRS

Subscription Data:

Published by Environmental Affairs, Inc., Boston College Law School, Brighton, Massachusetts 02135. Issued quarterly. Advertising is not accepted. Circulation: 1,500. Subscription: $18.00 per year. Founded: 1970.

Editorial Address:

The Editor, Environmental Affairs, Environmental Affairs Inc., Boston College Law School, Brighton, Massachusetts 02135.

Editorial Policy:

Includes environmental articles on the legal, scientific, political, and social aspects. The reading audience includes library patrons, scientists, students, and lawyers. Unsolicited manuscripts are welcome. Nine to twelve major articles are published per issue. Book reviews are ordinarily not included.

Manuscript Preparation:

Accepted manuscripts average a minimum of 4,500 words. One copy is required. Return postage and a self-addressed envelope are preferred. A style sheet will be sent on request to the editor. A background or explanatory cover letter is required, but not an outline, summary, or abstract. Biographical information about the author is required and should include a brief description of current position. Illustrations, pictures, graphs, etc., are discouraged, but accepted if necessary. No payment

is made for accepted manuscripts. Reprints are available at
request of the author.
Manuscript Disposition:
Receipt of a manuscript is acknowledged. Editorial decisions
are made within three to six weeks. Accepted articles usually
appear in print within one to three months. Unaccepted manuscripts are not returned.
Copyright:
Held by Environmental Affairs.

JOURNAL OF CRIMINAL LAW AND CRIMINOLOGY (formerly Journal of Criminal Law, Criminology, and Police Science)

Subscription Data:
Published by the Williams and Wilkins Company (for Northwestern
University School of Law), Baltimore, Maryland 21202. Issued
quarterly, in March, June, September, and December. Adver-
tising is not accepted. Circulation: 4,000. Subscription:
$15.00 per year; $16.00 foreign. Founded: 1910.
Editorial Address:
Editor-in-Chief, Journal of Criminal Law and Criminology, 357
East Chicago Avenue, Chicago, Illinois 60611.
Editorial Policy:
Includes lead articles in criminal law and criminology; notes and
comments on criminal law issues and problems; notes on recent
lower court decisions; and notes on important United States Supreme Court decisions (December issue only). The reading audience includes attorneys, law students, law enforcement officers,
sociologists, criminologists, graduate students, and educators.
Unsolicited manuscripts are welcome. Four to six lead articles
and two to four notes and comments are published per issue.
Book reviews are included.
Manuscript Preparation:
Accepted manuscripts range from 25 to 50 double-spaced, typewritten pages. Two copies are required. Return postage and
a self-addressed envelope are not required. Bibliographical
style should follow the citation form: "A Uniform System of
Citation," distributed by the Harvard Law Review Association.
Footnotes should be numbered serially on separate pages. Use
wide margins and double-space. A background or explanatory
cover letter and an outline, summary, or abstract of the article
are required. Biographical information about the author is required and should include degrees earned and present position.
Illustrations, pictures, graphs, etc., must be submitted in form
suitable for photocopying photographic reproduction, or type-
setting. No payment is made for accepted manuscripts. Fifty
free copies of each article, note, and comment are furnished
to each author. Additional copies are available at cost. One
copy of the issue in which article appears is furnished free to
the author.
Manuscript Disposition:
Receipt of a manuscript is acknowledged. Editorial decisions

are made within six to eight weeks. Accepted articles generally appear in the issue scheduled for publication six to nine months after acceptance. Unaccepted manuscripts are returned only upon request, generally without criticism or suggestions.

Copyright:
Held by the Northwestern University School of Law in Chicago, Illinois.

Additional Information:
Special features include a June issue devoted to interdisciplinary symposium and a December issue that contains a "Supreme Court Review," a review and analysis of important Supreme Court decisions handed down over the past term.

†JOURNAL OF LEGAL EDUCATION

Subscription Data:
Published by the School of Law, University of Kentucky, Lexington, Kentucky 40506. Sponsored by the Association of American Law Schools, 1521 New Hampshire Avenue, N.W., Washington, D.C. 20036. Issued four times each year, in March, June, September, and December. Advertising is not accepted. Circulation: 5,000 including complimentary copies to law professors, libraries, bar examiners, and selected foreign law schools. Subscription: $12.50 per year; slightly higher foreign. Founded: 1948.

Editorial Address:
The Editor, Journal of Legal Education, School of Law, University of Kentucky, Lexington, Kentucky 40506.

Editorial Policy:
Includes articles which relate to matters of interest to the legal education profession. The reading audience includes law professors, bar examiners, and attorneys. Unsolicited articles are welcome. Twelve to fifteen major articles are published per issue. Book reviews are included.

Manuscript Preparation:
No restrictions are placed upon manuscript length. One copy is required. Return postage and a self-addressed envelope are unnecessary. Footnoting and other bibliographical procedure may follow any widely used style manual. Use wide margins and double-space. A background or explanatory cover letter about the article is desired, but not an outline or summary. Biographical information about the author is desired and should include a summary of current position. Illustrations, pictures, and graphs may not be used. No payment is made for accepted articles. Reprints are not available.

Manuscript Disposition:
Receipt of a manuscript is acknowledged. Editorial decisions are made as soon as possible. Accepted articles usually appear in print from two to six months after acceptance. Unaccepted manuscripts are returned, occasionally with criticism and/or suggestions.

Copyright:
Held by the Association of American Law Schools.

*SCHOOL LAW REVIEW

Subscription Data:
Published by Stephen F. Roach, Box 25, Needham, Massachusetts 02192. Issued 10 times each year, September through June. Advertising is not accepted. Circulation: Privately circulated. Subscription: $8.00 per year; $15.00 for two years; $21.00 for three years. Founded: Eastern 1953; Western 1961; North Central 1966.

Editorial Address:
Stephen F. Roach, Editor, School Law Review, Box 25, Needham, Massachusetts 02192.

Editorial Policy:
Summarizes significant court decisions relating to public and private school, college, and university administration. The reading audience includes school system superintendents, business managers, school system attorneys, and college and university administrators. Unsolicited manuscripts cannot be used. Five major articles are published per issue. Book reviews are included (irregularly).

Copyright:
Held by Stephen F. Roach.

Additional Information:
Complete sets of back issues are maintained. School Law Review has separate Eastern, North Central, and Western editions.

STUDENT LAWYER

Subscription Data:
Published by the Law Student Division of the American Bar Association, 1155 East Sixtieth Street, Chicago, Illinois 60637. Issued nine times each year, September through May. Advertising is accepted. Circulation: 25,000. Subscription: $2.50 per year.

Editorial Address:
Tim Ayers, Editor, Student Lawyer, 1155 East Sixtieth Street, Chicago, Illinois 60637.

Editorial Policy:
Includes nontechnical articles dealing with social concerns which are of particular concern to law students. The reading audience is composed of 23,000 law students. Unsolicited manuscripts are welcome. Seven to ten major articles are published per issue. Book reviews are included.

Manuscript Preparation:
Accepted manuscripts should not exceed 3,000 words for articles and 1,500 words for reviews. One copy is required. Return postage and a self-addressed envelope are not required. Double or triple-space the manuscript and do not include footnotes. A background or explanatory cover letter and an outline, summary, or abstract are not required. Biographical information about the author is required and should include black and white photographs. Illustrations, photographs, etc., that accompany articles are

encouraged. No payment is made for accepted manuscripts.
There is a liberal reprint policy.

Manuscript Disposition:
　　Receipt of a manuscript is acknowledged. Editorial decisions
　　are made within three to four weeks. Accepted articles usually
　　appear in print within two to four months or longer. Unaccepted
　　manuscripts are returned, without criticism or suggestions.

Copyright:
　　Held by the American Bar Association.

Additional Information:
　　Prospective writers should see a copy of the journal for style
　　and treatment.

WISCONSIN LAW REVIEW

Subscription Data:
　　Published by the Wisconsin Law Review, University of Wisconsin
　　- Madison, Law School, Madison, Wisconsin 53706. Issued
　　quarterly. Advertising is accepted. Circulation: 2,500. Sub-
　　scription: $10.00 per year; $3.50 per issue. Founded: 1920.

Editorial Address:
　　The Editor, Wisconsin Law Review, University of Wisconsin -
　　Madison, Law School, Madison, Wisconsin 53706.

Editorial Policy:
　　Includes articles on law. The reading audience includes legal
　　scholars and lawyers. Unsolicited manuscripts are welcome.
　　Four or five major articles are published per issue. Book re-
　　views are included.

Manuscript Preparation:
　　Accepted manuscripts average 150 pages. One copy is required.
　　Return postage and a self-addressed envelope are not required.
　　Place footnotes on a separate page. Use 1-1/2 inch left margin
　　and triple-space. A background or explanatory cover letter is
　　helpful, but an outline, summary, or abstract is not required.
　　Biographical information about the author is required. Illustra-
　　tions, graphs, etc., are acceptable, but do not include pictures.
　　No payment is made for accepted manuscripts. Reprints are
　　available only on request.

Manuscript Disposition:
　　Receipt of a manuscript is acknowledged. Editorial decisions
　　are made within three weeks. Accepted articles usually appear
　　in print within three months. Unaccepted manuscripts are re-
　　turned, usually without criticism and/or suggestions.

Copyright:
　　Held by the Wisconsin Law Review.

LIBRARIES

*AMERICAN LIBRARIES (formerly ALA BULLETIN)

Subscription Data:
    Published by the American Library Association, 50 East Huron
    Street, Chicago, Illinois 60611. Issued monthly, except bimonth-
    ly during July-August. Advertising is accepted. Circulation:
    38,000. Subscription: Free with Association membership.
    Founded: 1907.
Editorial Address:
    The Editor, American Libraries, 50 East Huron Street, Chicago,
    Illinois 60611.
Editorial Policy:
    The reading audience includes librarians, publishers, trustees,
    and educators. Unsolicited manuscripts are not welcome but
    will answer inquiries from potential authors. One major article
    is published per issue. In house reviews of selected materials
    from all media are included.
Copyright:
    Held by the American Library Association unless otherwise
    specified in writing to the author.
Additional Information:
    A newsmagazine format requires correspondents and a limited
    number of stinger positions could be available upon inquiry to
    the editor.

AMERICAN SOCIETY FOR INFORMATION SCIENCE. JOURNAL

Subscription Data:
    Published by the American Society for Information Science,
    1155 Sixteenth Street, N.W., Washington, D.C. 20036. Issued
    six times each year, in January-February, March-April, May-
    June, July-August, September-October, and November-Decem-
    ber. Circulation: 5,000. Subscription: $35.00 per year;
    Free to membership in the Society. Founded: 1950.
Editorial Address:
    The Editor, Journal of the American Society for Information
    Science, 1155 Sixteenth Street, N.W., Washington, D.C. 20036.
Editorial Policy:
    Includes technical and scholarly articles on all aspects relating
    to information science-technology, book reviews, and brief com-
    munications. The reading audience includes information scien-
    tists (pure and applied), library administrators, librarians,
    computer scientists, etc. Unsolicited manuscripts are welcome.
    Six or seven major articles are published per issue. Book re-
    views are included.

277

Manuscript Preparation:

Two copies are required. List footnotes on page noted. References should be numbered in parenthesis and a full list of references should be on a separate sheet. Use one inch margins and double-space. A background or explanatory cover letter and an abstract are required. Figures should be camera-ready (offset); letters and numbers should be distinct. Figure numbers and captions should not appear on figures. No payment is made for accepted manuscripts.

Manuscript Disposition:

Receipt of a manuscript is not acknowledged. Editorial decisions are made within three to four weeks. Accepted articles usually appear in print within four to six months. Unaccepted manuscripts are not returned unless accompanied by stamped, self-addressed envelope. Criticism and/or suggestions are provided.

Copyright:

Held by the American Society for Information Science.

CATHOLIC LIBRARY WORLD

Subscription Data:

Published by the Catholic Library Association, 461 West Lancaster Avenue, Haverford, Pennsylvania 19041. Issued 10 times each year. Advertising is accepted. Circulation: 4,500. Subscription: $10.00 per year in the United States and Canada; $11.00 foreign. Founded: 1929.

Editorial Address:

Jane F. Hindman, Editor, Catholic Library World, 461 West Lancaster Avenue, Haverford, Pennsylvania 19041.

Editorial Policy:

Includes articles about books and libraries. The reading audience includes librarians and other interested persons and those interested in literature. Unsolicited articles are welcome. Four major articles are published per issue. Staff-written book reviews are included.

Manuscript Preparation:

Accepted manuscripts average 2,500 words. One copy is required. Return postage and a self-addressed envelope are required. Bibliographical procedure should follow the MLA Style Sheet. A background or explanatory cover letter is not required nor is an outline, summary, or abstract. Biographical information about the author is not required. Illustrations, pictures, graphs, etc., are welcome. No payment is made for accepted manuscripts. Catholic Library World has no reprint policy.

Manuscript Disposition:

Receipt of a manuscript is acknowledged. Editorial decisions are made within three weeks. Accepted articles usually appear in print within four months. Unaccepted manuscripts are returned, without criticism or suggestions.

Copyright:

Held by the Catholic Library Association.

COLLEGE AND RESEARCH LIBRARIES

Subscription Data:
Published by the Association of College and Research Libraries, American Library Association, 50 East Huron Street, Chicago, Illinois 60611. Issued bimonthly, in January, March, May, July, September, and November. Advertising is accepted. Circulation: 18, 000. Subscription: Free to members of the Association; $15. 00 to non-members. Founded: 1939.

Editorial Address:
The Editor, College and Research Libraries, James M. Milne Library, State University College, Oneonta, New York 13820.

Editorial Policy:
Includes manuscripts which report results of research or surveys, topical manuscripts, and bibliographical essays or bibliographies. The reading audience includes academic librarians. Unsolicited manuscripts are welcome. Six to eight major articles are published per issue. Book reviews are included.

Manuscript Preparation:
Accepted manuscripts average 2, 000 to 4, 000 words. Two copies are required. Return postage and a self-addressed envelope are required. Bibliographical procedure should follow the University of Chicago Manual of Style. List footnotes on a separate page. A background or explanatory cover letter is not required, but is sometimes useful. A 75 to 100 word abstract is required. Biographical information about the author is required and should include name, position, and institutional affiliation. Illustrations, pictures, graphs, etc., must be reproducible in quality. No payment is made for accepted manuscripts. Twenty-five offprints are provided authors; additional copies may be purchased.

Manuscript Disposition:
Receipt of a manuscript is acknowledged. Editorial decisions are made within six to eight weeks. Accepted articles usually appear in print within eight to fourteen months. Unaccepted manuscripts are returned with criticism and/or suggestions.

Copyright:
Held by the American Library Association.

*DREXEL LIBRARY QUARTERLY

Subscription Data:
Published by the Graduate School of Library Science, Drexel University, Philadelphia, Pennsylvania 19104. Issued quarterly, in January, April, July, and October. Advertising is not accepted. Circulation: 1, 000. Subscription: $10. 00 per year; $3. 00 per issue. Founded: 1965.

Editorial Address:
The Editor, Drexel Library Quarterly, Graduate School of Library Science, Drexel University, Philadelphia, Pennsylvania 19104.

Editorial Policy:
> Includes articles addressed to professional audience which might
> be technical and practical or of a research or scholarly nature.
> The total issue tries to provide a comprehensive survey of sub-
> jects not treated in depth elsewhere and is, in most cases, use-
> ful and informative for the practicing librarian. The reading
> audience includes librarians, information scientists, and educa-
> tors, including library science educators. Unsolicited manu-
> scripts are not welcome; however, someone with an idea for an
> entire issue can submit an outline, indicating possible contribu-
> tors. Seven to ten major articles are published per issue.
> Book reviews have been temporarily discontinued.

Manuscript Preparation:
> Each individual article is about 10 to 18 typewritten pages de-
> pending upon the number of articles comprising the entire issue.

Copyright:
> Held by the Graduate School of Library Science, Drexel Univer-
> sity.

Additional Information:
> Each issue is devoted to a single topic. A special editor is
> selected for each with articles solicited from several authors to
> make up the issue.

ILLINOIS. UNIVERSITY. GRADUATE SCHOOL OF LIBRARY SCI-
ENCE. NEWSLETTER ON LIBRARY RESEARCH

Subscription Data:
> Published by University of Illinois, Graduate School of Library
> Science, Publications Office, 249 Armory Building, Champaign,
> Illinois 61820. Issued quarterly, in March, June, September,
> and December. Advertising is not accepted. Circulation: 2,500.
> Subscription: $2.00 per year. Founded: 1972.

Editorial Address:
> The Editor, Newsletter on Library Research, University of Illi-
> nois, Graduate School of Library Science, Publications Office,
> 249 Armory Building, Champaign, Illinois 61820.

Editorial Policy:
> Includes short entries on news related to library research. The
> reading audience includes librarians, library school students,
> faculty, and researchers. Unsolicited manuscripts are welcome.
> Book reviews are included.

Manuscript Preparation:
> Accepted manuscripts average from a few lines to a few para-
> graphs. One copy is required. Return postage and a self-ad-
> dressed envelope are not required. A background or explanatory
> cover letter is not required nor is an outline, summary, or ab-
> stract. Biographical information about the author is not re-
> quired. There are no policies concerning illustrations, pictures,
> graphs, etc. No payment is made for accepted manuscripts.
> No reprints are available.

Manuscript Disposition:
> Receipt of a manuscript is not acknowledged. Editorial deci-

sions are made within 12 weeks. Accepted articles usually appear in print within three months. Unaccepted manuscripts are not returned.
Copyright:
Not copyrighted.

ILLINOIS. UNIVERSITY. GRADUATE SCHOOL OF LIBRARY SCIENCE. OCCASIONAL PAPERS

Subscription Data:
Published by University of Illinois, Graduate School of Library Science, Publications Office, 249 Armory Building, Champaign, Illinois 61820. Issued usually at least five times each year. Advertising is not accepted. Circulation: 1,000. Subscription: $5.00 per year. Founded: 1949.
Editorial Address:
The Editor, Occasional Papers, University of Illinois, Graduate School of Library Science, Publications Office, 249 Armory Building, Champaign, Illinois 61820.
Editorial Policy:
Includes articles relating to any aspect of librarianship. The reading audience includes librarians, educators, and others. Unsolicited manuscripts are welcome. One major article is published per issue. Book reviews are not included.
Manuscript Preparation:
Accepted manuscripts average 20 to 80 pages. One copy is required. Return postage and a self-addressed envelope are not required. Bibliographical procedure should follow a guide which is available upon request from the office of the editor. Use 1-1/2 inch margins and double-space. A background or explanatory cover letter is required, but not an outline, summary, or abstract. Biographical information about the author is required. Glossy eight by ten inch originals are required. No payment is made for accepted manuscripts. Reprints are available.
Manuscript Disposition:
Receipt of a manuscript is acknowledged. Editorial decisions are made within six weeks. Accepted articles usually appear in print within 12 months. Unaccepted manuscripts are returned with criticism and/or suggestions.
Copyright:
Not copyrighted.

JOURNAL OF EDUCATION FOR LIBRARIANSHIP

Subscription Data:
Published by the Association of American Library Schools, 471 Park Lane, State College, Pennsylvania 16801. Issued quarterly, in summer, fall, winter, and spring. Advertising is not accepted. Circulation: 1,900. Subscription: $8.00 per volume; all subscriptions on volume basis, beginning in July. Founded: 1960.

Editorial Address:
  Norman Horrocks, Editor, Journal of Education for Librarianship,
  471 Park Lane, State College, Pennsylvania 16801.
Editorial Policy:
  Includes articles on all phases of education for librarianship.
  The reading audience includes library educators. Unsolicited
  articles are invited. Six to ten articles are published per issue.
  Book reviews are occasionally included.
Manuscript Preparation:
  Accepted manuscripts are limited to approximately 20 manuscript
  pages. One copy is required. Return postage and a self-addressed envelope are required. Bibliographical procedure should
  follow the standard format. Use standard manuscript margin and
  spacing. An explanatory cover letter is required and an abstract
  is encouraged. Include biographical information about the author.
  No pictures should be used. No payment is made for accepted
  manuscripts. Permission must be secured for reprints.
Manuscript Disposition:
  Receipt of a manuscript is acknowledged. Editorial decisions
  are made within six to eight weeks. Accepted articles usually
  appear in print within six months. Unaccepted manuscripts are
  returned when rejected, sometimes with criticism.
Copyright:
  Held by the Association of American Library Schools.

JOURNAL OF LIBRARY HISTORY

Subscription Data:
  Published by the School of Library Science, Florida State Univer-
  sity, Tallahassee, Florida 32306. Issued quarterly, in January,
  April, July, and October. Advertising is accepted. Circulation:
  1,100. Subscription: $12.50 per year. Founded: 1966.
Editorial Address:
  Dr. Harold Goldstein, Editor, Journal of Library History,
  School of Library Science, Florida State University, Tallahassee,
  Florida 32306.
Editorial Policy:
  Includes documented scholarly articles, short, undocumented
  pieces, and book reviews. The reading audience includes librarians, library science students, and historians. Unsolicited manuscripts are welcome. Three major articles are published per
  issue. Book reviews are included.
Manuscript Preparation:
  Accepted manuscripts average 20 to 35 pages. Two copies are
  required. Return postage and a self-addressed envelope are
  not required. Bibliographical procedure should follow the Turabian Manual for Writers. Place all footnotes at the end of the
  article. Use one inch margins and double-space throughout. A
  background or explanatory cover letter is not required nor is an
  outline, summary, or abstract. Biographical information about
  the author is not required. Illustrations, pictures, graphs, etc.,
  are requested only if important to the text. No payment is
  made for accepted manuscripts. Reprints are not available.

Manuscript Disposition:
Receipt of a manuscript is acknowledged. Editorial decisions are made within eight to twelve weeks. Accepted articles usually appear in print within 12 months. Unaccepted manuscripts are returned with criticism and/or suggestions.

Copyright:
Held by the Journal of Library History.

LEARNING TODAY

Subscription Data:
Published by the Library-College Associates, Inc., Box 956, Norman, Oklahoma 73069. Issued four times each year. Advertising is accepted. Circulation: Learning Today 2,500; Supplement - Library-College Omnibus 20,000. Subscription: $10.00 per year. Founded: 1968.

Editorial Address:
The Editor, Learning Today, Box 956, Norman, Oklahoma 73069.

Editorial Policy:
Includes articles dealing with problems of the learner, and how a library-centered study/teaching method can facilitate personalized growth. The reading audience includes elementary, secondary, and college (interdisciplinary, with emphasis on media specialists and persons in professional education). Unsolicited manuscripts are welcome. Three or four major articles are published per issue in addition to regular departmental features. Book reviews are included.

Manuscript Preparation:
Accepted manuscripts average 1,500 to 2,500 words. One copy is required. Return postage and a self-addressed envelope are not required. Bibliographical procedure should follow the Turabian Manual for Writers. A background or explanatory cover letter is not required nor is an outline, summary, or abstract. Biographical information about the author is not required. Illustrations, pictures, graphs, etc., are welcomed. No payment is made for accepted manuscripts. All materials belong to Library-College Associates, Inc.

Manuscript Disposition:
Receipt of a manuscript is acknowledged. Editorial decisions are made within three to four weeks. Accepted articles usually appear in print within 18 months. Unaccepted manuscripts are returned without criticism and/or suggestions.

Copyright:
Held by the Library College Associates, Inc.

LIBRARY JOURNAL

Subscription Data:
Published by R. R. Bowker Company, 1180 Avenue of the Americas, New York, New York 10036. Issued twice monthly, September through June, monthly during July and August. Adver-

tising is accepted. Circulation: 40,000. Subscription: $16.20
per year. Founded: 1876.

Editorial Address:

The Editor, Library Journal, 1180 Avenue of the Americas,
New York, New York 10036.

Editorial Policy:

Includes articles and reports on librarianship, publishing, bibliography, documentation, education, and related topics. The reading audience includes librarians, librarian educators, and library
students. Unsolicited articles are welcome. Three or four major articles are published per issue. Book reviews are included.

Manuscript Preparation:

Accepted manuscripts average 2,500 words. One copy is required. Return postage and a self-addressed envelope are unnecessary. Footnotes should be placed at the end of the manuscript. Bibliographical procedure should follow the University
of Chicago Manual of Style. Use wide margins and double-space.
A background or explanatory cover letter and an outline or summary of the article are desired. Biographical information about
the author is required and should include a summary of current
position and indication of experience relative to the subject of the
article. Illustrations, pictures, graphs, etc., are sometimes
used. Payment is made for articles. Reprints are not normally
available.

Manuscript Disposition:

Receipt of a manuscript is acknowledged. Accepted articles appear in print from one month to one year after acceptance. Unaccepted manuscripts are returned, often with criticism or suggestions.

Copyright:

Held by the Xerox Corporation.

LIBRARY QUARTERLY

Subscription Data:

Published by the University of Chicago Press, 5801 Ellis Avenue,
Chicago, Illinois 60636. Sponsored by the Graduate Library
School of the University of Chicago. Issued four times each
year, in January, April, July, and October. Advertising is ac-
cepted. Circulation: 3,700. Subscription: $10.00 per year.
Founded: 1931.

Editorial Address:

Managing Editor, Library Quarterly, Graduate Library School,
University of Chicago, Chicago, Illinois 60637.

Editorial Policy:

Includes research articles on all topics related to libraries and
librarianship, including library planning, organization and management, information storage and retrieval, studies of library
use and library users, history of books, libraries, and printing.
The reading audience includes professional librarians and other
library workers. Unsolicited articles are welcome. Five major
articles are published per issue. Book reviews are included.

Manuscript Preparation:
    Accepted manuscripts average from 15 to 25 double-spaced type-
written pages. One copy is required. Return postage and a
self-addressed envelope are unnecessary. Incorporate footnotes
into the text where possible. Bibliographical procedure should
follow the University of Chicago Manual of Style. Use wide margins and double-space throughout. Neither a background or explanatory cover letter of the article is required. An abstract
of one paragraph is requested. Biographical information about
the author will be solicited by the editor via questionnaire.
Graphs may be used. No payment is made for accepted articles.
Reprints are available; 50 free copies are mailed to the author.
Cost of additional reprints varies with article length and order
volume; a cost summary is available.

Manuscript Disposition:
    Receipt of a manuscript is acknowledged. Editorial decisions
are made within two to four weeks. Accepted articles usually
appear in print within six months after acceptance. Unaccepted
manuscripts are returned, seldom with criticism or suggestions.

Copyright:
    Held by the University of Chicago Press.

†LIBRARY RESOURCES AND TECHNICAL SERVICES

Subscription Data:
    Published by the American Library Association, 50 East Huron
Street, Chicago, Illinois 60611. Sponsored by the Resources
and Technical Services Division of the American Library Association. Issued four times each year, in January, April, July,
and October. Advertising is accepted. Circulation: 9,000.
Subscription: Free to membership; $10.00 per year to non-
members. Founded: 1957.

Editorial Address:
    Wesley Simonton, Editor, Library Resources and Technical
Services, Library School, University of Minnesota, Minneapolis,
Minnesota 55455.

Editorial Policy:
    Includes articles which pertain to library service, especially the
building, organization, and control of collections. The reading
audience includes librarians in all phases of library work. Unsolicited articles are welcome. Ten major articles are published
per issue. Book reviews are included.

Manuscript Preparation:
    Accepted manuscripts average from eight to ten double-spaced
typewritten pages. Each manuscript should be in two copies.
Return postage and a self-addressed envelope are unnecessary.
Footnotes should be listed at the end of the article. Bibliographical procedure should follow the University of Chicago Manual of
Style. Preceding the article should be its title, the name and
affiliation of the author, and a 75 to 100 word abstract. The
article itself should be concise, simply written, and as free as
possible of jargon. Citations should be brief, easy to understand,

and consistent in form within the article. Illustrations, graphs, etc., may be used; however all must be submitted in finished form for the printer. No payment is made for accepted articles. Reprint costs vary with article length, use of cover, etc.

Manuscript Disposition:

Receipt of a manuscript is acknowledged. Editorial decisions are made jointly by the editor and the assistant editor using specific subject lists as a guide. Accepted articles usually appear in print within six months after acceptance. Unaccepted manuscripts are returned, often with criticism.

Copyright:

Not copyrighted; however, courtesy of citation to the original publication is requested when material is reprinted.

*LIBRARY TRENDS

Subscription Data:

Published by the University of Illinois Graduate School of Library Science, University Press, Urbana, Illinois 61801. Issued quarterly, in July, October, January, and April. Advertising is not accepted. Circulation: 6,000. Subscription: $8.00 per year. Founded: 1952.

Editorial Address:

The Editor, Library Trends, University of Illinois, Graduate School of Library Science, Publications Office, 249 Armory Building, Champaign, Illinois 61820.

Editorial Policy:

Includes articles related to a single topic of librarianship. The reading audience includes librarians, library science students, and educators. Unsolicited manuscripts are not welcome. Six to ten major articles are published per issue. Book reviews are not included.

Manuscript Preparation:

Accepted manuscripts average 10 to 20 double-spaced typewritten pages. One copy is required. Bibliographical procedure should follow the University of Chicago Manual of Style. Special manuscript footnoting recommendations are available upon request. Double-space the manuscript. A background or explanatory cover letter is not required nor is an outline, summary, or abstract. Biographical information about the author is required. Glossy originals that are eight by ten inches are required. No payment is made for accepted manuscripts. Fifty reprints are free to the author.

Manuscript Disposition:

Receipt of a manuscript is acknowledged. Accepted articles usually appear in print within six months. Criticism and/or suggestions are provided.

Copyright:

Held by the Board of Trustees, University of Illinois.

*PIONEER

Subscription Data:
    Published by the Library Bureau, 801 Park Avenue, Herkimer,
    New York 13350. Issued quarterly. Advertising is not accepted.
    Circulation: 20,000. Subscription: Complimentary. Founded:
    1937.
Editorial Address:
    The Editor, Pioneer, Library Bureau, 801 Park Avenue, Herki-
    mer, New York 13350.
Editorial Policy:
    Includes articles on all types of library work; primarily new li-
    brary building. The reading audience includes librarians, archi-
    tects, and others interested in library problems. Unsolicited
    manuscripts are seldom used. One to two major articles are
    published per issue. Book reviews are rarely included.
Copyright:
    Held by the Library Bureau Division of Remington Rand.

QUARTERLY JOURNAL OF THE LIBRARY OF CONGRESS

Subscription Data:
    Published by the Library of Congress, Washington, D.C. 20540.
    Issued quarterly, in January, April, July, and October. Ad-
    vertising is not accepted. Circulation: 5,300. Subscription:
    $4.75 per year; $5.95 foreign; $1.20 per issue. Founded: 1943.
Editorial Address:
    The Editor, Quarterly Journal of the Library of Congress, Pub-
    lications Office, Library of Congress, Washington, D.C. 20540.
Editorial Policy:
    Includes articles on the collections and activities of the Library
    of Congress. Occasional articles on LC-related collections and
    scholarly activities at other institutions are included. The read-
    ing audience includes the general reader interested in the human-
    ities and social sciences. Unsolicited manuscripts are welcome
    provided they are within the scope of the Journal's editorial pol-
    icy. Approximately three to five major articles are published
    per issue. Book reviews are not included.
Manuscript Preparation:
    Accepted manuscripts average 1,000 to 7,500 words. Longer
    articles are occasionally published. Two copies are required.
    Return postage and a self-addressed envelope are required. Bib-
    liographical procedure should follow the University of Chicago
    Manual of Style. List footnotes on a separate page. Pages must
    begin and end with a new paragraph. A background or explana-
    tory cover letter and an outline, summary, or abstract are re-
    quired. Biographical information about the author is required.
    All illustrations require an eight by ten inch glossy photograph.
    No payment is made for accepted manuscripts. Publisher does
    not supply reprints.

Manuscript Disposition:
  Receipt of a manuscript is acknowledged. Editorial decisions
  are made within eight to twelve weeks. Accepted articles usually appear in print within six to nine months. Unaccepted manuscripts are returned, if requested, with criticism and/or suggestions.
Copyright:
  Held by the author if specifically requested and if author regis-
  ters the article.

SCHOOL LIBRARY JOURNAL

Subscription Data:
  Published by the R. R. Bowker Company, 1180 Avenue of the
  Americas, New York, New York 10036. Issued three times each
  year, September through May. Advertising is accepted. Circulation: 29,500. Subscription: $10.80 per year. Founded:
  1954.
Editorial Address:
  The Editor, School Library Journal, R. R. Bowker Company,
  1180 Avenue of the Americas, New York, New York 10036.
Editorial Policy:
  Includes articles and reports on school and public libraries, library programs, children's literature, and audio-visual materials
  and equipment. The reading audience includes school and public
  librarians, and teachers. Unsolicited manuscripts are welcome.
  Six major articles are published per issue. Book reviews are
  included.
Manuscript Preparation:
  Accepted manuscripts average from 2,000 to 2,500 words. Two
  copies are required. Return postage and a return envelope are
  unnecessary. List all footnotes at the end of the article. Bibliographical style should follow the University of Chicago Manual
  of Style. A background or explanatory cover letter about the
  article is desired. An outline or summary of the article is required in advance of submission of the finished manuscript. Biographical information about the author is desired and should include a summary of professional background. Illustrations, pictures, etc., may be used; all must be marked for identification
  and will be returned only if requested. An honorarium is paid
  for accepted articles. Reprints are seldom available, but multiple copies of the Journal may be purchased at special rates.
Manuscript Disposition:
  Receipt of a manuscript is acknowledged. Editorial decisions
  are made as soon as possible; time required varies with plans
  for specific issues. Accepted manuscripts usually appear in
  print within one year after acceptance. Unaccepted manuscripts
  are returned; suggestions and criticism are given only if the
  author displays exceptional potential.
Copyright:
  Held by the R. R. Bowker Company.

SCHOOL MEDIA QUARTERLY (formerly School Libraries)

Subscription Data:
Published by the American Association of School Librarians, 50 East Huron Street, Chicago, Illinois 60611. Issued four times each year, in October, January, March, and May. Advertising which relates to instructional materials, supplies, media and equipment utilized in school library programs is accepted. Circulation: 15,000. Subscription: Only to Association members; $2.00 per copy for back issues. Founded: 1972 as School Media Quarterly; 1952 as School Libraries; 1951 as Newsletter.

Editorial Address:
The Editor, School Media Quarterly, American Association of School Librarians, 50 East Huron Street, Chicago, Illinois 60611.

Editorial Policy:
Includes professional and news articles on all phases of media library work. The reading audience includes school librarians, media specialists, public children's and young people's librarians, library school faculty members, and others concerned with school library services. Unsolicited articles are welcome. Four or five major articles are published per issue. Book reviews for professional workers are included.

Manuscript Preparation:
No policy regarding manuscript length has been established. The original and one carbon are required. Return postage and a self-addressed envelope are desired. Footnoting and other bibliographical procedure should follow the University of Chicago Manual of Style. Use wide margins and double-space. A background or explanatory cover letter about the article is desired, but not an outline or summary. Biographical information about the author is desired. Illustrations, pictures, graphs, etc., may be used. No payment is made for accepted articles. Reprint costs vary with article length and order volume.

Manuscript Disposition:
Receipt of a manuscript is acknowledged. Editorial decisions are made as soon as possible. Time from acceptance of a manuscript to its appearance in print varies with topic and editorial need. Unaccepted manuscripts are returned, sometimes with criticism and/or suggestions.

Copyright:
Not copyrighted.

Additional Information:
Articles which provide practical suggestions to school librarians, report trends in school library service, and help librarians discover new horizons are especially desired. Researched scholarly articles which summarize research results or important sources of library information for improved services are also welcomed. Various special columns focus on interests and news.

SPECIAL LIBRARIES

Subscription Data:
 Published by the Special Libraries Association, 235 Park Avenue
 South, New York, New York 10003. Issued 11 times each year.
 Advertising is accepted. Circulation: 10,000. Subscription:
 $22.50 per year. Founded: 1909.

Editorial Address:
 The Editor, Special Libraries, Special Libraries Association,
 235 Park Avenue South, New York, New York 10003.

Editorial Policy:
 Includes articles on documentation, library science, and information science. The reading audience includes special librarians
 and information experts. Unsolicited articles are welcome. Six
 to seven major articles are published per issue. Book reviews
 are included.

Manuscript Preparation:
 Accepted manuscripts average from 1,500 to 3,500 words. Two
 copies are required. Return postage and a self-addressed envelope are unnecessary. Bibliographical procedure should follow
 the University of Chicago Manual of Style. Use one inch margins
 and double-space. A background or explanatory cover letter
 about the article is not required, but a 50 to 100 word abstract
 is required in advance of or with submission of the finished manuscript. Biographical information about the author is desired
 and should include a summary of professional background. Illustrations, pictures, graphs, etc., will be used when appropriate.
 No payment is made for accepted articles. Reprint costs vary
 with article length and order quantity.

Manuscript Disposition:
 Receipt of a manuscript is acknowledged. Editorial decisions
 are made within six to eight weeks. Accepted articles appear
 in print from two to ten months after acceptance. Unaccepted
 manuscripts are returned, occasionally with suggestions and/or
 criticism. In cases of inappropriate articles the editor often
 recommends another journal.

Copyright:
 Held by the Special Libraries Association.

TOP OF THE NEWS

Subscription Data:
 Published by the American Library Association, 50 East Huron
 Street, Chicago, Illinois 60611. Issued quarterly, in January,
 April, June, and November. Advertising is accepted. Circula-
 tion: 13,500. Subscription: Available as part of ALA member-
 ship dues. Founded: 1942.

Editorial Address:
 The Editor, Top of the News, American Library Association,
 50 East Huron Street, Chicago, Illinois 60611.

Editorial Policy:
 Includes reports and articles which relate to librarians, library

work, and books. The reading audience includes children's librarians, young adult librarians, elementary and high school librarians, and public librarians. Unsolicited articles are welcome. Four or five major articles are published per issue. Bibliographies and book reviews which relate to reading, children, and young people are included.

Manuscript Preparation:
Accepted manuscripts average from 1,500 to 2,500 words. One copy is required. Return postage and a self-addressed envelope are desired. Footnoting and other bibliographical procedure should follow the University of Chicago Manual of Style. Use one inch margins and double-space. A background or explanatory cover letter about the article is desired, but not an outline or summary. Biographical information about the author is desired and should include a summary of current position. Illustrations, pictures, graphs, etc., will be used only if necessary to interpretation of the text. No payment is made for accepted articles. Reprints are available; costs vary with article length and order volume.

Manuscript Disposition:
Receipt of a manuscript is acknowledged. Editorial decisions are made within two to three weeks. Accepted articles usually appear in print within two to six months after acceptance. Unaccepted manuscripts are returned, often with criticism or suggestions.

Copyright:
Not copyrighted.

WILSON LIBRARY BULLETIN

Subscription Data:
Published by the H.W. Wilson Company, 950 University Avenue, Bronx, New York 10452. Issued monthly, except July and August. Advertising is accepted. Circulation: 38,000. Subscription: $9.00 per year. Founded: 1914.

Editorial Address:
The Editor, Wilson Library Bulletin, 950 University Avenue, Bronx, New York 10452.

Editorial Policy:
Includes articles and reports which relate to libraries, librarianship, and librarians. Many are solicited by the editor. The reading audience includes school, public, academic, and special librarians. Unsolicited articles are welcome. Special reports, news, features, columns, and pictorial items as well as six major articles are published in each issue. Reference books are reviewed by columnist.

Manuscript Preparation:
Accepted manuscripts average from 1,500 to 6,000 words. One copy, return postage, and a self-addressed envelope are required. Footnoting and other bibliographical procedure should follow Words Into Type. Spelling must conform to Webster's New International Dictionary. Use wide margins and double-space.

Absolutely no carbons or xerographic copies will be accepted as the first copy of a manuscript. Author's background is helpful. Small cash honorariums are paid contributors in addition to five copies. Reprints are not available from the publisher.

Manuscript Disposition:

Receipt of a manuscript is acknowledged. Editorial decisions are made within two to ten weeks. Time from acceptance of a manuscript to its appearance in print varies with topic and editorial need. Unaccepted manuscripts are returned, sometimes with criticism and/or suggestions.

Copyright:

Held by the H. W. Wilson Company.

Additional Information:

Several issues each year feature thematic sections such as children's literature, resources in a field, international activities, etc.

WISCONSIN LIBRARY BULLETIN

Subscription Data:

Published by the Division for Library Services, Wisconsin Department of Public Instruction, 126 Langdon Street, Madison, Wisconsin 53702. Issued bimonthly. Advertising is not accepted. Circulation: 4,100. Subscription: $3.50 per year; $.60 per issue. Founded: 1905.

Editorial Address:

Beryl E. Hoyt, Editor, Wisconsin Library Bulletin, 126 Langdon Street, Madison, Wisconsin 53702.

Editorial Policy:

Includes professional articles on libraries/media centers and their service; news of libraries/media centers, librarians and library associations in Wisconsin, and annotated materials lists. The reading audience includes librarians, media specialists, public library trustees, school district administrators in Wisconsin, library agencies in other states, and library schools and individuals around the world. Unsolicited manuscripts are welcome. Ten to twelve major articles are published per issue. Annotations are included, but full length reviews are not included.

Manuscript Preparation:

Accepted manuscripts generally average 300 to 1,700 words. One copy is required. Return postage and a self-addressed envelope are not required, but are appreciated for unsolicited manuscripts. Bibliographical procedure should generally follow the University of Chicago Manual of Style or the style sheet available from the editor. References are included within the text whenever possible rather than in footnotes; these are kept

to a minimum. Begin the articles three inches down on the
first page and on succeeding pages use one inch margins at top
and bottom. Number at the top and use 75 characters per line
(including spaces). Use ordinary type face (no script or italics)
and usual capitals and lower cases, and use a ribbon that gives
good black typed copy. Type on one side of 8-1/2 by 11 inch
bond paper and double-space throughout. A background or explanatory cover letter is not required, but is sometimes helpful.
An outline, summary, or abstract is not required. Biographical
information about the author is required and should include title,
professional position, and address; other pertinent data is welcome. Illustrations, pictures, graphs, etc., are used and are
welcome. If photographs are used, submit clear black and white
glossy prints (any size) with good contrast. Polaroids are acceptable. Identify photographs by a note taped to the back or by
very light pencil marking on the back. Estimate that a photograph replaces 100 words. No payment is made for accepted
manuscripts. Reprints are generally not available.

Manuscript Disposition:
    Receipt of a manuscript is acknowledged. Editorial decisions
are made usually within three weeks. Accepted articles usually
appear in print within a minimum of three months; it could be
a year if topic fits better in a later issue or space already is
planned. Unaccepted manuscripts are returned, usually without
criticism and/or suggestions.

Copyright:
    Not copyrighted.

LINGUISTICS - ENGLISH LANGUAGE

*CEA FORUM

Subscription Data:
Published by the College English Association, Inc., Centenary College, Shrereport, Louisiana 71104. Issued bimonthly, October through April. Advertising is accepted. Circulation: 2,800. Subscription: $8.00 per year; $10.00 to libraries and institutions. Founded: 1970.

Editorial Address:
The Editor, CEA Forum, Centenary College, Shrereport, Louisiana 71104.

Editorial Policy:
Includes "News and Views" of CEA members and short articles and poetry related to the teaching of college English. The reading audience includes college professors of English and humanities. Unsolicited manuscripts are not welcome. Two or three major articles are published per issue. Book reviews are included.

Manuscript Preparation:
Accepted manuscripts average under 1,500 words; 250 word mini-articles are preferred. One copy is required. Return postage and a self-addressed envelope are required. Avoid the use of footnotes. Use one inch margins and double-space. A background or explanatory cover letter is preferred, but not required. An outline, summary, or abstract is not required. Biographical information about the author is not required. Author must prepare camera-ready copies for illustrations, pictures, graphs, etc. No payment is made for accepted manuscripts. Reprints must be ordered in advance of publication.

Manuscript Disposition:
Receipt of a manuscript is acknowledged. Editorial decisions are made within four to six weeks. Accepted articles usually appear in print within two to twelve months. Unaccepted manuscripts are returned, sometimes with criticism and/or suggestions.

Copyright:
Held by the College English Association, Inc.

CLA JOURNAL

Subscription Data:
Published by the College Language Association, Morgan State College, Baltimore, Maryland 21239. Issued four times each year, in September, December, March, and June. Advertising

is accepted. Circulation: 1,000. Subscription: $6.00 per year; $6.50 in Canada; $7.00 elsewhere. Founded: 1957.

Editorial Address:

Therman B. O'Daniel, Editor, CLA Journal, Morgan State College, Baltimore, Maryland 21239.

Editorial Policy:

Includes articles which relate to the various aspects of language and literature in English and foreign language. The reading audience includes college and university faculty, and members of the general public who have interests in languages and literature. Unsolicited articles are welcome. Eight to twelve major articles are published per issue. Book reviews are included.

Manuscript Preparation:

Accepted manuscripts average 10 to 12 double-spaced typewritten pages. Two copies are required. Return postage and a self-addressed envelope are required. Bibliographical procedure should follow the revised MLA Style Sheet. Use one inch margins and double-space throughout except for single-spaced, indented long quotations. A background or explanatory cover letter about the article is not desired, but an abstract is required. Biographical information about the author is desired and should include a summary of his formal education, previous publications, and present position. Pictures, illustrations, graphs, etc., cannot be used. No payment is made for contributions. CLA Journal articles may be reprinted by permission and by payment of permission fees, which are shared equally by authors and the College Language Association.

Manuscript Disposition:

Receipt of a manuscript is acknowledged. Editorial decisions are made within three months. Accepted articles usually appear in print within one year after acceptance. Unaccepted manuscripts are returned, sometimes with criticism and suggestions.

Copyright:

Held by the College Language Association.

COLLEGE COMPOSITION AND COMMUNICATION

Subscription Data:

Published by the Conference on College Composition and Communication, 1111 Kenyon Drive, Urbana, Illinois 61801. Issued quarterly, in February, May, October, and December, plus a special November Directory of Assistantships and Fellowships for Graduate Study in English and the Teaching of English. Advertising is accepted. Circulation: 6,000. Subscription: $3.00 per year; $1.00 per issue; $2.50 for Directory. Founded: 1950.

Editorial Address:

Edward P.J. Corbett, Editor, College Composition and Communication, 1111 Kenyon Drive, Urbana, Illinois 61801.

Editorial Policy:

Includes (1) articles which pertain to the theory, practice, and teaching of composition and communication at all college levels, with emphasis on interrelationships among literature, language, and composition; (2) reports of research or notes on usage, grammar, rhetoric, and the logic of composition; (3) studies in linguistics of interest to the generalist; and (4) rhetorical, stylistic, thematic, or critical analysis of nonfiction prose commonly studied in composition courses. The reading audience includes college and junior college faculty and high school teachers of college preparatory students. Unsolicited articles are welcome. Twelve to fifteen major articles are published per issue. Book reviews are included.

Manuscript Preparation:
Accepted manuscripts average 2,500 words. One copy is required. Return postage and a self-addressed envelope are desired. Use 15 space margins and double-space. Place all footnotes on a separate page at the end of the article. Bibliographical procedure should follow the MLA Style Sheet. A background or explanatory cover letter about the article is not desired nor is an outline or summary. Biographical information about the author is unnecessary. Simple graphs may be used. Payment is occasionally made for solicited articles, but never for unsolicited work. Reprints are available; a reprint cost summary may be obtained from the office of the editor.

Manuscript Disposition:
Receipt of a manuscript is not acknowledged. Editorial decisions are made within two to three weeks. Accepted articles usually appear in print within four to eight months after acceptance. Unaccepted articles are returned, often with criticism.

Copyright:
Held by the National Council of Teachers of English.

COLLEGE ENGLISH

Subscription Data:
Published by the National Council of Teachers of English, 1111 Kenyon Road, Urbana, Illinois 61801. Issued monthly, October through May. Advertising is accepted. Circulation: 17,800. Subscription: $12.00 per year. Founded: 1939.

Editorial Address:
Richard Ohmann, Editor, College English, Wesleyan University, Middletown, Connecticut 06457.

Editorial Policy:
College English is particularly receptive to articles of general professional significance in the following areas: (1) the working concepts of criticism including structure, influence, period, etc.; (2) the nature of critical and scholarly reasoning, implicit standards of evidence and inference, and the nature of critical explanation; (3) the structure of the English field, implications of the way it is segmented, consequences of specialization, and the place of rhetoric and composition; and (4) the relevance of current thinking and research in related fields to the study and teaching of English. Critical articles or explications are no longer published, except for those calculated to have an impact

on critical theory, curriculum, and pedagogy. The reading audience includes both college and high school teachers of English. Unsolicited articles are welcome. Solicited book reviews are included.

Manuscript Preparation:
Manuscripts may contain up to 40 double-spaced typewritten pages, although shorter articles are welcome. Comments on published articles or reviews are welcome but should normally be limited to six typewritten pages. One copy is required. Return postage and a self-addressed envelope are desired. Avoid use of footnotes when possible; when necessary follow the MLA Style Sheet. Use wide margins and double-space throughout. A background or explanatory cover letter about the article is not desired nor is an outline or summary. Biographical information about the author is not usually required. No pictures can be used. No payment is made for accepted articles. Reprint costs vary with article length and number of copies ordered.

Manuscript Disposition:
Receipt of a manuscript is acknowledged. Editorial decisions are ordinarily made within three months. Accepted articles usually appear in print within one year after acceptance. Unaccepted manuscripts are returned with comment.

Copyright:
Held by the National Council of Teachers of English.

ETC.: A REVIEW OF GENERAL SEMANTICS

Subscription Data:
Published by the International Society for General Semantics, P.O. Box 2469, 509 Sansome Street, San Francisco, California 94126. Issued quarterly, in March, June, September, and December. Advertising is accepted. Circulation: 6,000. Subscription: $6.00 per year; $12.00 for two years; $15.00 for three years. Founded: 1943.

Editorial Address:
Dr. Thomas Weiss, Editor, ETC.: A Review of General Semantics, 108 Graduate Hall, College of Education, University of Wyoming, Laramie, Wyoming 82070.

Editorial Policy:
Includes articles on semantics, general semantics, communication related topics, and a limited amount of verse. The reading audience includes educators, students, librarians, and others interested in communication. Unsolicited manuscripts are welcome. Five to eight major articles are published per issue. Book reviews, poems, dates, and indexes are included.

Manuscript Preparation:
Manuscripts for publication must be sent in duplicate and accompanied by a stamped, self-addressed envelope. Footnoting and other bibliographical procedure should follow the APA Publication Manual. A background or explanatory cover letter is not required nor is an outline, summary, or abstract. Biographical information about the author is not required. Graphs

and line drawings may be used. No payment is made for accepted manuscripts. Reprints are not available.

Manuscript Disposition:

Receipt of a manuscript is acknowledged. Editorial decisions are made within 10 weeks. Accepted articles usually appear in print within 15 months. Unaccepted manuscripts are returned without criticism and/or suggestions.

Copyright:

Held by the International Society for General Semantics.

Additional Information:

The primary goal of the journal is to deal with problems of success and failure in communication as analyzed by psychologists, language experts, executives, foreign service officers, educators, and others who are dedicated to the improvement of communication. Because ETC is interdisciplinary in its readership, technical jargon must be kept to a minimum. In the text, refer to author by full name and descriptive label, not "as Maslow says," but "as the psychologist Abraham H. Maslow says."

ELEMENTARY ENGLISH

Subscription Data:

Published by the National Council of Teachers of English, 1111 Kenyon Road, Urbana, Illinois 61801. Issued monthly, September through May except December. Advertising is accepted. Circulation: 36,600. Subscription: $12.00 per year. Founded: 1924.

Editorial Address:

Iris M. Tiedt, Editor, Elementary English, 1111 Kenyon Road, Urbana, Illinois 61801.

Editorial Policy:

Includes articles on all phases of the language arts. The reading audience includes elementary teachers, and college professors of language arts, elementary education, and children's literature. Unsolicited articles are welcome. Twelve major articles are published per issue. Book reviews are included.

Manuscript Preparation:

Accepted manuscripts average from 1,500 to 3,500 words. One copy is required. Return postage and a self-addressed envelope are desired. Bibliographical procedure should follow the University of Chicago Manual of Style. Use one inch margins and double-space. Footnotes should be placed at the bottom of each page. A background or explanatory cover letter about the article is desired, but not an outline or summary. Biographical information about the author should be limited to a single sentence describing the author's current position. Illustrations, pictures, and graphs are occasionally used. No payment is made for accepted articles. A schedule of reprint costs is mailed to contributors whose works have been accepted.

Manuscript Disposition:

Acknowledgment of receipt of a manuscript is provided only if the manuscript is accepted, otherwise the article will be returned. Editorial decisions are made within two months. Accepted articles usually appear in print within one year after acceptance. Unaccepted manuscripts are returned without criticism.

Copyright:

Held by the National Council of Teachers of English. Release will be granted to the author for noncommercial republication.

*ENGLISH EDUCATION

Subscription Data:

Published by the National Council of Teachers of English, 1111 Kenyon Road, Urbana, Illinois 61801. Issued four times each year, in October, December, February, and May. Advertising is accepted. Circulation: 2,500. Subscription: $5.00 per year. Founded: 1970.

Editorial Address:

Dr. Ben F. Nelms, Editor, English Education, 2000 North Allen Drive, Columbia, Missouri 65201.

Editorial Policy:

Includes concise articles on all aspects of the preparation of teachers of English on the elementary, secondary, and college level. For further information, see English Education, V (December, 1973), 134-135. The reading audience includes college and university professors of English education, supervisors of English in high schools, elementary schools, and junior colleges, publishers, and teachers of English. Unsolicited manuscripts are welcome, but inquiries are appreciated. Five to eight major articles are published per issue. Book reviews are included only when assigned.

Manuscript Preparation:

Accepted manuscripts should not exceed 10 to 12 pages; brief "how-to-do-it" articles are encouraged and should average from three to five pages. One copy is required. Return postage and a self-addressed envelope are required if the manuscript is to be returned. Footnoting and bibliographical procedure should follow the MLA Style Sheet and should include documentation within the text whenever possible. A background or explanatory cover letter is not required nor is an outline, summary, or abstract. Biographical information about the author is not required, but encouraged. Illustrations, pictures, graphs, etc., are acceptable and flexible in regard to policy. No payment is made for accepted manuscripts. A copy of reprint policy will be provided upon request.

Manuscript Disposition:

Receipt of a manuscript is acknowledged. Editorial decisions are usually made within six weeks. Accepted articles usually appear in print within 12 months. Unaccepted manuscripts are returned only when accompanied by a stamped, self-addressed envelope. Criticism and/or suggestions are usually provided when manuscripts are provisionally accepted or when the author requests referees' critiques.

Copyright:
    Held by the National Council of Teachers of English.

ENGLISH JOURNAL

Subscription Data:
    Published by the National Council of Teachers of English, 1111
    Kenyon Road, Urbana, Illinois 61801. Issued monthly, September through May. Advertising is accepted. Circulation: 57,000.
    Subscription: $15.00 per year. Founded: 1912.
Editorial Address:
    The Editor, English Journal, P.O. Box 112, East Lansing,
    Michigan 48820.
Editorial Policy:
    Includes essays, articles, reviews, and editorials on theoretical
    and applied concern related to the teaching of English and the
    language arts in secondary schools. The reading audience includes English teachers, grades six to twelve, supervisory personnel, and college teachers of education. Unsolicited manuscripts are welcome. Eight to twelve major articles are published per issue. Book reviews are included.
Manuscript Preparation:
    Accepted manuscripts range from one to twenty pages with an
    average of 12 to 15 pages. One copy is required. Return postage and a self-addressed envelope are required. Bibliographical
    procedure should follow the MLA Style Sheet or the University
    of Chicago Manual of Style and should be scholarly consistent.
    A background or explanatory cover letter is not required nor is
    an outline, summary, or abstract. Biographical information
    about the author is not required. Photographs, drawings, and
    sketches related to essays are included. No payment is made
    for accepted manuscripts. Reprints are available from the
    printer at author's expense; a $50.00 charge for reprint permission is required from all others.
Manuscript Disposition:
    Receipt of a manuscript is acknowledged. Editorial decisions
    are made within nine weeks. Accepted articles usually appear
    in print within five to nine months. Unaccepted manuscripts are
    returned without criticism and/or suggestions.
Copyright:
    Held by the National Council of Teachers of English.
Additional Information:
    Prospective contributors may write for the English Journal style
    sheet which provides more guidance.

JOURNAL OF ENGLISH TEACHING TECHNIQUES

Subscription Data:
    Published by the Literature and American Language Department,
    Southwest Minnesota State College, Marshall, Minnesota 56258.
    Issued quarterly, in May, August, November, and February.

Advertising is not accepted. Circulation: 400. Subscription:
$3.00 per year; $5.50 for two years; $8.00 for three years;
$1.00 per issue. Founded: 1968.

Editorial Address:
Jack Hickerson or Delbert Wylder, Editors, Journal of English
Teaching Techniques, Literature and American Language Department, Southwest Minnesota State College, Marshall, Minnesota
56258.

Editorial Policy:
Includes articles dealing with the teaching of any aspect of English at all levels. The reading audience includes English teachers and students at all educational levels. Unsolicited manuscripts are welcome. Five or six major articles are published
per issue. Book reviews are included.

Manuscript Preparation:
Accepted manuscripts average approximately 2,500 words, but
policy is flexible. Two clear copies are required. Return
postage and a self-addressed envelope are required. Footnoting
and other bibliographical procedure should follow the MLA Style
Sheet. Use standard margins. A background or explanatory
cover letter is required, but not an outline, summary, or abstract. Pertinent biographical information about the author is
required. Use eight by ten inch glossy prints and black ink
drawings. No payment is made for accepted manuscripts. Authors are sent several complimentary copies of the issue in
which their article appears.

Manuscript Disposition:
Receipt of a manuscript is acknowledged. Editorial decisions
are made within ten weeks or sooner. Accepted articles usually
appear in print within three to six months. Unaccepted manuscripts are returned, without criticism and/or suggestions.

Copyright:
Held by the Literature and American Language Department,
Southwest Minnesota State College.

LANGUAGE

Subscription Data:
Published by the Linguistic Society of America, 1611 N. Kent
Street, Arlington, Virginia 22209. Issued four times each year,
in March, June, September, and December. Advertising is ac-
cepted. Circulation: 4,500. Subscription: $16.00 per year;
Free to Society members. Founded: 1924.

Editorial Address:
William Bright, Editor, Language, Department of Anthropology,
University of California, Los Angeles, California 90024.

Editorial Policy:
Includes articles and reports on all phases of research in linguistics. The reading audience includes linguists, educators,
and advanced students. Unsolicited articles are welcome, but
few from other than Society members can be used. Seven major
articles are published per issue. Book reviews are included.

Manuscript Preparation:
    No restrictions are placed upon manuscript length. One copy
    is required. Return postage and a self-addressed envelope are
    unnecessary. List footnotes alphabetically on a separate page;
    avoid their use where possible. All other bibliographical and
    format procedure should follow the LSA Publication Bulletin.
    Use wide margins and double-space. A background or explana-
    tory cover letter about the article is not desired, but an ab-
    stract is required. Biographical information about the author
    is unnecessary. Illustrations, pictures, graphs, etc., may be
    used. No payment is made for accepted articles. Reprints are
    available; 100 free copies are mailed to the author.
Manuscript Disposition:
    Receipt of a manuscript is acknowledged. Editorial decisions
    are made as soon as possible. Accepted articles usually appear
    in print within 18 months after acceptance. Unaccepted manu-
    scripts are returned, often with suggestions.
Copyright:
    Held by the Linguistic Society of America.

TEACHERS AND WRITERS COLLABORATIVE NEWSLETTER

Subscription Data:
    Published by the Teachers and Writers Collaborative, Inc., c/o
    P. S. 3, 490 Hudson Street, New York, New York 10014. Issued
    three times each year, in fall, winter, and spring. Advertising
    is not accepted. Circulation: 3, 000. Subscription: $5.00 for
    four issues; $1.50 per issue. Founded: 1967.
Editorial Address:
    The Editor, Teachers and Writers Collaborative Newsletter, c/o
    P. S. 3, 490 Hudson Street, New York, New York 10014.
Editorial Policy:
    Includes articles, diaries, other material by writers/artists, and
    teachers working on new approaches to the language arts in edu-
    cation. The reading audience includes teachers, teacher trainers,
    students, and writers/artists. Unsolicited manuscripts are wel-
    come. Eight major articles are published per issue. Book re-
    views are included.
Manuscript Preparation:
    Accepted manuscripts should not exceed 10,000 words. One copy
    is required. Return postage and a self-addressed envelope are
    required. Bibliographical procedure may vary. Double-space
    the manuscript. A background or explanatory cover letter is de-
    sired, but not an outline, summary, or abstract. Biographical
    information about the author is required. Illustrations, pictures,
    graphs, etc., should be in black on white background. No pay-
    ment is made for accepted manuscripts.
Manuscript Disposition:
    Receipt of a manuscript is not acknowledged. Editorial decisions
    are made within three weeks. Accepted articles usually appear
    in print within three months. Unaccepted manuscripts are re-
    turned, sometimes with criticism and/or suggestions.

Copyright:
    Held by the Teachers and Writers Collaborative, Inc.
Additional Information:
    Teachers and Writers Collaborative is a non-profit organization
    which sends writers and other artists into schools and other lo-
    cations to work with teachers and students to help break down
    the barriers which separate the arts from each other and from
    the remainder of a child's experience.

ADFL BULLETIN

Subscription Data:
Published by the Association of Departments of Foreign Languages, 62 Fifth Avenue, New York, New York 10011. Issued quarterly, in September, November, March, and May. Advertising is not accepted. Circulation: 1,200 except for September issue that includes 3,600. Subscription: $20.00 per year with membership in the Association; $5.00 for extras and libraries. Founded: 1969.

Editorial Address:
Richard Brod, Coordinator and Editor, ADFL Bulletin, 62 Fifth Avenue, New York, New York 10011.

Editorial Policy:
Includes articles on pedagogy, educational and professional policy, and administration, involving college and university foreign language departments in the United States and Canada. The reading audience includes chairmen of college and university foreign language departments. Unsolicited manuscripts are welcome. About eight major articles are published per issue. Book reviews are not included.

Manuscript Preparation:
Accepted manuscripts average eight to thirty double-spaced pages. The original is required. Return postage and a self-addressed envelope are not required. Bibliographical procedure should follow the MLA Style Sheet. Double-space manuscript and place footnotes on separate page. A background or explanatory cover letter is recommended, but not an outline, summary, or abstract. Biographical information about the author is not required; include only academic affiliation. Do not include photographs; there is a variable policy on graphs and tables. No payment is made for accepted manuscripts. Reprints may be ordered at author's expense.

Manuscript Disposition:
Receipt of a manuscript is acknowledged. Editorial decisions are made normally within four weeks. Accepted articles normally appear in print within nine months. Unaccepted manuscripts are returned, with criticism and/or suggestions provided in letter form.

Copyright:
Held by the Association of Departments of Foreign Languages.

Additional Information:
ADFL is a part of the Modern Language Association of America.

AMERICAN FOREIGN LANGUAGE TEACHER

Subscription Data:
  Published by the Advancement Press of America, Inc., 15 East
  Kirby, Suite 210, Detroit, Michigan 48202. Issued quarterly,
  in fall, winter, spring, and summer. Advertising is accepted;
  however, publisher reserves the right to refuse. Circulation:
  International. Subscription: $6.00 per year. Founded: 1970.
Editorial Address:
  The Editor, American Foreign Language Teacher, 15 East Kirby,
  Suite 210, Detroit, Michigan 48202.
Editorial Policy:
  Includes articles concerning the teaching of modern and classical
  languages. The reading audience includes language teachers at
  the high school and college level, people in libraries, publishing
  houses, institutes, etc. Unsolicited manuscripts are welcome.
  Approximately six major articles are published per issue. Book
  reviews are usually not included.
Manuscript Preparation:
  No restrictions are placed upon manuscript length. Two copies
  are required. Return postage and a self-addressed envelope
  are required. Bibliographical procedure should follow the MLA
  Style Sheet. List footnotes on last page. Double-space manuscripts and use at least 1/2 inch margin all around. A background or explanatory cover letter is helpful and recommended,
  but not always required. An outline, summary, or abstract of
  the article is not required. Biographical information about the
  author is required Illustrations, pictures, graphs, etc., are
  sometimes included, but each case is handled separately. No
  payment is made for accepted manuscripts. Reprints are available from the publisher at established rates.
Manuscript Disposition:
  Receipt of a manuscript is acknowledged; however, authors
  should expect some delay for evaluation. Accepted articles usually appear in print within six months or in accordance with
  the article's timeliness. Unaccepted manuscripts are returned,
  usually with criticism and suggestions.

ASSOCIATION OF TEACHERS OF JAPANESE.
JOURNAL-NEWSLETTER

Subscription Data:
  Published by the Association of Teachers of Japanese, 3068-70
  Frieze Building, University of Michigan, Ann Arbor, Michigan
  48104. Issued three times each year. Advertising is accepted.
  Circulation: 300. Subscription: $5.00 per year. Founded:
  1962.
Editorial Address:
  Marleigh Ryan, Editor, Journal-Newsletter of the Association
  of Teachers of Japanese, 316 Gilmore Hall, University of Iowa,
  Iowa City, Iowa 52242.

Editorial Policy:
   Includes articles on the Japanese language, literature, teaching
   methods and materials, and translations from the Japanese.
   The reading audience includes teachers of Japanese on all levels.
   Unsolicited manuscripts are welcome. Seven or eight major articles are published per issue. Book reviews are included.
Manuscript Preparation:
   No limitations are placed upon manuscript length. One copy is
   required. Return postage and a self-addressed envelope are
   not required. Bibliographical procedure should follow the Journal of Asian Studies Style Sheet. Use wide margins and double-
   space. A background or explanatory cover letter is not required
   nor is an outline, summary, or abstract. Biographical information about the author is required. Illustrations, pictures, graphs,
   etc., are limited only by photo offset process. No payment is
   made for accepted manuscripts. Reprints are available.
Manuscript Disposition:
   Receipt of a manuscript is acknowledged. Editorial decisions
   are made as soon as possible. Accepted articles usually appear
   in print within two to three months. Unaccepted manuscripts
   are returned with criticism and/or suggestions.
Copyright:
   Held by the Association of Teachers of Japanese.

FRENCH REVIEW

Subscription Data:
   Published by the American Association of Teachers of French,
   59 East Armory Avenue, Champaign, Illinois 61820. Issued six
   times each year, in October, December, February, March,
   April, and May. Advertising is accepted. Circulation: 13,400.
   Subscription: $10.00 per year. Founded: 1927.
Editorial Address:
   Jacques Hardré, Editor, French Review, P.O. Box 771, Chapel
   Hill, North Carolina 27514.
Editorial Policy:
   Includes articles on all phases of the French language, literature,
   and culture. The reading audience includes university, college,
   high school, and elementary school teachers. Unsolicited articles
   are welcome as long as the authors are members of the American Association of Teachers of French. Ten major articles are
   published per issue. Book or record reviews by members are
   included. Reviews are normally assigned, but unsolicited reviews of fewer than 500 words will be considered. When writing
   a review, the following data must always be furnished: author's
   name first, title, place of publication, publisher, date of publication, number of pages in the case of a book, size and "rpm" or
   "ips" in the case of discs or tapes, and price in the currency
   of the country of publication.
Manuscript Preparation:
   Manuscripts should not exceed 3,600 words, including footnotes.
   One copy is required. Return postage and a self-addressed

envelope are desired. Bibliographical procedure should follow the MLA Style Sheet. Use wide margins and double-space. Perfect legibility is essential, especially when the text is in French. Footnotes should be paragraphed on a separate page at the end of the article. Contributors to the special departments, especially reviewers of books and records, should study typographical arrangements used in the journal. A background or explanatory cover letter is desired, but not an outline or summary. A 200 word abstract in English of the article submitted, conforming to the "MLA Guidelines for Abstracting and Indexing Scholarly Articles," must be included. Illustrations are seldom used. No payment is made for accepted articles. Reprints are available from the printer.

Manuscript Disposition:
Receipt of a manuscript is acknowledged. Editorial decisions are made as soon as possible. Accepted articles usually appear in print within one year after acceptance. Unaccepted manuscripts are returned, often with criticism and suggestions.

Copyright:
Held by the American Association of Teachers of French.

Additional Information:
Contributions can be published either in English or French.

GERMAN QUARTERLY

Subscription Data:
Published by the American Association of Teachers of German, Inc., 239 Walnut Street, Philadelphia, Pennsylvania 19106. Issued five times each year, in January, March, May, September (membership directory), and November. Advertising is accepted. Circulation: 9,000. Subscription: $7.50 per year. Founded: 1927.

Editorial Address:
Professor William A. Little, Editor, German Quarterly, University of Virginia, Charlottesville, Virginia 22901.

Editorial Policy:
Includes articles on the German language and its literature, written in both German and English. The reading audience includes teachers of German at all levels of secondary school and college. Unsolicited manuscripts are welcome. Five or six major articles are published per issue. Book reviews are included.

Manuscript Preparation:
Accepted manuscripts average 10 to 30 double-spaced typewritten pages. The original typescript is preferred. Return postage and a self-addressed envelope are appreciated as a courtesy on the part of the author. Bibliographical procedure should follow the MLA Style Sheet. Use wide margins, double-space, and type legibly. A background or explanatory cover letter is desirable. No outline, summary, or abstract is required at the time of submission. Biographical information about the author is not required. Black and white pictures can be printed. No payment is made for accepted manuscripts. Author receives 10 free tear-sheets; reprint costs vary with the article length.

Manuscript Disposition:

Receipt of a manuscript is acknowledged. Editorial decisions are usually made within three months. Backlog of accepted manuscripts is large, but they usually appear in print within 18 months. Unaccepted manuscripts are returned, with valuable criticism from expert readers. Criticism is provided by outside readers.

Copyright:

Held by the American Association of Teachers of German, Inc.

HISPANIA

Subscription Data:

Published by the American Association of Teachers of Spanish and Portuguese. Issued five times each year, in March, May, September, October (membership issue), and December. Advertising is accepted. Circulation: 12,770. Subscription: Free with Association membership; $8.00 per year to others; $4.00 to students. Founded: 1917.

Editorial Address:

Irving P. Rothberg, Editor, Hispania, University of Massachusetts, Amherst, Massachusetts 01002.

Editorial Policy:

Includes articles on topics of interest to teachers of Spanish and Portuguese, with emphasis on the literary, linguistic, and methodological. The reading audience includes teachers of Spanish and Portuguese at all levels. Unsolicited articles from Association members are welcome. Ten major articles are published per issue. Book reviews are included. Some text books are re-reviewed by teachers who have used them.

Manuscript Preparation:

Papers on literary themes must be at least twelve pages, exclusive of notes. Accepted manuscripts average from seven to twenty double-spaced typewritten pages. One copy is required. Return postage and a self-addressed envelope are desired. Bibliographical procedure should follow the MLA Style Sheet or the Hispania style sheet printed in every issue. Use wide margins and double-space throughout. A background or explanatory cover letter about the article is desired, but not an outline or summary. Biographical information about the author is unnecessary. Use of illustrations, pictures, or graphs is discouraged. No payment is made for accepted articles. Reprints are available with costs determined by the printer.

Manuscript Disposition:

Receipt of a manuscript is acknowledged. Editorial decisions are made as soon as possible. Accepted articles usually appear in print within 24 months after acceptance. Unaccepted manuscripts are returned, often with criticism and/or suggestions.

Copyright:

Held by the American Association of Teachers of Spanish and Portuguese. Any article may be freely quoted if appropriate credit is given to Hispania. No article may be reproduced as a whole or in part except by special arrangement.

HISPANIC REVIEW

Subscription Data:
　Published by the University of Pennsylvania, Philadelphia, Pennsylvania 19174. Issued quarterly, in winter, spring, summer, and fall. Advertising is accepted. Circulation: Approximately 1,400. Subscription: $9.50 per year. Founded: 1933.

Editorial Address:
　The Editor, Hispanic Review, Williams Hall, University of Pennsylvania, Philadelphia, Pennsylvania 19174.

Editorial Policy:
　Includes articles on the Hispanic (Spanish and Portuguese -- both Peninsular and Latin-American) languages and literature. The reading audience includes teachers, professors, and students. Unsolicited articles are welcome. Five or six major articles are published per issue. Book reviews are included.

Manuscript Preparation:
　No policy regarding manuscript length has been established. Only the original typescript will be considered. Return postage (loose) and a self-addressed envelope are desired. Footnoting and other bibliographical procedure should follow the MLA Style Sheet (second edition, second printing, June, 1971). Use wide margins on a paper with a 1-1/2 inch top, bottom, and sides; include footnotes. Biographical information about the author is unnecessary. Illustrations, pictures, graphs, etc., are rarely used. No payment is made for accepted articles. Reprints are available; a cost sheet may be obtained through the office of the editor.

Manuscript Disposition:
　Receipt of a manuscript is acknowledged. Editorial decisions are made within two to six weeks. Accepted articles usually appear in print within 15 months after acceptance. Unaccepted manuscripts are returned, often with criticism and/or suggestions.

Copyright:
　Held by Hispanic Review.

ITALICA

Subscription Data:
　Published by the American Association of Teachers of Italian, Department of Italian, Rutgers University, New Brunswick, New Jersey 08903. Issued four times each year, in spring, summer, autumn, and winter. Advertising is accepted. Circulation: 1,900. Subscription: $8.00 per year. Founded: 1924.

Editorial Address:
　Professor Olga Ragusa, Editor, Italica, 601 Casa Italiana, Columbia University, New York, New York 10027.

Editorial Policy:
　Includes literary, linguistic, pedagogical, and cultural material which relates to Italy and to the Italian language. The reading audience includes teachers of Italian at all levels. Unsolicited articles are welcome. Four or five major articles are published per issue. Book reviews are included.

Manuscript Preparation:

Manuscripts should not exceed 20 typewritten pages. The original and one copy are required. Return postage and a self-addressed envelope are desired. Footnoting and other bibliographical procedure should follow the MLA Style Sheet. Place footnotes on a separate page. A background or explanatory cover letter about the article is not desired nor is an outline or summary. Biographical information about the author is usually unnecessary. Illustrations, pictures, and graphs will be published only upon special payment by the author. No payment is made for accepted articles. Reprints are available; authors can order offprints before publication.

Manuscript Disposition:

Receipt of a manuscript is not acknowledged unless solicited. Editorial decisions are made within one month. Accepted articles usually appear in print within 12 to 24 months after acceptance. Unaccepted manuscripts are returned; criticism and suggestions are not provided unless the article is accepted for publication.

Copyright:

Not copyrighted.

LANGUAGE LEARNING

Subscription Data:

Published by the Research Club in Language Learning, 2001 North University Building, University of Michigan, Ann Arbor, Michigan 48104. Issued twice each year. Advertising is not accepted. Circulation: 2,550. Subscription: $3.00 per year; $5.00 to libraries, schools, and other institutions. Founded: 1948.

Editorial Address:

The Editor, Language Learning, 2001 North University Building, University of Michigan, Ann Arbor, Michigan 48104.

Editorial Policy:

Includes articles on theoretical and practical research and experimentation in first and second language acquisition, psycholinguistics, socio-linguistics and other areas of applied linguistics. The reading audience includes high school and college language teachers, linguists, and other university faculty. Unsolicited articles are welcome. Eight to ten major articles are published per issue. Book reviews are included.

Manuscript Preparation:

Accepted manuscripts average from 12 to 25 double-spaced typewritten pages. One copy is required. Return postage and a self-addressed envelope are unnecessary. Footnoting and other bibliographical procedure should follow the LSA Publication Bulletin or the APA Publication Manual or Volume 22, Number 2, or the 1972 issue. Use wide margins and double-space throughout. A background or explanatory cover letter about the article is desired. An abstract is required in advance of or with submission of the finished manuscript. Biographical information about the author is not required, but is desirable. Illustrations, pictures, graphs, etc., are rarely used. No payment is made for accepted articles. Reprints are available; 50 free copies are mailed to authors upon publication.

Manuscript Disposition:
Receipt of a manuscript is acknowledged. Editorial decisions are made within six to eight weeks. Accepted articles appear in print within three to nine months after acceptance. Unaccepted manuscripts are returned, sometimes with criticism or suggestions.

Copyright:
Held by the Research Club in Language Learning.

MODERN LANGUAGE JOURNAL

Subscription Data:
Published by the National Federation of Modern Language Teachers Associations, Inc., 5500 Thirty-third Street, N.W., Washington, D.C. 20015. Issued six times each year, in September-October, November, December, January-February, March, and April. Advertising is accepted. Circulation: 9,241. Subscription: $6.00 per year; $8.00 to institutions and foreign. Founded: 1916.

Editorial Address:
Charles L. King, Editor, Modern Language Journal, University of Colorado, Boulder, Colorado 80302.

Editorial Policy:
Includes articles on all phases of foreign language learning and teaching, foreign cultures, literature, and comparative literature. Unsolicited articles are welcome. Usually five to eight major articles are published per issue. Solicited book reviews are included.

Manuscript Preparation:
No restrictions are placed upon manuscript length. One copy is required. Return postage and a self-addressed envelope are desired. Bibliographical procedure should follow the MLA Style Sheet. Place all footnotes and references at the end of the manuscript; they should be typed and double-spaced. Use a 1-1/2 inch left margin and double-space throughout. A background or explanatory cover letter about the article is desired, but not an outline or summary. Biographical information about the author will be solicited upon receipt of the manuscript. Illustrations, pictures, and graphs, in glossy original, India ink, and professional lettering, may be used. No payment is made for accepted articles. Reprints are available.

Manuscript Disposition:
Receipt of a manuscript is immediately acknowledged. Editorial decisions are made by the managing editor, with advice of selected readers, within six months. Accepted articles usually appear in print within six months after acceptance. Unaccepted manuscripts are returned, often with criticism and/or suggestions.

Copyright:
>Held by the National Federation of Modern Language Teachers
Associations, Inc.

MONATSHEFTE

Subscription Data:
>Published by the University of Wisconsin Press, Box 1379, Mad-
ison, Wisconsin 53701. Issued quarterly, in March, June, September, and December. Advertising is accepted. Circulation:
1,500. Subscription: $7.50 per year; $15.00 to institutions.
Founded: 1899.

Editorial Address:
>The Editor, Monatshefte, Department of German, Van Hise Hall,
University of Wisconsin, Madison, Wisconsin 53706.

Editorial Policy:
>Includes articles on German language, literature, and culture,
especially in its linguistic and literary relationships. The fall
issue includes Personalia: an annual listing of college and university teachers in the United States and Canada. The reading
audience includes mainly college and university teachers and
students. Unsolicited manuscripts are welcome. Five or six
major articles are published per issue. Book reviews are included.

Manuscript Preparation:
>Accepted manuscripts normally do not exceed 25 double-spaced
typewritten pages. Manuscripts in German are accepted, though
English is preferred. One copy is required. Return postage
and a self-addressed envelope are desired. Bibliographical procedure should follow the MLA Style Sheet. Footnotes should be
listed on a separate page at the end of the manuscript. Double-
space throughout the manuscript including lengthy quotes and footnotes and use an ample margin. A background or explanatory
cover letter is desired, but not an outline, summary, or abstract.
Abstracts should be 200 words or less in length and follow the
MLA Abstracts form. Biographical information about the author
is desired and should include the author's academic affiliation
and academic rank. Illustrations, pictures, graphs, etc., are
rarely used; special arrangement with the editor is required.
No payment is made for accepted manuscripts. Reprints are
available; a cost sheet is available from the editor.

Manuscript Disposition:
>Receipt of a manuscript is acknowledged. Editorial decisions
are made within two months. Accepted articles usually appear
in print within two years. Unaccepted manuscripts are returned
with criticism.

Copyright:
>Held by the University of Wisconsin Board of Regents.

Additional Information:
>Please note the special service provided to the profession: Per-
sonalia in the fall issue annually provides an up-to-date listing
of United States and Canadian college faculty by rank in their

respective departments, lists of promotions, visitors from abroad, and dissertations completed.

PMLA: PUBLICATIONS OF THE MODERN LANGUAGE ASSOCIA-TION OF AMERICA

Subscription Data:
Published by the Modern Language Association of America, 62 Fifth Avenue, New York, New York 10011. Issued six times each year, in January, March, May, September, October, and November. Advertising is accepted. Circulation: 33,500. Subscription: $25.00 per year to members in the Association; $7.00 to students; $18.00 foreign; $20.00 to libraries. Founded: 1884.

Editorial Address:
The Editor, PMLA, Modern Language Association of America, 62 Fifth Avenue, New York, New York 10011.

Editorial Policy:
Includes published articles on the modern languages and literatures which are of significant interest to the entire membership of the Association. Articles should normally (1) employ a widely applicable approach or methodology; or (2) use an interdisciplinary approach of importance to the interpretation of literature; or (3) treat a broad subject of theme; or (4) treat a major author or work; or (5) discuss a minor author or work in such a way as to bring insight to a major author, work, genre, period, or critical method. The reading audience includes members of the Association: college and university teachers of English and modern foreign languages and literatures. Only members of the Association may submit unsolicited manuscripts. Fifteen major articles are published per issue. Book reviews are not included.

Manuscript Preparation:
Accepted manuscripts average at least 2,500 words, but not more than 12,500. One copy is required. Return postage and a self-addressed envelope are not required. Footnoting, bibliographical procedure, and manuscript margin and spacing should follow the MLA Style Sheet. A background or explanatory cover letter is not required, but an outline, summary, or abstract is required on the standard form obtainable from the editor. Biographical information about the author is not required. There is no set policy on illustration, pictures, graphs, etc.; PMLA will include them if necessary. No payment is made for accepted manuscripts. Twenty-five "offprints" are supplied by the editorial office from disassembled issues which are stapled and rubber-stamped. Authors can purchase from the printer at cost professionally prepared offprints.

Manuscript Disposition:
Receipt of a manuscript is acknowledged. Editorial decisions are made within 60 days. Accepted articles usually appear in print within 24 months. Unaccepted manuscripts are returned with criticism and/or suggestions.

Copyright:
Held by the Modern Language Association.

Additional Information:

All articles are read by one consultant reader and one member of the advisory committee. If recommended by these readers, articles are forwarded to the editorial board for final decision. All articles must be written in English.

ROMANCE PHILOLOGY

Subscription Data:

Published by the University of California, Berkeley, California 94720. Issued quarterly, in February, May, August, and November. Advertising is not accepted. Circulation: 1,200. Subscription: $12.00 per year; $18.00 to institutions. Founded: 1947.

Editorial Address:

The Editor, Romance Philology, 4333 Dwinelle Hall, University of California, Berkeley, California 94720.

Editorial Policy:

Includes scholarly articles on all phases of Romance philology. The reading audience includes professors and graduate students. Unsolicited manuscripts are accepted only from subscribers. Five major articles are published per issue. Book reviews are included.

Manuscript Preparation:

Accepted manuscripts very rarely exceed 20 printed pages (unless institutionally subsidized). One copy is required; two are recommended. Return postage and a self-addressed envelope are not required, but are recommended. See a recent issue for bibliographical procedure. All footnotes must be typed on a separate page. Use wide margins and double-space. A background or explanatory cover letter about the article is desired in advance of or with submission of the finished manuscript. Biographical information about the author is required. Illustrations, graphs, etc., are rarely used. No payment is made for accepted articles. Reprints, including the complimentary quota and others at self-cost, are available through University of California Press.

Manuscript Disposition:

Receipt of a manuscript is acknowledged. Editorial decisions are made within one to two months. Accepted articles usually appear in print within twelve months after acceptance. Unaccepted manuscripts are returned, sometimes with criticism and/or suggestions.

Copyright:

Held by the Regents of the University of California.

RUSSIAN LANGUAGE JOURNAL

Subscription Data:

Published by N. P. Avtonomoff, 310 Twenty-ninth Avenue, San Francisco, California 94121. Sponsored by the Ivan V. Koulaieff

Educational Fund. Issued three times each year, in winter,
spring, and fall. Advertising is accepted. Circulation: 350 to
500. Subscription: $6.00 per year; $4.00 to students. Founded:
1947.
Editorial Address:
 Frank Ingram, Associate Editor, Russian Language Journal,
 717-A Wells Hall, Michigan State University, East Lansing,
 Michigan 48823.
Editorial Policy:
 Includes articles on the theory and methods of teaching the Russian language. The reading audience includes teachers and
 students at the university, college, and high school levels. Unsolicited articles are welcome. Five to seven major articles
 are published per issue. Book reviews are included.
Manuscript Preparation:
 Accepted manuscripts average from 1,000 to 3,200 words or
 from four to twelve manuscript pages. Return postage and a
 self-addressed envelope are unnecessary. Place all footnotes
 at the end of the article. Use wide margins and double-space.
 A background or explanatory cover letter about the article is
 required. Biographical information about the author is desired
 and should include a summary of his educational background and
 current position. No payment is made for accepted articles.
 Reprints are available; 15 free copies are mailed to the author.
Manuscript Disposition:
 Receipt of a manuscript is acknowledged. Editorial decisions
 are made within one to two months. Accepted articles usually
 appear in print within six months after acceptance.
Copyright:
 Held by N.P. Avtonomoff.

SCANDINAVIAN STUDIES

Subscription Data:
 Published by the Society for the Advancement of Scandinavian
 Study, Lawrence, Kansas 66044. Issued quarterly, in February,
 May, August, and November. Advertising is accepted. Circu-
 lation: 800. Subscription: $25.00 per year to libraries, in-
 stitutions, and non-members; $15.00 per year as part of the
 Society membership dues. Founded: 1911.
Editorial Address:
 Harald S. Naess, Editor, Scandinavian Studies, Department of
 Scandinavian, University of Wisconsin, 1370 Van Hise Hall,
 Madison, Wisconsin 53706.
Editorial Policy:
 Includes articles on the Scandinavian languages and literatures,
 and on the history, society, and culture of the North. The
 reading audience includes educators and students. Unsolicited
 manuscripts are welcome. Five major articles are published
 per issue. Book reviews are included.
Manuscript Preparation:
 Accepted manuscripts average from 20 to 25 double-spaced

typewritten pages. Two copies are desired. Return postage and
a self-addressed envelope are desired. Bibliographical procedure
should follow the MLA Style Sheet. Documentation should appear
in a Notes section following the article. Use wide margins and
double-space; single-space only in quoted passages of several
lines. A background or explanatory cover letter and a 200 word
abstract of the article are desired. Biographical information
about the author is required. Illustrations, pictures, graphs,
etc., are rarely used. No payment is made for accepted manuscripts; preference is given to contributions made by members
of the Society. Reprints are available; price list available
through Allen Press, Inc., Lawrence, Kansas.

Manuscript Disposition:
Receipt of a manuscript is acknowledged. Editorial decisions
are made within 10 weeks. Accepted articles usually appear in
print within one year after acceptance. Unaccepted manuscripts
are returned with criticism and/or suggestions for resubmission.

Copyright:
Held by the Society for the Advancement of Scandinavian Study.

SLAVIC AND EAST EUROPEAN JOURNAL

Subscription Data:
Published by the American Association of Teachers of Slavic and
East European Languages, AATSEEL of the United States, Inc.,
Foreign Languages 340, University of Arizona, Tucson, Arizona
85721. Issued quarterly, in March, June, September, and December. Advertising is accepted. Circulation: 2,000. Subscription: $15.00 per year with membership in the AATSEEL;
$7.50 to students for up to three years; $17.50 to institutions.
Founded: 1957.

Editorial Address:
Frank Y. Gladney, Editor, Slavic and East European Journal,
Department of Slavic Languages and Literatures, University of
Illinois, Urbana, Illinois 61801.

Editorial Policy:
Publishes articles on Slavic and East European languages, literatures, and language pedagogy. Includes no essays, but analytical or synthesizing studies which contain their own documentation and demonstrate a command of the basic materials of scholarship in the original languages. The reading audience includes
teachers and students of Slavic languages and literatures, plus
other interested individuals and organizations. Unsolicited manuscripts are welcome. Six to eight articles are published per
issue. Twenty-five to thirty book reviews are included in each
issue.

Manuscript Preparation:
Accepted manuscripts average 7,000 words or 20 pages of pica
typescript. The original copy is required. Return postage and
a self-addressed envelope are not required. Bibliographical
procedure should follow the current MLA Style Sheet or the
Slavic and East European Journal style sheet that is available

upon request. Footnotes should be double-spaced and placed
at the end of the article. Use 1-1/2 inch margins and double-
space throughout. A background or explanatory cover letter is
not required nor is an outline, summary, or abstract. Biographical information about the author is not required. No policies concerning illustrations, pictures, graphs, etc. No payment
is made for accepted manuscripts. Author receives a free copy
of the Journal plus 25 free offprints of the article and 12 of reviews, and additional copies may be purchased from the printer.

Manuscript Disposition:
Receipt of a manuscript is acknowledged. Editorial decisions
are made within two months. Accepted articles usually appear
in print within six to fifteen months. Unaccepted manuscripts
are returned with criticism and/or suggestions.

Copyright:
Held by the American Association of Teachers of Slavic and
East European Languages, Inc.

STUDIES IN PHILOLOGY

Subscription Data:
Published by the University of North Carolina Press, Box 2288,
Chapel Hill, North Carolina 27514. Issued five times each year,
in January, April, July, and October, plus a Texts & Studies
number in December. Advertising is accepted. Circulation:
2,000 to 2,200. Subscription: $10.00 per year. Founded:
1906.

Editorial Address:
The Editor, Studies in Philology, Department of English, Green-
law Hall, University of North Carolina, Chapel Hill, North Carolina 27514.

Editorial Policy:
Includes articles which relate to modern languages and literature,
and classical and medieval literature. The reading audience includes university professors, other scholars, and students. Unsolicited manuscripts are welcome. Six to eight major articles
are published per issue. Book reviews are not included.

Manuscript Preparation:
Accepted manuscripts average from 15 to 25 double-spaced typewritten pages. One copy is required. Return postage and a
self-addressed envelope are desired. Bibliographical procedure
should follow the MLA Style Sheet (use Roman numerals for
volume numbers). Use 1 to 1-1/2 inch margins and double-
space throughout. A background or explanatory cover letter is
not required. An abstract of not more than 150 words is required (e.g., MLA Abstract Form) and is published by MLA.
Biographical information about the author is not required. Illustrations, pictures, graphs, etc., are only used if absolutely
necessary. No payment is made for accepted manuscripts.
Twenty free copies are mailed to the author.

Manuscript Disposition:
Receipt of a manuscript is acknowledged. Editorial decisions

are made within one to three months. Accepted articles usually appear in print within 18 months. Unaccepted manuscripts are returned, sometimes with criticism and/or suggestions.

Copyright:

Held by the University of North Carolina Press.

CEA CRITIC

Subscription Data:
  Published by the College English Association, Inc., Centenary
  College, Shreveport, Louisiana 71104. Issued bimonthly, Novem-
  ber through May. Advertising is accepted. Circulation: 2,800.
  Subscription: $8.00 per year; $10.00 to libraries and institu-
  tions. Subscription includes the CEA Forum and occasional
  CEA chapbooks. Founded: 1939.
Editorial Address:
  The Editor, CEA Critic, Centenary College, Shreveport, Louisi-
  ana 71104.
Editorial Policy:
  Includes short critical essays which are directly useful in the
  teaching of literature. Poetry and fiction related to literature
  is also included. The reading audience includes college profes-
  sors of English and humanities. Unsolicited articles are welcome. Six major articles are published per issue. Book reviews are occasionally included.
Manuscript Preparation:
  Accepted articles average 2,000 words. One copy is required.
  Return postage and a self-addressed envelope are desired. Footnoting and other bibliographical procedure should follow the MLA
  Style Sheet. Footnotes should be incorporated into text. Use
  one inch margins and double-space all text material. A background or explanatory cover letter about the article is preferred,
  but not an outline or summary. Biographical information about
  the author is unnecessary. Illustrations, pictures, and graphs
  are used, but the author is responsible for preparing camera-
  ready copy. No payment is made for accepted articles. Reprints should be ordered in advance of publication.
Manuscript Disposition:
  Receipt of a manuscript is acknowledged. Editorial decisions
  are made within six to eight weeks. Accepted articles usually
  appear in print within six to twelve months after acceptance.
  Unaccepted manuscripts are returned, frequently with criticism
  and suggestions.
Copyright:
  Held by the College English Association.
Additional Information:
  This publication is reserved for members of the College English
  Association.

CHICAGO REVIEW

Subscription Data:
  Published by the University of Chicago, Chicago, Illinois 60637.
  Issued four times each year. Advertising is accepted with special rates for multiple insertions. Circulation: 5,000. Subscription: $5.00 per year; $9.50 for two years; $14.00 for
  three years. Founded: 1946.

Editorial Address:
  The Editor, Chicago Review, University of Chicago, 5757 South
  Drexel Avenue, Chicago, Illinois 60637.

Editorial Policy:
  Includes new fiction and poetry, illustrations, photography, essays, reviews, and interviews. The reading audience includes
  all 50 states of the United States, 39 foreign countries, and
  also many writers, professors of literature, library collections,
  and the interested public. Unsolicited manuscripts are very welcome. Several major articles are published per issue. Imagi-
  native book reviews are encouraged.

Manuscript Preparation:
  No restrictions are placed upon manuscript length. One copy is
  required. Return postage and a self-addressed envelope are always required. Bibliographical procedure is not restrictive,
  authors should generally stay within conventional stylistic frames
  only in bibliography, not in text. Dry, academic articles are not
  encouraged and are downgraded. Use one inch margins and
  double-space. A background or explanatory cover letter is not
  required, but is used only if the author feels it is necessary.
  An outline, summary, or abstract of the article is not required,
  but could be helpful. Biographical information about the author
  should be included as it is used in publication. Illustrations,
  pictures, graphs, etc., are always welcome, especially illustrations of high quality. The payment program is currently being
  expanded. There is no standard reprint policy.

Manuscript Disposition:
  Receipt of a manuscript is not acknowledged. Editorial decisions
  are made within four to eight weeks. Accepted articles usually
  appear in print within two to four months. Unaccepted manuscripts are always returned when appropriate postage and envelope are provided. Criticism and/or suggestions are often provided.

Copyright:
  Held by the Chicago Review. After publication the author can
  discuss transfer.

Additional Information:
  Chicago Review is a literary quarterly founded 29 years ago and
  has always sought out the innovative, experimental in writing.
  The Review was the first to publish excerpts from Naked Lunch,
  and brought out the first American material on concrete poetry.
  This anthology has been expanded and revised by a major publishing company. Any submissions or inquiries are welcome.

COLLEGE LITERATURE

Subscription Data:
  Published by West Chester State College, West Chester, Pennsylvania 19380. Issued three times each year, in winter, spring,
  and fall. Advertising is not accepted. Circulation: Not determined. Subscription: $3.00 per year; $5.00 for two years.
  Founded: 1974.

Editorial Address:
  Dr. Bernard Oldsey, Editor, College Literature, West Chester
  State College, West Chester, Pennsylvania 19380.

Editorial Policy:
  Includes articles dealing with those literary works most often
  taught in American colleges and universities; works which amount
  to a canon of Western culture from Homer to the present. The
  articles should contribute something to the actual teaching of literature courses. The reading audience includes mainly college
  and university teachers of literature, English language, and foreign languages. Unsolicited manuscripts are welcome. Six
  major articles are published per issue. Book reviews are included.

Manuscript Preparation:
  Accepted manuscripts average up to 20 to 25 pages in usual dou-
  ble-space typescript presentation. Two copies are required.
  Return postage and a self-addressed envelope are required.
  Footnoting and bibliographical procedure should follow the MLA
  Style Sheet. Endnotes are preferred over footnotes; also, prefer
  citations parenthetically within the text where possible. A background or explanatory cover letter is required, but not an outline, summary, or abstract until after acceptance of the article.
  Biographical information about the author is required. Illustrations, pictures, graphs, etc., are not pertinent. No payment
  is made for accepted manuscripts. Reprints are available at
  50% of the cost to the journal.

Manuscript Disposition:
  Receipt of a manuscript is acknowledged. Editorial decisions
  are made within six to ten weeks. Accepted articles usually
  appear in print within six to nine months. Unaccepted manuscripts are returned if accompanied by postage. Criticism and/
  or suggestions are sometimes provided.

Copyright:
  Held by College Literature at West Chester State College.

Additional Information:
  College Literature articles will be placed in the MLA abstract
  bank.

CRITIQUE: STUDIES IN MODERN FICTION

Subscription Data:
  Published by Critique, Department of English, Georgia Institute

of Technology, Atlanta, Georgia 30332. Issued three times each year, in August, December, and April. Advertising is not accepted. Circulation: 1,300. Subscription: $7.50 per year. Founded: 1956.

Editorial Address:
The Editor, Critique: Studies In Modern Fiction, Department of English, Georgia Institute of Technology, Atlanta, Georgia 30332.

Editorial Policy:
Includes critical essays on contemporary novels and novelists, particularly those who are alive and without great reputations. The reading audience includes scholars, critics, educators, and students. Unsolicited manuscripts are welcome. Eight major articles are published per issue. Book reviews are sometimes included.

Manuscript Preparation:
Accepted manuscripts average from 15 to 20 double-spaced typewritten pages. One copy is required. Return postage and a self-addressed envelope are desired. Place all footnotes on a separate page at the end of the article. Use normal margins and double-space. Bibliographical procedure should follow the MLA Style Sheet. A background or explanatory cover letter about the article is not required nor is an outline or summary. Biographical information about the author is not required. Illustrations, pictures, graphs, etc., cannot be used. No payment is made for accepted articles. Five free copies of the journal and 20 to 25 reprints are mailed to the author.

Manuscript Disposition:
Receipt of a manuscript is not acknowledged. Editorial decisions are made within one to four months. Accepted articles usually appear in print within one year after acceptance. Unaccepted manuscripts are returned, often with criticism or suggestions.

Copyright:
Held by Critique. Permission to reprint should be corroborated by the author when possible.

Additional Information:
Essays on established writers of the 20th century (Conrad, James, Joyce, Lawrence, Faulkner, Hemingway) are only rarely accepted; essays on writers who are alive and without great reputations are preferred.

ENGLISH RECORD

Subscription Data:
Published by New York State English Council, Union College, Schenectady, New York 11508. Issued quarterly. Circulation: 3,000. Subscription: $10.00 per year. Founded: 1948.

Editorial Address:
Richard L. Knudson, Editor, English Record, State University College, Oneonta, New York 13820.

Editorial Policy:
Includes articles about English education from grades kinder-

garten through college. The reading audience includes kinder-
garten through college language arts teachers. Unsolicited manuscripts are welcome. Ten major articles are published per
issue. Book reviews are included.

Manuscript Preparation:
   Accepted manuscripts average 1,500 to 5,000 words. One copy
is required. Return postage and a self-addressed envelope are
required. Bibliographical procedure should follow the MLA Style
Sheet. Use footnotes in text, and margins should be standard
size. A background or explanatory cover letter is not required
nor is an outline, summary, or abstract. Biographical information about the author is not required. Illustrations, pictures,
graphs, etc., are acceptable. No payment is made for accepted
manuscripts. The author contacts the printer for reprints.

Manuscript Disposition:
   Receipt of a manuscript is acknowledged. Editorial decisions
are made within six to eight weeks. Accepted articles usually
appear in print within two to six months. Unaccepted manuscripts are returned without criticism and/or suggestions.

Copyright:
   Held by English Record.

EXPLICATOR

Subscription Data:
   Published by the Explicator Literary Foundation, Inc., Virginia
Commonwealth University, 901 West Franklin Street, Richmond,
Virginia 23220. Issued 10 times each year, September through
June. Advertising is not accepted. Circulation: 2,600. Sub-
scription: $3.00 per year; $3.50 foreign, including Canada.
Founded: 1942.

Editorial Address:
   The Editor, Explicator, Virginia Commonwealth University, 901
West Franklin Street, Richmond, Virginia 23220.

Editorial Policy:
   Accepted articles average two journal pages. Contributions relevant to "explication de texte" in prose or poetry will be considered for publication. Materials concerned with genesis, par-
allelism, or biography cannot be accepted unless they have a
direct bearing upon interpretation of the text. The reading audience includes college professors, high school teachers, and
students of literature. Unsolicited articles are welcome. Eight
major articles are published per issue. Book reviews are not
included.

Manuscript Preparation:
   Accepted manuscripts average four double-spaced typewritten
pages. Two copies are required. Return postage and self-
addressed envelope are desired. Bibliographical procedure
should follow the MLA Style Sheet. Avoid use of footnotes and
use a 70 space line. A background or explanatory cover letter
about the article is not desired nor is an outline or summary.
An abstract is required only after acceptance. Biographical

information about the author is unnecessary. Illustrations, pictures, and graphs cannot be used. No payment is made for accepted articles. Ten free reprints are mailed to authors; a charge of $.15 per copy is made for additional reprints.

Manuscript Disposition:
Receipt of a manuscript is acknowledged. Editorial decisions are made within six months. Accepted articles usually appear in print approximately 12 months after acceptance. Unaccepted manuscripts are often returned, sometimes with criticism and/or suggestions.

Copyright:
Held by the Explicator Literary Foundation, Inc.

Additional Information:
Articles must be in English and explanatory in nature. The editor reserves the right to make stylistic changes necessary for format conformity and to omit matter not strictly relevant if space limitations so require.

GEORGIA REVIEW

Subscription Data:
Published by the University of Georgia, Lustrat House, University of Georgia, Athens, Georgia 30602. Issued quarterly, on the 15th of March, June, September, and December. Advertising is accepted. Circulation: 1,800. Subscription: $3.00 per year; $5.00 for two years. Founded: 1947.

Editorial Address:
The Editor, Georgia Review, Lustrat House, University of Georgia, Athens, Georgia 30602.

Editorial Policy:
Includes articles on literature, history, and ideas; fiction, poetry, and book reviews are in each issue. Heavily specialized writing is avoided. The reading audience includes the informed general reader. Unsolicited manuscripts are welcome. Five to eight major articles, depending on length, are published per issue. Book reviews are included.

Manuscript Preparation:
Accepted manuscripts average up to 12,000 words for articles on literary criticism and general learned interest, up to 4,500 words for fiction, and poetry of any length is considered. One copy is required. Return postage and a self-addressed envelope are required. Bibliographical procedure should follow the MLA Style Sheet. Avoid the use of footnotes; when necessary they should be listed at the end of the article. Use one inch margins and double-space. A background or explanatory cover letter is not required nor is an outline, summary, or abstract. Biographical information about the author is not required unless the material is accepted for publication. Illustrations, pictures, graphs, etc., are not used. Payment is made upon publication at the rate of $.01 per word for prose and $.50 per line for poetry. The contributor pays for reprints ordered. Each contributor receives two complimentary copies of the issue in which the work appears.

Manuscript Disposition:
Receipt of a manuscript is not acknowledged. Editorial decisions are made within an average of one to six weeks. Accepted articles usually appear in print within six to nine months. Unaccepted manuscripts are returned when accompanied by a stamped self-addressed envelope. Criticism and/or suggestions are provided at the editor's discretion.

Copyright:
Held by the University of Georgia.

JOURNAL OF ENGLISH AND GERMANIC PHILOLOGY

Subscription Data:
Published by the Graduate College, University of Illinois, Urbana, Illinois 61801. Issued four times each year, in January, April, July, and October. Advertising is accepted. Circulation: 1,800. Subscription: $7.50 per year. Founded: 1897.

Editorial Address:
The Editor, Journal of English and Germanic Philology, 100 English Building, University of Illinois-Urbana, Urbana, Illinois 61801.

Editorial Policy:
Includes scholarly and critical essays on English, German, and Scandinavian literature. The reading audience includes teachers and students of literature. Unsolicited articles are welcome. Five or six major articles are published per issue. Book reviews are included.

Manuscript Preparation:
Accepted articles average from 15 to 20 double-spaced typewritten pages. One copy is required. Return postage and a self-addressed envelope are desired. Place all footnotes at the end of the manuscript. Bibliographical procedure should follow the MLA Style Sheet. Avoid use of corrasable bond paper. Use wide margins and double-space throughout. A background or explanatory cover letter about the article is desired, but not an outline or summary. Biographical information about the author is unnecessary. Illustrations, pictures, and graphs should not be used. No payment is made for accepted articles. Reprints are available.

Manuscript Disposition:
Receipt of a manuscript is acknowledged. Editorial decisions are made within three months. Accepted articles usually appear in print within 12 to 18 months after acceptance. Unaccepted manuscripts are returned, often with criticism or suggestions.

Copyright:
Held by the Board of Trustees of the University of Illinois.

MODERN FICTION STUDIES

Subscription Data:
Published by the Department of English, Purdue University, West Lafayette, Indiana 47907. Issued four times each year,

in spring, summer, autumn, and winter. Advertising is not accepted. Circulation: 4,300. Subscription: $4.00 per year; $5.00 to libraries and institutions; $5.00 foreign. Founded: 1955.

Editorial Address:

The Editor, Modern Fiction Studies, Department of English, Purdue University, West Lafayette, Indiana 47907.

Editorial Policy:

Includes studies of modern American, British, and continental fiction since 1880. The reading audience includes professors, critics, and students. Unsolicited manuscripts are welcome. Seven to ten articles and notes are published per issue. Book reviews are included.

Manuscript Preparation:

Accepted manuscripts average from 3,000 to 5,000 words; none may exceed 10,000 words. One copy is required. Return postage and a self-addressed envelope are desired. Footnotes and other bibliographical procedure should follow the latest MLA Style Sheet. Use wide margins and double-space. A background or explanatory cover letter is sometimes useful. Accepted articles and notes must be abstracted for the MLA Abstract Center. Specific biographical information about the author is requested after a manuscript has been accepted for publication. Illustrations, pictures, graphs, etc., are occasionally used. No payment is made for accepted manuscripts. Two free copies of the journal and 20 to 40 off-prints are mailed to the contributors.

Manuscript Disposition:

Receipt of a manuscript is acknowledged. Editorial decisions are made within two to four months. Articles usually appear in print within one to three years after acceptance. Unaccepted manuscripts are returned, rarely with criticism and/or suggestions.

Copyright:

Held by the Purdue University Research Foundation.

NINETEENTH-CENTURY FICTION

Subscription Data:

Published by the University of California Press, Berkeley, California. Issued four times each year, in March, June, September, and December. Advertising is accepted. Circulation: 2,300. Subscription: $8.00 per year; $10.00 to institutions. Founded: 1945.

Editorial Address:

G. B. Tennyson, Editor, Nineteenth-Century Fiction, Department of English, Rolfe Hall 2319, UCLA, Los Angeles, California 90024.

Editorial Policy:

Includes articles on scholarly and critical articles and notes on nineteenth-century British and American fiction (English-language only). The reading audience includes scholars, teachers, students, and collectors. Unsolicited manuscripts are welcome. Six major articles are published per issue; two or three notes are published per issue. Book reviews are included.

Manuscript Preparation:

Accepted manuscripts should not exceed 25 typewritten double-spaced pages. One copy is required. Return postage and a self-addressed envelope are required. Bibliographical procedure should follow the revised MLA Style Sheet. All footnotes should be on a separate page, double-spaced throughout. Avoid oversize and legal-size paper. A background or explanatory cover letter is not required, nor is an outline, summary, or abstract required for submissions. Abstracts are required for articles after acceptance. Biographical information is required. Illustrations and graphs are very rarely used. No payment is made for accepted manuscripts. Twenty-five gratis offprints are provided authors of articles; authors of notes receive 10 tear sheets. Reprint rights are negotiated individually with the University of California Press.

Manuscript Disposition:

Receipt of a manuscript is acknowledged. Editorial decisions are made within three to four months. Accepted articles usually appear in print within one year to a year and a half. Unaccepted manuscripts are returned with criticism and/or suggestions.

Copyright:

Held by the Regents of the University of California.

Additional Information:

Most submissions are on a half-dozen major authors (see the September 1972 Nineteenth-Century Fiction for a breakdown on submissions), but submissions on all authors of the period are welcome. Also included are essays that treat more than one author or work or a theme and that show broad critical and background knowledge.

NOTRE DAME ENGLISH JOURNAL

Subscription Data:

Published by the Notre Dame English Association, Box 91, Notre Dame, Indiana 46556. Issued two times each year, in fall and spring. Advertising is not presently accepted. Circulation: 300. Subscription: $2.50 per year; $1.25 per issue. Founded: 1962.

Editorial Address:

The Editor, Notre Dame English Journal, 1116 Memorial Library, University of Notre Dame, Notre Dame, Indiana 46556.

Editorial Policy:

Includes primarily critical articles and book reviews on English/American language and literature. The reading audience includes college and university level teachers and students. Unsolicited manuscripts are welcome. Approximately five major articles are published per issue. Book reviews are included, but are usually assigned by the editors.

Manuscript Preparation:
    Accepted manuscripts average approximately 10 to 15 pages.
    One copy is required, but two are helpful. Return postage and
    a self-addressed envelope are required. Bibliographical proce-
    dure should follow the MLA Style Sheet. Double-space through-
    out including footnotes at the end of the manuscript. A back-
    ground or explanatory cover letter is not required, but an ab-
    stract is desired. Biographical information about the author is
    not required. Graphs or artwork are not acceptable. No pay-
    ment is made for accepted manuscripts. Contributors receive
    two copies of the issue and approximately 10 reprints.
Manuscript Disposition:
    Receipt of a manuscript is acknowledged. Editorial decisions
    are made within eight to twelve weeks. Accepted articles usual-
    ly appear in print within six to twelve months. Unaccepted man-
    uscripts are returned only if stamped self-addressed envelope is
    provided. Criticism and/or suggestions are usually not provided.
Copyright:
    Held by the Notre Dame English Association.
Additional Information:
    The Notre Dame English Journal is primarily a journal of liter-
    ary criticism; occasionally, it carries articles dealing with edu-
    cation-related topics.

QUARTERLY REVIEW OF LITERATURE

Subscription Data:
    Published by the Quarterly Review of Literature, 26 Haslet Ave-
    nue, Princeton, New Jersey 08540. Issued two times each year,
    two double issues. Advertising is accepted. Circulation: 2,000.
    Subscription: $5.00 per year. Founded: 1943.
Editorial Address:
    The Editor, Quarterly Review of Literature, 26 Haslet Avenue,
    Princeton, New Jersey 08540.
Editorial Policy:
    Includes creative writings in poetry and fiction. The Quarterly
    Review of Literature is a literary anthology of creative work and
    has for over the past 25 years, presented writings of many of
    the most significant foreign and American writers of our time.
    In addition to poems, short stories, and distinguished transla-
    tions, this journal features longer pieces including plays, nov-
    ellas, and long poems. The reading audience includes educators,
    literary scholars, students, and the general reading public. Un-
    solicited manuscripts are welcome if the author is familiar with
    the type of material printed in past issues. Book reviews are
    not included.
Manuscript Preparation:
    Check copies of the past issues for the length of accepted manu-
    scripts. One copy in the original typescript is required. Re-
    turn postage and a self-addressed envelope are required. Pay-
    ment is made for accepted manuscripts.
Manuscript Disposition:
    Receipt of a manuscript is not acknowledged. Editorial deci-

sions are made within several months. Unaccepted manuscripts are returned if the envelope and postage are included.

Copyright:
Held by the Quarterly Review of Literature.

Additional Information:
The contributor should be familiar with Quarterly Review of Literature issues before submitting manuscripts. Sample back issues are available for $1.50.

RENASCENCE

Subscription Data:
Published by the Catholic Renascence Society, Executive Secretary, Viterbo College, LaCrosse, Wisconsin 54601. Issued quarterly, in October, December, March, and June. Advertising is accepted. Circulation: 825. Subscription: $6.00 per year. Founded: 1948.

Editorial Address:
John D. MaCabe, Editor, Renascence, Marquette University, Milwaukee, Wisconsin 53233.

Editorial Policy:
Includes critical articles devoted to the study of values in literature. Primary emphasis is on modern and contemporary British and American writers; considerable attention is given to the tradition of French literature. The reading audience includes educators and students. Unsolicited manuscripts are welcome. Five to seven major articles are published per issue. Book reviews are not included.

Manuscript Preparation:
Accepted manuscripts average eight to fifteen double-spaced elite-typewritten pages. One copy is required. Return postage and a self-addressed envelope are desired. Bibliographical procedure should follow the MLA Style Sheet. Incorporation of references in the text is encouraged. Use 1-1/2 inch margins and double-space. A background or explanatory cover letter is not required and an outline, summary, or abstract is required only after acceptance for publication. Illustrations, pictures, graphs, etc., are rarely used. No payment is made for accepted manuscripts. Reprints are available; inquiries should be sent to the office of the editor.

Manuscript Disposition:
Receipt of a manuscript is acknowledged. Editorial decisions are made within six to eight weeks. Accepted articles usually appear in print within eighteen months after acceptance. Unaccepted manuscripts are returned with criticism and/or suggestions.

Copyright:
Held by the Catholic Renascence Society.

Additional Information:
Scholars may, without prior permission, quote from Renascence to document their own work, when proper acknowledgment is made. This waiver does not extend to the quotation of substantial parts of articles nor to direct quotations presented in

primary material. Where material is to be reproduced in an anthology or collection of essays undertaken with reasonable expectation of profit, permission to reprint must be obtained and a fee will be charged. Request for permission to reprint should be made to the editor, who will seek the author's concurrence.

SEWANEE REVIEW

Subscription Data:
 Published by the University of the South, Sewanee, Tennessee 37375. Issued four times each year, in January, April, July, and October. Advertising is accepted. Circulation: 4,000 United States; 700 foreign. Subscription: $7.00 per year domestic and foreign; $13.00 for two years; $18.00 for three years. Founded: 1892.

Editorial Address:
 The Editor, The Sewanee Review, University of the South, Sewanee, Tennessee 37375.

Editorial Policy:
 Includes articles on literary and related subjects, original verse and short fiction, and book reviews. The reading audience includes teachers, students, and others with interest in literature. Unsolicited manuscripts are welcome. Five or six major articles are published per issue. Book reviews are included.

Manuscript Preparation:
 Accepted manuscripts average 2,000 to 10,000 words. One copy, preferably an original, is required. Sufficient return postage and a self-addressed envelope are required. Bibliographical procedure should follow any reputable manual of style. Avoid or limit the use of footnotes wherever possible. A background or explanatory cover letter is not required nor is an outline, summary, or abstract. Biographical information about the author is required when galley proofs are checked and returned by the author. Illustrations, pictures, graphs, etc., are rarely used. Payment is made upon publication: $12.00 per printed page for essays and stories; $.60 per line for poetry. Reprints are not available.

Manuscript Disposition:
 Receipt of a manuscript is not acknowledged unless author requests and supplies a stamped envelope. Editorial decisions are made within two to ten weeks. Accepted articles appearance in print varies with editorial need. Unaccepted manuscripts are returned if postage has been supplied. Criticism and/or suggestions are rarely provided.

Copyright:
 Held by the University of the South.

STUDIES IN SHORT FICTION

Subscription Data:
 Published by Newberry College, 2100 College Street, Newberry,

South Carolina 29108. Issued four times each year, in October, January, April, and July. Advertising is not accepted. Circulation: 1,300. Subscription: $8.00 per year; $2.50 per issue. Founded: 1963.

Editorial Address:
The Editor, Studies in Short Fiction, 2100 College Street, Newberry, South Carolina 29108.

Editorial Policy:
Includes articles on fiction, "explication de texte," and short fiction. The reading audience includes college and university students and faculty, plus a growing number of high school students. Unsolicited articles are welcome. Forty articles are published per issue. Book reviews are included.

Manuscript Preparation:
Accepted manuscripts average from 12 to 15 double-spaced typewritten pages. One copy is required. Return postage and a self-addressed envelope are desired. Biographical procedure should follow the MLA Style Sheet. Footnotes may be placed at the bottom of each page or at the end of the article. Use a 1-1/2 inch left margin, one inch right, top, and bottom margins, and double-space throughout. A background or explanatory cover letter about the article is not desired nor is an outline or summary. Biographical information about the author is desired and should include a summary of his current position, publications, and works in progress. Illustrations, pictures, graphs, etc., may be used. No payment is made for accepted articles. Reprints are available.

Manuscript Disposition:
Receipt of a manuscript is acknowledged. Most editorial decisions are made within one month. Accepted articles usually appear in print within six months after acceptance. Unaccepted manuscripts are returned with criticism and/or suggestions if article is to be reconsidered when revised.

Copyright:
Held by Newberry College.

SYMPOSIUM

Subscription Data:
Published by the Department of Romance Languages, Syracuse University, Syracuse, New York 13210 (with the cooperation of the Centro de Estudios Hispanicos). Issued quarterly, in spring, summer, fall, and winter. Advertising is accepted. Circulation: 1,000. Subscription: $8.00 per year. Founded: 1946.

Editorial Address:
Secretary of the Editorial Board, Symposium, 205 H.B. Crouse Hall, Syracuse University, Syracuse, New York 13210.

Editorial Policy:
Includes articles which relate to modern foreign literature of all periods. The reading audience includes professors of modern foreign literature, other educators, and students. Unsolicited articles are welcome. Six or seven major articles are published per issue. Book reviews are included.

Manuscript Preparation:

No policy on manuscript length has been established. At least one copy is required. Return postage and a self-addressed envelope are necessary. Footnoting and other bibliographical procedure should follow the MLA Style Sheet. Use wide margins and double-space. A background or explanatory cover letter about the article is not desired nor is an outline or summary. Biographical information about the author is unnecessary. Illustrations are never used. No payment is made for accepted articles. Reprints are not available.

Manuscript Disposition:

Receipt of a manuscript is acknowledged. Editorial decisions are made as soon as possible, with time depending upon the number of editorial opinions sought. Accepted articles usually appear in print within one year after acceptance. Unaccepted manuscripts are returned with readers' criticism made available to authors.

Copyright:

Held by the Syracuse University Press.

TWENTIETH CENTURY LITERATURE

Subscription Data:

Published by the Immaculate Heart College, 2021 North Western Avenue, Los Angeles, California 90027. Issued quarterly, in January, April, July, and October. Advertising is not accepted. Circulation: 2,000. Subscription: $6.00 per year; $8.00 to institutions. Founded: 1955.

Editorial Address:

The Editor, Twentieth Century Literature, Immaculate Heart College, 2021 North Western Avenue, Los Angeles, California 90027.

Editorial Policy:

Articles should be on all aspects of modern and contemporary literature, including articles in English on writers in other languages. Unsolicited manuscripts are welcome. Four to six major articles are published per issue. Brief notes and unsolicited book reviews are not generally accepted.

Manuscript Preparation:

No limitations are placed upon manuscript length. One copy is required. Return postage and a self-addressed envelope are required. Manuscripts should be double-spaced (including quotations and footnotes) and follow an acceptable scholarly format-- the MLA Style Sheet is recommended. Footnotes should be numbered consecutively at the end of the article. A background or explanatory cover letter is not required nor is an outline, summary, or abstract. Biographical information about the author is not required. Payment is not made for accepted manuscripts. Permission for reprints is freely granted. Authors will receive 25 copies of their articles; additional copies are available at cost.

Manuscript Disposition:

Receipt of a manuscript is acknowledged. Editorial decisions

are made within eight to twelve weeks. Accepted articles usually appear in print within eight to twelve months. Unaccepted
manuscripts are returned with criticism and/or suggestions.
Copyright:
    Held by the Immaculate Heart College, Press.

WESTERN HUMANITIES REVIEW

Subscription Data:
    Published by the University of Utah, Salt Lake City, Utah 84112.
    Issued quarterly, in winter, spring, summer, and autumn. Ad-
    vertising is by exchange only, or $100 per page. Circulation:
    1, 000. Subscription: $5.00 per year. $5.50 foreign. Founded:
    1947.
Editorial Address:
    The Editor, Western Humanities Review, Orson Spencer Hall
    331, University of Utah, Salt Lake City, Utah 84112.
Editorial Policy:
    Includes articles on poetry, short stories, articles on the human-
    ities; book, film and poetry reviews. The reading audience in-
    cludes university students and faculty and well-educated persons.
    Unsolicited manuscripts are welcome. Three major articles are
    published per issue. Only solicited book reviews are included.
Manuscript Preparation:
    Accepted manuscripts should not exceed 5, 000 words. One copy
    is required. Return postage and a self-addressed envelope are
    required. Bibliographical procedure should follow the MLA
    Style Sheet. Use standard margins and double-space. A back-
    ground or explanatory cover letter is not required nor is an out-
    line, summary, or abstract. Biographical information about
    the author is required if the article is accepted. Illustrations,
    pictures, graphs, etc., are not used. Payment is made for ac-
    cepted manuscripts. Twenty-five complimentary copies are given
    to all contributors; reprints for articles and stories are avail-
    able at cost.
Manuscript Disposition:
    Receipt of a manuscript is not acknowledged. Editorial decisions
    are made within four to six weeks. Accepted articles usually
    appear in print within six months. Unaccepted manuscripts are
    returned without criticism or suggestions.
Copyright:
    Held by the Western Humanities Review.
Additional Information:
    The copyright can be transferred to the author upon request.
    Permission to reprint is also granted, but the Western Human-
    ities Review retains all reprint rights.

MATHEMATICS

AMERICAN MATHEMATICAL MONTHLY

Subscription Data:
Published by the Mathematical Association of America, 1225 Connecticut Avenue, N. W., Washington, D. C. 20036. Issued 10 times each year, in January, February, March, April, May, June-July, August-September, October, November, and December. Advertising is accepted. Circulation: 23,000. Subscription: $18.00 per year. Founded: 1894.

Editorial Address:
Professor Alex Rosenberg, Editor, American Mathematical Monthly, Department of Mathematics, Cornell University, Ithaca, New York 14850.

Editorial Policy:
Includes articles on all phases of mathematics. The reading audience includes college and high school teachers, graduate students, and industrial mathematicians. Unsolicited articles are welcome. Three to five major articles are published per issue. Book reviews are included.

Manuscript Preparation:
Accepted manuscripts average one to thirty double-spaced typewritten pages. Two copies are required. Return postage and a self-addressed envelope are unnecessary. See a recent issue for bibliographical procedure and style. Use one inch margins and double-space throughout. A background or explanatory cover letter about the article is not required nor is an outline or summary. Biographical information about the author is usually unnecessary. Illustrations, pictures, graphs, etc., will be used only if clearly drawn and suitable for reproduction. No payment is made for accepted articles. Reprints are available; 50 free copies are mailed to the author.

Manuscript Disposition:
Receipt of a manuscript is acknowledged. Editorial decisions are made within three to six months. Accepted articles usually appear in print within eight to eighteen months. Unaccepted manuscripts are returned, often with comments or criticism.

Copyright:
Held by the Mathematical Association of America.

AMERICAN METRIC JOURNAL

Subscription Data:
Published by the AMJ Publishing Company, P. O. Drawer L,

Oxnard Street, Tarzana, California 91356. Issued bimonthly, in January, March, May, July, September, and November. Advertising is accepted. Circulation: Varies due to promotional free copies. Subscription: $35.00 per year; Special bulk group rates. Founded: 1973.

Editorial Address:

The Editor, American Metric Journal, 18324 Oxnard Street, Tarzana, California 91356.

Editorial Policy:

Includes only articles on metric subjects. The reading audience includes persons in schools, industry, and government agencies. Unsolicited manuscripts are welcome. Five or six major articles are published per issue. Book reviews are included.

Manuscript Preparation:

Accepted manuscripts average one to four pages, but are flexible in length. Two copies are required. Return postage and a self-addressed envelope are required. Bibliographical procedure should follow the MLA Style Sheet. List footnotes separately and double-space manuscript. A background or explanatory cover letter is not required, but an outline, summary, or abstract is required. Biographical information about the author is required. The Journal screens illustrations, pictures, graphs, etc., for use. No payment is made for accepted manuscripts. Reprint policy is presently being established.

Manuscript Disposition:

Receipt of a manuscript is acknowledged. Editorial decisions are made within three to four weeks. Accepted articles usually appear in print within two months. Unaccepted manuscripts are returned without criticism or suggestions.

Copyright:

Held by the AMJ Publishing Company, except in certain cases.

AMERICAN STATISTICAL ASSOCIATION. JOURNAL

Subscription Data:

Published by the American Statistical Association, 806 Fifteenth Street, N.W., Washington, D.C. 20005. Issued quarterly. Advertising is accepted. Circulation: 13,500. Subscription: $25.00 per year; student members of the Association receive the Journal as part of an annual membership fee of $9.00; $6.50 per issue. Founded: 1888.

Editorial Address:

The Editor, Journal of the American Statistical Association, University of Illinois, Chicago Circle Campus, 4075 Behavioral Sciences Building, Chicago, Illinois 60680.

Editorial Policy:

Includes articles which report original contributions to statistical theory and method, interesting applications of statistics, criticism of published data and data sources, and reviews of the development of statistical ideas. The reading audience includes Association members and others interested in statistical theory, methodology, and application of statistics to fields of scientific endeavor. Unsolicited articles are welcome. Approximately 40 to 45 articles are published per issue. Unsolicited book reviews are not accepted.

Manuscript Preparation:

Accepted manuscripts average from 10 to 30 double-spaced type-written pages. Three copies are required for the review process. Bibliographical style should follow the JASA style sheet, available upon request from the Coordinating Editor. Use wide margins and double-space throughout. A background or explanatory cover letter about the manuscript is often helpful but not required. A short abstract of 100 words or fewer substantively summarizing the results is required. Biographical information about the author is not required. Tables must be submitted in camera-ready form and professionally drafted India ink drawings of all figures are required for accepted manuscripts. No payment is made for accepted articles. Authors have the opportunity to order reprints prior to publication and are entitled to four complimentary copies of the issue containing their article.

Manuscript Disposition:

Receipt of a manuscript is immediately acknowledged. Editorial decisions are generally made within three to four months. Accepted articles usually appear in print within four to five months on the average. Unaccepted manuscripts are returned, often with criticism.

Copyright:

Held by the American Statistical Association.

Additional Information:

Articles published in the Journal are subject to a voluntary page charge of $25.00 per printed page payable by the institution or granting agency supporting the research. Payment is not a prerequisite for publication nor is the author expected to pay these charges himself.

ARITHMETIC TEACHER

Subscription Data:

Published by the National Council of Teachers of Mathematics, 1906 Association Drive, Reston, Virginia 22091. Issued eight times each year, October through May. Advertising is accepted. Circulation: 44,000. Subscription: $9.00 per year as part of membership in the Council; $10.00 to institutions; $4.50 to students. Founded: 1954.

Editorial Address:

Managing Editor, Arithmetic Teacher, 1201 Sixteenth Street, N.W., Washington, D.C. 20036.

Editorial Policy:

Provides a means for communication of ideas that range over the broad spectrum of mathematics education in the elementary school. Contributions of novel content and viewpoint are often included as are expository articles and reports of research. The journal is an official publication of the National Council of Teachers of Mathematics and as such is devoted to the interests of elementary school personnel, teachers and consultants, administrators, elementary education majors in colleges and universities, and professors concerned with teacher education programs in mathematics for elementary teachers. Unsolicited articles are welcome. Ten to twelve major articles are published per issue. Book reviews are included.

Manuscript Preparation:

Accepted manuscripts should not exceed 15 double-spaced typewritten pages. The original and one clear copy are required. Return postage and a self-addressed envelope are unnecessary. Bibliographical procedure should follow the University of Chicago Manual of Style. Footnotes should be numbered consecutively and placed at the bottom of the page. Use 1-1/2 inch margins and double-space throughout. Neither an explanatory cover letter nor a summary of the article is necessary, but the author should submit a brief biography including a summary of professional background. Illustrations, pictures, and graphs may be used. All drawings should be produced on white paper in black India ink, somewhat larger than the final reproduction to appear in the periodical. No payment is made for accepted manuscripts. Reprints are provided at cost. Authors of feature articles receive four free copies of the journal and 50 complimentary reprints.

Manuscript Disposition:

Receipt of a manuscript is acknowledged. Editorial decision time varies from a few weeks to several months. Accepted articles usually appear in print within two years after acceptance. Unaccepted manuscripts are returned with criticism and reasons for rejection.

Copyright:

Held by the National Council of Teachers of Mathematics.

JOURNAL FOR RESEARCH IN MATHEMATICS EDUCATION

Subscription Data:

Published by the National Council of Teachers of Mathematics, 1906 Association Drive, Reston, Virginia 22091. Issued four times each year, in January, March, May, and November. Advertising is accepted. Circulation: 5,200. Subscription: $7.50 per year. Founded: 1970.

Editorial Address:

J. F. Weaver, Editor, Journal for Research in Mathematics Education, University of Wisconsin--Madison, School of Education, Department of Curriculum and Instruction, 225 North Mills Street, Madison, Wisconsin 53706.

Editorial Policy:

Includes reports of empirical studies, summaries of major research studies, and articles about current research in the field of mathematics education. The reading audience includes mathematics educators at all levels. Unsolicited manuscripts are welcome. Six major articles are published per issue. Book reviews are not included.

Manuscript Preparation:
  Accepted manuscripts average approximately 12 pages, including
  bibliography, tables, figures, and abstract. Manuscripts that
  exceed 20 pages will be given low priority for publication. Two
  copies are required. Return postage and a self-addressed envelope are not required. Bibliographical procedure should follow
  the APA Publication Manual. Footnotes should be kept to a minimum and a reference list should be used whenever possible.
  List essential footnotes on a separate page. Use one inch or
  larger margins and double-space. A background or explanatory
  cover letter is not required, but an abstract is required. Biographical information about the author is not required. The
  editorial office prepares finished artwork from author's roughs.
  No payment is made for accepted manuscripts. Reproductions
  of individual articles and microeditions of all volumes are available from University Microfilms, 300 North Zeeb Road, Ann
  Arbor, Michigan 48106.
Manuscript Disposition:
  Receipt of a manuscript is acknowledged. Editorial decisions
  are made within 15 weeks. Accepted articles usually appear in
  print within nine months. Unaccepted manuscripts are returned
  without criticism and/or suggestions.
Copyright:
  Held by the National Council of Teachers of Mathematics.

MATHEMATICAL LOG

Subscription Data:
  Published by Mu Alpha Theta, Room 423, Physical Science Center, 601 Elm, University of Oklahoma, Norman, Oklahoma
  73069. Issued three times each year, in September, January,
  and April. Advertising is not accepted. Circulation: 25,000.
  Subscription: $1.00 per year. Founded: 1958.
Editorial Address:
  The Editor, Mathematical Log, Box 1117, University of Oklahoma, Norman, Oklahoma 73069.
Editorial Policy:
  Includes articles on all phases of mathematics. The reading
  audience includes high school and junior college students, and
  their teachers. Unsolicited articles are welcome. Two or three
  major articles are published per issue. Book reviews are included.
Manuscript Preparation:
  No policy regarding manuscript length has been established. One
  copy is required. Return postage and a self-addressed envelope
  are desired. Use wide margins and double-space. A background
  or explanatory cover letter about the article is required. An
  outline or summary of the article is desired with submission of
  the finished manuscript. Biographical information about the author is desired and should include a summary of current work
  in mathematics. Simple illustrations and graphs can usually be
  used. No payment is made for accepted articles. Reprints are

not available, but each author receives 10 copies of the journal in which the article is published.

Manuscript Disposition:
Receipt of a manuscript is acknowledged. Editorial decisions are made within two to three months. Accepted articles usually appear in print within four to eight months after acceptance. Unaccepted manuscripts are returned if requested, but without criticism or suggestions.

Copyright:
Not copyrighted.

MATHEMATICS MAGAZINE

Subscription Data:
Published by the Mathematical Association of America, 1225 Connecticut Avenue, N. W., Washington, D. C. 20036. Issued five times each year, in January-February, March-April, May-June, September-October, and November-December. Advertising is accepted. Circulation: 7,800. Subscription: $7.00 per year. Founded: 1947.

Editorial Address:
Professor G. N. Wollan, Mathematics Magazine, Department of Mathematics, Purdue University, Lafayette, Indiana 47907.

Editorial Policy:
Includes articles on all branches of mathematics. The reading audience includes college students, and high school, junior college students, and teachers of high school, junior college, and university. Unsolicited articles are welcome. Eight to ten major articles are published per issue. Solicited book reviews are included.

Manuscript Preparation:
Accepted manuscripts average from two to ten double-spaced typewritten pages. Two copies are required. Return postage and a self-addressed envelope are unnecessary. Bibliographical procedure should follow a recent issue. Avoid use of footnotes where possible. Use one inch margins and double-space throughout. A background or explanatory cover letter about the article is not desired nor is an outline or summary. Biographical information about the author is unnecessary. Illustrations, pictures, graphs, etc., may be used; careful, clear, drawings are suitable for reproductions. No payment is made for accepted articles. Reprints are usually available; 50 free copies are mailed to the author.

Manuscript Disposition:
Receipt of a manuscript is acknowledged. Editorial decisions are made within three to six months. Accepted articles usually appear in print within eight to fourteen months after acceptance. Unaccepted manuscripts are returned, sometimes with criticism or suggestions.

Copyright:
Held by the Mathematical Association of America.

MATHEMATICS STUDENT JOURNAL

Subscription Data:
  Published by the National Council of Teachers of Mathematics,
  1906 Association Drive, Reston, Virginia 22091.   Issued quarterly, in October, December, February, and April.   Circulation:
  50,000.   Subscription: $2.50 per year.   Founded: 1954.
Editorial Address:
  Elroy J. Bolduc Jr., Editor, Mathematics Student Journal, College of Education, University of Florida, Gainesville, Florida
  32601.
Editorial Policy:
  Articles include mathematics for secondary school students and
  their teachers.   Unsolicited manuscripts are welcome.   One
  major article is published per issue.   Book reviews are rarely
  included.
Manuscript Preparation:
  Accepted manuscripts average about 2,000 words.   Two copies
  are required.   Return postage and a self-addressed envelope are
  not required, but desired.   Footnotes should be placed alphabetically at the end of the article.   Manuscripts should be double-spaced.   A background or explanatory cover letter is not
  required nor is an outline, summary, or abstract.   Biographical
  information should include a review of author's educational background, professional experience, and other accomplishments in
  mathematics.   Neat and clear illustrations, pictures, graphs,
  etc., may be used.   No payment is made for accepted manuscripts.   Ten free copies are given to authors; others are available at nominal cost through the Virginia office.
Manuscript Disposition:
  Receipt of a manuscript is acknowledged.   Editorial decisions
  are made within one month.   Unaccepted manuscripts are returned with criticism and/or suggestions.
Copyright:
  Held by the National Council of Teachers of Mathematics.

MATHEMATICS TEACHER

Subscription Data:
  Published by the National Council of Teachers of Mathematics,
  1906 Association Drive, Reston, Virginia 22091.   Issued eight
  times each year, October through May.   Advertising is accepted.
  Circulation: 48,000.   Subscription: $9.00 per year as part of
  Council membership; $10.00 to institutions; $4.50 to students;
  $1.25 per issue.   Founded: 1908.
Editorial Address:
  Carol V. McCamman, Managing Editor, Mathematics Teacher,
  1906 Association Drive, Reston, Virginia 22091.
Editorial Policy:
  Includes articles on all phases of mathematics education.   The
  reading audience includes teachers of mathematics in junior high
  schools, senior high schools, junior colleges, and teacher edu-

cation colleges. Unsolicited articles are welcome. Ten to fifteen major articles are published per issue. Book reviews are included.

Manuscript Preparation:
Accepted manuscripts average eight to ten double-spaced typewritten pages. Two copies are required. Return postage and a self-addressed envelope are desired. Bibliographical procedure should follow the University of Chicago Manual of Style. Use one inch margins and double-space throughout. A background or explanatory cover letter about the article is desired, but not an outline or summary. Biographical information about the author is unnecessary. Illustrations, pictures, and graphs may be used. No payment is made for accepted articles. Reprints are available from the Virginia office.

Manuscript Disposition:
Receipt of a manuscript is acknowledged. Editorial decisions are made as soon as possible. Time from acceptance of a manuscript to its appearance in print varies with editorial need. Unaccepted articles are returned, rarely with criticism.

Copyright:
Held by the National Council of Teachers of Mathematics.

SCHOOL SCIENCE AND MATHEMATICS

Subscription Data:
Published by the School Science and Mathematics Association, Inc., Lewis House, Box 1614, Indiana University of Pennsylvania, Indiana, Pennsylvania 15701. Issued monthly, October through May. Advertising is accepted. Circulation: 7,000. Subscription: $10.00 per year to institutions (United States and Canada); $12.00 per year elsewhere (United States Exchange); $7.00 per year to members; $1.50 per issue. Founded: 1900.

Editorial Address:
The Editor, School Science and Mathematics, 535 Kendall Avenue, Kalamazoo, Michigan 49007.

Editorial Policy:
Includes articles which emphasize improvement of teaching in the sciences and mathematics at all grade levels. The reading audience includes science and mathematics supervisors, experienced science and mathematics teachers, and college teachers of science and mathematics interested in teacher training. Unsolicited articles are welcome. Eight to ten major articles are published per issue. Book reviews are included.

Manuscript Preparation:
No limitations are placed upon manuscript length. Two copies are required. Return postage and a self-addressed envelope are required with unsolicited manuscripts. Bibliographical procedure may follow any widely used style manual. Use a 1-1/2 inch top margin with all others 1-1/4 inches; double-space throughout. A background or explanatory cover letter about the article is not desired nor is an outline or summary. Biographical information about the author is usually unnecessary. Illustrations, pictures,

and graphs may be used. All drawings must be prepared in India ink on white bond paper. No payment is made for accepted articles. Reprint costs vary with article length; a schedule is mailed to each author with galley proofs. See a recent issue for an abbreviated reprint cost summary.

Manuscript Disposition:

Receipt of a manuscript is acknowledged. Editorial decisions are usually made within two to three months although this process occasionally requires up to six months. Accepted articles usually appear in print within three to six months after acceptance. Unaccepted manuscripts are returned with complete comments of referees.

Copyright:

Held by the School Science and Mathematics Association, Inc.

MUSIC

AMERICAN MUSIC TEACHER

Subscription Data:
   Published by the Music Teachers National Association, 1831
   Carew Tower, Cincinnati, Ohio 45202. Issued six times each
   school year, in September-October, November-December, Jan-
   uary, February-March, April-May, and June-July. Advertising
   is accepted. Circulation: 14,000. Subscription: $4.00 per
   year. Founded: 1951.
Editorial Address:
   Mr. Homer Ulrich, Editor, American Music Teacher, 3587
   South Leisure World Boulevard, Silver Spring, Maryland 20906.
Editorial Policy:
   Includes articles on all phases of music, with emphasis on his-
   tory-literature, teaching, research, education, and the music
   industry. The reading audience includes college and private
   teachers at all levels and administrators. Most unsolicited manuscripts are welcome. Six to eight major articles are published
   per issue. Book reviews and reviews of music are included.
Manuscript Preparation:
   Accepted manuscripts average 1,500 to 3,000 words. One copy
   is required. Return postage and a self-addressed envelope are
   required. Bibliographical procedure should follow the University
   of Chicago Manual of Style. Footnotes should be numbered consecutively and listed on a separate page, and kept to a reasonable minimum. Use two inch margins and double-space. A
   background or explanatory cover letter is helpful, but not an
   outline, summary, or abstract. Brief biographical information
   about the author is required. Musical examples, illustrations,
   etc., are acceptable. No payment is made for accepted manuscripts. Reprints are available; a cost summary may be obtained from the Association office.
Manuscript Disposition:
   Receipt of a manuscript is acknowledged. Editorial decisions
   are made within three weeks. Accepted articles usually appear
   in print within six months or sooner. Unaccepted manuscripts
   are returned, usually without criticism or suggestions.
Copyright:
   Held by the Music Teachers National Association.

AMERICAN STRING TEACHER

Subscription Data:
   Published by the American String Teachers Association,

343

Executive Secretary, 2596 Princeton Pike, Trenton, New Jersey 08638. Issued quarterly, in October, January, April, and July. Advertising is accepted. Circulation: 4,200. Subscription: Available only through membership. Founded: 1947.

Editorial Address:
John Zurfluh, Sr., Editor, American String Teacher, 630 Kirkwood Avenue, Winthrop Harbor, Illinois 60096.

Editorial Policy:
Articles are professional in nature; includes articles related to string teaching with emphasis on violin, viola, violoncello, and string bass until 1972 when a "Classical Guitar" section was added. The reading audience includes teachers, artists and educators, and various persons interested in the maintenance and repair of string instruments. College students belong to student chapters. Unsolicited articles are welcome. Approximately six major articles are published in each issue. Reviews of books, music, and instructional material are included.

Manuscript Preparation:
Accepted manuscripts average about 1,000 words, but occasionally some of only 250 words or considerably more than 1,000 words are accepted. One typed copy is required. Return postage and a self-addressed envelope are desired. Bibliographical procedure may follow any widely used manual of style. Use 1-1/2 inch margins and double-space. A background letter is helpful, but an outline or summary is not required. Biographical material about the author is desired. A few photographs and illustrations are used. No payment is made for accepted manuscripts. Reprints are available at cost.

Manuscript Disposition:
Receipt of a manuscript is acknowledged. Editorial decisions are made usually within one month. Accepted articles usually appear in print within six months. Unaccepted manuscripts are returned, usually without criticism and/or suggestions.

Copyright:
Held by the American String Teachers Association.

Additional Information:
Occasional national scope reports are published.

CHORAL JOURNAL

Subscription Data:
Published by the American Choral Directors Association, P.O. Box 17736, Tampa, Florida 33612. Issued monthly, September through May. Advertising is accepted. Circulation: 5,500. Subscription: $4.00 per year to libraries only. Founded: 1959.

Editorial Address:
The Editor, Choral Journal, P.O. Box 17736, Tampa, Florida 33612.

Editorial Policy:
Includes choral and vocal articles and reports which contribute to the further education of choral conductors in elementary school, junior high, senior high, junior college, senior college,

university, church, community, and professional choir. Procedures, events, special presentations, specific works, lists, vocal
solutions, etc., are also included. The reading audience includes
members of the Association and other professionals. Unsolicited
articles are welcome. Four to six major articles are published
per issue. Book reviews are included.

Manuscript Preparation:
No policy regarding manuscript length has been established.
Two copies are required. Return postage and a self-addressed
envelope are desired. Bibliographical procedure should follow
the Turabian Manual for Writers. Use 1-1/2 inch margins and
double-space throughout. Place all footnotes at the end of the
article. Biographical information about the author should include
a summary of current position, general background, and choral
achievements. Illustrations, pictures, graphs, etc., may be
used. No payment is made for accepted articles.

Manuscript Disposition:
Receipt of a manuscript is acknowledged. Editorial decisions
are made by the editorial board within four to six weeks. Accepted articles appear in print as soon as space is available.
Unaccepted manuscripts are returned, often with suggestions
and/or criticism.

Copyright:
Held by the Choral Journal; however, an author may secure or
request a special copyright for a major article.

CLAVIER

Subscription Data:
Published by the Instrumentalist Company, Inc., 1418 Lake
Street, Evanston, Illinois 60204. Issued nine times each year,
in September, October, November, December, January, February, March, April, and May. Advertising is accepted. Circulation: 19,000. Subscription: $7.00 per year. Founded: 1962.

Editorial Address:
The Editor, Clavier, Instrumentalist Company, Inc., 1418 Lake
Street, Evanston, Illinois 60204.

Editorial Policy:
Includes articles related to keyboard music. The reading audience includes teachers of piano and organ. Unsolicited articles
are welcome. Seven major articles are published per issue.
Staff-written book reviews are included.

Manuscript Preparation:
Manuscripts may be of any reasonable length. One copy is required. Return postage and a self-addressed envelope are desired. Bibliographical procedure should follow the University
of Chicago Manual of Style. Use wide margins and double-space.
Avoid use of footnotes where possible. A background or explanatory cover letter about the article is not desired nor is an
outline or summary. Biographical information about the author
is desired and should include indication of formal education and
professional experience. Illustrations, pictures, and graphs

of $15.00 per printed page (about 1,200 words). Reprints are
sometimes available; cost varies with article length and order
volume.

Manuscript Disposition:
  Receipt of a manuscript is acknowledged. Editorial decisions
  are made as soon as possible. Accepted articles usually appear in print within 18 months after acceptance. Unaccepted
  manuscripts are returned without comment, unless the editor requests a rewrite.

Copyright:
  Held by the Instrumentalist Company, Inc.

INSTRUMENTALIST

Subscription Data:
  Published by the Instrumentalist Company, Inc., 1418 Lake
  Street, Evanston, Illinois 60204. Issued monthly, except July.
  Advertising is accepted. Circulation: 16,130. Subscription:
  $7.00 per year; $4.00 (five to nine subscriptions) and $3.50
  (10 or more subscriptions) for group subscriptions mailed to
  one address; $.80 per issue. Founded: 1946.

Editorial Address:
  The Editor, Instrumentalist, Instrumentalist Company, Inc.,
  1418 Lake Street, Evanston, Illinois 60204.

Editorial Policy:
  Includes articles which relate to all aspects of instrumental music. The reading audience includes musicians, teachers of music, and music and instrument dealers. Unsolicited articles are
  welcome. Twelve to fourteen major articles are published per
  issue. Book and record reviews are included.

Manuscript Preparation:
  Accepted manuscripts average from one to three journal pages.
  Return postage and a self-addressed envelope are desired. Use
  wide margins and double-space. Avoid use of footnotes. A
  background or explanatory cover letter about the article is desired, but not an outline or summary. Biographical information
  and author's photograph is desired. Illustrations, pictures,
  graphs, etc., may be used. Payment is made for published
  articles. Reprints are available.

Manuscript Disposition:
  Receipt of a manuscript is acknowledged. Editorial decisions
  are made as soon as possible. Accepted articles usually appear
  in print within one year after acceptance. Unaccepted manuscripts are returned, often with criticism and/or suggestions.

Copyright:
  Held by the Instrumentalist Company.

JOURNAL OF RESEARCH IN MUSIC EDUCATION

Subscription Data:
  Published by the Music Educators National Conference, 8150

Leesburg Pike, Vienna, Virginia 22180. Issued four times each year, in spring, summer, fall, and winter. Advertising is not accepted. Circulation: 9,000. Subscription: $8.00 per year. Founded: 1953.

Editorial Address:

Robert G. Petzold, Editor, Journal of Research in Music Education, School of Music, University of Wisconsin, Madison, Wisconsin 53706.

Editorial Policy:

Includes research articles on all phases of music education. The reading audience includes professional music educators at all levels. Unsolicited articles are welcome. Eight to ten major articles are published per issue. Book reviews are included.

Manuscript Preparation:

Accepted manuscripts average 6,000 words. One copy is required. Return postage and a self-addressed envelope are required. Bibliographical procedure should follow the University of Chicago Manual of Style. Use 1-1/2 inch margins and double-space. Type footnotes on a separate page at the end of the article, using consecutive numbers. A background or explanatory cover letter about the article is required. An outline or summary is desired in advance of or with submission of finished manuscript. Biographical information about the author is desired and should include a summary of his professional background. Illustrations, pictures, graphs, etc., should be prepared in black and white, ready for camera if possible. No payment is made for accepted articles. Reprints are available; 100 free copies are mailed to the author. A reprint cost list is available from the office of the editor.

Manuscript Disposition:

Receipt of manuscript is acknowledged. Editorial decisions are made within three to six months. Accepted articles usually appear in print within one year after acceptance. Unaccepted manuscripts are returned with criticism and suggestions provided for articles to be revised.

Copyright:

Held by the Music Educators National Conference. All rights are held for the author.

MUSIC EDUCATORS JOURNAL

Subscription Data:

Published by the Music Educators National Conference, 8150 Leesburg Pike, Vienna, Virginia 22180. Issued monthly, September through May. Advertising is accepted. Circulation: 70,000. Subscription: $4.00 per year; $6.00 per year to Canada; $8.00 foreign. Institutional subscriptions only; individuals must be members of Music Educators National Conference. Founded: 1914.

Editorial Address:

Malcolm E. Bessom, Editor, Music Educators Journal, Music Educators National Conference, 8150 Leesburg Pike, Vienna, Virginia 22180.

Editorial Policy:
 Includes articles on all aspects of music and music education,
 including performance, general music, elementary, secondary,
 and college curriculums, aesthetics, music education philosophy,
 new trends in music, educational innovations, etc. The reading
 audience includes music teachers at all levels, professional musicians, and music students. Unsolicited manuscripts are welcome. Ten to twelve major articles are published per issue.
 Book reviews are included.
Manuscript Preparation:
 Accepted manuscripts average eight to fifteen double-spaced typewritten pages. One copy is required. Return postage and a
 self-addressed envelope are unnecessary. Bibliographical procedure should follow the University of Chicago Manual of Style.
 Place footnotes on a separate page and include as few as possible. Use at least one inch margins and double-space throughout. A background or explanatory cover letter is desired, but
 not an outline, summary, or abstract. Biographical information
 about the author should include only current position. No payment is made for accepted manuscripts. Reprints can be made
 available at the author's expense.
Manuscript Disposition:
 Receipt of a manuscript is acknowledged within three days. Editorial decisions are made as soon as possible; editorial board
 reviews all manuscripts. Accepted articles usually appear in
 print within three to nine months. Unaccepted manuscripts are
 returned with reasons for rejection.
Copyright:
 Held by the Music Educators National Conference.

MUSIC JOURNAL

Subscription Data:
 Published by Sar-Les Music, Inc., 370 Lexington Avenue, New
 York, New York 10017. Issued monthly, except July when an
 anthology is published. Advertising is accepted. Circulation:
 60,000. Subscription: $9.00 per year. Founded: 1943.
Editorial Address:
 The Editor, Music Journal, 370 Lexington Avenue, New York,
 New York 10017.
Editorial Policy:
 Includes articles on all aspects of music. The reading audience
 includes musicians, teachers of music, dealers, and students.
 Unsolicited articles are welcome. Thirty articles are published
 per issue. Book reviews are included.
Manuscript Preparation:
 Accepted manuscripts average 1,000 words. Two copies are
 required. Return postage and a self-addressed envelope are
 required for immediate acknowledgment. See a recent issue for
 footnoting and other bibliographical procedure. Use one inch
 margins and double-space throughout. A background or explanatory cover letter about the article is desired, but not an outline

or summary. Biographical information about the author is desired. Illustrations, graphs, etc., are seldom used; photographs
are used when appropriate. Payment for accepted manuscripts
averages $25.00 per article. Reprints are available; costs vary
with article length.

Manuscript Disposition:
Receipt of a manuscript is acknowledged. Editorial decisions
are made within four to six weeks. Time from acceptance of a
manuscript to its appearance in print varies with editorial need.
Unaccepted manuscripts are returned, sometimes with criticism
and/or suggestions.

Copyright:
Held by the Music Journal.

NATS BULLETIN

Subscription Data:
Published by the National Association of Teachers of Singing,
430 South Michigan Avenue, Chicago, Illinois 60685. Issued
quarterly, in October, December, February, and May. Advertising is accepted. Circulation: 3,650. Subscription: $6.00
per year in the United States; $6.50 in Canada and in Mexico;
$7.00 elsewhere. Founded: 1944.

Editorial Address:
The Editor, NATS Bulletin, 430 South Michigan Avenue, Chicago,
Illinois 60685.

Editorial Policy:
Includes articles on voice pedagogy, voice research, repertoire,
and related fields. The reading audience includes voice teachers,
music educators, and advanced voice students. Unsolicited articles are welcome. Four to six major articles are published per
issue. Book, music, and record reviews are included.

Manuscript Preparation:
Accepted articles average from 10 to 15 double-spaced typewritten pages; longer articles will be divided for publication in
two issues. One copy is required. Return postage and a self-
addressed envelope are desired. For pica type set the left margin at 24 and the right margin at 62; adapt for elite. Use 25
double-spaced lines per page for pica type and 25 triple-spaced
lines for elite type. Footnoting and other bibliographical procedure may follow any widely used style manual which deals with
scholarly reporting. A background or explanatory cover letter
about the article is not desired nor is an outline or summary.
Biographical information about the author is desired and should
include a summary of past and present teaching positions, and
performance experience, if any. Pictures, graphs, and photographs may be used. No payment is made for accepted articles.
Reprint arrangements may be made with the printer.

Manuscript Disposition:
Receipt of a manuscript is acknowledged. Editorial decisions
are made as soon as possible. Accepted articles usually appear
in print within six months after acceptance. Unaccepted

manuscripts are returned, sometimes with suggestions and/or criticism.

Copyright:

Held by the National Association of Teachers of Singing.

SCHOOL MUSICIAN DIRECTOR AND TEACHER (formerly School Musician)

Subscription Data:

Published by Forrest L. McAllister, Four East Clinton Street, Joliet, Illinois 60431. Issued 10 times each year, September through June. Advertising is accepted. Circulation: 15,000. Subscription: $6.00 per year. Founded: 1929.

Editorial Address:

The Editor, School Musician Director and Teacher, Four East Clinton Street, Joliet, Illinois 60431.

Editorial Policy:

Includes technical, philosophical, and inspirational articles which relate to music and music education. The reading audience includes band, orchestra, and choral music directors, music teachers, music students, and parents. Unsolicited articles are welcome. Fourteen major articles are published per issue. Book reviews are included.

Manuscript Preparation:

Accepted manuscripts average from four to five double-spaced typewritten pages, or from 600 to 750 words. One copy on white bond paper is required. Return postage and a self-addressed envelope are desired. Bibliographical procedure may follow any widely used style manual. Use one inch margins and double-space throughout. Place footnotes at the bottom of the pages on which they occur. A background or explanatory cover letter about the article is desired but not an outline or summary. Biographical information about the author, limited to 60 to 80 words, should summarize formal education, and past and current positions. Illustrations, pictures, graphs, etc., may be used. Pictures should be eight by ten inch glossy prints, when possible. When drawings or music manuscripts are prepared, use black India ink and place each on a separate page. Illustrations and photographs are often used. No payment is made for accepted articles. Reprint costs vary with article length and order volume.

Manuscript Disposition:

Receipt of a manuscript is acknowledged. Editorial decisions are made within two to four weeks. Accepted articles usually appear in print within two to twelve months after acceptance. Unaccepted manuscripts are returned, often with reasons and/or criticism.

Copyright:

Held by the School Musician Director and Teacher.

Additional Information:

A detailed document entitled "How to Prepare Your Feature Article" may be obtained from the office of the editor.

PARAPSYCHOLOGY

*JOURNAL OF PARAPSYCHOLOGY

Subscription Data:
Published by the Parapsychology Press, Box 6847 College Station, Durham, North Carolina 27708. Issued quarterly, in March, June, September, and December. Advertising is not accepted. Circulation: 1,500. Subscription: $10.00 per year. Founded: 1937.

Editorial Address:
The Editor, Journal of Parapsychology, Box 6847, College Station, Durham, North Carolina 27708.

Editorial Policy:
Includes reports of experimental research, theoretical and statistical articles, and surveys which are closely associated with the research. The reading audience includes educated laymen and scientists. Unsolicited manuscripts are welcome, but previous correspondence is recommended. Four to six major articles are published per issue. Book reviews are included.

Manuscript Preparation:
Accepted manuscripts should not exceed 25 pages. Two copies are required. Return postage and a self-addressed envelope are required if the manuscript is to be returned. Bibliographical procedure should follow the APA Publication Manual. List footnotes at the bottom of page. Use 1-1/2 inch margins or wider. A background or explanatory cover letter and an outline, summary, or abstract are required. Copies of illustrations, pictures, graphs, etc., acceptable for printing, should be supplied by the author if the article is accepted for publication. No payment is made for accepted manuscripts. Twenty-five free copies are available; author pays half of additional cost up to 200 copies.

Manuscript Disposition:
Receipt of a manuscript is acknowledged. Editorial decisions are made within three weeks. Accepted articles usually appear in print within six months or more. Unaccepted manuscripts are returned if postage is included. Criticism and/or suggestions are provided if further work will make the paper publishable.

Copyright:
Not copyrighted.

PARAPSYCHOLOGY REVIEW

Subscription Data:
   Published by Parapsychology Foundation, 29 West Fifty-seventh
   Street, New York, New York 10019.   Issued six times each year.
   Advertising is not accepted.   Circulation: 3, 000.   Subscription:
   $4. 00 per year; $. 85 per issue.   Founded: 1953.
Editorial Address:
   The Editor, Parapsychology Review, 29 West Fifty-seventh
   Street, New York, New York 10019.
Editorial Policy:
   Includes the scientific approach to psychical phenomena; news
   of developments in the field and its leading figures and their research, from the academic and professional parapsychological
   community.   The reading audience includes the academic and
   law audience.   Unsolicited manuscripts are welcome.   Four or
   five major articles are published per issue.   Book reviews are
   included.
Manuscript Preparation:
   Accepted manuscripts average 500 to 3, 000 words.   One copy is
   required.   Return postage and a self-addressed envelope are required.   Bibliographical procedure should follow the University
   of Chicago Manual of Style.   Double-space manuscripts.   A background or explanatory cover letter and an outline, summary, or
   abstract are helpful.   Biographical information about the author
   is required.   Illustrations, pictures, and graphs are used.   Payment is made for accepted manuscripts.
Manuscript Disposition:
   Receipt of a manuscript is not acknowledged.   Editorial decisions
   are made within one to two weeks.   Accepted articles usually
   appear in print within two to six months.   Unaccepted manuscripts are returned, without criticism and/or suggestions except in special cases.
Copyright:
   Held by the Parapsychology Review.   Copyright is re-assigned
   to the author at publication date on request.

PHILOSOPHY

AMERICAN THEOSOPHIST

Subscription Data:
  Published by the Theosophical Society in America, P.O. Box
  270, Wheaton, Illinois 60187. Issued monthly. Advertising is
  not accepted. Circulation: 6,000. Subscription: $4.00 per
  year. Founded: 1886.

Editorial Address:
  The Editor, American Theosophist, P.O. Box 270, Wheaton,
  Illinois 60187.

Editorial Policy:
  Includes articles and reports on philosophy, religion, and science.
  The reading audience includes educators, scholars and others
  with interest in philosophy. Unsolicited articles are welcome.
  Two major articles are published per issue. Solicited book re-
  views are included.

Manuscript Preparation:
  Accepted manuscripts average from 1,500 to 3,000 words. Two
  copies are required. Return postage and a self-addressed envelope are desired. Bibliographical procedure may follow any
  widely used manual of style. Use wide margins and double-
  space. Footnotes should be placed at the bottom of each page
  or on a separate page at the end of the article. A background
  or explanatory cover letter about the article is not desired nor
  is an outline or summary. Biographical information about the
  author is desired and should include a summary of formal education, professional background, and previously published material. Illustrations, pictures, graphs, etc., may not be used.
  No payment is made for accepted articles.

Manuscript Disposition:
  Receipt of a manuscript is acknowledged. Editorial decisions
  are made within four weeks. All manuscripts are submitted to
  an advisory committee for critique. Accepted articles usually
  appear in print within six months after acceptance. Unaccepted
  manuscripts are returned, often with general suggestions and/or
  criticism.

Copyright:
  Not copyrighted.

Additional Information:
  This journal, as the major publication of TSA, publishes society
  business in 10 of its 12 annual issues and is therefore limited
  in the number of major articles it can use. In spring and fall,
  however, a special issue is published which deals with particular
  themes relating to man's spiritual, cultural, and intellectual life.

ETHICS: AN INTERNATIONAL JOURNAL OF SOCIAL, POLITICAL, AND LEGAL PHILOSOPHY

Subscription Data:
Published by the University of Chicago Press, 5801 South Ellis Avenue, Chicago, Illinois 60637. Issued quarterly, in October, January, April, and July. Advertising is accepted. Circulation: 2, 700. Subscription: $10. 00 per year; $19. 00 for two years; $28. 00 for three years; $12. 00 to institutions; $23. 00 for two years; $34. 00 for three years; $7. 00 to students with faculty signature. Founded: 1890.

Editorial Address:
The Editor, Ethics, University of Chicago, Cobb Hall, 5811 Ellis Avenue, Chicago, Illinois 60637.

Editorial Policy:
Includes articles in ethical theory, social science, and jurisprudence contributing to an understanding of the basic structure of civilization and society. Unsolicited manuscripts are welcome. Eight major articles, excluding book reviews, are published per issue. Book reviews are included.

Manuscript Preparation:
Accepted manuscripts average 15 to 30 pages for major articles and two to twenty pages for discussion articles. One copy is required. Return postage and a self-addressed envelope are required. Bibliographical procedure should follow the University of Chicago Manual of Style. List footnotes on a separate page and double-space. Use one inch margins and double-space throughout, including quotations. A background or explanatory cover letter is not required, nor is an outline, summary, or abstract. Biographical information about the author is not required. Illustrations, pictures, graphs, etc. , are not included. No payment is made for accepted manuscripts. Offprints may be ordered before publication.

Manuscript Disposition:
Receipt of a manuscript is acknowledged. Editorial decisions are made within 14 weeks. Accepted articles usually appear in print within nine months. Unaccepted manuscripts are returned if return postage is provided by author. Criticism and/or suggestions are not usually provided.

Copyright:
Held by the University of Chicago.

HUMANIST

Subscription Data:
Published by the American Humanist Association and American Ethical Union, 923 Kensington Avenue, Buffalo, New York 14215. Issued bimonthly. Circulation: 26, 500. Subscription: $8. 00 per year. Founded: 1941.

Editorial Address:
Paul Kurtz, Editor, Humanist, 923 Kensington Avenue, Buffalo, New York 14215.

Editorial Policy:
    Includes moral and social issues on the frontier of social change,
    with many articles on education. The reading audience includes
    professionals: educators, professors, etc. Unsolicited manu-
    scripts are welcome. Six to eight major articles are published
    per issue. Book reviews are included.
Manuscript Preparation:
    Accepted manuscripts average 2,000 to 3,000 words, but longer
    ones are acceptable. Four copies are required. Return postage
    and a self-addressed envelope are required. Bibliographical
    procedure should follow the MLA Style Sheet. Footnoting and
    manuscript margin and spacing recommendations are optional.
    A background or explanatory cover letter is helpful, but an out-
    line, summary, or abstract is not required. Biographical in-
    formation about the author is helpful. Payment is made for ac-
    cepted manuscripts. Ten copies are given to each author.
Manuscript Disposition:
    Receipt of a manuscript is acknowledged. Editorial decisions
    are made within six weeks. Accepted articles usually appear
    in print within six to nine months. Unaccepted manuscripts are
    returned, sometimes with criticism and/or suggestions.
Copyright:
    Held by Humanist.

NEW SCHOLASTICISM

Subscription Data:
    Published by the American Catholic Philosophical Association,
    Catholic University of America, Washington, D.C. 20017. Is-
    sued quarterly, in January, April, July, and October. Adver-
    tising is accepted. Circulation: 2,500. Subscription: $8.00
    per year. Founded: 1926.
Editorial Address:
    John A. Oesterle, Editor, New Scholasticism, University of
    Notre Dame, Notre Dame, Indiana 46556.
Editorial Policy:
    Includes articles on all aspects of philosophy. The reading au-
    dience includes ACPA members as well as others interested in
    philosophy. Unsolicited articles are welcome. Four or five
    major articles are published per issue; also discussion articles.
    Book reviews are included.
Manuscript Preparation:
    Accepted manuscripts average from 20 to 25 double-spaced type-
    written pages. One copy is required. Return postage and a
    self-addressed envelope are required with all unsolicited manu-
    scripts. Bibliographical procedure should follow the University
    of Chicago Manual of Style. A guide to writers is also avail-
    able through the office of the editor. Use two inch margins and
    double-space throughout. List footnotes on a separate page at
    the end of the article. A background or explanatory cover letter
    about the article is not desired, but a 150 word summary is re-
    quired. Biographical information about the author is desired

and should include information regarding academic training. Illustrations, pictures, graphs, etc., are rarely used. No payment is made for accepted articles. Reprints are available; 25
free copies are mailed to the author with additional copies available at cost.

Manuscript Disposition:
Receipt of a manuscript is acknowledged. Editorial decisions
are made within two to three months. Accepted articles usually
appear in print within six to twelve months after acceptance.
Unaccepted manuscripts are returned, often with criticism and/
or suggestions.

Copyright:
Held by the American Catholic Philosophical Association. Permission from the editor must be obtained for reproduction.

PHILOSOPHICAL FORUM

Subscription Data:
Published by the Department of Philosophy, Boston University,
232 Bay State Road, Boston, Massachusetts 02215. Issued quarterly, in September, December, March, and June. Advertising
is accepted. Circulation: 1,200. Subscription: $10.00 per
year; $15.00 to institutions; $6.00 to students; $2.75 per issue.
Founded: 1942 (annual); 1968 (quarterly).

Editorial Address:
Professor Marx W. Wartofsky, Editor, Philosophical Forum,
Department of Philosophy, Boston University, 232 Bay State
Road, Boston, Massachusetts 02215.

Editorial Policy:
Includes philosophical articles of breadth and includes contributions of all types: critical and constructive, systematic and
fragmentary, speculative and scholarly, substantive and historical. The Forum welcomes applied philosophy: the philosophical
critique, an analysis of questions arising in politics and society,
the sciences, art, religion, and education. The reading audience
includes scholars and philosophers of all kinds. Unsolicited manuscripts are welcome. Eight or more major articles are published per issue. Book reviews are included.

Manuscript Preparation:
Accepted manuscripts should not exceed 100 pages. Three copies are required. Return postage is required. Bibliographical
procedure should follow the MLA Style Sheet. Use large margins and double-space. A background or explanatory cover letter is required, but not an outline, summary, or abstract.
Biographical information about the author is not required. Illustrations, pictures, graphs, etc., are welcome. No payment
is made for accepted manuscripts. Reprints are generally acceptable, but must seek permission.

Manuscript Disposition:
Receipt of a manuscript is acknowledged. Accepted articles usually appear in print within six to nine months. Original manuscripts are returned with criticism and suggestions.

Copyright:
   Held by Philosophical Forum.

PHILOSOPHICAL REVIEW

Subscription Data:
   Published by the Philosophical Review, 218 Goldwin Smith Hall,
   Cornell University, Ithaca, New York 14850. Issued quarterly,
   in January, April, July, and October. Advertising is accepted.
   Circulation: 4,000. Subscription: $5.00 per year; $8.00 to
   libraries and other institutions. Founded: 1892.
Editorial Address:
   The Editor, Philosophical Review, 218 Goldwin Smith Hall,
   Cornell University, Ithaca, New York 14850.
Editorial Policy:
   Includes articles, reports, and discussions of general philosophy.
   The reading audience includes teachers and students of philosophy.
   Unsolicited articles are welcome. Six major articles are pub-
   lished per issue. Book reviews are included.
Manuscript Preparation:
   Accepted articles average from 20 to 30 double-spaced typewrit-
   ten pages. Accepted reports or discussion manuscripts average
   from five to fifteen double-spaced pages. One copy is required.
   Return postage and a self-addressed envelope are unnecessary.
   Bibliographical procedure should follow the University of Chicago
   Manual of Style. Use 1-1/2 inch margins and double-space
   throughout. Footnotes should be incorporated into the body of
   the text or listed at the end of the article. A background or explanatory cover letter about the article is not desired nor is an
   outline or summary. Biographical information about the author
   is unnecessary. Use of illustrations, pictures, and graphs
   should be kept to a minimum. No payment is made for accepted
   articles. Reprints are available; a reprint cost summary is
   available through the office of the editor.
Manuscript Disposition:
   Receipt of a manuscript is acknowledged. Editorial decisions
   are made within six weeks. Accepted articles usually appear
   in print within one year after acceptance. Unaccepted manuscripts are returned.
Copyright:
   Not copyrighted.

REVIEW OF METAPHYSICS

Subscription Data:
   Published by the Philosophy Education Society, Inc., Catholic
   University of America, Washington, D.C. 20017. Issued quarterly, in September, December, March, and June. Advertising is
   accepted. Circulation: 3,700. Subscription: $7.00 per year;
   $12.00 to institutions; $5.00 to students. Founded: 1947.

Editorial Address:

The Editor, Review of Metaphysics, Catholic University of America, Washington, D. C. 20017.

Editorial Policy:

Includes articles on all aspects of philosophy. Original and critical work, rather than historical reporting, is encouraged. The reading audience includes the professional philosophical community plus other educators and students. Unsolicited articles are welcome. Seven or eight major articles are published per issue. Capsule reviews of all books received and feature-length critical studies of important books are included.

Manuscript Preparation:

Manuscripts should not exceed 20 to 25 double-spaced typewritten pages. One copy is required. Return postage and a self-addressed envelope are desired. Footnoting and other bibliographical procedure should follow the University of Chicago Manual of Style. Use 1-1/2 inch margins and double-space throughout. A background or explanatory cover letter about the article is desired. An outline or summary may be submitted for critique prior to completion of the article. Biographical information about the author is desired. Illustrations and graphs may be used, but photographs may not. No payment is made for accepted articles. Reprints are available; costs vary with article length and order volume. Twenty-five free copies are mailed to the author.

Manuscript Disposition:

Receipt of a manuscript is acknowledged. Editorial decisions are made within three weeks. Accepted articles usually appear in print within three to six months after acceptance. Unaccepted manuscripts are returned, often with reasons for rejection and criticism.

Copyright:

Held by the Philosophy Education Society. Permission is required, and granted, for reproduction of articles by authors.

PHYSICAL EDUCATION AND RECREATION

ATHLETIC JOURNAL

Subscription Data:
Published by the Athletic Journal Publishing Company, 1719 Howard Street, Evanston, Illinois 60202. Issued monthly, except July and August. Advertising is accepted. Circulation: 32,000. Subscription: $4.00 per year. Founded: 1921.

Editorial Address:
The Editor, Athletic Journal, 1719 Howard Street, Evanston, Illinois 60202.

Editorial Policy:
Includes articles and reports which relate to coaching and the administration of athletics. The reading audience includes high school and college coaches, and athletic directors. Unsolicited articles are welcome. Twenty major articles are published per issue. Book reviews are included.

Manuscript Preparation:
Accepted manuscripts average five double-spaced typewritten pages. One copy is required. Return postage and a self-addressed envelope are unnecessary. Footnotes should be avoided when possible. Use wide margins and double-space throughout. A background or explanatory cover letter about the article is desired, but not an outline or summary. Biographical information about the author is desired and should include current position, a summary of all schools at which coaching has been done, and coaching record. Pictures, graphs, and diagrams may be used. Payment for accepted articles varies from $10.00 to $25.00. Reprints are available; costs vary with article length and order volume.

Manuscript Disposition:
Receipt of a manuscript is acknowledged. Editorial decisions are made within two weeks. Accepted articles usually appear in print within one year after acceptance, depending upon the sport involved. Unaccepted manuscripts are returned, often with criticism and/or suggestions.

Copyright:
Held by the Athletic Journal Publishing Company.

Additional Information:
Articles must be prepared by people actively engaged in coaching or administration of high school or college athletics.

JOURNAL OF HEALTH, PHYSICAL EDUCATION, RECREATION

Subscription Data:
Published by the American Association for Health, Physical

Education, and Recreation, 1201 Sixteenth Street, N.W., Washington, D.C. 20036. Issued monthly, September through May. Advertising is accepted. Circulation: 45,000. Subscription: Free to Association members with $25.00 dues. Founded: 1896.

Editorial Address:

Managing Editor, Journal of Health, Physical Education, Recreation, 1201 Sixteenth Street, N.W., Washington, D.C. 20036.

Editorial Policy:

The Journal considers manuscripts on any aspect of physical education, outdoor education, safety and driver education, athletics, and recreation, including professional preparation in health, physical education, and recreation. All types of articles including practical, theoretical, technical, philosophical, controversial, and inspirational are suitable. The reading audience includes educators at all levels. Unsolicited articles are welcome. Eight to ten major articles are published per issue. Book reviews are included.

Manuscript Preparation:

Accepted manuscripts average from three to six double-spaced typewritten pages, or approximately 750 to 1,500 words; longer articles are considered only if quality warrants. One copy is required. Return postage and a self-addressed envelope are not required. Footnoting and bibliographical procedure should follow the University of Chicago Manual of Style. Manuscripts must be typewritten, double-spaced, preferably six inches wide and nine inches long to the page, on one side of the paper, 8-1/2 by 11. A background or explanatory cover letter about the article is not desired nor is a summary. A brief biographical summary about the author is desired. To give the article a better presentation, photographs are desirable. Photographs should be glossy prints, eight by ten, if possible, and should be accompanied by captions, giving complete information about picture, and also credit lines. Photographs are returned only when author requests. No payment can be made. Articles in the Journal are considered a contribution to the profession. No remuneration can be made. The author receives complimentary copies of the issue containing the article.

Manuscript Disposition:

Receipt of a manuscript is acknowledged. Editorial decisions are made within six to eight weeks. Accepted articles usually appear in print within two to three months after acceptance. Galley proofs are sent only upon written request. Unaccepted manuscripts are returned, usually without criticism or suggestions.

Copyright:

Held by the American Association for Health, Physical Education, and Recreation.

JOURNAL OF PHYSICAL EDUCATION

Subscription Data:

Published by Burt Printing Company, Inc., 88 Industry Avenue,

P. O. Box 2633, Springfield, Massachusetts 01101. Publication
of the National Physical Education Society (a section of the Association of Professional Directors of the YMCAs of the United
States). Issued bimonthly. Advertising is accepted. Subscription: $6.00 per year in the United States and Canada; $6.50
foreign; $3.00 per year to men in armed forces and college stu-
dents. Circulation: 2,500. Founded: 1902 as Physical Training.

Editorial Address:
  Leonard Rosewarren, Editor, Journal of Physical Education,
  YMCA of York & York County, 90 North Newberry Street, York,
  Pennsylvania 17401.
Editorial Policy:
  Includes articles and reports which relate to physical and health
  education, research, outdoor activity, or dance. The reading
  audience includes YMCA professionals, coaches, and physical
  educators in schools and colleges, in the United States and
  abroad. Unsolicited articles are welcome. From 10 to 14 major
  articles are published per issue. Book reviews are included.
Manuscript Preparation:
  No restrictions are placed on manuscript length. One copy is
  acceptable though two copies are preferred. A full column outline, "Advice to Authors," is included in each issue. A background or explanatory cover letter is helpful and even may pre-
  cede the article if some special treatment is possible. First
  time authors may include a biographical sketch that includes
  professional work experience, honors, professional affiliations,
  and age. Illustrations and pictures can be used; they will be
  returned. No payment is made for articles. Reprints are
  available; costs vary with article length and number of illustrations. Reprints are most speedily available if ordered when the
  article is accepted.
Manuscript Disposition:
  Receipt of a manuscript is acknowledged. Editorial decisions
  are made within one month. Accepted articles usually appear
  within one year after acceptance. Unaccepted manuscripts are
  returned, often with criticism.
Copyright:
  Held by the National Physical Education Society.

PARKS AND RECREATION

Subscription Data:
  Published by the National Recreation and Park Association, 1601
  North Kent Street, Arlington, Virginia 22209. Issued monthly.
  Advertising is accepted. Circulation: 22,500. Subscription:
  $7.50 per year; $10.00 foreign. Founded: 1907.
Editorial Address:
  The Editor, Parks and Recreation, 1601 North Kent Street,
  Arlington, Virginia 22209.
Editorial Policy:
  Includes articles and reports on outdoor education, parks, and

recreation. The reading audience includes park and recreation
leaders and outdoor educators in the schools. Unsolicited articles are welcome. Eight to ten major articles are published
per issue. Book reviews are included.

Manuscript Preparation:
    Accepted manuscripts average 2,000 words preferably. Two
    copies are required. Return postage and a self-addressed envel-
    ope are desired. Bibliographical procedure should follow the
    U.S. Government Printing Office Style Manual. Use one inch
    margins and double-space. Footnotes should be incorporated in-
    to the article wherever possible. A background or explanatory
    cover letter about the article is not desired nor is an outline
    or summary. Biographical information about the author is re-
    quired. Illustrations, pictures, graphs, etc., are desirable.
    No payment is made for accepted manuscripts. Reprints are
    available; costs vary with length and volume.

Manuscript Disposition:
    Receipt of a manuscript is acknowledged. Editorial decisions
    are made as soon as possible. Accepted articles usually appear
    in print within three to five months. Unaccepted manuscripts
    are returned without criticism or suggestions.

Copyright:
    Held by the National Recreation and Park Association.

*PHYSICAL EDUCATOR

Subscription Data:
    Published by the Phi Epsilon Kappa fraternity, 6919 East Tenth
    Street, Indianapolis, Indiana 46219. Issued four times each
    year, in March, May, October, and December. Advertising is
    not accepted. Circulation: 12,000. Subscription: $4.00 per
    year; $7.00 for two years; $10.00 for three years. Founded:
    1940.

Editorial Address:
    The Editor, Physical Educator, 1004 South Foley Street, Cham-
    paign, Illinois 61820.

Editorial Policy:
    Includes articles on health and safety at the elementary, second-
    ary, and college levels. The reading audience includes profes-
    sionals in the fields of health, safety, and recreation. Unsolic-
    ited articles are not welcome. Twelve to fifteen major articles
    are published per issue. Book reviews are included. Sections
    on Teaching Techniques, Dances, and Elsewhere in the World
    are included; also two noteworthy people are presented in each
    issue.

Manuscript Preparation:
    Accepted manuscripts average 1,500 words, but often range
    from 1,000 to 2,000 words. Two copies are required. Return
    postage and a self-addressed envelope are desired. Footnoting
    and other bibliographical procedure may follow any widely used
    style manual. Use wide margins and double-space. A back-
    ground or explanatory cover letter about the article is desired,

but not an outline or summary. Biographical information about
the author is desired and should include a summary of current position, professional experience, and earned degrees. Illustrations and pictures may be used. No payment is made for
accepted articles. Reprints are not available.

Manuscript Disposition:
    Receipt of a manuscript is acknowledged. Editorial decisions
    are made within six to eight weeks. Accepted articles usually
    appear in print within 10 to 14 months after acceptance. Unac-
    cepted manuscripts are returned with criticism and/or sugges-
    tions often given if return postage has been included.

Copyright:
    Held by the Phi Epsilon Kappa fraternity.

Additional Information:
    Physical Educator is not a fraternity magazine, but strictly a
    professional publication.

RESEARCH QUARTERLY

Subscription Data:
    Published by the American Alliance for Health, Physical Edu-
    cation, and Recreation, 1201 Sixteenth Street, N. W., Washington,
    D. C. 20036. Issued quarterly, in March, May, October, and
    December. Advertising is accepted. Circulation: 15, 000. Sub-
    scription: Free to members; $15.00 to institutions; $10.00 to
    students. Founded: 1930.

Editorial Address:
    John S. Mitchem, Editor, Research Quarterly, American Al-
    liance for Health, Physical Education and Recreation, Baruch
    College, 17 Lexington Avenue, New York, New York 10010.

Editorial Policy:
    Includes articles which report research in health education and
    physical education, with emphasis on recent research studies,
    reviews of research, critical comment of published research,
    and descriptions of new research apparatus or techniques. The
    reading audience includes health, physical education, and recrea-
    tion educators. Unsolicited articles are welcome. Fifteen ma-
    jor articles are published per issue.

Manuscript Preparation:
    Accepted manuscripts average from 10 to 15 double-spaced type-
    written pages, or from 4, 500 to 5, 000 words including tabular
    material. Three copies are required. Return postage and a
    self-addressed envelope are not required. Footnoting and other
    bibliographical procedure follow style manual that is available
    from editor upon request. Indent the first line of each para-
    graph and number paragraphs consecutively throughout the manu-
    script. A brief abstract of not more than 200 words (including
    purpose, procedure, and findings) should be typed on a separate
    page. Biographical information about the author is required.
    Illustrations, graphs (in India ink), and pictures may be used.
    Policies concerning illustrations, pictures and graphs are in
    guide for contributors. Extended tabular material or other

supplementary information may be deposited with the American
Documentation Institute. Type each table on a separate page and
indicate its approximate location in the article. Photographs
must be clear black and white prints on glossy paper. Identify
all photographs. No payment is made for accepted manuscripts.
Reprints are available to the author from another printer.

Manuscript Disposition:
Receipt of a manuscript is acknowledged. Editorial decisions
are made within six months. All manuscripts are read by at
least three members of the editorial board. Accepted articles
usually appear in print within ten to twelve months. Unaccepted
manuscripts are returned, often with criticism and/or suggestions.

Copyright:
Held by the American Alliance for Health, Physical Education,
and Recreation.

SCHOLASTIC COACH

Subscription Data:
Published by Scholastic Magazines, Inc., 50 West Forty-fourth
Street, New York, New York 10036. Issued 10 times each year,
September through June. Advertising is accepted. Circulation:
39,000. Subscription: $4.00 per year. Founded: 1931.

Editorial Address:
The Editor, Scholastic Coach, 50 West Forty-fourth Street, New
York, New York 10036.

Editorial Policy:
Includes technical how-to articles on all phases of school athletics. The reading audience includes college and high school
coaches. Unsolicited articles are welcome. Fifteen major articles are published per issue. Book reviews are included.

Manuscript Preparation:
Accepted manuscripts average from four to ten double-spaced
typewritten pages. One copy is required. Return postage and a
self-addressed envelope are unnecessary. See a recent issue
for footnoting and other bibliographical procedure. Use wide
margins and double-space throughout. A background or explanatory cover letter about the article is not desired nor is an outline or summary. Biographical information about the author is
unnecessary. Illustrations, graphs, etc., are welcome. Payment for accepted articles is made at a rate of $30.00 per man-
uscript. Reprints are sometimes available.

Manuscript Disposition:
Editorial decisions are made within two weeks. Accepted articles appear in print within one year after acceptance. Unaccepted
manuscripts are returned, often with suggestions or detailed criticism.

Copyright:
Held by Scholastic Magazines, Inc.

POLITICAL SCIENCE

†*AMERICAN ACADEMY OF POLITICAL AND SOCIAL SCIENCE. AN-
NALS

Subscription Data:
    Published by the American Academy of Political and Social Sci-
    ence, 3937 Chestnut Street, Philadelphia, Pennsylvania 19104.
    Issued six times each year, in January, March, May, July,
    September, and November. Advertising is accepted. Circula-
    tion: 24,000. Subscription: $12.00 per year. Founded: 1890.
Editorial Address:
    The Editor, Annals of the American Academy of Political and
    Social Science, 3937 Chestnut Street, Philadelphia, Pennsylvania
    19104.
Editorial Policy:
    Includes articles in the fields of the social sciences. The read-
    ing audience includes professional and lay people. Unsolicited
    manuscripts are not published as each issue's special editor se-
    lects contributors for a given theme. Approximately 14 major
    articles are published per issue. Seventy-five book reviews are
    included per issue; also included is a listing of approximately
    250 books.

AMERICAN POLITICAL SCIENCE REVIEW

Subscription Data:
    Published by the American Political Science Association, 1527
    New Hampshire Avenue, N.W., Washington, D.C. 20036. Is-
    sued quarterly, in March, June, September, and December.
    Advertising is accepted. Circulation: 20,000. Subscription:
    $20.00 to $30.00 per year based on income; $10.00 to graduate
    and undergraduate students; $50.00 per year to institutions; add
    $1.00 for foreign subscriptions. Founded: 1906.
Editorial Address:
    Nelson Polsby, Managing Editor, American Political Science Re-
    view, Department of Political Science, University of California,
    Berkeley, California 94720.
Editorial Policy:
    Includes articles on all phases of political science and other
    closely related topics. The reading audience includes political
    scientists, other social scientists, and students. Unsolicited
    articles are welcome. Nine or ten major articles are published
    per issue. Book reviews are included. Address books intended
    for review to Philip Siegeman, 210 Barrones Hall, University of
    California, Berkeley, Berkeley, California 94720.

Manuscript Preparation:

Accepted manuscripts range from 20 to 30 double-spaced typewritten pages. Two copies are required. Return postage and
a self-addressed envelope are desired. Bibliographical procedure should follow the University of Chicago Manual of Style.
Use one inch margins and double-space throughout. Place all
footnotes on a separate page at the end of the article. A background or explanatory cover letter about the article is desired,
but not an outline or summary. The author's name and professional affiliation should appear only on a separate covering page;
other biographical information is unnecessary. Illustrations,
graphs, etc., are rarely used. No payment is made for accepted articles. Reprints are available through the Johnson Reprint Corporation, 111 Fifth Avenue, New York, New York
10003. Fifty free reprints are mailed to the author.

Manuscript of Disposition:

Receipt of a manuscript is acknowledged. Editorial decisions
are made within two to three months. Accepted articles usually
appear in print within three to six months after acceptance. Unaccepted manuscripts are returned, often with criticism.

Copyright:

Held by the American Political Science Association.

*COMPACT

Subscription Data:

Published by the Education Commission of the States, 1860 Lincoln Street, Denver, Colorado 80203. Issued bimonthly, in January, March, May, July, September, and November. Advertising is accepted. Circulation: 15,000. Subscription: $6.00 per
year. Founded: 1967.

Editorial Address:

Robert L. Jacobson, Managing Editor, Compact, Education Commission of the States, 1860 Lincoln Street, Denver, Colorado
80203.

Editorial Policy:

The reading audience includes educators and political leaders,
especially at the state level. Unsolicited manuscripts are not
accepted; however, queries are welcome. Twelve major articles are published per issue. Book reviews are included.

Manuscript Preparation:

Accepted manuscripts average length depends on content. Payment is made for accepted manuscripts.

Manuscript Disposition:

Receipt of a manuscript is acknowledged.

Copyright:

Held by the Education Commission of the States.

FORUM ON PUBLIC AFFAIRS

Subscription Data:

Published by the Institute of Public Affairs, University of

Wisconsin - Platteville, Platteville, Wisconsin 53818. Issued semi-annually. Advertising is not accepted. Circulation: 400. Subscription: $2.00 donation to the Institute for the two issues per year. Founded: 1964.

Editorial Address:

The Editor, Forum on Public Affairs, Institute of Public Affairs, University of Wisconsin - Platteville, Platteville, Wisconsin 53818.

Editorial Policy:

Includes articles on current issues in public affairs which report or have been the result of empirical and scholarly study. Addresses presented by participants attending each semi-annual Forum on Public Affairs conducted by the Institute is selectively included. The reading audience includes major university libraries in addition to interested individuals and research centers. Unsolicited manuscripts are welcome. Two to four major articles are published per issue. Book reviews are included.

Manuscript Preparation:

Accepted manuscripts average 40 double-spaced typewritten pages, but length may vary with author requirements. Two copies are required. Return postage and a self-addressed envelope are not required. Bibliographical procedure should follow the Turabian Manual for Writers. Footnotes should be placed at the end of the article. Use one wide margin for editing. Double-space throughout. A background or explanatory cover letter is not required, but a short abstract is preferred. Biographical information about the author is required. All illustrations and graphs will be produced directly from the author's copy and none may be larger than five by eight inches. Pictures will be used. Reprints are not available.

Manuscript Disposition:

Receipt of a manuscript is acknowledged. Editorial decisions require at least eight weeks. Time from acceptance of a manuscript to its appearance in print varies with editorial need and available space. Unaccepted manuscripts are returned with criticism and suggestions.

Copyright:

Not copyrighted.

Additional Information:

Permission is granted to reproduce articles and parts of articles published in the journal. In addition to crediting the author with his "by-line," please acknowledge reproduction as follow: "Reprinted by courtesy of Forum on Public Affairs, University of Wisconsin - Platteville, Platteville, Wisconsin." Reproductions of all or substantial parts of any article for commercial purpose must receive the approval of the author.

JOURNAL OF POLITICS

Subscription Data:

Published by the Southern Political Science Association, Peabody Hall, University of Florida, Gainesville, Florida 32601. Issued quarterly, in February, May, August, and November.

Advertising is accepted. Circulation: 4, 000. Subscription:
$8.00 per year (add $1.00 per year for foreign postage); $5.00
to students; $10.00 to institutions. Founded: 1939.

Editorial Address:
Donald Strong, Editor, Journal of Politics, Department of Political Science, University of Alabama, University, Alabama 35486.

Editorial Policy:
Includes articles on all phases of political science and related
fields. The reading audience includes political scientists, students, and other interested persons. Unsolicited manuscripts
are welcome. Eight major articles are published per issue.
Book reviews are included.

Manuscript Preparation:
Accepted manuscripts range from 25 to 50 double-spaced typewritten pages. One copy is required. Return postage and a
self-addressed envelope are desired. Use wide margins and
double-space throughout. Avoid use of footnotes where possible.
A background or explanatory cover letter about the article is unnecessary and no outline or summary is required. Biographical
information about the author is required and should include an
indication of current position and qualifications as a writer. Illustrations, graphs, and charts can be used, but pictures cannot.
No payment is made for accepted articles. Reprints are available at cost.

Manuscript Disposition:
Receipt of a manuscript is acknowledged. Editorial decisions
are made as soon as possible. Time from acceptance of a
manuscript to its appearance in print varies with the backlog of
accepted articles. Unaccepted manuscripts are returned, often
with criticism and/or suggestions.

Copyright:
Held by the Southern Political Science Association.

*MIDDLE EAST JOURNAL

Subscription Data:
Published by the Middle East Institute, 1761 North Street, N.W.,
Washington, D.C. 20036. Issued quarterly, in winter, spring,
summer, and autumn. Advertising is accepted. Circulation:
3, 800. Subscription: $10.00 per year. Founded: 1947.

Editorial Address:
The Editor, Middle East Journal, 1761 North Street, N.W.,
Washington, D.C. 20036.

Editorial Policy:
Includes articles on contemporary Middle East, politics, economics, sociology, anthropology, covering from North Africa to
Pakistan. The reading audience includes professors, advanced
students, interested government officials and businessmen, whose
specialty is Middle East. Unsolicited manuscripts are not welcome. Four major articles are published per issue. Book reviews and a Bibliography of Periodical Literature are included.

Manuscript Preparation:
Accepted manuscripts average 5, 000 words. One copy is

required. Return postage and a self-addressed envelope are not
required. Bibliographical procedure should follow the University
of Chicago Manual of Style. Double-space and place footnotes
at the end of each manuscript. A background or explanatory
cover letter is required, but not an outline, summary, or abstract. Biographical information about the author is helpful.
An occasional graph is used. No payment is made for accepted
manuscripts. One-hundred reprints are available to each author.
Manuscript Disposition:
 Receipt of a manuscript is acknowledged. Editorial decisions
are made within eight weeks. Accepted articles usually appear
in print within six months. Unaccepted manuscripts are returned,
sometimes with criticism and/or suggestions.
Copyright:
 Held by the Middle East Institute.

NEW REPUBLIC

Subscription Data:
 Published by Robert Myers, 1244 Nineteenth Street, N.W., Wash-
ington, D.C. 20036. Issued weekly, except combined issue in
January and July and two in August. Advertising is accepted.
Circulation: 150,000. Subscription: $15.00 per year. Founded:
1914.
Editorial Address:
 The Editor, New Republic, 1244 Nineteenth Street, N.W., Washington, D.C. 20036.
Editorial Policy:
 Includes articles which relate to public affairs, literature, and
the arts. The reading audience includes well educated persons
from many disciplines including education. Unsolicited articles
are welcome. Six major articles are published per issue. Book
reviews are included.
Manuscript Preparation:
 Accepted manuscripts range from 1,000 to 1,500 words. One
copy is required. Return postage and a self-addressed envelope
are desired. Do not use footnotes. Use wide margins and double-space. A background or explanatory cover letter is required.
An outline or summary of the article is desired in advance of or
with submission of the finished manuscript. Biographical information about the author is desired and should include a summary
of professional qualifications. Illustrations, pictures, and graphs
may not be used. Payment of $.08 per word is made for ac-
cepted articles. Reprints are sometimes available; costs vary
with article length and order volume.
Manuscript Disposition:
 Receipt of a manuscript is acknowledged. Editorial decisions
are made as soon as possible. Accepted articles usually appear
in print within two weeks after acceptance. Unaccepted manuscripts are returned.
Copyright:
 Held by New Republic.

PARTISAN REVIEW

Subscription Data:
 Published by Partisan Review, Inc., Rutgers University, One
 Richardson Street, New Brunswick, New Jersey 08903. Issued
 quarterly, in February, May, July, and October. Advertising
 is accepted. Circulation: 10,000. Subscription: $5.50 per
 year; $4.50 to students. Founded: 1934.
Editorial Address:
 The Editor, Partisan Review, Rutgers University, One Richardson Street, New Brunswick, New Jersey 08903.
Editorial Policy:
 Includes articles and book reviews on contemporary political,
 social, and cultural topics. Readers have an informed and serious interest in books, art, general cultural, and political subjects. Unsolicited manuscripts are welcome. Number of major
 articles varies. Book reviews are included.
Manuscript Preparation:
 Accepted manuscripts average 2,000 words. One copy is required. Return postage and a self-addressed envelope are required. Avoid footnotes and use double-spacing. A background
 or explanatory cover letter is not required nor is an outline,
 summary, or abstract. Biographical information about the author
 is not required. Illustrations, pictures, graphs, etc., are rarely used. Payment of $.015 per word is made for accepted
 manuscripts. Reprint policy can be arranged.
Manuscript Disposition:
 Receipt of a manuscript is not acknowledged. Editorial decisions are made within five months. Unaccepted manuscripts are
 returned if they include return postage. Criticism and/or suggestions are not provided.
Copyright:
 Held by Partisan Review.

POLITICAL SCIENCE QUARTERLY

Subscription Data:
 Published by the Academy of Political Science, 2852 Broadway,
 New York, New York 10025. Issued four times each year, in
 March, June, September, and December. Advertising is ac-
 cepted. Circulation: 10,700. Subscription: $12.00 per year.
 Founded: 1880.
Editorial Address:
 The Editor, Political Science Quarterly, 2852 Broadway, New
 York, New York 10025.
Editorial Policy:
 Includes articles which relate to contemporary and historical
 aspects of government, politics, and public affairs. The read-
 ing audience includes professors, businessmen, government of-
 ficials, lawyers, and students. Unsolicited manuscripts are
 welcome. Six major articles are published per issue. Book
 reviews are included.

Manuscript Preparation:
Accepted manuscripts average 6,000 words. Two copies are required. Return postage and a self-addressed envelope are required. List footnotes on a separate page; double-space within footnote. Use wide margins, double-space throughout. A background or explanatory cover letter and an abstract are required. Biographical information about the author is required. Illustrations, pictures, graphs, etc., may be used when submitted on a separate page. No payment is made for accepted manuscripts. Reprints are available at cost; author receives 50 complimentary reprints.

Manuscript Disposition:
Receipt of a manuscript is acknowledged. Editorial decisions are made within four to five weeks. Accepted articles usually appear in print within three to six months. Unaccepted manuscripts are not returned.

Copyright:
Held by the Academy of Political Science.

†PUBLIC OPINION QUARTERLY

Subscription Data:
Published by the Columbia University Press, 136 South Broadway, Irvington-on-Hudson, New York 10533. Sponsored by the Advisory Committee on Communication, Columbia University. Issued quarterly. Advertising is accepted. Circulation: 5,300. Subscription: $8.50 per year; $15.00 for two years; $19.50 for three years; $8.80 foreign; $15.50 foreign for two years; $20.40 foreign for three years; $3.50 per issue. Founded: 1937.

Editorial Address:
Bernard Roshco, Editor, Public Opinion Quarterly, Journalism Building, Columbia University, 116th Street and Broadway, New York, New York 10027.

Editorial Policy:
Includes articles which report public opinion on a wide variety of topics. The Quarterly is hospitable to all points of view provided that the material presented will help to illuminate problems of communication and public opinion. The reading audience includes personnel from academic, business, and governmental fields. Unsolicited articles are welcome. Seven major articles are published per issue. Book reviews are included.

Manuscript Preparation:
Accepted manuscripts average 5,000 words. Two copies are required. Return postage and a self-addressed envelope are desired. Bibliographical procedure may follow any widely used style manual. Use one inch margins and double-space. Place footnotes at the bottom of the page on which the reference occurs. A background or explanatory cover letter about the article is not desired nor is an outline or summary. Biographical information about the author is desired and should include a summary of present position and major accomplishments. Illustrations, pictures, graphs, etc., may be used. No payment is made for accepted manuscripts. Reprints are not often available.

Manuscript Disposition:

Receipt of a manuscript is acknowledged. Editorial decisions are made within two months. Accepted articles usually appear in print within six months after acceptance. Unaccepted manuscripts are returned, often with criticism and/or suggestions.

Copyright:

Held by the Columbia University Press.

Additional Information:

Statements of fact and opinion are made on the responsibility of the authors alone and do not necessarily represent the views of the editors, sponsor, or publisher.

REVIEW OF POLITICS

Subscription Data:

Published by the University of Notre Dame, Box B, Notre Dame, Indiana 46556. Issued quarterly, in January, April, July, and October. Advertising for books and journals is accepted. Circulation: 2,400. Subscription: $7.00 per year. Founded: 1939.

Editorial Address:

The Editor, Review of Politics, Box B, Notre Dame, Indiana 46556.

Editorial Policy:

Includes articles and reports on politics, political theory, and related topics. The reading audience includes educators, students, governmental officials, and other interested persons. Unsolicited articles are welcome. Five or six major articles are published per issue. Book reviews are included.

Manuscript Preparation:

Accepted manuscripts range from 2,500 to 10,000 words, depending on the topic covered. One copy is required. Return postage and a self-addressed envelope are desired. Footnoting and other bibliographical procedure should follow the University of Chicago Manual of Style. Use wide margins and double-space. A background or explanatory cover letter about the article is not desired nor is an outline or summary. Biographical information about the author is unnecessary. Illustrations, pictures, graphs, etc., may not be used. No payment is made for accepted articles. Reprints are available; 50 free copies are mailed to the author.

Manuscript Disposition:

Receipt of a manuscript is acknowledged. Editorial decisions are made within three months. Accepted articles usually appear in print within four to twenty-four months after acceptance. Unaccepted manuscripts are returned, sometimes with criticism and/or suggestions.

Copyright:

Held by Review of Politics.

RUSSIAN REVIEW

Subscription Data:
Published by the Russian Review, Inc., Hoover Institution, Stanford, California 94305. Issued quarterly, in January, April, July, and October. Advertising is accepted. Circulation: 2,000. Subscription: $9.00 per year; $16.00 for two years (domestic rate). Founded: 1941.

Editorial Address:
The Editor, Russian Review, Hoover Institution, Stanford, California 94305.

Editorial Policy:
Includes articles on Russian and Soviet history, literature, culture, politics and education. The reading audience consists of scholars, teachers, and students. Unsolicited articles should be accompanied by return postage. Six major articles are published in each issue. An extensive book review section is included in each issue.

Manuscript Preparation:
Accepted manuscripts average 3,500 to 5,000 words. One copy is required. Return postage and a self-addressed envelope are required. Double-space manuscripts; footnotes should follow the University of Chicago Manual of Style. Do not use footnotes for book reviews. An outline, summary, or abstract of the article is not required. Biographical information about the author is required and should contain background, present academic rank, and publications. No illustrations are accepted. No payment is made for accepted manuscripts; 25 free reprints are available for each author. Editor's permission is required for reprints.

Manuscript Disposition:
Receipt of a manuscript is acknowledged. Editorial decisions are made within two to three weeks. Accepted articles appearance in print depends on how the material lines up. Unaccepted manuscripts are returned if return postage is supplied by the author. Criticism and/or suggestions are sometimes provided.

Copyright:
Held by the Russian Review, Inc.

TEACHING POLITICAL SCIENCE

Subscription Data:
Published by Sage Publications, Inc., 275 South Beverly Drive, Beverly Hills, California 90212. Issued semiannually. Advertising is accepted. Circulation: Not determined. Subscription: $8.00 per year; $16.00 to institutions; $1.00 more for foreign mailing. Founded: October, 1973.

Editorial Address:
The Editor, Teaching Political Science, 1414 Social Sciences Building, University of Minnesota, Minneapolis, Minnesota 55455.

Editorial Policy:
Seeks empirical research articles, reports, and essays which emphasize teaching with direct application to the subject matter of political science. The overall objective is to contribute to the recognition of the teaching function as an important part of the academic profession. The reading audience includes teachers of political science at the college level, and graduate students, and teachers of political science and social science at the pre-collegiate level. Unsolicited manuscripts are welcome. Two to four major articles are published per issue. Book reviews are included.

Manuscript Preparation:
Articles should not exceed 25 to 30 double-spaced typewritten pages with footnotes, references, tables, and charts on separate pages. Teaching Notes should average three to four pages. Two copies are required. Return postage and a self-addressed envelope are not required. Bibliographical procedure should follow the Sage style sheet available on request from Sage Publications or editors. All footnotes and references should be listed on separate pages at end of the manuscript. Use six inch lines and double-space. A background or explanatory cover letter is not required, nor is an outline, summary, or abstract. Biographical information about the author is required upon acceptance of the manuscript for publication. Artwork should be prepared for maximum size of 4-1/2 inches wide by 6 inches deep and should be clean and sharp black on white paper. Glossy photostats are best. No payment is made for accepted manuscripts. Reprint information is available from the publisher's address.

Manuscript Disposition:
Receipt of a manuscript is acknowledged. Editorial decisions are made within eight weeks. Accepted articles usually appear in print within 18 months. Unaccepted manuscripts are returned upon request with criticism and/or suggestions.

Copyright:
Held by Sage Publications, Inc.

WORLD POLITICS

Subscription Data:
Published by the Princeton University Press, William Street, Princeton, New Jersey 08540. Sponsored by the Center of International Studies, Princeton University. Issued quarterly, in October, January, April, and July. Advertising is accepted. Circulation: 4,000. Subscription: $9.00 per year; $15.00 for two years; $20.50 for three years; foreign postage is $.50 additional per year. Founded: 1948.

Editorial Address:
Corwin Hall, Editor, World Politics, Princeton University, Princeton, New Jersey 08540.

Editorial Policy:
Includes articles which report scholarly research having broad

theoretical significance in interantional relations. The reading
audience includes professors, researchers, and graduate students.
Unsolicited manuscripts are welcome. Approximately five major
articles are published per issue. Book review articles are included in addition to major articles.

Manuscript Preparation:

Accepted manuscripts average from 3,000 to 5,000 words. Preferably two copies are required. Return postage and a self-addressed envelope are not required. See a recent issue for bibliographical procedure. Footnotes should be double-spaced and
listed at the end of the article. A style sheet will be sent on
request. Use wide margins and double-space throughout. A
background or explanatory cover letter is not required. An abstract is appreciated and is needed at time of publication. Biographical information about the author is required at time of publication only--not at time of manuscript submission. Illustrations,
pictures, graphs, etc., are used only where copy is suitable for
line cuts. Payment of $50.00 per article is made for accepted
manuscripts. Reprint permissions are handled by the Princeton
University Press. One-hundred free offprints are available at
time of publication with additional offprints available at cost, in
multiples of 100, at time of publication.

Manuscript Disposition:

Receipt of a manuscript is acknowledged. Editorial decisions
are made within one to three months. Accepted articles usually
appear in print within four to ten months. Unaccepted manuscripts are returned, without criticism or suggestions.

Copyright:

Held by the Princeton University Press.

PSYCHIATRY

AMERICAN ACADEMY OF CHILD PSYCHIATRY. JOURNAL

Subscription Data:
  Published by Yale University Press, 92A Yale Station, New Haven, Connecticut 06520. Sponsored by the American Academy of Child Psychiatry. Issued quarterly, in winter, spring, summer, and fall. Advertising is accepted. Circulation: 4,000. Subscription: $17.50 per year; $19.50 foreign; $6.00 per issue. Founded: 1962.

Editorial Address:
  Eveoleen N. Rexford, M.D., Editor, Journal of the American Academy of Child Psychiatry, 100 Memorial Drive, Suite 2-9B, Cambridge, Massachusetts 02142.

Editorial Policy:
  Includes valid articles relevant to maturational patterns, child development, and childhood problems that will serve to increase or integrate knowledge concerning the psychological aspects of childhood. The reading audience includes child psychiatrists, social workers, psychologists, educators, and others concerned with childhood emotional development and disorder. Unsolicited manuscripts are welcome. A variable number of major articles are published per issue. Book reviews are included.

Manuscript Preparation:
  No limitations are placed upon length of accepted manuscripts. One original and three carbons are required. Return postage and a self-addressed envelope are not required, but desired. Specific instructions regarding footnoting and other bibliographical procedure are sent to potential authors upon request. Use 1-1/2 inch margins and double-space. A background or explanatory cover letter is desired, but an outline, summary, or abstract is not required. Biographical information about the author is desired and should include a summary of his current professional affiliations. Illustrations, pictures, graphs, etc., may be used, but publication costs must be paid by the author. No payment is made for accepted manuscripts. Reprints are available; costs vary with length and order volume.

Manuscript Disposition:
  Receipt of a manuscript is acknowledged. Editorial decisions are made within three to six months. Accepted articles usually appear in print within one year after acceptance. Unaccepted manuscripts are returned, with criticism and/or suggestions.

Copyright:
  Held by the American Academy of Child Psychiatry.

AMERICAN JOURNAL OF PSYCHIATRY

Subscription Data:
 Published by the American Psychiatric Association, 1700 Eighteenth Street, N. W. , Washington, D. C. 20009. Issued monthly. Advertising is accepted. Circulation: 26, 682. Subscription: $15. 00 per year; $15. 75 to Canada and South America; $18. 00 foreign; $1. 75 plus postage per issue. Founded: 1844.

Editorial Address:
 The Editor, American Journal of Psychiatry, American Psychiatric Association, 1700 Eighteenth Street, N. W. , Washington, D. C. 20009.

Editorial Policy:
 Includes original psychiatry material only with articles on research, general psychiatry, and mental health. The reading audience includes psychiatrists and other mental health professionals. Unsolicited manuscripts are welcome. Twenty-two major articles are published per issue. Book reviews are included.

Manuscript Preparation:
 Accepted manuscripts should not exceed 10 to 12 typewritten pages. Two copies are required. Return postage and a self-addressed envelope are not required. Bibliographical procedure should follow the style according to Index Medicus. There are no special manuscript footnoting recommendations as this is done in editing. Double-space the manuscript. A background or explanatory cover letter is required. An outline, summary, or abstract is preferred, but can be done in editing. Biographical information about the author is required. All tables should read vertically and all figures should be glossy prints suitable for photographing. No payment is made for accepted manuscripts. Reprints must be ordered by authors; none are furnished free.

Manuscript Disposition:
 Receipt of a manuscript is acknowledged. Editorial decisions are made within four weeks. Accepted articles usually appear in print within six to eight months. Unaccepted manuscripts are returned with criticism and/or suggestions.

Copyright:
 Held by the American Psychiatric Association.

AMERICAN PSYCHOANALYTIC ASSOCIATION. JOURNAL

Subscription Data:
 Published by the International Universities Press, Inc. , 239 Park Avenue, South, New York, New York 10003, for the American Psychoanalytic Association. Issued quarterly. Selected advertising is accepted. Circulation: 5, 000. Subscription: $17. 50 per year. Founded: 1953.

Editorial Address:
 The Editor, Journal of the American Psychoanalytic Association, 23 The Hemlocks, Roslyn Estates, New York 11576.

Editorial Policy:
  Includes contributions to the psychoanalytic literature whether
  clinical, theoretical, historical, or an application of psychoanalysis. Contributions to psychoanalytic education and research
  are also welcome. The reading audience includes psychoanalysts
  and people in the mental health professions. Unsolicited manuscripts are welcome. Seven to eight major articles are published per issue. Book reviews are included.

Manuscript Preparation:
  Accepted manuscripts vary in length, but are usually under 40
  typewritten pages. Three or four copies are required. Return
  postage and a self-addressed envelope are not required. See
  style instruction on inside cover for bibliographical procedure,
  footnoting, and manuscript margin and spacing recommendations.
  A background or explanatory cover letter is not required, but an
  outline, summary, or abstract is required. Biographical information about the author is not required. Author may have to pay
  for utilization of illustrations, pictures, graphs, etc. No payment is made for accepted manuscripts. Reprints can be obtained at author's option and expense.

Manuscript Disposition:
  Receipt of a manuscript is acknowledged. Editorial decisions
  are made within eight weeks. Accepted articles usually appear
  in print within 12 months. Unaccepted manuscripts are returned
  with criticism and/or suggestions.

Copyright:
  Held by the American Psychoanalytic Association.

CHILD PSYCHIATRY AND HUMAN DEVELOPMENT

Subscription Data:
  Published by Behavioral Publications, 72 Fifth Avenue, New York,
  New York 10011. Issued quarterly. Advertising is accepted.
  Circulation: 2,000. Subscription: $15.00 per year; $30.00 to
  institutions. Founded: 1970.

Editorial Address:
  John S. Duffy, M.D., Medical Director, Editor, Child Psychiatry
  and Human Development, Tucson Child Guidance Center, 1415
  North Fremont Avenue, Tucson, Arizona 85719.

Editorial Policy:
  The journal was created to serve the allied professional groups
  represented by the specialities of child psychiatry, pediatrics,
  psychology, social science, and human development in their task:
  to define the developing child and adolescent in health and con-
  flict. CPHD is open to all points of view and articles accepted
  are determined only by the quality of scholarship. The reading
  audience includes child psychiatrists, pediatricians, and psychologists. Unsolicited manuscripts are welcome. Five major
  articles are published per issue. Book reviews are included.

Manuscript Preparation:
  Accepted manuscripts should not exceed more than 20 double-
  spaced pages. Three copies are required. Return postage and

a self-addressed envelope are required. Citations are to appear within the text, in parentheses. Use only the author's last name and publication date. Footnotes are discouraged. Use one inch margins on the top, sides, and bottom and double-space. A background or explanatory cover letter and an outline, summary, or abstract are required. Biographical information about the author is required. Illustrations, pictures, graphs, etc., should be placed on separate pages at the end of manuscripts and marked with Arabic numerals, indicate where placed in the manuscript. No payment is made for accepted manuscripts. No free reprints are available; cost varies with length of article.

Manuscript Disposition:
    Receipt of a manuscript is acknowledged. Editorial decisions are made within six months to one year. Accepted articles usually appear in print within six months to one year. Unaccepted manuscripts are returned if stamped self-addressed envelope is provided. Criticism and/or suggestions are provided upon request.

Copyright:
    Held by Behavioral Publications.

*FOREIGN PSYCHIATRY

Subscription Data:
    Published by the International Arts and Sciences Press, 901 North Broadway, White Plains, New York 10603. Issued quarterly, in fall, winter, spring, and summer. Advertising is accepted and consists of mainly exchange ads. Circulation: Not determined. Subscription: $15.00 per year; $55.00 to institutions. Founded: 1972.

Editorial Address:
    Nathan S. Kline, M.D., Director, Editor, Foreign Psychiatry, Research Center, Rockland State Hospital, Orangeburg, New York 10962.

Editorial Policy:
    Foreign Psychiatry is a translation journal covering all aspects of psychiatry. The reading audience includes professionals. Unsolicited manuscripts are generally not welcome. Approximately six to eight major articles are published per issue. Book reviews are not included at the present time.

Copyright:
    Held by the International Arts and Sciences Press.

HOSPITAL AND COMMUNITY PSYCHIATRY

Subscription Data:
    Published by the American Psychiatric Association, 1700 Eighteenth Street, N.W., Washington, D.C. 20009. Issued monthly. Advertising is accepted. Circulation: 18,200. Subscription: $12.00 per year; or through membership in the Hospital and Community Psychiatry Service. Founded: 1950.

Editorial Address:

The Editor, Hospital and Community Psychiatry, American Psychiatric Association, 1700 Eighteenth Street, N.W., Washington, D.C. 20009.

Editorial Policy:

Includes articles in the field of psychiatry, mental health, and mental retardation, especially those related to organization, administration, or operation of programs in mental health facilities or agencies. The reading audience includes psychiatrists, social workers, administrators of mental health programs, and various other workers in the mental health field. Unsolicited manuscripts are welcome. Approximately ten full-length papers and five shorter papers are published per issue. Book reviews are included, but unsolicited reviews are generally not included.

Manuscript Preparation:

The journal has no fixed length restriction, but generally papers longer than 20 typed pages are not suitable. The content of the paper determines its ultimate edited length. Shorter contributions of two to eight pages are welcomed for the program briefs section or for open forum, which emphasizes opinion and comment. Two copies are required. Return postage and a self-addressed envelope are not required. Bibliographical procedure should follow the journal's own style sheet, which is similar to the MLA Style Sheet. For footnote style and content, check recent issues. List footnotes chronologically on a separate page. Use 1-1/2 inch margins and double-space throughout. A background or explanatory cover letter is not required. A 50 to 150 word summary is suggested, but not required. Biographical information about the author is required and should include job title and affiliation. Tables are used in limited numbers; figures and graphs are rarely used and to be considered they must be camera-ready and of professional quality. Photographs illustrating manuscripts are welcome. They must be clear, unmarked, black-and-white prints, five by seven or eight by ten inches. No payment is made for accepted manuscripts. All authors receive two to five complimentary copies of the issue containing their paper. A price list and order form for obtaining reprints is enclosed with the complimentary copies.

Manuscript Disposition:

Receipt of a manuscript is acknowledged. Editorial decisions are made generally within eight weeks. Accepted articles usually appear in print within six to twelve months. Unaccepted manuscripts are returned, generally without criticism and/or suggestions.

Copyright:

Held by the American Psychiatric Association.

INTERNATIONAL JOURNAL OF GROUP PSYCHOTHERAPY

Subscription Data:

Published by the American Group Psychotherapy Association, Box 230, 150 Christopher Street, New York, New York 10014.

Issued quarterly. Advertising is accepted. Circulation: 5,000.
Subscription: $15.00 per year. Founded: 1950.

Editorial Address:
Dr. Saul Scheidlinger, Editor, International Journal of Group
Psychotherapy, Box 230, 150 Christopher Street, New York,
New York 10014.

Editorial Policy:
Includes clinical and research articles on group psychotherapy.
The reading audience includes group therapists. Unsolicited
manuscripts are welcome. Twelve major articles are published
per issue. Book reviews are included.

Manuscript Preparation:
Accepted manuscripts average 20 pages in length. Two copies
are required. Return postage and a self-addressed envelope are
not required. See a recent issue for bibliographical procedure.
Footnotes are numbered consecutively on text pages, 8-1/2 by
11 inch paper and double-space. A background or explanatory
cover letter is required, but not an outline, summary, or abstract. Biographical information about the author should include
professional affiliation. Illustrations are not acceptable; tables
and graphs should be kept to a minimum. No payment is made
for accepted manuscripts. Authors may buy reprints.

Manuscript Disposition:
Receipt of a manuscript is acknowledged. Editorial decisions
are made within three months. Accepted articles usually appear
in print within six to nine months. Unaccepted manuscripts are
returned without criticism and/or suggestions.

Copyright:
Held by the American Group Psychotherapy Association.

*INTERNATIONAL JOURNAL OF MENTAL HEALTH

Subscription Data:
Published by the International Arts and Sciences Press, Inc.,
901 North Broadway, White Plains, New York 10603. Issued
quarterly. Advertising is accepted mostly on an exchange basis.
Circulation: Not known. Subscription: $15.00 per year; $35.00
to institutions. Founded: 1972.

Editorial Address:
The Editor, International Journal of Mental Health, 901 North
Broadway, White Plains, New York 10603.

Editorial Policy:
Each issue is devoted to one subject. "Mental health scientists
are still much too often not aware of what happens outside their
own backyard. The Journal bridges gaps in knowledge globally,
conceptually speaking, as well as geographically, and thus fills
an important need," states Leopold Bellak, M.D. The reading
audience is interdisciplinary. Unsolicited manuscripts are generally not welcome. A variable number of major articles are
published per issue. Book reviews are included.

Manuscript Preparation:
Manuscripts should not greatly exceed the maximum length

specified in the editor's invitation to the contributor. One original and one copy are required. Bibliographical procedure should follow the contributor's guide furnished upon request or by the modified APA Publication Manual. Footnotes should be avoided whenever possible. If they are essential and there are three or less, use an asterisk, a dagger, and a double dagger, in that order; if there are more than three footnotes, use superscript numbers. Manuscripts should be typewritten and triple-spaced throughout. Footnotes, legends, and title pages should be typed on separate sheets. Regular, hard, typewriter paper is preferred to erasable bond. Changes or corrections on the typed manuscript should be made in ink. Authors are requested to furnish a brief, identifying note concerning degree(s), professional affiliation or position, address to which requests for reprints may be directed, and other pertinent information. Drawings in black ink on white paper (graphs, diagrams, etc.) and glossy prints of photographs are acceptable. Each illustration should be accompanied by an identifying legend typed on a separate sheet. No payment is made for accepted manuscripts. Authors receive one copy and 20 offprints.

Copyright:
Held by the International Arts and Sciences Press, Inc.

JOURNAL OF GERIATRIC PSYCHIATRY

Subscription Data:
Published by the International Universities Press, Inc., 239 Park Avenue South, New York, New York 10003. Issued two times each year, in spring and fall. Advertising is not accepted. Circulation: 700. Subscription: $12.00 per volume; $7.00 per issue. Founded: 1967.

Editorial Address:
Martin A. Berezin, M.D., Editor, Journal of Geriatric Psychiatry, 90 Forest Avenue, West Newton, Massachusetts 02165.

Editorial Policy:
Includes papers on geriatric psychiatry and allied disciplines. The reading audience includes psychiatrists, psychologists, social workers, and nursing home personnel. Subscribers include medical schools and university libraries, schools of social work, and hospital libraries. Unsolicited manuscripts are welcome. Six to ten major articles are published per issue. Book reviews are included.

Manuscript Preparation:
Accepted manuscript length varies according to material and each paper is judged individually. Four copies are required. Return postage and a self-addressed envelope are not required. Bibliographical procedure should follow the International Universities Press style sheet on the preparation of manuscripts. Footnotes are to be numbered consecutively within each paper or chapter, and should appear at the bottom of the page on which the reference is made. Manuscripts must be typewritten on heavy bond paper with at least 1-1/2 inch margins. All parts should be

double-spaced, including references, footnotes, and extracts. A background or explanatory cover letter is required, but not an outline, summary, or abstract. Biographical information about the author is not required. Tables must be presented in camera-ready form, each separately. Each chart must be on a separate page and should be drawn in black India ink on white glazed paper. The costs for the publication of charts, tables, and pictures are to be paid by the author. No payment is made for accepted manuscripts. Publisher will contact author regarding reprints at time galleys are submitted.

Manuscript Disposition:
Receipt of a manuscript is acknowledged. Editorial decisions are made within six weeks. Accepted articles usually appear in print within six to twelve months. Unaccepted manuscripts are returned with criticism and/or suggestions.

Copyright:
Held by the International Universities Press, Inc.

LIFE THREATENING BEHAVIOR

Subscription Data:
Published by Behavioral Publications, 72 Fifth Avenue, New York, New York 10011. Issued quarterly. Advertising is accepted. Circulation: 2,000. Subscription: $12.00 per year; $30.00 to institutions. Founded: 1971.

Editorial Address:
Edwin S. Shneidman, Ph.D., Editor, Life Threatening Behavior, U.C.L.A. Neuropsychiatric Institute, 760 Westwood Plaza, Los Angeles, California 90024.

Editorial Policy:
Includes articles devoted to emergent approaches in theory and practice relating to self destructive and life threatening behaviors. It is multidisciplinary and concerned with a variety of subjects: suicide, suicide prevention, death, accidents, subintended death, threats to life's length and breadth from within and without. The reading audience includes psychologists, psychotherapists, and psychiatrists. Unsolicited manuscripts are welcome. Five to seven major articles are published per issue. Book reviews are included.

Manuscript Preparation:
Accepted manuscripts should not exceed 20 double-spaced pages. Three copies are required. Return postage and a self-addressed envelope are required. Bibliographical procedure should follow the APA Publication Manual. Avoid the use of footnotes. Use one inch margins on the top, sides, and bottom; double-space throughout. A background or explanatory cover letter is optional, but an outline, summary, or abstract is required. Biographical information about the author is required. Illustrations, pictures, graphs, etc., are to be placed on separate pages at the end of the manuscript and marked with Arabic numerals and also indicated where placed in the manuscript. No payment is made for accepted manuscripts. No free reprints are available; cost varies with length of the article.

384 / Psychiatry

Manuscript Disposition:
Receipt of a manuscript is acknowledged. Editorial decisions
are made within six months to one year. Accepted articles usually appear in print within six months to one year. Unaccepted
manuscripts are returned if postage is provided. Criticism and/
or suggestions are provided upon request.

Copyright:
Held by Behavioral Publications.

MH (formerly Mental Hygiene)

Subscription Data:
Published by the National Association for Mental Health, 1800
North Kent Street, Arlington, Virginia 22209. Issued quarterly,
in January, April, July, and October. Advertising is accepted.
Circulation: 6,700. Subscription: $10.00 per year; $17.00 for
two years; $25.00 for three years. Founded: 1917.

Editorial Address:
The Editor, MH, National Association for Mental Health, 1800
North Kent Street, Arlington, Virginia 22209.

Editorial Policy:
Includes articles on the social-action, treatment, and prevention
of mental illness. The reading audience includes lay and professional policymakers in the mental health field. Unsolicited manuscripts are welcome. Six to eight major articles are published
per issue. Book reviews are included.

Manuscript Preparation:
Accepted manuscripts average 3,000 words. Two copies are required. Return postage and a self-addressed envelope are required. Bibliographical procedure is not required. Manuscripts
should be double-spaced. A background or explanatory cover
letter and an outline, summary, or abstract are required. Biographical information about the author is required. Eight by ten
inch glossies or line art are acceptable. No payment is made
for accepted manuscripts. Permission is granted for reprints.

Manuscript Disposition:
Receipt of a manuscript is acknowledged. Editorial decisions
are made within three weeks. Accepted articles usually appear
in print within one year. Unaccepted manuscripts are returned
without criticism or suggestions.

Copyright:
Held by the National Association for Mental Health.

Additional Information:
Permission to use material in the journal should be obtained both
from the Association and the author, where practical, and credit
given to the source.

PSYCHIATRY

Subscription Data:
Published by the William Alanson White Psychiatric Foundation,

1610 New Hampshire Avenue, N. W., Washington, D. C. 20009.
Issued quarterly, in February, May, August, and November.
Advertising is accepted. Circulation: 3,500. Subscription:
$12.50 per year; $20.00 to institutions; Add $1.00 for foreign
postage excluding Canada and Mexico. Founded: 1938.

Editorial Address:

The Editor, Psychiatry, 1610 New Hampshire Avenue, N. W.,
Washington, D. C. 20009.

Editorial Policy:

The journal seeks to provide a medium for effective communication between psychiatry, the social sciences, and all other
branches of the study of man and his individual and collective
problems in living. Psychiatry is addressed to all serious students of these problems, to all who are applying current remedial measures, and to all who are searching for more effective
solutions. The aim is to encourage an integrative and truly
cumulative growth of knowledge by facilitating mutual understanding among various disciplines and overcoming tendencies toward
insularity. The journal attempts to be broadly communicative
without sacrificing technical quality. It is designed to present
accounts of clinical and field observations, reports of original
research, surveys and critiques of scientific literature, and
studies concerning methodology, epistemology, and philosophy.
The reading audience includes psychiatrists, psychologists, sociologists, nurses, anthropologists, etc. Unsolicited manuscripts
are welcome and form the bulk of the content. Approximately
nine major articles are published per issue. Book reviews are
included.

Manuscript Preparation:

Accepted manuscripts average 10 to 50 pages. Two copies are
required. Return postage and a self-addressed envelope are required. See a recent issue for bibliographical procedure. Avoid
the use of footnotes if possible; list them on a separate page.
Double-space throughout, including quotations. A background or
explanatory cover letter is not required, nor is an outline, summary, or abstract. Biographical information about the author is
required and should include highest degree, school, and year.
Use few illustrations, pictures, graphs, etc., as possible. Only
camera-ready material is to be supplied; author is to assume
any unusual expense. No payment is made for accepted manuscripts. No complimentary copies are available; reprints can be
ordered.

Manuscript Disposition:

Receipt of a manuscript is acknowledged. Editorial decisions
are made within three or four months. Accepted articles usually appear in print within 11 to 12 months. Unaccepted manuscripts are returned if return envelope is enclosed. Criticism
and/or suggestions are provided if relevant and helpful.

Copyright:

Held by the William Alanson White Psychiatric Foundation, Inc.

Additional Information:

Manuscripts are not to be submitted if being considered by other
publications.

PSYCHIATRY IN MEDICINE

Subscription Data:
Published by Baywood Publishing Company, 43 Central Drive, Farmingdale, New York 11735. Issued quarterly, in winter, spring, summer, and fall. Exchange advertising for other professional journals is accepted. Circulation: 600. Subscription: $25.00 per year. Founded: 1970.

Editorial Address:
The Editor, Psychiatry in Medicine, Department of Psychiatry, Mount Auburn Hospital, 330 Mount Auburn Street, Cambridge, Massachusetts 02138.

Editorial Policy:
Includes mostly clinical articles that are about application of psychiatric principles to medical practice, psychological aspects of illness and hospitalization, and case conferences. The reading audience includes psychiatrists, general practitioners, nurses, mental health professionals, and social workers. Unsolicited manuscripts are welcome. Forty to fifty-five major articles are published per issue. Book reviews are included.

Manuscript Preparation:
Accepted manuscripts average 10 to 30 double-spaced typewritten pages. One original and two copies are required. Return postage and a self-addressed envelope are not required. References are to be prepared according to the style of the American Psychosomatic Society, Inc., as exemplified in Psychosomatic Medicine. Footnotes should be numbered consecutively throughout the article. Do not use printer's symbols. Footnotes should be placed on separate pages at the end of the manuscript, following references. Manuscripts must be typed on one side only of white paper, 8-1/2 by 11 inches, double-spaced with wide margins, and numbered consecutively, beginning with the first page. A background or explanatory cover letter is not required, but an abstract of 250 words or less is required. Biographical information about the author is not required. Tables should be placed on separate pages at the end of the manuscript, following the references. Figures should be submitted in a final form, suitable for photographing. They should be drawn with India ink and placed on separate pages at the end of the manuscript, following the references. Legends for both tables and figures should be supplied on separate pages, clearly labeled, at the end of the manuscript, following the references. No payment is made for accepted manuscripts. Reprints are available at cost to the author.

Manuscript Disposition:
Receipt of a manuscript is acknowledged. Editorial decisions are made within three months. Accepted articles usually appear in print within six to nine months. Unaccepted manuscripts are returned, usually with criticism and/or suggestions.

Copyright:
Held by Baywood Publishing Company.

PSYCHOANALYTIC QUARTERLY

Subscription Data:
Published by the Psychoanalytic Quarterly, Inc., 57 West Fifty-seventh Street, New York, New York 10019. Issued quarterly, in January, April, July, and October. Advertising is not accepted. Circulation: 4,600. Subscription: $15.00 per year; $16.00 foreign. Founded: 1932.

Editorial Address:
Jacob A. Arlow, M.D., Editor, The Psychoanalytic Quarterly, Psychoanalytic Quarterly, Inc., 57 West Fifty-seventh Street, New York, New York 10019.

Editorial Policy:
Includes articles on psychoanalysis, psychiatry, psychology, and related disciplines. The reading audience includes professional clinicians, educators, and advanced students. Unsolicited manuscripts are welcome. Five major articles are published per issue. Book reviews, abstracts of articles from other journals, and notes on scientific meetings are included.

Manuscript Preparation:
Accepted manuscripts average 2,500 to 5,000 words. An original and one copy are required. Return postage and a self-addressed envelope are desired. See a recent issue for bibliographical procedure. Footnotes should be typed in the body of the manuscript directly after the line containing the reference number. Use 10 space margins and double-space throughout. A background or explanatory cover letter and a summary are required. Biographical information about the author is desired. Illustrations, pictures, and graphs are used when absolutely necessary to support the text and are reproduced at the author's expense. No payment is made for accepted manuscripts. Reprints are available.

Manuscript Disposition:
Receipt of a manuscript is acknowledged. Editorial decisions are made within three months. Accepted articles usually appear in print within six months. Unaccepted manuscripts are returned, usually with criticism and/or suggestions.

Copyright:
Held by the Psychoanalytic Quarterly, Inc.

PSYCHOLOGICAL - DEVELOPMENTAL AND CLINICAL

AMERICAN ACADEMY OF PSYCHOANALYSIS. JOURNAL

Subscription Data:
  Published by John Wiley and Sons, Inc., 605 Third Avenue, New York, New York 10016. Issued quarterly. Circulation: Not known. Subscription: $21.00 per year. Founded: 1973.
Editorial Address:
  The Editor, Journal of the American Academy of Psychoanalysis, 40 Gramercy Park North, New York, New York 10010.
Editorial Policy:
  Includes articles of psychoanalytic interest. The reading audience includes all members of behavioral sciences. Unsolicited manuscripts are welcome. Approximately seven major articles are published per issue. Book reviews are not included.
Manuscript Preparation:
  No limitations are placed upon manuscript length. Three copies are required. Return postage and a self-addressed envelope are not required. Bibliographical procedure should follow the "Information for Contributors" that is available from the editor. Manuscripts should be typewritten, double-spaced (including footnotes, references, and extracts) on one side of 8-1/2 by 11 inch heavy bond paper, with at least 1-1/2 inch margins all around. Footnotes should be avoided if possible. If used, they should be numbered consecutively and typed in the body of the manuscript directly after the line containing the reference number. Initial footnotes referring to the title or author are not numbered. A background or explanatory cover letter is not required nor is an outline, summary, or abstract. Biographical information about the author is required. Tables, charts, and photographs should be submitted on separate pages. They should be self-explanatory. Photographs submitted should be eight by ten inch glossy prints. For line drawings (graphs, etc.), the figures must be drawn clearly with India ink on heavy white paper, Bristol board drawing linen, or coordinate paper with a very light blue background. No payment is made for accepted manuscripts. The author will receive with the proofs a reprint form which must be completed and returned with the proofs. Senior authors will receive 20 reprints of their articles without charge.
Manuscript Disposition:
  Receipt of a manuscript is acknowledged. Editorial decisions are made within two months. Unaccepted manuscripts are returned, with criticism and/or suggestions.
Copyright:
  Held by John Wiley and Sons, Inc.

AMERICAN IMAGO

Subscription Data:
   Published by the Wayne State University Press, Detroit, Michigan 48202. Issued quarterly, in April, July, and October. Advertising is not accepted. Circulation: 1,500. Subscription: $10.00 per year. Founded: 1939.
Editorial Address:
   Dr. Harry Slochower, American Imago, 46 East Seventy-third Street, New York, New York 10021.
Editorial Policy:
   Includes articles on psychoanalysis as applied to art, science, and other aspects of culture. The reading audience includes psychologists, educators, and students. Unsolicited articles are welcome. About four major articles are published per issue. Book reviews are included.
Manuscript Preparation:
   Accepted manuscripts average 20,000 words. Two copies are required. Return postage and a self-addressed envelope are desired. Bibliographical procedure should follow the MLA Style Sheet. A background or explanatory cover letter about the article is not desired nor is an outline, summary, or abstract. Biographical information about the author is unnecessary. No payment is made for accepted articles. Reprints are available; 25 free copies are given to each author.
Manuscript Disposition:
   Receipt of a manuscript is acknowledged. Editorial decisions are made within four weeks. Accepted articles usually appear in print within twelve months after acceptance. Unaccepted manuscripts are returned with criticism and/or suggestions.
Copyright:
   Held by the Wayne State University Press.

AMERICAN JOURNAL OF CLINICAL HYPNOSIS

Subscription Data:
   Published by the North Central Publishing Company, St. Paul, Minnesota 55107. Issued quarterly, in January, April, July, and October. Advertising is not accepted. Circulation: 3,300. Subscription: $8.50 per year; $2.50 per issue. Founded: 1957.
Editorial Address:
   William E. Edmonston, Jr., Ph.D., Editor, American Journal of Clinical Hypnosis, Department of Psychology, Colgate University, Hamilton, New York 13346.
Editorial Policy:
   Unsolicited manuscripts are welcome. Seven to twelve major articles are published per issue. Book reviews are included.
Manuscript Preparation:
   Three copies are required. Bibliographical procedure should follow the APA Publication Manual. An abstract of no more than 150 words is required.
Copyright:
   Held by the American Society of Clinical Hypnosis.

*ART PSYCHOTHERAPY

Subscription Data:
Published by Pergamon Press, Maxwell House, Elmsford, New York 10523. Issued quarterly. Advertising is accepted. Circulation: Not determined. Subscription: $10.00 per year; $30.00 to libraries. Founded: 1973.

Editorial Address:
Dr. Ernest Harms, Editor, Art Psychotherapy, 158 East Ninety-fifth Street, New York, New York 10025.

Editorial Policy:
Includes scientific articles emphasizing the therapeutic aspect of the art and pathology relationship. The reading audience includes professionals: M.D.s, psychiatrists, psychologists, occupational therapists, educators, and social workers. Solicited manuscripts are preferred. A maximum of 10 major articles are published per issue. Book reviews are included.

Manuscript Preparation:
Accepted manuscripts average 25 pages. Two copies are required. Return postage and a self-addressed envelope are not required. Bibliographical procedure should follow the APA Publication Manual. Avoid the use of footnotes. Use regular margins and spacing. A background or explanatory cover letter is welcome, but not required. An abstract is required when the author sends an unsolicited manuscript. Biographical information about the author is welcome. Use no colored illustrations; line drawings and half-tones are welcome, but do not use more than six to eight per paper. One journal copy and 25 free reprints are provided.

Manuscript Disposition:
Receipt of a manuscript is acknowledged. Editorial decisions are made within one to two months. Accepted articles usually appear in print when suitable according to the contents. Unaccepted manuscripts are returned without criticism and/or suggestions.

Copyright:
Held by Pergamon Press.

FAMILY THERAPY

Subscription Data:
Published by Libra Publishers, Inc., P.O. Box 165, 391 Willets Road, Roslyn Heights, Long Island, New York 11577. Issued triannually, in spring, fall, and winter. Advertising is accepted. Circulation: Not determined. Subscription: $16.00 per year; $30.00 for two years; $44.00 for three years; $17.00 foreign; $32.00 for two years; $47.00 for three years; $20.00 to institutions; $38.00 for two years to institutions; $56.00 for three years to institutions. Founded: 1974.

Editorial Address:
Martin G. Blinder, MD., Editor, Family Therapy, Libra Publishers, Inc., P.O. Box 165, 391 Willets Road, Roslyn Heights, Long Island, New York 11577.

Editorial Policy:

Family Therapy is a clinical journal devoted to the practice of
family, group, and other interactional therapies. Although the
family unit is considered as the base in terms of nurturing and
stimulating growth, the needs of the individual must also be met.
Therefore, a variety of directions with different treatment approaches and techniques are called for - depending on an assessment of the most effective way of proceeding. The articles
selected reflect this multi-faceted approach. The reading audience includes professionals dealing with family therapy. Unsolicited manuscripts are welcome. Approximately eight major articles are published per issue. Book reviews are not presently
included.

Manuscript Preparation:

Accepted manuscripts average 1, 200 to 6, 000 words. Two copies are required. Return postage and a self-addressed envelope
are required. Bibliographical procedure should follow any widely used style manual. List footnotes on a separate page. Use
one inch margins on all sides and double or triple-space. A
background or explanatory cover letter is not required nor is an
outline, summary, or abstract. Biographical information about
the author is required. Illustrations, pictures, graphs, are included, but camera-ready copies are preferred. No payment is
made for accepted manuscripts. Authors may purchase reprints.

Manuscript Disposition:

Receipt of a manuscript is acknowledged. Editorial decisions
are made within four weeks. Accepted articles usually appear
in print within eight months. Unaccepted manuscripts are returned, sometimes with criticism and/or suggestions.

Copyright:

Held by Libra Publishers, Inc.

GENETIC PSYCHOLOGY MONOGRAPHS

Subscription Data:

Published by the Journal Press, 2 Commercial Street, Provincetown, Massachusetts 02657. Issued four times each year, in
February, May, August, and November. Advertising is not accepted. Circulation: 1, 175. Subscription: $26. 00 per year.
Founded: 1925.

Editorial Address:

Managing Editor, Genetic Psychology Monographs, Journal Press,
2 Commercial Street, Provincetown, Massachusetts 02657.

Editorial Policy:

Includes articles which relate to developmental and clinical psychology. The reading audience includes professionals in psychology and related fields. Unsolicited articles are welcome.
Three or four major articles are published per issue. Book reviews are not included.

Manuscript Preparation:

Manuscripts should be at least 50, but not more than 300, double-spaced typewritten pages. One original typewritten version
and one copy are required. Return postage and a self-addressed

envelope are desired. See a recent issue for bibliographical procedure. Use one inch margins and double-space throughout. Footnotes should be submitted on a separate page, with insertion points indicated in the text. A background or explanatory cover letter about the article is not desired; however, each article requires a short summary at the beginning. Biographical information about the author, including a summary of education, is desired if the author is unknown to the editor. Illustrations, pictures, and graphs may be used. Figures should be submitted as clean glossy prints of approximate size of the final reproduction. Each author receives 200 free bound reprints of the article; no other payment is made. Quotations for additional reprints are made when the article is at the page-proof stage.

Manuscript Disposition:
Receipt of a manuscript is not usually acknowledged. Editorial decisions are ordinarily made within one month. Accepted articles usually appear in print within one year after acceptance. Unaccepted manuscripts are returned, often with criticism and/ or suggestions.

Copyright:
Held by the Journal Press. Authors may obtain release for any specific purpose.

INTERNATIONAL JOURNAL OF CLINICAL AND EXPERIMENTAL HYPNOSIS

Subscription Data:
Published by the Society of Clinical and Experimental Hypnosis, 205 West End Avenue, Suite 1P, New York, New York 10023. Issued quarterly, in January, April, July, and October. Advertising is not encouraged, but scientifically relevant material may be submitted. Circulation: 1,480. Subscription: $18.00 per year. Founded: 1953.

Editorial Address:
The Editor, International Journal of Clinical and Experimental Hypnosis, 111 North Forty-nineth Street, Philadelphia, Pennsylvania 19139.

Editorial Policy:
Includes papers dealing with hypnosis in psychology, psychiatry, the medical and dental specialties, and allied areas of science. Articles include clinical and experimental studies, discussion of theory, significant historical and cultural material, and related data. The reading audience is unlimited. Unsolicited manuscripts are welcome. Approximately eight major articles are published per issue. Book reviews are included.

Manuscript Preparation:
Accepted manuscripts average from five to twenty double-spaced typewritten pages, but this depends on the subject matter. Four copies are required. Return postage and a self-addressed envelope are not required. Bibliographical procedure should follow the APA Publication Manual. Footnotes should be numbered consecutively throughout the article with superscript Arabic

numerals and should be typed on a separate sheet of paper. Use 1-3/4 inch left margins and 1-1/4 inch right margins; double-space throughout on one side of the paper. A background or explanatory cover letter and an abstract that does not exceed 120 words are required. Biographical information about the author is not required. Figures and graphs must be submitted in glossy form; black and white pictures are occasionally included at author's expense. No payment is made for accepted manuscripts. Reprints may be ordered from printer at author's expense with no complimentary reprints furnished.

Manuscript Disposition:
Receipt of a manuscript is acknowledged. Editorial decisions are made within an average of 16 weeks. Accepted articles usually appear in print within 14 months from date of acceptance of final revision. Three unaccepted manuscripts are returned with comments provided by at least two peer consultants. The editor's letter, as well, discusses the paper and reviewers' comments.

Copyright:
Held by the Society for Clinical and Experimental Hypnosis.

JOURNAL OF CONTEMPORARY PSYCHOTHERAPY

Subscription Data:
Published by Long Island Consultation Center, 97-29 Sixty-fourth Road, Forest Hills, New York 11374. Issued semiannually, in summer and winter. Advertising is accepted. Circulation: 3,000. Subscription: $5.00 per year; $9.00 for two years. Founded: 1966.

Editorial Address:
The Editor, Journal of Contemporary Psychotherapy, 97-29 Sixty-fourth Road, Forest Hills, New York 11374.

Editorial Policy:
The Journal is multidisciplinary and includes brief, original papers in individual and group psychotherapy, psychoanalysis, psychiatry, casework, and allied mental health disciplines. The reading audience includes psychotherapists, psychologists, psychiatrists, social workers, students, library patrons, and hospital personnel. Unsolicited manuscripts are welcome. A variable number of major articles are published per issue. Book reviews are included.

Manuscript Preparation:
Accepted manuscripts average 10 to 15 double-spaced typewritten pages. Two copies are required. Return postage and a self-addressed envelope are not required. Bibliographical procedure should follow the APA Publication Manual. Manuscripts should be double-spaced. A background or explanatory cover letter is not required, nor is an outline, summary, or abstract. Biographical information about the author is required. Illustrations, pictures, graphs, etc., are acceptable and can be flexible. No payment is made for accepted manuscripts. Reprints are furnished to the author at a modest price.

Manuscript Disposition:

Receipt of a manuscript is acknowledged. Editorial decisions are made within eight to twelve weeks. Accepted articles usually appear in print within six to twelve months. Unaccepted manuscripts are returned, occasionally with criticism and/or suggestions.

Copyright:

Held by the Journal of Contemporary Psychotherapy. If the author specifically requests copyright, it will be granted.

JOURNAL OF COUNSELING PSYCHOLOGY

Subscription Data:

Published by the American Psychological Association, Inc., 1200 Seventeenth Street, N.W., Washington, D.C. 20036. Issued bimonthly, in January, March, May, July, September, and November. Advertising is not accepted. Circulation: 3,300. Subscription: $15.00 per year; $16.00 foreign; $3.00 per issue; $5.00 with APA membership rate. Founded: 1954.

Editorial Address:

Dr. Ralph F. Berdie, Editor, Journal of Counseling Psychology, 408 Morrill Hall, University of Minnesota, Minneapolis, Minnesota 55455.

Editorial Policy:

The Journal is a primary publication medium for theory, research, and practice concerning counseling and related activities of counselors and personnel workers. Particular attention is given to articles dealing with the developmental aspects of counseling, as well as to diagnostic, group, remedial, and therapeutic approaches. Occasionally includes topical reviews of research and other systematic surveys and also measurement and research methodology studies directly related to counseling. Reviews of tests used by counselors and basic theoretical contributions are published periodically. The Journal is designed to be of interest to psychologists and counselors in schools, colleges, and universities; public and private agencies; business and industry; and religious and military agencies. Unsolicited articles are welcome. Twenty-one major articles are published per issue. Book reviews are included.

Manuscript Preparation:

Manuscripts should not exceed 15 double-spaced typewritten pages. Two copies are required. Return postage and a self-addressed envelope are unnecessary. Bibliographical procedure should follow the instructions provided in each Journal. Use wide margins and double-space throughout. A background or explanatory cover letter about the article is unnecessary. An abstract of 100 to 200 words is required with the manuscript. Biographical information about the author is usually unnecessary. Illustrations, pictures, and graphs, suitable for reproduction, may be used. No payment is made for accepted articles. Authors may order reprints of their articles from the printer when they receive galley proofs.

Copyright:

Held by the American Psychological Association. Written permission must be obtained from the APA for copying or reprinting tables, figures, or text of more than 500 words. Permission is normally granted contingent upon like permission of the author, inclusion of the APA copyright notice on the first page of reproduced material, and payment of $10.00 per page of APA material. Permission fees are waived for authors who wish to reproduce their own articles, or when material is reproduced in limited quantities for instructional purposes.

JOURNAL OF EMOTIONAL EDUCATION

Subscription Data:

Published by the Institute for Emotional Education, Inc., 112 East Nineteenth Street, New York, New York 10003. Issued quarterly, in February, March, August, and November. Advertising is accepted. Circulation: Not known. Subscription: $5.00 per year; $9.00 for two years; $12.00 for three years; $1.25 per issue. Founded: 1961.

Editorial Address:

The Editor, Journal of Emotional Education, Institute for Emotional Education, Inc., 112 East Nineteenth Street, New York, New York 10003.

Editorial Policy:

Includes articles related to milieu therapy or articles relevant to therapists practicing milieu therapy. The reading audience includes educated laymen and professionals in the helping professions. Unsolicited manuscripts are welcome. Five major articles are published per issue. Book reviews are included.

Manuscript Preparation:

Accepted manuscripts average six to ten pages. Three copies are required. Return postage and a self-addressed envelope are required for return of manuscript. A background or explanatory cover letter is not required nor is an outline, summary, or abstract. Biographical information about the author is required. No payment is made for accepted manuscripts. Reprints of individual articles are available upon request at cost.

Manuscript Disposition:

Receipt of a manuscript is not acknowledged. Editorial decisions are made within two to three weeks. Unaccepted manuscripts are returned if requested.

Copyright:

Held by the Institute for Emotional Education, Inc.

JOURNAL OF GENETIC PSYCHOLOGY

Subscription Data:

Published by the Journal Press, 2 Commercial Street, Provincetown, Massachusetts 02657. Issued four times each year, in March, June, September, and December. Advertising is not

accepted. Circulation: 1,630. Subscription: $26.00 per year.
Founded: 1891.

Editorial Address:
Managing Editor, Journal of Genetic Psychology. Journal Press,
2 Commercial Street, Provincetown, Massachusetts 02657.

Editorial Policy:
Includes short articles on developmental and clinical psychology.
The reading audience includes psychologists and others interested
in the field. Unsolicited articles are welcome. Eighteen major
articles are published per issue. Current book listings are included with occasional book reviews.

Manuscript Preparation:
Accepted manuscripts range up to 30 double-spaced typewritten
pages, but more concise works are preferred. One copy is required. Return postage and a self-addressed envelope are desired. See a recent issue for format and bibliographical style.
Use one inch margins and double-space throughout. Place footnotes on a separate page and indicate insertion points in the
text. A background or explanatory cover letter about the article
is not desired nor is an outline. All articles begin with a summary. Biographical information about the author is desired only
if the author is unknown to the editor, in which case it should
include a summary of formal education. Illustrations, pictures,
graphs, etc., may be used and should be submitted as clear
glossy prints of approximate size of final reproduction. No payment is made for accepted articles. Each author receives 100
free reprints. Cost quotations for additional reprints are made
when the article is at the page-proof stage.

Manuscript Disposition:
Receipt of a manuscript is acknowledged. Editorial decisions
are ordinarily made within two to three weeks. The managing
editor will make a final decision based on two reports: one
from the editor or a member of an editorial board on merit and
significance of the manuscript, and one from the copy editing
department on mechanical, editorial, and stylistic problems involved in publication of the paper. Accepted articles usually appear in print within one year after acceptance. Unaccepted manuscripts are returned, often with criticism and/or suggestions.

Copyright:
Held by the Journal Press.

Additional Information:
A document entitled "Preparation of Manuscripts" may be obtained from the managing editor and should be consulted for additional detail.

JOURNAL OF INDIVIDUAL PSYCHOLOGY

Subscription Data:
Published by the American Society of Adlerian Psychology, University of Vermont, John Dewey Hall, Burlington, Vermont
05401. Sponsored by the University of Vermont. Issued twice
each year, in May and November. Selected advertising is

accepted. Circulation: 1,400. Subscription: $5.00 per year.
Founded: 1940.

Editorial Address:

The Editor, Journal of Individual Psychology, University of Vermont, John Dewey Hall, Burlington, Vermont 05401.

Editorial Policy:

Includes articles on goal-oriented, humanistic psychology, psychotherapy, and related topics. The reading audience includes clinical psychologists, educators, and advanced students. Unsolicited articles are welcome. Ten to twelve major articles are published per issue. Book reviews are included.

Manuscript Preparation:

Accepted manuscripts average 3,000 words. Two copies are required. Return postage and a self-addressed envelope are optional. Footnoting and other bibliographical procedure should follow the APA Publication Manual. Use wide margins and double-space. A background or explanatory cover letter about the article is required. An outline or summary of the article is desired with submission of the finished manuscript. Biographical information about the author is required. Illustrations, graphs, etc., are sometimes used. No payment is made for accepted articles. Reprints are available; a cost sheet may be obtained through the office of the editor.

Manuscript Disposition:

Receipt of a manuscript is acknowledged. Editorial decisions are made within two months. Accepted articles usually appear in print within three months after acceptance. Unaccepted manuscripts are returned, often with criticism and/or suggestions.

Copyright:

Held by the American Society of Adlerian Psychology.

JOURNAL OF PERSONALITY ASSESSMENT

Subscription Data:

Published by the Society for Personality Assessment, Inc., 1071 East Angeleno Avenue, Burbank, California 91501. Issued bimonthly, in February, April, June, August, October, and December. Advertising is accepted. Circulation: 2,500. Subscription: $15.00 per year. Founded: 1938.

Editorial Address:

Walter G. Klopfer, Editor, Journal of Personality Assessment, 7840 S.W. Fifty-first Avenue, Portland, Oregon 97219.

Editorial Policy:

Includes articles related to all aspects of the measurement and assessment of human personality. The reading audience includes psychologists and students of psychology. Unsolicited articles are welcome. Twelve to fifteen major articles are published per issue. Book reviews are included.

Manuscript Preparation:

Two copies are required. Bibliographical procedure should follow the APA Publication Manual. Manuscripts should be typewritten and double-spaced. An abstract of 100 to 120 words is required. All illustrative material should be submitted in finished form for photographic reproduction without retouching. Original drawings should be submitted and not tracings or photographs. The cost of such illustrations, tables, and special type must be paid for by the author at cost. Basic publication costs are gratis. Reprints can be ordered upon return of the galley proofs. Rates for reprints are determined by the length of the paper. A reprint cost-and-order blank will accompany each galley.

Copyright:
Held by the Society for Personality Assessment.

Additional Information:
The editors reserve the right to refuse any manuscript submitted and to make minor deletions and condensations. No major changes will be made without the author's permission.

PSYCHOANALYTIC REVIEW

Subscription Data:
Published by the National Psychological Association for Psychoanalysis, Inc., 150 West Thirteenth Street, New York, New York 10011. Issued quarterly, in March, June, September, and December. Advertising is accepted. Circulation: 2,000. Subscription: $14.00 per year. Founded: 1913.

Editorial Address:
The Editor, Psychoanalytic Review, National Psychological Association for Psychoanalysis, Inc., 150 West Thirteenth Street, New York, New York 10011.

Editorial Policy:
Includes articles on psychoanalytic psychology, with emphasis on theoretical and clinical reports and essays relative to culture and social science. The reading audience includes professional clinicians and educators. Unsolicited articles are welcome. Eight major articles are published per issue. Book reviews are included.

Manuscript Preparation:
Accepted manuscripts range from 3,000 to 5,000 words. Three copies are required. Return postage and a self-addressed envelope are unnecessary. Footnotes and other bibliographical procedure should follow the University of Chicago Manual of Style. Use wide margins and double-space. A background or explanatory cover letter about the article is not desired nor is an outline or summary. Biographical information about the author is desired and should include a summary of current professional affiliations. Illustrations, pictures, graphs, etc., may be used, but the author must pay for their publication. No payment is made for accepted articles. Reprints are available.

Manuscript Disposition:
Receipt of a manuscript is acknowledged. Editorial decisions are made by three readers within three months. Accepted articles usually appear in print within two years after acceptance. Unaccepted manuscripts are returned and criticism is supplied only at the author's request.

Copyright:
   Held by the National Psychological Association for Psychoanalysis, Inc.

REHABILITATION PSYCHOLOGY

Subscription Data:
   Published by Rehabilitation Psychology, P. O. Box 26034, Tempe, Arizona 85282. Issued quarterly, in March, June, September, and December. Advertising is not presently accepted. Circulation: 3,000. Subscription: $15.00 per volume per year; $7.50 special professional rate. Founded: 1953.
Editorial Address:
   The Editor, Rehabilitation Psychology, P. O. Box 26034, Tempe, Arizona 85282.
Editorial Policy:
   Includes original investigations, theoretical papers, and evaluative reviews relating to the psychological aspects of illness, disability, retardation and deprivation; and application to rehabilitation. The reading audience includes psychologists, educators, and rehabilitation personnel. Unsolicited manuscripts are welcome. Five to seven major articles are published per issue. Book reviews are included.
Manuscript Preparation:
   Accepted manuscripts average four to forty double-spaced typewritten pages. Three copies are required. Return postage and a self-addressed envelope are required if author wants return of manuscript. Bibliographical procedure should follow the APA Publication Manual. Use one inch margins on 8-1/2 by 11 inch paper and double-space throughout. A background or explanatory cover letter is not required, but an outline, summary, or abstract is required. Biographical information about the author is required and should include highest degree and current position only. Illustrations, pictures, graphs, etc., are encouraged and papers containing data are given priority. Generally, no payment is made for accepted articles. A charge may be made for excess tabular material or a large number of figures. Author may order reprints; an order blank is sent after manuscript is in type.
Manuscript Disposition:
   Receipt of a manuscript is acknowledged. Editorial decisions are made within three months. Accepted articles usually appear in print within nine months or less. Unaccepted manuscripts are returned only if requested. Criticism and/or suggestions are provided.
Copyright:
   Held by Rehabilitation Psychology.

SMALL GROUP BEHAVIOR

Subscription Data:
   Published by Sage Publications, Inc., 275 South Beverly Drive,

Beverly Hills, California 90212. Issued quarterly, in February, May, August, and November. Advertising is accepted. Circulation: 1,000. Subscription: $10.00 per year; $15.00 to institutions; $8.00 to students. Founded: 1970.

Editorial Address:

William F. Hill, Ph.D., Editor, Small Group Behavior, Department Behavioral Science, California State Polytechnic University, Pomona, California 91766.

Editorial Policy:

Includes articles on theory, research, programs, clinical practice, and training in small group fields. The reading audience includes group therapists, social workers, school counselors, clinical psychologists, psychiatrists, RNs, and other group workers. Unsolicited manuscripts are welcome. Ten major articles are published per issue. Book reviews are usually included.

Manuscript Preparation:

Accepted manuscripts average under 40 pages. Two copies are required. Return postage and a self-addressed envelope are not required. Bibliographical procedure should follow the Sage style sheet that is available from the editor. All copy, including indented matter, notes, and references, should be typed double-spaced on white standard paper. Lines should not exceed six inches in length. Type only on one side of a sheet and number all pages. Avoid the use of footnotes. A background or explanatory cover letter is not required nor is an outline, summary, or abstract. Biographical information about the author is required. Camera-ready illustrations, pictures, graphs, etc., are acceptable. Type each table on a separate sheet, showing only a marginal reference line in the text for placement. In general, artwork should be prepared for same-size use at a maximum size of 4-1/2 inches wide by 6 inches deep. Oversize artwork should be prepared to the same proportions taking into consideration that any lettering should be somewhat oversize so as to remain legible when reduced. As with tables, use a marginal reference line for placement of figures. Artwork should be clean, sharp, preferably black on white paper. Light blue linework does not photograph at all. Most office copying machine work reproduces very poorly and should be avoided. Glossy photostats are best, preferably furnished to final size. Photographs should be large glossies rather than small snapshots and have high contrast. No payment is made for accepted manuscripts. Reprints should be ordered before publication.

Manuscript Disposition:

Receipt of a manuscript is acknowledged. Editorial decisions are made within eight weeks. Accepted articles usually appear in print within 12 to 18 months. Unaccepted manuscripts are returned, usually without criticism and/or suggestions.

Copyright:

Held by Sage Publications, Inc.

PSYCHOLOGICAL - GENERAL AND APPLIED
(EXCLUDING CLINICAL)

AMERICAN PSYCHOLOGIST

Subscription Data:
Published by the American Psychological Association, 1200 Seventeenth Street, N. W., Washington, D. C. 20036. Issued monthly. Advertising is accepted. Circulation: 40,000. Subscription: $12.00 per year. Founded: 1946.

Editorial Address:
The Editor, American Psychologist, 1200 Seventeenth Street, N. W., Washington, D. C. 20036.

Editorial Policy:
Includes articles on archival documents and broad general articles. The reading audience includes psychologists - students, MAs, PhDs. Unsolicited articles are welcome. Six to eight major articles are published per issue. Book reviews are not included.

Manuscript Preparation:
Accepted manuscripts average length varies. Three copies are required. Return postage and a self-addressed envelope are unnecessary. Footnotes and other bibliographical procedure should follow the APA Publication Manual. Use 1-1/2 inch margins and double-space throughout. A background or explanatory cover letter about the article is desired, and an abstract of 100 to 120 words is required. Biographical information about the author is unnecessary. Illustrations, pictures, graphs, etc., may be used, but must be ready for the printer. Glossy prints are desired. No payment is made for accepted articles. Reprints are available from the printer, but no free reprints are provided.

Manuscript Disposition:
Receipt of a manuscript is acknowledged. Editorial decisions are made within four to six weeks. Accepted articles usually appear in print within six to eight months after acceptance. Unaccepted manuscripts are returned, usually with brief suggestions and/or criticism.

Copyright:
Held by the American Psychological Association.

JOURNAL OF APPLIED BEHAVIOR ANALYSIS

Subscription Data:
Published by the Society for the Experimental Analysis of

Behavior, Inc., Department of Human Development, University
of Kansas, Lawrence, Kansas 66044. Issued quarterly. Advertising is accepted. Circulation: 7,000. Subscription: $10.00
per year; $18.00 to institutions; $6.00 to students. Founded:
1968.

Editorial Address:
Todd Risley, Editor, Journal of Applied Behavior Analysis,
Johnney Cake Child Study Center, Route 1, Mansfield, Arkansas
72944.

Editorial Policy:
The reading audience includes those individuals interested in
sociology-psychology, special education, social work, speech and
hearing, criminology, and juvenile problems. All received manuscripts are reviewed. Twelve to fifteen major articles are
published per issue. Book reviews are included.

Manuscript Preparation:
Five copies are required. Return postage and a self-addressed
envelope are not required, but appreciated. Bibliographical
procedure should follow the APA Publication Manual. An outline, summary, or abstract is required. No payment is made
for accepted manuscripts. The Journal holds the copyright
privileges.

Manuscript Disposition:
Receipt of a manuscript is acknowledged. Editorial decisions
are made within two to six months. Accepted articles usually
appear in print within three months. Unaccepted manuscripts
are returned with criticism and/or suggestions.

Copyright:
Held by the Journal of Applied Behavior Analysis.

JOURNAL OF APPLIED PSYCHOLOGY

Subscription Data:
Published by the American Psychological Association, 1200 Seventeenth Street, N.W., Washington, D.C. 20036. Issued bimonthly. Advertising is not accepted. Circulation: 6,000. Subscription: $24.00 per year. Founded: 1917.

Editorial Address:
Dr. Edwin A. Fleishman, Editor, Journal of Applied Psychology,
American Institutes for Research, 8555 Sixteenth Street, Silver
Spring, Maryland 20910.

Editorial Policy:
Includes articles on all phases of applied psychology; includes
regular articles, monographs, and short notes. The reading audience includes psychologists and other behavioral scientists.
Unsolicited manuscripts are welcome. An average of 15 regular
articles and four to eight short notes are published per issue.
Book reviews are not included.

Manuscript Preparation:
Accepted manuscripts average from 2,500 to 5,000 words. Three
manuscript copies are preferred. Return postage and a self-

addressed envelope are not required. Bibliographical procedure
should follow the APA Publication Manual. Use wide margins
and double-space. Place footnotes on a separate page. A background or explanatory cover letter is desired. An abstract of
no more than 120 words is required; detailed instructions for
preparation may be obtained from the editor or from the APA
central office. Biographical information about the author is unnecessary. Graphs, figures, and tables may be included; figures
must be submitted with one original drawing or an eight by ten
inch glossy print along with the photographic or pencil-drawn
copy. No payment is made for accepted manuscripts. Contributors are charged $45.00 per printed page if early publication is
requested. Reprints are available; they may be ordered from
the printer prior to publication. No gratis reprints are supplied.

Manuscript Disposition:
Receipt of the manuscript is acknowledged. Editorial decisions
are made within eight to twelve weeks. Accepted articles usually appear in print within 15 months. Unaccepted manuscripts
are returned, often with suggestions and/or criticism.

Copyright:
Held by the American Psychological Association.

JOURNAL OF APPLIED SOCIAL PSYCHOLOGY

Subscription Data:
Published by the Scripta Publishing Corporation, 1511 K Street,
Washington, D.C. 20005. Issued quarterly. Advertising is ac-
cepted. Circulation: 1,600. Subscription: $16.00 per year;
$30.00 to libraries. Founded: 1971.

Editorial Address:
Dr. Siegfried Streufert, PhD., Editor, Journal of Applied Social
Psychology, Department of Psychology Sciences, Purdue Univer-
sity, West Lafayette, Indiana 47907.

Editorial Policy:
The Journal disseminates findings from behavioral science research which have applications to current problems of society
by publishing relevant research and emphasizing excellence of
experimental results, that bridge the theoretical and applied
areas of social research. The Journal serves as a means of
communication among scientists, as well as between researchers
and those engaged in the task of solving social problems. Preference is given to manuscripts reporting laboratory and field
research in primarily three areas: 1) problems of society, 2)
problems of human development, learning, and education, and
3) problems of political, social, and industrial organizations.
The reading audience includes professionals and applied workers.
Unsolicited manuscripts are welcome. Approximately eight to
ten major articles are published per issue. Book reviews are
not included.

Manuscript Preparation:
Accepted manuscripts should not exceed 15 typewritten pages.
Two copies are required. Return postage and a self-addressed

envelope are not required. Footnoting and other bibliographical procedure should follow the APA Publication Manual. A cover letter and an abstract are required. Biographical information about the author is not required. Original graphs are required. No payment is made for accepted manuscripts. Reprints are available for a charge.

Manuscript Disposition:

Receipt of a manuscript is acknowledged. Editorial decisions are made within two weeks to three months. Accepted articles usually appear in print within three to six months after receipt. Unaccepted manuscripts are returned with criticism and/or suggestions.

Copyright:

Held by the Scripta Publication Corporation.

JOURNAL OF COMMUNITY PSYCHOLOGY

Subscription Data:

Published by the Clinical Psychology Publishing Company, Inc., 4 Conant Square, Brandon, Vermont 05733. Issued quarterly, in January, April, July, and October. Advertising is accepted. Circulation: 1,500. Subscription: $20.00 per year. Founded: 1973.

Editorial Address:

J. R. Newbrough, Ph. D., Editor, Journal of Community Psychology, Box 319, George Peabody College, Nashville, Tennessee 37203.

Editorial Policy:

Includes papers with implications for community psychology. The reading audience includes mental health workers and psychologists. Unsolicited manuscripts are welcome. Thirty major articles are published per issue. Book reviews are not included.

Manuscript Preparation:

Accepted manuscripts average six to eight typewritten pages. Two copies are required. Return postage and a self-addressed envelope are required. Special Journal style reprint is available from the editor. List footnotes on a separate page. Use 1-1/2 inch margins. A background or explanatory cover letter and a summary are required. Biographical information about the author is not required. Camera-ready illustrations, pictures, graphs, etc., are acceptable. No payment is made for accepted manuscripts. Reprints are available at cost.

Manuscript Disposition:

Receipt of a manuscript is acknowledged. Editorial decisions are made within four weeks. Accepted articles usually appear in print within six months. Unaccepted manuscripts are returned with criticism and/or suggestions.

Copyright:

Held by Clinical Psychology Publishing Company, Inc.

JOURNAL OF CREATIVE BEHAVIOR

Subscription Data:
Published by the Creative Education Foundation, Inc., State University College (Buffalo), 1300 Elmwood Avenue, Buffalo, New York 14222. Issued quarterly, in March, June, September, and December. Advertising is not accepted. Circulation: 4,000. Subscription: $9.00 per year in the United States and Canada; $10.00 elsewhere. Founded: 1966.

Editorial Address:
The Editor, Journal of Creative Behavior, Chase Hall, State University College (Buffalo), 1300 Elmwood Avenue, Buffalo, New York 14222.

Editorial Policy:
Includes articles on creativity, intelligence, problem-solving, concept formation, language and thought process, perception, and related topics. Articles should be of interest to individuals who have either a vocational or avocational interest in these areas. The reading audience includes behavioral scientists from all disciplines. Unsolicited manuscripts are welcome. Five to eight major articles are published per issue. Book reviews are not regularly included.

Manuscript Preparation:
Accepted manuscripts should not exceed 8,000 words in length; however, consideration will be given to longer articles of special interest. Two copies should be submitted, and a third retained by the author. Manuscripts should be typed on one side only, double-spaced. For preparation of manuscripts use a guide which may be obtained from the managing editor. Papers should be as concise as possible with illustrations and tables kept to a minimum. No payment is made for accepted manuscripts. Author will receive two copies of the Journal. Reprints may be ordered for a nominal cost. Authors will be granted permission for non-profit reprinting.

Manuscript Disposition:
Receipt of a manuscript is acknowledged. Editorial decisions are made within three to six months. Accepted articles usually appear in print shortly after acceptance. Unaccepted manuscripts are returned without criticism and/or suggestions.

Copyright:
Held by Creative Education Foundation, Inc.

JOURNAL OF EDUCATIONAL PSYCHOLOGY

Subscription Data:
Published by the American Psychological Association, 1200 Seventeenth Street, N.W., Washington, D.C. 20036. Issued bimonthly. Advertising is accepted. Circulation: 6,000. Subscription: $10.00 per year; $10.50 foreign; $2.00 per issue. Founded: 1910.

Editorial Address:

Joanna Williams, Journal of Educational Psychology, Teachers College, Columbia University, New York, New York 10027.

Editorial Policy:

Includes original investigations and theoretical papers which deal with problems of learning, teaching, and the psychological development, relationships, and adjustment of the individual. Preference is given to studies of the more complex types of behavior which relate to all age groups and all levels of education. The reading audience includes educators and psychologists. Unsolicited articles are welcome. Ten or eleven major articles are published per issue. Book reviews are included.

Manuscript Preparation:

Accepted manuscripts range from four to ten Journal pages in length. Two copies are required. Return postage and a self-addressed envelope are desired. Use wide margins and double-space throughout. Bibliographical procedure should follow the APA Publication Manual. Place references on a separate page at the end of the article. A background or explanatory cover letter about the article is desired. An abstract of 100 to 120 words, prepared to conform with Psychological Abstracts, is required on a separate page. Detailed information on preparation of abstracts appears in Volume 16 of the American Psychologist, or may be obtained from the APA Washington office. Biographical information about the author is desired and should include a summary of formal education and professional experience. Graphs, tables, etc., may be used. No payment is made for accepted articles. Reprints are available.

Manuscript Disposition:

Receipt of a manuscript is acknowledged. Editorial decisions are made as soon as possible. Accepted articles usually appear in print within one year after acceptance. Unaccepted manuscripts are returned, sometimes with criticism and/or suggestions.

Copyright:

Held by the American Psychological Association.

Additional Information:

The following policies govern reprinting: (a) approval is required to reprint tables and figures, and text only if more than 500 words are taken from one article; (b) permission is usually granted, contingent upon the author's approval, to reprint entire articles or major parts of articles; (c) where possible, royalties from commercial publishers will be negotiated to the American Psychological Foundation.

JOURNAL OF GENERAL PSYCHOLOGY

Subscription Data:

Published by the Journal Press, 2 Commercial Street, Provincetown, Massachusetts 02657. Issued four times each year, in January, April, July, and October. Advertising is not accepted. Circulation: 1,700. Subscription: $26.00 per year. Founded: 1927.

Editorial Address:
   Managing Editor, Journal of General Psychology, Journal Press,
   2 Commercial Street, Provincetown, Massachusetts 02657.
Editorial Policy:
   Includes articles on experimental, physiological, and comparative
   psychology. The reading audience includes professional psychologists and other social scientists. Unsolicited articles are welcome. Eighteen major articles are published per issue. Current book listings are included, but not book reviews.
Manuscript Preparation:
   Manuscripts of any length up to 50 double-spaced typewritten
   pages will be considered, but concise works are preferred. One
   copy is required. Return postage and a self-addressed envelope
   are desired. See a recent issue for bibliographical procedure.
   Use one inch margins and double-space throughout. Place all
   footnotes on a separate page with insertion points indicated in the
   text. A background or explanatory cover letter about the article
   is not desired. All articles begin with a summary. Biographical information about the author is desired only if unknown to
   the editor. Illustrations, pictures, graphs, etc., should be submitted as clear glossy prints of approximate final-reproduction
   size. No payment is made for accepted articles. Reprints are
   available; 100 free copies are mailed to the author. Reprint
   cost quotations are made at the page-proof stage.
Manuscript Disposition:
   Receipt of a manuscript is acknowledged. Editorial decisions
   are made within two to three weeks. Each is based upon a report from a member of the editorial board regarding merit and
   significance of the manuscript and a report from the copy department regarding mechanical, editorial, and stylistic problems
   involved in publishing the paper. Accepted articles usually appear in print within one year after acceptance. Unaccepted manuscripts are returned, often with suggestions and/or criticism.
Copyright:
   Held by the Journal Press. Authors may obtain release for any
   specific purpose.
Additional Information:
   A document entitled "Preparation of Manuscripts" may be obtained
   from the managing editor and should be consulted for additional
   detail.

JOURNAL OF INSTRUCTIONAL PSYCHOLOGY

Subscription Data:
   Published by V-U Publishing Company, P.O. Box 5630, Milwaukee, Wisconsin 53211. Issued quarterly, in winter, spring,
   summer, and fall. Advertising is accepted. Circulation: 500.
   Subscription: $7.50 per year; $10.00 to institutions; $19.00
   for two years to institutions; $26.00 for three years to institu-
   tions. Founded: 1973.
Editorial Address:
   The Editor, Journal of Instructional Psychology, Vásquez Associates, Ltd., P.O. Box 5630, Milwaukee, Wisconsin 53211.

Editorial Policy:
    Includes original investigations and theoretical papers dealing
    with learning and psychology. The reading audience includes
    college and university instructional personnel and, to a lesser
    extent, appropriate high school personnel. Unsolicited manu-
    scripts are welcome. Approximately eight to ten major articles
    are published per issue. Book reviews are included.
Manuscript Preparation:
    Accepted manuscripts average 1,500 to 2,500 words. The origi-
    nal and two copies are required. Return postage and a self-
    addressed envelope are not required. Bibliographical procedure
    should follow the APA Publication Manual. Use one inch mar-
    gins on top, bottom, left, and right. Quotations of five lines or
    more should be indented five additional spaces at both ends. A
    background or explanatory cover letter is not required, but an
    outline, summary, or abstract is required. Biographical infor-
    mation about the author is not required. Illustrations, pictures,
    graphs, etc., are discouraged. No payment is made for accepted
    manuscripts. Publisher does not enter into reprint decisions as
    this is considered between the author and printer.
Manuscript Disposition:
    Receipt of a manuscript is not acknowledged. Editorial decisions
    are made within 16 weeks. Accepted articles usually appear in
    print within six to twelve months. Unaccepted manuscripts are
    returned, usually with criticism and/or suggestions.
Copyright:
    Held by V-U Publishing Company.

JOURNAL OF PSYCHOLOGY

Subscription Data:
    Published by the Journal Press, 2 Commercial Street, Province-
    town, Massachusetts 02657. Issued six times each year, in
    January, March, May, July, September, and November. Adver-
    tising is not accepted. Circulation: 1,750. Subscription:
    $39.00 per year. Founded: 1935.
Editorial Address:
    Managing Editor, Journal of Psychology, Journal Press, 2 Com-
    mercial Street, Provincetown, Massachusetts 02657.
Editorial Policy:
    Includes articles and reports on all branches of psychology. The
    reading audience includes psychologists, advanced students, and
    scholars in related fields. Unsolicited articles are welcome.
    Eighteen major articles are published per issue. Book reviews
    are not included.
Manuscript Preparation:
    Accepted manuscripts should not exceed 50 double-spaced type-
    written pages. Two copies are required. Return postage and
    a self-addressed envelope are desired. See a recent issue for
    bibliographical and format procedure. Use one inch margins
    and double-space throughout. Footnotes should be submitted on
    a separate page, with insertion points indicated in the text. A

background or explanatory cover letter about the article is not desired. All articles begin with a summary. Biographical and educational information is desired if author is unknown to the editor. Illustrations, pictures, graphs, etc., may be used and should be submitted as clear glossy prints of approximate size of final reproduction. Tables must be typed on separate pages using Arabic numbers; omit all vertical lines. Drawings should be prepared on white drawing paper using India ink. Legends must be typed on separate pages. No payment is made for accepted articles. Two-hundred free reprints, plus cost quotation for additional copies, are mailed to the author. A detailed cost summary and order forms are available to others through the office of the editor.

Manuscript Disposition:
Receipt of a manuscript is acknowledged. Editorial decisions are made within two weeks. Accepted articles usually appear in print within two months after acceptance. Unaccepted manuscripts are returned, often with comments and/or suggestions.

Copyright:
Held by the Journal Press.

Additional Information:
A document entitled "Preparation of Manuscripts" may be obtained from the office of the managing editor and should be consulted for additional detail.

JOURNAL OF SCHOOL PSYCHOLOGY

Subscription Data:
Published by the Behavioral Publications, Inc., 72 Fifth Avenue, New York, New York 10011. Issued quarterly, in March, June, September, and December. Advertising is accepted. Circulation: 2,500. Subscription: $12.00 per year; $30.00 to institutions. Founded: 1962.

Editorial Address:
Beeman N. Phillips, Editor, Journal of School Psychology, College of Education, Department of Educational Psychology, University of Texas, Austin, Texas 78712.

Editorial Policy:
The Journal publishes articles on research, opinion, and practice in school psychology, with the aim of fostering its continued development as a scientific and professional speciality. The reading audience includes school psychologists and psychiatrists, special educators, school administrators, and counselors. Unsolicited manuscripts are welcome. Twelve to fifteen major articles are published per issue. Book reviews are included.

Manuscript Preparation:
Manuscripts average five to fifteen typewritten pages or between 1,500 and 4,500 words. Two copies are required. Return postage and a self-addressed envelope are not required. Bibliographical procedure should follow the APA Publication Manual. References should refer only to material cited within the text; list in alphabetical order on separate pages following the text. The

entire manuscript should be double-spaced, including quotations, footnotes, references, and tables. Use a minimum of one inch margins. Footnotes should be numbered consecutively throughout the article and placed on separate pages at the end of the manuscript, following the references. Do not use printer's symbols. A background or explanatory cover letter and an abstract of not more than 100 words are required. The authors' names, titles, and affiliations with complete addresses should be included on a separate sheet with each manuscript. Tables should be placed on separate pages at the end of the manuscript. Use arabic numerals and indicate approximate placement within text. Figures should be professional drafted and submitted in final form on glossy paper, suitable for photographic reproduction. All drawings and graphs should be distinct enough to allow substantial reduction without loss in clarity. Indicate the placement of figures within the text in the same manner as tables. No payment is made for accepted manuscripts. Reprints may be ordered through the publisher.

Manuscript Disposition:
Receipt of a manuscript is acknowledged. Editorial decisions are made within two months. Accepted articles usually appear in print within nine to twelve months. Unaccepted manuscripts are returned usually with criticism and/or suggestions.

Copyright:
Held by the Journal of School Psychology, Inc.

Additional Information:
See inside back cover of a recent issue for editorial policies and procedures. Authors are responsible for authenticity of all quoted matter and bibliographical citations, and for obtaining permission from the original source for quotes of 100 or more words.

JOURNAL OF THE HISTORY OF THE BEHAVIORAL SCIENCES

Subscription Data:
Published by the Clinical Psychology Publishing Company, Inc., 4 Conant Square, Brandon, Vermont 05733. Issued quarterly, in January, April, July, and October. Advertising is accepted. Circulation: 1,100. Subscription: $20.00 per year. Founded: 1965.

Editorial Address:
Robert Weyant, Ph.D., Dean, Editor, Journal of the History of the Behavioral Sciences, University of Calgary, Calgary, Alberta, Canada.

Editorial Policy:
Includes historical papers. The reading audience includes historians and psychologists. Unsolicited manuscripts are welcome. Eight major articles are published per issue. Book reviews are included.

Manuscript Preparation:
Accepted manuscripts average 15 to 20 typewritten pages. Two copies are required. Return postage and a self-addressed envelope are required. Bibliographical procedure should follow

the authors appropriate style of the discipline. Place footnotes on a separate page. Use a 1-1/2 inch margin. A background or explanatory cover letter is required, but an outline, summary, or abstract is not required. Biographical information about the author is required. Illustrations, pictures, graphs, etc., should include camera-ready copies. No payment is made for accepted manuscripts. Reprints are available at cost.

Manuscript Disposition:
Receipt of a manuscript is acknowledged. Editorial decisions are made within four weeks. Accepted articles usually appear in print within 12 months. Unaccepted manuscripts are returned with criticism and/or suggestions.

Copyright:
Held by the Clinical Psychology Publishing Company, Inc.

JOURNAL OF VOCATIONAL BEHAVIOR

Subscription Data:
Published by Academic Press, Inc., 111 Fifth Avenue, New York, New York 10003. Issued bimonthly, in January, March, May, July, September, and November. Advertising is not accepted. Circulation: 800. Subscription: $15.00 per year; $44.00 to institutions. Founded: 1971.

Editorial Address:
Dr. Samuel H. Osipow, Editor, Journal of Vocational Behavior, Department of Psychology, Ohio State University, 1945 North High Street, Columbus, Ohio 43210.

Editorial Policy:
Includes empirical research, literature, reviews, and theoretical articles. The reading audience includes mainly specialists in vocational choice, behavior, adjustment in industry, education counseling, and government. Unsolicited manuscripts are welcome. Seventy to seventy-five major articles are published per issue. Book reviews are not included.

Manuscript Preparation:
No limitations are placed on manuscript length; however, accepted manuscripts average from four to thirty typewritten pages. Two copies are required. Return postage and a self-addressed envelope are not required. Bibliographical procedure should follow the APA Publication Manual; also see a style note within the periodical. Minimize footnotes and place them on a separate page. Indicate address for reprint requests as footnote one. Use 1-1/2 inch margins on both sides and double-space. A cover letter is required as the author's name should not appear on the manuscript. An abstract of approximately 100 words is required. Biographical information about the author is not required except for institutional affiliation. Figures must be submitted that are acceptable for photographic reproduction. No payment is made for accepted manuscripts. Fifty free reprints are given to each author; additional reprints are available.

Manuscript Disposition:
Receipt of a manuscript is acknowledged. Editorial decisions

are made within approximately eight to ten weeks. Accepted articles usually appear in print within 10 to 14 months. Unaccepted manuscripts are returned with criticism and/or suggestions.

Copyright:

Held by Academic Press, Inc.

Additional Information:

A blind review procedure is used; therefore, authors must not put their names on the manuscript.

MERRILL-PALMER QUARTERLY OF BEHAVIOR AND DEVELOPMENT

Subscription Data:

Published by the Merrill-Palmer Institute, 71 East Ferry Avenue, Detroit, Michigan 48202. Issued quarterly, in January, April, July, and October. Advertising is not accepted. Circulation: 2,000. Subscription: $11.50 per year. Founded: 1954.

Editorial Address:

Martin L. Hoffman, Ph.D., Editor, Merrill-Palmer Quarterly of Behavior and Development, Department of Psychology, University of Michigan, Ann Arbor, Michigan 48104.

Editorial Policy:

Includes theoretical articles, critical reviews, and research reports. The reading audience includes primarily developmental psychologists, child-based professionals, and sociologists. Unsolicited manuscripts are welcome. Five to seven major articles are published per issue. Book reviews are included.

Manuscript Preparation:

Accepted manuscripts average approximately 20 double-spaced typewritten pages. Two copies are required. Return postage and a self-addressed envelope are not required. Footnoting and other bibliographical procedure should follow the APA Publication Manual. A background or explanatory cover letter is not required nor is an outline, summary, or abstract. Biographical information about the author is not required. Illustrations, pictures, graphs, etc., should follow the APA Publication Manual. No payment is made for accepted manuscripts. Fifty free reprints are given each author; more can be ordered at a nominal cost.

Manuscript Disposition:

Receipt of a manuscript is acknowledged. Editorial decisions are made within approximately four to eight weeks. Accepted articles usually appear in print within eight to twelve months. One unaccepted manuscript is returned, usually with criticism and/or suggestions.

Copyright:

Held by the Merrill-Palmer Institute.

PERSONNEL PSYCHOLOGY

Subscription Data:
 Published by Personnel Psychology, Inc., Box 6965, College Station, North Carolina 27708. Issued quarterly, in March, June, September, and December. Advertising is not accepted. Circulation: 2,800. Subscription: $15.00 per year. Founded: 1948.
Editorial Address:
 The Editor, Personnel Psychology, Box 6965, College Station, Durham, North Carolina 27708.
Editorial Policy:
 Includes articles which report methods, research results, and the application of research results to the solution of personnel problems in business, industry, education, and government. Also included are critical surveys of literature relative to various phases of personnel psychology such as training, job and worker analysis, organizational behavior, employee relations, and morale. The reading audience includes personnel directors, in business, industry, and education, and teachers of management and personnel in colleges and universities. Unsolicited articles are welcome. Ten to twelve major articles are published per issue. Book reviews are included.
Manuscript Preparation:
 No policy regarding manuscript length has been established. Accepted articles average from 10 to 15 double-spaced typewritten pages. Three copies are required. Return postage and a self-addressed envelope are not required. Footnoting and other bibliographical procedure should follow the APA Publication Manual. Use wide margins and double-space throughout. A background or explanatory cover letter about the article is unnecessary. An outline or summary of the article is desired with submission of finished manuscript. Biographical information about the author is unnecessary. Illustrations, pictures, graphs, etc., may be used. No payment is made for accepted articles.
Manuscript Disposition:
 Receipt of a manuscript is acknowledged. Editorial decisions are made within three months. Accepted articles usually appear in print within six months after acceptance. Unaccepted manuscripts are usually returned without criticism or suggestions.
Copyright:
 Held by Personnel Psychology, Inc.

PROFESSIONAL PSYCHOLOGY

Subscription Data:
 Published by the American Psychological Association, 1200 Seventeenth Street, N.W., Washington, D.C. 20015. Issued quarterly, in February, May, August, and November. Advertising is

accepted. Circulation: 6,000. Subscription: $5.00 to members of the Association; $12.00 to non-members. Founded: 1959.

Editorial Address:
Donald K. Freedheim, Ph.D., Editor, Professional Psychology, Department of Psychology, Case Western Reserve University, Cleveland, Ohio 44106.

Editorial Policy:
Includes articles concerning professional affairs and issues across the broad spectrum of psychological specialities. The reading audience includes psychologists, students, and guidance counselors. Unsolicited manuscripts are welcome. Approximately 12 major articles are published per issue. Book reviews are not included; however, films, tests, reviews and bibliographies are included.

Manuscript Preparation:
Accepted manuscripts should not exceed 20 pages. Three copies are required. Return postage and a self-addressed envelope are not required. Bibliographical procedure should follow the APA Publication Manual. List footnotes on a separate page. Footnotes indicating addresses for reprints are required. Use one inch margins and double-space. A background or explanatory cover letter is not required, but an abstract is required. Biographical information about the author is not required with submission of the manuscript; however, a biography is published with the article and should be sent upon acceptance. Use separate pages for illustrations, pictures, graphs, etc.; camera-ready material is required. No payment is made for accepted manuscripts. Reprints may be purchased and ordered with galley proofs.

Manuscript Disposition:
Receipt of a manuscript is acknowledged. Editorial decisions are made within an average of eight weeks. Accepted articles usually appear in print within 12 months. Unaccepted manuscripts are returned with criticism and/or suggestions.

Copyright:
Held by the American Psychological Association.

*PSYCHOLOGICAL ISSUES

Subscription Data:
Published by the International Universities Press, 239 Park Avenue South, New York, New York 10003. Issued four times each year, irregularly. Advertising is not accepted. Circulation: 1,400 subscribers. Single issues are also advertised and sold separately and very widely in their sales. Subscription: $15.00 for Volume VIII; $20.00 for Volume IX; individual issues are priced according to length. Founded: 1958.

Editorial Address:
The Editor, Psychological Issues, Department of Psychiatry, University of Colorado Medical Center, 4200 East Ninth Avenue, Denver, Colorado 80220.

Editorial Policy:
Psychological Issues is a publishing outlet for works of high
scholarship or scientific merit that are relevant to psychoanalysis but too long for publication in an ordinary journal, and would
appeal to too limited a readership to interest a trade publisher,
or would require, in order to be published by a trade publisher,
that the author compromise on matters of detailed, scholarly reporting. The reading audience includes behavioral scientists and
professionals. Unsolicited manuscripts are not welcome. Usually one major article is published per issue. Some issues consist of collections of papers that may include as many as ten.
Book reviews are not included.

Manuscript Preparation:
Length of a printed monograph is normally 160 printed pages.
Lengthy manuscripts can be published as a double issue. Manuscripts that would yield a printed monograph of under 80 pages
are rarely accepted. Three copies are required. Return postage and a self-addressed envelope are desired. Bibliographical
procedure should follow the "Instructions to Authors and Typists"
which is available from the editor. Number all footnotes serially
in the text. Footnotes can be placed at the bottom of the page
on which reference to them appears, or collected at the end of
the manuscript. In either case, double-space. Use adequate
margins of at least 1-1/4 inches on right and left, and one inch
at top and bottom. Double-space everything, especially quoted
material, footnotes, and references. A background or explanatory cover letter is required, and an outline, summary, or abstract is desired. Biographical information about the author is
required. Illustrations, pictures, graphs, etc., are welcome
if they contribute to the clarity of the manuscript. Authors are
not charged for these. Type each table on a separate page and
place it at the end of the manuscript. Figures must be submitted in final reproducible form. Payment is not made for accepted manuscripts. Psychological Issues is organized as a non-
profit corporation and any surplus of income over expenses is
returned to authors in proportion to the individual sales of their
monographs. Reprints are available from the publisher for those
monographs that consist of a collection of individually authored
papers. Authors are entitled to five free copies of the monograph in which their work appears and may purchase additional
copies at 40% discount.

Manuscript Disposition:
Receipt of a manuscript is acknowledged. The length of time
to make an editorial decision depends on the length and com-
plexity of the manuscript. Accepted articles usually appear in
print within 18 months. Unaccepted manuscripts are returned
with criticism and/or suggestions. The editorial policy is to
help the author produce the best possible manuscript.

Copyright:
Held by the International Universities Press.

PSYCHOLOGICAL REVIEW

Subscription Data:
  Published by the American Psychological Association, 1200 Seventeenth Street, N. W., Washington, D. C. 20036. Issued six times each year, in January, March, May, July, September, and November. Advertising is accepted. Circulation: 11,000. Subscription: $12.00 per year. Founded: 1894.

Editorial Address:
  Dr. George Mandler, Editor, Psychological Review, Department of Psychology, University of California, La Jolla, California 92037.

Editorial Policy:
  Includes theoretical articles and theoretical notes, as well as brief letters on theoretical issues generally in the area of psychology. The reading audience includes psychologists in universities, schools, industry, and clinics. Unsolicited manuscripts are welcome. Four or five major articles are published per issue. Book reviews are not included.

Manuscript Preparation:
  Accepted manuscripts average 7,600 words or less. Three copies are required. Return postage and a self-addressed envelope are not required. Bibliographical procedure should follow the APA Publication Manual. Place footnotes on a separate page. Use wide margins and double-space. A background or explanatory cover letter is not required. An abstract is required and should follow the style of Psychological Abstracts. Biographical information about the author is not required. Illustrations, pictures, graphs, etc., are accepted as appropriate for manuscript. No payment is made for accepted manuscripts. Reprints are available; cost sheet is available from the American Psychological Association.

Manuscript Disposition:
  Receipt of a manuscript is acknowledged. Editorial decisions are made within one to eight weeks. Accepted articles usually appear in print within six to eight months. Unaccepted manuscripts are returned, often with criticism and/or suggestions.

Copyright:
  Held by the American Psychological Association.

Additional Information:
  Detailed policy statements on form and content of appropriate manuscripts may be found in any issue of the Review. At the present, the Review publishes about 20% of submitted manuscripts.

PSYCHOLOGY IN THE SCHOOLS

Subscription Data:
  Published by the Clinical Psychology Publishing Company, Inc., 4 Conant Square, Brandon, Vermont 05733. Issued quarterly, in January, April, July, and October. Advertising is accepted. Circulation: 2,500. Subscription: $20.00 per year; $15.00

per year to professionals in the school psychology field for personal subscriptions. Founded: 1964.

Editorial Address:

Gerald B. Fuller, Editor, Psychology in the Schools, Department of Psychology, Central Michigan University, Mount Pleasant, Michigan 48858.

Editorial Policy:

Includes papers dealing with theoretical and other problems of the school psychologist, teacher, counselor, and administrator in schools and colleges. Preference is given to articles that clearly describe implications for the practitioner. The reading audience includes school psychologists, teachers, counselors, administrators, and other personnel workers in schools and colleges. Unsolicited manuscripts are welcome. Twenty major articles are published per issue. Book reviews are included.

Manuscript Preparation:

Accepted manuscripts average one to twelve printed pages. Three copies are required. Return postage and a self-addressed envelope are not required. Bibliographical procedure should follow the APA Publication Manual. Tables, figures, and footnotes should be listed on separate sheets. Use one inch margins and double-space. A background or explanatory cover letter is not required, but an outline, summary, or abstract is required. Biographical information about the author is not required. Illustrations, pictures, graphs, etc., are used as necessary. The journal has a standard publication charge. Reprints are available at cost.

Manuscript Disposition:

Receipt of a manuscript is acknowledged. Editorial decisions are made within four weeks. Accepted articles usually appear in print within six to nine months. Unaccepted manuscripts are returned with criticism and suggestions.

Copyright:

Held by the Clinical Psychology Publishing Co., Inc.

SIMULATION AND GAMES

Subscription Data:

Published by Sage Publications, Inc., 275 South Beverly Drive, Beverly Hills, California 90212. Issued quarterly, in March, June, September, and December. Advertising is accepted. Circulation: Not known. Subscription: $12.00 per year; $20.00 to institutions; $9.00 to students. Founded: 1970.

Editorial Address:

The Editor, Simulation and Games, c/o Academic Games Associates, Inc., 430 East Thirty-third Street, Baltimore, Maryland 21218.

Editorial Policy:

Includes theoretical and empirical papers related to man, man-machine, and machine simulations. The reading audience is interdisciplinary. Unsolicited manuscripts are welcome. Approximately five major articles are published per issue. Book reviews and simulation-game reviews are included.

Manuscript Preparation:

Accepted manuscripts average from 10 to 30 double-spaced type-written pages for major articles and three to ten double-spaced typewritten pages for brief communications. Three copies are required. Return postage and a self-addressed envelope are not required. Bibliographical procedure should follow the American Statistical, Psychological, and Sociological Associations. Copies of the style sheet may be obtained upon request. List footnotes on a separate page. All copy, including indented matter, notes and references, should be typed double-spaced on white standard paper. Lines should not exceed five or six inches. Type only on one side of a page. A cover letter and an abstract are required. Biographical information about the author is required only if the manuscript is accepted for publication. Prepare each figure, diagram, or chart on a separate sheet of paper. In general, artwork should be a maximum size of 4-1/2 by 7 inches. Artwork should be clear, sharp black and white originals. Photographs should be large glossies, rather than snapshots--and the contrast should be sharp for best reproduction. For tabular style, see current issues of the journal. No payment is made for accepted manuscripts.

Manuscript Disposition:

Receipt of a manuscript is acknowledged. Editorial decisions are made within approximately 10 to 15 weeks. Accepted articles usually appear in print within five to eight months. Unaccepted manuscripts are returned, with criticism and/or suggestions.

Copyright:

Held by Sage Publications, Inc.

PSYCHOLOGICAL - RESEARCH

AMERICAN JOURNAL OF PSYCHOLOGY

Subscription Data:
  Published by the University of Illinois Press, Urbana, Illinois
  61801. Issued quarterly, in March, June, September, and De-
  cember. Advertising is accepted. Circulation: 3,200. Sub-
  scription: $15.00 per year; $15.50 foreign. Founded: 1887.
Editorial Address:
  Lloyd G. Humphreys, American Journal of Psychology, Psychology Building, University of Illinois at Urbana, Sixth and Daniel,
  Champaign, Illinois 61801.
Editorial Policy:
  Includes original research in general experimental psychology.
  The reading audience includes advanced graduate students and
  specialists in experimental psychology and closely related disci-
  plines in both the physical and social science sides of psychology,
  though primarily the former. Unsolicited manuscripts are welcome. From 15 to 20 major articles are published per issue.
  Book reviews are included. Books intended for review must be
  sent to the Book Review Editor, Dr. Carl P. Duncan, Department of Psychology, Northwestern University, Evanston, Illinois
  60201.
Manuscript Preparation:
  Accepted manuscripts vary in length, but brevity is encouraged.
  Return postage and a self-addressed envelope are required. Footnoting and other bibliographical procedure should follow the APA
  Publication Manual. A background or explanatory cover letter is
  not required, but an outline, summary, or abstract of the article
  is required and should be limited to five lines, if possible. Biographical information about the author is not required. Illustrations, pictures, graphs, etc., should follow the APA Publication
  Manual; there are no charges. No payment is made for accepted
  manuscripts. Authors may order offprints at the time of publication only; charge is $2.00 per page of the article for 200 off-
  prints.
Manuscript Disposition:
  Receipt of a manuscript is acknowledged. Editorial decisions
  are made within 60 days. Accepted articles usually appear in
  print within nine to twelve months, but lag is decreasing substantially. Unaccepted manuscripts are returned with criticism
  and/or suggestions.
Copyright:
  Held by the Board of Trustees of the University of Illinois.

BEHAVIORAL BIOLOGY

Subscription Data:
Published by Academic Press, 111 Fifth Avenue, New York, New York 10003. Issued monthly. Advertising is accepted. Circulation: 1,000. Subscription: $30.00 per year to institutions. Founded: 1972.

Editorial Address:
Dr. James L. McGaugh, Editor, Behavioral Biology, Department of Psychobiology, School of Biological Sciences, University of California, Irvine, California 92664.

Editorial Policy:
Includes original contributions to the scientific literature. Brief reports should report original research findings and notes should consist of critical comments dealing with methodological and/or theoretical issues raised by papers published in Behavioral Biology. The reading audience includes comparative and physiological psychologists, animal behavior neurobiologists, and neuroscientists. Unsolicited manuscripts are welcome. Book reviews are not included.

Manuscript Preparation:
Accepted articles should not exceed 35 pages. Brief reports are limited to 1,500 words and three tables and/or figures. Ordinarily, notes should not exceed 800 words, including references. Three copies are required. Return postage and a self-addressed envelope are not required. Footnotes in the text should be identified by superscript Arabic numerals and should be typed double-spaced on a separate sheet of paper in the order of their appearance in the text. Manuscripts should be typewritten and double-spaced throughout (including tables, footnotes, references, and figure captions); the original typescript should be prepared on one side of a good grade 8-1/2 by 11 inch white paper, with one inch margins on all sides. A background or explanatory cover letter is suggested, and an outline, summary, or abstract is required. Biographical information about the author is not required. Number tables consecutively with Arabic numerals in order of their appearance in the text. Type a short descriptive title above the table. Footnotes to tables should be identified by superscript lower case letter and should appear at the end of the table. All figures should be denoted by Arabic numerals and cited consecutively in the text, with figure legends typed double-spaced on a separate sheet. It is essential that all illustrations be in finished form ready for reproduction. Lettering on the original drawing should be large enough to be legible after reduction of 50 to 60%. Graphs should be plotted with black India ink on light blue coordinate paper, no larger than 8-1/2 by 11 inches, with coordinates properly labeled. Photographs should be submitted as glossy prints. Original drawings that are no larger than 8-1/2 by 11 inches are preferred. No payment is made for accepted manuscripts. Fifty reprints of each article will be supplied free of charge. Additional reprints may be ordered on the form accompanying galley proof.

Manuscript Disposition:
  Receipt of a manuscript is acknowledged. Editorial decisions
  are made within five weeks. Accepted articles usually appear in
  print within six months. Unaccepted manuscripts are returned
  with criticism and/or suggestions.
Copyright:
  Held by Academic Press.

BEHAVIORAL SCIENCE

Subscription Data:
  Published by Behavioral Science, P.O. Box 1055, Louisville,
  Kentucky 40201. Issued bimonthly, in January, March, May,
  July, September, and November. Advertising is accepted.
  Circulation: 4,500. Subscription: $16.00 per year; $30.00
  to institutions; $19.00 foreign, excluding Canada. Founded:
  1956.
Editorial Address:
  James G. Miller, M.D., Ph.D., Editor, Behavioral Science,
  P.O. Box 1055, Louisville, Kentucky 40201.
Editorial Policy:
  Includes articles on general systems research, both living and
  nonliving, at all levels and especially cross-level. The reading
  audience is primarily the scientific professional; however, the
  interdisciplinary approach provides important contributions to
  others interested in research in the behavioral sciences. Unsolicited manuscripts are welcome. Five to six major articles
  are published per issue. Book reviews are included.
Manuscript Preparation:
  Accepted manuscripts average 30 double-spaced typewritten pages.
  Three copies are required. Return postage and a self-addressed
  envelope are required. Bibliographical procedure should follow
  the APA Publication Manual. Avoid the use of footnotes for the
  tendency is to edit them. Never use mathematical notations in
  footnotes. Leave wide margins on all edges and double-space
  throughout. A background or explanatory cover letter is not required, but an abstract is required. Biographical information
  is not required with submission. Author must provide original
  artwork from a professional draftsman. Glossy prints are acceptable. No payment is made for accepted manuscripts. Authors may order reprints at time of publication at cost. Reprints are made from printer's plates.
Manuscript Disposition:
  Receipt of a manuscript is acknowledged. Editorial decisions
  are made within two to twelve weeks. Accepted articles usually
  appear in print approximately 10 to 11 months from submission.
  Unaccepted manuscripts are returned if the author sends the
  postage. Criticism and/or suggestions are usually sent to the
  author.
Copyright:
  Held by James G. Miller, M.D., Ph.D., Editor.

DEVELOPMENTAL PSYCHOBIOLOGY

Subscription Data:
  Published by Interscience, John Wiley and Sons, Inc. , 605 Third
  Avenue, New York, New York 10016. Issued bimonthly, in Jan-
  uary, March, May, July, September, and November. Advertis-
  ing is not accepted. Circulation: 1, 000. Subscription: $25.00
  per volume. Founded: 1968.
Editorial Address:
  Dr. Gilbert W. Meier, Editor, Developmental Psychobiology, Meyer
  Children's Rehabilitation Institute, University of Nebraska Medical
  Center, 444 South Forty-fourth Street, Omaha, Nebraska 68131.
Editorial Policy:
  Includes 1) research reports, research reviews, and theoretical
  statements, and 2) short notes, miscellany, announcements. The
  reading audience includes researchers and advanced students in
  psychology, zoology, obstetrics, and pediatrics. Unsolicited
  manuscripts are welcome. Ten to twelve major articles are
  published per issue. Book reviews are usually not included.
Manuscript Preparation:
  Accepted manuscripts average 15 pages for reports, reviews,
  and statements, and three pages for notes, miscellany, and announcements. Three copies are required. Return postage and
  a self-addressed envelope are not required. Bibliographical procedure should follow the AIBS Manual or the APA Publication
  Manual. "Suggestions to Authors" is available from the editor
  upon request. Text footnotes should be numbered consecutively
  throughout the paper with superscripts in Arabic numerals.
  Table footnotes should be lettered consecutively within each table
  with superscripts in lower case Roman. List footnotes and acknowledgments on separate page. Articles should be typewritten
  on one side of 8-1/2 by 11 inch paper of good quality, double-
  spaced throughout and have wide margins. A background or explanatory cover letter is not required, but an abstract is required.
  Biographical information about the author is not required. Illustrations should be identified on the back with number, author's
  name, and "top" indicated lightly in pencil. Prints of figures
  should be sharp, clear, and glossy. Half-tones should be glossy,
  strongly contrasted prints. Captions should be typed on a separate sheet at the end of the manuscript. Indicate approximate
  point of insertion in the text. Each table should be typed on a
  separate sheet, indicating approximate point of insertion in the
  text. No payment is made for accepted manuscripts. The author
  will receive with galley proofs a reprint order form which
  must be completed and returned with the proofs. Senior authors
  will receive 50 reprints of their articles without charge.
Manuscript Disposition:
  Receipt of a manuscript is acknowledged. Editorial decisions
  are made within six weeks. Accepted articles usually appear
  in print within 12 months. Two unaccepted manuscripts are returned with criticism and/or suggestions.
Copyright:
  Held by Interscience, John Wiley and Sons, Inc.

EDUCATIONAL AND PSYCHOLOGICAL MEASUREMENT

Subscription Data:
　　Published by Educational and Psychological Measurement, Box
　　6907, College Station, Durham, North Carolina 27708. Issued
　　quarterly. Advertising is not accepted. Circulation: 2,600.
　　Subscription: $16.00 per year; $4.00 per issue. Founded:
　　1941.

Editorial Address:
　　The Editor, Educational and Psychological Measurement, Box
　　6907, College Station, Durham, North Carolina 27708.

Editorial Policy:
　　Includes articles on all phases of the measurement field includ-
　　ing problems of measuring individual differences, reports on the
　　development and use of tests and measurements in education,
　　industry, and government, and descriptions of various testing
　　programs in use. The reading audience includes educators, psy-
　　chologists, school counselors, and personnel managers. Unsolic-
　　ited articles are welcome. Twelve major articles are published
　　per issue. Book reviews are accepted.

Manuscript Preparation:
　　Accepted manuscripts average from five to eight double-spaced
　　typewritten pages. Two copies are required. Return postage
　　and a self-addressed envelope are unnecessary. Bibliographical
　　procedure should follow the APA Publication Manual. Use wide
　　margins and double-space throughout. A background or explana-
　　tory cover letter about the article is desired and an abstract is
　　required. Authors should put tables, footnotes, and abstracts on
　　pages separate from the text. Biographical information about
　　the author is unnecessary. Tables and graphs may be used. No
　　payment is made for accepted articles. Contributors are charged
　　only when they request early publication. Authors are granted
　　permission to have reprints made of their own articles for their
　　own use at their own expense.

Manuscript Disposition:
　　Receipt of a manuscript is acknowledged within two weeks. Edi-
　　torial decisions are made within two to three months. Accepted
　　articles usually appear in print within eight to twelve months
　　after acceptance. Unaccepted manuscripts are returned with sug-
　　gestions and/or criticism.

Copyright:
　　Held by Educational and Psychological Measurement.

JOURNAL OF APPLIED BEHAVIORAL SCIENCE

Subscription Data:
　　Published by the National Training Laboratories Institute for Ap-
　　plied Behavioral Science, National Training Laboratory Institute,
　　P.O. Box 9155, Rosslyn Station, Arlington, Virginia 22209. Is-
　　sued quarterly, in February, May, August, and November. Ad-
　　vertising is accepted. Circulation: 5,000. Subscription: $15.00
　　per year. Founded: 1965.

Editorial Address:
　　The Editor, Journal of Applied Behavioral Science, National
　　Training Laboratories, P.O. Box 9155, Rosslyn Station, Arling-
　　ton, Virginia 22209.
Editorial Policy:
　　Includes articles which develop and test new theories and con-
　　cepts of change; examine new social institutions, social inven-
　　tions and practices, and methods of intervention; make direct
　　explicit analysis of values ... practice of planned change. The
　　reading audience includes sociologists, psychologists, consultants
　　and those concerned with planned change for groups, and organ-
　　izations, individuals in business and industry, and libraries.
　　Unsolicited manuscripts are welcome. Six to eight major arti-
　　cles are published per issue. Book reviews are included.
Manuscript Preparation:
　　Accepted manuscripts average 1, 500 to 7, 500 words or six to
　　thirty double-spaced typewritten pages. Three copies are re-
　　quired. Return postage and a self-addressed envelope are re-
　　quired if manuscript is to be returned. List footnotes on a
　　separate page numbered to correspond with the text. Use wide
　　margins and double-space on white 8-1/2 by 11 inch paper. A
　　background or explanatory cover letter is not required, but an
　　abstract is required. Biographical information about the author
　　is not required. Pictures are not acceptable; charts, graphs,
　　etc., that are able to be reduced to a page size of six by nine
　　inches are acceptable. No payment is made for accepted man-
　　uscripts. Reprints may be ordered directly from the printer,
　　but a minimum of 100 must be ordered.
Manuscript Disposition:
　　Receipt of a manuscript is acknowledged. Editorial decisions
　　are made within eight to ten weeks. Accepted articles usually
　　appear in print within 16 months. Unaccepted manuscripts are
　　returned if postage and envelope is provided. Criticism and/or
　　suggestions are not provided unless the manuscript is to be re-
　　vised.
Copyright:
　　Held by the National Training Laboratories Institute, Journal of
　　Applied Behavioral Science.

JOURNAL OF CLINICAL PSYCHOLOGY

Subscription Data:
　　Published by Clinical Psychology Publishing Company, Inc., 4
　　Conant Square, Brandon, Vermont 05733. Issued quarterly, in
　　January, April, July, and October. Advertising is accepted.
　　Circulation: 2, 500. Subscription: $20.00 per year. Founded:
　　1946.
Editorial Address:
　　Dr. Vladimir Pishkin, Editor, Journal of Clinical Psychology,
　　VA Hospital, 921 Northeast Thirteenth Street, Oklahoma City,
　　Oklahoma 73104.

Editorial Policy:
   Includes objective research reports. The reading audience includes clinical psychologists. Unsolicited manuscripts are welcome. Thirty major articles are published per issue. Book reviews are not included.
Manuscript Preparation:
   Accepted manuscripts average six to eight typewritten pages. Two copies are required. Return postage and a self-addressed envelope are required. See Journal reprints on accepted style. List footnotes on separate page. Use 1-1/2 inch margins. A background or explanatory cover letter and a summary are required. Biographical information about the author is not required. Illustrations, pictures, graphs, etc., are acceptable, but should include only camera-ready copies. No payment is made for accepted manuscripts. Reprints are available at cost.
Manuscript Disposition:
   Receipt of a manuscript is acknowledged. Editorial decisions are made within four weeks. Accepted articles usually appear in print within six months. Unaccepted manuscripts are returned with criticism and/or suggestions.
Copyright:
   Held by Clinical Psychology Publishing Company, Inc.

†JOURNAL OF COMPARATIVE AND PHYSIOLOGICAL PSYCHOLOGY

Subscription Data:
   Published by the American Psychological Association, 1200 Seventeenth Street, N.W., Washington, D.C. 20036. Issued monthly in two volumes, six issues per volume. Advertising is accepted. Circulation: 3,900. Subscription: $60.00 per year; $61.00 foreign, $25.00 per year with Association membership; $6.00 per issue. Founded: 1947.
Editorial Address:
   Professor Garth J. Thomas, Journal of Comparative and Physiological Psychology, Center for Brain Research, Medical Center, University of Rochester, Rochester, New York 14642.
Editorial Policy:
   Publishes research reports that make a substantial and significant contribution to the literature. Preference is given to experimental reports that elucidate physiological mechanisms of behavior or truly comparative aspects of behavior. Authors should seriously weigh whether their paper is chiefly directed toward clarification of physiological, anatomical, or chemical mechanisms of behavior (for the physiological emphasis of the Journal) or biological (genetic and species-specific) mechanisms of behavior (for the comparative emphasis of the Journal). The reading audience includes psychologists, physiologists, and others interested in the topics covered. Unsolicited manuscripts are welcome. Twenty-five major articles are published per issue. Book reviews are not included.
Manuscript Preparation:
   Accepted manuscripts average 10 double-spaced typewritten pages.

Two copies are required. Return postage and a self-addressed envelope are desired. Bibliographical procedure should follow the APA Publication Manual. Use 1-1/2 inch margins and double-space throughout. Place footnotes on a separate page at the end of the manuscript. A background or explanatory cover letter about the article and a short abstract are required. Biographical information about the author is unnecessary. Illustrations, pictures, and graphs are not often used. No payment is made for accepted articles. Authors may order reprints of their articles from the printer when they receive galley proofs.

Manuscript Disposition:
Receipt of a manuscript is acknowledged. Editorial decisions are made within four months. Accepted articles usually appear in print within one year after acceptance. Unaccepted manuscripts are returned, sometimes with suggestions and/or criticism.

Copyright:
Held by the American Psychological Association.

JOURNAL OF CROSS-CULTURAL PSYCHOLOGY

Subscription Data:
Published by Sage Publications, Inc., 275 South Beverly Drive, Beverly Hills, California 90212. Issued quarterly, in March, June, September, and December. Advertising is accepted. Circulation: 1,500. Subscription: $10.00 per year; $18.00 to institutions; $9.00 to students. Founded: 1970.

Editorial Address:
Walter J. Lonner, Editor, Journal of Cross-Cultural Psychology, Department of Psychology, Western Washington State College, Bellingham, Washington 98225.

Editorial Policy:
Includes empirical research dealing with differential cultural conditioning of human behavior and occasional theoretical papers. The reading audience includes psychologists, anthropologists, and educators. Unsolicited manuscripts are welcome. Nine or ten major articles are published per issue. Book reviews are included.

Manuscript Preparation:
Accepted manuscripts average 10 to 25 double-spaced typewritten pages. Three copies are required. Return postage and a self-addressed envelope are not required. Bibliographical procedure should follow the APA Publication Manual or the style sheet provided by the publisher. List footnotes on separate pages. Use 1-1/2 inch margins and double-space. A background or explanatory cover letter is not required, but an abstract that does not exceed 125 words is required. Biographical information about the author is required if article is accepted. Camera-ready illustrations, pictures, graphs, etc., must be supplied by the author. Each author receives 24 copies of the article and two copies of the issue.

Manuscript Disposition:
Receipt of a manuscript is acknowledged. Editorial decisions

are made within four to eight weeks. Accepted articles usually
appear in print within six to nine months. Unaccepted manuscripts are returned with criticism and/or suggestions.

Copyright:
Held by the Western Washington State College.

Additional Information:
Journal of Cross-Cultural Psychology is a publication affiliated
with the International Association for Cross-Cultural Psychology.

JOURNAL OF EXPERIMENTAL CHILD PSYCHOLOGY

Subscription Data:
Published by the Academic Press, Inc., 111 Fifth Avenue, New
York, New York 10003. Issued six times each year, in February, April, June, August, October, and December. Advertising is accepted. Circulation: 2,000. Subscription: $12.00
per year; $24.00 to institutions. Founded: 1964.

Editorial Address:
Dr. Harry Beilin, Journal of Experimental Child Psychology,
City University of New York Graduate School, 33 West Forty-
second Street, New York, New York 10036.

Editorial Policy:
Includes research reports, theoretical articles, technical notes,
critical notes and letters; addressed to experimental studies of
child behavior and development. The reading audience includes
developmental psychologists, educational psychologists, medical
researchers, and others interested in child psychology. Unsolicited manuscripts are welcome. Ten to twelve major articles
are published per issue. Book reviews are not included.

Manuscript Preparation:
Accepted manuscripts average 15 typewritten pages. Two copies
are required. Return postage and a self-addressed envelope
are not required. Bibliographical procedure should follow the
APA Publication Manual and instructions on the back cover of a
recent Journal issue. Use one inch margins and double-space
throughout. Footnotes should be placed on a separate page at
the end of the manuscript. A background or explanatory cover
letter about the article is not desired nor is an outline or summary. An abstract of not more than 150 words is required.
Biographical information about the author is unnecessary. Illustrations, pictures, and graphs may be used. When large original drawings are used they should be photographed and submitted
as 8-1/2 by 11 inch glossy prints mounted on cardboard. No
payment is made for accepted articles. Fifty free reprints are
available; additional copies may be ordered when galleys are
received.

Manuscript Disposition:
Receipt of a manuscript is acknowledged. Editorial decisions
are made within four to eight weeks. Accepted articles usually
appear in print within eight months. Unaccepted manuscripts
are returned with one or two reviews provided in addition to
the editor's suggestions.

Copyright:
Held by the Academic Press, Inc.

JOURNAL OF EXPERIMENTAL PSYCHOLOGY

Subscription Data:
Published by the American Psychological Association, 1200 Seventeenth Street, N. W., Washington, D. C. 20036. Issued monthly. Advertising is not accepted. Circulation: 4,100. Subscription: $50.00 per year; $25.00 to Association members and to members of the Student Journal Group; $5.00 per issue. Founded: 1916.

Editorial Address:
David A. Grant, Editor, Journal of Experimental Psychology, Psychology Building, West Johnson and Charter Streets, University of Wisconsin, Madison, Wisconsin 53706.

Editorial Policy:
Includes original experimental investigations which are judged by the editors to contribute substantially and significantly toward the development of psychology as an experimental science. Studies with normal human subjects are favored over studies involving abnormal or animal subjects, except when the latter are specifically oriented toward the extension of general psychological theory. Experimental psychometric studies and studies in applied experimental psychology or engineering psychology may be accepted if they have broad implications for experimental and theoretical psychology. The reading audience includes experimental psychologists and others interested in psychological research. Unsolicted articles are welcome. Twenty major articles are published per issue. Book reviews are not included.

Manuscript Preparation:
Accepted manuscripts average from 2,800 to 3,800 words. Two copies are required. Return postage and a self-addressed envelope are desired. Bibliographical procedure should follow the APA Publication Manual. Use wide margins and double-space throughout. A background or explanatory cover letter about the article is desired. An abstract of 100 to 120 words is required. Biographical information about the author is unnecessary. Illustrations, tables, graphs, etc., are sometimes used. No payment is made for accepted articles. Contributors are charged per page when early publication is requested. There are no free reprints.

Manuscript Disposition:
Receipt of a manuscript is acknowledged immediately. Editorial decisions are made within four to eight weeks. Normally papers are published in order of their receipt, and the current publication lag is about seven months. All of the cost of an author's alterations in galley proof is charged to the author. Unaccepted manuscripts are returned, usually with criticism.

Copyright:
Held by the American Psychological Association.

JOURNAL OF HUMANISTIC PSYCHOLOGY

Subscription Data:
Published by the Association for Humanistic Psychology, 325
Ninth Street, San Francisco, California 94103. Issued quarter-
ly, in January, April, July, and October. Advertising is ac-
cepted. Circulation: 4,500. Subscription: $10.00 per year;
$14.00 to libraries and institutions. Founded: 1961.
Editorial Address:
Thomas Greening, Editor, Journal of Humanistic Psychology,
Psychological Services Associates, 1314 Westwood Boulevard,
Los Angeles, California 94024.
Editorial Policy:
Includes experimental reports, theoretical papers, research
studies, applications of humanistic psychology, and humanistic
analysis of contemporary culture. The reading audience includes
professionals, laymen, and students. Unsolicited manuscripts
are welcome. Approximately seven major articles are published
per issue. Book reviews are not included.
Manuscript Preparation:
Accepted manuscripts average 25 to 40 pages. One copy is required. Return postage and a self-addressed envelope are not
required. Footnoting and bibliographical procedure should follow
the APA Publication Manual. Use one inch margins and double-
space. A background or explanatory cover letter is required,
but not an outline, summary, or abstract. Biographical information about the author is required and should include a photograph of the author. Illustrations, pictures, graphs, etc., must
be approved by the editor. No payment is made for accepted
manuscripts. One-hundred free reprints of the article are mailed
to the author.
Manuscript Disposition:
Receipt of a manuscript is acknowledged. Editorial decisions
are made within 12 weeks. Accepted articles usually appear in
print within one year. Unaccepted manuscripts are returned
without criticism or suggestions.
Copyright:
Held by the Association for Humanistic Psychology.

JOURNAL OF MOTOR BEHAVIOR

Subscription Data:
Published by Journal Publishing Affiliates, 726 State Street,
Santa Barbara, California 93103. Issued quarterly, in March,
June, September, and December. Advertising is accepted. Cir-
culation: 960. Subscription: $10.00 per year; $25.00 to insti-
tutions. Founded: 1968.
Editorial Address:
Richard A. Schmidt, Editor, Journal of Motor Behavior, Barbour
Gym, University of Michigan, Ann Arbor, Michigan 48104.
Editorial Policy:
Includes reviews, research reports, and notes. The reading

audience includes scientists in motor behavior. Unsolicited manuscripts are welcome. Book reviews are not included.

Manuscript Preparation:
Accepted manuscripts should not exceed 50 typewritten pages. Three copies are required. Return postage and a self-addressed envelope are not required. Bibliographical procedure should follow the APA Publication Manual. Place footnotes on a separate page. Use standard margin and spacing. A background or explanatory cover letter is not required, but an outline, summary, or abstract is required. Biographical information about the author is not required. No payment is made for accepted manuscripts. Reprints may be purchased.

Manuscript Disposition:
Receipt of a manuscript is acknowledged. Editorial decisions are usually made within eight weeks. Accepted articles usually appear in print within three to six months. Unaccepted manuscripts are returned with criticism and/or suggestions.

Copyright:
Held by Journal Publishing Affiliates.

†JOURNAL OF PERSONALITY

Subscription Data:
Published by the Duke University Press, P.O. Box 6697, College Station, Durham, North Carolina 27708. Issued quarterly, in March, June, September, and December. Advertising is included. Circulation: 2,300. Subscription: $12.00 per year; $3.00 per issue; $8.00 to members of the American Psychological Association. Founded: 1932.

Editorial Address:
Philip R. Costanzo, Journal of Personality, Department of Psychology, Duke University, Durham, North Carolina 27706.

Editorial Policy:
Includes articles which report scientific investigations in the field of personality, with emphasis on experimental studies of behavior dynamics and character structure, personality-related consistencies in cognitive processes, and the development of personality in its cultural context. The scope of the Journal is not fixed and is intended that it reflect the areas of current significant research. Most contributions will be empirical in character. The reading audience includes psychologists, clinicians in related fields, educators, and students. Unsolicited articles are welcome. Ten or eleven articles are published per issue. Book reviews are not included.

Manuscript Preparation:
Accepted manuscripts range from six to twenty-five double-spaced typewritten pages or from 5,000 to 8,000 words. Two copies are required. Return postage and a self-addressed envelope are desired. Footnoting and other bibliographical procedure should follow the APA Publication Manual. Use wide margins and double-space throughout. A background or explanatory cover letter about the article and an abstract of not more than 200 words

are desired. Biographical information about the author is required. Illustrations, graphs, etc., are sometimes used. No
payment is made for accepted articles. Contributors are
charged $12.50 per page for articles in excess of 20 printed
pages. Reprints are available at cost; 50 offprints are supplied
without charge.

Manuscript Disposition:
    Receipt of a manuscript is acknowledged. Editorial decisions
    are made within four months. Accepted articles usually appear
    in print within nine to twelve months after acceptance. Unac-
    cepted manuscripts are returned, often with criticism and/or
    suggestions.

Copyright:
    Held by the Duke University Press.

JOURNAL OF PERSONALITY AND SOCIAL PSYCHOLOGY

Subscription Data:
    Published by the American Psychological Association, 1200 Sev-
    enteenth Street, N.W., Washington, D.C. 20036. Issued month-
    ly. Advertising is accepted. Circulation: 6,990. Subscription:
    $40.00 per year. Founded: 1965.

Editorial Address:
    John T. Lanzetta, Editor, Journal of Personality and Social Psy-
    chology, Department of Psychology, Dartmouth College, Hanover,
    New Hampshire 03755.

Editorial Policy:
    The Journal publishes original research reports in the areas of
    social psychology and personality dynamics. The reading audi-
    ence includes psychologists, sociologists, workers in related
    disciplines such as education, and students. Unsolicited articles
    are welcome. Fifteen to twenty major articles are published
    per issue. Book reviews are not included.

Manuscript Preparation:
    The length of manuscripts should normally not exceed 45 type-
    written pages. Two copies are required. Return postage and
    a self-addressed envelope are not required. Footnoting, biblio-
    graphical procedure, and manuscript margin and spacing should
    follow the APA Publication Manual. A background or explanatory
    cover letter and an abstract are required. Biographical informa-
    tion about the author is not required. Illustrations, pictures,
    graphs, etc., must conform in style to that described in the
    APA Publication Manual. No payment is made for accepted arti-
    cles. Reprints are available.

Manuscript Disposition:
    Receipt of a manuscript is acknowledged. Length of time re-
    quired for editorial decisions averages about 12 weeks. Accepted
    articles usually appear in print within 16 months. Unaccepted
    manuscripts are returned with criticism and/or suggestions.

Copyright:
    Held by the American Psychological Association.

JOURNAL OF SOCIAL PSYCHOLOGY

Subscription Data:
Published by the Journal Press, 2 Commercial Street, Province-town, Massachusetts 02657. Issued six times each year, in February, April, June, August, October, and December. Advertising is not accepted. Circulation: 2,400. Subscription: $39.00 per year. Founded: 1930.

Editorial Address:
Managing Editor, Journal of Social Psychology, Journal Press, 2 Commercial Street, Provincetown, Massachusetts 02657.

Editorial Policy:
Includes studies of persons in group settings and of culture and personality. Special attention is given to cross-cultural articles and notes, and to briefly reported replications and refinements. The reading audience includes professional psychologists and professionals in related fields. Unsolicited articles are welcome. Eighteen major articles are published per issue. Book listings are included, but not book reviews.

Manuscript Preparation:
Manuscripts should not exceed 30 double-spaced typewritten pages. Two copies are required. Return postage and a self-addressed envelope are desired. See a recent issue for bibliographical procedure. Use one inch margins and double-space throughout. Footnotes must be prepared on a separate page with insertion points indicated in the text. A background or explanatory cover letter about the article is usually unnecessary. All articles begin with a summary. Biographical information is desired if the author is unknown to the editor, and should include a summary of his formal education. Illustrations, pictures, graphs, etc., should be submitted as clear glossy prints of approximate final reproduction size. No payment is made for accepted articles. Reprints are available; 100 free copies are mailed to authors. Reprint cost quotations are provided at the page-proof stage.

Manuscript Disposition:
Receipt of a manuscript is acknowledged. Editorial decisions are made within two to three weeks. Accepted articles usually appear in print within one year after acceptance. Unaccepted manuscripts are returned, occasionally with suggestions and/or criticism.

Copyright:
Held by the Journal Press. Authors may obtain release for any specific purpose.

Additional Information:
A document entitled "Preparation of Manuscripts" may be obtained from the managing editor and should be consulted for additional detail.

JOURNAL OF TRANSPERSONAL PSYCHOLOGY

Subscription Data:
Published by Transpersonal Institute, 2637 Marshall Drive, Palo

Alto, California 94303. Issued twice each year, in spring and
fall. Advertising is not accepted. Circulation: 1,400. Subscription: $7.50 per year; $4.00 per issue; $9.50 foreign.
Founded: 1969.

Editorial Address:
The Editor, Journal of Transpersonal Psychology, 2637 Marshall
Drive, Palo Alto, California 94303.

Editorial Policy:
The Journal is concerned with the publication of theoretical and
applied research, empirical papers, articles and studies in meta-
needs, transpersonal values and states, unitive consciousness,
peak experiences, ecstasy, mystical experience, being, essence,
bliss, awe, wonder, self-actualization, self-transcendence, spirit,
sacralization of everyday life, oneness, cosmic awareness, cosmic play, individual and species-wide synergy, the theories and
practices of meditation, spiritual paths, transpersonal actualiza-
tion, compassion; and related concepts, experiences and activities. The reading audience includes professional and non-pro-
fessional interest groups. Unsolicited manuscripts are welcome.
Four or five major articles are published per issue. Book reviews are included.

Manuscript Preparation:
Accepted manuscripts average 10 to 80 double-spaced typewritten
pages. Two copies are required. Return postage and a self-
addressed envelope are required. Bibliographical procedure
should follow the APA Publication Manual. Use one inch margins throughout and double-space. A background or explanatory
cover letter is preferred, and an outline, summary, or abstract
is required. Biographical information about the author is required. Illustrations, pictures, graphs, etc., are acceptable
if specific to material. No payment is made for accepted manuscripts. Fifty free reprints are given to the author; permission to reprint is required.

Manuscript Disposition:
Receipt of a manuscript is acknowledged. Editorial decisions
are made within two months. Accepted articles usually appear
in print within eight months. Unaccepted manuscripts are returned with criticism and/or suggestions.

Copyright:
Held by Transpersonal Institute.

JOURNAL OF VERBAL LEARNING AND VERBAL BEHAVIOR

Subscription Data:
Published by Academic Press, Inc., 111 Fifth Avenue, New
York, New York 10003. Issued bimonthly. Advertising is ac-
cepted. Circulation: 2,300. Subscription: $35.00 per year.
Founded: 1962.

Editorial Address:
Edwin Martin, Editor, Journal of Verbal Learning and Verbal
Behavior, Human Performance Center, University of Michigan,
330 Packard Road, Ann Arbor, Michigan 48104.

434 / Psychological - Research

Editorial Policy:
    Includes experimental and theoretical articles on human memory,
    verbal learning, and psycholinguistics. The reading audience in-
    cludes researchers and teachers in the areas of human memory,
    verbal learning, and psycholinguistics. Unsolicited manuscripts
    are welcome. The number of major articles published per issue
    varies. Book reviews are not accepted.
Manuscript Preparation:
    No limitations are placed upon manuscript length. Four copies
    are required. Return postage and a self-addressed envelope
    are not required. Bibliographical procedure should follow the
    APA Publication Manual. Use one inch margins and double-
    space. A background or explanatory cover letter about the arti-
    cle is not desired. An abstract of 120 words or less is re-
    quired. Biographical information about the author is not re-
    quired. See the APA Publication Manual for policies concerning
    illustrations, pictures, graphs, etc. No payment is made for
    accepted articles. Fifty free prints are mailed to the author;
    additional copies may be ordered.
Manuscript Disposition:
    Receipt of a manuscript is acknowledged. Editorial decisions
    are made within four weeks. Accepted articles usually appear
    in print within eight months after acceptance. Unaccepted man-
    uscripts are returned with criticism and suggestions.
Copyright:
    Held by Academic Press, Inc.

PSYCHOLOGICAL RESEARCH

Subscription Data:
    Published by Springer-Verlag, 175 Fifth Avenue, New York,
    New York 10010. Issued irregulary, with one volume consist-
    ing of four issues. Advertising is accepted. Subscription:
    $64.30 for four issues (in 1974). Founded: 1921.
Editorial Address:
    Professor H. W. Leibowitz, Editor, Psychological Research,
    417 Psychology Building, University Park, Pennsylvania 16802.
Editorial Policy:
    Invites contributions in general experimental psychology. Since
    psychology is concerned with problems of behavior and percep-
    tual processes, contributions from related behavior-oriented dis-
    ciplines such as zoology, ethology, psysiology, psychiatry, soci-
    ology, and neurology are accepted. Manuscripts submitted to
    Psychological Research should be firmly based on experimenta-
    tion and may, at the same time, explore the theoretical rele-
    vance of the data obtained. Especially favored are articles in
    which theoretical considerations lead to experimentation, the
    data of which are then re-integrated into theory. Contributions
    from developmental psychology will be published only if they im-
    prove one's understanding of fundamental psychological mecha-
    nisms. The reading audience includes specialists in advanced
    behavioral sciences. Unsolicited manuscripts are welcome.

Approximately seven major articles are published per issue.
Book reviews are not included.

Manuscript Preparation:

Accepted manuscripts should not exceed 32 printed pages which
equals 41 typewritten pages of 35 lines each. Two copies are
required. Return postage and a self-addressed envelope are not
required. Bibliographical procedure should follow the "Instructions for Authors" found in each issue. Footnotes except those
referring to the head of the article are to be numbered consecutively. Manuscripts must be typewritten on one side of the page
only. Use broad margins and double-space. A summary is required as each paper should be preceded by a summary of the
main points (of not more than 3/4 of a typed page). Biographical information about the author should include name, title, and
affiliation. Authors should mark in the margin of the manuscript
the desired position of figures and tables. All figures including
graphs are to be numbered consecutively as text figures (Arabic
numerals). They must be submitted in finished form on separate
sheets. All should have descriptive and concise legends. These
must be typed in numerical order and added as an appendix to
the manuscript. The number of illustrations must be kept to a
minimum required for clarification of the text. Line drawings
in graphs should be drawn with India ink. Photographs must be
clean, glossy prints in sharp focus and with strong contrast.
Halftone drawings must be submitted in the original. For each
paper 75 offprints are provided free of charge. Additional copies may be ordered at cost.

Copyright:

Held by Springer-Verlag.

JOURNAL OF READING

Subscription Data:
Published by the International Reading Association, Six Tyre Avenue, Newark, Delaware 19711. Issued eight times each year, October through May. Advertising is accepted. Circulation: 15,000. Subscription: $15.00 per year as part of Association membership; $15.00 to libraries and institutions; $2.00 per issue. Founded: 1955.

Editorial Address:
Dr. Lloyd W. Kline, Editor, Journal of Reading, International Reading Association, Six Tyre Avenue, Newark, Delaware 19711.

Editorial Policy:
Includes articles about reading and related fields. The Journal welcomes material of special interest to the teacher of reading at the secondary school, college, and adult levels, and to others who share that interest. The reading audience includes professionals in reading. Unsolicited manuscripts are welcome. Six to eight major articles are published per issue. Solicited book reviews are included.

Manuscript Preparation:
Accepted manuscripts vary in length. Three copies are required. Return postage and a self-addressed envelope are required. Bibliographical procedure should follow the MLA Style Sheet. A background or explanatory cover letter is not required nor is an outline, summary, or abstract. Biographical information about the author is not required. Illustrations, pictures, graphs, etc., can be included if they are at no cost to the Journal. Free copies are given to each author, but no payment is made for accepted articles. Use of the International Reading Association's copyright to reproduce articles protects the author.

Manuscript Disposition:
Receipt of a manuscript is acknowledged. Editorial decisions are made within four to six weeks. Accepted articles usually appear in print within two to six months. Unaccepted manuscripts are returned with criticism and/or suggestions.

Copyright:
Held by the International Reading Association.

Additional Information:
Because the Journal of Reading serves as an open forum, its contents do not necessarily reflect or imply advocacy or endorsement by the International Reading Association, its officers, or its members.

JOURNAL OF READING BEHAVIOR

Subscription Data:
Published by the National Reading Conference, Appalachian State University, Boone, North Carolina 28607. Issued quarterly, in February, May, August, and November. Advertising is not accepted. Circulation: 1,500. Subscription: $10.00 per year. Founded: 1969.

Editorial Address:
J. Jaap Tuinman, Editor, Journal of Reading Behavior, Institute for Child Study, Indiana University, Bypass 46, Bloomington, Indiana 47401.

Editorial Policy:
Includes articles dealing with basic and applied research in reading, reading instruction, and learning from reading. The reading audience includes college faculty and reading specialists. Unsolicited manuscripts are welcome. Eight to ten major articles are published per issue. Book reviews are included.

Manuscript Preparation:
No limitations are placed on manuscript length; however, the typical manuscript averages between 1,500 to 4,000 words. Five copies are required. Return postage and a self-addressed envelope are required. Bibliographical procedure should follow the APA Publication Manual. A background or explanatory cover letter is not required, but an abstract is required. Biographical information about the author is not required. No payment is made for accepted manuscripts. Reprints are available at cost.

Manuscript Disposition:
Receipt of a manuscript is acknowledged. Editorial decisions are made within eight to twelve weeks. Accepted articles usually appear in print within nine months. Unaccepted manuscripts are returned only if requested. Criticism and/or suggestions are provided.

Copyright:
Held by the National Reading Conference.

Additional Information:
"Information for Authors" is available from the editor.

READING IMPROVEMENT

Subscription Data:
Published by PROJECT INNOVATION, 1402 West Capital Drive, Milwaukee, Wisconsin 53206. Issued three times each year, in September, December, and April. Advertisement related to reading is accepted. Circulation: 2,500. Subscription: $5.00 per year; $7.00 to institutions. Founded: 1963.

Editorial Address:
The Editor, Reading Improvement, 1402 West Capital Drive, Milwaukee, Wisconsin 53206.

Editorial Policy:
 Includes reports of investigations and creative theoretical papers
 dealing with every aspect of reading improvement, and at all
 different levels of instruction. The reading audience includes
 teachers of reading, educators, teachers, and persons interested
 in the improvement of reading in our schools and colleges. Unsolicited manuscripts are welcome. From 12 to 15 articles are
 published in each issue. Book reviews are published.

Manuscript Preparation:
 Accepted manuscripts average 2,000 to 4,000 words. Two copies are required. Return postage is requested. Procedure and
 style sheet is available on request and follows the APA Publication Manual. Footnotes are not desired; margins and spacing
 should follow the APA Publication Manual. A cover letter is not
 essential, but an abstract of 120 words or less is required.
 Biographical information about the author should include only address and institution affiliation. Illustrations, figures, half-
 tones, and dense tables require a lithographic plate be made at
 cost to the author. No payment is made for manuscripts. Reprints are available from the printer at nominal charges.

Manuscript Disposition:
 Receipt of a manuscript is acknowledged. Editorial decisions
 are made within four to six weeks. Accepted articles are published generally within the year. Unaccepted manuscripts are
 returned to authors, but criticism is given only for those to be
 re-submitted.

Copyright:
 Held by PROJECT INNOVATION.

Additional Information:
 Uninvited articles and articles not classed as "priority" require
 authors to share in publication costs.

READING RESEARCH QUARTERLY

Subscription Data:
 Published by the International Reading Association, Six Tyre
 Avenue, Newark, Delaware 19711. Issued quarterly, in fall,
 winter, spring, and summer. Advertising is not accepted. Cir-
 culation: 10,000. Subscription: $15.00 per year to institutions;
 Free with $15.00 Association membership; $7.50 to students.
 Founded: 1965.

Editorial Address:
 The Editors, Reading Research Quarterly, 231 Pine Hall, Indiana University, Bloomington, Indiana 47401.

Editorial Policy:
 Includes experimental, statistical, and technical articles and
 critical reviews of research in reading. The primary goal of
 the Quarterly is to provide a forum for current research and
 theory which relates to the reading process. The reading audience includes researchers and professionals in the field of reading. Unsolicited articles are welcome. Four to six major articles are published per issue.

Manuscript Preparation:

No limitations are placed upon manuscript length. Accepted
articles average 30 triple-spaced pages. Four copies are required. Return postage and a self-addressed envelope are unnecessary. Bibliographical procedure should follow Author's
Guide to the Reading Research Quarterly, available through the
office of the editor. Use 1-1/2 inch margins and triple-space.
Only content footnotes will be published; all should be numbered
consecutively and should be double-spaced. A background or explanatory cover letter about the article is not desired nor is an
outline or summary. Biographical information about the author
is required and should be prepared as outlined in the Author's
Guide. Pictures are not often used. Graphs, charts, and illustrations should be submitted ready for the camera or as glossy
photographs. Drawings should be proportioned for reduction to
page size. Lettering must be clear and uniform with sharp contrast. No payment is made for accepted articles. Reprints
are available.

Manuscript Disposition:

Receipt of a manuscript is acknowledged. Editorial decisions
are made within 90 days. Accepted articles usually appear in
print within six to twelve months after acceptance. Unaccepted
manuscripts are returned, sometimes with suggestions and/or
criticism.

Copyright:

Held by the International Reading Association, Inc.

READING TEACHER

Subscription Data:

Published by the International Reading Association, 800 Barks-
dale Road, Newark, Delaware 19711. Issued eight times each
year, October through May. Advertising is accepted. Circulation: 46,500. Subscription: $15.00 per year as part of Asso-
ciation membership; $15.00 to libraries and institutions; $2.00
per issue. Founded: 1954.

Editorial Address:

Dr. Lloyd W. Kline, Editor, Reading Teacher, International
Reading Association, Six Tyre Avenue, Newark, Delaware 19711.

Editorial Policy:

The Reading Teacher is published as a service to its members
and to all others who are concerned with reading, especially as
it is practiced and encouraged through instruction and supervision in schools. The journal provides a forum for the exchange
of information and opinion in the pursuit and exploration of such
interests. Material of special interest to the elementary classroom teacher of reading and to others who share that interest
are welcome. Unsolicited manuscripts are welcome. Eight to
twelve major articles are published per issue. Book reviews
are included.

Manuscript Preparation:

Accepted manuscripts should not exceed 15 pages. Three

copies are required. Return postage and a self-addressed envelope are required. Bibliographical procedure should follow the MLA Style Sheet. Keep footnotes to a minimum and give references by author's last name and date in parentheses within the bibliography. Request authors' guide for manuscript margin and spacing recommendations. A background or explanatory cover letter is not required nor is an outline, summary, or abstract. Biographical information about the author is not required. Request authors' guide for policies concerning illustrations, pictures, graphs, etc. No payment is made for accepted manuscripts.

Manuscript Disposition:
Receipt of a manuscript is acknowledged. Editorial decisions are made within four to eight weeks. Accepted articles usually appear in print within two to twelve months. Unaccepted manuscripts are returned with criticism and/or suggestions.

Copyright:
Held by the International Reading Association.

Additional Information:
Because Reading Teacher serves as an open forum, its contents do not necessarily reflect or imply advocacy or endorsement by the International Reading Association, its officers, or its members.

READING WORLD (formerly Journal of the Reading Specialist)

Subscription Data:
Published by the College Reading Association, c/o Dr. Leonard S. Braam, Reading and Language Arts Center, Syracuse University, Syracuse, New York 13210. Issued quarterly, in October, December, March, and May. Advertising is accepted. Circulation: 3,000. Subscription: $15.00 per year. Founded: 1961.

Editorial Address:
Dr. Samuel S. Zeman, Editor, Reading World, College Reading Association, Shippensburg State College, Shippensburg, Pennsylvania 17257.

Editorial Policy:
Includes manuscripts which relate to all aspects of reading at all levels, including college and clinical disability programs. The reading audience includes professionals in reading at the college and university level, reading specialists in the schools, elementary school supervisors and elementary and secondary school teachers. Unsolicited articles are welcome. Six to seven major articles are published per issue. Book reviews are included.

Manuscript Preparation:
Accepted manuscripts average 2,000 to 3,500 words, and sometimes more. Two copies are required. Return postage and a self-addressed envelope are not required. Bibliographical procedure need follow no particular style. Double-space the manuscript. A background or explanatory cover letter about the article is not desired, but an abstract is desired. Biographical

information about the author is desired. Illustrations, pictures, graphs, etc., may be used, with no specific policy. No payment is made for accepted articles. Reprints are available on request.

Manuscript Disposition:

Receipt of a manuscript is acknowledged. Editorial decisions are made within four weeks. Accepted articles usually appear in print within six to twelve months after acceptance. Unaccepted manuscripts are returned, often with suggestions and/or criticism.

Copyright:

Held by the College Reading Association.

WISCONSIN STATE READING ASSOCIATION JOURNAL

Subscription Data:

Published by the United Scholars Associated, LTD., La Salle at Abbe Hill Road, Eau Claire, Wisconsin 54701. Issued four times each year, in October, January, March, and May. Advertising is accepted. Circulation: 4,000. Subscription: $4.00 per year; $1.00 per back issue. Founded: 1957.

Editorial Address:

The Editor, Wisconsin State Reading Association Journal, Box 42, School of Education, University of Wisconsin - Oshkosh, Oshkosh, Wisconsin 54901.

Editorial Policy:

Includes all articles pertaining to the entire field of reading. The reading audience includes primarily reading teachers in elementary and secondary schools. Unsolicited manuscripts are welcome. Ten major articles are published per issue. Book reviews are normally not included; however, they are acceptable.

Manuscript Preparation:

Accepted manuscripts should not exceed 10 double-spaced typewritten 8-1/2 by 11 inch bond pages. Two copies are required. Return postage and a self-addressed envelope are not required. Footnoting and other bibliographical procedure are individualized. A background or explanatory cover letter is not required nor is an outline, summary, or abstract. Biographical information about the author is not required. The policies used for illustrations, pictures, graphs, etc., are variable. No payment is made for accepted manuscripts. Reprints are available at acceptance of the author.

Manuscript Disposition:

Receipt of a manuscript is acknowledged. Editorial decisions are made within four weeks. Accepted articles usually appear in print within two months. Unaccepted manuscripts are returned without criticism and/or suggestions.

Copyright:

Held by the Wisconsin State Reading Association.

RELIGION AND THEOLOGY

*CHURCH AND STATE (formerly Church and State Review)

Subscription Data:
Published by Americans United for Separation of Church and
State, 8120 Fenton Street, Silver Spring, Maryland 20910. Is-
sued monthly, except August. Advertising is not accepted.
Circulation: 135,000. Subscription: $5.00 per year; $6.00
foreign. Founded: 1948.
Editorial Address:
The Editor, Church and State, Americans United for Separation
of Church and State, 8120 Fenton Street, Silver Spring, Maryland 20910.
Editorial Policy:
Includes articles of interest to persons who are concerned with
developments in church-state relations in all areas, especially
government funding of church enterprises and church-related
institutions. The reading audience includes scholars and the
lay public. Unsolicited articles cannot be used. Four articles
are published per issue. Book reviews are included.
Copyright:
Held by Church and State.

CHURCH HISTORY

Subscription Data:
Published by the American Society of Church History, 305 East
Country Club Lane, Wallingford, Pennsylvania 19086. Issued
quarterly, in March, June, September, and December. Adver-
tising is accepted. Circulation: 2,900. Subscription: $10.00
per year; $6.00 to students upon recommendation of professor.
Founded: 1932.
Editorial Address:
The Editor, Church History, Swift Hall, University of Chicago,
Chicago, Illinois 60637.
Editorial Policy:
Includes articles which relate to the history of the churches
in all places at all times. The reading audience includes professors and students of ecclesiastical history, religion, and
religious studies. Unsolicited manuscripts are welcome. Approx-
imately seven articles are published per issue. Book reviews are
included.
Manuscript Preparation:
Accepted manuscripts should average not more than 25 to 30

442

double-spaced typewritten pages of text. One copy is required.
Return postage and a self-addressed envelope are not required.
Bibliographical procedure should follow the University of Chicago
Manual of Style. All footnotes should be on separate sheets following the text and should be double-spaced and typewritten. A
style sheet is available from the editorial office. Use one inch
margins and double-space throughout. A background or explanatory cover letter is required, but not an outline, summary, or
abstract. Biographical information about the author is required
and should include especially formal education and current position. No illustrations or pictures, but graphs may be used if
crucial to a particular article. No payment is made for accepted manuscripts. Reprints are available; cost depends on
article length and order volume.

Manuscript Disposition:
Receipt of a manuscript is acknowledged. Editorial decisions
are made generally within three months. Accepted articles appear in print usually within one year. Unaccepted manuscripts
are returned. All articles are subject to revision when accepted, but no criticism or suggestions are provided for unaccepted materials.

Copyright:
Held by the American Society of Church History.

HARVARD THEOLOGICAL REVIEW

Subscription Data:
Published by the Harvard University Press, 19 Gorden Street,
Cambridge, Massachusetts 02138. Issued quarterly, in January,
April, July, and October. Advertising is not accepted. Circula-
tion: 1,180. Subscription: $8.00 per year. Founded: 1908.

Editorial Address:
The Editor, Harvard Theological Review, Divinity School, Harvard University, 45 Francis Avenue, Cambridge, Massachusetts
02138.

Editorial Policy:
Includes articles on theology, ethics, history, philosophy of religion, and cognate subjects. The reading audience includes specialists in the various fields and areas of religion, religious
educators, and students. The journal has wide international distribution to libraries. Unsolicited articles are welcome. Four
or five major articles are published per issue. Although book
reviews are not included, a quarterly list of books received is
published.

Manuscript Preparation:
Accepted manuscripts range from 15 to more than 40 double-
spaced typewritten pages. One copy is required. Return postage and a self-addressed envelope are desired. See a recent
issue for bibliographical procedure. Use two inch margins and
double-space throughout. Place all footnotes on a separate page
at the end of the manuscript. A background or explanatory
cover letter about the article is desired, but not an outline or

summary. Biographical information about the author is desired.
Illustrations, pictures, graphs, etc., may be used. No payment
is made for accepted articles. Complimentary reprints are
mailed to the author. Reprints may be ordered only at the time
of printing, at a cost which varies with article length and order
volume.

Manuscript Disposition:
Receipt of a manuscript is acknowledged. Editorial decisions
are made within two to three months. Accepted articles usually
appear in print within six to twelve months after acceptance.
Unaccepted manuscripts are returned, often with criticism and/
or suggestions.

Copyright:
Held by the President and Fellows of Harvard University.

INTERDENOMINATIONAL THEOLOGICAL CENTER. JOURNAL

Subscription Data:
Published by the Interdenominational Theological Center, 671
Beckwith Street, S. W., Atlanta, Georgia 30314. Issued semi-
annually. Paid advertising is accepted. Circulation: 3,000.
Subscription: $5.00 per year; $6.00 to institutions. Founded:
1973.

Editorial Address:
The Editor, Journal of the Interdenominational Theological Center, 671 Beckwith Street, S. W., Atlanta, Georgia 30314.

Editorial Policy:
Includes articles which deal with any aspect of religion and
philosophy; however, there is a particular interest in the Black
religious experience. Unsolicited manuscripts are welcome.
Ten major articles are published per issue. Book reviews are
included.

Manuscript Preparation:
Accepted manuscripts average 10 to 25 typewritten pages. One
copy is required. Return postage and a self-addressed envelope
are not presently required. List footnotes at the bottom of each
page. Bibliographical procedure and manuscript margin and
spacing should follow the Turabian Manual For Writers. A
background or explanatory cover letter is required, but not an
outline, summary, or abstract. Biographical information about
the author is helpful for editorial purposes. No pictures, graphs,
etc., are acceptable. Currently no payment is made for accepted manuscripts, but eventually payment will be made for
manuscripts. Ten reprints for each accepted article are provided.

Manuscript Disposition:
Receipt of a manuscript is acknowledged. Editorial decisions
are made within four weeks. Accepted articles usually appear
in print within six months. Unaccepted manuscripts are returned
with criticism and/or suggestions.

Copyright:
Held by the Interdenominational Theological Center.

INTERPRETATION

Subscription Data:
   Published by the Union Theological Seminary, 3401 Brook Road,
   Richmond, Virginia 23227. Issued quarterly, in January, April,
   July, and October. Book publisher advertising is accepted.
   Circulation: 6,805. (This journal is international and inter-
   denominational, with readers in all states and Canadian prov-
   inces and approximately 85 other foreign countries.) Subscription: $7.00 per year; $18.00 for three years; $7.70 foreign
   for one year; $20.10 foreign for three years. Founded: 1947.
Editorial Address:
   The Editor, Interpretation, 3401 Brook Road, Richmond, Virginia 23227.
Editorial Policy:
   Includes articles on the Bible, theology, exegesis, interpretation,
   and homiletics. The reading audience includes ministers, min
   isterial students, professors in seminaries and colleges, and
   laymen. Unsolicited articles are welcome. Four or five major
   articles are published per issue. Four to six major-length book
   review articles and a varying number of shorter reviews and
   notices are published per issue. Most book reviews are assigned to known reviewers, but requests for reviewing assign-
   ments will be entertained.
Manuscript Preparation:
   Accepted manuscripts range from 4,000 to 10,000 words, including footnotes. One copy, typewritten on bond paper, is required.
   See a recent issue for footnoting and other bibliographical procedure. Use wide margins and double-space throughout. Translations of foreign-language articles should carry the original publication style. The editor appreciates author queries prior to
   submission of manuscripts. A background or explanatory cover
   letter about the article is desired. Biographical information
   about the author is required and should include official title and
   a summary of current position. Illustrations, pictures, graphs,
   etc., may not be used. Payment for accepted articles varies,
   is nominal, and is paid upon publication. Offprints in small
   quantities may be ordered from the printer prior to publication.
Manuscript Disposition:
   Receipt of a manuscript is acknowledged. Editorial decisions
   are made within one month. Accepted articles usually appear
   in print within 12 to 18 months after acceptance. Unaccepted
   manuscripts are returned without editorial comment.
Copyright:
   Held by the Union Theological Seminary. Reprint rights are
   usually granted willingly upon specific request.

JOURNAL OF RELIGIOUS THOUGHT

Subscription Data:
   Published by the School of Religion, Howard University, Washington, D.C. 20001. Issued twice each year, in January and

July. Advertising is accepted. Circulation: 500. Subscription: $3.00 per year. Founded: 1945.

Editorial Address:
  The Editor, Journal of Religious Thought, School of Religion, Howard University, Washington, D.C. 20001.

Editorial Policy:
  Includes articles, reports, and other general works on religion, particularly as it relates to the Black experience, including non-Christian ideas. The reading audience includes students of religion, pastors, and teachers. Unsolicited articles are welcome. Six major articles are published per issue. Book reviews are included.

Manuscript Preparation:
  Accepted manuscripts range from 15 to more than 25 double-spaced typewritten pages. One copy is required. Return postage and a self-addressed envelope are required. Footnoting and other bibliographical procedure should follow the University of Chicago Manual of Style. Use one inch margins and double-space throughout. A background or explanatory cover letter is about the article is not desired nor is an outline or summary. Biographical information about the author is required and should include a summary of educational background, employment, and recent publications. Illustrations, pictures, graphs, etc., may not be used. No payment is made for accepted articles. Reprints are available; costs are determined on a sliding scale established by the printer which varies with article length and style of binding used.

Manuscript Disposition:
  Receipt of a manuscript is acknowledged. Editorial decisions are made as soon as possible. Accepted articles usually appear in print within six months after acceptance. Unaccepted manuscripts are returned, often with criticism and/or suggestions.

Copyright:
  Held by Howard University.

RELIGION AND SOCIETY

Subscription Data:
  Published by Religion and Society, Inc., Box 244, Stillwater, Minnesota 55082. Issued bimonthly. Only exchange advertising is accepted. Circulation: 2,500. Subscription: $10.00 per year; $16.00 for two years. Founded: 1968.

Editorial Address:
  The Editor, Religion and Society, Box 244, Stillwater, Minnesota 55082.

Editorial Policy:
  Includes articles of good taste on religion and society. The reading audience is very broad. Unsolicited manuscripts are welcome. Two major articles are published per issue. Book reviews are included.

Manuscript Preparation:
  No limitations are placed upon manuscript length. One copy is

required. Return postage and a self-addressed envelope are desired. Prefer footnotes be placed on the same page. Use 1-1/2 inch margins. A background or explanatory cover letter is not required nor is an outline, summary, or abstract. Biographical information about the author is not required. Do not include illustrations, pictures, graphs, etc. No payment is made for accepted manuscripts.

Manuscript Disposition:
Receipt of a manuscript is acknowledged. Editorial decisions are made within one to two weeks. Accepted articles usually appear in print within 12 months. Unaccepted manuscripts are returned with criticism and/or suggestions.

Copyright:
Held by Religion and Society, Inc.

SOUNDINGS (formerly Christian Scholar)

Subscription Data:
Published jointly by Vanderbilt University and the Society for Religion in Higher Education, Nashville, Tennessee 37203. Issued quarterly, in March, June, September, and December. Advertising is accepted. Circulation: 2,000. Subscription: $9.00 per year; $20.00 for three years; $6.00 to students. Founded: 1968.

Editorial Address:
The Editor, Soundings, Box 6309, Station B, Nashville, Tennessee 37235.

Editorial Policy:
Includes articles on all fields and disciplines, especially articles pertinent to other fields. Articles are published that combine boldness with professional competence and that highlight issues and insights from many fields disclosing serious humane concerns. The reading audience includes college and university teachers, administrators, and laymen. Unsolicited manuscripts are welcome. Six to eight major articles are published per issue. Review essays that are commissioned are included.

Manuscript Preparation:
Accepted manuscripts average 6,000 words. One copy is required. Return postage and a self-addressed envelope are required. Bibliographical procedure should follow the MLA Style Sheet. List explanatory notes at bottom of the page and bibliographical notes on page at the end of the article. No manuscript margin and spacing recommendations. A background or explanatory cover letter is desirable, but not an outline, summary, or abstract. Biographical information about the author is desired. Illustrations, pictures, graphs, etc., are limited in use. No payment is made for accepted manuscripts. Authors may order offprints; 10 free copies are given to each author.

Manuscript Disposition:
Receipt of a manuscript is acknowledged. Editorial decisions are made within four weeks. Accepted articles usually appear

in print within six months. Unaccepted manuscripts are returned if postage is included.
Copyright:
Held by Soundings.

THEOLOGICAL STUDIES

Subscription Data:
Published by Theological Studies, Inc., Mount Royal and Guilford Avenues, Baltimore, Maryland 21202. Issued quarterly, in March, June, September, and December. Advertising is accepted. Circulation: 7,000. Subscription: $8.00 per year; $8.50 Canada and foreign. Founded: 1940.
Editorial Address:
The Editor, Theological Studies, 475 Riverside Drive, Room 244, New York, New York 10027.
Editorial Policy:
Includes scholarly research in the various theological disciplines. The reading audience includes mostly readers of some theological background. Unsolicited manuscripts are welcome. Six major articles are published per issue. Book reviews are included.
Manuscript Preparation:
Accepted manuscripts average from 2,000 to 20,000 words. One copy is required. Return postage and a self-addressed envelope are desired. Theological Studies does not conform totally to any style sheet; advisable to consult current issues. List footnotes on a separate page and double-space. Use one inch margins and double-space throughout. A background or explanatory cover letter is not required but desirable. An outline, summary, or abstract is not required. Biographical information about the author is required. No payment is made for accepted manuscripts. There are 100 offprints gratis to each author.
Manuscript Disposition:
Receipt of a manuscript is acknowledged. Editorial decisions are made within six weeks. Accepted articles usually appear in print within nine months. Unaccepted manuscripts are returned, usually with criticism and/or suggestions.
Copyright:
Held by Theological Studies, Inc.

THOUGHT

Subscription Data:
Published by the Fordham University Press, Fordham University, Bronx, New York 10458. Issued quarterly, in March, June, September, and December. Advertising is accepted. Circulation: 1,770. Subscription: $10.00 per year. Founded: 1926.
Editorial Address:
The Editor, Thought, Fordham University, Bronx, New York 10458.

Editorial Policy:
Includes articles on all aspects of learning and culture in literature, theology, philosophy, etc. The reading audience includes university and college professors, advanced students, professional people (doctors, lawyers, etc.), clergy. Unsolicited manuscripts are welcome. Five major articles are published per issue. Book reviews are included.

Manuscript Preparation:
Accepted manuscripts average 4,000 to 10,000 words. One copy is required. Return postage and a self-addressed envelope are desired. Use any widely used style manual. Footnotes are not encouraged and should be as brief as possible. Use wide margins and double-space. A background or explanatory cover letter is desired, but not an outline, summary, or abstract. Biographical information about the author is required and should include a summary of academic background, current position, and recent publications. Illustrations, pictures, graphs, etc., can occasionally be used. No payment is made for accepted manuscripts. Seventy-five bound copies are mailed free to the author.

Manuscript Disposition:
Receipt of a manuscript is acknowledged. Editorial decisions are made within four weeks. Accepted articles usually appear in print within one year after acceptance. Unaccepted manuscripts are returned without criticism or suggestions.

Copyright:
Held by the Fordham University Press.

RELIGIOUS EDUCATION

JEWISH EDUCATION

Subscription Data:
Published by the National Council for Jewish Education, 114 Fifth Avenue, New York, New York 10011. Issued four times each year, in November, January, April, and July. Advertising is accepted. Circulation: 3,500. Subscription: $7.00 per year. Founded: 1930.

Editorial Address:
Dr. Alvin I. Schiff, Editor, Jewish Education, 426 West Fifty-eighth Street, New York, New York 10019.

Editorial Policy:
Includes articles on both general and Jewish education. The reading audience includes professionals and laymen in the field of Jewish education. Unsolicited articles are welcome. Four or five major articles are published per issue. Book reviews are included.

Manuscript Preparation:
Accepted manuscripts average from six to twenty double-spaced typewritten pages. Two copies are required. Return postage and a self-addressed envelope are desired. Use one inch margins and double-space throughout. Footnotes should appear at the end of the article, unless few are used, in which case they may be placed at the bottom of each page. A background or explanatory cover letter about the article is not desired nor is an outline or summary. Biographical information about the author is required and should include title and the name of the university or other agency. Authors unknown to the editor should submit a summary of their scholarly background. Illustrations, pictures, and graphs are rarely used. No payment is made for accepted articles. Reprints are available; costs vary with article length and order volume.

Manuscript Disposition:
Receipt of a manuscript is acknowledged. Editorial decisions are made as soon as possible. Accepted articles usually appear in print within six to twelve months after acceptance. Unaccepted manuscripts are returned, often with criticism and/or suggestions.

Copyright:
Held by the National Council for Jewish Education.

JEWISH PARENT MAGAZINE

Subscription Data:
Published by the National Association of Hebrew Day School

PTA's, 229 Park Avenue South, New York, New York 10003.
Issued quarterly, in October, January, March, and June. Ad-
vertising is accepted. Circulation: 4,000 to 5,000. Subscrip-
tion: $2.00 per year. Founded: 1948.
Editorial Address:
The Editor, Jewish Parent Magazine, National Association of
Hebrew Day School PTA's, Torah Umesorah, 156 Fifth Avenue,
New York, New York 10010.
Editorial Policy:
Includes articles on mental hygiene, psychology, and general
education. The reading audience includes parents of Hebrew
day school students, educators, and PTA officials. Unsolicited
articles are welcome. Seven or eight major articles are published per issue. Book reviews are included.
Manuscript Preparation:
Accepted manuscripts average from two to six double-spaced
typewritten pages. Three copies are required. Return postage
and a self-addressed envelope are desired. Footnoting and other
bibliographical procedure may follow any widely used style manual. Use wide margins and double-space. A background or explanatory cover letter about the article is required. An outline
or summary is desired in advance of the finished manuscript.
Biographical information about the author is desired and should
include a summary of his professional background and current
position. Illustrations, pictures, graphs, etc., are rarely used.
No payment is made for accepted articles. Reprints are available.
Manuscript Disposition:
Receipt of a manuscript is acknowledged. Editorial decisions
are made within two weeks. Accepted articles usually appear
in print within one year after acceptance. Unaccepted manuscripts are returned, sometimes with criticism.
Copyright:
Held by the National Association of Hebrew Day School PTA's.

JOURNAL OF ADVENTIST EDUCATION (formerly Journal of True
Education)

Subscription Data:
Published by the General Conference of Seventh-Day Adventists,
Department of Education, 6840 Eastern Avenue, N.W., Washing-
ton, D.C. 20012. Issued bimonthly, September through June.
Advertising is not accepted. Circulation: 7,100. Subscription:
$4.00 per year. Founded: 1939.
Editorial Address:
The Editor, Journal of Adventist Education, 6840 Eastern Ave-
nue, N.W., Washington, D.C. 20012.
Editorial Policy:
Includes articles on administration, pedagogy, research, and
staff and student personnel services. The reading audience in-
cludes teachers and administrators in parochial school systems.
Unsolicited articles are welcome. Nine or ten major articles
are published per issue. Book reviews are included.

Manuscript Preparation:

Accepted manuscripts average from 1,500 to 2,200 words. Two copies are required. Return postage and a self-addressed envelope are desired. Bibliographical procedure should follow Campbell's Form and Style or any other standard style manual. Use 3/4 inch margins and double-space. Place numbered footnotes at the end of the article. A background or explanatory cover letter is desired and an outline or summary is required. Biographical information about the author is desired and should include a summary of his professional position and academic degrees. Illustrations, pictures, graphs, etc., may be used if needed for clarity. No payment is made for accepted articles. Reprints are not available, but extra copies of the Journal are available at $.80 per copy.

Manuscript Disposition:

Receipt of a manuscript is acknowledged. Editorial decisions are made within four months. Accepted articles usually appear in print within two to twenty-four months after acceptance. Unaccepted manuscripts are usually returned with reasons and/or suggestions.

Copyright:

Held by the Journal of Adventist Education.

LUTHERAN EDUCATION

Subscription Data:

Published by the Lutheran Church--Missouri Synod, Concordia Publishing House, 3558 South Jefferson Avenue, St. Louis, Missouri 63118. Issued bimonthly, September through May. Advertising is not accepted. Circulation: 4,800. Subscription: $5.00 per year. Founded: 1864.

Editorial Address:

Merle L. Radke, Editor, Lutheran Education, Concordia Teachers College, River Forest, Illinois 60305.

Editorial Policy:

Includes articles which relate to elementary education, educational administration, and theology. The reading audience includes Lutheran elementary school teachers and administrators. Unsolicited articles are welcome. Ten major articles are published per issue. Book reviews are included.

Manuscript Preparation:

Accepted manuscripts average from 10 to 12 double-spaced typewritten pages. One copy is required. Return postage and a self-addressed envelope are desired. Footnoting and other bibliographical procedure should follow the MLA Style Sheet. Use 1-1/2 inch margins and double-space throughout. A background or explanatory cover letter about the article is desired, but not an outline or summary. Biographical information about the author is desired and should include a summary of academic background, professional experience, and major publications. Illustrations, pictures, graphs, etc., may be used but must be suitable for reproduction. No payment is made for accepted articles. Reprints are available.

Manuscript Disposition:
Receipt of a manuscript is acknowledged. Editorial decisions are made within six weeks. Accepted articles usually appear in print from three to twelve months after acceptance. Unaccepted manuscripts are returned, often with criticism and/or suggestions.

Copyright:
Held by Lutheran Education.

Additional Information:
Materials accepted for publication must be in keeping with the policies and practices of education as conducted in schools of the Lutheran Church--Missouri Synod.

MIDSTREAM

Subscription Data:
Published by the Theodor Herzl Foundations, Inc., 515 Park Avenue, New York, New York 10022. Issued monthly. Advertising is accepted. Circulation: 10,000. Subscription: $7.00 per year; $13.00 for two years; $1.00 per issue. Founded: 1955.

Editorial Address:
The Editor, Midstream, 515 Park Avenue, New York, New York 10022.

Editorial Policy:
Includes articles pertaining to Jewish interest, fiction, book reviews, and poetry. The reading audience is varied. Unsolicited manuscripts are welcome. Three major articles are published per issue. Book reviews are included.

Manuscript Preparation:
Accepted manuscripts average 4,000 to 10,000 words. One copy is required. Return postage and a self-addressed envelope are required. A background or explanatory cover letter is helpful, but an outline, summary, or abstract is not required. Biographical information about the author is required. Illustrations, pictures, graphs, etc., are used infrequently. Payment is made for accepted manuscripts. Generally 30 tearsheet copies are available to the author.

Manuscript Disposition:
Receipt of a manuscript is not acknowledged. Editorial decisions are made within two to three weeks. Accepted articles usually appear in print within two to three months. Unaccepted manuscripts are returned, generally without criticism and/or suggestions.

Copyright:
Held by Theodor Herzl Foundations, Inc.

MOMENTUM (formerly National Catholic Educational Association Bulletin)

Subscription Data:
Published by the National Catholic Educational Association,

Suite 350, One Dupont Circle, Washington, D. C. 20036. Issued quarterly, in February, May, October, and December. Advertising is not accepted. Circulation: 16, 000. Subscription: $7. 00 per year. Founded: 1970.

Editorial Address:

The Editor, Momentum, National Catholic Educational Association, Suite 350, One Dupont Circle, Washington, D. C. 20036.

Editorial Policy:

Includes articles on innovative programs in Catholic schools, as well as articles on current topics of interest to Catholic educators. The reading audience includes Catholic educators and people interested in Catholic education. Unsolicited manuscripts are welcome. Seven or eight major articles are published per issue. Book reviews are included.

Manuscript Preparation:

Accepted manuscripts average 2, 000 to 2, 500 words. One copy is required. Return postage and a self-addressed envelope are required. Use standard margins and double-space. A background or explanatory cover letter is not required nor is an outline, summary, or abstract. Biographical information about the author is required. If possible, the author should submit five or six eight by ten inch glossy black and white photographs to illustrate the article. Payment of $. 02 per word is made for accepted manuscripts. Reprints are available.

Manuscript Disposition:

Receipt of a manuscript is acknowledged. Editorial decisions are made within two weeks. Accepted articles usually appear in print within two to three months. Unaccepted manuscripts are returned, usually without criticism and/or suggestions.

Copyright:

Held by the National Catholic Educational Association.

PEDAGOGIC REPORTER

Subscription Data:

Published by the American Association for Jewish Education, 114 Fifth Avenue, New York, New York 10011. Issued three times each year. Advertising is not accepted. Circulation: 2, 000. Subscription: $4. 50 per year. Founded: 1950.

Editorial Address:

The Editor, Pedagogic Reporter, American Association for Jewish Education, 114 Fifth Avenue, New York, New York 10011.

Editorial Policy:

Includes articles on Jewish education and round-up of programs and experimentations in the field. The reading audience includes principals, teachers, rabbis, and group workers. Publications received are listed with short description.

Copyright:

Held by the American Association for Jewish Education.

RELIGIOUS EDUCATION

Subscription Data:
Published by the Religious Education Association, 545 West
111th Street, New York, New York 10025. Issued bimonthly.
Advertising is accepted. Circulation: 5,000. Subscription:
$12.50 per year to Association members; $6.00 to students.
Founded: 1906.

Editorial Address:
The Editor, Religious Education, 409 Prospect Street, New
Haven, Connecticut 06510.

Editorial Policy:
Includes articles which relate to religious education. The reading audience includes professionals in religious education and
others interested in the field. Unsolicited articles are welcome.
Ten major articles are published per issue. Book reviews are
included.

Manuscript Preparation:
Accepted manuscripts average from 3,000 to 5,000 words. One
copy is required. Return postage and a self-addressed envelope
are desired. All long quotes should be indented and single-
spaced. Bibliographical procedure should follow the University
of Chicago Manual of Style. Use standard margins and double-
space. Footnotes should be placed at the bottom of each page.
A brief background or explanatory cover letter about the article
is desired, but not an outline or summary. Biographical information about the author is desired and should include title or
position and experience. Illustrations and pictures may not be
used; graphs may be used in research reporting if kept simple.
No payment is made for accepted articles. Reprints are available; minimum order is 100 copies.

Manuscript Disposition:
Receipt of a manuscript is acknowledged. Manuscripts are held
for possible publication, without formal decision, for several
months. Accepted articles usually appear in print within three
to twelve months after acceptance. Unaccepted manuscripts are
returned, rarely with criticism and/or suggestions.

Copyright:
Copyrighted. Arrangements for use of material should be made
with the author.

SOUTHERN BAPTIST EDUCATOR

Subscription Data:
Published by the Education Commission of the Southern Baptist
Convention in cooperation with the Association of Southern Baptist Colleges and Schools, 460 James Robertson Parkway, Nashville, Tennessee 37219. Issued bimonthly. Advertising is not
accepted. Circulation: 8,000. Subscription: $1.50 per year.
Founded: 1947.

Editorial Address:
    The Editor, *Southern Baptist Educator*, 460 James Robertson
Parkway, Nashville, Tennessee 37219.

Editorial Policy:
    Includes articles on all phases of higher education. The read-
ing audience includes faculty, administrators, trustees, and
others interested in higher education. Unsolicited articles are
welcome. Two or three major articles are published per issue.
Book reviews are occasionally included.

Manuscript Preparation:
    Accepted manuscripts average from 1,500 to 1,800 words. One
copy is required. Return postage and a self-addressed envelope
are desired. Bibliographical procedure should follow the University of Chicago *Manual of Style.* Type 55 characters per line
and double-space. A background or explanatory cover letter is
desired, but not an outline, summary, or abstract. Biographical
information about the author is desired. Illustrations, pictures,
graphs, etc., will be considered for publication when submitted
as part of a manuscript. No payment is made for accepted manuscripts. Reprints are available with up to 15 free copies for
authors.

Manuscript Disposition:
    Receipt of a manuscript is acknowledged. Editorial decisions
are made within six weeks. Accepted articles usually appear
in print within two to five months after acceptance. Unaccepted
manuscripts are returned, often with criticism.

Copyright:
    Not copyrighted.

SYNAGOGUE SCHOOL

Subscription Data:
    Published by the United Synagogue Commission on Jewish Educa-
tion, 218 East Seventieth Street, New York, New York 10021.
Issued quarterly. Advertising is accepted. Circulation: 2,200.
Subscription: $2.50 per year. Founded: 1946.

Editorial Address:
    The Editor, *Synagogue School*, United Synagogue Commission on
Jewish Education, 218 East Seventieth Street, New York, New
York 10021.

Editorial Policy:
    Includes theoretical and operational articles on all phases of
Jewish education. The reading audience includes educators and
informed laity. Unsolicited articles are welcome. Three major
articles are published per issue. Book reviews are included.

Manuscript Preparation:
    No limitations are placed upon manuscript length. One copy is
required. Return postage and a self-addressed envelope are desired. Bibliographical procedure may follow any accepted style
manual. Use wide margins and double-space. A background or
explanatory cover letter about the article is desired, but not an
outline or summary. Biographical information about the author

is desired including a summary of current position and professional training. Illustrations, pictures, graphs, etc., are not often used. No payment is made for accepted articles. Reprint costs vary with article length.

Manuscript Disposition:
Receipt of a manuscript is acknowledged. Editorial decisions are made within two weeks. Accepted articles usually appear in print within six weeks after acceptance. Unaccepted manuscripts are returned without comment.

Copyright:
Held by the United Synagogue Commission on Jewish Education.

TODAY'S CATHOLIC TEACHER

Subscription Data:
Published by Peter Li, Inc., 2451 East River Road, Suite 200, Dayton, Ohio 45439. Issued monthly, September through May, excluding December. Advertising is accepted. Circulation: 72,000. Subscription: $6.00 per year; $7.00 Canada. Founded: 1967.

Editorial Address:
The Editor, Today's Catholic Teacher, 2451 East River Road, Suite 200, Dayton, Ohio 45439.

Editorial Policy:
Includes articles on philosophy, innovations, methods, school practices and experiences, accounts of outstanding teachers, etc., particularly in Catholic schools of the country. The reading audience includes teachers, principals, administrators, religious educators, school boards, and others interested in Catholic education. Unsolicited manuscripts are welcome. Five or six major articles are published per issue. Book reviews are included.

Manuscript Preparation:
Accepted manuscripts average 1,000 to 1,200 words and 1,800 to 2,000 words. One copy is required. Return postage and a self-addressed envelope are required. Bibliographical procedure may vary. Use generous margins and double-space. A background or explanatory cover letter and an outline, summary, or abstract are not required. Brief current information about the author is required. Good black and white photographs are welcome. Payment is made on publication. Today's Catholic Teacher retains all reprint rights, but occasionally reprints articles. Permission for reprinting is required.

Manuscript Disposition:
Receipt of a manuscript is not usually acknowledged. Editorial decisions are made usually within four to six weeks. Accepted articles usually appear in print within three months. Unaccepted manuscripts are returned, if stamped self-addressed envelope is included. Criticism and/or suggestions are occasionally provided.

Copyright:
Held by Peter Li, Inc.

SAFETY

ASSE JOURNAL (formerly Journal of the American Society of Safety Engineers)

Subscription Data:
Published by the American Society of Safety Engineers, 850 Busse Highway, Park Ridge, Illinois 60068. Issued monthly. Advertising is accepted. Circulation: 10,000. Subscription: $10.00 per year; $1.00 per issue. Founded: 1956.

Editorial Address:
The Editor, ASSE Journal, 850 Busse Highway, Park Ridge, Illinois 60068.

Editorial Policy:
Includes articles on all phases of safety and safety engineering. The reading audience includes safety engineers, hygienists, fire protection engineers, supervising engineers, and others in industry, education, etc. Unsolicited articles are welcome. Two or three major articles are published per issue. Book reviews are included.

Manuscript Preparation:
Accepted manuscripts average from 1,500 to 5,000 words, or six to twenty double-spaced typewritten pages. At least two copies are required. Return postage and a self-addressed envelope are necessary. Bibliographical procedure may follow any widely used style guide. Use wide margins and double-space throughout. All articles should be well documented. Study of previous issues should be undertaken before finished writing is begun. A background or explanatory cover letter about the article is usually desired. An outline or summary is required in advance of or with submission of the finished manuscript. Biographical information about the author is desired and should include a summary of education, current position, and membership in professional organizations. Illustrations, pictures, graphs, etc., may be used, but must be of reproduction quality. Photographs must be prepared as glossy prints. No payment is made for accepted articles. Reprints are usually available.

Manuscript Disposition:
Receipt of a manuscript is acknowledged. Editorial decisions are made by an editorial board within six to eight weeks. Accepted articles usually appear in print within two to six months after acceptance. Unaccepted manuscripts are returned with suggestions when the article will be reconsidered.

Copyright:
Held by the American Society of Safety Engineers.

Additional Information:
The Journal is published to keep the professional Safety Spe-

cialist informed on developments in the research and technology
of accident prevention. It is also the official publication of the
American Society of Safety Engineers, its chapters, and members.

†SAFETY JOURNAL

Subscription Data:
   Published by Safety Journal, Inc., Box 4189, Station B, Ander-
   son, South Carolina 29621. Issued bimonthly. Advertising is
   accepted. Circulation: 21,000. Subscription: $3.00 per year.
   Founded: 1950.
Editorial Address:
   The Editor, Safety Journal, Box 4189, Station B, Anderson,
   South Carolina 29621.
Editorial Policy:
   Includes technical reports and articles on all phases of safety
   and safety education, with emphasis on general safety, first aid,
   school safety, fire prevention, and industrial hygiene. The reading audience includes safety educators and others interested in
   safety education. Unsolicited articles are welcome. Five major
   articles are published per issue. Book reviews are included.
Manuscript Preparation:
   Accepted manuscripts average three double-spaced typewritten
   pages. One copy is required. Return postage and a self-addressed envelope are desired. Use no footnotes. Use one inch
   margins and double-space throughout. A background or explanatory cover letter about the article is desired, but not an outline
   or summary. Biographical information about the author is required. Illustrations, pictures, graphs, etc., are occasionally
   used. No payment is made for accepted articles. Reprints are
   available.
Manuscript Disposition:
   Receipt of a manuscript is acknowledged. Editorial decisions
   are made within two months. Accepted reports and articles are
   made within two months. Accepted reports and articles usually
   appear in print within three months after acceptance. Unaccepted
   manuscripts are returned without suggestions or criticism.
Copyright:
   Not copyrighted.

AMERICAN SCIENTIST

Subscription Data:
    Published by the Society of the Sigma Xi, 345 Whitney Avenue,
New Haven, Connecticut 06511. Issued monthly. Advertising
is accepted. Circulation: 130, 000. Subscription: $12. 00 per
year. Founded: 1913.

Editorial Address:
    The Editor, American Scientist, 345 Whitney Avenue, New Haven,
Connecticut 06511.

Editorial Policy:
    Includes articles in all areas of science and engineering describ-
ing the results of research. The reading audience includes scientists in many different fields. Unsolicited manuscripts are
welcome. Eight to ten articles are published per issue. Book
reviews are included with approximately 80 per issue.

Manuscript Preparation:
    Accepted manuscripts average 15 to 25 double-spaced typewritten
pages. Two copies are required. Return postage and a self-
addressed envelope are required. References should follow the
accepted form in each discipline. List footnotes on a separate
page. Double-space and use ample margins. A background or
explanatory cover letter is not required, but useful. An outline,
summary, or abstract of the article is not required. Biographical information about the author is required. Illustrations of
all kinds will be considered. No payment is made for accepted
manuscripts. One-hundred free reprints are available; an additional 100 are available at cost.

Manuscript Disposition:
    Receipt of a manuscript is acknowledged. Editorial decisions
are made within four to eight weeks. Accepted articles usually
appear in print within one to two issues after acceptance. Unaccepted manuscripts are returned on request. Articles are
sometimes criticized, when appropriate.

Copyright:
    Held usually by the American Scientist.

†ASTRONOMICAL JOURNAL

Subscription Data:
    Published by the American Institute of Physics, 335 East Forty-
fifth Street, New York, New York 10017. Sponsored by the
American Astronomical Society. Issued monthly, except January and July. Advertising is not accepted. Circulation: 2, 200.
Subscription: $40. 00 per year. Founded: 1849.

Editorial Address:
 The Editor, Astronomical Journal, Yale University Observatory,
 Box 2023, Yale Station, New Haven, Connecticut 06520.
Editorial Policy:
 Includes reports of original observation and research in astrono-
 my. The reading audience includes astronomers and students.
 Unsolicited articles are welcome. Twelve major articles are
 published per issue. Book reviews are not included.
Manuscript Preparation:
 No limitations are placed upon manuscript length. Two copies
 are required. Return postage and a self-addressed envelope
 are unnecessary. Bibliographical procedure should follow the
 American Institute of Physics Style Manual. Avoid use of footnotes where possible. Use one inch margins and double-space.
 A background or explanatory cover letter about the article is
 not desired nor is an outline or summary. Biographical information about the author is unnecessary. Illustrations, pictures,
 graphs, etc., may be used. No payment is made for accepted
 articles. Reprints are available; costs vary with article length
 and order volume.
Manuscript Disposition:
 Receipt of a manuscript is acknowledged. Editorial decisions
 are made within one month. Accepted articles usually appear
 in print within five months after acceptance. Unaccepted manuscripts are returned, often with criticism and/or suggestions.
Copyright:
 Not copyrighted.

FRONTIERS

Subscription Data:
 Published by the Academy of Natural Sciences, Nineteenth and
 the Parkway, Philadelphia, Pennsylvania 19103. Issued four
 times each year, in September, December, March, and June.
 Advertising is accepted. Circulation: 4,600. Subscription:
 $4.00 per year. Founded: 1936.
Editorial Address:
 The Editor, Frontiers, Academy of Natural Sciences, Nineteenth
 and the Parkway, Philadelphia, Pennsylvania 19103.
Editorial Policy:
 Includes articles and reports on natural history. The reading
 audience includes students of natural history, including both
 teen-agers and adults. Unsolicited articles are welcome. Twenty-five to thirty major articles are published per issue. Book
 reviews are included.
Manuscript Preparation:
 Accepted manuscripts average from five to ten double-spaced
 typewritten pages. One copy is required. Return postage and
 a self-addressed envelope are desired. Bibliographical procedure may follow any widely used style manual. Use one inch
 margins and double-space throughout. A background or explanatory cover letter about the article is not desired nor is
 an outline or summary. Biographical information about the

author is desired and should include an indication of educational background and interest in natural history, and a list of published works. Photographs are usually required with accepted articles. Payment of from $25.00 to $90.00 is made upon acceptance of a manuscript. Reprints are sometimes available.

Manuscript Disposition:
  Editorial decisions are made as soon as possible. Accepted articles usually appear in print from four to eight months after acceptance. Unaccepted manuscripts are returned without criticism and/or suggestions.

Copyright:
  Held by the Academy of Natural Sciences.

JOURNAL OF COLLEGE SCIENCE TEACHING

Subscription Data:
  Published by the National Science Teachers Association, 1201 Sixteenth Street, N.W., Washington, D.C. 20036. Issued five times each year, September through May in alternate months. Advertising is accepted. Circulation: 3,200. Subscription: $12.00 per year included with Association membership. Founded: 1971.

Editorial Address:
  The Editor, Journal of College Science Teaching, 1201 Sixteenth Street, N.W., Washington, D.C. 20036.

Editorial Policy:
  Includes articles relating to science or education which would be of interest to college science teachers of introductory courses. The reading audience includes junior college, college, and university professors in all sciences. Unsolicited manuscripts are welcome. Approximately eight major articles are published per issue. Book reviews are reviewed by a special editor.

Manuscript Preparation:
  Accepted manuscripts should not exceed 4,000 words. Three copies are required. Return postage and a self-addressed envelope are required. Bibliographical procedure should follow a guide which is available through the office of the editor. A background or explanatory cover letter is not required nor is an outline, summary, or abstract. Biographical information about the author is required. Illustrations, pictures, graphs, etc., are welcome. No payment is made for accepted manuscripts. Reprints are available to authors at low cost.

Manuscript Disposition:
  Receipt of a manuscript is acknowledged. Editorial decisions are made within eight weeks. Accepted articles usually appear in print within seven months. Unaccepted manuscripts are returned, sometimes with criticism and/or suggestions.

Copyright:
  Held by the National Science Teachers Association.

JOURNAL OF GEOLOGICAL EDUCATION

Subscription Data:
    Published by the National Association of Geology Teachers, Inc.,
    2201 M Street, N. W. , Washington, D. C. 20037.   Issued five
    times each year, in January, March, May, September, and No-
    vember.   Advertising is not accepted.   Circulation: 3, 700.
    Subscription: $10. 00 per year.   Founded: 1951.
Editorial Address:
    The Editor, Journal of Geological Education, Geology Depart-
    ment, Colorado State University, Fort Collins, Colorado 80521.
Editorial Policy:
    Includes articles which deal with geology and earth science ma-
    terial and teaching information.   The reading audience includes
    geology and earth science teachers at all levels.   Unsolicited
    articles are welcome.   Several major and minor articles are
    published per issue.   Book reviews and film reviews are in-
    cluded.
Manuscript Preparation:
    Accepted manuscripts average from 3, 000 to 4, 000 words for
    major articles.   The original and one carbon are required.   Re-
    turn postage and a self-addressed envelope are unnecessary.
    See a recent issue for format style and bibliographical proce-
    dure.   Use wide margins and double-space throughout, including
    quotations and reference citations.   A background or explanatory
    cover letter about the article is desired.   Abstracts are re-
    quired with major articles but are unnecessary with brief re-
    ports.   Biographical information about the author is unnecessary.
    Illustrations, pictures, graphs, etc. , may be used.   Drafted
    illustrations should be prepared in waterproof black ink on white
    paper or tracing cloth.   Lettering must be done with the aid of
    lettering guides.   All photographs must be sharp glossy prints.
    No payment is made for accepted articles.   Reprints are avail-
    able; a cost summary is available from the office of the editor.
Manuscript Disposition:
    Receipt of a manuscript is acknowledged.   Editorial decisions
    are made with the aid of two referees as soon as possible.   Ac-
    cepted articles usually appear in print from four to six months
    after acceptance.   Unaccepted manuscripts are returned, often
    with criticism and/or suggestions.
Copyright:
    Held by the National Association of Geology Teachers, Inc.
Additional Information:
    Upon acceptance of a manuscript the author is requested to fur-
    nish a small photograph that is to be published with the article.

JOURNAL OF RESEARCH IN SCIENCE TEACHING

Subscription Data:
    Published by John Wiley and Sons, 605 Third Avenue, New York,

New York 10016. Sponsored by the National Association for Research in Science Teaching. Issued quarterly, in April, June, September, and November. Advertising is not accepted. Circulation: 2,000. Subscription: $10.00 per year. Founded: 1962.

Editorial Address:

Prof. O. Roger Anderson, Editor, Journal of Research in Science Teaching, Teachers College Columbia University, 525 W. 120 Street, New York, New York 10027.

Editorial Policy:

Includes articles and reports which relate to theory and research in science education. The reading audience includes science educators and educational researchers. Unsolicited articles are welcome. Ten major articles are published per issue. Book reviews are included.

Manuscript Preparation:

Accepted manuscripts average from six to ten double-spaced typewritten pages. The original and one copy are required. Return postage and a self-addressed envelope are desired. Footnoting and other bibliographical procedure may follow any widely used style manual and "Information for Contributors," available from the office of the editor. Use one inch margins and double-space throughout. Number references consecutively at the end of the article. A background or explanatory cover letter about the article is desired. An outline or summary of 100 to 150 words is required. Biographical information about the author is unnecessary. Illustrations, graphs, etc., may be used; all figures must be submitted in form suitable for reproduction. Clear positive photographs are required for half-tone reproduction. Line drawings, graphs, etc., must be prepared in India ink on heavy white paper, bristol board, drawing linen, or coordinate paper with light blue background. Drawings should be prepared so that upon reduction final size will not exceed three by five inches. Where possible, submit drawings twice the size of final engravings. Legends are required for all figures and must be compiled on a separate page. No payment is made for accepted articles. Reprints are available; twenty-five free copies are mailed to the author.

Manuscript Disposition:

Receipt of a manuscript is acknowledged. Editorial decisions are made within three months. Accepted articles usually appear in print from nine to twelve months after acceptance. Unaccepted manuscripts are returned only if requested by the author at the time they are submitted, often with criticism and/or suggestions.

Copyright:

Held by the National Association for Research in Science Teaching.

†*LAB WORLD

Subscription Data:

Published by the Sidale Publishing Company, 2525 West Eighth

Street, Los Angeles, California 90057. Issued monthly. Advertising is accepted. Circulation: 15,000. Subscription: $5.00 per year. Founded: 1949.

Editorial Address:

The Editor, Lab World, Sidale Publishing Company, 2525 West Eighth Street, Los Angeles, California 90057.

Editorial Policy:

Includes articles on all phases of the clinical-scientific laboratory field. The reading audience includes clinicians, technicians, educators, and advanced students from clinical, pathological, medical, research, hospital, private, and other health related organizations and institutions in the clinical laboratory field. An outline must be submitted to the editor prior to formal submission of a manuscript. On the basis of this outline the editor will either solicit the article for examination by an editorial board or the outline will be rejected. Ten to fifteen major articles are published per issue. Book reviews are included.

Manuscript Preparation:

Accepted manuscripts average from 750 to 1,000 words. One copy is required. Return postage and a self-addressed envelope are desired. Footnotes, lists of references, etc., should not be used. Use wide margins and double-space. A background or explanatory cover letter about the article is required. Biographical information about the author is desired and should include information regarding educational background, current position, and title(s). Glossy photographs, illustrations, and graphs may be used. Payment for accepted articles is individually determined. Reprints are sometimes available.

Manuscript Disposition:

Receipt of a manuscript is acknowledged. Editiorial decisions are made as soon as possible. Accepted articles usually appear in print from one to six months after acceptance. Unaccepted manuscripts are returned, sometimes with criticism and/or suggestions.

Copyright:

Held by the Sidale Publishing Company.

Additional Information:

Articles must be both timely and directly pertinent to the clinical laboratory field.

NATURAL HISTORY

Subscription Data:

Published by the American Museum of Natural History, Central Park West at Seventy-ninth Street, New York, New York 10024. Issued 10 times each year, bimonthly in June-September. Advertising is accepted. Circulation: 325,000. Subscription: $8.00 per year. Founded: 1900.

Editorial Address:

The Editor, Natural History, Central Park West at Seventy-ninth Street, New York, New York 10024.

Editorial Policy:

Includes articles on biological sciences, ecology, anthropology,

earth science, and astronomy. The reading audience includes
scientists, teachers, students, and an intelligent lay audience
interested in natural history. Unsolicited manuscripts are welcome. Six to eight major articles are published per issue.
Book reviews are included.

Manuscript Preparation:
Accepted manuscripts average 2, 000 to 3, 500 words. One copy
is required. Return postage and a self-addressed envelope are
desired, but not required. Footnotes are not used. Bibliography is requested if manuscript is accepted for publication.
Double-space manuscripts and use one inch margins. A background or explanatory cover letter is required and an outline,
summary, or abstract of the article may be submitted. Biographical information about the author is required. Illustrations,
color transparencies, and photographs may be used if supplied
by the author. Payment is made for accepted manuscripts. Reprints are not available, but copies of the magazine may be purchased at half price.

Manuscript Disposition:
Receipt of a manuscript is acknowledged. Editorial decisions
are made within two to six weeks. Time from acceptance of
a manuscript to its appearance in print varies with editorial
need. Unaccepted manuscripts are returned without criticism
or suggestions.

Copyright:
Held by the American Museum of Natural History.

SCIENCE

Subscription Data:
Published by the American Association for the Advancement of
Science, 1515 Massachusetts Avenue, N. W. , Washington, D. C.
20005. Published weekly. Advertising is accepted. Circulation: 153, 606. Subscription: $30. 00 per year; $18. 00 to members. Founded: 1880.

Editorial Address:
The Editor, Science, American Association for the Advancement
of Science, 1515 Massachusetts Avenue, N. W. , Washington,
D. C. 20005.

Editorial Policy:
Includes articles and reports on the scientific disciplines. The
reading audience includes specialists practicing in all areas of
scientific study, science educators, and advanced students. Unsolicited articles are welcome. Twenty-five to thirty articles
are published per issue. Five types of signed papers are published: articles, reports, letters, technical comments, and
book reviews.

Manuscript Preparation:
Accepted manuscripts range from 2, 000 to 5, 000 words. Short
reports may vary in length from one to seven double-spaced
manuscript pages of text, including the bibliography. Three
copies are required. Return postage and a self-addressed

envelope are unnecessary. Footnotes should be listed at the end
of the article. Bibliographical procedure should follow recent
biological journals and the form entitled "Instructions for Contributors" by the editors of Science. Use one inch margins and
double-space throughout. A background or explanatory cover
letter is not desired nor is an outline or summary. Biographical information about the author is unnecessary. Illustrations,
pictures, graphs, etc., may be used. Submit three copies of
each diagram, graph, map, or photograph. Cite all illustrations
in the text and provide a brief legend, to be set in type, for
each. Photographs should have a glossy finish with sharp contrast between black and white areas. Do not submit more than
one illustration (table or figure) for each 800 words unless author
has planned carefully for grouping them. Type each table on a
separate sheet, number it with an Arabic numeral, give it a
title, and cite it in the text. No payment is made for accepted
articles. One-hundred reprints are supplied gratis for each article published. An order blank for additional reprints accompanies proofs.

Manuscript Disposition:
Receipt of a manuscript is acknowledged. Authors will usually
be notified of acceptance, rejection, or need for revision in four
to six weeks for reports and within six to ten weeks for articles.
Accepted reports usually appear in print within two and one-half
to three months, and accepted articles appear in print within six
months. Unaccepted manuscripts are returned without criticism
or suggestions.

Copyright:
Held by the American Association for the Advancement of Science.

SCIENCE AND CHILDREN

Subscription Data:
Published by the National Science Teachers Association, 1201
Sixteenth Street, N. W., Washington, D. C. 20036. Issued eight
times a year, except June, July, and August; January/February
issue is combined. Advertising is accepted. Circulation:
28, 000. Subscription: $8. 00 per year; Free to membership in
the elementary section of the National Science Teachers Association; $1. 00 per issue. Founded: 1963.

Editorial Address:
The Editor, Science and Children, National Science Teachers Association, 1201 Sixteenth Street, N. W., Washington, D. C. 20036.

Editorial Policy:
Includes articles designed to stimulate and improve science instruction. The reading audience includes elementary school
teachers, principals, and supervisors. Unsolicited articles are
welcome. Six to ten major articles are published per issue.
Book reviews are included.

Manuscript Preparation:
Accepted manuscripts average from 800 to 1, 500 words. Two

copies are required. Return postage and a self-addressed envelope are not required. Use 1-1/2 inch right, top, and bottom margins and a 1/2 inch left margin. Double-space all text material. See a recent issue for bibliographical procedure. Place single footnotes at the bottom of the page to which they refer. If more than two publications are cited use a reference list. A background explanatory cover letter is not required nor is an outline or summary. Biographical information about the author is unnecessary. Illustrations, pictures, and graphs may be used. No payment is made for accepted articles. Reprints are available; a cost summary may be obtained from the office of the editor.

Manuscript Disposition:
    Receipt of a manuscript is acknowledged. Editorial decisions are made as soon as possible. Time from receipt of a solicited manuscript to its appearance in print averages six weeks; others are used as appropriate. Unaccepted articles are returned, sometimes with criticism and/or suggestions.

Copyright:
    Held by the National Science Teachers Association.

Additional Information:
    NSTA is an associated organization of the National Education Association and an affiliate of the American Association for the Advancement of Science. All articles published represent the personal expressions of the author and do not necessarily represent the policies of the Association.

SCIENCE EDUCATION

Subscription Data:
    Published by Wiley-Interscience, a division of John Wiley and Sons, Inc., 605 Third Avenue, New York, New York 10016. Issued quarterly, in January-March, April-June, July-September, and October-December. Advertising is not accepted. Subscription: $12.00 per volume. Founded: 1916.

Editorial Address:
    Professor Emeritus N. Eldred Bingham, Editor, Science Education, 1718 N.W. Tenth Avenue, Gainesville, Florida 32601.

Editorial Policy:
    The journal is directed toward science education from the kindergarten through junior college levels and to the preparation of teachers to teach science serving general education at these levels. Graduate students in curriculum, in instruction, in educational psychology, in child development, in science education, and in educational research, will profit from the research articles. Includes innovations in curricula, in methods, in materials, in teacher education and in evaluative procedures; also includes articles dealing with international education. The reading audience includes teacher educators, graduate students, supervisors, and teachers. Unsolicited manuscripts are welcome. Eighteen to twenty major articles are published per issue. Book reviews are included.

Manuscript Preparation:
    Accepted manuscripts vary in length, but are usually from 1,500
to 3,000 words. Manuscripts should be submitted in duplicate.
Return postage and a self-addressed envelope are not required.
Bibliographical procedure should follow the MLA Style Sheet.
Footnotes are printed at the bottom of the page where the reference is made. Use wide margins and double-space throughout.
A background or explanatory cover letter is not required nor is
an outline, summary, or abstract. Biographical information
about the author is not required. Print graphs, tables, and
figures are acceptable, but not photographs. No payment is made
for accepted manuscripts. Reprints are available to the authors
if ordered at the time proof is read; 25 free reprints are provided for each author.

Manuscript Disposition:
    Receipt of a manuscript is acknowledged. Editorial decisions
are refereed and usually made within six to ten weeks. Accepted
articles usually appear in print within six to nine months after
acceptance. Unaccepted manuscripts are returned with criticism
and/or suggestions.

Copyright:
    Held by John Wiley and Sons, Inc.

Additional Information:
    Science Education is the official journal for the Association for
the Education of Teachers in Science. It serves as a forum for
science educators with major emphasis on research.

*SCIENCE NEWS

Subscription Data:
    Published by Science Service, Inc., 1719 North Street, N.W.,
Washington, D.C. 20036. Issued weekly. Advertising is ac-
cepted. Circulation: 97,297. Subscription: $10.00 per year.
Founded: 1922.

Editorial Address:
    The Editor, Science News, Science Service, Inc., 1719 North
Street, N.W., Washington, D.C. 20036.

Editorial Policy:
    Includes articles on all aspects of current science. The reading
audience includes scientists and engineers, teachers, students,
and others interested in current science. Unsolicited articles
are not welcome. Two to three major articles are published
per issue. Book listings are included.

Manuscript Preparation:
    Accepted manuscripts average from one to two journal pages.
Two copies are required. Return postage and a self-addressed
envelope are desired. Use wide margins and double-space.
Avoid use of footnotes. A background or explanatory cover letter about the article is desired, but not an outline or summary.
Biographical information about the author is desired. Illustrations, pictures, graphs, etc., are sometimes used. Payment is
rarely made for accepted articles. Reprints are seldom available.

Manuscript Disposition:
    Receipt of a manuscript is acknowledged. Editorial decisions
    are made as soon as possible. Accepted articles usually appear
    in print within six months. Unaccepted manuscripts are re-
    turned, sometimes with criticism and/or suggestions.
Copyright:
    Held by Science Service, Inc.

SCIENCE TEACHER

Subscription Data:
    Published by the National Science Teachers Association, 1201
    Sixteenth Street, N. W., Washington, D. C. 20036. Issued month-
    ly, September through May. Advertising is accepted. Circula-
    tion: 23,000. Subscription: $15.00 per year; $1.70 per issue.
    Founded: 1950.
Editorial Address:
    The Editor, Science Teacher, 1201 Sixteenth Street, N. W.,
    Washington, D. C. 20036.
Editorial Policy:
    Includes articles which relate to the teaching of science, admin-
    istration and supervision of science programs, and science teach-
    er education. The reading audience includes school and college
    science teachers and administrators. Unsolicited articles are
    welcome. Eight to twelve major articles are published per is-
    sue. Book reviews are included.
Manuscript Preparation:
    Accepted articles average from 2,000 to 2,500 words. Two
    copies are required. Return postage and a self-addressed envel-
    ope are desired. Footnoting and other bibliographical procedure
    should follow Words Into Type or the University of Chicago Man-
    ual of Style. Identify each page with the author's name and num-
    ber each page at the top using Arabic numerals. All material
    must be typewritten using double-spacing and a seventy-five space
    line on bond paper. A background or explanatory cover letter is
    required, including a statement that the manuscript is not being
    considered elsewhere. An outline or summary of the article is
    desired. Biographical information about the author is desired
    on a separate page and should include a summary of present
    position. Illustrations, pictures, and graphs prepared in India
    ink may be used and will be returned. All tabular material
    must be prepared on separate pages; always indicate its place-
    ment in the text. Photographs should be 8-1/2 by 11 inch black
    and white glossy prints. Reprints are available; a cost summary
    may be obtained through the office of the editor. Costs vary
    with article length, use of color, and order volume. Orders of
    less than 100 reprints are not accepted. Three free copies of
    the journal are sent to each author.
Manuscript Disposition:
    Receipt of a manuscript is acknowledged. Editorial decisions
    are made within two months. Accepted articles usually appear
    in print within four to eight months after acceptance. Unaccepted
    articles are returned, often with criticism and/or suggestions.

Copyright:
Held by the National Science Teachers Association.

SCIENTIFIC AMERICAN

Subscription Data:
Published by Scientific American, Inc., 415 Madison Avenue,
New York, New York 10017. Issued monthly. Advertising is
accepted. Circulation: 500,700. Subscription: $10.00 per
year. Founded: 1845.

Editorial Address:
Dennis Flanagan, Editor, Scientific American, 415 Madison
Avenue, New York, New York 10017.

Editorial Policy:
Includes articles about current advances in science, technology,
and medicine. The articles are addressed to the educated layman, including scientists, engineers, and physicians who are
interested in advances in disciplines outside their own. Reprints
of certain articles are used for teaching purposes in colleges and
universities. Eight feature articles are published in each issue,
with the exception of an annual single-topic issue in September,
which may contain a larger number of articles. Book reviews
are normally written by the book editor.

Manuscript Preparation:
Published articles average about 4,000 words in length. Each
article is accompanied by about 10 illustrations. Payment is
made for all accepted articles.

Manuscript Disposition:
Receipt of a manuscript is acknowledged. Editorial decisions
are made as soon as possible. Accepted manuscripts are used
as needed. Unaccepted manuscripts are returned, sometimes
with criticism and/or suggestions.

Copyright:
Held by Scientific American, Inc.

SKY AND TELESCOPE

Subscription Data:
Published by the Sky Publishing Corporation, Harvard Observa-
tory, 49 Bay State Road, Cambridge, Massachusetts 02138.
Issued monthly. Advertising is accepted. Circulation: 57,000.
Subscription: $8.00 per year in the United States and its poses-
sions. Founded: 1941.

Editorial Address:
The Editor, Sky and Telescope, 49 Bay State Road, Cambridge,
Massachusetts 02138.

Editorial Policy:
Includes articles and reports on astronomy and space science.
The reading audience includes amateur and professional astronomers, teachers, students, and interested laymen. Unsolicited
articles are welcome. Five or six major articles are published
per issue. Book reviews are included.

Manuscript Preparation:

No policy regarding manuscript length has been established.
The original and one carbon are required. Return postage and
a self-addressed envelope are desired. Bibliographical procedure may follow any widely used style manual. Use one inch
margins and double-space. Number footnotes consecutively at
the end of the article. A background or explanatory cover letter about the article is required. An outline or summary is
desired in advance of or with submission of the finished manuscript. Biographical information about the author is unnecessary. Pictures, graphs, etc., may be used. Pictures must
be prepared as five by seven or eight by ten inch glossy prints.
Line-drawings may be submitted from which the editorial staff
will prepare final illustrations. Payment for accepted articles
is made by special arrangement through the office of the editor.
Reprints are available; costs vary with article length and order
volume.

Manuscript Disposition:

Receipt of a manuscript is acknowledged. Editorial decisions
are made within two weeks. Accepted articles usually appear
in print from three to four months after acceptance. Unaccepted
manuscripts are returned, rarely with detailed criticism and/or
suggestions.

Copyright:

Held by the Sky Publishing Corporation. Permission for reprinting or reproduction is made upon request.

*SKYLIGHTS

Subscription Data:

Published by the National Aerospace Education Association, 806
Fifteenth Street, N. W., Washington, D. C. 20005. Issued nine
times each year, September through May. Advertising is not
accepted. Circulation: 15,000. Subscription: $2.00 per year;
Free to members. Founded: 1954.

Editorial Address:

The Editor, Skylights, National Aerospace Education Association, 806 Fifteenth Street, N. W., Washington, D. C. 20005.

Editorial Policy:

Includes nontechnical articles on aviation, space exploration, and
aerospace education. The reading audience includes teachers at
all grade levels and students, grade seven through college. Unsolicited articles cannot be used. One or two major articles are
published per issue. Book announcements, but not reviews, are
included.

Copyright:

Held by the National Aerospace Education Association.

SECONDARY EDUCATION

BEHAVIORAL AND SOCIAL SCIENCE TEACHER

Subscription Data:
   Published by Behavioral Publications, 72 Fifth Avenue, New
   York, New York 10011. Issued biannually, in spring and fall.
   Advertising is accepted. Circulation: 2,000. Subscription:
   $5.00 per year; $10.00 to institutions. Founded: 1973.
Editorial Address:
   Professor Harwood Fisher, Editor, Behavioral and Social Science Teacher, City College, School of Education, Klapper Hall
   303, 135th Street and Convent Avenue, New York, New York
   10031.
Editorial Policy:
   Includes articles that emphasize curriculum issues and new developments in the teaching of psychology, sociology, and anthropology at the high school level. The first several issues feature
   contemporary problems in American society as they affect high
   school age youth. These issues, usually associated with college
   youth but now reaching downward, include alienation, drugs, ag-
   gression, rebellion, and the question of what constitutes meaning-
   ful learning. The reading audience includes psychologists, psychotherapists, and psychiatrists. Unsolicited manuscripts are
   welcome. Twelve major articles are published per issue. Book
   reviews are included.
Manuscript Preparation:
   Accepted manuscripts should not exceed 20 double-spaced pages.
   Three copies and return postage are required. Bibliographical
   procedure should follow the APA Publication Manual. Avoid the
   use of footnotes. Use one inch margins on the top, sides, and
   bottom and double-space. A background or cover letter is optional, but an outline, summary, or abstract of the article is required. Biographical information about the author is required.
   Illustrations, pictures, and graphs are to be placed on separate
   pages at the end of manuscript marked with Arabic numerals.
   The body of the manuscript should contain the location of illustrative material. No payment is made for accepted manuscripts.
   No free reprints are available; cost varies with length of article.
Manuscript Disposition:
   Receipt of a manuscript is acknowledged. Editorial decisions
   are made within six months to one year. Accepted articles us-
   ually appear in print within six months to one year. Criticism
   and/or suggestions are provided if postage is provided.
Copyright:
   Held by Behavioral Publications.

473

HIGH SCHOOL JOURNAL

Subscription Data:
Published by the University of North Carolina Press, Chapel
Hill, North Carolina 27514. Issued eight times each year, October through May. Advertising is not accepted. Circulation:
3,000. Subscription: $5.00 per year. Founded: 1917.

Editorial Address:
The Editor, High School Journal, School of Education, University of North Carolina, Chapel Hill, North Carolina 27514.

Editorial Policy:
Includes articles which relate to theory and practice in secondary education. The reading audience includes college, university, high school, and foreign educators. Unsolicited articles
are welcome. Four to six major articles are published per
issue. Book reviews are included.

Manuscript Preparation:
Accepted manuscripts average 3,000 words. The original and
one copy are required. Return postage and a self-addressed
envelope are desired. Bibliographical procedure may follow any
widely used style manual. Footnotes should be placed at the
bottom of each page. A background or explanatory cover letter
about the article is not desired nor is an outline or summary.
Biographical information about the author is desired; data collection cards are mailed to each author. Pictures cannot be
used and graphs are seldom used. No payment is made for accepted articles. Reprints are available; a reprint cost summary
may be obtained through the office of the editor.

Manuscript Disposition:
Receipt of a manuscript is acknowledged. Editorial decisions
are made within 60 days. Accepted articles usually appear in
print from 12 to 18 months after acceptance. Unaccepted manuscripts are returned.

Copyright:
Held by the University of North Carolina Press.

STUDENT ADVOCATE (formerly Student Life Highlights)

Subscription Data:
Published by the National Association of Secondary School Principals, 1904 Association Drive, Reston, Virginia 22091. Issued
monthly, September through May. Advertising is accepted. Circulation: 15,000. Subscription: $3.00 per year. Founded:
1974.

Editorial Address:
The Editor, Student Advocate, National Association of Secondary
School Principals, 1904 Association Drive, Reston, Virginia
22091.

Editorial Policy:
Includes articles on the high school student's general interest,
with focus on student government, student councils, leadership
issues, and student activities in secondary schools. The reading

audience includes high school students (some junior high), high school student activity advisors, and school principals. Unsolicited manuscripts are very welcome. Three to five major articles are published per issue. Book reviews are included.

Manuscript Preparation:

Accepted manuscripts average 1,500 to 2,000 words. One copy is required. Return postage and a self-addressed envelope are not required. Bibliographical procedure should follow any generally accepted style manual. Double-space and use one inch margins. A background or explanatory cover letter is required, but not an outline, summary, or abstract. Biographical information about the author should include present position and brief background information. Black and white photographs and drawings are acceptable and cartoons are welcome. No payment is made for accepted manuscripts. Reprints are not generally available.

Manuscript Disposition:

Receipt of a manuscript is acknowledged. Editorial decisions are made within four weeks. Accepted articles usually appear in print within three to four months. Unaccepted manuscripts are returned with criticism and/or suggestions.

Copyright:

Held by the National Association of Secondary School Principals.

Additional Information:

Student Advocate replaces the newsletter Student Life Highlights, founded 1962.

SOCIAL SCIENCES

AMERICAN QUARTERLY

Subscription Data:
 Published by the University of Pennsylvania, American Studies
 Association, Philadelphia, Pennsylvania 19174. Issued five
 times each year, in March, May, August, October, and December. Advertising is accepted. Circulation: 3,500. Subscription: $15.00 per year; $10.00 to libraries; $7.50 to students;
 $3.00 per issue. Founded: 1949.
Editorial Address:
 The Editor, American Quarterly, Box 1, Logan Hall, University of Pennsylvania, Philadelphia, Pennsylvania 19174.
Editorial Policy:
 Includes articles which provide a sense of direction to studies
 of the culture of the United States, both past and present. Contributors should concern themselves not only with areas of American life which they know best, but also with the relation of those
 areas to the entire American scene and to world society. Most
 articles accepted for publication are interdisciplinary in nature.
 The reading audience includes scholarly readers from all disciplines. Unsolicited articles are welcome. Eight to ten major articles are published per issue. Book reviews are included.
Manuscript Preparation:
 Accepted manuscripts may not exceed 25 double-spaced typewritten pages. Two copies are required; do not use onionskin for
 the second copy. Return postage and a self-addressed envelope
 are desired. Bibliographical procedure should follow the MLA
 Style Sheet. Allow sufficient margin for comment and double-
 space throughout. A background or explanatory cover letter
 about the article is not desired nor is an outline or summary.
 Biographical information about the author is unnecessary. Illustrations, pictures, and graphs may be used. No payment is
 made for accepted articles. Twenty-five reprints and one issue
 are mailed to the author free of charge.
Manuscript Disposition:
 Receipt of a manuscript is acknowledged. Editorial decisions
 are made within five months. Accepted articles usually appear
 in print from two to three months after acceptance. Unaccepted
 manuscripts are returned, often with criticism and/or suggestions.
Copyright:
 Held by the University of Pennsylvania.

AMERICAN SCHOLAR

Subscription Data:
 Published by Phi Beta Kappa, 1811 Q Street, N. W., Washington, D. C. 20009. Issued quarterly, in March, June, October, and December. Advertising is accepted. Circulation: 47,000. Subscription: $6.50 per year. Founded: 1932.

Editorial Address:
 The Editor, The American Scholar, 1811 Q Street, N. W., Washington, D. C. 20009.

Editorial Policy:
 Includes articles on a variety of subjects of general interest, plus nontechnical articles and essays on current national affairs, the cultural scene, politics, the arts, religion, science, and poetry. The reading audience includes all who are interested in the current cultural scene. Unsolicited articles are welcome. Eight major articles are published per issue. Book reviews are included.

Manuscript Preparation:
 Articles of approximately 4,000 words are preferred. One copy is required. Return postage and a self-addressed envelope are required. No specific format demands are made other than legibility and double-spacing. Try not to use lists of reference materials as these should be worked into the text. Footnotes are rarely used; prefer that documentation be worked into the text. An outline is desired in advance of the finished article, in addition to a cover letter of general information about its content. Biographical information, including the author's address and a list of recent publications, is required. Illustrations, pictures, and graphs are rarely used. Payment of $150.00 is made upon acceptance. Reprints are available; costs vary with article length and number of copies ordered. Three free copies of the issue are mailed to the author.

Manuscript Disposition:
 Receipt of a manuscript is acknowledged. Editorial decisions are made within two to five weeks. Each accepted article must be approved by two members of the editorial board and the editor. Accepted articles usually appear in print from four to six months after acceptance. Unaccepted manuscripts are returned; no criticism is made unless the editor requests resubmission.

Copyright:
 Held by the American Scholar until the author wishes to have the copyright transferred.

†*CURRENT

Subscription Data:
 Published by Heldref Publications, 4000 Albemarle Street, N. W., Suite 302, Washington, D. C. 20016. Issued 11 times per year. Advertising is accepted. Circulation: 8,500. Subscription: $10.00 per year; $12.00 to libraries. Founded: 1960.

Editorial Address:
    The Editor, Current, Plainfield, Vermont 05667.
Editorial Policy:
    Current is a reprint magazine. The reading audience includes
students, educators, and concerned citizens. Unsolicited manuscripts are not welcome. Seven to nine major articles are published per issue. Book reviews are not included.
Copyright:
    Held by Helen Dwight Reid Educational Foundation.

HUMAN BEHAVIOR

Subscription Data:
    Published by Manson Western Corporation, 12031 Wilshire Boule-
vard, Los Angeles, California 90025. Issued monthly. Advertising is accepted. Circulation: 100, 000. Subscription: $14.00
per year. Founded: 1972.
Editorial Address:
    The Editor, Human Behavior, 12031 Wilshire Boulevard, Los
Angeles, California 90025.
Editorial Policy:
    Includes reports on work, trends, and new ideas in the social
sciences. Fifty percent of the reading audience consists of
professionals or advanced degree holders. Unsolicited manuscripts are welcome. Five major articles are published per
issue. Staff written book reviews are included.
Manuscript Preparation:
    Accepted manuscripts average 1, 500 to 4, 000 pages. One copy
is required. Return postage and a self-addressed envelope are
required. A background or explanatory cover letter is desired,
but not an outline, summary, or abstract. Biographical information about the author is required. Illustrations, pictures, graphs,
etc., are acceptable if pertinent to the article. Payment is made
for accepted manuscripts. Human Behavior controls reprint
rights.
Manuscript Disposition:
    Receipt of a manuscript is not acknowledged. Editorial deci-
sions are made within four weeks. Accepted articles usually appear in print within two to four months. Unaccepted manuscripts
are returned, sometimes with criticism and/or suggestions.
Copyright:
    Held by Human Behavior.

†HUMAN ORGANIZATION

Subscription Data:
    Published by the Society for Applied Anthropology, 1703 New
Hampshire Avenue, N.W., Washington, D.C. 20009. Issued
four times each year, in March, June, September, and December. Advertising is not accepted. Circulation: 3, 500. Subscription: $14.00 per year; $21.00 to institutions; $16.00 to
fellows; $7.00 to students. Founded: 1941.

Editorial Address:
 Deward E. Walker, Jr., Editor, Human Organization, Institute
 of Behavioral Science No. 1, University of Colorado, Boulder,
 Colorado 80302.
Editorial Policy:
 Includes articles which report applications of social research
 findings to mental health, industry and other work organizations,
 both urban and rural community organizations, political behavior,
 social welfare, public health, and cultural and technological
 change. The specific goals of the journal are promotion of scientific investigation of principles which influence relations among
 human beings and the encouragement of the wide application of
 these principles to practical problems. Because Human Organization is devoted to applied social science, contributors are encouraged to submit only manuscripts that deal with this area of
 the social sciences. The reading audience includes sociologists,
 educators, anthropologists, social workers, mental health workers, and professionals from related disciplines. Unsolicited
 articles are welcome. Ten to twelve major articles are published per issue. Book reviews are not included.
Manuscript Preparation:
 No limitations are placed upon manuscript length. Four copies
 are required. Return postage and a self-addressed envelope are
 unnecessary. Manuscripts should be typed on non-erasable bond
 paper 8-1/2 by 11 inches (use one side of the sheet only). Double space all typed matter, including titles, text, quotations, footnotes, legends for illustrations, etc., leaving two inch margins
 on all four sides of the typed page. Consult the University of
 Chicago Manual of Style in matters of punctuation and usage.
 See a recent issue for "Information For Authors." Footnotes
 appear as "Notes" at the end of articles. Authors are advised
 to include footnote material in the text wherever possible. Notes
 are to be numbered consecutively throughout the paper and are
 to be typed on a separate sheet. References to literature are
 not cited in footnotes but carried within the text in parentheses.
 References cited should be typed on a separate page. A 200
 word abstract and an author's statement (including present affiliation and research acknowledgments) must be included for publication with each manuscript. All tables, graphs, diagrams, and
 illustrative materials should appear on separate pages following
 the text. No payment is made for accepted manuscripts. Reprints are available; 50 free copies are mailed to authors.
Manuscript Disposition:
 Receipt of a manuscript is acknowledged. Editorial decisions
 are made within one month. Accepted articles usually appear in
 print within one year after acceptance. Unaccepted manuscripts
 are returned, often with criticism.
Copyright:
 Held by the Society for Applied Anthropology.
Additional Information:
 The editor strongly recommends that each author submit with the
 manuscript a publishable commentary of not more than 750 words
 by either one or all of the following: the sponsors of the research, a representative(s) of the research population, and/or

agencies concerned with the research population (e.g., the Bureau of Indian Affairs).

*JOURNAL OF CONTEMPORARY ISSUES

Subscription Data:
   Published by the Atlantic Consultants, 95 St. Mary's Street, Boston, Massachusetts 02215. Issued monthly, except combined July-August and November-December. Advertising is not accepted. Circulation: Undetermined. Subscription: $72.00 per year. Founded: 1973.
Editorial Address:
   The Editor, Journal of Contemporary Issues, 95 St. Mary's Street, Boston, Massachusetts 02215.
Editorial Policy:
   The Journal is a bibliographic review; issues of contemporary concern are researched for the purpose of compiling all pertinent material on an issue. Topics cover the spectrum of contemporary issues whose significance is also of historical import. The reading audience includes teachers, professional researchers, librarians, students, and generally any segment of the public interested in comprehensive bibliographic reviews of the important issues in our society. All research is done by in-house staff to insure accuracy and comprehensiveness; therefore, unsolicited manuscripts cannot be accepted. Two to four major articles are published per issue. The Journal employs one standard format. Book reviews are incorporated only as reviews of the information of importance to the topic being researched from pertinent sources.
Copyright:
   Held by the Atlantic Consultants.

JOURNAL OF HUMAN RESOURCES

Subscription Data:
   Published by University of Wisconsin Press, Box 1379, Madison, Wisconsin 53701. Issued quarterly, in winter, spring, summer, and fall. Advertising is accepted. Circulation: 2,200. Subscription: $10.00 per year; $20.00 to institutions. Founded: 1966.
Editorial Address:
   Barbara B. Dennis, Managing Editor, Journal of Human Resources, University of Wisconsin - Madison, 4315 Social Science Building, 1180 Observatory Drive, Madison, Wisconsin 53706.
Editorial Policy:
   Includes articles that offer new quantitative information and which relate clearly to empirical work. Areas covered are manpower policies, welfare policies, health economics, and costs and returns to education (primarily higher and vocational). The reading audience is composed of the scholarly. Unsolicited manuscripts are welcome. Six to nine major articles are published per issue. Book reviews are not included.

Manuscript Preparation:
    Accepted manuscripts average 20 to 30 manuscript pages for ar-
    ticles with preference given to shorter papers and up to 10 pages
    for communications. Three copies are required. Return postage
    and a self-addressed envelope are required only if the author
    wishes to have a rejected manuscript returned. Bibliographical
    procedure should follow the University of Chicago Manual of
    Style. Reference footnotes should be placed in brackets and
    refer to the list of references at end of text. Explanatory foot-
    notes should be numbered consecutively on separate pages. Use
    generous margins and double-space. A background or explana-
    tory cover letter and an abstract of no more than 100 words are
    required. Biographical information about the author is not re-
    quired. Illustrations, pictures, graphs, etc., must be clear and
    readable. No payment is made for accepted manuscripts. Au-
    thor receives 25 free tearsheets; reprints must be ordered from
    reprint house.
Manuscript Disposition:
    Receipt of a manuscript is acknowledged. Editorial decisions
    are made within approximately 12 weeks. Accepted articles
    usually appear in print within six to twelve months. Unaccepted
    manuscripts are returned only if author sends postage. Criti-
    cism and/or suggestions are provided unless the manuscript is
    clearly unsuitable for the Journal. Most manuscripts are ref-
    ereed.
Copyright:
    Held by the Regents of the University of Wisconsin System.

OCCASIONAL REVIEW

Subscription Data:
    Published by World Research, Inc., 11722 Sorrento Valley Road,
    San Diego, California 92121. Issued occasionally. Advertising
    is accepted. Circulation: 5,000. Subscription: $3.00 per is-
    sue. Founded: 1974.
Editorial Address:
    The Editor, Occasional Review, 11722 Sorrento Valley Road,
    San Diego, California 92121.
Editorial Policy:
    Includes articles on philosophy, literature, political science,
    economics, religion, history, etc. The reading audience in-
    cludes academicians and students. Unsolicited manuscripts are
    welcome. Six to twelve major articles are published per issue.
    Book reviews are included.
Manuscript Preparation:
    Accepted manuscripts average under 8,000 words. Two copies
    are required. Return postage and a self-addressed envelope are
    required. Bibliographical procedure should follow the MLA
    Style Sheet or Strunk Elements of Style. Use ample margins.
    A background or explanatory cover letter is required, and an
    outline, summary, or abstract is recommended. Biographical
    information about the author is required. Line drawings and
    half-tones are acceptable. Payment is made for accepted

manuscripts. Author can reprint with written permission and
if proper credit is given.

Manuscript Disposition:

Receipt of a manuscript is not acknowledged. Editorial decisions are made within four weeks. Accepted articles usually
appear in print within nine months. Unaccepted manuscripts
are returned, without criticism and/or suggestions.

Copyright:

Held by World Research, Inc.

SOCIAL RESEARCH

Subscription Data:

Published by the New School for Social Research, 65 Fifth Avenue, New York, New York 10003. Issued four times each year;
in spring, summer, autumn, and winter. Advertising is accepted. Circulation: 3,500. Subscription: $10.00 per year;
$18.00 for two years; $12.00 to libraries and institutions;
$11.00 to booksellers and book agents; $9.50 with membership
in the ASA and APA; $10.00 to $12.00 foreign; $3.00 per issue.
Founded: 1933.

Editorial Address:

The Editor, Social Research, New School for Social Research,
65 Fifth Avenue, New York, New York 10003.

Editorial Policy:

Includes articles involving the social sciences. The reading audience is international - varied, but mostly scholarly. Unsolicited manuscripts are welcome. Approximately 36 major articles
are published per issue. Book reviews are sometimes included.

Manuscript Preparation:

Accepted manuscripts do not exceed 25 double-spaced pages.
One copy is required. Return postage and a self-addressed envelope are required. Bibliographical procedure will be indicated
upon acceptance for publication. Copy editor will edit footnotes.
A background or explanatory cover letter is not required nor is
an outline, summary, or abstract. Illustrations, pictures,
graphs, etc., are not acceptable. No payment is made for accepted manuscripts. Author has permission to reprint; a fee of
$150.00 is required for others to reprint. Author receives 50
reprints without charge.

Manuscript Disposition:

Receipt of a manuscript is acknowledged. Editorial decisions
are made within approximately three weeks. Accepted articles
appear in print within approximately nine months. Unaccepted
manuscripts are returned upon receipt of self-addressed, stamped
envelope. Criticism and/or suggestions are rarely provided.

Copyright:

Held by Social Research.

SOCIAL SCIENCE

Subscription Data:

Published by the Social Science Publishing Company, 1719 Ames Street, Winfield, Kansas 67156. Sponsored by Pi Gamma Mu, the National Social Science Honor Society. Issued four times each year, in January, April, June, and October. Advertising is not accepted. Circulation: 8,000. Subscription: $3.00 per year. Founded: 1925.

Editorial Address:

Panos D. Bardis, Editor, Social Science, Toledo University, Toledo, Ohio 43606.

Editorial Policy:

Includes articles on all aspects of the social sciences. The reading audience includes educators and social scientists from all disciplines. Unsolicited articles are welcome. About seven major articles are published per issue. Book reviews are included.

Manuscript Preparation:

Accepted manuscripts average 15 double-spaced typewritten pages. One original copy is required. Return postage and a self-addressed envelope are desired. Use wide margins and double-space throughout. Place all footnotes at the end of the manuscript, as NOTES, double-spaced. A background or explanatory cover letter about the article is desired. An 80 word abstract is required with submission of the finished manuscript. Biographical information about the author is desired and should include a summary of formal education, current position, and recent publications. Few illustrations, pictures, or graphs can be used. No payment is made for accepted articles. Reprints are available; costs vary with order volume.

Manuscript Disposition:

Receipt of a manuscript is usually acknowledged. Editorial decisions are made within 10 to 15 days. Accepted articles usually appear in print within six to twelve months after acceptance. Unaccepted manuscripts are returned, occasionally with suggestions.

Copyright:

Held by Social Science.

SOCIAL SCIENCE QUARTERLY

Subscription Data:

Published by the Southwestern Social Science Association, Louisiana State University, Baton Rouge, Louisiana 70803. Issued quarterly, in June, September, December, and March. Advertising is accepted. Circulation: 3,000. Subscription: $8.00 per year; $15.00 to libraries. Founded: 1920.

Editorial Address:
    The Editor, Social Science Quarterly, University of Texas at
Austin, Austin, Texas 78712.

Editorial Policy:
    Includes articles and reports on all phases of the social sciences
and business-oriented disciplines. The reading audience served
includes educators at all levels and mature students. Unsolicited
articles are welcome. Six to eight major articles are published
per issue. Book reviews are included.

Manuscript Preparation:
    Accepted manuscripts average 30 pages maximum, including foot-
notes and tables, and 15 pages maximum for research notes.
Three copies are required. Return postage and a self-addressed
envelope are not required. Bibliographical procedure should follow the editor's style sheet. Write for style sheet for special
manuscript footnoting recommendations, etc. Use a 60 space
line. A background or explanatory cover letter is not required,
but an abstract is required. Rank and affiliation of the author are required. Camera-ready line drawings for figures and
graphs are required. No payment is made for accepted manuscripts. Author receives 25 gratis reprints and may order others at cost and postage.

Manuscript Disposition:
    Receipt of a manuscript is acknowledged. Editorial decisions
are made within five to eight weeks. Accepted articles usually
appear in print within three to six months. Unaccepted manuscripts are returned with criticism and/or suggestions.

Copyright:
    Held by the Social Science Quarterly.

SOCIAL STUDIES

†JEWISH SOCIAL STUDIES

Subscription Data:
Published by the Conference on Jewish Social Studies, Inc.,
2929 Broadway, New York, New York 10025. Issued four times
each year, in January, April, July, and October. Advertising
is not accepted. Circulation: 1,250. Subscription: $15.00
per year. Founded: 1939.

Editorial Address:
The Editor, Jewish Social Studies, Conference on Jewish Social
Studies, Inc., 2929 Broadway, New York, New York 10025.

Editorial Policy:
Includes articles and reports which deal with historical and sociological aspects of Jewish life. The reading audience includes
university faculty, students and scholars, and special interest
groups. Unsolicited articles are welcome. Nine to twelve major articles are published per issue. Book reviews are included.

Manuscript Preparation:
Manuscripts of any reasonable length will be considered. Three
copies are required. Return postage and a self-addressed envelope are desired. A detailed statement of format, to be used in
manuscript preparation, is available to authors through the office
of the editor. This document must be consulted before a manuscript is prepared in final form. Use wide margins and double-
space throughout. List footnotes on a separate page. A background or explanatory cover letter is optional. A summary of
the nature of the article is desired in advance of submission of
the finished manuscript. Biographical information about the
author is desired and should include indication of present position and a list of published works. Illustrations, pictures,
graphs, etc., may be used. Payment is made for accepted
articles. Reprints are available; 50 free copies are mailed to
the author. Additional copies are available at cost.

Manuscript Disposition:
Receipt of a manuscript is acknowledged. Editorial decisions
are made within two to three months. Time from acceptance
of a manuscript to its appearance in print varies with editorial
need. Accepted manuscripts are returned, occasionally with
criticism.

Copyright:
Held by the Conference on Jewish Social Studies, Inc.

Additional Information:
Essay articles are not often used. Informational articles which
have something new to offer in interpretation or appraisal of
new subject matter are especially desired.

SOCIAL EDUCATION

Subscription Data:
 Published by the National Council for the Social Studies, 1201
 Sixteenth Street, N. W., Washington, D. C. 20036. Issued eight
 times each year, October through May. Advertising is accepted.
 Circulation: 25,000. Subscription: $10.00 per year; Free with
 membership dues of $12.00. Founded: 1937.
Editorial Address:
 Dr. Daniel Roselle, Editor, Social Education, National Council
 for the Social Studies, 1201 Sixteenth Street, N. W., Washington,
 D. C. 20036.
Editorial Policy:
 Includes articles of interest and value to social studies teachers
 at every level--elementary, secondary, college, and university.
 The reading audience includes teachers of social studies at all
 levels. Unsolicited manuscripts are welcome. Approximately
 10 major articles are published per issue. Book reviews are
 included.
Manuscript Preparation:
 Accepted manuscripts average from 1,000 to 4,000 words. One
 copy is required. Return postage and a self-addressed envelope
 are required. Bibliographical procedure should follow the University of Chicago Manual of Style. Footnotes should be listed
 on a separate page or at the bottom of the page on which the
 reference occurs. Use wide margins and double-space. A background or explanatory cover letter is useful, but not required.
 An outline, summary, or abstract of the article is not required.
 A brief statement about the author is necessary. Illustrations,
 pictures, graphs, etc., should be sent along with manuscript,
 if author wishes to include them. In general, no payment for
 accepted manuscripts is made. Reprints are available; a cost
 summary is available from the office of the editor.
Manuscript Disposition:
 Receipt of a manuscript is acknowledged. Editorial decisions
 are made within three weeks. Accepted articles usually appear
 in print within four months. Unaccepted manuscripts are returned, sometimes with suggestions.
Copyright:
 Held by the National Council for the Social Studies.

SOCIAL STUDIES REVIEW

Subscription Data:
 Published by the California Council for the Social Studies, 2205
 Sixteenth Street, Sacramento, California 95818. Issued quarter-
 ly, in fall (October), winter (December), conference (February),
 and spring (May). Advertising is accepted. Circulation: 5,000.
 Subscription: $6.00 per year. Founded: 1962.
Editorial Address:
 The Editor, Social Studies Review, California Council for the
 Social Studies, 2205 Sixteenth Street, Sacramento, California
 95818.

Editorial Policy:

Includes articles of general interest to social studies educators.
Emphasis is put on practical classroom implementation, but occasionally articles of a more theoretical nature may appear.
The reading audience includes classroom teachers of elementary
and secondary; college and university students and faculty; supervisors and curriculum consultants; and administrators, and other
interested individuals and library patrons. Solicited manuscripts
are welcome. Twelve to fifteen major articles are published
per issue. Book reviews are included only on rare occasions.

Manuscript Preparation:

Accepted manuscripts should not exceed 10 to 12 pages (including
bibliographies and footnotes). One copy is required. Return
postage and a self-addressed envelope are required. Bibliographical procedure should follow the MLA Style Sheet. List all footnotes on a separate page. Use one inch margins throughout and
double-space. Title of article and author's name and address
should be at the top of the first page of copy. A background or
explanatory cover letter is required, but not an outline, summary or abstract. Biographical information about the author is
requested. Illustrations, pictures, graphs, etc., must be camera-ready or easily reducible to page size. No payment is made
for accepted manuscripts. Three copies are given to the author.
California Council for the Social Studies retains all rights to all
articles that appear in Social Studies Review.

Manuscript Disposition:

Receipt of a manuscript is acknowledged. Editorial decisions
are made no later than 15 days prior to publication. Accepted
articles usually appear in print within ten months. Unaccepted
manuscripts are returned, sometimes with criticism and/or
suggestions at editor's discretion.

Copyright:

Held by the California Council for the Social Studies.

THEORY AND RESEARCH IN SOCIAL EDUCATION

Subscription Data:

Published by the Michigan State University Printing Office,
Michigan State University, East Lansing, Michigan 48824. Issued irregularly, one to three times per year. Advertising is
accepted. Circulation: 300. Subscription: $7.00 per year;
$9.00 to institutions. Founded: 1973.

Editorial Address:

Cleo H. Cherryholmes, Editor, Theory and Research in Social
Education, Department of Political Science, Michigan State University, East Lansing, Michigan 48824.

Editorial Policy:

Includes articles on theory and research in social studies education, effects thereof, different models of, relationship to different student populations, school characteristics, etc. Authors
are social scientists, educators, philosophers, and historians.
The reading audience includes social scientists and educators
concerned with teacher training and curriculum development in

social studies education. Unsolicited manuscripts are welcome.
All manuscripts, whether solicited or unsolicited, are reviewed
anonymously by two reviewers. Four to six major articles
are published per issue. Book reviews are included.

Manuscript Preparation:

Accepted manuscripts average 10 to 50 double-spaced pages.
Three copies are required. Return postage and a self-addressed
envelope are not required. Bibliographical procedure should follow the APA Publication Manual. Manuscripts should be typed
with a dark black ribbon, clearly mimeographed, or multilithed.
Everything should be double-spaced including footnotes and references. Only substantive footnotes should be sequentially numbered within the text and located at the end of the manuscript.
Manuscript should be clean. A background or explanatory cover
letter is not required, but an abstract is required. Biographical information about the author is not required. All artwork
must be prepared by the author. Each table should be placed
on a separate page and placed in a separate section at the end
of the manuscript. Arabic numbers should be used for number-
ing tables consecutively throughout the manuscript. Figures
should be submitted in final form. Use India ink and place figures on separate pages in a separate section at the end of the
manuscript. Number them and locate them in the text in the
same way as tables. No payment is made for accepted manuscripts. Reprints are available at cost to the author. Costs of
$100.00 per article are required for inclusion in books of readings,
etc.

Manuscript Disposition:

Receipt of a manuscript is acknowledged. Editorial decisions
are made within eight weeks. Accepted articles usually appear
in print in the next issue. Unaccepted manuscripts are returned
with criticism and/or suggestions.

Copyright:

Held by the College and University Faculty Assembly of the National Council for the Social Studies.

SOCIAL WORK

ABSTRACTS FOR SOCIAL WORKERS

Subscription Data:
> Published by the National Association of Social Workers, 1425
> H Street, N.W., Suite 600, Washington, D.C. 20005. Publica-
> tion office located at 49 Sheridan Avenue, Albany, New York
> 12210. Issued quarterly, in spring, summer, fall, and winter.
> Advertising is not accepted. Circulation: 7,500. Subscription:
> $20.00 per year. Founded: 1965.

Editorial Address:
> Inez L. Sperr, Editor, Abstracts for Social Workers, National
> Association of Social Workers-Editorial Office, Box 504, Murray
> Hill Station, New York, New York 10016.

Editorial Policy:
> Includes articles on theory, research, and practice on social
> work/social welfare. Disciplines related to human service
> from about 200 professional journals are abstracted. Coverage
> includes anthropology, economics, medicine, philosophy, psy-
> chiatry, psychology, and sociology. The reading audience in-
> cludes social workers and counselors, social welfare practition-
> ers and administrators, educators, legal and medical personnel,
> and social planners. Abstracts are obtained directly from
> editors of source journals, or from authors of original articles,
> or prepared by the staff. Content regularly consists of abstracts
> of 250 articles (minimum). Occasional full-length review articles
> are published. Mainly periodical literature is included; abstracts
> of books do not exceed 10% of the total items in any single issue.

Manuscript Preparation:
> Accepted abstracts average 250 words. Information on manu-
> script preparation is supplied with the request for an abstract.
> Journal content consists solely of abstracts (informative summa-
> ries); the occasional reviews of the literature are prepared by
> special arrangement. Professional affiliation and address of au-
> thors of original articles are required. Illustrations are not ac-
> ceptable. No payment is made for abstracts. No reprints are
> available.

Copyright:
> Held by the National Association of Social Workers.

CHILD WELFARE

Subscription Data:
> Published by the Child Welfare League of America, Inc., 67
> Irving Place, New York, New York 10003. Published monthly,

except August and September. Advertising is accepted. Circulation: 9,500. Subscription: $6.00 per year. Founded: 1921.

Editorial Address:

The Editor, Child Welfare, Child Welfare League of America, Inc., 67 Irving Place, New York, New York 10003.

Editorial Policy:

Includes articles on all phases of child welfare, social services to children and their families, and social conditions affecting children. The reading audience includes social workers and lay people connected with child welfare services and other social agencies, psychiatrists, and students. Unsolicited articles are welcome. Seven major articles are published per issue. Book reviews are included.

Manuscript Preparation:

Accepted manuscripts range from 3,000 to 4,000 words or from 12 to 16 double-spaced typewritten pages. The original and one carbon are required. Return postage and a self-addressed envelope are necessary. Standardized bibliography is not required. A style sheet on documentation can be supplied. Use one inch margins and double-space throughout. A background or explanatory cover letter about the article is not required nor is an outline or summary. Biographical information about the author is required. There is no policy concerning illustrations, pictures, graphs, etc., beyond keeping the number of tables limited. No payment is made for accepted articles. Reprints are available; authors receive rate sheets and order forms.

Manuscript Disposition:

Receipt of a manuscript is acknowledged promptly. Editorial decisions are made within two to four weeks. Time from acceptance of a manuscript to its appearance in print varies from nine to twelve months. Unaccepted manuscripts are returned if postage is received. Suggestions and criticism are not usually provided.

Copyright:

Held by the Child Welfare League of America, Inc.

CLINICAL SOCIAL WORK JOURNAL

Subscription Data:

Published by Behavioral Publications, 72 Fifth Avenue, New York, New York 10011. Issued quarterly. Advertising is accepted. Circulation: 2,000. Subscription: $12.00 per year; $25.00 to institutions. Founded: 1973.

Editorial Address:

Mary L. Gottesfeld, M.S.S., Editor, Clinical Social Work Journal, 285 West End Avenue, New York, New York 10023.

Editorial Policy:

The Journal's main objectives are to broaden the understanding and skill of the clinical social work practitioner or teacher concerned with individuals, couples, families, and groups. The reading audience includes psychologists, psychotherapists, and psychiatrists. Unsolicited manuscripts are welcome. Five ma-

jor articles are published per issue. Book reviews are included.
Manuscript Preparation:
Accepted manuscripts should not exceed 20 double-spaced pages.
Three copies are required. Return postage and a self-addressed
envelope are required. Bibliographical procedure should follow
the APA Publication Manual. Avoid the use of footnotes. Use
one inch margins on the top, sides, and bottom and double-space.
A background or explanatory cover letter is optional, but an outline, summary, or abstract is required. Biographical information about the author is required. Illustrations, pictures, graphs,
etc., should be placed on separate pages at the end of the manuscript, marked with Arabic numerals, and indicated where placed
in the manuscript. No payment is made for accepted manuscripts.
No free reprints are available; cost varies with length of article.
Manuscript Disposition:
Receipt of a manuscript is acknowledged. Editorial decisions
are made within six months to one year. Accepted articles usually appear in print within six months to one year. Unaccepted
manuscripts are returned if author provides postage. Criticism
and/or suggestions are provided upon request.
Copyright:
Held by Behavioral Publications.

JOURNAL OF EDUCATION FOR SOCIAL WORK

Subscription Data:
Published by the Council on Social Work Education, 345 East
Forty-sixth Street, New York, New York 10017. Issued three
times each year, in fall, winter, and spring. Advertising is
not accepted. Circulation: 5,500. Subscription: Available to
members only. Founded: 1965.
Editorial Address:
The Editor, Journal of Education for Social Work, 345 East
Forty-sixth Street, New York, New York 10017.
Editorial Policy:
Includes articles on social work education. The reading audience includes social work educators. Unsolicited manuscripts
are welcome. Fifteen to eighteen major articles are published
per issue. Book reviews are included by request only.
Manuscript Preparation:
Accepted manuscripts average 3,500 words. Three copies are
required. Return postage and a self-addressed envelope are
not required. A background or explanatory cover letter and an
outline, summary, or abstract are required. Biographical information about the author is not required. Use as few illustrations, pictures, graphs, etc., as possible. No payment is
made for accepted manuscripts.
Manuscript Disposition:
Receipt of a manuscript is acknowledged. Editorial decisions
are made within four to five months. Accepted articles usually
appear in print within 12 to 18 months. Unaccepted manuscripts
are returned without criticism and/or suggestions.

Copyright:
  Held by the Council on Social Work Education.

SOCIAL WORK

Subscription Data:
  Published by the National Association of Social Workers, 1425
  H Street, N.W., Washington, D.C. 20005. Issued bimonthly,
  in January, March, May, July, September, and November. Advertising is accepted. Circulation: 65,000. Subscription:
  $15.00 per year; $7.50 to students; $3.00 per issue. Founded:
  1956.
Editorial Address:
  Editorial Office, Social Work, P.O. Box 504, Murray Hill Station, New York, New York 10016.
Editorial Policy:
  Includes manuscripts that yield new insight into established practices, evaluate new techniques and research, examine current
  social problems; or bring serious, critical analysis to bear on
  the problems, or bring serious, critical analysis to bear on
  literary piece is welcome when it concerns issues significant to
  social workers. The reading audience includes social workers,
  lawyers, doctors, nurses, educators, ministers, students, researchers, journalists, and leaders of community organizations.
  Unsolicited manuscripts are welcome. Ten to twelve major articles are published per issue. Book reviews are included, but
  unsolicited reviews are not used.
Manuscript Preparation:
  Articles should be 14 to 16 double-spaced typewritten pages.
  Book reviews should be two double-spaced typewritten pages.
  Brief notes should be no more than four to six double-spaced
  typewritten pages. Points and viewpoints should be no more
  than four to six double-spaced typewritten pages. Letters to
  the editor should be as short as possible. The journal prefers
  shorter to longer articles because of the need to achieve variety
  in subject matter. Three copies are required. Return postage
  and a self-addressed envelope are not required. Footnoting and
  other bibliographical procedure should follow the "Information
  for Authors" that is available from the editor. A style manual
  has been prepared by the members of the Publications Department for the use of the journal's staff editors. The manual
  is available to authors on request. Footnotes should appear at
  the end of the manuscript and be typed double-spaced. They
  should be numbered consecutively throughout, with numbers
  keyed to numbers in the text. A background or explanatory
  cover letter is not required, but an outline, summary, or abstract is required. Biographical information about the author
  is required and should include author's highest degree, titles,
  current organizational connection as well as affiliation at the
  time the article was written. Camera-ready illustrations, pictures, graphs, etc., are acceptable and must be furnished by
  the author. No payment is made for accepted manuscripts

except on assignment for special issues.   Five copies of the issue in which the article appears are sent to the author upon publication along with a form for ordering reprints of the article.
Manuscript Disposition:
  Receipt of a manuscript is acknowledged.   Editorial decisions are
  made within approximately two to three months.   Accepted articles usually appear in print within four to eight months.   Unaccepted manuscripts are returned, without criticism and/or suggestions, unless revision is requested.
Copyright:
  Held by the National Association of Social Workers.

SOCIOLOGY

†AMERICAN JOURNAL OF SOCIOLOGY

Subscription Data:
Published by the University of Chicago Press, 5750 Ellis Avenue, Chicago, Illinois 60637. Issued six times each year, in July, September, November, January, March, and May. Advertising is accepted. Circulation: 7,200. Subscription: $10.00 per year, $19.00 for two years, $28.00 for three years; $15.00 to institutions, $29.00 for two years, $43.00 for three years; $7.50 per year to members of the American Sociological Association; $2.50 per issue to individuals, $3.50 per issue to institutions. Founded: 1895.

Editorial Address:
The Editor, American Journal of Sociology, 1130 East Fifty-ninth Street, University of Chicago, Chicago, Illinois 60637.

Editorial Policy:
Includes technical articles which emphasize sociological analysis, research, and theory. The reading audience includes social scientists, educators, and students. Unsolicited articles are welcome. Eight major articles are published per issue. Book reviews are included.

Manuscript Preparation:
No policy regarding manuscript length has been established. Two copies are required. Return postage and a self-addressed envelope are desired. See a recent issue for bibliographical procedure. Use wide margins and double-space. List footnotes on a separate page at the end of the article. A background or explanatory cover letter about the article is desired. An abstract of not more than 100 words should be included with the finished manuscript. Biographical information about the author is desired. Illustrations, graphs, etc., may be used; tables must be prepared on separate pages. No payment is made for accepted articles. Reprints are available; 50 free copies are mailed to the author. A detailed reprint cost summary and additional copies are available through the office of the editor.

Manuscript Disposition:
Receipt of a manuscript is acknowledged. Each article is submitted to at least two qualified readers for editorial recommendations. Editorial decisions are made within three to four months. Accepted manuscripts usually appear in print from four to five months after acceptance. Unaccepted manuscripts are returned, often with criticism and/or suggestions.

Copyright:
Held by the University of Chicago. Requests for permission to quote from the Journal should be submitted directly to the University of Chicago Press. All rights reserved.

AMERICAN SOCIOLOGICAL REVIEW

Subscription Data:
Published by the American Sociological Association, 1722 N
Street, N. W., Washington, D. C. 20036. Issued six times each
year, in February, April, June, August, October, and Decem-
ber. Advertising is accepted. Circulation: 18, 000. Subscrip-
tion: $15.00 per year to non-members; $30.00 per year to in-
stitutions. Founded: 1936.
Editorial Address:
James F. Short, Jr., Editor, American Sociological Review,
Department of Sociology, Washington State University, Pullman,
Washington 99163.
Editorial Policy:
Includes articles on sociology and related aspects of the social
sciences. The reading audience includes research workers in
the social sciences, educators, and students. Unsolicited articles are welcome. Ten to twelve major articles are published
per issue. Book reviews are not included.
Manuscript Preparation:
Accepted manuscripts should not exceed 30 double-spaced typewritten pages. Two copies are required; do not mimeograph or
ditto. Return postage and a self-addressed envelope are unnecessary. Bibliographical procedure should follow the ASA Style
Manual. Use one inch margins and double-space throughout.
Place footnotes on a separate page at the end of the article. A
background or explanatory cover letter is unnecessary. An abstract of the article is desired with submission of the finished
manuscript. Biographical information about the author is unnecessary. Illustrations and pictures may not be used, but graphs
and tables are acceptable. No payment is made for accepted
articles. Reprints are available; a cost summary may be obtained from the office of the editor.
Manuscript Disposition:
Receipt of a manuscript is acknowledged. Editorial decisions
are made within three months. Accepted articles usually appear
in print within six months after acceptance. Unaccepted manuscripts are returned, often with criticism and/or suggestions.
Copyright:
Held by the American Sociological Association.

CRIME AND DELINQUENCY

Subscription Data:
Published by the National Council on Crime and Delinquency,
Continental Plaza, 411 Hackensack Avenue, Hackensack, New
Jersey 07601. Issued quarterly, in January, April, July, and
October. Advertising is accepted. Circulation: 10, 000.
Subscription: $15.00 per year; $4.00 per issue. Founded:
1955.
Editorial Address:
The Editor, Crime and Delinquency, Continental Plaza, 411
Hackensack Avenue, Hackensack, New Jersey 07601.

Editorial Policy:
Includes articles which deal with all phases of crime, delinquency, correction, and criminal justice. The reading audience includes employees of youth-serving and family agencies, lawyers, educators, social workers, sociologists, and students of the behavioral sciences. Unsolicited articles are welcome. All articles for thematic issues are solicited. Other issues consist of unsolicited articles which cover a variety of topics. Ten major articles are published per issue. Book reviews are included.

Manuscript Preparation:
Accepted manuscripts average from 12 to 20 double-spaced typewritten pages. Two copies, both on bond paper, are required. Return postage and a self-addressed envelope are desired. See a recent issue for bibliographical procedure and format. Use one inch margins and double-space throughout. Number footnotes consecutively on a separate page at the end of the article. A background or explanatory cover letter about the article is desired. A 300 word abstract is required with submission of the finished manuscript. Biographical information about the author is desired and should include a summary of formal education and professional background. Illustrations, pictures, graphs, etc., may be used, but half-tones may not. No payment is made for accepted articles. Reprints are available; a cost summary may be obtained through the office of the editor. Five free copies of the issue are mailed to the author.

Manuscript Disposition:
Receipt of a manuscript is acknowledged. Editorial decisions are made within three to twelve weeks. Accepted articles usually appear in print within two years after acceptance. Unaccepted manuscripts are returned, sometimes with criticism and/or suggestions.

Copyright:
Held by the National Council on Crime and Delinquency.

Additional Information:
Technical terminology should be used only where it is necessary for precision. Include case materials when possible. A guide entitled "Information to Contributors" is available through the office of the editor.

EDUCATION AND URBAN SOCIETY

Subscription Data:
Published by Sage Publications, 275 South Beverly Drive, Beverly Hills, California 90212. Issued quarterly, in November, February, May, and August. Advertising is accepted. Circulation: 2,000. Subscription: $10.00 per year; $18.00 to institutions; $9.00 to students; Add $1.00 for subscriptions outside the United States and Canada. Founded: 1968.

Editorial Address:
Jay Scribner, Editor, Education and Urban Society, Graduate School of Education, UCLA, Los Angeles, California 90024.

Editorial Policy:
  Provides a multidisciplinary forum for social scientific research
  on education as a social institution within urban environments.
  During recent years an increasing number of social scientists
  have been conducting research on education as a social institution. Research studies have not been limited to the working of
  the institution, but have begun to explore educational institutions
  and processes as agents of social change. Not only does much
  of this work center on the problems and needs resulting from
  the national concern with improving the urban environment, but
  it also involves the role of education in a society which is urban.
  Education and Urban Society exists to foster such research and
  to provide a multidisciplinary forum for communication. The
  reading audience includes educators, administrators, and urban
  specialists. Unsolicited manuscripts are welcome. Eight to
  ten major articles are published per issue. Book reviews are
  included.
Manuscript Preparation:
  Accepted articles average 25 to 30 double-spaced typewritten
  pages. Three copies are required. Return postage and a self-
  addressed envelope are not required. Footnoting and bibliographical procedure should follow the Sage style manual which
  is available from the publisher upon request. Double-space manuscript. A background or explanatory cover letter is not required nor is an outline, summary, or abstract. Biographical
  information about the author is not required. Camera-ready
  artwork is required. Graphs, tables, and charts should be
  placed on separate pages. No payment is made for accepted
  manuscripts. Authors may purchase a minimum of 100 reprints.
Manuscript Disposition:
  Receipt of a manuscript is acknowledged. Editorial decisions
  are made within eight to twelve weeks. Accepted articles usually appear in print within six to nine months. Unaccepted manuscripts are returned with criticism and/or suggestions.
Copyright:
  Held by Sage Publications.

ENVIRONMENT AND BEHAVIOR

Subscription Data:
  Published by Sage Publications, Inc., 275 South Beverly Drive,
  Beverly Hills, California 90212. Issued quarterly, in March,
  June, September, and December. Advertising is accepted.
  Circulation: 1,700. Subscription: $12.00 per year to profes-
  sionals and teachers; $20.00 to institutions. Founded: 1969.
Editorial Address:
  Gary H. Winkel, Editor, Environment and Behavior, Environ-
  mental Psychology Program, Graduate Center of the City Uni-
  versity of New York, 33 West Forty-second Street, New York,
  New York 10036.
Editorial Policy:
  Includes theoretical, methodological, and empirical papers con-

cerning the relationship between the physical environment and behavior. The reading audience includes sociologists, psychologists, architects, planners, geographers, and natural resource researchers. Unsolicited manuscripts are welcome. Five to seven major articles are published per issue. Book reviews are not presently included.

Manuscript Preparation:

Accepted manuscripts average five to forty pages. Three copies are required. Return postage and a self-addressed envelope are not required. Bibliographical procedure should follow the Sage style sheet. List footnotes on a separate page. All copy, including indented matter, notes, and references, should be typed double-spaced on white standard paper. Lines should not exceed six inches in length. Type only on one side of a sheet and number all pages. A background or explanatory cover letter is not required, but an abstract is required. Biographical information about the author is required. Illustrations, pictures, graphs, etc., should be limited to those absolutely essential. No payment is made for accepted manuscripts. Twenty-five reprints are available.

Manuscript Disposition:

Receipt of a manuscript is acknowledged. Editorial decisions are made within six months. Accepted articles usually appear in print within 12 months. Unaccepted manuscripts are returned with detailed criticism and/or suggestions.

Copyright:

Held by Sage Publications, Inc.

HOMOSEXUAL COUNSELING JOURNAL

Subscription Data:

Published by the Homosexual Community Counseling Center, Inc., 921 Madison Avenue, New York, New York 10021. Issued quarterly, in January, April, July, and October. Advertising is accepted. Circulation: Not determined. Subscription: $10.00 per year; $15.00 to institutions. Founded: 1974.

Editorial Address:

Ralph Blair, D. Ed., Editor, Homosexual Counseling Journal, 921 Madison Avenue, New York, New York 10021.

Editorial Policy:

Includes articles on research, practice, and theory in counseling and psycho-therapy. Also included are book and journal reviews, news, professional placement, and questions and answers. The reading audience includes professional counselors and psychotherapists. Unsolicited manuscripts are welcome. Two or three major articles are published per issue. Book reviews are included.

Manuscript Preparation:

Accepted manuscripts average 2,400 words. Three copies are required. Return postage and a self-addressed envelope are required. Footnoting and other bibliographical procedure should follow the APA Publication Manual. Triple-space manuscript.

A background or explanatory cover letter and an outline, summary, or abstract are required. Biographical information about
the author is required. Illustrations and pictures are not acceptable; graphs and tables are welcome. No payment is made
for accepted manuscripts. Reprints will be negotiated.

Manuscript Disposition:

Receipt of a manuscript is acknowledged. Editorial decisions
are made within eight to ten weeks. Accepted articles usually
appear in print within three to nine months. Unaccepted manuscripts are returned without criticism and/or suggestions if
self-addressed, stamped envelope is enclosed.

Copyright:

Held by the Homosexual Community Counseling Center, Inc.

INTERNATIONAL MIGRATION REVIEW

Subscription Data:

Published by the Center for Migration Studies of New York, Inc.,
209 Flagg Place, Staten Island, New York 10304. Issued quarterly, in March, June, September, and December. Advertising
is accepted. Circulation: 2,000. Subscription: $12.00 per
year, $22.00 for two years, $33.50 for three years; $12.50 to
Canada and Pan American Postal Union, $24.00 for two years,
$35.00 for three years; $13.00 per year to other countries,
$25.00 for two years, $36.50 for three years; $3.50 per issue.
Founded: 1966.

Editorial Address:

The Editor, International Migration Review, 209 Flagg Place,
Staten Island, New York 10304.

Editorial Policy:

The journal studies sociological, demographic, historical, and
legislative aspects of human migration movements and ethnic
group relations. It makes available the most authoritative and
up-to-date research and extensive bibliographical service on
migration and ethnicity through original articles, documentary
reports, legislative notes, statistics, review of reviews, and
book reviews. The reading audience includes professionals,
scholars, students of migration movements and ethnicity, etc.
Unsolicited manuscripts are welcome. Five major articles are
published per issue. Book reviews are included.

Manuscript Preparation:

Accepted manuscripts average approximately 25 double-spaced
typewritten pages. Two copies are required. Return postage
and a self-addressed envelope are required. See a current issue for bibliographical procedure. Do not use footnotes. Double-space manuscript. A background or explanatory cover letter
is not required, but an outline, summary, or abstract is preferred. Biographical information about the author is not required. Camera-ready graphs are acceptable. No payment is
made for accepted manuscripts. Reprints are available at author's expense.

Manuscript Disposition:
Receipt of a manuscript is acknowledged. Editorial decisions
are made within six to eight weeks. Accepted articles usually
appear in print within 12 months. Unaccepted manuscripts are
returned with criticism and/or suggestions.

Copyright:
Held by the Center for Migration Studies of New York, Inc.

JOURNAL OF HUMAN RELATIONS

Subscription Data:
Published by Central State University, Wilberforce, Ohio 45384.
Issued quarterly, in January, April, July, and October. Advertising is accepted. $4.00 per year; $4.50 foreign. Founded:
1952.

Editorial Address:
The Editor, Journal of Human Relations, P.O. Box 307, Central
State University, Wilberforce, Ohio 45384.

Editorial Policy:
Includes articles and reports on all phases of human relations;
an interdisciplinary approach to human relations in the world
today; view to understanding the human condition; a search for
scientific enlightenment toward psychosocial awareness; and
practical programs which may lead to improvement of the human
condition in the world. The reading audience is from all disciplines but mostly from the field of education; suitable for laymen as well as scholars and students. Unsolicited manuscripts
are welcome. Seven or eight major articles are published per
issue. Book reviews are included.

Manuscript Preparation:
Accepted manuscripts average from 15 to 18 double-spaced typewritten pages. Two copies are required. Return postage and
a self-addressed envelope are desired. Footnoting and other
bibliographical procedure may follow the University of Chicago
Manual of Style. Use 1-1/4 inch margins and double-space
throughout. A "Notes and References" heading should be placed
at the end of the manuscript with all pertinent information included under that heading. A background or explanatory cover
letter about the article is desired, but not an outline or summary. Biographical information about the author is desired and
should include a short statement of current professional status.
No cash payments are made for accepted articles. Two copies
of the issue are mailed to each author along with 15 free reprints of the article. Reprints are available; costs vary with
order volume and type of binding.

Manuscript Disposition:
Receipt of a manuscript is acknowledged. Editorial decisions
are made within four to eight weeks. Accepted articles usually
appear in print within six to nine months. Unaccepted manuscripts are returned, usually with constructive criticism.

Copyright:
Held by the Central State University.

JOURNAL OF MARRIAGE AND THE FAMILY

Subscription Data:
> Published by the National Council on Family Relations, 1219 University Avenue, Southeast, Minneapolis, Minnesota 55414. Issued quarterly, in February, May, August, and November. Advertising is accepted. Circulation: 9,800. Subscription: $20.00 per year which includes membership in NCFR; $12.00 per year without membership. Founded: 1938.

Editorial Address:
> The Editor, Journal of Marriage and the Family, Department of Sociology, University of Southern California, Los Angeles, California 90007.

Editorial Policy:
> Includes research, theoretical, and descriptive sociological articles which relate to marriage and the family. The reading audience includes sociologists, family life educators, and students. Unsolicited articles are welcome. Sixteen major articles are published per issue. Book reviews are included; however, unsolicited book reviews are not included.

Manuscript Preparation:
> Accepted manuscripts average 20 double-spaced typewritten pages. Two copies are required. Return postage and a self-addressed envelope are unnecessary. Bibliographical procedure should follow "Manuscript Preparation Requirements" which appear in each issue or the University of Chicago Manual of Style or ASA Style Manual. Use 1-1/2 inch margins and double-space throughout. List all footnotes on separate pages at back and use as few as possible. A background or explanatory cover letter about the article is not desired nor is an outline or summary. A one paragraph abstract is required. Biographical information about the author is not required and only the current position is needed. Tables set by printers can be used; all other illustrations, pictures, and graphs must be black-white, camera-ready format. No payment is made for accepted articles. Reprints are available with a cost summary obtainable through the NCFR Office.

Manuscript Disposition:
> Receipt of a manuscript is acknowledged. Editorial decisions are made within two months. Accepted articles usually appear in print within six months after acceptance. Unaccepted manuscripts are returned, often with criticism and/or suggestions.

Copyright:
> Held by the National Council on Family Relations.

JOURNAL OF POLITICAL AND MILITARY SOCIOLOGY

Subscription Data:
> Publisher is not determined. Issued twice each year, in spring and fall. Advertising is accepted. Circulation: Not determined. Subscription: $7.50 per year to individuals and institutions; $6.50 to students. Founded: 1973.

Editorial Address:

Dr. George A. Kourvetaris, Editor, Journal of Political and Military Sociology, c/o Department of Sociology, Northern Illinois University, DeKalb, Illinois 60115.

Editorial Policy:

Includes articles of a theoretical, methodological, and empirical nature, which explore the relationship between political and social structure in general and/or political and military in particular. The reading audience includes professional sociologists, political scientists, and persons in related fields; university libraries, army libraries, ROTC units, military personnel, and persons in non-academic fields interested in political and military affairs. Unsolicited manuscripts are accepted. Approximately eight or nine major articles are published per issue. Book reviews are included.

Manuscript Preparation:

Short and quality articles that do not exceed 15 to 20 double-spaced typewritten pages in length, including footnotes and references, are preferable to long ones. Three copies are required. Return postage and a self-addressed envelope are not required. Bibliographical procedure should follow the ASA Style Manual or the Journal's editorial procedures that are provided by the editor upon request. Footnotes should be used only for substantive comments not included in the main text. They should be numbered serially and typed double-spaced on separate sheets at the end of the text before the references. Type all copy on white bond 8-1/2 by 11 inch paper, double-spaced, and on only one side of the page. Lines should not exceed six inches and use one inch margins at the top and bottom. A cover letter is preferred. An abstract that does not exceed 150 to 200 words is required. Biographical information about the author is requested only after paper is accepted. Type each table on a separate page and insert a location note in numerical order in the text. Draw figures, in India ink, send copies, but retain original until the paper is accepted. No payment is made for accepted manuscripts. Twenty free reprints are given to the author with an option to order and pay for more.

Manuscript Disposition:

Receipt of a manuscript is acknowledged. Editorial decisions are made normally within 10 to 12 weeks. Accepted articles usually appear in print within three to seven months. Unaccepted manuscripts are returned with criticism and/or suggestions.

Copyright:

Held by the Journal of Political and Military Sociology.

*JOURNAL OF SOCIAL ISSUES

Subscription Data:

Published by the Society for the Psychological Study of Social Issues, P.O. Box 1248, Ann Arbor, Michigan 48106. Issued quarterly. Advertising is accepted on an exchange basis only. Circulation: 7,000. Subscription: $9.00 per year; $15.00 to institutions and organizations. Founded: 1944.

Editorial Address:
> Jacqueline D. Goodchilds, General Editor, Journal of Social Issues, Department of Psychology, University of California, Los Angeles, California 90024.

Editorial Policy:
> Includes thematically organized articles. The reading audience includes professionals in the social sciences and interested others. Mostly solicited manuscripts are accepted, but others are welcome. Ten to twelve major articles are published per issue. Book reviews are not included.

Manuscript Preparation:
> No limitations are placed upon manuscript length. Three copies are required. Return postage and a self-addressed envelope are required. Footnoting and bibliographical procedure should follow the APA Publication Manual. Use standard manuscript margin and spacing. A background or explanatory cover letter is not required, but an outline, summary, or abstract of the article is required. Biographical information about the author is required. Illustrations, pictures, graphs, etc., may be used. No payment is made for accepted manuscripts. Reprints are available at time of publication.

Manuscript Disposition:
> Receipt of a manuscript is acknowledged. Editorial decisions are made as soon as possible. Time from acceptance of a manuscript to its appearance in print varies with editorial need. Unaccepted manuscripts are returned, sometimes with criticism and/or suggestions.

Copyright:
> Held by the Journal of Social Issues.

Additional Information:
> The primary goal of the Journal is to bring behavioral and social science theory, empirical evidence, and practice into focus as they relate to problems of groups and communities from local to international. Each issue is devoted to a single topic, the objective of which is to communicate scientific findings and interpretations.

RURAL SOCIOLOGY

Subscription Data:
> Published by the Rural Sociological Society, 207 Weaver Building, Pennsylvania State University, University Park, Pennsylvania 16802. Issued quarterly, in March, June, September, and December. Advertising is accepted. Circulation: 3,000. Subscription: $12.00 per year. Founded: 1936.

Editorial Address:
> Robert C. Bealer, Editor, Rural Sociology, 207 Weaver Building, Penn State University, University Park, Pennsylvania 16802.

Editorial Policy:
> Includes articles and reports on rural sociology, community development, directed change, and comparative structure. The reading audience includes sociologists, anthropologists, educators,

and students. Unsolicited articles are welcome. Six or seven
major articles are published per issue. Book reviews are included.

Manuscript Preparation:
Accepted manuscripts may not exceed 25 double-spaced typewritten pages. Four copies are required. Return postage and
a self-addressed envelope are unnecessary. Bibliographical
procedure should follow the University of Chicago Manual of
Style and "Notice to Contributors," published in each issue.
Use 1-1/2 inch margins and double-space throughout. A background or explanatory cover letter about the article is desired.
An abstract of approximately 150 words is required with the
completed manuscript. Biographical information about the author is unnecessary. Illustrations, graphs, etc., are not often
used. No payment is made for accepted articles. Reprints
are available.

Manuscript Disposition:
Receipt of a manuscript is acknowledged. Editorial decisions
are made within four months. Accepted articles usually appear
in print within six to nine months after acceptance. Unaccepted
manuscripts are returned, often with the comments and/or suggestions of reviewers.

Copyright:
Held by the Rural Sociological Society.

SOCIAL POLICY

Subscription Data:
Published by the Social Policy Corporation, 184 Fifth Avenue,
New York, New York 10010. Issued bimonthly, in January-
February, March-April, May-June, July-August, September-
October, and November-December. Advertising is accepted.
Circulation: 4,500. Subscription: $8.00 per year; $14.00 for
two years; $19.00 for three years; $6.00 to students. Founded:
1970.

Editorial Address:
The Editor, Social Policy, 184 Fifth Avenue, New York, New
York 10010.

Editorial Policy:
Includes articles on education, sociology, economics, welfare,
community development, and health (quantitative, qualitative,
personal). The reading audience includes sociologists, educators, political scientists, economists, movement people - trade
union, black and minority liberation, women's rights, students,
and professionals. Unsolicited manuscripts are welcome. Approximately seven or eight major articles are published per
issue. Book reviews are included.

Manuscript Preparation:
Accepted manuscripts average approximately 2,000 to 4,000
words. Two copies are required. Return postage and a self-
addressed envelope are required if the author wants manuscript
returned. List footnotes on a separate page and be sure they

are complete. Use adequate margins for notations and double-space. A background or explanatory cover letter is required, but not an outline, summary, or abstract. Biographical information about the author is required. Illustrations, pictures, and graphs are welcome, but not required. No payment is made for accepted manuscripts. Reprints are available at cost; six issues of the magazine are sent to the author.

Manuscript Disposition:
Receipt of a manuscript is acknowledged. Editorial decisions are made within two weeks. Accepted articles usually appear in print within two to six months. Unaccepted manuscripts are returned if stamped, self-addressed envelope is provided. Limited suggestions are provided.

Copyright:
Held by the Social Policy Corporation.

SOCIAL PROBLEMS

Subscription Data:
Published by the Society for the Study of Social Problems, Inc., a non-profit scholarly educational society, P.O. Box 533, Notre Dame, Indiana 46556. Issued quarterly. Advertising is accepted. Circulation: 4,300. Subscription: Subscription prices available from the Society for the Study of Social Problems Executive Office, Irenea Horning, P.O. Box 533, Notre Dame, Indiana 46556. Founded: 1953.

Editorial Address:
The Editor, Social Problems, c/o P.O. Box 533, Notre Dame, Indiana 46556.

Editorial Policy:
Includes articles which pertain to social problems. The reading audience includes sociologists and others interested in social problems. Unsolicited manuscripts are welcome. Nine major articles are published per issue. Book reviews are included.

Manuscript Preparation:
No limitations are placed upon manuscript length. Two copies are required. Return postage and a self-addressed envelope are desired. Bibliographical procedure should follow the ASA Style Manual. Use wide margins and double-space throughout. A background or explanatory cover letter about the article is desired, but not an outline or summary. Biographical information about the author is unnecessary. Avoid use of illustrations. No payment is made for accepted articles. Reprints are available; 25 free copies are mailed to the author.

Manuscript Disposition:
Receipt of a manuscript is acknowledged within 10 days. Editorial decisions are made within two months. Accepted articles usually appear in print within six months after acceptance. Unaccepted manuscripts are returned, often with criticism and/or suggestions.

Copyright:
Held by the Society for the Study of Social Problems, Inc.

SOCIOLOGICAL QUARTERLY

Subscription Data:
Published by the University of Missouri--Columbia, Columbia, Missouri 65201, for the Midwest Sociological Society. Issued quarterly, in spring, summer, winter, and fall. Advertising is accepted. Circulation: 2,300. Subscription: $10.00 per year; $12.00 to institutions; $8.50 to American Sociological Association members. Founded: 1959.
Editorial Address:
The Editor, Sociological Quarterly, 1004 Elm, University of Missouri, Columbia, Missouri 65201.
Editorial Policy:
Includes articles on all phases of sociological study. The reading audience includes sociologists, other social scientists, and students. Unsolicited articles are welcome. Eight to ten major articles are published per issue. Book reviews are included.
Manuscript Preparation:
Accepted manuscripts average 20 double-spaced typewritten pages. The original and two carbons are required. Return postage and a self-addressed envelope are desirable. Footnotes should be numbered consecutively throughout the paper and should be listed on a separate page at the end of the article. Use one inch margins and double-space throughout. Consult ASA Style Manual for reference format. An abstract is required. Biographical information about the author is unnecessary. Illustrations, graphs, etc., may be used, but authors are charged for art work. No payment is made for accepted articles. Reprints are available; a cost summary is available through the office of the editor.
Manuscript Disposition:
Receipt of a manuscript is acknowledged. Editorial decisions are made by two readers and the editor within two to three months. Accepted articles usually appear in print from six to eight months after acceptance. Unaccepted manuscripts are returned, sometimes with criticism and/or suggestions.
Copyright:
Held by the Midwest Sociological Society.
Additional Information:
Articles which offer a new viewpoint, approach, or insight and which contribute either to elucidation of recent theory or to establishment of new theory are given preference.

SOCIOLOGY AND SOCIAL RESEARCH

Subscription Data:
Published by the University of Southern California, University Park, Los Angeles, California 90007. Issued four times each year, in January, April, July, and October. Advertising is not accepted. Circulation: 1,930. Subscription: $5.00 per year. Founded: 1916.
Editorial Address:
The Editor, Sociology and Social Research, University of

Southern California, University Park, Los Angeles, California
90007.

Editorial Policy:
Includes articles on sociology, social research, and related aspects of the social sciences. The reading audience includes
sociologists and other social scientists. Unsolicited articles
are welcome. Nine or ten major articles are published per
issue. Book reviews are included.

Manuscript Preparation:
Accepted manuscripts average 4,000 words. Two copies are
required. Return postage and a self-addressed envelope are
unnecessary. See a recent issue for footnoting and other bibliographical procedure. Use 15 space left margins and 10 space
right margins. Double-space manuscript, except quotations
which may be single spaced. A background or explanatory cover letter is not desired, but a short abstract of the article is
required. Biographical information about the author is desired
and should include a summary of current position. Tables and
simple graphs can be used, but pictures cannot. No payment
is made for accepted articles. Reprints are available; costs
vary with article length.

Manuscript Disposition:
Receipt of a manuscript is acknowledged. Editorial decisions
are made within two months. Accepted articles usually appear
in print within four to six months after acceptance. Unaccepted
manuscripts are returned, often with criticism and/or suggestions.

Copyright:
Held by Sociology and Social Research.

SOCIOLOGY OF EDUCATION

Subscription Data:
Published by the American Sociological Association, 1722 N
Street, N.W., Washington, D.C. 20036. Issued quarterly, in
January, March, June, and October. Selected advertising is
accepted. Circulation: 3,000. Subscription: $7.00 per year;
$5.00 to Association members. Founded: 1963.

Editorial Address:
Dr. John I. Kitsuse, Editor, Sociology of Education, American
Sociological Association, 1722 N Street, N.W., Washington,
D.C. 20036.

Editorial Policy:
Includes articles which report studies of education conducted
by social scientists from all parts of the world. The reading
audience includes anthropologists, economists, historians, political scientists, psychologists, sociologists, and educators. Unsolicited articles are welcome. Four or five major articles are
published per issue. Book reviews are not included.

Manuscript Preparation:
No limitations are placed upon manuscript length. Two copies
are required. Return postage and a self-addressed envelope

are unnecessary. Footnoting and other bibliographical procedure should follow the ASA Style Manual. Use 1-1/2 inch margins and double-space. Footnotes, numbered serially, should be listed at the end of the article. A background or explanatory cover letter about the author is required. An abstract of 100 to 125 words should accompany each article. Biographical information about the author is desired. Illustrations, graphs, and pictures may be used. Tables must be typed on separate pages; figures must be drawn on white paper in India ink. Mathematical notation should be provided in both symbols and words. No payment is made for accepted articles. Reprints are available.

Manuscript Disposition:

Receipt of a manuscript is acknowledged. Editorial decisions are made as soon as possible. Accepted articles usually appear in print within 14 months after acceptance. Unaccepted manuscripts are returned, often with criticism and/or suggestions.

Copyright:

Held by the American Sociological Association.

Additional Information:

Contributors are asked to attach a cover page including the title, the author's name, and institutional affiliation; the manuscript should bear only the title as a menas of identification. Copy for "News Notes Concerning Research in Progress" should be prepared as a short article and should contain approximately 150 words of concise description, including indication of both content and design.

SOCIOLOGY OF WORK AND OCCUPATIONS

Subscription Data:

Published by Sage Publications, Inc., P.O. Box 776, Beverly Hills, California 90210. Issued quarterly, in February, May, August, and November. Advertising is accepted. Circulation: Not determined. Subscription: $12.00 per year; $20.00 to institutions. Founded: February, 1974.

Editorial Address:

Rue Bucher, Editor, Sociology of Work and Occupations, University of Illinois at the Medical Center, P.O. Box 6998, Chicago, Illinois 60680.

Editorial Policy:

Includes articles pertaining to empirical research and theoretical essays pertinent to the general, substantive area of work and occupations. The reading audience is international and includes mainly sociologists, industrial relations people, and others. Unsolicited manuscripts are welcome. Approximately six major articles are published per issue. Book reviews are included.

Manuscript Preparation:

No limitations are placed on manuscript length as whatever is necessary for the author to effectively communicate material is acceptable. Three copies are required. Return postage and a self-addressed envelope are appreciated. Bibliographical procedure should follow the Sage style manual. List footnotes on

a separate page. Use one inch margins on either side. A
background or explanatory cover letter is not required, but must
have author's most efficient mailing address. Abstracts are required. Biographical information about the author is required if
manuscript is accepted; information is requested by the publisher.
Illustrations, pictures, graphs, etc., should follow the Sage
style manual. No payment is made for accepted manuscripts.
Twenty-four free reprints and two copies of the issue are given
to each author.

Manuscript Disposition:
Receipt of a manuscript is acknowledged. Editorial decisions
are made within six to fourteen weeks. Accepted articles usually appear in print within four months. Unaccepted manuscripts
are returned, usually with criticism and/or suggestions.

Copyright:
Held by Sage Publications, Inc.

Additional Information:
Authors may obtain permission to have papers reprinted in other
sources.

TEACHING SOCIOLOGY

Subscription Data:
Published by Sage Publications, Inc., 275 South Beverly Drive,
Beverly Hills, California 90121. Issued semiannually, in Octo-
ber and April. Advertising is accepted. Circulation: 1,200.
Subscription: $8.00 per year; $16.00 to institutions. Founded:
1973.

Editorial Address:
The Editor, Teaching Sociology, Department of Sociology, 512
Chafee Social Science Center, University of Rhode Island, Kings-
ton, Rhode Island 02881.

Editorial Policy:
Teaching Sociology seeks to present a range of articles dealing
with the teaching of the discipline. New courses and innovations
in course organization, teaching techniques and teaching technology, brief (four to five pages) reports of class projects and
demonstrations, evaluation of teaching techniques and teaching
are some of the areas of focus. The journal is particularly
interested in addressing the content of teaching in addition to the
technology. Toward this end, articles which review a particular
field or subfield in sociology are encouraged. The reading audience include sociologists teaching at colleges, universities,
junior colleges, and secondary schools. Unsolicited manuscripts
are welcome. Six to nine major articles are published per issue. Book reviews are included, but unsolicited book reviews
are discouraged.

Manuscript Preparation:
Accepted manuscripts average 12 to 20 pages. Three copies are
required. Return postage and a self-addressed envelope are not
required. Bibliographical procedure should follow the Sage style
sheet. All copy, including indented matter, notes, and references,

should be typed double-spaced on white standard paper. Lines
should not exceed six inches in length. Type only on one side of
a sheet and number all pages. A background or explanatory
cover letter is not required, but an abstract is required. Biographical information about the author is not required. Type
each table on a separate sheet, showing only a marginal reference line in the text for placement. In general, artwork should
be prepared for same-size use at a maximum size of 4-1/2
inches wide by 6 inches deep. Oversize artwork should be prepared to the same proportions taking into consideration that any
lettering should be somewhat oversize so as to remain legible
when reduced. Artwork should be clear, sharp, preferably
black on white paper. Photographs should be large glossies
rather than small snapshots, and have high contrast. No payment is made for accepted manuscripts. Twenty-four free tear-
sheets are given to each author. Reprints are available; price
sheet may be obtained from the editor.

Manuscript Disposition:
Receipt of a manuscript is acknowledged. Editorial decisions
are made within 12 to 16 weeks. Accepted articles usually appear in print within four to eight months. Unaccepted manuscripts are returned with criticism and/or suggestions.

Copyright:
Held by Sage Publications, Inc.

YOUTH AND SOCIETY

Subscription Data:
Published by Sage Publications, Inc., 275 South Beverly Drive,
Beverly Hills, California 90212. Issued quarterly, in Septem-
ber, December, March, and June. Advertising is accepted.
Circulation: 1,000. Subscription: $15.00 per year; $10.00
to professionals; $7.50 to students. Founded: 1969.

Editorial Address:
A. W. McEachern, Editor, Youth and Society, c/o School of
Public Administration, University of Southern California, Los
Angeles, California 90007.

Editorial Policy:
Youth and Society is an interdisciplinary journal concerned
with the social and political implications of youth culture and
development. Concentrates primarily on the age span from
mid-adolescence through young adulthood - bringing together
significant empirical and theoretical studies relevant to the processes of youth development, political socialization, the impact
of youth culture on society, and patterns of acquisition of adult
roles. The reading audience includes sociologists, professors,
students, and others interested in youth behavior patterns in
society. Unsolicited manuscripts are welcome. Approximately
six major articles are published per issue. Book reviews are
not included.

Manuscript Preparation:
Accepted manuscripts average 30 double-spaced typewritten

pages. Two copies are required. Footnoting and other bibliographical procedure should follow the Sage style sheet. A background or explanatory cover letter should contain only name and address of author. An outline, summary, or abstract is not required. Biographical information about the author is not required. Contributors should type each table on a separate sheet and furnish cleanly typed tables suitable for photographing as artwork. Artwork should be clean, sharp, preferably black on white paper. Light blue linework does not photograph at all. Glossy photostats are best, preferably finished to final size. Photographs should be large glossies rather than small snapshots, and have high contrast. No payment is made for accepted manuscripts. Twenty-four reprints are furnished to each author upon publication of article; additional reprints may be purchased in quantities of 100.

Manuscript Disposition:

Receipt of a manuscript is acknowledged. Unaccepted manuscripts are returned.

Copyright:

Held by Sage Publications, Inc.

AMERICAN FORENSIC ASSOCIATION. JOURNAL

Subscription Data:
  Published by the American Forensic Association, James Weaver, Secretary, Iowa State University, Department of Speech, Ames, Iowa 50010. Issued four times each year, in August, November, February, and May. Advertising is accepted. Circulation: 1,500. Subscription: $12.00 per year to libraries. Founded: 1964.

Editorial Address:
  George Ziegelmueller, Editor, Journal of the American Forensic Association, Department of Speech, Communication and Theatre, Wayne State University, Detroit, Michigan 48201.

Editorial Policy:
  Includes articles related to debate, oratory, extemporaneous speaking, and other speech contests. Also includes articles related to the theory of argument and debate. Unsolicited manuscripts are welcome. Two to five major articles are published per issue. Book reviews are included.

Manuscript Preparation:
  Accepted manuscripts average 4,000 words. Two copies are required. Return postage and a self-addressed envelope are not required. Bibliographical procedure should follow the MLA Style Sheet. Use 1-1/2 inch margins and double-space. A background or explanatory cover letter is not required nor is an outline, summary, or abstract. Biographical information about the author is required. Illustrations and pictures are not accepted. Statistical tables are used, but graphs are discouraged. No payment is made for accepted manuscripts. Reprints must be ordered in advance. The printer contacts the author before publication.

Manuscript Disposition:
  Receipt of a manuscript is acknowledged. Editorial decisions are made within three to four weeks. Accepted articles usually appear in print within four to six months. Unaccepted manuscripts are returned with criticism and/or suggestions.

Copyright:
  Held by the American Forensic Association.

CENTRAL STATES SPEECH JOURNAL

Subscription Data:
  Published by the Central States Speech Association, Lawrence, Kansas. Issued four times each year, in spring, summer, fall,

and winter. Advertising is accepted. Circulation: 2,200. Subscription: Provided with $6.00 Association membership. Founded: 1950.

Editorial Address:

James W. Gibson, Editor, Central States Speech Journal, Department of Speech, University of Missouri--Columbia, Columbia, Missouri 65201.

Editorial Policy:

Includes articles on all aspects of speech, including theatre, radio-TV, speech pathology, and speech education. The reading audience includes secondary and college speech teachers. Unsolicited articles are welcome. Eight major articles are published per issue. Book reviews are not included.

Manuscript Preparation:

Articles should not exceed 4,000 words. Contributions to the "Special Reports" section should not exceed 1,000 words. Type the total number of words used in the upper right corner of page one. Two copies are required. Return postage and a self-addressed envelope are not required. Bibliographical procedure should follow the MLA Style Sheet. Use 1/2 inch margins and double-space. Place footnotes on a separate page. A background or explanatory cover letter about the article is desired and an outline, summary, or abstract is required. Biographical information about the author is required. Use a minimum of pictures and graphs. No payment is made for accepted manuscripts. Contact printer for reprints.

Manuscript Disposition:

Receipt of a manuscript is acknowledged. Editorial decisions are made within five weeks. Accepted articles usually appear in print within four months. Unaccepted manuscripts are returned with criticism and/or suggestions.

Copyright:

Held by the Central States Speech Association.

Additional Information:

Printer's address is: Standard Printing Company, 201-09 North Third Street, Hannibal, Missouri 63401.

QUARTERLY JOURNAL OF SPEECH

Subscription Data:

Published by the Speech Communication Association, Statler Hilton Hotel, New York, New York 10001. Issued quarterly, in October, December, February, and April. Advertising is accepted. Circulation: 8,500. Subscription: $15.00 per year; $7.50 to students. Founded: 1915.

Editorial Address:

Robert L. Scott, Quarterly Journal of Speech, Department of Speech-Communication, University of Minnesota, Minneapolis, Minnesota 55455.

Editorial Policy:

Includes articles on theatre, drama, interpretation, rhetoric, public address, radio, television, films, phonetics, linguistics, and voice science. The reading audience includes basically college teachers and some secondary teachers. Unsolicited manuscripts are welcome. Approximately ten major articles are published per issue. Book reviews are included.

Manuscript Preparation:
Accepted manuscripts range from 2,500 to 6,000 words. Two copies are required. Return postage and a self-addressed envelope are not required, but are appreciated. Footnoting and other bibliographical procedure should follow the MLA Style Sheet. Footnotes should be listed on separate page. Manuscript margin and spacing should be generous. A background or explanatory cover letter about the article is not required, but an outline, summary, or abstract is required if the article is accepted. Illustrations, pictures, graphs, etc., can be accepted; however, use of pictures is especially limited. No payment is made for accepted manuscripts. Approximately 25 copies are mailed to the author; additional offprints may be purchased from the printer.

Manuscript Disposition:
Receipt of a manuscript is acknowledged. Editorial decisions are made within six weeks. Accepted articles usually appear in print within nine months. Unaccepted manuscripts are returned with criticism and/or suggestions.

Copyright:
Held by the Speech Communication Association.

Additional Information:
The Journal prefers author's identification on a separate sheet and that the author not identify him/herself in any other place in the typescript.

SPEECH MONOGRAPHS

Subscription Data:
Published by the Speech Communication Association, Statler Hilton Hotel, New York, New York 10001. Issued quarterly, in March, June, August, and November. Advertising is not accepted. Circulation: 3,500. Subscription: $15.00 per year. Founded: 1934.

Editorial Address:
Thomas M. Scheidel, Editor, Speech Monographs, 6138 Vilas Hall, Department of Communication Arts, University of Wisconsin, Madison, Wisconsin 53706.

Editorial Policy:
Includes reports of research on all aspects of human speech communication. The reading audience includes research oriented scholars and educators in speech, social science, philosophy, and English. Unsolicited articles are welcome. The number of major articles published per issue varies. Book reviews are not included.

Manuscript Preparation:
Manuscripts normally should not exceed 10,000 words. Three copies are required. Return postage and a self-addressed

envelope are required, except from Association members. Footnotes and other bibliographical procedure should follow the MLA Style Sheet (second edition). Use wide margins and double-space. A background or explanatory cover letter about the article is desired, but not an outline or summary. Biographical information about the author is required and should include a summary of present position. Graphs and tables may be used; pictures are occasionally used. No payment is made for accepted articles. Reprints are available and may be secured by special arrangement with Standard Printing Company, 201 North Third Street, Hannibal, Missouri 63401.

Manuscript Disposition:
Receipt of a manuscript is acknowledged, with immediate decision on article appropriateness. Final editorial decisions are made within twelve weeks. Accepted articles usually appear in print within nine to twelve months after acceptance. Unaccepted manuscripts are returned with reasons for rejection.

Copyright:
Held by the Speech Communication Association.

SPEECH TEACHER

Subscription Data:
Published by the Speech Communication Association, Statler Hilton Hotel, New York, New York 10001. Issued four times each year, in January, March, September, and November. Advertising is accepted. Circulation: 5,780. Subscription: $15.00 per year with Association membership. Founded: 1952.

Editorial Address:
Mary M. Roberts, Editor, Speech Teacher, Department of Speech, Kansas State College of Pittsburg, Pittsburg, Kansas 66762.

Editorial Policy:
Includes articles dealing with practical or theoretical matters of interest to teachers of speech communication at all levels of public and private education. The reading audience includes speech communication teachers and students. Unsolicited manuscripts are welcome. Six to twelve major articles are published per issue. Book reviews are included.

Manuscript Preparation:
Accepted manuscripts average no more than eight double-spaced pages for Teachers' Potpourri and nine to twenty-five pages for regular length articles. Included are short book reviews and reviews of nonprint materials. Two copies are required. Return postage and a self-addressed envelope are required. Bibliographical procedure should follow the MLA Style Sheet. Double-space all entries, including quotations that are indented. A background or explanatory cover letter is not required, but an 80 word abstract is required for all articles except Teachers' Potpourri. Biographical information about the author should contain only author's name, address, rank, and institutional connection on a separate sheet from the manuscript. Essential tables

should be placed at the end of manuscript before footnotes. No
payment is made for accepted manuscripts. Reprints may be
ordered from the printer.

Manuscript Disposition:
Receipt of a manuscript is acknowledged. Editorial decisions
are made within four to ten weeks. Accepted articles usually
appear in print within three to five months. Criticism and/or
suggestions are provided for articles for which resubmission is
requested.

Copyright:
Held by the Speech Communication Association.

TODAY'S SPEECH

Subscription Data:
Published by the Eastern Communication Association, Executive
Secretary, University of Rhode Island, Kingston, Rhode Island
02881. Issued quarterly, in winter (February), spring (April),
summer (July), and fall (October). Advertising is accepted.
Circulation: 3,000. Subscription: $10.00 per year. Founded:
1953.

Editorial Address:
Editor, Today's Speech, Department of Speech, University of
Massachusetts, Amherst, Massachusetts 01002.

Editorial Policy:
Includes articles on all phases of communication: historical
and experimental studies of the processes and effects of writer-
speaker and reader-listener transactions, including essays on
the theatre and mass communication, film, theatre, etc. The
reading audience includes college and high school teachers of
speech, English, film, and broadcasting (radio and television).
Unsolicited manuscripts are welcome. Six to ten major articles
are published per issue. Book reviews are included.

Manuscript Preparation:
Accepted manuscripts average from 3,000 to 5,000 words. Two
copies are required. Return postage and a self-addressed envelope are not required. Bibliographical information about the
author should follow the second edition of the MLA Style Sheet.
Use one inch margins. A background or explanatory cover letter is not required, but an outline, summary, or abstract of
the article is required. Biographical information about the author is not required. Graphs, tables, etc., are acceptable,
however, no pictures. No payment is made for accepted manuscripts. Reprints are available at the rate of $15.00 per 50;
$20.00 per 100.

Manuscript Disposition:
Receipt of a manuscript is acknowledged. Editorial decisions
are made within six to eight weeks. Accepted articles usually
appear in print within six months. Unaccepted manuscripts are
returned with criticism and/or suggestions.

Copyright:
Held by the Eastern Communication Association.

TECHNICAL EDUCATION

AGRICULTURAL EDUCATION

Subscription Data:
   Published by the Lawhead Press, Inc., 900 East State Street,
   Athens, Ohio 45701. Issued monthly. Advertising is not ac-
   cepted. Circulation: 10,000. Subscription: $5.00 per year;
   $6.00 foreign.
Editorial Address:
   Includes articles on all phases of professional education in agriculture. The reading audience includes teachers of agriculture,
   supervisors, and teacher trainers in agricultural education. Unsolicited articles are welcome. Ten to fourteen major articles
   are published per issue. Book reviews are included.
Manuscript Preparation:
   Accepted manuscripts average 500 or fewer words. One copy is
   required. Return postage and a self-addressed envelope are required only if the author desires to have the manuscript returned. Use wide margins and double-space. Footnoting procedure may follow any accepted documentation style. A background or explanatory cover letter is not desired nor is an outline or summary. Biographical information about the author is
   desired and should include a brief statement of his relationship
   to education and/or agriculture. Illustrations, pictures, and
   graphs may be used. No payment is made for accepted articles.
   Reprint costs vary with article length and order volume.
Manuscript Disposition:
   Receipt of a manuscript is acknowledged. Editorial decisions
   are made within one to three months. Accepted articles usually
   appear in print within three to six months after acceptance.
   Unaccepted manuscripts are returned, often without suggestions
   or criticism.
Copyright:
   Not copyrighted.

ENGINEERING EDUCATION (formerly Journal of Engineering Educa-
tion)

Subscription Data:
   Published by the American Society for Engineering Education,
   One Dupont Circle, Suite 400, Washington, D.C. 20036. Issued
   eight times each year, October through May. Advertising is
   accepted. Circulation: 16,000. Subscription: $20.00 per year
   in the United States and Canada; $22.00 foreign. Founded:
   1894.

Editorial Address:
   The Editor, Engineering Education, One Dupont Circle, Suite
   400, Washington, D. C. 20036.
Editorial Policy:
   Includes articles which relate to all phases of engineering education, with emphasis on teaching and learning at the graduate and
   undergraduate levels.   The reading audience includes engineering
   educators, industrial personnel, and professional engineers.   Unsolicited manuscripts are welcome.   Six to ten major articles
   are published per issue.   Book reviews are occasionally included.
Manuscript Preparation:
   Accepted manuscripts average six to twelve double-spaced typewritten pages.   Three copies are required.   Return postage and
   a self-addressed envelope are not required.   Bibliographical procedure should follow the University of Chicago Manual of Style
   and/or the U. S. Government Printing Office Style Manual.   Footnotes must be listed on a separate page.   A background or explanatory cover letter is not required nor is an outline, summary,
   or abstract.   Biographical information about the author is required.   Illustrations, pictures, graphs, etc., may be used but
   must be submitted as original line-drawings.   Black and white
   glossy eight by ten inch prints are required for photograph reproduction.   No payment is made for accepted manuscripts.
   Reprints are available, but must be ordered when galley proofs
   are returned.   Reprint costs vary with article length and order
   volume.
Manuscript Disposition:
   Receipt of a manuscript is acknowledged.   Editorial decisions
   are made within eight to twelve weeks.   Accepted articles usually appear in print within three to twelve months.   Unaccepted
   manuscripts are returned, sometimes with criticism and/or suggestions.
Copyright:
   Held by the American Society for Engineering Education.

JOURNAL OF AEROSPACE EDUCATION

Subscription Data:
   Published by the National Aeronautic Association, 806 Fifteenth
   Street, N. W., Washington, D. C. 20005.   Issued 10 times each
   year, September through June.   Advertising is not presently
   accepted.   Circulation: 5,000.   Subscription: $5.00 per year.
   Founded: 1974.
Editorial Address:
   The Editor, Journal of Aerospace Education, National Aeronautic
   Association, 806 Fifteenth Street, N. W., Washington, D. C.
   20005.
Editorial Policy:
   Includes articles on any classroom or extracurricular activity
   involving aviation and space, either as specific subjects or as
   enrichment in the standard curriculum at all age levels.   The
   reading audience includes educators, elementary through univer-

sity. Unsolicited manuscripts are welcome. Approximately four major articles are published per issue. Book reviews are not presently included, but will be in the future.

Manuscript Preparation:

Accepted manuscripts average 1,000 to 3,000 words, plus black and white pictures if available. One copy is required. Return postage and a self-addressed envelope are required. Bibliographical procedure may follow whatever is clear and convenient. A background or explanatory cover letter is preferred, but an outline, summary, or abstract is not required. Biographical information about the author is required. Black and white photographs, preferably of student activity, are included. Line drawings in finished form are acceptable. No payment is made for accepted manuscripts. Reprints are available.

Manuscript Disposition:

Receipt of a manuscript is not acknowledged. Editorial decisions are made within six weeks. Accepted articles usually appear in print within four months. Unaccepted manuscripts are returned without criticism and/or suggestions.

Copyright:

Held by the National Aeronautic Association.

Additional Information:

News items of teachers and their organizations and their activities involving aerospace are welcome. Curriculum suggestions at all age levels are eagerly received.

JOURNAL OF ARCHITECTURAL EDUCATION

Subscription Data:

Published by the Association of Collegiate Schools of Architecture, Inc., 1735 New York Avenue, N. W., Washington, D. C. 20006. Issued quarterly, in August, November, March, and June. Advertising is accepted. Circulation: 5,000. Subscription: $5.00 per year. Founded: 1912.

Editorial Address:

Art Hacker, Editor, Journal of Architectural Education, School of Architecture, University of Houston, Houston, Texas 77004.

Editorial Policy:

Includes articles on subjects of built-environment, design, decision process, education, sense of place, environmental psychology or sociology, morphology, form, process, ecology, cultural geography, etc. Unsolicited manuscripts are welcome. Two or three major articles are published per issue. Book reviews are included.

Manuscript Preparation:

Accepted manuscripts are open in regard to length. Four copies are required. Return postage and a self-addressed envelope are required. Bibliographical procedure is very informal. A background or explanatory cover letter is required, but not an outline, summary, or abstract. Biographical information about the author is required. Illustrations, pictures, graphs, etc., are welcome. No payment is made for accepted manuscripts.

Manuscript Disposition:
　　Receipt of a manuscript is not acknowledged. Editorial decisions
　　are made within six weeks. Accepted articles usually appear in
　　print within four months. Unaccepted manuscripts are returned,
　　without criticism or suggestions.
Copyright:
　　Held by the Association of Collegiate Schools of Architecture,
　　Inc.

JOURNAL OF ENVIRONMENTAL EDUCATION

Subscription Data:
　　Published by Dembar Educational Research Services, Inc., Box
　　1605, 2101 Sherman Avenue, Madison, Wisconsin 53701. Issued
　　quarterly. Advertising is accepted. Circulation: 2,500. Sub-
　　scription: $10.00 per year, $18.00 for two years; $7.00 to
　　students; $3.00 per issue. Founded: 1969.
Editorial Address:
　　The Editor, Journal of Environmental Education, Box 1605,
　　2101 Sherman Avenue, Madison, Wisconsin 53701.
Editorial Policy:
　　Includes primarily research articles, project reports, and criti-
　　cal essays designed to advance the scientific study of conserva-
　　tion communications and improve field practice in environmental
　　education. The reading audience includes educators, profes-
　　sionals, library patrons, people in public agencies and environ-
　　mental groups, etc. Unsolicited manuscripts are welcome. Ap-
　　proximately 20 major articles are published per issue. Book re-
　　views are included.
Manuscript Preparation:
　　Articles are usually relatively short, within a range of 1,500 to
　　3,500 words; longer treatises will be considered if they repre-
　　sent a signal contribution to the field. Two copies are required.
　　Return postage and a self-addressed envelope are not required.
　　Bibliographical procedure should follow the University of Chicago
　　Manual of Style. The Journal does not prescribe any set order
　　of presentation, but should possess evident elements of structure
　　in a clearly organized sequence. Strive for simplicity and clari-
　　ty of expression. "Guidelines for Contributors" is available from
　　the editor. Avoid explanatory footnotes by incorporating their
　　content in the text. For essential footnotes, identify them with
　　consecutive superscripts and list them in a section entitled
　　FOOTNOTES, at the end of the text, but preceding the REFER-
　　ENCES. References should be listed alphabetically, according
　　to the author's last name, at the end of the manuscript. Only
　　references actually cited in the article should be included. Copy
　　should be double-spaced with adequate margins. A background
　　or explanatory cover letter is not required nor is an outline,
　　summary, or abstract. Biographical information about the au-
　　thor is preferred. Draw any graphs and charts in black ink on
　　good quality paper, title each, and number consecutively. Send
　　the original copy, for mimeographed figures or charts are unac-

ceptable. Prepare tables precisely as they are to appear in print, caption each with a brief and to-the-point title, and number consecutively with Arabic numerals. No payment is made for accepted manuscripts. Each contributor will receive five complimentary copies of the issue in which the article appears. Reprints are charged at cost; a price schedule will be sent to each contributor in advance of publication.

Manuscript Disposition:

Receipt of a manuscript is acknowledged. Editorial decisions are made within three to six weeks. Accepted articles usually appear in print within nine months. Unaccepted manuscripts are returned with criticism and/or suggestions.

Copyright:

Held by Dembar Educational Research Services, Inc.

NATIONAL ASSOCIATION OF COLLEGES AND TEACHERS OF AGRICULTURE. JOURNAL

Subscription Data:

Published by the National Association of Colleges and Teachers of Agriculture, Box 5136 Tech Station, Ruston, Louisiana 71270. Issued four times each year, in March, June, September, and December. Advertising is accepted. Circulation: 1,200. Subscription: $5.00 per year. Founded: 1957.

Editorial Address:

The Editor, Journal of the National Association of Colleges and Teachers of Agriculture, P.O. Box 5136, Tech Station, Ruston, Louisiana 71270.

Editorial Policy:

Presents articles covering topics that treat all aspects of college teaching of agriculture, such as methods, problems, philosophy and rewards. The reading audience includes college teachers of agriculture. Unsolicited articles are welcome. Twelve to fifteen major articles are published per issue. Book reviews are included.

Manuscript Preparation:

Major articles should not exceed 3,000 words unless special arrangements are made. Four copies are required. Return postage and a self-addressed envelope are required. Bibliographical procedure should follow a recent issue of NACTA Journal or consult the latest edition of the University of Chicago Manual of Style. Footnotes should be double-spaced. A background or explanatory cover letter about the article is required. If there are doubts of suitability of an article, an outline should be submitted. A summary or conclusion should be included in the article. Biographical information about the author is not required. Photographs, tables, or figures may be used when they aid communication. Payment is not made for accepted manuscripts. Reprints are available only if you contact printer (address in Journal).

Manuscript Disposition:

Receipt of a manuscript is acknowledged. Editorial decisions

are made as soon as possible. Accepted articles usually appear
in print within twelve months after acceptance. Unaccepted manuscripts are returned, sometimes with criticism and/or suggestions.

Copyright:
    Not copyrighted.

TECHNICAL EDUCATION NEWS

Subscription Data:
    Published by the Gregg/Community College Division, McGraw-
    Hill Book Company, 1221 Avenue of the Americas, New York,
    New York 10020. Issued periodically during the school year.
    Advertising is not accepted. Circulation: 50,000. Subscrip-
    tion: Free to technical and occupational educators and to those
    working with training programs in business, industry, and the
    government. Founded: 1941.

Editorial Address:
    Mrs. Susan S. Schrumpf, Editor, Technical Education News,
    McGraw-Hill Book Company, 1221 Avenue of the Americas,
    New York, New York 10020.

Editorial Policy:
    Includes articles on innovative technical and occupational pro-
    grams and related teaching methodology. The reading audience
    includes teachers, teacher educators, and administrators. Un-
    solicited manuscripts are welcome. About seven major articles
    are published per issue. Book reviews are not included.

Manuscript Preparation:
    Accepted manuscripts average from 1,600 to 2,500 words. Two
    copies are required. Return postage and a self-addressed en-
    velope are desired. All footnotes should appear at the end of
    the article. Manuscripts should be typed and double-spaced on
    a 60-space line, with the first page including the title and the
    author's name and professional affiliation. A background or
    explanatory cover letter is required, but not an outline, sum-
    mary, or abstract. Biographical information about the author
    should include only author's professional affiliation. Graphs
    and photographs are published when they are an integral part
    of the editorial content. Payment is made for accepted manu-
    scripts. McGraw-Hill holds all reproduction rights but will re-
    assign rights to author after publication.

Manuscript Disposition:
    Receipt of a manuscript is acknowledged. Editorial decisions
    are made within six to eight weeks. Accepted articles appear
    in print within six months to one year. Unaccepted manuscripts
    are returned, sometimes with criticism and/or suggestions.

Copyright:
    Held by McGraw-Hill Book Company.

STYLE MANUALS

Style manuals cited in the Guide are listed below with bibliographical information or the address where the manual may be obtained.

American Chemical Society. Handbook for Authors of Papers in the Journals of the American Chemical Society. Washington, D. C.: American Chemical Society, 1967.

American Educational Research Association. Style Manual.
American Educational Research Association
1126 Sixteenth Street, N. W.
Washington, D. C. 20036

American Institute of Physics. Publications Board. Style Manual for Guidance in the Preparation of Papers for Journals Published by the American Institute of Physics. Revised Edition. New York: American Institute of Physics, 1970.

American Physical Therapy Association. Physical Therapy Style Manual.
American Physical Therapy Association
1156 Fifteenth Street, N. W.
Washington, D. C. 20005

American Psychological Association. Publication Manual of the American Psychological Association. Second Edition. Washington, D. C.: American Psychological Association, 1974.

American Psychosomatic Society. Style Manual.
American Psychosomatic Society, Inc.
265 Nassal Road
Roosevelt, New York 11575

American Sociological Association. Style Manual.
American Sociological Association
1722 "N" Street, N. W.
Washington, D. C. 20036

Campbell, William Giles. Form and Style: Theses, Reports, Term Papers. Fourth Edition. Boston: Houghton-Mifflin, 1974.

Chicago. University. Press. Manual of Style for Authors, Editors, and Copywriters. Twelfth Edition Revised. Chicago: University of Chicago Press, 1969.

Council of Biology Editors. Committee on Form and Style. CBE Style Manual. Third Edition. Washington, D.C.: Published for the Council of Biology Editors by the American Institute of Biological Sciences, 1972.

Dugdale, Kathleen. Manual of Form for Theses and Term Reports. Fifth Edition. Bloomington, Indiana: The Author, 1972.

Education Index. New York: H. W. Wilson.

Harvard Law Review Association. Uniform System of Citation: Forms of Citation and Abbreviations. Eleventh Edition. Cambridge, Massachusetts: Harvard Law Review Association, 1967.

Hunt Botanical Library. B-P-H; Botanico - Periodicum - Huntianum. Pittsburgh, Pennsylvania: Hunt Botanical Library, 1968.

International Universities Press. Style Sheet.
    International Universities Press, Inc.
    239 Park Avenue South
    New York, New York 10003

Linguistic Society of America. Publication Bulletin.
    Linguistic Society of America
    1611 North Kent Street
    Arlington, Virginia 22209

Modern Language Association of America. MLA Style Sheet. Second Edition. New York: Modern Language Association of America, 1971.

National Education Association of the United States. NEA Style Manual for Writers and Editors. Revised Edition. Washington, D.C.: National Educational Association of the United States, 1966.

National Library of Medicine. Index Medicus.
    Chief, Bibliographic Services Division
    National Library of Medicine
    8600 Rockville Pike
    Bethesda, Maryland 20014

New York Times. Style Book for Writers and Editors. Revised Edition. New York: McGraw-Hill, 1962.

Skillin, Marjorie E. Words Into Type. Third Edition Englewood Cliffs, New Jersey: Prentice-Hall, 1974.

Strunk, William. Elements of Style. Second Edition. New York: Macmillan, 1972.

Turabian, Kate L. Manual for Writers of Term Papers, Theses, and Dissertations. Fourth Edition. Chicago: University of Chicago Press, 1973.

United States Government Printing Office. Style Manual. Revised Edition. Washington, D. C.: U. S. Government Printing Office, 1973.

Webster's Third New International Dictionary of the English Language. Unabridged. Springfield, Massachusetts: G. & C. Merriam, 1964.

Winkler, G. P. Associated Press Style Book. Revised Edition. New York: Associated Press, 1970.

MASTER LIST OF SUBJECT HEADINGS

ADMINISTRATION AND SUPER-
VISION

ADULT EDUCATION

AEROSPACE. See TECHNICAL
EDUCATION

AGRICULTURE. See TECHNI-
CAL EDUCATION

AMERICAN INDIAN

ANTHROPOLOGY AND ARCHAE-
OLOGY

ARCHAEOLOGY. See ANTHRO-
POLOGY AND ARCHAEOL-
OGY

ARCHITECTURE. See TECH-
NICAL EDUCATION

ART

ASTRONOMY. See SCIENCE -
GENERAL

ATHLETICS. See PHYSICAL
EDUCATION AND RECREA-
TION

AUDIO VISUAL. See INSTRUC-
TIONAL MEDIA AND TECH-
NIQUES

AUDITORY HANDICAPPED. See
HANDICAPPED - AUDITORY

BIOLOGY

BLACK STUDIES

BOTANY. See BIOLOGY

BUSINESS EDUCATION

CATHOLIC INTEREST

CHEMISTRY AND PHYSICS

CHILDREN AND YOUTH

CLASSICAL STUDIES

COMMUNICATIONS

COUNSELING, GUIDANCE, AND
PERSONNEL. See also
PSYCHOLOGICAL - DEVEL-
OPMENTAL AND CLINICAL

DATA PROCESSING

DEAF. See HANDICAPPED -
AUDITORY

DRAMATICS

DRUGS

ECONOMICS

EDUCATION - GENERAL

EDUCATIONAL RESEARCH

ELEMENTARY EDUCATION

ENGINEERING. See TECHNI-
CAL EDUCATION

ENGLISH. See LINGUISTICS -
ENGLISH LANGUAGE

ENVIRONMENT

ETHNIC GROUPS. See ETH-
NOLOGY AND ETHNIC
GROUPS

ETHNOLOGY AND ETHNIC
GROUPS

EXTENSION EDUCATION. See
ADULT EDUCATION

FILMS. See INSTRUCTIONAL
MEDIA AND TECHNIQUES

FOREIGN LANGUAGE. See
LINGUISTICS - FOREIGN
LANGUAGE

GEOGRAPHY

GIFTED CHILDREN

GUIDANCE. See COUNSELING,
GUIDANCE, AND PERSONNEL

HANDICAPPED - AUDITORY

527

HANDICAPPED - MENTAL. See also PSYCHOLOGICAL - DEVELOPMENTAL AND CLINICAL

HANDICAPPED - PHYSICAL

HANDICAPPED - SPEECH

HANDICAPPED - VISUAL

HEALTH

HIGHER EDUCATION

HISTORY

HOME ECONOMICS

INDIAN. See AMERICAN INDIAN

INDUSTRIAL EDUCATION

INSTRUCTIONAL MEDIA AND TECHNIQUES

INTERNATIONAL EDUCATION

INSTRUCTIONAL EDUCATION

JEWISH EDUCATION

JOURNALISM

LAW

LIBRARIES

LINGUISTICS - ENGLISH LANGUAGE

LINGUISTICS - FOREIGN LANGUAGE

LITERATURE

MATHEMATICS

MEDICAL SCIENCES

MENTALLY HANDICAPPED. See HANDICAPPED - MENTAL

METEOROLOGY. See GEOGRAPHY

MUSIC

NEGRO INTEREST. See BLACK STUDIES

PARAPSYCHOLOGY. See also PSYCHOLOGICAL - RESEARCH

PARENT-TEACHER ORGANIZA-

TIONS

PERSONNEL. See COUNSELING, GUIDANCE, AND PERSONNEL

PHILOSOPHY

PHYSICAL EDUCATION AND RECREATION

PHYSICALLY HANDICAPPED. See HANDICAPPED - PHYSICAL

PHYSICS. See CHEMISTRY AND PHYSICS

POLITICAL SCIENCE

PSYCHIATRY. See also PSYCHOLOGY

PSYCHOLOGICAL - DEVELOPMENTAL AND CLINICAL

PSYCHOLOGICAL - GENERAL AND APPLIED (excluding CLINICAL)

PSYCHOLOGICAL - RESEARCH

PSYCHOLOGY. See PSYCHOLOGICAL - DEVELOPMENTAL AND CLINICAL; PSYCHOLOGICAL - GENERAL AND APPLIED; PSYCHOLOGICAL - RESEARCH

READING

RECREATION. See PHYSICAL EDUCATION AND RECREATION

RELIGION AND THEOLOGY

RELIGIOUS EDUCATION

RESEARCH. See EDUCATIONAL RESEARCH; PSYCHOLOGICAL - RESEARCH

SAFETY

SCIENCE - GEOGRA-

SECONDARY EDUCATION

SOCIAL SCIENCES

SOCIAL STUDIES

SOCIAL WORK

SOCIOLOGY

SPECIAL EDUCATION. See specific field.

SPEECH

SPEECH HANDICAPPED. See HANDICAPPED - SPEECH

SUPERVISION. See ADMINISTRATION AND SUPERVISION

TECHNICAL EDUCATION

THEOLOGY. See RELIGION AND THEOLOGY

VISUALLY HANDICAPPED. See HANDICAPPED - VISUAL

VOCATIONAL EDUCATION

YOUTH. See CHILDREN AND YOUTH

ZOOLOGY. See BIOLOGY

SUBJECT INDEX

TITLE INDEX

AAUP Bulletin (American Association of University Professors) 222

AAUW Journal (American Association of University Women) 222

ADFL Bulletin (Association of Departments of Foreign Language) 304

AMS Bulletin (American Montessori Society) 166

AMS News (American Montessori Society) 166

ASSE Journal (American Society of Safety Engineers) 458

AV Communication Review 253

AV Guide: The Learning Media Magazine 254

Abstracts for Social Workers 489

Academic Therapy 58

Administrative Science Quarterly 3

Administrator's Notebook 3

Administrator's Swap Shop 16

Adolescence 58

Adult Education 16

Adult Jewish Education 17

Adult Leadership 18

Agricultural Education 517

American Academy of Child Psychiatry. Journal 376

American Academy of Political and Social Science. Annals 365

American Academy of Psychoanalysis. Journal 388

American Annals of the Deaf 196

American Anthropologist 22

American Antiquity 23

American Artist 26

American Biology Teacher 37

American Economic Review 111

American Education 124

American Educational Research Journal 158

American Ethnologist 175

American Foreign Language Teacher 305

American Forensic Association. Journal 512

American Historical Review 238

American Imago 389

American Indian Culture and Research Journal 175

American Jewish Historical Quarterly 238

American Journal of Clinical Hypnosis 389

American Journal of Comparative Law 270

American Journal of Economics and Sociology 112

American Journal of International Law 271

American Journal of Mental Deficiency 189

American Journal of Nursing 210

American Journal of Occupational Therapy 197

American Journal of Pharmaceutical Education 211

American Journal of Physics 53

American Journal of Psychiatry 377

American Journal of Psychology 419

American Journal of Public Health 212

American Journal of Sociology 494

American Libraries 277

American Mathematical Monthly 334

American Metric Journal 334

American Music Teacher 343

American Political Science Re-

Journal of Heredity 42
Journal of Higher Education 234
Journal of Home Economics 248
Journal of Human Relations 500
Journal of Human Resources 480
Journal of Humanistic Psychology 429
Journal of Individual Psychology 396
Journal of Industrial Teacher Education 250
Journal of Instructional Psychology 407
Journal of Interdisciplinary History 242
Journal of Learning Disabilities 202
Journal of Legal Education 274
Journal of Library History 282
Journal of Marketing 118
Journal of Marriage and the Family 501
Journal of Medical Education 213
Journal of Motor Behavior 429
Journal of Negro Education 181
Journal of Negro History 242
Journal of Nursing Education 215
Journal of Nutrition Education 215
Journal of Parapsychology 351
Journal of Personality 430
Journal of Personality and Social Psychology 431
Journal of Personality Assessment 397
Journal of Physical Education 360
Journal of Political and Military Sociology 501
Journal of Politics 367
Journal of Psychedelic Drugs 108
Journal of Psychology 408
Journal of Reading 436
Journal of Reading Behavior 437
Journal of Rehabilitation 202
Journal of Religious Thought 445
Journal of Research and Development in Education 163
Journal of Research in Music Education 346

Journal of Research in Science Teaching 463
Journal of Retailing 119
Journal of Risk and Insurance 119
Journal of School Health 216
Journal of School Psychology 409
Journal of Social Issues 502
Journal of Social Psychology 432
Journal of Southern History 243
Journal of Special Education 141
Journal of Speech and Hearing Disorders 203
Journal of Speech and Hearing Research 204
Journal of Teacher Education 235
Journal of the ... See name of the association, institution, organization, society, etc.
Journal of the History of Ideas 244
Journal of the History of the Behavioral Sciences 410
Journal of Transpersonal Psychology 432
Journal of Verbal Learning and Verbal Behavior 433
Journal of Vocational Behavior 411
Journalism Quarterly 267

Lab World 464
Language 301
Language Learning 310
Learning 172
Learning Today 283
Liberal Education 235
Library Journal 283
Library Quarterly 284
Library Resources and Technical Services 285
Library Trends 286
Life and Health 218
Life Threatening Behavior 383
Lutheran Education 452